THE
HUTCHINSON
ILLUSTRATED ENCYCLOPEDIA
—— OF ——
BRITISH HISTORY

THE
HUTCHINSON
ILLUSTRATED ENCYCLOPEDIA

— OF —

BRITISH HISTORY

Helicon

First published in Great Britain in 1995 by:
Helicon Publishing Limited
42 Hythe Bridge street
Oxford OX1 2EP

ISBN 1-85986-127-X

British Library Cataloguing in Publication Data

A catalogue record for this book is available
from the British Library

Papers used in this publication are natural recyclable products made from wood grown in sustainable forests. The manufacturing process of both raw materials and paper conform to the environmental regulations of the country of origin.

Designed and typeset by Roger Walker/Graham Harmer

Printed and bound in Great Britain by
The Bath Press Ltd, Bath, Avon

Title page illiustration: Queen Victoria (after Baron von Angeli)
by E M Ward (1816–79), Forbes Magazine Collection, New York.
Bridgeman Art Library

Contents

Contributors and editors

Contributors

Matthew Bennett, Royal Military Academy Sandhurst
Jeremy Black, University of Exeter
Michael Brown, University of Strathclyde
Christopher Durston, St Mary's College, Twickenham
Simon Esmonde Cleary, University of Birmingham
Raymond Gillespie, St Patrick's College, Maynooth
Reg Grant, freelance editor and historical writer
Simon Hall, freelance editor and historical writer
Martin Henig, Institute of Archaeology, Oxford
Ian V Hogg, freelance historical writer
John Haywood, University of Lancaster
Ronald Hutton, University of Bristol
Peter Martland, Corpus Christi College, Cambridge
Janet L Nelson, King's College, University of London
Robert Peberdy, formerly of Merton College Oxford and the
   University of Leicester
Michael Prestwich, University of Durham
Glyn Redworth, formerly of Christ Church College, Oxford
Sasha Roberts, Roehampton Institute, London
Adrian Room, freelance historical writer
Joe Staines, freelance historical writer
Jason Tomes, formerly of Nuffield College, Oxford

Editorial team

Acquisitions director
Anne-Lucie Norton

Project editor
Simon Hall

Text editor
Paul Davis

Proofreader
Avril Cridlan

Chronologies compiler
Robert Peberdy

Quotations compiler
Chris Murray

Cartographic editor
Olive Pearson

Cartographers
European Map Graphics Ltd

Picture researcher
James Nash

Picture resources manager
Terry Caven

Design & make-up
Roger Walker/
Graham Harmer

Production manager
Tony Ballsdon

Introduction

The *Hutchinson Illustrated Encyclopedia of British History* has been compiled with the intention of providing a practical and attractive source of quick reference for the non-specialist reader to the people, events, and ideas that have shaped the history of Britain and Ireland.

Yet from the first conception of the project, the editors have sought to acknowledge – and indeed to emphasize – the truth that history is more than simply a compilation of facts from the past. The reader who looks up the *South Sea Bubble*, or *Hadrian's Wall*, or *Winston Churchill*, wants to know more than the dates and factual details of an 18th-century financial scandal, a Roman fortification system, or a 20th-century prime minister. He or she wants some guide to the importance of these subjects, some understanding of their immediate historical context, some sense of the vanished world in which they featured. Increasingly, and at all levels of historical interest, we have become aware that the proper subject of history is the totality of past human experience, cultural influences and common habits of thought as much as dramatic events or prominent individuals.

We have addressed the problem of conveying this sense of British and Irish history as a totality in a number of ways in this *Encyclopedia*. First, the facts are essential, and we have included as much factual information as possible in each A–Z entry, as many tables and statistics as possible, and as many specially-created maps and plans as we could manage. Second, the chronological relationships of past events or lives must be clear, so we have included detailed subject chronologies throughout the *Encyclopedia*, attached to the relevant A–Z entries. Third, the cultural context of as many entries as possible must be brought to life – so we have included a wide range of illustrations, mostly contemporary, which provide a wealth of visual detail and, often, a key to past perceptions. A generous selection of quotations also allows the past to speak in its own voice, often more simply human than the rush of historical events allows us to expect. The large thematic chronology which follows the A–Z text provides a visual reference to the relationship between the events of British and Irish history and events elsewhere in the world, but also to the British and Irish social, economic, and scientific developments and achievements in literature, art, and music which interweave with conventional history.

Last and by no means least, we are fortunate enough to have been able to include a number of feature articles, many by historians of the very highest reputation in their fields. These articles provide the analysis and the sense of the broad sweep of history which are otherwise impossible to convey in an A–Z reference book. Read in chronological order, they provide an authoritative and up-to-date overview of British and Irish history – but also, by their variety of subjects and approaches, they emphasize the wide scope of historical enquiry and the extraordinary, fascinating wealth of the past we share.

Some practical considerations in the use of this book are essential. First, readers should note that some categories of entry have been excluded, for reasons of space. With the exception of some towns listed under their Roman names, placenames and the names of historic buildings are generally not listed. Similarly, individuals significant for cultural rather than conventionally historical reasons are also largely excluded, no matter how eminent. Although there are some entries relating to the prehistory of these islands, the focus of the *Encyclopedia* is largely on the period conventionally accepted as historical, that is from the Roman occupation of Britain onwards. None of these exclusions is in any way intended to imply that the omitted subjects lack historical significance.

Readers should also note that the many cross-references in the A–Z text are intended to refer users to related entries which they might otherwise not consult: cross-references are not usually provided to obviously related entries. Feature articles, tables, maps, chronologies, illustrations, and quotations are not cross-referenced, since they appear in close proximity to the relevant A–Z headword.

Simon Hall

List of feature articles

List of chronologies

List of maps and battle plans

List of genealogies

List of colour plates

abdication crisis the constitutional upheaval of the period 16 Nov 1936 to 10 Dec 1936, brought about by the British king Edward VIII's decision to marry Wallis Simpson, a US divorcee.

The marriage of the 'Supreme Governor' of the Church of England to a divorced person was considered unacceptable by the prime minister Stanley Baldwin and the king was finally forced to abdicate 10 Dec and left for voluntary exile in France. He was succeeded by his brother, the Duke of York, who came to the throne as King George VI. Edward was created Duke of Windsor and married Mrs Simpson 3 June 1937.

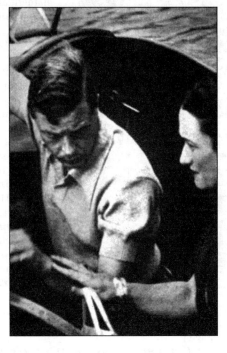

abdication crisis
King Edward VIII and Wallis Simpson holidaying on board the *Nahlin* during the summer of 1936. Edward reigned for just 11 months before giving up the throne to marry the twice-divorced American.
Image Select

Abercromby Ralph 1734–1801. British general. He served in Flanders and the West Indies during the French Revolutionary Wars, capturing Trinidad 1797. In 1801 he commanded an expedition to the Mediterranean, charged with the liquidation of the French forces left behind by Napoleon in Egypt. He fought a brilliant action against the French at Aboukir Bay in 1801, but was mortally wounded at the battle of Alexandria a few days later.

Aberdeen George Hamilton Gordon, 4th Earl of Aberdeen 1784–1860. British Tory politician, prime minister 1852–55 when he resigned because of the criticism aroused by the miseries and mismanagement of the ◊Crimean War.

Aberdeen began his career as a diplomat and was ambassador to Vienna 1813–14. He was foreign secretary under the Duke of Wellington 1828 and again 1841 under Robert Peel. He resigned with Peel over the Corn Laws 1846 and succeeded him as leader of the 'Peelite' wing of the Tories. He became prime minister 1852 in a government of Peelites and Whigs (Liberals), but resigned 1855 because of the Crimean War losses. Although a Tory, he supported Catholic emancipation and followed Peel in his conversion to free trade.

Aboukir Bay, Battle of (also known as the ***Battle of the Nile***) naval battle during the Napoleonic Wars between Great Britain and France, in which Admiral Horatio Nelson defeated Napoleon Bonaparte's fleet at the Egyptian seaport of Aboukir 1 Aug 1798. The defeat put an end to French designs in the Middle East.

Abraham, Plains of plateau near Québec, Canada, where the British commander ◊Wolfe defeated the French under Montcalm, 13 Sept 1759, during the Seven Years' War (1754–63). The outcome of the battle established British supremacy in Canada.

absolutism or ***absolute monarchy*** system of government in which the ruler or rulers have unlimited power. The principle of an absolute monarch, given a right to rule by God (the divine right of kings), was extensively used in Europe during the 17th and 18th centuries. Absolute monarchy is contrasted with limited or constitutional monarchy, in which the sovereign's powers are defined or limited.

I have found it impossible to carry the heavy burden of responsibility and to discharge my duties as King as I would wish to do, without the help and support of the woman I love.
ABDICATION CRISIS
abdication speech of Edward VIII, 11 Dec 1936

Anno xxvii. Reginæ Elizabethæ.

¶ At the Parliament

begunne and holden at Weſtminſter, the xxiij. day of Nouember, in the xrbii. yeere of the reigne of our moſt gracious Soueraigne Lady Elizabeth, by the grace of God, of England, France, and Ireland Queene, defender of the Faith, &c. and there continued, vntill the xxix, of March following:

To the high pleaſure of Almightie God, and the weale publike of this Realme, were enacted as followeth.

Imprinted at London by Chriſtopher Barker, Printer to the Queenes moſt excellent Maieſtie.

1 5 8 5.

act of Parliament
Title page of an Elizabethan act of Parliament 1585.
Philip Sauvain

That the king can do no wrong, is a necessary and fundamental principle of the English constitution.

ABSOLUTISM
English jurist William Blackstone,
Commentaries *book 3*

The absolute power of the monarch in England was effectively challenged in the 13th century by the Barons who imposed a series of legal restrictions on the sovereign with the ◊Magna Carta. In the 17th century, the struggle for power between parliament and King Charles I led to the ◊Civil War and the temporary overthrow of the monarchy, the ◊interregnum. Finally, in the reign of William III, a constitutional monarchy was established by the ◊Bill of Rights 1689.

act of Parliament a change in the law originating in Parliament and called a statute. Before an act receives the royal assent and becomes law it is a *bill*. An act of Parliament may be either public (of general effect), local, or private. The body of English statute law comprises all the acts passed by Parliament: the existing list opens with the Statute of Merton, passed in 1235. An act (unless it is stated to be for a definite period and then to come to an end) remains on the statute book until it is repealed.

How an act of Parliament becomes law:

1 first reading of the bill The title is read out in the House of Commons (H of C) and a minister names a day for the second reading.

2 The bill is officially printed.

3 second reading A debate on the whole bill in the H of C followed by a vote on whether or not the bill should go on to the next stage.

4 committee stage A committee of MPs considers the bill in detail and makes amendments.

5 report stage The bill is referred back to the H of C which may make further amendments.

6 third reading The H of C votes whether the bill should be sent on to the House of Lords.

7 House of Lords The bill passes through much the same stages in the Lords as in the H of C. (Bills may be introduced in the Lords, in which case the H of C considers them at this stage.)

8 last amendments The H of C considers any Lords' amendments, and may make further amendments which must usually be agreed by the Lords.

9 royal assent The Queen gives her formal assent.

10 The bill becomes an act of Parliament at royal assent, although it may not come into force until a day appointed in the act.

Adams Gerry (Gerard) 1948– . Northern Ireland politician, president of Provisional Sinn Féin (the political wing of the Irish Republican Army) from 1978. He was elected member of Parliament for Belfast West 1983 but never took his seat, saying he did not believe in the British government. (He lost his seat 1992.) In 1991 he started moving Sinn Féin's strategy toward peace talks, and began a series of talks with John Hume, leader of the SDLP, which had always opposed the IRA. In 1993, when the UK premier John Major and the Irish premier Albert Reynolds agreed on a strategy for the future of Northern Ireland, Adams stepped up his campaign to win international support. He visited the USA Jan 1994 where he appeared on radio and television, although at the time he was barred from these media in Britain. The ceasefire announced by the IRA 31 Aug 1994 was a breakthrough to which Adams had largely contributed.

Addington Henry, 1st Viscount Sidmouth 1757–1844. British Tory politician and prime minister 1801–04. As prime minister, he was responsible for the peace of ◊Amiens 1802 which ended the French Revolutionary Wars. He was forced to resign 1805 when he lost the support of ◊Pitt the Younger but became home secretary 1812–1822. In this post, he introduced much repressive legislation, including the notorious ◊Six Acts, and his attempts to suppress political radicalism have been held partly responsible for the ◊Peterloo Massacre 1819.

Addison Joseph 1672–1719 English writer and Whig MP. In 1704 he celebrated ◊Marlborough's victory at Blenheim in a poem, *The Campaign*, and subsequently held political appointments, including undersecretary of state and secretary to the Lord-Lieutenant of Ireland 1708. In 1709 he contributed to the *Tatler* magazine, begun by Richard Steele, and was cofounder, with Steele, of the *Spectator* 1711–12 . His essays set a new standard of easy elegance in English prose.

Addled Parliament name given to the English Parliament that met for two months 1614 but failed to pass a single bill. It was dissolved by James I for failing to vote supplies and for attacking 'impositions', customs duties levied by the king.

Adelaide 1792–1849. Queen consort of ◊William IV of England. Daughter of the Duke of Saxe-Meiningen, she married William, then Duke of Clarence, 1818. No children of the marriage survived infancy.

Aden (Arabic *'Adan*) former British colony on the southwest coast of the Arabian Peninsula, where it is now part of Yemen. It was held by the British and governed as part of India 1839–1937, and in the latter year separated from India and made a crown colony. It was a fortified naval base in World War II and gained independence 1968.

Admiralty, Board of the the administrative department of state for the Royal Navy from 1832 until 1964, when most of its functions – apart from that of management – passed to the Ministry of Defence. The board was established 1832 when the office of Lord High Admiral was divided between six Lords Commissioners: one from government (the First Sea Lord); four from the navy; and one Civil Lord. It replaced the Navy Board, established in the reign of Henry VIII.

Adrian IV (Nicholas Breakspear) *c.*1100–1159. Pope 1154–59, the only English pope. He secured the execution of Arnold of Brescia, crowned Frederick I Barbarossa as German emperor, refused Henry II's request that Ireland should be granted to the English crown in absolute ownership, and was at the height of a quarrel with Frederick I about papal supremacy when he died.

Adullamite a person who is disaffected or secedes from a political party. The term was applied to about 40 British Liberal MPs who voted against their leaders to defeat the 1866 Reform Bill. It comes from the name of a biblical city with nearby caves in which David and those who had some grievance took refuge (1 Samuel 22).

advowson right to nominate clergy to a vacant church living or benefice, especially in Church of England; a form of ◊patronage. Dating from Anglo-Saxon times, when landowners built their own churches, it was recognized as a heritable property right by the 1164 Constitutions of Clarendon. Advowsons are still held by some individual landowners and colleges. An association was formed Jan 1995 to protect private patronage in the Church, partly in response to the Anglican ordination of women.

Aelfric *c.*955–1020. Anglo-Saxon writer and abbot. He became a priest and taught at Cernel monastery (now Cerne Abbas) in Dorset, and was abbot of Eynsham from 1005. He was the author of two collections of *Catholic Homilies* 990–92, sermons, and the *Lives of the Saints* 996–97, written in vernacular Old English prose, some of the best quality examples still extant.

Afghan Wars three wars waged between Britain and Afghanistan to counter the threat to British India from expanding Russian influence in Afghanistan.

    First Afghan War 1838–42, the British invaded Afghanistan to restore an unpopular emir, Shashoja, to the throne. An Afghan rebellion wiped out the British garrison at Kabul and forced their withdrawal. The previous emir was restored

    Second Afghan War 1878–80, Emir Shir Ali received a Russian mission but would not accept a mission from the British. British forces invaded Nov 1878 and the Afghans came to terms, accepting British interests in the Treaty of Gandamak May 1879. However the murder of the British envoy Sept 1879 led to the British occupation of Kabul Oct 1879 and the British replaced the emir with their own nominee March 1880. The war came to an end when General ◊Roberts marched from Kabul to relieve ◊Kandahar and routed the Afghans 1 Sept 1880.

When vice prevails, and impious men bear sway/The post of honour is a private station.

JOSEPH ADDISON
Cato 1713

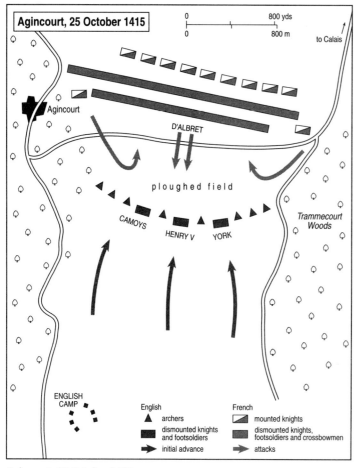

Agincourt, 25 October 1415

English		French	
▲	archers	◩	mounted knights
■	dismounted knights and footsoldiers	■	dismounted knights, footsoldiers and crossbowmen
➡	initial advance	➡	attacks

Agincourt, 25 October 1415

Facing a large French force under d'Albret, Henry V took up a defensive position in a ploughed field outside Agincourt, with his army's flanks protected by forests. Successive attacks by French footsoldiers and knights were cut down by concentrated English archery as they struggled across the broken ground.

You speak like a fool... Do you not believe that God, with this small force of men on his side, can conquer the hostile arrogance of the French, who pride themselves on their numbers and their strength?

AGINCOURT

comment attributed to Henry V before the battle, on being asked if he needed more soldiers.

Third Afghan War May–Aug 1919, a month of fighting broke out when Afghan forces invaded British India. After the dispatch by the UK of the first aeroplane ever seen in Kabul, the Indian government and Afghanistan agreed terms at a peace conference at Rawalpindi 26 July and the treaty was signed 8 Aug. Under the terms of the peace, Afghanistan gained full independence.

Agincourt, Battle of battle of the Hundred Years' War in which Henry V of England defeated the French 25 Oct 1415, mainly through the overwhelming superiority of the English longbow. The French lost more than 6,000 troops to about 1,600 English casualties. As a result of the battle, Henry gained France and the French princess, Catherine of Valois, as his wife. The village of Agincourt (modern ***Azincourt***) is south of Calais, in northern France.

Agricola Gnaeus Julius AD 37–93. Roman general and politician. Born in Provence, he became consul AD 77, and then governor of Britain AD 78–85. He successfully Romanized the south of England and extended Roman rule to the Firth of Forth in Scotland, defeating the Scots at the battle of ◊Mons Graupius. His fleet sailed round the north of Scotland and proved that Britain was an island. He was the first Roman general to subdue Britain effectively, but he was recalled to Rome *c*. AD 85 by the emperor Domitian, who was jealous of his success.

agricultural revolution sweeping changes that took place in British agriculture over the period 1750–1850 in response to the increased demand for food from a rapidly expanding population. Recent research has shown these changes to be only part of a much larger, ongoing process of development.

Changes of the latter half of the 18th century included the enclosure of open fields, the introduction of crop rotation, the use of new fodder crops such as turnips which enabled more stock to be kept over winter, and the development of improved breeds of livestock through experiments with in-breeding. Pioneers of this new style of farming included Viscount ◊Townshend (known as 'Turnip' Townshend), Jethro ◊Tull, Robert Bakewell, and enlightened landowners such as Thomas Coke of Norfolk (1752–1842).

Many of the changes were in fact underway before 1750 and other breakthroughs, such as farm mechanization, did not occur until after 1859. Scientific and technological advances in farming during the second half of the 20th century have further revolutionized agriculture.

Aidan, St *c*.600–651. Irish monk from Iona who converted Northumbria to Christianity at the invitation of its king, St ◊Oswald. He founded Lindisfarne monastery on Holy Island off the northeast coast of England, becoming its first abbot and bishop. His feast day is 31 Aug.

Alamein, El, Battles of in World War II, two decisive battles in the western desert, northern Egypt. In the First Battle of El Alamein 1–27 July 1942, the British 8th Army under Auchinleck held off the German and Italian forces under Rommel. In the Second Battle of El Alamein 24 Oct–4 Nov 1942, ◊Montgomery defeated Rommel.

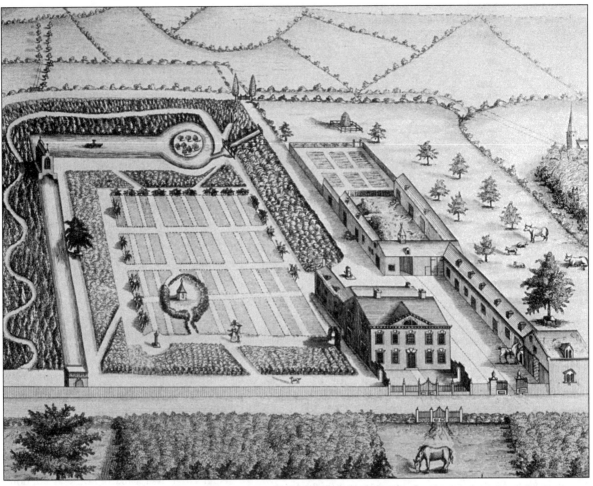

agricultural revolution
An estate at Burbage, Leicestershire, *c.* 1750 showing some of the innovations of the agricultural revolution such as enclosed fields, a model farm, and separate parkland and woodland.
Image Select

Agricultural revolution: chronology

*c.*1600	Spread of water-meadows, increasing availability of grass for grazing.
1640s	Sir Richard Weston, while in exile, studied the agriculture of the Low Countries and on returning to England wrote an influential account of clover-growing.
c. 1650	Widespread adoption of turnips in east and south England as extra course in crop rotations.
1669	John Worlidge designed a seed drill.
1701	Jethro Tull invented a horse-drawn seed drill.
1730	The Rotherham plough, based on Dutch designs, was patented.
1745	Robert Bakewell, one of many breeders in north Leicestershire, began a series of experiments to improve livestock.
1760s	Start of widespread enclosure of common fields and wastes by means of parliamentary act.
1776	Publication of the *Farmer's Magazine*.
1780	John Ellman in Sussex started breeding programme to improve downland sheep.
1786	Introduction of the first effective threshing machine.
1812	John Common, a Northumberland millwright, designed a horse-drawn reaper, on which the later McCormick reaper was based.
1835	Sir John Lawes and J H Gilbert began studying the effects of fertilizers on crops; from 1842 they manufactured superphosphate fertilizers at Deptford.
1843	Sir John Lawes founded the Rothamsted agricultural research station.
1845	Foundation of the Royal Agricultural College, Cirencester, the first institution providing specialist courses.
1846	Improved techniques led to the lowering of drainage schemes.
1856	Agricultural engineer John Fowler patented ploughing with two traction engines.

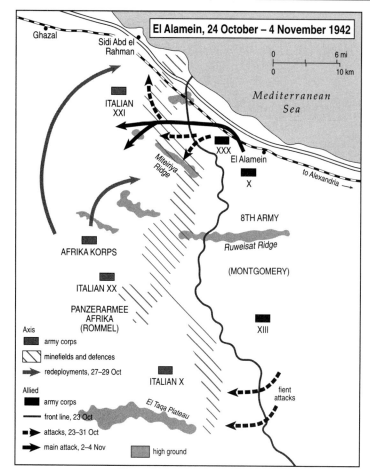

El Alamein, 24 October – 4 November 1942

Ghazal
Sidi Abd el Rahman

Mediterranean Sea

ITALIAN XXI

Miteiriya Ridge

XXX
El Alamein

to Alexandria

X

8TH ARMY

Ruweisat Ridge

AFRIKA KORPS

(MONTGOMERY)

ITALIAN XX

PANZERARMEE AFRIKA (ROMMEL)

XIII

Axis
- army corps
- minefields and defences
- redeployments, 27–29 Oct

Allied
- army corps
- front line, 23 Oct
- attacks, 23–31 Oct
- main attack, 2–4 Nov

ITALIAN X

El Taqa Plateau

fient attacks

high ground

El Alamein, 24 October – 4 November 1942
The second Battle of El Alamein was a grim struggle in which the 8th Army's numerical superiority, particularly in armour, was the decisive factor. The X Corps attack north of Miteiriya Ridge finally exhausted Rommel's armoured reserves, and the Panzerarmee Afrika never again regained the strategic initiative.

The ***first battle*** was inconclusive but strategically vital: Rommel attacked the British line in a series of engagements, but Auchinleck kept him at bay. Neither side can be said to have won, but the British had the strategic advantage of short supply lines and so could reinforce faster than the Germans.

Montgomery began the ***second battle*** with a diversionary attack in the south to draw Axis forces into the area so that the main attack in the north could create a gap for the British armoured divisions to pass through German minefields. Progress was slow however and Montgomery changed tactics, constantly switching the main emphasis of his attack to wear down Rommel's front line. The decisive phase of the battle came with an Australian attack along the coastal road 26 Oct which diverted Axis forces while Montgomery launched a fresh attack further south which developed into a major tank battle. By 3 Nov Rommel had only 30 serviceable tanks in action and on the following day began organizing his withdrawal. He was able to escape, as the British were hampered by heavy rain and a shortage of fuel, but this was a crushing blow for the Axis campaign in North Africa.

Albany Robert Stewart, 1st Duke of *c.*1340–1420. Scottish noble and governor of Scotland 1402–20. His brother, Robert III of Scotland, was an invalid and so deemed unable to rule. Albany vied with Robert's elder son, David, Duke of Rothesay, for dominance and became de facto ruler after Rothesay's disgrace and death 1402. He increased his power after the capture by the English of Robert's second son, the future James I, and Robert's subsequent death 1406, ruling as governor of Scotland until his death 1420 when he was succeeded by his son, Murdoch.

Albany Alexander Stewart, 3rd Duke of Albany *c.*1454–1485. A son of James II of Scotland, he usurped the throne of Scotland with English help. He was arrested by his brother, King James III, 1479 but escaped to England and was recognized as king of Scotland June 1482 by the English king Edward IV who invaded in support of his claim. In return he acknowledged English suzerainty over Scotland and did so when he again held the throne 1484. He was forced to flee to France where he died.

Albany John Stewart, 4th Duke of Albany 1484–1536. Son of Alexander, 3rd Duke of Albany, he was made regent for the infant king James V 1514 acting as an agent for the French king Francis I. He fled to France 1517 where he was detained for a time under an agreement with the English but was allowed to return to Scotland when the English declared war on France and Scotland 1521. He led two invasions of England 1522 and 1523, but was finally forced to leave Scotland for France May 1524.

Albert, Prince Consort 1819–1861. Husband of British queen ◊Victoria from 1840; a patron of the arts, science, and industry. Albert was the second son of Ernst I, the Duke of Saxe Coburg-Gotha, and first cousin to Queen Victoria. He married Queen Victoria 1840 and became in effect her chief adviser, although he was regarded with groundless suspicion by the British people because of his German connections, a factor which limited his political influence. He was given the title of Prince Consort 1857 and his early death from typhoid 1861 led Victoria to withdraw from public life for 10 years.

Much of his energy went into social and artistic projects. He planned the Great Exhibition of 1851, the profits of which were used to buy the sites in London of all the South Kensington museums and colleges and the Royal Albert Hall, built 1871. The **Albert Memorial** 1872, designed by Sir Gilbert Scott, in Kensington Gardens, London, typifies Victorian decorative art. Albert is also remembered for popularizing the Christmas tree in Britain.

Albion ancient name for Britain used by the Greeks and Romans. It was mentioned by Pytheas of Massilia (4th century BC), and is probably of Celtic origin, but the Romans, thinking of the white cliffs of Dover, assumed it to be derived from *albus* (white).

Alcock John William 1892–1919. British aviator. On 14 June 1919, he and Arthur Whitten Brown (1886–1948) made the first nonstop transatlantic flight, from Newfoundland to Ireland in a Vickers-Vimy biplane. They completed the trip in $16\frac{1}{2}$ hrs. Alcock died after an aeroplane accident in the same year.

Alcuin (Flaccus Albinus Alcuinus) 735–804. English scholar. Born in York, he became master of the cathedral school 778 but left to go to Rome 780. At Charlemagne's request, he moved to his court in Aachen 782. From 796 he was abbot of Tours. He disseminated Anglo-Saxon scholarship, organized education and learning in the Frankish empire, gave a strong impulse to the Carolingian Renaissance, and produced the standard medieval version of the Bible.

alderman (Old English *ealdor mann* 'older man') Anglo-Saxon term for the noble governor of a shire (see ◊ealdorman); after the Norman Conquest the office was replaced with that of sheriff. From the 19th century aldermen were the senior members of the borough or county councils in England and Wales, elected by the other councillors, until the abolition of the office 1974; the title is still used in the City of London, and for members of a municipal corporation in certain towns in the USA.

Alexander three kings of Scotland:

Alexander I *c*.1078–1124. King of Scotland from 1107, known as **the Fierce**. He ruled to the north of the rivers Forth and Clyde while his brother and successor David ruled to the south. He was married to Sybilla, an illegitimate daughter of Henry I of England whom he assisted in his campaign against Wales 1114. He was notably religious, defending the independence of the church in Scotland and founding several monasteries, including the abbeys of Inchcolm and Scone.

Alexander II 1198–1249. King of Scotland from 1214, when he succeeded his father William the Lion. Alexander supported the English barons in their struggle with King John after ◊Magna Carta, hoping to claim the three northern counties of England. He gave up this claim in the treaty of York 1237 and by the treaty of Newcastle 1244 he pledged allegiance to Henry III of England. In the 1240s he concentrated on consolidating his power in the north and west of Scotland and died on an expedition to win the Western Isles from Norway.

Alexander II
The great seal of King Alexander II of Scotland. Much of his reign (1214–49) was spent trying to free his country from the Vikings. He died on the eve of a military campaign to drive them out of the Hebrides.
Hulton Deutsch

Alexander III 1241–1285. King of Scotland from 1249, son of Alexander II. In 1263, he defeated the Norwegians at the battle of Largs and extended his authority over the Western Isles, which had been dependent on Norway. He gained the Hebrides and the Isle of Man under the treaty of Perth 1266 and the rest of his reign was reputedly a period of peace and stability in which he did much to strengthen his power as a central Scottish ruler.

He died as the result of a fall from his horse, leaving his granddaughter Margaret, the Maid of Norway, to become queen of Scotland.

Alexander Harold Rupert Leofric George, 1st Earl Alexander of Tunis 1891–1969. British field marshal, a commander in World War II in France, Burma (now Myanmar), North

The voice of the people is the voice of God.
Vox populi, vox dei.

ALCUIN
letter to the Emperor Charlemagne,
AD 800

Africa, and the Mediterranean. He was governor general of Canada 1946–52 and UK minister of defence 1952–54.

Third son of the 4th Earl of Caledon, he was commissioned in the Irish Guards and served in World War I. In World War II he commanded the 1st Division in France 1939 and was the last person to leave in the evacuation of ◊Dunkirk 1940. In Burma 1942 he fought a delaying action for five months against superior Japanese forces. In Aug 1942 he went to North Africa as commander in chief, Middle East, and defeated the Axis forces in Egypt, Libya and Tunisia 1943. After the fall of Rome 1944, Alexander became supreme Allied commander in the Mediterranean, and later a field marshal.

Alexander Sir William, 1st Earl of Stirling c.1576–1640. Scottish soldier, poet and courtesan. In the 1620s he led unsuccessful attempts to establish a Scottish colony in Nova Scotia. He was Scottish secretary to Charles I 1626–40 and was made an earl 1633. His poetry includes the sonnets collected in *Aurora* 1604.

Alfred *the Great* c.848–c.900. King of Wessex from 871. He defended England against Danish invasion, founded the first English navy, and put into operation a legal code, the 'Dooms' of Alfred. He encouraged the translation of works from Latin (some he translated himself), and promoted the development of the ◊*Anglo-Saxon Chronicle*.

Alfred was born at Wantage, Oxfordshire, the youngest son of Ethelwulf (died 858), king of the West Saxons. In 870 Alfred and his brother Ethelred fought many battles against the Danes. He gained a victory over the Danes at Ashdown 871, and succeeded Ethelred as king April 871 after a series of defeats. Five years of uneasy peace followed while the Danes were occupied in other parts of England. The Danes attacked again 876, and in 878 Alfred was forced to retire to the stronghold of ◊Athelney, from where he finally emerged to win the victory of Edington, Wiltshire. By the Peace of Wedmore 878 the Danish leader Guthrum (died 890) agreed to withdraw from Wessex and from Mercia west of Watling Street. A new landing in Kent encouraged a revolt of the East Anglian Danes, which was suppressed 884–86, and after the final foreign invasion was defeated 892–96, Alfred strengthened the navy and the fortification of Wessex to prevent fresh incursions. His court at Wessex was famed for its learning and his reign was chronicled by his tutor, the Welsh monk Asser.

The tale that Alfred burned the cakes he was supposed to be watching while they baked is apocryphal and is first recorded in the 11th century.

Aliens Act legislation passed by the Conservative government 1905 to restrict the immigration of 'undesirable persons' into Britain; it was aimed at restricting Jewish immigration.

Undesirable persons were defined as people who might be a charge on the poor rates because they were without means or infirm. Since the act appeared to be stimulated by the arrival of large numbers of impoverished Europeans, many of them Jews from the Russian Empire, Prime Minister Balfour was accused of anti-Semitism.

All the Talents, Ministry of coalition 1806–07 formed after Pitt the Younger's death to abolish the slave trade. Although the coalition was predominantly Whig – with William Wyndham, Lord Grenville, as prime minister and Charles James Fox as foreign secretary – some conservatives were also represented. Wilberforce's bill outlawing the slave trade in the British empire was passed 1807 but the coalition's conduct of the Napoleonic Wars was not a success. The coalition broke up March 1807 over Grenville's refusal to permit Catholics to become officers in the army.

Allenby Edmund Henry Hynman, 1st Viscount Allenby 1861–1936. British field marshal. In World War I he served in France before taking command 1917–19 of the British forces in the Middle East. In his campaign against the Turks he captured Jerusalem 1917 then drove the Turkish army through Syria before securing the armistice of Mudros Sept 1918. He was made a viscount 1919 and served as high commissioner in Egypt 1919–35.

Alliance, the loose union 1981–87 formed by the ◊Liberal Party and ◊Social Democratic Party (SDP) for electoral purposes.

Allies, the in World War I, the 23 countries allied against the Central Powers (Germany, Austria-Hungary, Turkey, and Bulgaria), including France, Italy, Russia, the UK, Australia and other Commonwealth nations, and, in the latter part of the war, the USA; and in World War II, the 49 countries allied against the ◊Axis Powers (Germany, Italy, and Japan), including France, the UK, Australia and other Commonwealth nations, the USA, and the USSR. In the

Many Franks, Gauls, Pagans, Britons, Scots, and Armoricans, nobles and poor men alike, submitted voluntarily to his dominion; all of whom he ruled, loved, honoured and enriched as if they were his own people.

ALFRED THE GREAT
Anglo-Saxon chronicler
Asser, Life of Alfred
c. 900

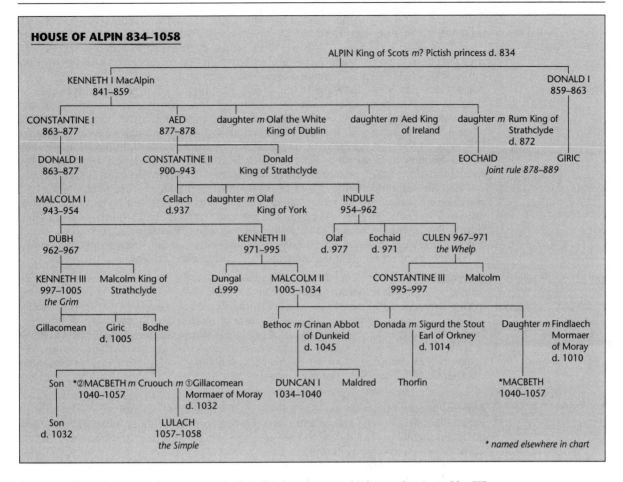

HOUSE OF ALPIN 834–1058

1991 Gulf War, there were 28 countries in the Allied coalition, which was dominated by US forces, but Britain and France were also prominent.

almshouse private institution providing shelter to the poor or indigent, often founded and endowed by wealthy individuals as institutionalized fulfilment of a religious duty to give charity. (See also ◊poor laws).

Alpin, House of the first identifiable royal house of Scotland, c.841–1034. ◊Kenneth I MacAlpin, son of a chieftain of the (Irish) Scots of Dalriada, married a Pictish princess early in the 830s. The unified kingdom of Picts and Scots was known as Scotia or Alba. During the reign of the Alpins the Pictish culture was entirely assimilated, the kingdom of the Strathclyde Britons destroyed, and under the last Alpin king, Malcolm II, the southern frontier of Scotia was established near the modern English–Scots border. The kingdom withstood extensive Scandinavian incursions in the north and west throughout the period.

Ambrosius Aurelianus 5th century. Romano-British military leader. He led the resistance of the British against the Saxons and it may have been him who led them to a significant military victory at the Battle of ◊Mons Badonicus. He belonged to a prominent Romano-British family and in the Welsh tradition is known as Emrys (a form of Ambrosius).

American Revolution also known as the *American War of Independence* revolt 1775–83 of the British North American colonies, resulting in the establishment of the United States of America. It was caused by colonial opposition to British economic exploitation and by the unwillingness of the colonists to pay for a standing army. It was also fuelled by the colonists' antimonarchist sentiment and a desire to participate in the policies affecting them.

Resentment had been growing in the American colonies from 1763 onward as a result of high-handed British legislation, like the ◊Stamp Act 1765, which levied a tax on all official

If I were an American, as I am an Englishman, while a foreign troop was landed in my country I would never lay down my arms – never, never, never!

AMERICAN
REVOLUTION
*Pitt the Elder, speech in
House of Commons,
1777*

documents, and the Townshend Acts 1767 which imposed taxes on various goods including tea. The first casualties occurred in the Boston Massacre 1770 when British troops opened fire on protesters. In the Boston Tea Party 1773, protesters disguised as Indians emptied 342 chests of cheap imported tea into the harbour, to which Britain responded with the punitive Intolerable Acts 1774. In 1775 fighting broke out at Lexington and Concord and in the same year the Americans invaded Canada and George Washington was appointed commander in chief of the American forces. The Declaration of Independence was issued 1776 but Washington's troops suffered a series of defeats at the hands of General Howe. The turning point in the war came with the decisive American victory at the Battle of Saratoga Springs 1777 which prompted the French to enter the war on the American side. American military success culminated in British defeat and surrender at Yorktown 1781. The defeat forced the resignation of the British prime minister, Lord ◊North, one of the war's main advocates.

Under the Peace of Versailles 3 Sept 1783 Britain recognized the independence of the USA and in return was allowed to retain Canada and recovered its West Indian territories; France recovered St. Lucia, Tobago, Senegal, and Goree; and Spain retained Minorca and recovered Florida. During the war many British politicians, including ◊Shelburne and ◊Fox, had sought conciliation rather than war with the colonists. The success of the American Revolution had an enormous impact on the spread of democratic and republican ideas.

Amiens, battles of series of battles in World War I around a city in northeast France at the confluence of the rivers Somme and Avre. An important rail junction, Amiens was occupied by the German army for several days before the battle of the ◊Marne Sept 1914 but thereafter remained in French hands and became the hub of military communications in northern France. The German Spring Offensive 1918 brought it within the sound of gunfire and it was in some danger for several weeks, during which the main railway line to Paris was cut. The danger was finally lifted when British field marshal Douglas Haig launched his victorious counteroffensive Aug 1918. The town was awarded the *Croix de Guerre* after the end of the war.

Amiens, peace of treaty signed March 1802 which ended the Revolutionary Wars, a series of wars 1791–1802 between France and the combined armies of Britain, Austria, Prussia, and other continental powers, during the period of the French Revolution and Napoleon's subsequent campaign to conquer Europe.

Under the terms of the treaty Britain was to restore all maritime conquests, except Trinidad and Ceylon, to France, Spain, and Holland; France agreed to evacuate Naples; the integrity of Portugal was recognized; the independence of the Ionian Islands was agreed upon; both French and British armies evacuated Egypt which was restored to Turkey; and Malta was similarly restored to the Knights of Malta.

Amritsar Massacre also called *Jallianwallah Bagh massacre* the killing of 379 Indians (and wounding of 1,200) in Amritsar, at the site of a Sikh religious shrine in the Punjab 1919. British troops under General Edward Dyer (1864–1927) opened fire without warning on a crowd of some 10,000, assembled to protest against the arrest of two Indian National Congress leaders. A government enquiry subsequently censured Dyer and he was forced to resign his commission. However, he won popular support in the UK for his action, spurring Mahatma ◊Gandhi to a policy of active noncooperation with the British.

Anabaptist (Greek 'baptize again') member of any of various 16th-century radical Protestant sects. They believed in adult rather than child baptism, and sought to establish utopian communities. Anabaptist groups spread rapidly in northern Europe, particularly in Germany, and were widely persecuted.

Anderson Elizabeth Garrett 1836–1917. The first English woman to qualify in medicine. Refused entry into medical school, Anderson studied privately and was licensed by the Society of Apothecaries in London 1865. She was physician to the Marylebone Dispensary for Women and Children (later renamed the Elizabeth Garrett Anderson Hospital), a London hospital now staffed by women and serving women patients, and helped found the London School of Medicine.

She supported her sister Millicent ◊Fawcett in the campaign for female suffrage and was the first woman member of the British Medical Association and the first woman mayor in Britain.

THE DEVIL'S BROOD

The Angevin Kings and their Empire

A notable feature of much of medieval Europe was the weakness of royal authority. Effective government often lay in the hands of counts, dukes, or even knights. Their territories could pass from family to family by marriage, inheritance, or warfare, and large, diverse territories could thus be accumulated. Between 1066 and 1205, England's history was shaped by just such a process. From 1066 the kings of England, as dukes of Normandy, were also feudal vassals of the king of France, and in 1154 England was drawn into a new grouping of territories whose heartland lay in Anjou in western France. These territories have been known since the 19th century as the Angevin Empire ('Angevin' being derived from 'Anjou'). At its greatest extent, the Empire reached from the River Tweed in northern England to the Pyrenees in southern France. The relatively brief lengths of time spent by Henry II and Richard I in their English lands suggest that ideologically at least the Angevin Empire was at heart a French, not English, territorial grouping. Moreover, its 50-year history shows that it was a grouping prone to instability, from many sources.

The making of an empire

The Angevin Empire came into being in 1150–54, through a combination of war, inheritance and marriage centred on Henry of Anjou (born 1133). Warfare should have been unnecessary: Henry should have inherited Anjou from his father, Geoffrey, count of Anjou, and England and Normandy from his mother, Matilda, the daughter and designated successor of Henry I, king of England and duke of Normandy. But his eventual succession to Normandy and England was blocked by his nephew Stephen of Blois, who seized England and Normandy when Henry I died in 1135. Matilda had to fight for both her own and Henry's inheritance.

The first Angevin success was in Normandy, which Geoffrey conquered in 1144. He was invested as duke, and was succeeded by Henry in 1150. In 1151, on Geoffrey's death, Henry succeeded as count of Anjou. The following year he married Eleanor of Aquitaine, thereby adding southwest France to his lands. Henry then renewed his efforts to secure England: he landed in England in January 1154 and forced King Stephen to accept him as heir. Stephen died in October 1154, and Henry was crowned on 19 December.

Henry's empire remained a loose group of individual territories. He improved the management of his personal estates, but made no attempt to introduce common institutions. He respected the traditions of each territory, encouraging development separately within each. Hence it happened that a French king of England, whose territories were centred on Anjou, presided over the development of English common law and improvements in English royal government.

Disunity and disaster

The empire's integrity was threatened by disputes in a ruling family popularly regarded as diabolical, discontented feudal subordinates, and the king of France. All three factors caused trouble in the period 1173–74. In 1173, Henry gave three castles in Anjou to his youngest son John as part of a marriage settlement. His eldest son, Henry, objected, demanding a part of his own inheritance. When his father refused, he fled to King Louis VII of France. They organized invasions of Normandy, northern England, and eastern England, and a revolt broke out in Anjou. King Henry managed to suppress the revolt and defeat the invasion of Normandy, while his magnates in England successfully fought off the invasions there. The following year, two invasions of England were defeated. Henry faced a similar revolt in 1189, when his discontented second son and now heir Richard joined the king of France, now Philip II (Philip Augustus). Henry died while defeating the new revolt.

Henry was succeeded by his son, Richard I (the Lion-Heart). As ruler of the Angevin lands, Richard faced similar problems to his father. In 1193, while he was being held captive in Germany when returning from Crusade, his brother John attempted to seize the English throne and in 1194 ceded part of Normandy to Philip II. Ransomed at great expense, Richard hurried back to England and then spent the years until his death in 1199 recovering most of the lost Norman lands.

The disintegration of the Angevin Empire began at Richard's death. Anjou and Maine rejected John as ruler and instead recognized John's nephew Arthur of Brittany. John circumvented this, in 1200, by doing homage to Philip for his French territories. But he thereby affirmed his dependent position on the king of France. Within two years, Philip had declared John's French territories forfeit and invaded Normandy. John's forces were quickly defeated.

By 1205, John was left, in France, with just part of Aquitaine. With the loss of the French lands, England reverted from being a peripheral part of a French-based empire to the central base from which future royal ambitions would have to be launched.

ROBERT PEBERDY

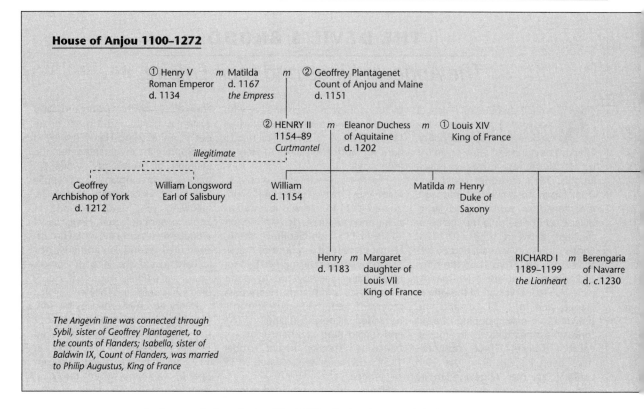

House of Anjou 1100–1272

① Henry V *m* Matilda *m* ② Geoffrey Plantagenet
Roman Emperor d. 1167 Count of Anjou and Maine
d. 1134 *the Empress* d. 1151

② HENRY II *m* Eleanor Duchess *m* ① Louis XIV
1154–89 of Aquitaine King of France
Curtmantel d. 1202

illegitimate

Geoffrey William Longsword William Matilda *m* Henry
Archbishop of York Earl of Salisbury d. 1154 Duke of
d. 1212 Saxony

Henry *m* Margaret RICHARD I *m* Berengaria
d. 1183 daughter of 1189–1199 of Navarre
Louis VII *the Lionheart* d. *c.*1230
King of France

*The Angevin line was connected through
Sybil, sister of Geoffrey Plantagenet, to
the counts of Flanders; Isabella, sister of
Baldwin IX, Count of Flanders, was married
to Philip Augustus, King of France*

Anderson shelter during World War II, simple air raid shelter comprising an arched piece of corrugated metal partly buried in domestic gardens and covered with earth for added protection. It was named after Sir John Anderson, home secretary 1939–40.

Andrew, St New Testament apostle. A native of Bethsaida, he was Simon Peter's brother. With Peter, James, and John, who worked with him as fishers at Capernaum, he formed the inner circle of Jesus' 12 disciples. According to tradition, he went with John to Ephesus, preached in Scythia, and was martyred at Patras on an X-shaped cross (***St Andrew's cross***) which became his symbol.

According to legend, several of his relics were brought to Scotland in the 4th century by Rule, a native of Patras. They were supposedly deposited at a site in Fife which was subsequently named St Andrews. He is the patron saint of Scotland and his cross, in white on a blue background, is the central component of the Scottish flag. Feast day 30 Nov.

angel English gold coin introduced 1465, named after the image of the Archangel Michael embossed on the face. They were worth 6 shillings and 8 pence, and half-angels were minted into the 17th century.

Angevin relating to the reigns of the English kings Henry II, Richard I, and John (also known, with the later English kings up to Richard III, as the ***Plantagenets***). The name Angevin derives from Anjou, a region in northern France as Henry II was the son of Geoffrey Plantagenet, Count of Anjou. The ***Angevin Empire*** comprised the territories (including England) that belonged to the Anjou dynasty and John is generally considered the last Angevin king, as it was during his reign that most of the Angevin territories were lost.

Angle member of the Germanic tribe that invaded Britain in the 5th century along with the Saxons and the Jutes; see ◊Anglo-Saxon. The Angles settled mainly in the north and east of England and eventually gave their name to the whole of the country ('Angle-land').

Anglesey Henry William Paget, 1st Marquis of 1768–1854. English field marshal. He commanded the British cavalry during the Napoleonic Wars. He was twice Lord Lieutenant of

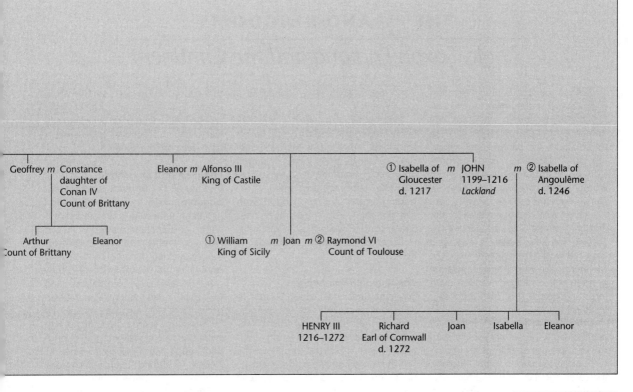

Geoffrey *m* Constance
daughter of
Conan IV
Count of Brittany

Eleanor *m* Alfonso III
King of Castile

① Isabella of *m* JOHN   *m* ② Isabella of
Gloucester   1199–1216   Angoulême
d. 1217   *Lackland*   d. 1246

Arthur   Eleanor
Count of Brittany

① William   *m* Joan *m* ② Raymond VI
King of Sicily   Count of Toulouse

HENRY III   Richard   Joan   Isabella   Eleanor
1216–1272   Earl of Cornwall
                 d. 1272

Ireland, and succeeded his father as Earl of Uxbridge 1812. At the Battle of Waterloo he led an unsuccessful charge in which he lost a leg.

Anglo-American War war between the USA and Britain 1812–1814; see ◊War of 1812.

Anglo-Catholicism the 'high church' wing of the Anglican Church, which stresses the Catholic heritage of faith and liturgical practice. The term was first used 1838 to describe the ◊Oxford Movement, which began in the wake of pressure from the more Protestant wing of the Church of England. Since the Church of England voted 1992 to ordain women as priests, some Anglo-Catholics have found it difficult to remain within the Church of England.

Anglo-Dutch Wars series of conflicts between Britain and the Netherlands in the period 1650–75. There was continual tension between the two countries for much of the 17th century arising from their rivalry for the same trade markets.

  First Anglo-Dutch War (1652–54), the war was sparked by the Navigation Act Oct 1651 which restricted the import of foreign goods into Britain to British vessels or vessels of the country of origin of the goods. The Act was aimed at minimizing the role of the Netherlands in maritime trade. Hostilities broke out at the Battle of Downs, off Folkstone, May 1652, although war was not formally declared until the start of July. The British won several victories, notably at the Battle of ◊Texel 1653 and the war was ended by the Treaty of Westminster April 1654. The Dutch agreed to accept the Navigation Act and also made several other concessions, including payment for fishing in British waters and compensation for the Dutch massacre of British settlers on Amboina in the East Indies 1623.

  Second Anglo-Dutch War (1665–67) again caused by commercial rivalry, but in the colonies rather than domestic markets. Hostilities in Africa June 1664 led to the loss of British forts on the Gold Coast but in Aug the British annexed the New Netherlands (Dutch colonies in North America) from Connecticut to Delaware, and renamed New Amsterdam as New York. War was formally declared Feb 1665 after the Dutch captured a Swedish ship laden with masts en route to Britain in the Straits of Dover. The French declared for the Dutch 1666 and this, combined with financial difficulties forced Charles II to open negotia-

Becoming an Anglo-Catholic must surely be a sad business – rather like becoming an amateur conjurer.

ANGLO-CATHOLICISM
John Strachey, The Coming Struggle for Power....

Our business is to break with them and yet to lay the breache [sic] at their door.

ANGLO-DUTCH WARS
Earl of Arlington, describing British diplomacy on the eve of the Third Dutch War, 1672 (attributed)

THE ISLAND KINGDOMS
Anglo-Saxon England and the Continent

In the 5th century, invaders and settlers from north Germany turned most of the Roman province of Britannia into an Anglo-Saxon and pagan zone, enslaving and expelling many Britons (though sometimes marrying British women). New concentrations of political power emerged, some with connections well beyond the former Roman province. The occupant of the Sutton Hoo ship burial, c. 630, had amassed wealth from Scandinavia, the Mediterranean world, and Francia: he perhaps acknowledged Frankish overlordship, despite his own imposing insignia.

Other Continental influences resulted from the sending of Christian missionaries by Pope Gregory I in 597. Christianity offered kings literacy, increased social control, and territorial organization. The first Anglo-Saxon royal convert, Ethelbert of Kent, was also the first Anglo-Saxon king to issue a law-code, imitating Roman models. Charismatic holy men like Cuthbert (d. 687), founder of the church of Lindisfarne off the Northumbrian coast, had universal appeal. In the late 7th-century Lindisfarne Gospels, diverse artistic influences were wonderfully blended, reflecting cultural contacts with wider worlds. Bede's *Ecclesiastical History of the English People* (completed in 731, also in Northumbria) embodied the idea of an English identity.

The reality was of several independent kingdoms, all prey to succession disputes and the hostility of their neighbours. Northumbrian power yielded to the Midlands kingdom of Mercia, whose warlike kings overawed their contemporaries. Offa (757–96) dealt especially harshly with Kent. His reach also extended far afield. He sent money-payments to the pope in return for church privileges. Offa even sought, unsuccessfully, the daughter of the Frankish ruler Charlemagne as a bride for his son. He shed much blood to secure his son's succession, but the son's death, soon after, unleashed a Kentish revolt.

In the 9th century, Wessex, the dark horse among the leading Anglo-Saxon kingdoms, emerged as Mercia's chief rival. Wessex's advantages included flourishing Continental connections. Hamwih (Southampton) was a great trading-centre; another, London, with a major mint, also came under West Saxon control, while West Saxon kings replaced Mercians as overlords of Kent.

The Scandinavian impact

Scandinavians attacked Lindisfarne in 793, but such raids were sporadic until the mid-9th century, when Scandinavian warlords, redirecting their attention from Francia, turned on the British Isles. A *micel here* ('great army') of heathen Danes led by several 'kings' landed in East Anglia 865. Within nine years, sections of the *here* had attacked and taken over the kingdoms of Northumbria and East Anglia, killing their kings, and won control of much of Mercia, driving its ruler overseas.

Alfred, king of Wessex (871–99), exploited this situation. He gained overlordship of southwest Mercia, as well as London and the Thames valley, securing a Danish truce. He then built up a defensive system of fortified burghs, and mounted a vigorous ideological offensive on the hearts and minds of other Anglo-Saxons. He stressed his personal links with the papacy and engaged in prestigious gift-exchange with successive popes. He issued a law-code, borrowing from the Franks (and ultimately from the Romans) the idea of treason, with capital punishment for traitors. Adopting Bede's notion of one English people, and offering rewards for loyalty, Alfred persuaded the aristocracies of the old kingdoms south of the Humber to acknowledge his rule. He avoided conflict within the royal family and arranged his daughter's marriage to the count of Flanders. In the 890s, renewed Scandinavian attacks were repelled. Alfred has been overrated as a war leader: his political achievements have been underestimated.

Conquest and unification

By 954, all the formerly independent kingdoms under Scandinavian control had been subjected to Wessex's domination and England existed in fact as well as theory. Alfred's successors mostly avoided dynastic conflict, they cajoled and browbeat aristocrats, they were indefatigable legislators, and they maintained friendly relations with popes and foreign potentates. By 10th-century standards, England was an exceptionally well-integrated kingdom under strong central rule, its wealth, including church resources, tapped by royal government.

These traits made it the magnet of a new phase of Danish attacks, now on a much larger scale. That King Ethelred II 'the Unready' sustained English resistance for over twenty years was a remarkable feat. Canute's eventual conquest in 1017 was of one single, unified kingdom. His regime imitated those of his English predecessors: he maintained Ethelred's Norman alliance and married Ethelred's widow Emma, sister of the count of Normandy and descendant of Scandinavian settlers in northern Francia.

Ethelred's son (and Emma's stepson) Edward had sought refuge in Normandy in 1016. When Canute's descent-line failed in 1042, Edward returned to England to become king. His later saintly reputation (whence his nickname, 'the Confessor') masked his failure to engender a son. The succession dispute of 1066 pitted his brother-in-law Harold against his erstwhile patron William of Normandy. The prize was a kingdom whose unity owed much to long contact with the political and cultural worlds of Continental Europe.

JANET L NELSON

Anglo-Saxon England: chronology

from c. 430	Germanic migrants arrived in east and southeast England. The main groups were: Jutes from the Jutland Peninsula (modern Denmark); Angles from Angeln in southwest Jutland; Saxons from northwest Germany.
c.450–600	Expansion of the area settled by Anglo-Saxons and emergence of several large kingdoms: Kent; Sussex (south Saxons); Wessex (west Saxons); Essex (east Saxons); East Anglia; Mercia (based in the west Midlands); and Deira (Yorkshire) and Bernicia (Durham, Northumberland and southeast Scotland), sometimes combining as Northumbria.
597	Arrival of St Augustine in Kent, sent by Pope Gregory the Great. King Ethelbert of Kent accepted Christianity.
601	Augustine enthroned as first archbishop of Canterbury.
627	King Edwin of Northumbria and his court accepted Christianity from St Paulinus, but in 632 his successor, Osric, apostasized.
633	King Oswald of Northumbria requested a Christian missionary from the Celtic Catholic monastery of Iona, off west Scotland. Aidan was sent, who established a monastery and bishop's see on Lindisfarne 635.
635	King Cynegils of Wessex was converted to Christianity and baptized.
642	King Oswald of Northumbria killed at Oswestry by the pagan King Penda of Mercia.
653	Penda allowed his son Peada to be baptized a Christian.
655	Penda of Mercia killed by King Oswy of Northumbria at the Battle of Winwaed.
664	Dispute over the time of Easter settled at the Synod of Whitby, which preferred the modern Catholic practice to the older practice maintained by the Celtic Church.
668–90	Theodore of Tarsus served as archbishop of Canterbury; he created new sees and improved Church discipline.
685–8	King Caedwalla absorbed Sussex, Surrey, and Kent into the kingdom of Wessex.
690	Northumbrian missionaries landed in Frisia, including Willibrord who became archbishop of Frisia 695.
716–57	King Ethelbald expanded Mercia rule over much of southern England.
718–54	Mission of Boniface of Wessex to the Frisians, Germans, and Franks, ending with martyrdom.
731	The Northumbrian monk Bede completed his *Ecclesiastical History of the English People*.
757–96	Reign of Offa, king of Mercia, who issued silver pennies, corresponded with Charlemagne, and tried to make Lichfield an archbishopric.
793–5	First recorded Viking raids on Britain. Vikings attacked monasteries at Lindisfarne, Jarrow, and Iona.

---

tions for peace. In June 1667, the Dutch fleet under Admiral de Ruyter burned Sheerness, sailed up the River Medway, raided Chatham dockyard, and towed away the British flagship the *Royal Charles*. There was widespread panic in Britain at this sign of vulnerability and the peace of Breda was concluded the following month. The Dutch were able to minimize British demands, retaining the island of Pulo Run, but were forced to acknowledge the loss of the American colonies, New York, Delaware, and New Jersey.

Third Anglo-Dutch War 1672–74. The British declared war on the Dutch March 1672 at the instigation of Louis XIV in accordance with the terms of the secret Treaty of ◊Dover 1670, and attacked Dutch vessels in the Atlantic and the North Sea. The Great Elector of Brandenburg concluded an alliance with the Dutch in May, forming the First Coalition against France. There were a series of indecisive naval battles in the Channel and the North Sea 1672 and the Dutch held off an Anglo-French invasion 1673, as well as recapturing New York from the British Aug 1673. The First Coalition collapsed June 1673 when the Great Elector concluded the Peace of Vossem with France, but the Dutch were then joined by Leopold I and Spain. Britain withdrew from the war Feb 1674 by the Treaty of Westminster, under which the Dutch recognized New York as British, but the war continued as a coalition effort against France.

Anglo-Irish Agreement or **Hillsborough Agreement** concord reached 1985 between the then UK premier Margaret Thatcher and Irish premier Garret FitzGerald. A consequence of the improved relations between the two countries was increased cooperation between police and security forces across the border with Northern Ireland. The pact also gave the Irish Republic a greater say in the affairs of Northern Ireland. However, the agreement was rejected by Northern Ireland Unionists as a step toward the renunciation of British sovereignty.

Kingdoms in Britain and Ireland c. AD 600
The Anglo-Saxon conquest of Britain was a slow process. By AD 600 the invaders were firmly established in the southeast, the Midlands, and the northeast of England, but Wales, Scotland, and the southwest remained in the hands of the Celts, Picts, or British inheritors of Roman Britain. The small British kingdom of Elmet still separated the Northumbrian kingdoms of Bernicia and Deira from the rest of Anglo-Saxon England.

Kingdoms in Britain and Ireland c. AD 600

DEIRA Anglo-Saxon kingdom
ELMET Celtic or British kingdom

They came from three very powerful nations of the Germans: that is, from the Saxones, Angli, and Iutae.

ANGLO-SAXON
Bede Ecclesiastical History of the English People, *early 8th century.*

Following further talks 1988, the UK premier John Major and the Irish premier Albert Reynolds issued a joint statement 1993, the so called Downing Street Declaration, setting out principles for a settlement in Northern Ireland.

The statement did not envisage any particular outcome, but specified that the consent of the majority of the people of Northern Ireland was required before there could be any constitutional change. Following the IRA's announcement of a ceasefire 1994, John Major said the outcome of any talks between the Northern Ireland political parties would be put to the people there in a referendum. He added that the government could move toward the beginning of dialogue with Sinn Féin. Exploratory talks between the two sides were held 1995.

Anglo-Saxon one of the several Germanic invaders (Angles, Saxons and Jutes) who conquered much of Britain between the 5th and 7th centuries. They set up seven kingdoms, commonly known as the ◊Heptarchy, and these were united in the early 9th century under the overlordship of Wessex. The Norman conquest 1066 brought the Anglo-Saxon rule to an end.

The Jutes probably came from the Rhineland rather than Jutland, as formerly believed. The Angles and Saxons came from Schleswig-Holstein, and may have united before the invasion. The Angles settled largely in East Anglia, Mercia and Northumbria; the Saxons in Essex, Sussex and Wessex; and the Jutes in Kent and southern Hampshire. The invaded country could have been named after any of the three tribes, but in the event it was the Angles who gave the name of England. There was probably intermarriage with the Romanized Celts of ancient Britain, although the latter's language and civilization virtually disappeared.

Anglo-Saxon Chronicle history of England from the Roman invasion to 1154, in the form of a series of chronicles written in Old English by monks. It was begun in the 9th century, during the reign of King Alfred, and continued to the 12th century. The Chronicle survives in seven manuscripts arranged by historians in four groups: the Parker Chronicle, named after Archbishop Parker (1504–75); the Abingdon Chronicles; the Worcester Chronicle; and the Laud Chronicle, named after Archbishop Laud (1573–1645). The most important and most detailed are the Parker and Laud Chronicles. It forms a unique annalistic record of early English history and of the development of Old English prose up to its final stages in the year 1154, by which date it had been superseded by Middle English.

Anglo-Scottish wars series of conflicts between England and Scotland 1293–1346. The wars began when John Balliol, the reigning Scots king, renounced his allegiance to Edward I of England 1295. Edward defeated the Scots at Dunbar 1296 and assumed sovereignty over Scotland. Sir William Wallace led a rebellion against English rule 1297 but this was crushed by 1303. The struggle for independence was revived by Robert the Bruce, whose forces inflicted a decisive defeat on Edward II at the Battle of ◊Bannockburn 1314. Edward III recognized the independence of Scotland on his accession 1328, but resumed hostilities against the Scots in the 1340s. He was subsequently diverted by wars with France and no longer opposed Scotland seriously, although border strife continued.

Anglo-Zulu War conflict between British forces in South Africa and the Zulu nation 1878–79. The Zulus formed a powerful kingdom in the early 19th century under Shaka (died 1828) and built up an empire in Natal, displacing other peoples of southern Africa. As the British extended their South African colonies, pushing the Boers north, they also came into conflict with the Zulus under their king Cetshwayo. A British force was massacred by Zulus at ◊Isandhlwana Jan 1879. Cetshwayo was defeated and captured by the British army at Ulundi Aug 1879 and a peace treaty was signed 1 Sept 1879. Zululand became a British protectorate 1887 and part of the British colony of Natal 1897.

Anne 1665–1714. Queen of Great Britain and Ireland 1702–14. She was the second daughter of James, Duke of York, who became James II, and Anne Hyde. She received a Protestant upbringing, and in 1683 married Prince George of Denmark (1653–1708). Of their many children only one survived infancy, William, Duke of Gloucester (1689–1700). For the greater part of her life Anne was a close friend of Sarah ◊Churchill (1650–1744), wife of John Churchill (1650–1722), afterwards Duke of Marlborough; the Churchills' influence helped lead her to desert her father for her brother-in-law, William of Orange, during the Revolution of 1688, although she was later to engage in Jacobite intrigues.

She succeeded William III to become queen 1702 and replaced the Tories with a Whig government 1703–04. Events of her reign include the War of the Spanish Succession, Marlborough's victories at Blenheim, Ramillies, Oudenarde, and Malplaquet, and the union of the English and Scottish parliaments 1707. She broke with the Marlboroughs 1710, when Mrs Masham succeeded the duchess as her favourite, and supported the Tory government of the same year. Anne was succeeded by George I.

Anne of Bohemia 1366–94. first wife of Richard II of England from 1382 until her death from the plague 1394. The eldest daughter of Emperor Charles IV by his fourth wife, Elizabeth of Pomerania, she married Richard Jan 1382 as part of attempts by her brother, Emperor Wenceslas, to form an anti-French alliance to promote his candidate for the papacy. Despite threats of French interception, Anne reached England Dec 1381. There is no evidence that she promoted the religious teachings of John Wycliffe, but her Bohemian servants introduced his writings to the early Protestant thinker, John Huss. She died of pestilence and was given a sumptuous funeral by her husband.

The Anglo–Scottish wars: chronology

1286	Death of King Alexander III of Scotland, leaving his granddaughter Margaret (the Maid of Norway), aged 3, as heir.
1290	Death of Margaret, creating succession crisis. Leading men invited King Edward I of England to select the new ruler from 13 candidates.
1292	*17 Nov* At Berwick-on-Tweed, Edward I chose John Balliol as king of Scots.
1294	Four Scottish bishops, four earls, and four barons, opposed to Balliol's deference to King Edward, formed a council; in Oct 1295 they made a treaty with France.
1296	*March* King Edward invaded Scotland and defeated the Scots at the Battle of Dunbar 27 April.
	July 10 John Balliol abdicated; on 28 Aug, Scots did homage to Edward who then began the introduction of English government.
1297	*May* Following the killing of an English sheriff by William Wallace, rebellion broke out in Scotland.
	11 Sept Battle of Stirling: Wallace defeated an English army. In Oct, the Scots raided north England.
1298	*22 July* Battle of Falkirk: English army under King Edward defeated Scottish army under Wallace.
1300, 1301, 1303	King Edward mounted further campaigns in Scotland. English government was established in south Scotland.
1305	English captured and executed William Wallace; in Sept King Edward issued legal ordinances for Scotland.
1306	*10 Feb* Robert the Bruce (a claimant in 1292) killed John Comyn (another claimant); on 25 March Bruce was crowned king at Scone.
	26 June Battle of Methven Park: English scattered the Scots; Bruce later fled to Rathlin Island off Ulster.
1307	*10 May* Battle of Loudoun Hill: Robert the Bruce defeated English army.
	7 July Death of King Edward I; succeeded by son Edward.
1307–8	Bruce established rule in north and west Scotland.
1308–14	Bruce captured many English-held towns and castles in Scotland.
1314	*24 June* Battle of Bannockburn: Scots inflicted a heavy defeat on an English army that was attempting to relieve English forces in Stirling.
1320	*26 April* Scottish earls and barons sealed the Declaration of Arbroath: in a letter to Pope John XXII they declared their rejection of English rule.
1322	English army commanded by King Edward II raided the Scottish lowlands.
1323	Edward II agreed 13-year truce.
1327	In England, deposition of Edward II; accession of son Edward (III).
1328	*4 May* In Treaty of Northampton, ratifying Treaty of Edinburgh, King Edward III recognized Robert the Bruce as king of Scots.
1329	*7 June* Death of Robert the Bruce; succeeded by son David (II), aged 5.
1332	*6 Aug* Edward Balliol, son of former King John Balliol, and supporters invaded Scotland; 12 Aug, defeated Scots army at Dupplin and was crowned at Scone on 24 Sept.
	12 Dec Scots loyal to King David II defeated Balliol at Annan; Balliol fled to England.
1333	*19 July* Battle of Halidon Hill: Scots attempting to relieve Berwick-on-Tweed (under siege from the English) are defeated; the English captured Berwick.
1334	*May* King David II fled to France.
June	Edward Balliol recognized Edward III as overlord of Scotland and ceded the counties of southern Scotland to England.
1337	*Oct* Edward III made formal claim to French throne, starting the Hundred Years' War.
1341	*June* King David II returned to Scotland; Edward Balliol returned to England.
1346	*17 Oct* Battle of Neville's Cross: Scots invading England (at French request) are defeated near Durham; King David is captured.
1356	*Jan* Edward Balliol surrendered Scotland to Edward III. English raided south Scotland.
1357	*6 Nov* General Council of Scots ratified Treaty of Berwick, agreeing to pay ransom for release of David II.
1363	*Nov* David II agreed with Edward III that Edward would succeed him; agreement was repudiated by Scottish parliament 4 March 1364.
1371	*22 Feb* Death of David II; succeeded by Robert II, cousin of David, grandson of Robert the Bruce and the first Stewart ruler.

Anne of Cleves 1515–1557. Fourth wife of ◊Henry VIII of England 1540. She was the daughter of the Duke of Cleves, and was recommended to Henry as a wife by Thomas ◊Cromwell, who wanted an alliance with German Protestantism against the Holy Roman Empire. Henry was disappointed with her and had the marriage declared void after six months on the grounds of non-consummation. Anne was awarded a substantial pension and remained in England for the rest of her life.

Anne of Denmark 1574–1619. Queen consort of James VI of Scotland (later James I of Great Britain 1603). She was the daughter of Frederick II of Denmark and Norway, and married James 1589. Anne was suspected at the time of having Catholic leanings. She was a flamboyant character, appearing in person in Ben Jonson's masques, and was noted for her extravagance, dying in debt as a result.

Anselm, St c.1033–1109. Medieval Benedictine monk and philosopher. As abbot from 1078, he made the abbey of Bec in Normandy, France, a centre of scholarship in Europe. He was appointed archbishop of Canterbury by William II of England 1093, but was later forced into exile. He holds an important place in the development of scholasticism.

As archbishop of Canterbury St Anselm was recalled from exile by Henry I, with whom he bitterly disagreed on the investiture of the clergy; a final agreement gave the king the right of temporal investiture and the clergy that of spiritual investiture. Anselm was canonized 1494. Feast day 21 Aug.

Anson George, 1st Baron Anson 1697–1762. English admiral. In 1740 he commanded the squadron attacking the Spanish colonies and shipping in South America and returned home by circumnavigating the world, with £500,000 of Spanish treasure. As first lord of the Admiralty, he carried out a series of reforms, which increased the efficiency of the British fleet and contributed to its success in the Seven Years' War (1756–63) against France.

Anti-Corn Law League extra-parliamentary pressure group formed Sept 1838 by Manchester industrialists, to campaign against the ◊Corn Laws. Led by British Liberals Richard ◊Cobden and John ◊Bright, the league argued for free trade and campaigned successfully against duties on the import of foreign corn to Britain imposed by the Corn Laws, which were repealed 1846.

The league initiated strategies for popular mobilization and agitation including mass meetings, lecture tours, pamphleteering, opinion polls, and parliamentary lobbying. Reaction by the conservative landed interests was organized with the establishment of the Central Agricultural Protection Society, nicknamed the Anti-League. In June 1846 political pressure, the state of the economy, and the Irish situation prompted Prime Minister Robert ◊Peel to repeal the Corn Laws.

Antonine Wall Roman line of fortification built AD 142, stretching between the Clyde and Forth rivers in Scotland. Named after the emperor Antoninus Pius, it was Roman Britain's most northerly frontier. The wall was made of turf and defended by 19 forts and remained in use until c.200.

Anzio, Battle of in World War II, Allied attempt to bypass German defences at Monte ◊Cassino by an amphibious landing 22 Jan–23 May 1944. The failure to use information gained by deciphering German codes in the 'Ultra' project led to Allied troops being stranded temporarily after German attacks. Allied troops were held on the beachhead for five months before the breakthrough after Monte Cassino allowed the US 5th Army to dislodge the Germans from the Alban Hills and allow the Anzio force to begin its advance on Rome.

appeasement conciliatory policy adopted by the British government, in particular under Neville Chamberlain, toward the Nazi and Fascist dictators in Europe in the 1930s in an

You have sent me a Flanders mare.

ANNE OF CLEVES
Henry VIII on seeing Anne for the first time. (attributed)

If our forefathers two hundred years ago... refused to be bondmen of a king, shall we be born thralls of an aristocracy like ours? Shall we, who struck the lion down, shall we pay homage to the wolf?

ANTI-CORN LAW LEAGUE
John Bright, speech at an Anti-Corn Law meeting, London, December 1845

Anson
English admiral George Anson who circumnavigated the globe with a fleet of six ships 1740. He returned after nearly four years with only one ship but nearly £500,000 in looted Spanish treasure.
Michael Nicholson

effort to maintain peace. It was strongly opposed by Winston Churchill, but the ◊Munich Agreement 1938 was almost universally hailed as its justification. Appeasement ended when Germany occupied Bohemia–Moravia March 1939. War was declared after Germany attacked Poland Sept 1939, the beginning of World War II.

Aquae Sulis (Latin, 'waters of Sul'– the British goddess of wisdom) Roman name for the city of Bath, from the natural springs found there which made it a prosperous spa town under the Roman Empire. When Roman rule in Britain collapsed at the end of the 4th century, the city faded into relative obscurity until the 18th century when its springs made it once more a fashionable health resort.

The ruins of the Roman baths, as well as a great temple, are the finest Roman remains in Britain. Excavations 1979 revealed thousands of coins and 'curses', offered at a place which was thought to be the link between the upper and lower worlds.

Arbroath, declaration of declaration 26 April 1320 by Scottish nobles of their loyalty to King Robert the Bruce and of Scotland's identity as a kingdom independent of England. A response to papal demands that the Scots should yield to English claims, the document was probably composed by Robert the Bruce's chancellor, Bernard de Linton. It claimed that Scotland had enjoyed an 'uninterrupted succession of 113 kings, all of our own native and royal stock'. It was cleverly asserted that the Scots would depose even King Robert if he capitulated to the English, 'for it is not for glory, riches nor honours that we fight, but for freedom alone'. In the 20th century, it has become a manifesto for Scottish nationalism.

Arch Joseph 1826–1919. English Radical member of Parliament and trade unionist, founder of the National Agricultural Union (the first of its kind) 1872.

archbishop in the Christian church, a bishop of superior rank who has authority over other bishops in his jurisdiction and often over an ecclesiastical province. The Church of England is presided over by two archbishops: the archbishop of Canterbury, who is 'primate of All England', and the archbishop of York, who is 'primate of England'. The archbishop of Canterbury has the privilege of crowning the kings and queens of England and takes precedence immediately after the princes of royal blood.

In the time of St Augustine (5th century) the plan was to divide England into two provinces with two archbishops, one at London and one at York, with precedence depending on seniority. Canterbury gained supremacy, however, when in the period before the Reformation (16th century) the metropolitan of Canterbury exercised the powers of papal legate throughout England.

Arctic convoys in World War II, series of supply convoys sailing from the UK to the USSR around the North Cape to Murmansk, commencing Oct 1941.

The natural hazards of sailing in these waters were greatly increased by the activity of German submarines and surface ships, together with German aircraft operating from bases in northern Norway, and casualties were often heavy. In spite of such losses, the convoys delivered thousands of tanks and aircraft, 356,000 trucks, 50,000 jeeps, 1,500 locomotives, and 9,800 freight wagons in the course of the war.

Argyll line of Scottish peers who trace their descent to the Campbells of Lochow. The earldom dates from 1457. They include:

Argyll Archibald Campbell, 5th Earl of Argyll 1530–1573. Adherent of the Scottish presbyterian John ◊Knox. A supporter of Mary Queen of Scots from 1561, he commanded her forces after her escape from Lochleven Castle 1568. He revised his position and became Lord High Chancellor of Scotland 1572.

Argyll Archibald Campbell, 1st Marquess and 8th Earl of Argyll, 1598–1661. Scottish ◊Covenanter. He opposed Charles I in Scotland in the 1630s and during the Civil War fought against the royalists, suffering heavy losses against Montrose's Highlanders 1644–45. After Charles' execution 1649 he broke with the English Parliamentarians and attended the coronation of Charles II 1650. He submitted to parliamentarian forces 1652 and from 1658 was an MP in the Commonwealth parliament. He was beheaded for treason after the Restoration of Charles II 1660.

Argyll Archibald Campbell, 9th Earl of Argyll 1629–1685. Scottish royalist. He supported the royalist cause in Scotland in the 1650s and was imprisoned 1661–63 after the conviction of his father, the 8th Earl, on charges of treason. He was appointed 1667 to appease the Highlanders but his opposition to extreme measures, such as the Scottish Test Act, incurred the enmity of the Duke of York (later James II), who sentenced him to death on dubious charges 1681 and Argyll fled to Holland. On the accession of James II, he conspired with ◊Monmouth, and invaded Scotland 1685. He failed to rouse the Covenanters and Monmouth's planned invasion of England did not proceed and so the rebellion failed and he was executed.

Argyll Archibald Campbell, 10th Earl and 1st Duke of Argyll, d. 1703. Scottish nobleman who largely restored his family's fortune. He failed to win the favour of James II who had executed his father, the 9th earl, and so did not regain the family estates confiscated after the Monmouth rebellion 1685. He supported William III's claim to the throne, and was one of the commissioners who offered him the Scottish crown. Following William's accession to the throne in the ◊Glorious Revolution 1688, Argyll's estates were returned 1689. He continued his loyalty to the new regime and was associated with the massacre of suspected Jacobite members of the MacDonald clan at ◊Glencoe 1692. He subsequently gained many honours, notably a dukedom 1701.

Argyll Archibald Campbell, 3rd Duke of Argyll 1682–1761. Scottish soldier and politician. He became Lord High Treasurer of Scotland and Earl of Islay 1705 and promoted the union of Scotland with England 1707. He fought against the Jacobites at Sheriffmuir 1715 and later became Walpole's chief adviser on Scottish affairs. He became Duke of Argyll 1743.

Argyll John, 2nd Duke of Argyll 1678–1743. Scottish soldier. He played a leading part in bringing about the union between Scotland and England 1707. He fought in the War of the ◊Spanish Succession, serving with distinction under Marlborough in Flanders 1706–09 and returned to become commander in chief in Scotland 1712. He suppressed the Earl of Mar's Jacobite rebellion at ◊Sheriffmuir 1715 and was created Duke of Westminster 1719.

Arkwright Richard 1732–1792. English inventor and manufacturing pioneer who developed a machine for spinning cotton (he called it a 'spinning frame') 1768. He was one of the pioneers of the industrial revolution and set up a water-powered spinning factory 1771 and installed steam power in a Nottingham factory 1790.

In 1773 Arkwright produced the first cloth made entirely from cotton; previously, the warp had been of linen and only the weft was cotton. A special act of Parliament was passed 1774 to exempt Arkwright's fabric from the double duty imposed on cottons by an act of 1736. By 1782 Arkwright employed 5,000 workers.

Armada fleet sent by Philip II of Spain against England 1588. See ◊Spanish Armada.

Arminianism a ◊high church school of Christian theology opposed to Calvin's doctrine of predestination which flourished under James I and Charles I and later formed the basis of Wesleyan ◊Methodism. Named after a Dutch Protestant theologian, Jacob Arminius 1560–1609, it was associated in England with William ◊Laud, bishop of London and later archbishop of Canterbury. It was first promoted by Charles, as Prince of Wales, and the Duke of ◊Buckingham, to the annoyance of James I. With its emphasis on free will, the divine institution of bishops, and 'the beauty of holiness', Arminianism undermined central tenets of the Puritanism or ◊Calvinism which hitherto dominated the Elizabethan and Jacobean Church. Arminians were also perceived as supporting many of Charles's more unpopular policies, such as the imposition of ship money and the ◊Bishops' Wars in Scotland. Arminianism was denounced when Parliaments were called again in 1640, after the 11-year period of Charles's personal rule.

Arnhem, Battle of in World War II, airborne operation by the Allies, 17–26 Sept 1944, to secure a bridgehead over the Rhine, thereby opening the way for a thrust toward the Ruhr and a possible early end to the war. It was only partially successful, with 7,600 casualties.

Arnhem itself was to be taken by the British while US troops were assigned bridges to the south of the city. Unfortunately, two divisions of the SS Panzer Corps were refitting in Arnhem when the British landed and penned the British troops in, while the US force captured the bridge at Nijmegen but were unable to secure the bridge at Elst. Despite the arrival of Polish reinforcements 21 Sept, Montgomery ordered a withdrawal four days later.

Arnold Thomas 1795–1842. English schoolmaster, father of the poet and critic Matthew Arnold. He was headmaster of Rugby School 1828–42 where he broadened the traditional

My object will be, if possible, to form Christian men, for Christian boys I can scarcely hope to make.

THOMAS ARNOLD
letter on appointment to the headmastership of Rugby, 1828

classical curriculum and introduced a system of prefects as a means of curbing brutality. His regime has been graphically described in Thomas Hughes's *Tom Brown's Schooldays* 1857. He emphasized training of character based on Christian principles and had a profound influence on public school education.

Arran James Hamilton, 2nd Earl of Arran *c*.1516–1575. Scottish nobleman. He was appointed Governor of Scotland for the infant Mary Queen of Scots 1542 and initially favoured religious reform and pro-English policies. He was later won back to Roman Catholicism and an alliance with France. He resigned his governorship 1554 in favour of Mary of Guise and was created Duke of Châtelherault by Henry II of France. He then changed sides again, supporting the Protestant ◊Lords of the Congregation in their successful attempt to oust Mary of Guise 1559–60.

Arran James Stewart, Earl of Arran *c*.1545–1596. Scottish magnate. He spent most of his life on the Continent, but returned to Scotland 1577 and won the favour of James VI, who created him earl 1581. After James escaped from the extreme Protestant Ruthven raiders 1583, Arran became his closest adviser. His power collapsed, however, on the return of extreme Protestant leaders from exile 1585, and James deserted him.

Arras, Battle of in World War I, April–May 1917, an effective but costly British attack on German forces in support of a French offensive, which was only partially successful, on the Siegfried Line. British casualties totalled 84,000 as compared to 75,000 German casualties.

Arras, Battle of in World War II, Allied attack on German forces holding the French town of Arras 21 May 1940. Although the Allies were eventually beaten off, the German general Rommel's report of being attacked by 'hundreds of tanks' led to a 24-hour delay in the German advance which gave the British vital time to organize their retreat through Dunkirk.

array, commission of system of universal military conscription dating from the 13th century, when the obligation to serve the king was extended to serfs. Able-bodied men between the ages of 15 and 60 in each shire were selected by local commissioners to serve in a force paid for by the county. Although hired soldiers predominated in royal armies by the following century, in the 16th century the power of array was accorded to lords-lieutenant. During the Civil War, Charles I issued commissions to raise troops for the royalist armies.

Arthur, King legendary British king and hero in the stories of ◊Camelot and the quest for the Holy Grail. He is said to have been born in Tintagel, Cornwall, and to have died in Glastonbury, Somerset. He may have been a 6th-century Romano-Celtic leader against pagan Saxon invaders. Nennius, a 9th-century Welsh chronicler, identifies him with the British military commander (though not yet king) who was the victor at the Battle of ◊Mons Badonicus (Mount Badon).

The legends of Arthur were developed in the 12th century by Geoffrey of Monmouth, who in his *Historia Regum Britanniae* relates the birth and conquests of Arthur, the infidelity of his wife Queen Guinevere, his final defeat by Mordred, and his translation when mortally wounded to the Isle of Avalon. The 12th-century Norman writer Wace adds further details, including the earliest known reference to the Knights of the Round Table. The French subsequently borrowed the stories as a vehicle for tales of courtly love. Later writers to popularize the Arthurian stories include Thomas Malory in the 15th century, Tennyson in the 19th century, and T H White in the 20th century.

One to mislead the public, another to mislead the Cabinet, and the third to mislead itself.

H H Asquith
remark quoted in Alistair Horne Price of Glory *on the War Office's sets of figures*

Arthur Duke of Brittany 1187–1203. Grandson of Henry II of England and nephew of King ◊Richard I, who named him as his heir but later changed his decision in favour of his brother John. When Richard died, Arthur claimed the throne but was captured and probably murdered by John April 1203.

Articles, Lords of see ◊Lords of the Articles.

Ascension British island colony in the south Atlantic. Since 1922 it has administratively been part of St Helena. Its airfield, built by US engineers in World War II, is used as a refuelling base on transatlantic flights to southern Europe, North Africa, and the Near East.

Ascham Roger *c*.1515–1568. English scholar and royal tutor, author of *The Scholemaster* 1570 on the art of education. After writing a treatise on archery, King Henry VIII's favourite sport, Ascham was appointed tutor to Princess Elizabeth in 1548. He retained favour under Edward

VI and Queen Mary (despite his Protestant views), and returned to Elizabeth's service as her secretary after she became queen.

Ashanti Wars four British expeditions 1873–1901 to the interior of modern Ghana to wrest control of trade in West Africa from the indigenous Ashanti people and end the slave trade which thrived in the area.

The first Ashanti War broke out April 1873 when Garnet Wolseley was sent with 2,500 troops to defeat the Ashanti ruler, the Asantehene Kofi Karikari, and free the coastal regions from further incursions. This was settled by the Treaty of Fomena 14 March 1874 under which the Asantehene promised free trade, an open road to Kumasi, an end to human sacrifices, and to pay an indemnity to Britain. The agreement was broken and further expeditions followed: the area was declared a British protectorate Aug 1896 and the Asantehene was deported. The Ashanti territory was incorporated into the neighbouring Gold Coast colony Sept 1901.

Ashingdon, Battle of or ***Assandun*** victory 18 Oct 1016 of King Canute's Danish army over King Edmund II ('Ironside') at the village of Ashingdon, Essex. Following the battle, only Wessex remained in English hands and when Edmund died 30 Nov, Canute ruled the whole kingdom. See also ◊Danelaw.

Ashmole Elias 1617–1692. English antiquary, whose collection forms the basis of the Ashmolean Museum, Oxford. He was one of the first English freemasons and wrote books on alchemy and on antiquarian subjects. He amassed a fine library and a collection of curiosities, both of which he presented to Oxford University 1682. His collection was housed in the 'Old Ashmolean' (built 1679–83); the present Ashmolean Museum was erected 1897.

Asiento agreement or ***Asiento de Negros*** agreement between the UK and Spain as part of the Treaty of Utrecht 1713, whereby British traders were permitted to introduce 144,000 black slaves into the Spanish-American colonies in the course of the following 30 years. In 1750 the right was bought out by the Spanish government for $100,000.

Asquith Herbert Henry, 1st Earl of Oxford and Asquith 1852–1928. British Liberal politician, prime minister 1908–16. As chancellor of the Exchequer he introduced old-age pensions 1908. He limited the powers of the House of Lords and attempted to give Ireland Home Rule.

Asquith was born in Yorkshire. Elected a member of Parliament 1886, he was home secretary in Gladstone's 1892–95 government. He was chancellor of the Exchequer 1905–08 and succeeded Campbell-Bannerman as prime minister. Forcing through the radical budget of his chancellor ◊Lloyd George led him into two elections 1910, which resulted in the Parliament Act 1911, limiting the right of the Lords to veto legislation. His endeavours to pass the Home Rule for Ireland Bill led to the ◊Curragh 'Mutiny' and incipient civil war. Unity was re-established by the outbreak of World War I 1914, and a coalition government was formed May 1915. However, his attitude of 'wait and see' was not suited to all-out war, and he was replaced by Lloyd George Dec 1916. The Liberal election defeat 1918 led to the eclipse of the party. He was created 1st Earl of Oxford and Asquith 1925.

assize in medieval Europe, the passing of laws, either by the king with the consent of nobles, or as a complete system, such as the ***Assizes of Jerusalem***, a compilation of the law of the feudal kingdom of Jerusalem in the 13th century.

Assize courts were introduced in England and Wales by Henry II, primarily to settle disputes over land ownership. After the Statute of Westminster 1285, judges were sent 'on circuit' to hear cases all round the country. The term remained in use in the UK for the courts held by judges of the High Court in each county. They were abolished under the Courts Act 1971 – their civil jurisdiction was taken over by the High Court and their criminal jurisdiction was taken over by the Crown Court.

Astor Nancy Witcher Langhorne, Lady 1879–1964. US-born British politician, the first woman member of Parliament. She succeeded her

Two thousand Ashantis, under the leadership of an intelligent British officer, would soon extend the power of the English from Cape Coast castle across the Thogoshi mountains to Timbuctoo, and from Mandingo Land to Benin.

ASHANTI WARS
Henry Morton Stanley,
Coomassie and Magdala
1874

Astor
Nancy Astor, Britain's first woman MP, shortly after her election as member for Plymouth Nov 1919. She stood for the seat, previously held by her husband William Waldorf Astor, as a Conservative in support of Lloyd George's coalition
Hulton Deutsch

husband as Conservative MP for the constituency of Plymouth when he entered the Lords as Viscount Astor 1919. She remained in parliament until 1945, as an active champion of women's rights, educational issues, and temperance.

Athelney, Isle of area of firm ground in marshland near Taunton in Somerset, in 878 the headquarters of King ◊Alfred the Great when he was in hiding from the Danes. It was from Athelney that he launched the counterattack that led to his victory at Edington, and he later endowed a monastery there. It was also the setting of the legend of the burnt cakes.

Athelstan c.895–939. King of the Mercians and West Saxons. Son of Edward the Elder and grandson of Alfred the Great, he was crowned king 925 at Kingston upon Thames. By 927, he was regarded as the first king of England, after successfully invading Northumbria. He defeated a coalition of Welsh, Scots, and Danes at Brunanburh 937; the exact location is unclear, but it appears to have been somewhere in northern England.

Atholl John Murray, 2nd Earl and 1st Marquess of Atholl, c.1635–1703. Scottish politician. As Justice General of Scotland 1670–78, he initially supported Charles II's commissioner for Scotland, Lauderdale, but withdrew his allegiance after the defeat of the ◊Covenanters at Bothwell Bridge 1679. He was responsible for the capture of Archibald Campbell, 9th Earl of Argyll after the Monmouth rebellion against James II 1685. Atholl then professed his loyalty to William III following the Glorious Revolution 1688, but this did not secure the advancement he had hoped for and he became preoccupied with a series of intrigues against William which came to nothing.

Atlantic, Battle of the German campaign during World War I to prevent merchant shipping from delivering food supplies from the USA to the Allies, chiefly the UK. By 1917, some 875,000 tons of shipping had been lost. The odds were only turned by the belated use of naval convoys and depth charges to deter submarine attack.

Atlantic, Battle of the during World War II, continuous battle fought in the Atlantic Ocean by the sea and air forces of the Allies and Germany, to control the supply routes to the UK. The Allies destroyed nearly 800 U-boats during the war and at least 2,200 convoys of 75,000 merchant ships crossed the Atlantic, protected by US naval forces.

The battle opened 4 Sept 1939, the first night of the war, when the ocean liner *Athenia*, sailing from Glasgow to New York, was torpedoed by a German U-boat off the Irish coast. The Germans employed a variety of tactics in the course of the campaign such as U-boats, surface-raiders, indiscriminate minelaying, and aircraft, but the Allies successfully countered all of them, although they suffered some significant reverses such as the sinking of the armed merchant ships *Rawalpindi* (23 Nov 1939) and *Jervis Bay* (5 Nov 1940) by German warships.

U-boats remained the greatest menace to Allied shipping, especially after the destruction of the German battleship *Bismarck* by the British 27 May 1941. Prior to the US entry into the war 1941, destroyers were supplied to the British under the Lend-Lease Act.

Atlantic Charter declaration issued during World War II by the British prime minister Winston Churchill and the US president Franklin Roosevelt after meetings Aug 1941. It stressed their countries' broad strategy and war aims and was largely a propaganda exercise to demonstrate public solidarity among the Allies.

The Atlantic Charter stated that the UK and the USA sought no territorial gains; desired no territorial changes not acceptable to the peoples concerned; respected the rights of all peoples to choose their own form of government; wished to see self-government restored to the occupied countries; would promote access by all states to trade and raw materials; desired international collaboration for the raising of economic standards; hoped to see a peace affording security to all nations, enabling them to cross the seas without hindrance; and proposed the disarmament of the aggressor states as a preliminary step to general disarmament. The charter was incorporated by reference into the Declaration of the United Nations 1941.

Atlantic triangle 18th century trade route; goods were exported from Britain to Africa where they were traded for slaves which were shipped to either Spanish colonies in South America or British colonies in North America, in return for staple goods for Europe such as cotton. The triangle trade boomed after the granting of the ◊Asiento concessions.

Atrebates Belgic tribe which settled in southeast England about 80 BC and predominated in that area prior to the arrival of the Romans. They maintained contact with their continental

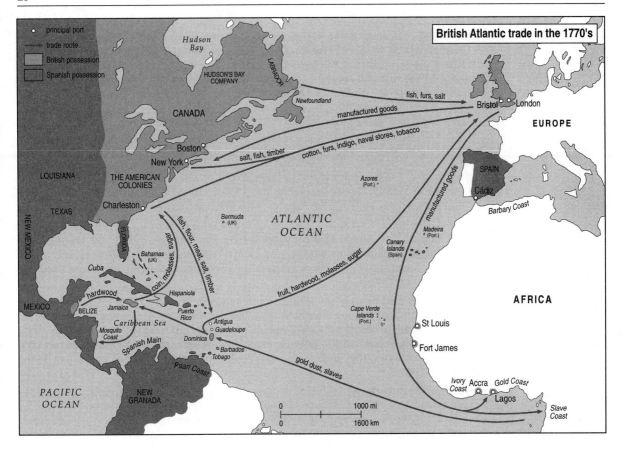

British Atlantic trade in the 1770's

counterparts so that in 55 BC Julius Caesar was still able to use a continental Belgic chieftain as an intermediary with those who had settled in England. They later came under pressure from another tribe, the Catuvellauni, which made them more amenable to the Roman invasion AD 43 and they were later recognized by the Romans as a tribal corporation or ◊*civitas*. They settled principally south of the river Thames to the west of Kent and their main settlements were at Silchester (the capital), Winchester, and Chichester where a variety of coins have been found.

attainder, bill of legislative device that allowed the English Parliament to declare guilt and impose a punishment on an individual without bringing the matter before the courts. Such bills were used intermittently from the Wars of the Roses until 1798. The guilty party was deemed to be 'tainted' and so could neither inherit property nor bequeath it to an heir. Some acts of attainder were also passed by US colonial legislators during the American Revolution to deal with 'loyalists' who continued to support the English crown but were later expressly forbidden by the US Constitution.

Henry VIII employed bills of attainder arbitrarily against his political opponents and they were later revived by James I and Charles I, whose best-known bill of attainder involved the Earl of ◊Strafford 1641. The last bill of attainder was passed against Lord Edward Fitzgerald (1763–1798) for leading a rebellion in Ireland. The use of the device has generally been deplored as it does not require the accusers to prove their case and was usually employed to punish 'new' crimes of treason that were detrimental to those in power.

Attlee Clement (Richard), 1st Earl Attlee 1883–1967. British Labour politician. In the coalition government during World War II he was Lord Privy Seal 1940–42, dominions secretary 1942–43, and Lord President of the Council 1943–45, as well as deputy prime minister from 1942. As prime minister 1945–51 he introduced a sweeping programme of nationalization and a whole new system of social services.

Attlee was educated at Oxford and practised as a barrister 1906–09. Social work in London's East End and cooperation in poor-law reform led him to become a socialist; he

British Atlantic trade in the 1770s
British trade across the Atlantic in the 18th century was based on the two-way trade of raw materials for manufactured goods between Great Britain and the colonies in North America and the Caribbean, but the trade in slaves and gold from the British bases in Africa to the British and Spanish plantations in the Americas added a new, lucrative dimension.

joined the Fabian Society and the Independent Labour Party 1908. He was secretary to Toynbee Hall 1910 and became lecturer in social science at the London School of Economics 1913. After service in World War I he was mayor of Stepney, East London, 1919–20 and served as Labour member of Parliament for Limehouse 1922–50 and for West Walthamstow 1950–55. In the first and second Labour governments he was undersecretary for war 1924 and chancellor of the Duchy of Lancaster and postmaster general 1929–31. In 1935 he became leader of the opposition.

In July 1945 he became prime minister after a Labour landslide in the general election. His government carried out a radical programme of social welfare reform, including the establishment of the National Health Service 1948, and nationalization. In foreign affairs, both India 1947 and Burma (now Myanmar) 1948 gained their independence under Attlee's administration. The government was returned to power with a much reduced majority 1950 and was defeated 1951. He was created 1st Earl 1955 on his retirement as leader of the opposition.

Attwood Thomas 1783–1856. British ◊Chartist politician. He founded the Birmingham Political Union 1830 and was member of parliament for Birmingham 1832–39. He presented the first Chartist Petition to parliament July 1839 which was rejected, leading to riots across the country. A banker by profession, he favoured the introduction of paper money and the easier availability of credit.

Aughrim, Battle of final defeat of the Jacobite forces in Ireland 12 July 1691 southwest of Ballinasloe, Co Galway in the aftermath of William III's victory at the ◊Boyne. The English army scattered the Jacobite forces and Limerick capitulated, marking the end of Jacobite resistance. The battle was a turning point in Irish history, and left Ireland in the hands of a Protestant ascendancy, the 'English in Ireland' who were mostly the descendants of Tudor and Stuart settlers.

Augustine of Canterbury, St d. 605. First archbishop of Canterbury. Originally prior of the Benedictine monastery of St Andrew, Rome, he was sent from Rome to convert England to Christianity by Pope Gregory I. He landed at Ebbsfleet in Kent 597 and soon after baptized Ethelbert, king of Kent, along with many of his subjects. He was consecrated bishop of the English at Arles in the same year, and appointed archbishop 601, establishing his see at Canterbury. In 603 he attempted unsuccessfully to unite the Roman and native Celtic churches at a conference on the Severn. He founded Christ Church, Canterbury 603, and the abbey of Saints Peter and Paul, now the site of Saint Augustine's Missionary College. Feast day 26 May.

auld alliance intermittent alliance between Scotland and France that lasted from the end of the 13th century until 1560, when Protestantism displaced Catholicism as the dominant faith in Scotland.

Auldearn, Battle of victory of the royalist Marquess of Montrose over a numerically superior army of Covenanters 9 May 1645 east of Nairn, Scotland. Although the Covenanters had the numerical advantage and managed to take Montrose by surprise, his Highland and Irish troops managed to hold them off and were defeated. Montrose went on to win a further series of victories against the Covenanters before being defeated himself and forced to flee to France later in the year.

Austin Herbert, 1st Baron 1866–1941. English industrialist and philanthropist. He began manufacturing cars 1905 in Northfield, Birmingham, notably the Austin Seven, the 'Baby Austin', 1921. His Austin series of cars did much to popularize motoring in Britain, bringing cars within the reach of many more people, much as Henry Ford did in the USA. He was Conservative member of parliament for King's Norton 1918–24.

Australia (officially Commonwealth of Australia) independent state in the southern hemisphere, and the world's smallest continent. An independent sovereign nation within the Commonwealth, Australia formally retains the British monarch as head of state, represented by a governor general, although pressure was growing in 1994–95 to declare the country a republic by the year 2000.

Its eastern part was claimed for Britain by Capt James ◊Cook 1770, who named it New South Wales. The first English settlement was built by convicts as a penal colony at Port Jackson 1788.

I should be a sad subject for any publicity expert. I have none of the qualities which create publicity.

CLEMENT ATTLEE
quoted in Harold Nicolson, Diary
14 January 1949

The entire continent was claimed by Britain 1829 and given limited self-government through the Australian Colonies Government Act 1850. British imperial forces left Australia 1870 after which it became self-dependent for defence. The separate colonies were federated into a commonwealth by a British act of Parliament 1901. Constitutional ties with Britain allowing British intervention in government were formally abolished 1986. The Native Title Act 1993 restored land rights to the Aborigines which had been lost after British settlement.

Austrian Succession, War of the 1740–48 war between Austria (supported by Britain and Holland) and Prussia (supported by France and Spain). Its immediate cause was the death of the Holy Roman Emperor Charles VI of Austria, who had promised his territorial possessions to his daughter, Maria Theresa, and her husband, the Grand Duke Francis. Britain and its allies tried to enforce the succession of Maria Theresa and her husband, but Francis' claim to the Imperial title was disputed by Charles Albert of Bavaria, with support from France and Prussia.

The war began when the Prussians, led by Frederick II, seized the Austrian province of Silesia 1740 and Charles Albert was installed as Charles VII. After Prussia had temporarily withdrawn from the war, an allied army, under the direct command of King George III, defeated the French at the Battle of ◊Dettingen 1743. When Charles VII died 1745, his son, Maximilian Joseph, agreed to recognize Francis as Emperor and in return Maria Theresa ceded Silesia to the Prussians. In the same year, an Austro-English army was defeated at Fontenoy by the French who proceeded to occupy the Austrian Netherlands.

The war was one of several conflicts among the European powers at the time, including the War of ◊Jenkins' Ear between Britain and Spain 1739, fighting between the British and French in North America and India, and the Jacobite rebellion in Scotland 1745–46 in which the French supported the Stuart claim to the throne of Scotland.

The war was ended with an unsatisfactory compromise by the Treaty of Aix-la-Chapelle 1748 under which Francis I was recognized as Holy Roman Emperor, Maria Theresa's right to her father's territories, apart from Silesia and Glatz which she had already ceded, was upheld, and the French recognized the Hanoverian succession and restored Madras, which they had seized Sept 1746 in a subsidiary action in India, to Britain. Several other territorial issues remained unresolved and the conflict was effectively restarted eight years later as the ◊Seven Years' War 1756.

Avebury Europe's largest stone circle (diameter 412 m/1,352 ft), in Wiltshire. It was probably constructed in the Neolithic period 3,500 years ago for some ritual purpose, and is linked with nearby ◊Silbury Hill. The village of Avebury was built within the circle, and many of the stones were used for building material.

Avebury John Lubbock, 1st Baron Avebury 1834–1913. British banker. A Liberal (from 1886 Liberal Unionist) member of Parliament 1870–1900, he was responsible for the Bank Holidays Act 1871 introducing statutory public holidays.

axe factories neolithic and later (*c.* 3500–1400 BC) sites of volcanic rock where axe-heads were shaped. Some 550 axe factories have been identified in the Lake District of Cumbria, and it is thought that scree at Pike O'Stickle in the Langdales represents the debris from as many as 75,000 stone axe-heads. Elsewhere, axe factories have been identified in the Lleyn Peninsula in Wales and in Cornwall. They are rare in southern and eastern England, where axe-heads were made chiefly from flint.

Axis alliance of Nazi Germany and Fascist Italy before and during World War II. The **Rome–Berlin Axis** was formed 1936, when Italy was being threatened with sanctions because of its invasion of Ethiopia (Abyssinia). It became a full military and political alliance May 1939. A ten-year alliance between Germany, Italy, and Japan (**Rome–Berlin–Tokyo Axis**) was signed Sept 1940 and was subsequently joined by Hungary, Bulgaria, Romania, and the puppet states of Slovakia and Croatia. The Axis collapsed with the fall of Mussolini and the surrender of Italy 1943 and Germany and Japan 1945.

B

Babington Anthony 1561–1586. English Catholic who hatched a plot to assassinate Elizabeth I and replace her with ◊Mary Queen of Scots. Details of the plot were intercepted by Elizabeth's secretary of state, ◊Walsingham. Babington was arrested and executed 1586; Mary's collusion in the plot led to her trial and execution the following year.

Bacon Francis 1561–1626. English politician, philosopher, and essayist. Bacon studied law at Cambridge from 1573, was part of the embassy in France until 1579, and became a member of Parliament 1584. He was the nephew of Queen Elizabeth's adviser Lord ◊Burghley, but turned against him when he failed to provide Bacon with patronage. He helped secure the execution of the Earl of Essex as a traitor 1601, after formerly being his follower. Bacon was accused of ingratitude, but he defended himself in *Apology* 1604. He became Lord Chancellor 1618, and the same year confessed to bribe-taking, was fined £40,000 (which was later remitted by the king), and spent four days in the Tower of London.

His works include *Essays* 1597, characterized by pith and brevity; *The Advancement of Learning* 1605, a seminal work discussing scientific method; *Novum organum* 1620, in which he redefined the task of natural science, seeing it as a means of empirical discovery and a method of increasing human power over nature; and *The New Atlantis* 1626, describing a utopian state in which scientific knowledge is systematically sought and exploited.

Bacon Roger *c.* 1214–1292. English philosopher and scientist. He studied alchemy, the biological and physical sciences, and magic, and is credited with many discoveries, including the magnifying lens. He described a hypothetical diving apparatus and some of the properties of gunpowder. Bacon promoted the use of latitude and longitude in mapmaking, and suggested the changes necessary to improve the Western calendar that were finally carried out by Pope Gregory XIII in 1582.

He became a Franciscan monk and lectured in Paris about 1241–47, then at Oxford University. In 1266, at the invitation of his friend Pope Clement IV, he began his *Opus maius/Great Work*, a compendium of all branches of knowledge and sent it, along with his *Opus minus/Lesser Work* and other writings, to the pope 1268. Bacon was condemned and imprisoned by the Christian church for 'certain novelties' (heresy) 1277 and not released until 1292.

Baden-Powell Robert Stephenson Smyth, 1st Baron Baden-Powell 1857–1941. British general, founder of the Scout Association. He fought in defence of Mafeking (now Mafikeng) during the Second South African War. After 1907 he devoted his time to developing the Scout movement, which rapidly spread throughout the world.

Baden-Powell
Sir Robert Baden-Powell, founder of the Boy Scouts, with his son Peter at a rally of Scouts in Cape Town, South Africa, 1906.
Hulton Deutsch

Born in London, he was educated at Charterhouse. After failing to gain a place at Oxford University he joined the Indian army, being commissioned in the Hussars in 1876; he became its youngest colonel by the age of 40. His defence of Mafikeng brought him worldwide fame.

Baden-Powell began the Scout movement in 1907 with a camp for 20 boys on Brownsea Island, Poole Harbour, Dorset. He published *Scouting for Boys* 1908 and about thirty other books. He was World Chief Scout from 1920. He was created a peer 1929 and received the Order of Merit 1937.

Baedeker raids series of German air raids during World War II directed at British provincial towns and cities April–Oct 1942. They were so named because the targets were all places of cultural interest which appeared to have been selected from *Baedeker's Guide to Britain*.

Bahamas former British colony, a chain of islands southeast of Florida and north of Cuba. They were granted by the British Crown to Sir Robert Heath 1629, and surrendered to him that year. They were constantly attacked by the Spanish but the British Parliament authorized their settlement by the company of Eleutherian Adventurers 1649. The islands were granted to the lords proprietors of Carolina 1649 but civil and military government was assumed by the British Crown 1717. The Bahamas capitulated to Spain 1782. They were restored to Great Britain by the Treaty of Versailles 1783. The Bahamas received internal self-government 1964 and became independent 1973.

Bahrein independent state in the western Persian Gulf. The islands have been ruled since 1782 by a member of a Kuwait family, but their defence was the responsibility of the British 1820–1971. Persian possession was denied by the British 1928.

bailiff officer of the court whose job, usually in the county courts, is to serve notices and enforce the court's orders involving seizure of the goods of a debtor.

The term originated in Normandy as the name for a steward of an estate. It retained this meaning in England throughout the Middle Ages and could also denote a sheriff's assistant. In France, the royal *bailli* or *bayle* was appointed to administer a large area of territory, the *baillage*, and was a leading local official.

Baird John Logie 1888–1946. Scottish electrical engineer who pioneered television. In 1925 he gave the first public demonstration of television and in 1926 pioneered fibre optics, radar (in advance of Robert Watson-Watt), and 'noctovision', a system for seeing at night by using infrared rays.

Baird began working on television possibly as early as 1912, and took out his first provisional patent 1923. He also developed video recording on both wax records and magnetic steel discs (1926–27), colour TV (1925–28), 3-D colour TV (1925–46), and transatlantic TV (1928). In 1944 he developed facsimile television, the forerunner of Ceefax, and demonstrated the world's first all-electronic colour and 3-D colour receiver.

Balaclava, Battle of in the Crimean War, failed Russian attack on British positions 25 Oct 1854, near a town in Ukraine, 10 km/6 mi southeast of Sevastopol. It was the scene of the ill-timed *Charge of the Light Brigade* of British cavalry against the Russian entrenched artillery, a futile action arising from misunderstood orders. Of the 673 soldiers who took part, there were 272 casualties. *Balaclava helmets* were knitted hoods worn here by soldiers in the bitter weather.

The Russian army broke through Turkish lines 25 Oct and entered the valley of Balaklava, intending to attack the British supply base in the harbour and relieve the encirclement of Sevastopol by attacking British positions from the rear. The battlefield consisted of two valleys divided by low hills; the British cavalry's Heavy Brigade were positioned in the south valley, while the Light Brigade were in the north valley. The first Russian advance broke into the south valley and was immediately driven back over the hill by the Heavy Brigade, forcing the Russians to fall back on their line of artillery.

The Light Brigade were ordered to 'prevent the enemy carrying away the guns' – it seems that this was intended to direct them to the hills where the

Make yourselves good scouts and good rifle shots in order to protect the women and children of your country if it should ever become necessary.

ROBERT
BADEN-POWELL
Scouting for Boys, *1908*

Baird
Scottish television pioneer John Logie Baird (centre) recording the matineé idol Jack Buchanan (left) 1929. He had given the first public demonstration of his television system four years earlier.
Topham Picture Library

They dashed on towards that thin red line tipped with steel.

BALACLAVA
Journalist William Russell
The British Expedition in
the Crimea

I look forward to a time when Irish patriotism will as easily combine with British patriotism as Scottish patriotism combines now.

ARTHUR BALFOUR
speech, 1889

Russians had captured some Turkish guns, but the order was badly phrased, leading the Light Brigade's commander to assume his target was the Russian guns about a mile away up the north valley. Erroneously obeying what he assumed to be his instructions, he led the infamous 'Charge of the Light Brigade' up the length of the valley between two rows of Russian artillery, sustaining heavy casualties. A charge by French cavalry saved the Light Brigade from total destruction, and the 93rd Highland Regiment broke up a Russian cavalry attack. The battle ended with the Russians retaining their guns and their position.

Baldwin Stanley, 1st Earl Baldwin of Bewdley 1867–1947. British Conservative politician, prime minister 1923–24, 1924–29, and 1935–37; he weathered the general strike 1926, secured complete adult suffrage 1928, and dealth with the ◊abdication crisis of Edward VIII 1936, but failed to prepare Britain for World War II.

Born in Bewdley, Worcestershire, the son of an iron and steel magnate, in 1908 he was elected Unionist member of Parliament for Bewdley, and in 1916 he became parliamentary private secretary to Bonar ◊Law. He was financial secretary to the Treasury 1917–21, and then appointed to the presidency of the Board of Trade. In 1919 he gave the Treasury £50,000 of War Loan for cancellation, representing about 20% of his fortune. He was a leader in the disruption of the Lloyd George coalition 1922, and, as chancellor under Bonar Law, achieved a settlement of war debts with the USA.

As prime minister 1923–24 and again 1924–29, Baldwin passed the Trades Disputes Act of 1927 after the general strike, granted widows' and orphans' pensions, and complete adult suffrage 1928. He joined the national government of Ramsay MacDonald 1931 as Lord President of the Council. He handled the abdication crisis during his third premiership 1935–37, but was later much criticized for his failures to anticipate and prepare adequately for the coming war in Europe. Specifically, he is accused of failing to resist the popular wish for an accommodation with the dictators Hitler and Mussolini, and failing to rearm more effectively.

Balfour
Arthur Balfour, British statesman, formulator of the Balfour Declaration. An intellectual – he delivered the Gifford Lectures on *Theism and Humanism* 1915 – he was sometimes considered too detached to excel in politics.
Michael Nicholson

Balfour Arthur James, 1st Earl of Balfour 1848–1930. British Conservative politician, prime minister 1902–05 and foreign secretary 1916–19, when he issued the Balfour Declaration 1917 and was involved in peace negotiations after World War I, signing the Treaty of Versailles.

Son of a Scottish landowner, Balfour was elected a Conservative member of Parliament 1874. In Lord Salisbury's ministry he was secretary for Ireland 1887, and was called 'Bloody Balfour' by Irish nationalists for his ruthless vigour. In 1891 and again in 1895 he became First Lord of the Treasury and leader of the Commons, and succeeded Salisbury as prime minister 1902. Despite the success of the Education Act 1902, which made local education authorities responsible for elementary education, his cabinet was fatally divided over Joseph Chamberlain's tariff-reform proposals, and suffered a crushing defeat in the 1905 elections.

Balfour retired from the party leadership 1911 and joined the Asquith coalition as First Lord of the Admiralty 1915. As foreign secretary 1916–19 he issued the Balfour Declaration in favour of a national home in Palestine for the Jews. He was Lord President of the Council 1919–22 and 1925–29. Created 1st Earl of Balfour 1922. He also wrote books on philosophy.

Balfour Declaration letter, dated 2 Nov 1917, from British foreign secretary A J Balfour to Lord Rothschild (chair, British Zionist Federation) stating: 'HM government view with favour the establishment in Palestine of a national home for the Jewish people ... it being understood that nothing shall be done which may prejudice the civil and religious rights of existing non-Jewish communities.' It helped form the basis for the foundation of Israel 1948.

Baliol (or ***Balliol***) John de c.1250–1314. King of Scotland 1292–96. As an heir to the Scottish throne on the death of Margaret, the Maid of Norway, his cause was supported by the English king, Edward I, against 12 other claimants. Baliol paid homage to Edward and was proclaimed king but soon rebelled. He gave up the kingdom when English forces attacked Scotland.

Ball John English priest, one of the leaders of the ◊Peasants' Revolt 1381, known as 'the mad priest of Kent'. A follower of John Wycliffe and a believer in social equality, he was imprisoned for disagreeing with the archbishop of Canterbury. During the revolt he was released from prison, and when in Blackheath, London, incited people against the ruling classes by preaching from the text 'When Adam delved and Eve span, who was then the gentleman?' When the revolt collapsed he escaped but was captured near Coventry and executed.

Ball
Late 15th-century manuscript showing the rebels in the Peasant's Revolt 1381 led by John Ball (on horseback) and Wat Tyler (front left). The uprising was sparked by the introduction of the much-hated poll tax.
Hulton Deutsch

ballot act legislation introduced by Gladstone's Liberal administration 1872, providing for secret ballots in elections. The measure was opposed by landowners who would no longer be able to monitor, and hence control, the voting of their tenants. They defeated the measure when it was first presented in the Lords 1871 but William Forster eventually secured its passage July 1872.

Bank of England UK central bank founded by act of Parliament 1694 to finance William III' s wars in France. It was entrusted with issuing bank notes under the Bank Charter Act 1844 and by the end of the 19th century was the UK's central clearing bank and keeper of the central gold reserve. It was nationalized by Attlee's Labour government 1946.

As the government's bank, it manages and arranges the financing of the public sector borrowing requirement and the national debt, implements monetary policy and exchange-rate policy by intervening in foreign-exchange markets, and supervises the UK banking system.

Bank of Ireland Ireland's first joint-stock bank, founded in Dublin 1783. All restrictions on other joint-stock banks in Ireland were removed 1845, so that the Bank of Ireland did not become a true central bank. The Irish government established the Central Bank 1943 as the only bank with the right to issue Irish banknotes.

Bank of England
Known as 'the Old Lady of Threadneedle Street', the Bank of England acts as banker to the government and to other banks. It stands at the heart of the City, London's financial and banking centre.
Anthony Lambert

Bank of Scotland Scotland's first joint-stock bank, established in Edinburgh 1695. It had a monopoly of banking in Scotland for 21 years until 1716, after which various other joint-stock banks were set up. It retains the right of issuing Scottish banknotes, as do the other Scottish banks.

Bannockburn, Battle of 23–24 June 1314 battle in which ◊Robert (I) the Bruce of Scotland defeated the English under Edward II, who had come to relieve the besieged Stirling Castle. Named after the town of Bannockburn, south of Stirling, central Scotland.

On 23 June the English vanguard attempted to force the road to Stirling, but their mounted attack was broken up by a combination of stakes, concealed pits, and resolute Scottish defence. The English knights then attempted to bypass the Scottish position via the low, boggy ground known as the Carse, but were driven back by a Scottish counter-attack, and the main army camped below the Scottish position. The next morning, Bruce launched the schiltrons (tightly packed formations) of Scottish pikemen in an attack downhill on the cramped English position. The battle hung in the balance until Scottish reserves (possibly including refugee Templar knights) came up, and the English position collapsed. English losses are reckoned at about 10,000 troops against about 4,000 Scots.

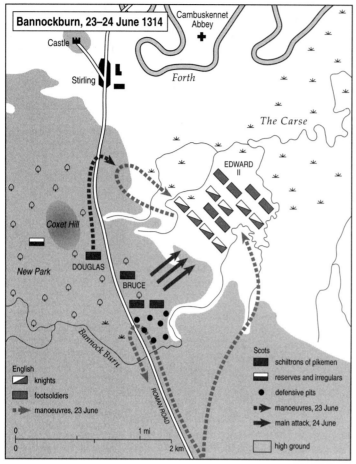

Bannockburn, 23–24 June 1314

Bannockburn, 23–24 June 1314
Edward II's advance on Stirling was blocked by Bruce's forces, protected by concealed pits which broke up the English cavalry attacks. The English attempted to bypass the Scottish position, but were driven back by Douglas and camped for the night near the boggy Carse. The next morning Bruce's pikemen, possibly supported by refugee Templar knights, advanced downhill to rout the hemmed-in English force.

Baptist member of any of several Protestant and evangelical Christian sects that practise baptism by immersion only upon profession of faith. Baptists seek their authority in the Bible. They originated among English Dissenters who took refuge in the Netherlands in the early 17th century. The first Baptist church was founded by Reverend John Smyth, a Cambridge scholar and an ordained minister of the Church of England, in Amsterdam 1609, and the movement spread rapidly by emigration, especially later on to the USA, and missionary activity. The Baptist Missionary Society, formed 1792 in Britain, pioneered the 19th-century missionary movement which spread the Baptist creed through Europe and to British colonies. Of the world total of approximately 31 million, some 26.5 million are in the USA and 265,000 in the UK.

Barbados former British colony, an island in the West Indies, east of the Windward group. It was claimed for England 1605 and a party of English settlers landed 1627, when it was granted to the Earl of Carlisle. It was taken over by the Crown 1663, and became prosperous as a sugar producer. Slaves were brought in from Africa to work in the sugar plantations. All the slaves in Barbados were freed by 1838 following abolition of slavery in the British Empire 1833. Barbados joined the West Indies Federation 1958 and gained independence 1966.

barbarian conspiracy joint attack AD 367 on Roman Britain from the north by Picts, Scots and Attacotti, and from continental Europe by Franks and Saxons. Nectaridus, probably *comes* (count) of the Roman coastal defences known as the Saxon Shore, was killed in the raids. The Roman commanders in Britain, Jovinus and Severus, were unable to repel the raiders and the Emperor Valentinian sent Theodosius to restore order. He landed at Richborough 368, marched on London, and reorganized Britain's defences. Despite his capable efforts, the attack was a great shock to Britain's defence system, and the country never recovered from the severe damage caused.

They glory in their warhorses and equipment. For us the name of the Lord must be our hope of victory in battle.

BANNOCKBURN
Robert the Bruce addressing his troops before the battle, 1314

Barebones Parliament English assembly called by Oliver ◊Cromwell to replace the 'Rump Parliament' July 1653. It consisted of 140 'godly men' nominated by the army and derived its name from one of its members, Praise-God Barbon. Although they attempted to pass sensible legislation (civil marriage; registration of births, deaths, and marriages; custody of lunatics), its members' attempts to abolish tithes, patronage, and the court of chancery, and to codify the law, led to the resignation of the conservative members and its dissolution Dec 1653.

Barnet, Battle of in the Wars of the ◊Roses, the defeat of Lancastrian forces, led by the Earl of ◊Warwick by the Yorkists, under King Edward IV, at Barnet (now in NW London) 14 April 1471.

baron rank in the ◊peerage of the UK, above a baronet and below a viscount. Historically, any member of the higher nobility, a direct vassal (feudal servant) of the king, not bearing other titles such as duke or count. The term originally meant the vassal of a lord, but acquired its present meaning in the 12th century.

The first English barony by patent was created 1387, but barons by 'writ' existed earlier. Life peers, created under the Act of 1958, are always of this rank. The wife of a baron, or a woman holding a title in her own right, is a **baroness**.

baronet British order of chivalry below the rank of baron, but above that of knight, created 1611 by James I to finance the settlement of Ulster. It is a hereditary honour, although women cannot succeed to a baronetcy. A baronet does not have a seat in the House of Lords but is entitled to the style *Sir* before his name. The sale of baronetcies was made illegal 1937.

Barons' Wars two civil wars between the barons and the Crown in England during the 13th century:

1215–17 between King ◊John and his barons, over his failure to honour the terms of ◊Magna Carta. In response the barons offered the throne to Prince Louis of France. After the death of King John 1216 and the accession of his son Henry III, the barons were defeated at ◊Lincoln 1217.

1264–67 between ◊Henry III (and the future ◊Edward I) and his barons (led by Simon de ◊Montfort). The barons attempted to limit the King's power and consequently he declared them to be rebels but was defeated and captured by Simon de Montfort at the Battle of ◊Lewes 14 May 1264. Simon de Montfort then effectively ruled England until he was defeated and killed by Edward at the Battle of ◊Evesham 4 Aug 1265.

barrow burial mound, usually composed of earth but sometimes of stones, examples of which are found in many parts of the world. The two main types are *long*, dating from the New Stone Age, or Neolithic, and *round*, dating from the later Mesolithic peoples of the early Bronze Age.

Long barrows may be mere mounds, but usually they contain a chamber of wood or stone slabs in which were placed the bodies of the deceased. They are common in southern England from Sussex to Dorset. The earthen (or unchambered) long barrows belong to the early and middle Neolithic, while others were constructed over Megalithic tombs.

Round barrows belong mainly to the Bronze Age, although in historic times some of the Saxon and most of the Danish invaders were barrow-builders. The commonest type is the bell barrow, consisting of a circular mound enclosed by a ditch and an outside bank of earth. Other types include the bowl barrow, pond barrow, and saucer barrow, all of which are associated with the Wessex culture (the Early Bronze Age culture of southern England dating to approximately 2000–1500 BC). Many barrows dot the Wiltshire downs in England.

Basutoland former British colony (now Lesotho) in southern Africa. It first received British protection 1843. It was annexed by the British 1868 and made part of Cape Colony 1871. It separated from Cape Colony and became a British colony 1884. It achieved independence 1966, when it adopted its present name.

Bayeux Tapestry linen hanging made about 1067–70 which gives a vivid pictorial record of the life of King Harold I and the invasion of England by William I (the Conqueror) 1066. It is an embroidery rather than a true tapestry, sewn with woollen threads in blue, green, red, and yellow, 70 m/231 ft long and 50 cm/20 in wide, and containing 72 separate scenes with descriptive wording in Latin. It was traditionally reputed to have been made by Queen Matilda, the wife of William I, but there is no evidence to support this. It is exhibited at the museum of Bayeux in Normandy, France.

Beachy Head, Battle of English naval defeat in the Channel 30 June 1690 by a French force sailing to London in support of a proposed Jacobite rebellion. The English army at the time under William of Orange was almost entirely occupied in Ireland where the exiled King James II was based. Taking advantage of this weakness, Louis XIV of France prepared a large fleet to attack London, raise a Jacobite rebellion in support of James II, and invade England. Despite this victory, James suffered a series of reverses and was forced to flee to France, so the proposed invasion never took place.

Beaconsfield title taken by Benjamin ◊Disraeli, prime minister of Britain 1868 and 1874–80.

Beaker people people thought to be of Iberian origin who spread out over Europe from the 3rd millennium BC. They were skilled in metalworking, and are identified by their use of distinctive earthenware beakers with various designs, of which the bell-beaker type was widely distributed throughout Europe. They favoured inhumation (burial of the intact body), often

Becket
The murder of Thomas à Becket, archbishop of Canterbury, depicted by the artist and chronicler Matthew Paris. After his death, Becket's tomb at Canterbury became one of the most important English pilgrimage sites of the middle ages.
Philip Sauvain

round ◊barrows, or secondary burials in some form of chamber tomb. A beaker accompanied each burial, possibly to hold a drink for the deceased on their final journey. They have been associated with the later stages of the construction of ◊Stonehenge.

bearbaiting baiting by dogs of a chained bear, often for gambling. Popular in Europe in the 16th century, it was outlawed in Britain 1835, although it still continues in many parts of the world, even if technically illegal. The Master of Bears was at one time a Crown appointment.

Beaton David 1494–1546. Scottish cardinal and politician, adviser to James V. Under Mary Queen of Scots, he supported closer ties with France and was opposed to the alliance with England. He persecuted Scottish Protestants; the supporters of George Wishart, who was condemned by Beaton to the stake, later murdered him.

Beatty David, 1st Earl 1871–1936. British admiral in World War I. He commanded the battle cruiser squadron 1912–16 and bore the brunt of the Battle of ◊Jutland 1916. In 1916 he became commander of the fleet, and in 1918 received the surrender of the German fleet.

Beaufort Henry 1375–1447. English priest, bishop of Lincoln from 1398, of Winchester from 1405. As chancellor of England, he supported his half-brother Henry IV and made enormous personal loans to Henry V to finance war against France. As a guardian of Henry VI from 1421, he was in effective control of the country until 1426. In the same year he was created a cardinal. In 1431 he crowned Henry VI as king of France in Paris.

Beaufort Margaret, Countess of Richmond and Derby 1443–1509. English noblewoman. She married Edmund Tudor, Earl of Richmond 1455. Their son, ◊Henry VII, claimed the English throne through his mother's descent from ◊John of Gaunt. Her third husband, Thomas Stanley, defected from the Yorkists to the Lancastrians, aiding Henry's victory at the Battle of ◊Bosworth 1485.

Beaverbrook (William) Max(well) Aitken, 1st Baron Beaverbrook 1879–1964. British financier, newspaper proprietor, and politician, born in Canada. He bought a majority interest in the *Daily Express* 1919, founded the *Sunday Express* 1921, and bought the London *Evening Standard* 1929. He served in Lloyd George's World War I cabinet as minister of information and Churchill's World War II cabinet as minister of aircraft production.

Between the wars he used his newspapers, in particular the *Daily Express*, to campaign for empire and free trade and against Prime Minister Baldwin.

Bechuanaland former British colony (now Botswana) in southern Africa. The region was occupied by the British 1884 at the instigation of Cecil Rhodes. It was organized as a British protectorate 1885 and divided into British Bechuanaland (south of the Molopo) and Bechuanaland Protectorate (north of it). When British Bechuanaland was attached to the Cape of Good Hope 1895, the northern part remained a protectorate until it became an independent republic 1966, when it adopted its present name.

Becket St Thomas à 1118–1170. English priest and politician. He was chancellor to ◊Henry II 1155–62, when he was appointed archbishop of Canterbury. The interests of the church soon conflicted with those of the crown and Becket was assassinated; he was canonized 1173.

A friend of Henry II, Becket was a loyal chancellor, but on becoming archbishop of Canterbury transferred his allegiance to the church. In 1164 he opposed Henry's attempt to curtail the independence of ecclesiastical courts, and had to flee the country; he returned 1170, but the reconciliation soon broke down. Encouraged by a hasty outburst from the king, four knights murdered Becket before the altar of Canterbury cathedral.

He was declared a saint, and his shrine became the busiest centre of pilgrimage in England until the Reformation.

Bede *c*.673–735. English theologian and historian, known as ***the Venerable Bede***, active in Durham and Northumbria. He wrote many scientific, theological, and historical works. His *Historia Ecclesiastica Gentis Anglorum/Ecclesiastical History of the English People* 731 is a seminal source for early English history.

Born at Monkwearmouth, Durham, he entered the local monastery at the age of seven, later transferring to Jarrow, where he became a priest in about 703. He devoted his life to writing and teaching; among his pupils was Egbert, archbishop of York. He was canonized 1899. Much of our knowledge of England in the Dark Ages prior to the 8th century depends on Bede's historical works and his painstaking efforts to research and validate original sources, both documentary and oral testimony. He popularized the system of dating events from the birth of Christ (*anno domini*).

Bedlam (abbreviation of ***Bethlehem***) one of the first European mental institutions. The hospital was opened in the 14th century in London and is now sited in Surrey.

Beeching Report 1963 official report on the railway network of Britain, which recommended the closure of loss-making lines and the improvement of money-making routes. Hundreds of lines and several thousand stations were closed as a result. It was named after Dr Richard Beeching who was chair of the British Railways Board 1963–65.

Bedlam
A scene from Hogarth's *A Rake's Progress* 1735 set in Bedlam, London's main hospital for the insane at the time. Sightseers, such as the two women in the background, could pay to look at the inmates chained up in their cells. *Philip Sauvain*

Belgae name given by Roman authors to people who lived in Gaul, north of the Seine and Marne rivers. They were defeated by Caesar 57 BC. Many of the Belgae settled in southeast England during the 2nd century BC. Belgic remains in Britain include coins, minted in Gaul, pottery made on a wheel, and much of the finest Iron Age Celtic art.

Benbow John 1653–1702. English admiral, hero of several battles with France. He ran away to sea as a boy, and from 1689 served in the navy. He fought at the battles of Beachy Head 1690 and La Hogue 1692, and died of wounds received in an engagement with a superior French force off Jamaica.

Benedictine order religious order of monks and nuns in the Roman Catholic Church, founded by St Benedict at Subiaco, Italy, in the 6th century, combining a communal life with regular prayer. It had a strong influence on medieval learning and reached the height of its prosperity early in the 14th century.

St ◊Augustine of Canterbury brought the order to England. A number of Oxford and Cambridge colleges have a Benedictine origin. The need for royal or noble landed endowments meant that the Benedictines were inextricably bound up with the aristocracy, and recruitment was largely from noble families. By the 10th century, the order was in need of reform which was carried out by Aethelwode, Oswald, and Dunstan, the abbot of Glastonbury. Aethelwode's *Regularis Concordia* was an attempt to provide one form of the Benedictine Rule, based on the best practice observed on the continent, for all English houses. This monastic revival greatly increased royal patronage at the expense of the nobility and in return the great abbots provided prayers for the king and quotas for his army. Several English cathedrals, notably Winchester and Ely, began to convert their chapters into monasteries, with the bishop also functioning as abbot. The 'Black Monks' now dominated the religious life of medieval England, and St Benedict's rule influenced many other forms of monasticism, including the ◊Cistercian order.

... as if, when you are sitting at dinner with your chiefs and ministers in wintertime... a sparrow from outside flew quickly through the hall... having come out of the winter it returns to the winter. Man's life appears like this: of what came before, and what follows, we are ignorant.

BEDE
Ecclesiastical History of the English People
early 8th century.

Bentham
English Utilitarian philosopher Jeremy Bentham. His failure to appreciate quality and poetry was criticized by John Stuart Mill, among others, but his radical social reformism greatly influenced subsequent practice.
Michael Nicholson

Bentinck
Lord George Bentinck, English Tory politician, supporter of emancipation. A keen sportsman, he reformed abuses in horse racing and field sports. He was greatly admired by Disraeli.
Michael Nicholson

By the time of the ◊Reformation in the 1530s, there were nearly 300 Benedictine monasteries and nunneries in England, all of which were suppressed by Henry VIII. Benedictinism was re-introduced into England by both the Catholic and Anglican Churches in the 19th century, and a number of notable public schools, such as Ampleforth and Downside, are connected to Benedictine monasteries, as are several colleges of Oxford and Cambridge.

benefit of clergy immunity from lay jurisdiction granted to members of the clergy. The benefit was granted by the Constitutions of ◊Clarendon 1164 which laid down that members of the clergy should be exempt from the jurisdiction of lay courts, except in the case of infringement of royal forest laws. They were to be handed over instead to an ecclesiastical court, where it was widely felt that they would receive more lenient treatment.

By the 15th century it was sufficient to be able to read to claim benefit, as the church had a strong association with learning, and literacy was taken to be sufficient proof of being a member of the clergy. Those claiming this right would normally be asked to read Psalm 51 i, the so-called 'neck verse', and so this passage was often allegedly memorised by those who could not in fact read. During the early Reformation, the rights to benefit were severely restricted, although it was only actually abolished 1825.

Bengal former British colony; part of British ◊India.

Bentham Jeremy 1748–1832. English philosopher, legal and social reformer, and founder of utilitarianism. The essence of his moral philosophy is found in the pronouncement of his *Principles of Morals and Legislation* (written 1780, published 1789): that the object of all legislation should be 'the greatest happiness for the greatest number'.

He made suggestions for the reform of the poor law 1798, which formed the basis of the reforms enacted 1834, and in his *Catechism of Parliamentary Reform* 1817 he proposed annual elections, the secret ballot, and universal male suffrage. He was also a pioneer of prison reform.

Bentinck Lord William Cavendish 1774–1839. British colonial administrator, son of the 3rd Duke of Portland. He was the first governor general of India 1828–35 where he acted against the ancient Hindu customs of thuggee and suttee, and established English as the language of instruction.

Bentinck Lord William George Frederick Cavendish 1802–1848. (known as Lord George Bentinck) English nobleman and politician, son of the 4th Duke of Portland. An advocate of protectionism, he was a leading opponent of the repeal of the ◊Corn Laws 1848 but after the repeal helped defeat ◊Peel's government. During his lifetime, he was better known as a racehorse owner than as a politician.

Berkeley William 1606–1677. British colonial administrator in North America, governor of the colony of Virginia 1641–77. He was removed from the governorship by Oliver Cromwell 1652 due to his Royalist sympathies but was reappointed 1660 by Charles II. However, growing opposition to him in the colony culminated in Bacon's Rebellion 1676 and in 1677 Berkeley was removed from office for his brutal repression of that uprising.

Berlin, Conference of conference 1884–85 of the major European powers (France, Germany, the UK, Belgium, and Portugal together with the USA and Turkey) called by German chancellor Otto von Bismarck to decide on the colonial partition of Africa.

Britain recognized German claims to the Cameroons and New Guinea in return for support against the French in Nigeria. The conference as a whole agreed on a neutral Congo Basin with free trade, and recognized the Congo Free State as the personal possession of King Leopold II of Belgium. The conference also sought to end slavery and prohibited the slave trade in Africa.

Bermuda British colony, a group of islands in the western North Atlantic. The islands were visited by the Spanish 1515 who named them after Juan de Bermúdez. The English called them the Somers Islands, after Sir George Somers who was shipwrecked here en route to Virginia 1609. They were first colonized by the English 1612 and taken over by the British Crown 1684. Internal self-goverment was introduced 1968.

Bernicia, kingdom of 6th-century Anglo-Saxon kingdom stretching from the Firth of Forth in the north down to its southern boundary either on the Tyne or the Tees. It was established by Ida at Bamburgh AD 547, founding a dynasty that reigned for most of the 6th century. It was combined with the neighbouring kingdom of ◊Deira by ◊Edwin to form Northumbria 616. The name is tribal in origin and has left no trace on the modern map.

Berwick James Fitzjames, Duke of Berwick 1670–1734. French marshal, illegitimate son of the Duke of York (afterwards James II of England) and Arabella Churchill (1648–1730), sister of the Duke of ◊Marlborough, his enemy in battle. He was made Duke of Berwick in 1687. After the revolution of 1688 he served under his father in Ireland, joined the French army, fought against William III and Marlborough, and in 1707 defeated the English at Almansa in Spain. He was killed at the siege of Philippsburg.

Berwick, treaties of three treaties between the English and the Scots, signed at Berwick on the border of the two countries. In the first treaty Jan 1560, Queen Elizabeth I of England and the Calvinist ◊Lords of the Congregation in Scotland agreed to an alliance, and the expulsion from Scotland of French troops who were supporting the Catholic regent, Mary of Guise, mother of ◊Mary Queen of Scots.

In the second treaty July 1586, James VI of Scotland signed a treaty with Elizabeth by which, in return for an English pension of £4,000, both sides agreed to maintain their established religions, and cooperate in case of an invasion of Britain by Catholic forces.

The third treaty June 1639 ended the first ◊Bishops' War. King Charles I of England agreed with the Scottish rebels that a General Assembly of the Scottish Church, the Kirk, would determine religious matters and a parliament would be summoned in Edinburgh, and in return they stood down their forces.

Besant Annie 1847–1933. English socialist and feminist activist. She was associated with the radical atheist Charles Bradlaugh and the socialist ◊Fabian Society. She and Bradlaugh published a treatise advocating birth control and were prosecuted; as a result she lost custody of her daughter. In 1889 she became a disciple of the theosophist Madame Blavatsky and went to India, where she campaigned for Indian independence. She founded the Central Hindu College 1898 and the Indian Home Rule League 1916 and became president of the Indian National Congress 1917.

Bessemer Henry 1813–1898. British engineer and inventor who developed a simple method of converting molten pig iron into steel by blowing cold air through the molten metal (the **Bessemer process**) 1856.

Bevan Aneurin (Nye) 1897–1960. British Labour politician. Son of a Welsh miner, and himself a miner at 13, he became member of Parliament for Ebbw Vale 1929–60. As minister of health 1945–51, he inaugurated the National Health Service (NHS); he was minister of labour Jan–April 1951, when he resigned (with Harold Wilson) on the introduction of NHS charges and led a Bevanite faction against the government. In 1956 he became chief Labour spokesperson on foreign affairs, and deputy leader of the Labour party 1959. He was an outstanding orator.

Beveridge William Henry, 1st Baron Beveridge 1879–1963. British economist and social reformer. A civil servant, he acted as Lloyd George's prime adviser in the social legislation of the Liberal government before World War I. The **Beveridge Report** 1942 formed the basis of the welfare state in Britain.

Beveridge Report, the popular name of *Social Insurance and Allied Services*, a report written by William Beveridge 1942 that formed the basis for the social-reform legislation of the Labour government of 1945–50. Also known as the *Report on Social Security*, it identified five 'giants': illness, ignorance, disease, squalor, and want. It proposed a scheme of social insur-

All punishment is mischief: all punishment in itself is evil.

JEREMY BENTHAM
Principles of Morals and Legislation

We have been the dreamers, we have been the sufferers, now we are the builders... We want to complete political extinction of the Tory Party and twenty-five years of Labour government. We cannot do in five years what requires to be done.

ANEURIN (NYE)
BEVAN
speech, two months before Labour's landslide victory, Labour Party Conference, 1945.

Bevin

During World War II, all able-bodied men between the ages of 18 and 51 were eligible for national service under a scheme devised by Ernest Bevin, minister of labour. Some 30,000 men under the age of 25, known as 'Bevin boys', were sent to work in the mines.
Image Select

ance from 'the cradle to the grave', and recommended a national health service, social insurance and assistance, family allowances, and full-employment policies.

Bevin Ernest 1881–1951. British Labour politician. Chief creator of the Transport and General Workers' Union, he was its general secretary from 1921 to 1940, when he entered the war cabinet as minister of labour and national service. He organized the 'Bevin boys', men chosen by ballot to work in the coal mines as war service. As foreign secretary in the Labour government 1945–51 he supported the acceptance of the Marshall Plan for reviving Western Europe and the creation of NATO.

Bible (Greek *ta biblia*, 'the books') the sacred book of the Jewish and Christian religions. The earliest attempts to translate the Bible into English are the 9th-century and 10th-century versions of the Psalms and the Gospels, together with Aelfric's translation of the Old Testament in the late 10th century. Wycliffe and his followers were the first to render the complete Scriptures into English in the 14th century, working from a Latin text that was itself a translation. In the 16th century, Tyndale was the first to translate the New Testament into English from the original Greek. The complete English Bible that bears the name of Miles Coverdale was printed in 1535. It was not a translation from the original, but from Luther's German Bible of 1534.

Following further English versions, the Authorized Version, or King James Bible, was issued in 1611, and became established as the standard English Bible, famous for the clarity and

My [foreign] policy is to be able to take a ticket at Victoria Station and go anywhere I damn well please.

ERNEST BEVIN
The Spectator, *April 1951*

beauty of its language. The Revised Version of the New Testament was published 1881 and of the Old Testament 1885. A modern English translation of the New Testament was published 1969, with the Old Testament following 1970. The two were combined as the New English Bible. There have been further modern English versions since.

Bill of Rights act of Parliament 1689 which established it as the primary governing body of the country. The Bill of Rights embodied the Declarations of Rights which contained the conditions on which William and Mary were offered the throne. It made provisions limiting royal prerogative with respect to legislation, executive power, money levies, courts, and the army and stipulated Parliament's consent to many government functions.

The act made illegal the suspension of laws by royal authority without Parliament's consent; the power to dispense with laws; the establishment of special courts of law; levying money by royal prerogative without Parliament's consent; and the maintenance of a standing army in peacetime without Parliament's consent. It also asserted a right to petition the

Bible

Title page of the first complete English Bible, printed in Zurich 1535. Miles Coverdale's translation, of Luther's German Bible, was based on the Vulgate edition and Tyndale's translation of the New Testament.
Philip Sauvain

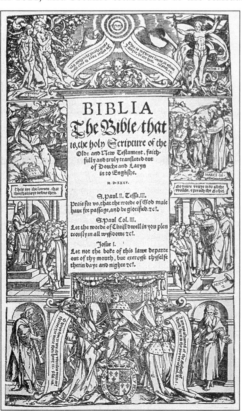

sovereign, freedom of parliamentary elections, freedom of speech in parliamentary debates, and the necessity of frequent parliaments.

Birkenhead Frederick Edwin Smith, 1st Earl of Birkenhead 1872–1930. British Conservative politician and lawyer. A flamboyant character, known as 'FE', he joined with Edward ◊Carson in organizing armed resistance in Ulster to Irish Home Rule. He was Lord Chancellor 1919–22 and a much criticized secretary for India 1924–28.

Birkbeck George 1776–1841. English doctor and pioneer of workers' education. Born in Settle, Yorkshire, he studied medicine and philosophy in Edinburgh. As professor of natural philosophy at Anderson's College, Glasgow, he started giving free lectures to workers 1799 and these classes later became the Glasgow Mechanics' Institution. He moved to London as a doctor 1804 and established a similar scheme of free classes for workers there. This scheme became the London Mechanics' Institute 1824 and then evolved to become Birkbeck College, a college offering part-time degrees in the new University of London, which he also helped found.

Bishops' Wars struggles between King Charles I of England and Scottish Protestants 1638–40 over Charles' attempt to re-impose royal authority over the church in Scotland. The name derives from the ◊Arminian bishops in England who were seen as the driving force behind Charles' attempt.

The dispute began with Archbishop ◊Laud's attempt to introduce the new Anglican prayer book into Scottish churches – there were riots in Edinburgh when the prayer book was first used July 1637. This resistance led Charles to issue a proclamation defending the new book and upholding its use. The Scottish Protestants viewed this as a challenge to the integrity of their church and issued the National Covenant March 1638, in which they agreed to resist Charles's imposition of a the new prayer book. The General Assembly of the Kirk met in Glasgow Nov 1638 without Charles permission and passed resolutions abolishing Scottish bishops and rejecting the new Prayer Book. The Scots began mobilizing their forces for war and took Edinburgh and other key towns March 1639. Charles was reluctant to call an English Parliament to fund a war against the rebels, and so his forces were gathered hastily and were obviously no match for the Covenanters. The first Bishops' War was ended without a battle by the Treaty of ◊Berwick June 1639.

However, the Scots continued to defy Charles who turned to the Irish for help after being refused assistance by the Short Parliament April 1640. The second Bishops' War started Aug 1640 when the Scots invaded England, defeating Charles at Newburn and occupying Newcastle-upon-Tyne. Charles withdrew to York and concluded the Treaty of ◊Ripon with the Scots Oct 1640. Charles was obliged to pay £3,600,000 to the Scots, who by then controlled six English counties, and agree to reform of the English Church. To raise this huge sum, payable in three instalments, Charles was forced to call the Long Parliament and largely accede to its wishes.

Black and Tans nickname of a special auxiliary force of the Royal Irish Constabulary employed by the British 1920–21 to combat the Sinn Féinners (Irish nationalists) in Ireland; the name derives from the colours of the uniforms, khaki with black hats and belts. They were notorious for their brutal reprisals for terrorist activity which caused much resentment in the nationalist community.

Black Death great epidemic of bubonic plague that ravaged Europe in the mid-14th century, killing between one-third and half of the population. The cause of the plague was the bacterium *Yersinia pestis*, transmitted by fleas borne by migrating Asian black rats.

It was recognized in England at Weymouth Aug 1348, and before waning in the winter of 1349 had reduced the population of England by a third. The dramatic impact on localities is perpetuated in accounts which have entered folklore, such as the Reverend Mompesson's handling of the outbreak in the village of Eyam, Derbyshire, and commemorated in some playground dances of children, for example, 'Ring a' Roses'. Labour shortages caused by the Black Death led to spiralling wage rises which the government struggled to control with measures such as the Statute of ◊Labourers 1351. Popular resentment at these measures after the immense suffering of the plague helped cause the ◊Peasants' Revolt.

Black Prince nickname of ◊Edward, Prince of Wales, eldest son of Edward III of England.

They constituted ticket-of-leave men, city toughs, soldiers unable to settle down and ambitious nonentities who had failed to get on – rogues, fools and disappointed men.

BLACK AND TANS
historian C Desmond Greaves
Liam Mellowes and the Irish Revolution, *1971*

The flower of the world's knighthood at that time and the finest soldier of his age.

BLACK PRINCE
described in Jean Froissart's Chronicles

Blackshirts term widely used to describe fascist paramilitary organizations. Originating with Mussolini's fascist Squadristi in the 1920s, it was also applied to the Nazi SS (*Schutzstaffel*). In Britain, the name was applied to the followers of Oswald ◊Mosley's British Union of Fascists (BUF), founded Oct 1932, who adopted the black shirt in imitation of the Italian and German fascists. The Public Order Act 1936 prohibited the wearing of uniforms by political parties after several violent clashes involving the blackshirts during 1936, especially in Jewish areas of East London.

Blair Tony (Anthony Charles Lynton) 1953– . British politician, leader of the Labour Party from 1994. A centrist in the manner of his predecessor John ◊Smith, he became Labour's youngest leader by a large majority in the first fully democratic elections to the post July 1994.

Blair practised as a lawyer before entering the House of Commons 1983 as member for the Durham constituency of Sedgfield. He was elected to Labour's shadow cabinet 1988 and given the energy portfolio; he shadowed employment from 1991 and home affairs from 1992. Like John Smith, he did not ally himself with any particular faction and, in drawing a distinction between 'academic and ethical socialism', succeeded in winning over most sections of his party, apart from the extreme left.

Blake George 1922– . British double agent who worked for the British overseas intelligence service MI6 and also for the USSR. Blake was unmasked by a Polish defector 1960 and imprisoned, but escaped to the Eastern bloc 1966. He is said to have betrayed at least 42 British agents to the Soviet side.

Blake Robert 1599–1657. English admiral of the Parliamentary forces during the English ◊Civil War. Appointed 'general-at-sea' 1649, he destroyed Prince Rupert's privateering fleet off Cartagena, Spain, in the following year. In 1652 he won several engagements against the Dutch navy. In 1654 he bombarded Tunis, the stronghold of the Barbary corsairs, and in 1657 captured the Spanish treasure fleet in Santa Cruz.

blanketeers Manchester hand-loom weavers who began a march on London March 1817, in protest against the suspension of the Habeas Corpus Act and the economic slump after the end of the Napoleonic Wars; so named as the marchers were carrying their blankets. The march was broken up in Stockport, Cheshire, the day after it began. See also ◊Peterloo Massacre.

Blenheim, Battle of in the War of the Spanish Succession, decisive victory 13 Aug 1704 of Allied troops under ◊Marlborough over French and Bavarian armies near the Bavarian village of Blenheim (now in Germany) on the left bank of the Danube, about 25 km/18 mi northwest of Augsburg. Although the war was to continue for a further eight years, Blenheim marked the turning point at which the power of France was first broken.

The French planned to send an army to unite with the Bavarians and then march down the Danube to capture Vienna. To preempt this, the British under the Duke of Marlborough and the Austrians under Prince Eugène of Savoy decided on a joint attack on Bavaria. Several groups of German troops joined the Austro-British force during its advance and the opposing armies met at the village of Blindheim, better known as Blenheim.

The French had fortified the village, where they based their right flank with their line extending some 5 km/3 mi along a ridge protected to the front by marshy ground bisected by a stream. The Allies marched overnight to gain the element of surprise and attacked at about noon on 13 Aug 1704. Eugène attacked the Bavarians on the French left flank, while Marlborough attacked Blenheim directly, without immediate success. Assuming that the attacks against the flanks would also have weakened the French centre, Marlborough drove a massive force – 90 squadrons of horse, 23 battalions of infantry, and supporting artillery – straight through the centre of the French line. Eugène moved his advance in turn, taking the French in their flank and splitting them from the Bavarians so that both could be dealt with separately. Marlborough then completed the move against Blenheim and captured most of the garrison, although most of the Bavarian forces were able to escape.

Bligh William 1754–1817. English sailor who accompanied Captain James ◊Cook on his second voyage around the world 1772–74, and in 1787 commanded HMS *Bounty* on an expedition to the Pacific.

On the return voyage the crew mutinied against his allegedly brutal treatment 1789, and Bligh was cast adrift in a small boat with the 18 members of the crew who remained loyal to him. Despite having no map and few provisions, they survived and reached Timor, near Java after many weeks, having drifted 5,822 km/3,618 mi. He was appointed governor of New South Wales 1805, where his discipline again provoked a mutiny 1808 (the Rum Rebellion). He returned to Britain, and was made an admiral 1811.

Blitz, the (anglicization of *Blitzkrieg*) German air raids against Britain during World War II, following the German's failure to establish air superiority in the Battle of ◊Britain. It has been estimated that about 40,000 civilians were killed, 46,000 injured, and more than a million homes destroyed and damaged in the Blitz, together with an immense amount of damage caused to industrial installations.

The first raid was against London 7–8 Sept 1940, and raids continued on all but ten nights until 12 Nov. The raids then targeted industrial cities such as Coventry (14 Nov), Southampton, Birmingham, Bristol, Cardiff, Portsmouth, and Liverpool, with occasional raids on London. In spring 1941 the air defences began to take a larger toll of the attackers, due to improvements in radar for night fighters and for artillery control. The raids fell away during the early summer as Luftwaffe forces were withdrawn from the west in preparation for the invasion of the USSR. However, German air raids on Britain continued throughout the war.

Blood Thomas 1618–1680. Irish adventurer, known as Colonel Blood, who attempted to steal the crown jewels from the Tower of London, 1671. After failing to capture Dublin Castle 1663, he fled to Holland. He later tried to assassinate the Duke of Ormonde 1670, before his infamous attempt on the crown jewels. He and three accomplices succeeded in stealing the crown and orb, but were captured not long after. He was later pardoned by Charles II and his estates restored.

Bloody Assizes courts held by judges of the High Court in the west of England under the Lord Chief Justice, Judge ◊Jeffreys, after ◊Monmouth's rebellion 1685. Over 300 rebels were executed, many more were flogged or imprisoned, and about 800 were transported.

Bloody Sunday dispersion by the police of a meeting in Trafalgar Square, London, Sunday 13 Nov 1887, with over 100 casualties and two deaths. The meeting, which had been prohibited by the Commissioner of Police, was organized by the Social Democratic Federation to demand the release from prison of the Irish nationalist William O'Brien. Two members of Parliament were arrested during the confrontation: Robert Cunninghame-Graham and John Burns.

Bloody Sunday outrage in the Bogside, Londonderry, Northern Ireland, 30 Jan 1972 when British paratroopers opened fire on unarmed civil rights demonstrators. The order to fire was given after violence broke out at an anti-internment march: 13 people were killed and many wounded. The incident provoked outrage both in Britain and abroad and led to serious unrest in Ireland. The British Embassy in Dublin was burnt down and the IRA extended its bombing campaign to mainland Britain; disorders in Northern Ireland itself led to direct rule from Westminster being imposed on the province. An enquiry under Lord Widgery

Bligh
Aquatint by Robert Dodd of William Bligh and officers cast adrift from HMS *Bounty* 4 April 1789 by mutineers, National Maritime Museum, Greenwich, London. A skilled and courageous sailor, Capt Bligh does not seem to have been unduly tyrannical, though his abusive and overbearing manner made him deeply unpopular.
E T Archive

Blitz
The intensive German bombing campaign of London, known as the Blitz, began 7 Sept 1940. Extensive damage was caused and the 2,000 regular members of the London Fire Brigade were supplemented by 20,000 auxiliaries.
Image Select

accepted the security forces' account that they had themselves been under fire, although this version of events had often been challenged.

Blount Charles, Earl of Devonshire, 8th Baron Mountjoy 1562–1606. English soldier, a friend of the 2nd Earl of ◊Essex. Blount accompanied him and ◊Raleigh on their unsuccessful expedition to the Azores 1597. He became Lord Deputy of Ireland 1600 and quelled the revolt led by the Irish chief Hugh O'Neill, 2nd Earl of Tyrone, when the Irish failed in their attempt to reach a Spanish force that had arrived at Kinsale 1601. He subdued most of Ireland and was created earl 1603.

blue books official reports presented to Parliament, so named for their blue paper covers. They are usually the reports of a royal commission or a committee, but short Acts of Parliament are also sometimes known as blue books, even when they have no cover. The 'treachery of the Blue Books' relates to the 1847 report on education in Wales, which associated religious nonconformity and ignorance of the English language with immorality.

Blunt Anthony 1907–1983. British art historian and double agent. As a Cambridge lecturer, he recruited for the Soviet secret service and, as a member of the British Secret Service 1940–45, passed information to the USSR. In 1951 he assisted the defection to the USSR of the British agents Guy ◊Burgess and Donald Maclean (1913–1983). He was unmasked 1964 and given immunity after his confession, although when the affair became public 1979 he was stripped of his knighthood.

Boadicea alternative spelling of British queen ◊Boudicca.

Bodley Thomas 1545–1613. English scholar and diplomat, after whom the Bodleian Library in Oxford is named. After retiring from Queen Elizabeth I's service 1597, he restored the university's library, which was opened as the Bodleian Library 1602. The library had originally been founded in the 15th century by Humphrey, Duke of Gloucester (1391–1447). He was knighted in 1604.

Boer War the second of the ◊South African Wars 1899–1902, waged between Dutch settlers in South Africa and the British.

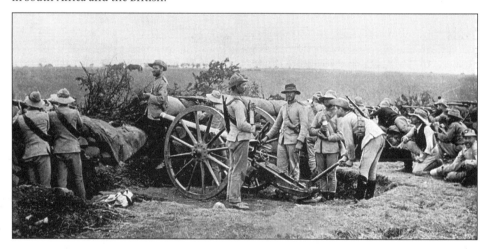

Boer War
Boer forces bombarding Ladysmith with long-range French Creusot guns, known as 'Long Toms', during the 2nd South African, or Boer, War.
Hulton Deutsch

Boleyn Anne 1507–1536. Queen of England 1533–36. Henry VIII broke with the pope (see ◊Reformation) in order to divorce his first wife and marry Anne, the daughter of Sir Thomas Boleyn. She was married to Henry 1533 and gave birth to the future Queen Elizabeth I in the same year and a stillborn son three years later. Accused of adultery and incest with her half-brother (a charge invented by Thomas ◊Cromwell), she was beheaded at the Tower of London 19 May 1536.

Bolingbroke Henry St John, Viscount Bolingbroke 1678–1751. British Tory politician and political philosopher. He was foreign secretary 1710–14 and a Jacobite conspirator. His books, such as *Idea of a Patriot King* 1738, which argued for leadership independent of party politics, and *The Dissertation upon Parties* 1735, laid the foundations for 19th-century Toryism.

The Boers said the war was for liberty. The British said it was for equality. The majority of the inhabitants, who were not white at all, gained neither liberty nor equality.

BOER WARS
historian Rayne Kruger, Goodbye Dolly Gray 1959

Never had a prince a more dutiful wife than you have in Anne Boleyn; with which name and place I could willingly have contented myself, if God and your Grace's pleasure had so been pleased.

ANNE BOLEYN
last letter to Henry VIII, May 1536

Secretary of war 1704–08, he became foreign secretary in Robert ◊Harley's ministry 1710, and in 1713 negotiated the Treaty of Utrecht. His plans to restore the 'Old Pretender' James Francis Edward Stuart were ruined by Queen Anne's death only five days after he had secured the dismissal of Harley 1714. He fled abroad, returning 1723, when he worked to overthrow Robert Walpole.

Bonar Law British Conservative politician; see ◊Law, Andrew Bonar.

Bondfield Margaret Grace 1873–1953. British socialist who became a trade-union organizer to improve working conditions for women. She was a Labour member of Parliament 1923–24 and 1926–31, and was the first woman to enter the cabinet – as minister of labour 1929–31.

Bonnie Prince Charlie Scottish name for ◊Charles Edward Stuart, pretender to the throne.

Booth William 1829–1912. British founder of the ◊Salvation Army 1878, and its first 'general'.

Booth was born in Nottingham. He experienced religious conversion at the age of 15. In 1865 he founded the Christian Mission in Whitechapel, East London, which became the Salvation Army 1878. *In Darkest England, and the Way Out* 1890 contained proposals for the physical and spiritual redemption of the many down-and-outs. His wife Catherine (1829–1890, born Mumford), whom he married 1855, became a public preacher about 1860, initiating the ministry of women.

borough unit of local government in the UK from the 8th century until 1974, when it continued as an honorary status granted by royal charter to a district council, entitling its leader to the title of mayor.

The term, which derives from the Anglo-Saxon 'burgh', a town or settlement fortified against Viking invasion, was originally applied to an area entitled to send a representative to Parliament. A 'pocket borough' was one in which the nomination of a candidate was 'in the pocket' of a local wealthy family. A 'rotten borough' was one which had so few electors that their votes could be bought or influenced. Such abuse was ended by the Reform Act 1932. The term today especially applies to the 32 boroughs of Greater London and to any town or district that has been granted a royal charter.

Bosworth, 22 August 1485
The last act of the Wars of the Roses, the Battle of Bosworth was a small-scale action which saw the final defeat of the House of York and the first death in battle of an English king since 1066. The decision of the Stanley family to support Henry Tudor at the last minute was crucial: it was their troops who killed Richard III as he led the counter-charge against Henry's advance.

Booth
Portrait of English evangelist William Booth by Hubert Herkomer. Booth founded the Salvation Army and became its first 'general', modelling its operations on those of the British army. His movement grew rapidly, and its work soon extended to the USA, Australia, India, and elsewhere, and Booth's standing was such that he was invited to the coronation of Edward VII 1901.
Library of Congress

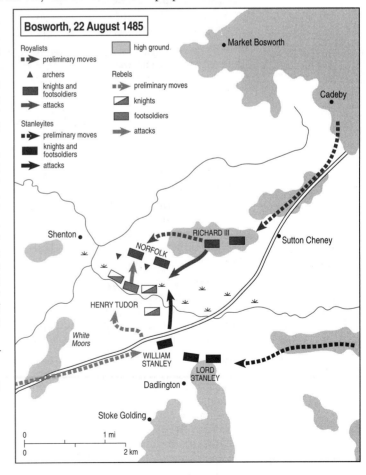

Bosworth, 22 August 1485

Royalists
■▶ preliminary moves
▲ archers
■ knights and footsoldiers
➤ attacks

Stanleyites
■▶ preliminary moves
■ knights and footsoldiers
➤ attacks

high ground

Rebels
■▶ preliminary moves
▱ knights
■ footsoldiers
➤ attacks

Market Bosworth
Cadeby
Shenton
RICHARD III
Sutton Cheney
NORFOLK
HENRY TUDOR
White Moors
WILLIAM STANLEY
LORD STANLEY
Dadlington
Stoke Golding

0   1 mi
0   2 km

Bosworth, Battle of last battle of the Wars of the ◊Roses, fought on 22 Aug 1485. Richard III, the Yorkist king, was defeated and slain by Henry of Richmond, who became Henry VII. The battlefield is near the village of Market Bosworth, 19 km/12 mi west of Leicester.

Richard's oppressive reign ensured that Henry, landing in Wales, gathered an army of supporters as he marched into England to meet Richard's army which was drawn up on a hill at Bosworth. A third, smaller, army led by Lord Stanley stood off from both sides, undecided upon which to join. Henry opened the battle by advancing up the hill and charging into the opposition. Lord Stanley now made his decision and fell on the rear of King Richard's position, causing the King's force to break and flee. Richard was unhorsed in the rush and beaten to death as he lay. As the battle ended, Lord Stanley crowned Henry as king; Henry later married Edward IV's daughter Elizabeth, uniting the houses of York and Lancaster to bring the Wars to an end.

Bothwell Francis Stewart, 5th Earl of Bothwell *c.*1563–1611. Scottish nobleman, an opponent of James VI. He was involved in various plots and conspiracies against James, in alliance with both Protestant and Roman Catholic interests, culminating after 1590 in a series of attempts to seize the king. He forfeited his title 1592 and was obliged to escape abroad 1595. He died in Italy.

Bothwell James Hepburn, 4th Earl of Bothwell *c.*1536–1578. Scottish nobleman, third husband of ◊Mary Queen of Scots, 1567–70, alleged to have arranged the explosion that killed Darnley, her previous husband, 1567. Tried and acquitted a few weeks after the assassination, he abducted Mary and married her 15 May. A revolt ensued, and Bothwell was forced to flee. Mary obtained a divorce 1570, and Bothwell was confined in a castle in the Netherlands where he died insane.

Bothwell Bridge, Battle of final defeat of the rebel Covenanters of southwest Scotland by the Duke of ◊Monmouth 22 June 1679 at a site southeast of Glasgow. Some 4,000 rebels faced Monmouth's 10,000-strong army: about 200 to 400 were killed and 1,200 captured.

Boudicca 1st century AD. Queen of the ◊Iceni, a British tribe in modern East Anglia, she is often referred to by the Latin form ***Boadicea***. Her husband, King Prasutagus, had been a tributary of the Romans, but on his death AD 60 the territory of the Iceni was violently annexed. Boudicca was scourged and her daughters raped. Boudicca raised the whole of southeast England in revolt, and before the main Roman armies could return from campaigning in Wales she burned Londinium (London), Verulamium (St Albans), and Camulodunum (Colchester). Later the Romans under governor Suetonius Paulinus defeated the British between London and Chester; they were virtually annihilated and Boudicca poisoned herself.

***Bounty*, Mutiny on the** naval mutiny in the Pacific 1789 against British captain William ◊Bligh.

Bow Street Runners informal police force organized 1749 by Henry ◊Fielding, chief magistrate at Bow Street in London. The scheme was initially established as a force of detectives to aid the Bow Street Magistrates' court but from 1757 it was funded by the government to cover the rest of London and formed the basis for the Metropolitan police force established by Robert ◊Peel's government 1829.

Boycott Charles Cunningham 1832–1897. English land agent in County Mayo, Ireland, who strongly opposed the demands for agrarian reform by the Irish Land League 1879–81, with the result that the peasants refused to work for him. His name is the origin of the word ***boycott***, meaning to socially or commercially isolate an individual, organization, or country, a tactic much used by modern pressure groups.

Boyle Richard, 1st Earl of Cork 1566–1643. Anglo-Irish business magnate and administrator. Born in Canterbury, he arrived in Dublin 1588 and by means of a judicious marriage and shrewd manoeuvring became the wealthiest landowner in southwest Ireland, with large plantations in Munster. He won the favour of Elizabeth I and did much to encourage the immigration of English Protestants to Ireland. He was created Earl of Cork 1620 and became Lord High Treasurer 1631. During the 1630s he lost royal favour through his intrigues against Wentworth, the future Earl of Strafford, but took revenge by testifying against Wentworth at his impeachment. He successfully repressed a Catholic rebellion in Munster late 1641.

Boyne, Battle of the battle fought 1 July 1690 in eastern Ireland, in which the exiled king James II was defeated by William III and fled to France. It was the decisive battle of the War of English Succession, confirming a Protestant monarch. It took its name from the river Boyne which rises in County Kildare and flows 110 km/69 mi northeast to the Irish Sea.

After obtaining aid from Louis XIV of France, James landed in Ireland where he had numerous supporters. King William also landed an army in Ireland, collected more forces from Londonderry, and marched south with about 36,000 troops. James' forces had taken up a position on the south side of the river Boyne, and William launched the attack by sending a force to cross the river some miles upstream so as to turn the Irish flank. The French turned to oppose this attack, and William then sent his cavalry across the river in a frontal assault on James' position. After fierce fighting the Irish foot soldiers broke but their cavalry continued to fight for some time before being routed. James fled to Dublin while his army largely became fugitives; any hopes of James' restoration to the English throne were finally dashed.

Bradlaugh Charles 1833–1891. British freethinker and radical politician. In 1880 he was elected Liberal member of Parliament for Northampton, but was not allowed to take his seat until 1886 because, as an atheist, he (unsuccessfully) claimed the right to affirm instead of taking the oath. He was associated with the feminist Annie ◊Besant.

He served in the army, was a lawyer's clerk, became well known as a speaker and journalist under the name of Iconoclast, and from 1860 ran the *National Reformer*. He advocated the freedom of the press, contraception, and other social reforms.

Bramham Moor, Battle of final defeat of Henry ◊Percy, Earl of Northumberland, by Henry IV 19 Feb 1408 near Tadcaster, Yorkshire. Percy had been forced to flee to Scotland 1405 and early 1408 invaded England to meet Henry at Bramham Moor. Percy was killed in the battle and the family's rebellion against Henry was crushed.

Breda, Treaty of 1667 treaty that ended the Second Anglo-Dutch War (1665–67). By the terms of the treaty, England gained New Amsterdam, which was renamed New York, but abandoned its claim to the Moluccan islands.

Brétigny, Treaty of or *Treaty of Calais* treaty made between Edward III of England and John II of France in 1360 following the failure of Edward's campaign of 1359–60 at the end of the first phase of the Hundred Years' War. John, who had been captured at the battle of Poitiers, was ransomed for £500,000, and Edward received Aquitaine and its dependencies in exchange for renunciation of his claim to the French throne. Although Edward never formally renounced his claim to the French throne, there was a lull in the fighting for nine years.

Bretwalda (from Old English *Bretenanwealda*, 'ruler of Britain') 9th-century Anglo-Saxon title for a powerful king who exercised authority over England south of the Humber. The term was initially used in Bede's list of hegemonic rulers, but also extended to include more recent kings, such as ◊Egbert of Wessex. Other powerful kings holding much the same sway, such as Offa of Mercia, were not included. The existence of the title provides important evidence for the early concept of an English 'nation'.

bridewell jail or house of correction. The word comes from the royal palace of Bridewell, built 1522 by Henry VIII. In 1555 it was converted to a type of prison where the 'sturdy and idle' as well as certain petty criminals were made to labour. Various other towns set up their own institutions following the same regime.

Bridgewater Francis Egerton, 3rd Duke of 1736–1803. Pioneer of British inland navigation. With James ◊Brindley as his engineer, he constructed 1762–72 the Bridgewater canal from his coal mine at Worsley to Manchester, cutting the price of coal by half. In 1776, the canal was extended to the Mersey, a distance of 67.5 km/42 mi.

Bright John 1811–1889. British Liberal politician, a campaigner for free trade, peace, and social reform. A Quaker millowner, he was among the founders of the Anti-Corn Law League in 1839, and was largely instrumental in securing the passage of the Reform Bill of 1867.

Bright
John Bright, British Victorian politician and humanitarian campaigner against the Corn Laws and the Crimean War. A stirring orator, he said of the Crimean War: 'The angel of death has been abroad throughout the land; you may almost hear the beating of his wings'.
Michael Nicholson

*Beginning reform
is beginning
revolution.*

BRISTOL RIOTS
*remark by the Duke of
Wellington to Mrs
Arbuthnot,
7 November 1830*

After entering Parliament 1843 Bright led the struggle there for free trade, together with Richard ◊Cobden, which achieved success 1846. His *laissez-faire* principles also made him a prominent opponent of factory reform. He constantly exerted his influence on behalf of peace, and opposed the Crimean War, Palmerston's aggressive policy in China, Disraeli's anti-Russian policy, and the bombardment of Alexandria. He sat in Gladstone's cabinets as president of the Board of Trade 1868–70 and chancellor of the Duchy of Lancaster 1873–74 and 1880–82, but broke with him over the Irish Home Rule Bill.

Brighton Pavilion alternative name for the ◊Royal Pavilion, Brighton.

Brindley James 1716–1772. British canal builder, the first to employ tunnels and aqueducts extensively, in order to reduce the number of locks on a direct-route canal. His 580 km/360 mi of canals included the ◊Bridgewater (Manchester–Liverpool) and Grand Union (Manchester–Potteries) canals.

Bristol Riots public protests in Bristol 1831. The disturbances arose at the time of the rejection in Parliament of the Reform Bill 1831 (eventually passed 1832), and were largely prompted by the visit of Sir Charles Wetherell, recorder of the city, who was an opponent of reform and had voted against the Bill. Rioters burned down several buildings, including the Mansion House, Custom House, Bishop's Palace and town gaol. The disturbances were quelled by the intervention of the army. The destruction of property was so great (some £200,000) that the city was obliged to charge a heavy annual rate on its residents in order to compensate the victims.

Britain island off the northwest coast of Europe, one of the British Isles. It comprises England, Scotland, and Wales (together officially known as *Great Britain*), and is part of the United Kingdom. The name is derived from the Roman name Britannia, which in turn is derived from the ancient Celtic name of the inhabitants, *Bryttas*.

Britain, ancient period in the British Isles (excluding Ireland) extending through prehistory to the Roman occupation (1st century AD). Settled agricultural life evolved in Britain during the 3rd millennium BC. Neolithic society reached its peak in southern England, where it was capable of producing the great stone circles of Avebury and Stonehenge early in the 2nd millennium BC. It was succeeded in central southern Britain by the Early Bronze Age Wessex culture, with strong trade links across Europe. The Iron Age culture of the Celts was predominant in the last few centuries BC, and the ◊Belgae (of mixed Germanic and Celtic stock) were partially Romanized in the century between the first Roman invasion of Britain under Julius Caesar (54 BC) and the Roman conquest (AD 43). See also ◊Roman Britain.

At the end of the last Ice Age, Britain had a cave-dwelling population of Palaeolithic hunter-gatherers, whose culture was called Creswellian, after Creswell Crags, Derbyshire, where remains of flint tools were found. Throughout prehistory successive waves of migrants from continental Europe accelerated or introduced cultural innovations. Important Neolithic remains include: the stone houses of Skara Brae, Orkney; so-called causewayed camps in which hilltops such as Windmill Hill, Wiltshire, were enclosed by concentric fortifications of ditches and banks; the first stages of the construction of the ritual monuments known as henges (for example, Stonehenge, Woodhenge); and the flint mines at Grimes Graves, Norfolk. Burial of the dead was in elongated earth mounds (long barrows).

Aircraft Losses in the Battle of Britain

aircraft losses 10 July–31 Oct 1940

| period | RAF | | Luftwaffe | | |
	fighter	other	bomber[1]	fighter[2]	other
10–30 July	75 (27)	8 (1)	116 (31)	49	9 (6)
31 July–27 Aug	284 (30)	30 (7)	306 (53)	268 (35)	21 (9)
28 Aug–1 Oct	471 (32)	12 (5)	345 (78)	400 (41)	28 (18)
2–31 Oct	174 (57)	11 (7)	194 (68)	162 (36)	19 (9)

figures in brackets indicate aircraft lost in accidents (included in totals)
[1] Luftwaffe bombers include Ju 87 dive-bombers
[2] Luftwaffe fighters include Me110 twin-engine fighters

The ◊Beaker people probably introduced copper working to the British Isles. The aristocratic society of the Bronze Age Wessex culture of southern England is characterized by its circular burial mounds (round barrows); the dead were either buried or cremated, and cremated remains were placed in pottery urns. Later invaders were the ◊Celts, a warrior aristocracy with an Iron Age technology; they introduced horse-drawn chariots, had their own distinctive art forms, and occupied fortified hilltops. The Belgae, who buried the ashes of their dead in richly furnished flat graves, were responsible for the earliest British sites large and complex enough to be called towns; settled in southern Britain, the Belgae resisted the Romans from centres such as Maiden Castle, Dorset.

Britain, Battle of World War II air battle between German and British air forces over Britain lasting 10 July–31 Oct 1940.

At the outset the Germans had the advantage because they had seized airfields in the Netherlands, Belgium, and France, which were safe from attack and from which southeast England was within easy range. On 1 Aug 1940 the Luftwaffe had about 4,500 aircraft of all kinds, compared to about 3,000 for the RAF. The Battle of Britain had been intended as a preliminary to the German invasion plan *Seelöwe* (Sea Lion), which Hitler indefinitely postponed 17 Sept and abandoned 10 Oct, choosing instead to invade the USSR.

The Battle of Britain has been divided into five phases: 10 July–7 Aug, the preliminary phase; 8–23 Aug, attack on coastal targets; 24 Aug–6 Sept, attack on Fighter Command airfields; 7–30 Sept, daylight attack on London, chiefly by heavy bombers; and 1–31 Oct, daylight attack on London, chiefly by fighter-bombers. The main battle was between some 600 Hurricanes and Spitfires and the Luftwaffe's 800 Messerschmitt 109s and 1,000 bombers (Dornier 17s, Heinkel 111s, and Junkers 88s). Losses Aug–Sept were, for the RAF: 832 fighters totally destroyed; for the Luftwaffe: 668 fighters and some 700 bombers and other aircraft.

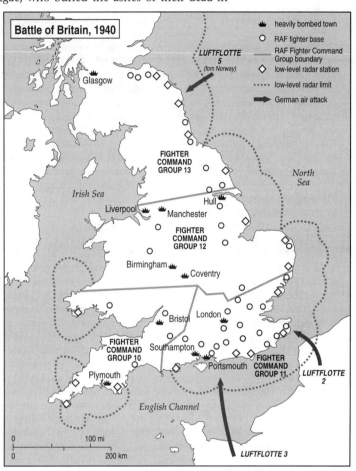

The Battle of Britain, 1940
From July to October 1940, sustained German air attacks were made on a variety of British targets, including industrial cities, by three German air fleets. The incoming formations were picked up by British coastal radar stations, and RAF fighter aircraft were directed against them. Aircraft losses on both sides were huge, but the inability of air power alone to inflict a decisive strategic defeat was clearly demonstrated.

Britain since 1945 period of British history characterized by the loss of traditional industries and markets and the search for a new, European role for Britain. ◊feature

British Antarctic Territory colony created 1962 and comprising all British territories south of latitude 60° S: the South Orkney Islands, the South Shetland Islands, the Antarctic Peninsula and all adjacent lands, and Coats Land, extending to the South Pole; total land area 660,000 sq km/170,874 sq mi; population (exclusively scientific personnel) about 300.

British Broadcasting Corporation (BBC) the UK state-owned broadcasting network. It operates television and national and local radio stations, and is financed by the sale of television viewing licences; it is not allowed to carry advertisements but it has an additional source of income through its publishing interests and the sales of its programmes. Overseas radio broadcasts (World Service) have a government subsidy.

The BBC was converted from a private company (established 1922) to a public body under royal charter 1927. Under the Charter, news programmes were required to be politically impartial. The first director-general 1922–1938 was John Reith.

British East India Company see ◊East India Company, British.

BREAKING WITH THE PAST

Britain since 1945

Britain emerged victorious from World War II, with its Empire intact. 'Now Win the Peace', said the election posters. The new Labour Government promised planned economic growth, Keynesian remedies for unemployment, modernization of industry by nationalization, and welfare 'From the Cradle to the Grave'. It was little short of a social revolution, but high hopes were soon tempered by reality.

The end of Empire

Internationally, the 'Big Three' were at best the 'Two-and-a-half'. The USA and USSR had contributed most to victory. When their rivalry turned into Cold War, Britain could not hope to compete in the arms race for long. At home, the staple British export industries (coal, steel, textiles, and shipbuilding) were in long-term decline. Markets lost during the War would never be fully recovered, and economic problems seemed endemic. These issues were linked: how could a nation with chronic balance of payments difficulties afford to remain a global power?

Despite austerity policies, by 1949 Britain had been forced to devalue the pound and reduce its overseas commitments by withdrawing from India and Palestine. Departure from these trouble-spots did not mean wholesale retreat. The government hoped to transform the British Empire into a freely co-operating Commonwealth of Nations with real political and economic significance. The aim was to satisfy colonial nationalism, while preserving a network of military bases and a trading bloc making international payments in sterling.

The weakness of this strategy was revealed by the Suez Crisis. When Britain attempted to exercise neo-imperial dominance in the Middle East by force, it failed and unleashed a wave of anti-British feeling. Harold Macmillan accelerated decolonization and accepted that the Commonwealth was going to be a very loose association. By 1964 most of the Empire had become independent. The 'special relationship' with the USA suffered as a result: Britain minus the colonies was simply not so valuable an ally. Fearing isolation, Britain turned to the European Community, only to find its application for membership vetoed by France. 'Great Britain has lost an Empire and has not yet found a role', observed Dean Acheson in 1962.

'East of Suez'

Britain meanwhile shared in the remarkable post-war economic recovery of the western world. 'Most of our people have never had it so good', said Macmillan in 1957. Both Conservatives and Labour were broadly committed to maintaining the mixed economy, the welfare state, and full employment. While living standards rose, governments shrank from tackling the underlying problems of an uncompetitive economy with high wage demands and low investment. The Treasury merely operated short-term 'stop-go' policies as each spurt of growth ended in balance of payments deficits. These necessitated a second devaluation in 1967 and drastic cuts in overseas defence spending. All significant commitments 'East of Suez' were to be abandoned by 1971. Thus Britain broke through the status barrier: it was a world power no longer. Late-1960s society may have been affluent and permissive, but the nation seemed in decline – the word itself was becoming a cliché.

Edward Heath swung foreign policy decisively toward Europe. Britain entered the EC in 1973 but found it difficult to adjust to its institutions and policies. EC membership did not bring the dramatic material benefits expected. Nor did the discovery of North Sea oil. Rising unemployment, record levels of inflation, an energy crisis, widespread industrial disputes, and violence in Northern Ireland all deepened the mood of demoralization.

The Thatcher years

The post-war consensus crumbled as politicians in both parties tried to find new policies. This plunged Labour into a decade of internal strife and permanent opposition from 1979. The Conservatives, led by Margaret Thatcher, adopted a radical 'monetarist' programme intended to revitalize the economy through rapid deflation, deregulation, privatization, and the reduction of trade union power. But this economic shock treatment coincided with a global recession. British unemployment topped 3 million, amid signs of a growing divide between the depressed North and relatively prosperous South. Productivity improved and enterprise was encouraged in an economy increasingly based on services, but the 'economic miracle' of the mid-1980s proved short-lived, and unemployment remained high.

Thatcher sought to re-assert British influence in international affairs, but the prestige derived from the Falklands War and a revival of the 'special relationship' was not sustainable. When the end of the Cold War prompted further European integration British doubts about the EC resurfaced in the politics of the 1990s.

Britain has been transformed since 1945. The British Empire, built up over four centuries, came to an end in the 1960s. Traditional industries, chief sources of national wealth since the Industrial Revolution, withered away and all but died in the 1980s. The nation faced these historic changes with some reluctance, but the era of empire and industry is now over. A new era has begun.

JASON TOMES

British Expeditionary Force (BEF) British army serving in France in World War I 1914–18. Also the 1939–40 army in Europe in World War II, which was evacuated from Dunkirk, France.

In World War I the BEF was first commanded by General Sir John French and then General Sir Douglas Haig. It consisted of five infantry and one cavalry division, numbering about 100,000 troops. A sixth infantry division joined this force in Sept. The term 'BEF' strictly referred only to the forces initially sent to France in 1914, but it continued to be commonly applied to the British forces operating in France and Flanders.

In World War II Field Marshal John Gort commanded the BEF sent to France in 1939. By May 1940 it consisted of 10 infantry divisions, one tank brigade, and an RAF element of about 500 fighters and light bombers. After sustaining heavy losses during the French and Belgian campaigns of 1940 the remains were evacuated from Dunkirk in June, leaving much of their equipment behind.

British Guiana former British colony (now Guyana) in northern South America. Following settlement by the Dutch *c.* 1620, the territory was visited by many non-Dutch, including several English, in the 18th century. It was first captured by the British 1781, when they founded Georgetown. It was recaptured by the Dutch but finally regained by the British 1803 and ceded to Britain 1814. The crown colony of British Guiana was established 1831. The colony gained independence 1966, when it adopted its present name.

British Honduras former British colony (now Belize) in Central America. It was settled *c.* 1638 by English foresters from Jamaica, but was subject to frequent attacks by the Spanish, who claimed sovereignty. The Spanish were decisively defeated by the Royal Navy in the Battle of St George's Caye 1798. The area was recognized by Britain as a colony 1871 and renamed Belize (after its main river) 1973. It gained independence 1981.

British Indian Ocean Territory British colony in the Indian Ocean. It was formed 1965 from islands formerly belonging to Mauritius (notably the Chagos Archipelago) and the Seychelles. All the islands apart from the Chagos Archipelago were returned to the Seychelles 1976.

British Library national library of the UK. Created 1973, it comprises the reference division (the former library departments of the British Museum, being rehoused in Euston Road, London); lending division at Boston Spa, Yorkshire, from which full text documents and graphics can be sent by satellite link to other countries; bibliographic services division (incorporating the British National Bibliography); and the National Sound Archive in South Kensington, London.

British Museum largest museum of the UK. Founded in 1753, it opened in London in 1759. Rapid additions led to the construction of the present buildings (1823–47). In 1881 the Natural History Museum was transferred to South Kensington.

The museum began with the purchase of Hans Sloane's library and art collection, and the subsequent acquisition of the Cottonian, Harleian, and other libraries. It was first housed at Montagu House in Bloomsbury. Its present buildings were designed by Robert Smirke, with later extensions in the circular reading room 1857, and the north wing or Edward VII galleries 1914.

British National Party (BNP) extreme right-wing political party. Initially a small but violent offshoot of the ◊National Front, it has now taken the latter's place as the leading far-right party in the UK, achieving national prominence 1993 when Dereck Beacon became the first BNP councillor in by-elections for the Tower Hamlets council. The party is heavily implicated in the rise in racial violence in the area and near its Bexhill head-quarters.

British New Guinea former British colony, southeastern New Guinea. The south coast of New Guinea (Papua) was visited from the 16th century by Portuguese and Spanish navigators and later by the French and English. The territory was proclaimed British 1883 and 1884 but not annexed, as British New Guinea, until 1888. British New Guinea was placed under the authority of Australia 1906, who administered it together with Papua until 1975, when the joint territories gained their independence.

British North Borneo former British colony (now Sabah) in northeastern Borneo. The English unsuccessfully attempted to settle the region in the 17th and 18th centuries. The first concession was granted to Sir James Brooke 1841. New concessions were granted by the Sultans of Brunei and Sulu to the British North Borneo Company, chartered 1881. The territory was proclaimed a British protectorate 1888 but continued to be administered by the Company to 1941, when it was occupied by the Japanese. It became a British colony 1946 and an independent state of Malaysia 1963, when it took its present name.

British Somaliland former British protectorate (now Somali) in East Africa. The coast came under British influence in the 19th century but the region remained under Egyptian control to 1884. It was administered by the Government of India 1884–98 and by the British Foreign Office 1898–1905, when it was transferred to the British Colonial Office. It was occupied by Italy 1940–41, and united with the former Italian Somaliland to form the Somali Democratic Republic 1960.

broad church term used to describe Anglicans who accept the legitimacy of both Protestant and Catholic traditions within the Established Church. See also ◊tractarianism.

Brooke James 1803–1868. British administrator who became rajah of Sarawak, on Borneo, 1841. Born near Varanasi, Uttar Pradesh, Brooke served in the army of the East India Company. Wounded in the first Burmese War, he went to Britain, and from there set out for Borneo 1838 at the head of a private expedition. He helped to suppress a revolt, for which the sultan gave him the title of rajah of Sarawak. Brooke became known as the 'the white rajah'. He was succeeded as rajah by his nephew, Sir Charles Johnson (1829–1917), whose son Sir Charles Vyner (1874–1963), in 1946 arranged for the transfer of Sarawak to the British crown.

Brougham
Scottish-born English politician, lawyer, and reformer, Henry Brougham was often considered arrogant and eccentric. He campaigned vigorously for Benthamite legal reforms and co-founded London University. The carriage specially built for him became the prototype of the 'brougham'.
Michael Nicholson

Brougham Henry Peter, 1st Baron Brougham and Vaux 1778–1868. British Whig politician and lawyer. From 1811 he was chief adviser to the Princess of Wales (afterwards Queen Caroline), and in 1820 he defeated the attempt of George IV to divorce her. He was Lord Chancellor 1830–34, supporting the Reform Bill.

Born in Edinburgh, he was a founder of the *Edinburgh Review* 1802. He sat in Parliament 1810–12 and from 1816, and supported the causes of public education, the abolition of slavery, and law reform. He was one of the founders of University College, London, 1828. When the Whigs returned to power 1830, Brougham accepted the chancellorship and a peerage a few weeks later. His allegedly dictatorial and eccentric ways led to his exclusion from office when the Whigs next assumed power 1835. From 1837 he was active in the House of Lords.

Browne Robert 1550–1633. English Puritan leader, founder of the Brownists. He founded communities in Norwich, East Anglia, and in the Netherlands which practised non-ritualistic worship and which developed into present-day ◊Congregationalism.

Browne, born in Stamford, Lincolnshire, preached in Norwich and then retired to Middelburg in the Netherlands, but returned after making his peace with the church and became head of Stamford Grammar School. In *A Book which Sheweth the Life and Manner of all True Christians* 1582 Browne advocated Congregationalist doctrine; he was imprisoned several times in 1581–82 for attacking Episcopalianism (church government by bishops). From 1591 he was a rector in Northamptonshire.

Bruce, House of royal house of Scotland 1306–1371. After the humiliation of ◊John Balliol at the hands of Edward (I) of England in 1296, Scotland recovered its independence under the two kings of the house of Bruce, ◊Robert I the Bruce (1306–1329), the victor at ◊Bannockburn, and ◊David II (1329–1371).

Brummell Beau (George Bryan) 1778–1840. British dandy and leader of fashion. He introduced long trousers as conventional day and evening wear for men. A friend of the Prince of Wales, the future George IV, he later quarrelled with him. In 1816, gambling losses drove him to exile in France, where he died in an asylum.

Brunel Isambard Kingdom 1806–1859. British engineer and inventor. In 1833 he became engineer to the Great Western Railway, which adopted the 2.1-m/7-ft gauge on his advice. He built the Clifton Suspension Bridge over the river Avon at Bristol and the Saltash Bridge over the river Tamar near Plymouth. His ship-building designs include the *Great Western* 1837, the first steamship to cross the Atlantic regularly; the *Great Britain* 1843, the first large iron ship to have a screw propeller; and the *Great Eastern* 1858, which laid the first transatlantic telegraph cable.

In all, Brunel was responsible for building more than 2,600 km/ 1,600 mi of the permanent railway of the west of England, the Midlands, and South Wales. He also constructed two railway lines in Italy, acted as adviser on the construction of the Victoria line in Australia and on the East Bengal railway in India. The son of Marc Brunel, he made major contributions in shipbuilding and bridge construction, and assisted his father in the Thames tunnel project. Brunel University in Uxbridge, London, is named after both father and son.

Brussels, Treaty of pact of economic, political, cultural, and military alliance established 17 March 1948, for 50 years, by the UK, France, and the Benelux countries, joined by West Germany and Italy 1955. It was the forerunner of the North Atlantic Treaty Organization and the European Community (now the European Union).

Bruton John 1947– . Irish politician, leader of Fine Gael (United Ireland Party)

Brunel
English engineer and inventor Isambard Kingdom Brunel. Perhaps the greatest of the 19th-century engineers, he designed railways for the Great Western Railway, with bridges, tunnels, and viaducts; ships, including the *Great Western* 1838, the first steamship to cross the Atlantic, and the *Great Britain* 1843.
Topham Picture Library

from 1990 and prime minister from 1994. The collapse of Albert ◊Reynolds' Fianna Faíl–Labour government Nov 1994 thrust Bruton, as a leader of a new coalition with Labour, into the prime ministerial vacancy. He pledged himself to the continuation of the Anglo-Irish peace process as pursued by his predecessor.

A Dublin-trained lawyer and working farmer, Bruton entered parliament 1969 and, as party spokesman, made steady progress through the departments of agriculture, industry and commerce, and education. He served in the government of Garret FitzGerald 1982–87 before succeeding him as party leader.

Buckingham George Villiers, 1st Duke of Buckingham 1592–1628. English courtier, powerful adviser to James I and later Charles I. Introduced to the court of James I 1614, he soon became his favourite and was made Earl of Buckingham 1617 and a duke 1623. He failed to arrange the marriage of Prince Charles and the Infanta of Spain 1623, but on returning to England negotiated Charles's alliance with Henrietta Maria, sister of the French king. After Charles's accession, Buckingham attempted to form a Protestant coalition in Europe, which led to war with France. His policy on the French Protestants was attacked in Parliament, and he failed to relieve the Protestants (◊Huguenots) besieged in La Rochelle 1627. This added to his unpopularity with Parliament, and he was assassinated in Portsmouth when about to sail again for La Rochelle.

Buckingham George Villiers, 2nd Duke of Buckingham 1628–1687. English politician and playwright, a member of the ◊Cabal under Charles II. He helped bring about the downfall of ◊Clarendon. A dissolute son of the first duke, he was brought up with the royal children. His play *The Rehearsal* satirized the style of the poet Dryden, who portrayed him as Zimri in *Absalom and Achitophel*.

bull-baiting the setting of dogs to attack a chained bull, a one-time 'sport' popular in the UK and Europe. It became illegal in Britain 1835.

Who's your fat friend?

BEAU BRUMMEL
speaking to Lord Alvanley and referring to the Prince Regent (quoted in Gronow's Reminiscences)

Houses of Bruce and Balliol

Other claimants to the throne of Scotland in this period were Edward II of England, who claimed descent from Malcolm III through Malcolm's daughter Matilda, and John Comyn the Red (died 1306), who was descended from a daughter of Donald III of the House of Dunkeld

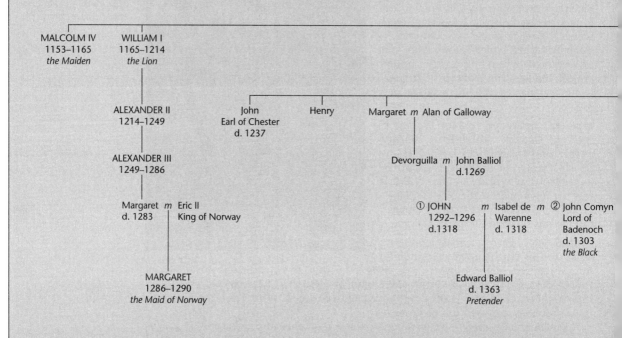

Bull John. Imaginary figure personifying England.

Buller Redvers Henry 1839–1908. British commander against the Boers in the South African War 1899–1902. He was defeated at Colenso and Spion Kop 1900, but relieved Ladysmith; he was superseded by British field marshal Lord Roberts.

Bunker Hill, Battle of the first significant engagement in the ◊American Revolution, 17 June 1775, near a small hill in Charlestown (now part of Boston), Massachusetts, USA; the battle actually took place on Breed's Hill, but is named after Bunker Hill as this was the more significant of the two. Although the colonists were defeated, they were able to retreat to Boston in good order and lost only 450 casualties against British losses of 226 killed and 828 wounded.

The two hills had a commanding position over Boston and so the British commander Thomas Gage decided to occupy them but was pre-empted by a party of about 1,200 American militiamen who seized Breed's Hill on the night of 16 June and erected a stockade

You must drive these farmers from the hill or it will be impossible for us to remain in Boston.

BUNKER HILL
William, Viscount Howe addressing his troops before the battle

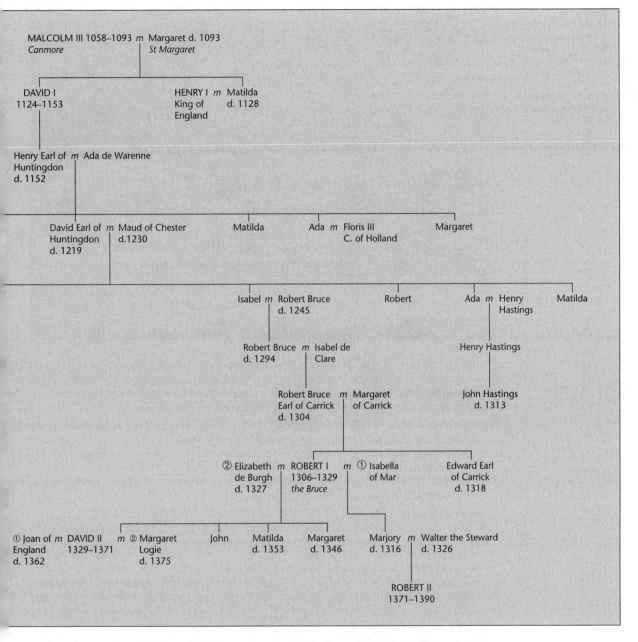

MALCOLM III 1058–1093 *m* Margaret d. 1093
Canmore   *St Margaret*

DAVID I   HENRY I *m* Matilda
1124–1153   King of   d. 1128
                           England

Henry Earl of *m* Ada de Warenne
Huntingdon
d. 1152

David Earl of *m* Maud of Chester   Matilda   Ada *m* Floris III   Margaret
Huntingdon   d.1230   C. of Holland
d. 1219

Isabel *m* Robert Bruce   Robert   Ada *m* Henry   Matilda
          d. 1245   Hastings

Robert Bruce *m* Isabel de   Henry Hastings
d. 1294   Clare

Robert Bruce *m* Margaret   John Hastings
Earl of Carrick   of Carrick   d. 1313
d. 1304

② Elizabeth *m* ROBERT I   *m* ① Isabella   Edward Earl
de Burgh   1306–1329   of Mar   of Carrick
d. 1327   *the Bruce*   d. 1318

① Joan of *m* DAVID II *m* ② Margaret   John   Matilda   Margaret   Marjory *m* Walter the Steward
England   1329–1371   Logie   d. 1353   d. 1346   d. 1316 │ d. 1326
d. 1362   d. 1375

                                                                         ROBERT II
                                                                         1371–1390

to protect them from the fire of British warships in the harbour. The following morning Gage ordered a 2,000-strong force of infantry to clear the hill. The British made two advances which suffered heavy losses due to strong barrages from the American position; a third, better-planned attack, succeeded in taking the top of the hill and driving off the Americans, who retired in good order. Gage's failure to defeat the rebels soundly led to his replacement as British commander.

Burgess Guy (Francis de Moncy) 1910–1963. British spy, a diplomat recruited by the USSR as an agent. He was linked with Kim ◊Philby, Donald Maclean (1913–1983), and Anthony ◊Blunt.

burgh former unit of Scottish local government, referring to a town enjoying a degree of self-government, abolished 1975; the terms ***burgh*** and ***royal burgh*** once gave mercantile privilege but are now only an honorary distinction.

Bunker Hill, Battle of
British ships bombarding
American positions on
Breed's Hill during the
Battle of Bunker Hill
1775. Although the
British won, they
sustained heavy losses
and the battle was a
moral victory for the
American rebels.
Image Select

Burgh is also an Anglo-Saxon term for a fortified town (also spelt 'burh'), which came to mean any built-up area and hence evolved into the modern conception of a borough. Alfred the Great undertook a widespread programme of building and strengthening burghs in Wessex against the threat of Danish invasion in the 9th century.

Burgh Hubert de. d. 1243 English ⟡justiciar and regent of England. He began his career in the administration of Richard I, and was promoted to the justiciarship by King John; he remained in that position under Henry III from 1216 until his dismissal 1232. He was a supporter of King John against the barons, and ended French intervention in England by his defeat of the French fleet in the Strait of Dover 1217. He became the most powerful figure in Henry III's minority following the death of the regent, William Marshall, 1219.

Burghley William Cecil, Baron Burghley 1520–1598. English politician, chief adviser to Elizabeth I as secretary of state from 1558 and Lord High Treasurer from 1572. He was largely responsible for the religious settlement of 1559, and took a leading role in the events preceding the execution of Mary Queen of Scots 1587.

One of Edward VI's secretaries, he lost office under Queen Mary, but on Queen Elizabeth's succession became her most trusted minister. He carefully avoided a premature breach with Spain in the difficult period leading up to the attack by the Spanish Armada 1588, did a great deal toward abolishing monopolies and opening up trade, and was created Baron Burghley 1571.

Burke Edmund 1729–1797. British Whig politician and political theorist, born in Dublin, Ireland. In Parliament from 1765, he opposed the government's attempts to coerce the American colonists, for example in *Thoughts on the Present Discontents* 1770, and supported the emancipation of Ireland, but denounced the French Revolution, for example in *Reflections on the Revolution in France* 1790.

Burke wrote *A Philosophical Inquiry into the Origin of our Ideas on the Sublime and Beautiful* 1756, on aesthetics. He was paymaster of the forces in Rockingham's government 1782 and in the Fox–North coalition 1783, and after the collapse of the latter spent the rest of his career in opposition. He attacked Warren Hastings's misgovernment in India and promoted his impeachment. Burke defended his inconsistency in supporting the American but not the French Revolution in his *Appeal from the New to the Old Whigs* 1791 and *Letter to a Noble Lord* 1796, and attacked the suggestion of peace with France in *Letters on a Regicide Peace* 1795–97. He retired 1794. He was a skilled orator and is regarded by British Conservatives as the greatest of their political theorists.

*Magnanimity in
politics is not
seldom the truest
wisdom; and a great
empire and little
minds go ill
together.*

EDMUND BURKE
*speech on conciliation
with America, 1775*

Burma former British colony, now the republic of Myanmar, southeast of India. It fought three wars with the British 1824–6, 1852–3, 1885–6, and the British gained increasing portions of its territory as a result of these. It was first a province of British India, then a crown colony from 1937. A pact signed with Britain 1947 brought it independence 1948.

Burns John 1858–1943. British labour leader, sentenced to six weeks' imprisonment for his part in the Trafalgar Square demonstration on 'Bloody Sunday' 13 Nov 1887, and leader of the strike in 1889 securing the 'dockers' tanner' (wage of 6d per hour). An Independent Labour member of Parliament 1892–1918, he was the first working-class person to be a member of the cabinet, as president of the Local Government Board 1906–14. At the outbreak of World War I he opposed British involvement in the war, and withdrew from political life shortly after.

Bute John Stuart, 3rd Earl of Bute 1713–1792. British Tory politician, prime minister 1762–63. Bute succeeded his father as earl 1723, and in 1737 was elected a representative peer for Scotland. On the accession of George III in 1760, he became the chief instrument in the king's policy for breaking the power of the Whigs and establishing the personal rule of the monarch through Parliament. His position as the king's favourite and supplanter of the popular prime minister Pitt the Elder made him hated in the country. He resigned 1763 after the Seven Years' War.

Butler Josephine (born Gray) 1828–1906. English social reformer. She promoted women's education and the Married Women's Property Act, and campaigned against the Contagious Diseases Acts of 1862–70, which made women in garrison towns and seaports suspected of prostitution liable to compulsory examination for venereal disease. Refusal to undergo examination meant imprisonment. As a result of her campaigns, the acts were repealed 1883.

Butler Richard Austen ('Rab'), Baron Butler 1902–1982. British Conservative politician. As minister of education 1941–45, he was responsible for the 1944 Education Act which established universal secondary education. He was chancellor of the Exchequer 1951–55, Lord Privy Seal 1955–59, and foreign minister 1963–64. As a candidate for the prime ministership, he was defeated 1957 by Harold Macmillan (under whom he was home secretary 1957–62), and by Alec Douglas Home 1963.

The term 'butskellism' was used to describe the similar moderate policies advocated by Butler and the Labour leader Hugh ◊Gaitskell.

Butt Isaac 1813–1879. Irish Protestant lawyer who founded the idea of Home Rule for Ireland. He became a lawyer 1838 and Tory MP for Youghal 1851, and defended Fenian prisoners from 1865–69. He was converted to nationalism and popularized the slogan 'Home Rule', founding the Home Government Association (Home Rule League) 1870 and leading it until 1878.

Buxar, Battle of 1764 at Buxar, in Bihar, northeast India, battle in which the British ◊East India Company secured dominance of northern India. It defeated the triple forces of the Mogul emperor Shah Alam II (reigned 1759–1806); Mir Qasim, the recently dispossessed governor of Bengal; and Shuja-ud Daula, governor of the Ganges valley province of Oudh and *wazir* (chief minister) to the emperor.

Byng George, Viscount Torrington 1663–1733. British admiral. He captured Gibraltar 1704, commanded the fleet that prevented an invasion of England by the 'Old Pretender' James Francis Edward Stuart 1708, and destroyed the Spanish fleet at Messina 1718. John ◊Byng was his fourth son.

At the Battle of ◊Beachy Head 1690 he advised protecting the Thames and awaiting the return of the rest of the fleet, but Queen Mary ordered him to give battle. He was subsequently court-martialled but acquitted; he said '...while we had a fleet in being they would not dare to make an attempt' and from this came the strategic doctrine of the 'fleet in being' whereby the existence of a powerful fleet becomes a deterrent in itself.

Byng John 1704–1757. British admiral. Byng failed in the attempt to relieve Fort St Philip when the island of Minorca was invaded by France 1756. He was court-martialled and shot. The French writer Voltaire ironically commented 'Dans ce pays-ci il est bon de tuer de temps en temps un amiral pour encourager les autres' (In this country [England] it is considered a good idea to kill an admiral from time to time to encourage the others).

But, as a servant, I will obey her majesty's commandment... Presuming that she, being God's chief minister, it shall be God's will to have her commandments obeyed... You see I am a mixture of divinity and policy.

LORD BURGHLEY
letter to his son,
March 1596

Politics is the art of the possible.

'RAB' BUTLER
(attributed)

Cabal, the (from *kabbala*) group of politicians, the English king Charles II's counsellors 1667–73, whose initials made up the word by coincidence – Clifford (Thomas Clifford 1630–1673), Ashley (Anthony Ashley Cooper, 1st Earl of ◊Shaftesbury), ◊Buckingham (George Villiers, 2nd Duke of Buckingham), Arlington (Henry Bennett, 1st Earl of Arlington 1618–1685), and ◊Lauderdale (John Maitland, Duke of Lauderdale). They are sometimes seen as an early form of cabinet but they did not have a unified policy and could be dismissed at the King's discretion.

cabinet (a small room, implying secrecy) in politics, the group of ministers holding a country's highest executive offices who decide government policy. In Britain the cabinet system originated under the Stuarts. Under William III it became customary for the king to select his ministers from the party with a parliamentary majority. The US cabinet, unlike the British, does not initiate legislation, and its members, appointed by the president, must not be members of Congress.

The first British 'cabinet councils' or subcommittees of the ◊Privy Council undertook special tasks. When George I ceased to attend cabinet meetings, the office of prime minister, not officially recognized until 1905, came into existence to provide a chair (Robert Walpole was the first). Cabinet members are chosen by the prime minister; policy is collective and the meetings are secret, minutes being taken by the secretary of the cabinet, a high civil servant. Secrecy has been infringed in recent years by 'leaks', or unauthorized disclosures to the press.

Caboto Giovanni or **John Cabot** *c.* 1450–1498. Italian navigator and explorer, the first European to reach North America. He came to England 1484 and settled in Bristol *c.* 1490. He was commissioned, with his three sons, by Henry VII of England to discover unknown lands and find a new maritime route to Asia. He arrived at Cape Breton Island, Nova Scotia, 24 June 1497, thus becoming the first European to reach the North American mainland, which he claimed for England although he thought he was in northeast Asia. In 1498 he sailed again, reaching Greenland, and probably died on the voyage.

Cade Jack d. 1450 English rebel, although according to some accounts born in Ireland. He was a prosperous landowner, but led a revolt 1450 in Kent against the high taxes and court corruption of Henry VI and demanded the recall from Ireland of Richard, Duke of York. The rebels defeated the royal forces at Sevenoaks and occupied London. After being promised reforms and pardon they dispersed, but Cade was hunted down and killed near Heathfield in Sussex.

Cadwallon d. 634. King of Gwynedd, N Wales, from *c.* 625. He invaded Northumbria with Penda of Mercia and defeated and killed Edwin of Northumbria at the battle of Heathfield 633. About a year later he was himself killed in battle by Oswald of Bernicia.

Caesar Gaius Julius 100–44 BC. Roman statesman and general. During his conquest of Gaul, he crossed into Britain 55 BC to discourage British Celts from sending aid to their cousins in Gaul. He landed in Kent but was forced to leave after a few weeks when storms threatened the safety of his fleet. He returned the following year for a more substantial campaign and defeated the Britons under ◊Cassivellaunus. After extracting tribute and assurances that the Britons would not interfere in Gaul, he left and returned to his main business of conquering Gaul. Neither expedition was planned as an invasion: the first was a show of strength; the second a punitive expedition.

Caledonia Roman term for Scottish Highlands, inhabited by Caledones. The tribes of the area remained outside Roman control – they were defeated but not conquered by ◊Agricola

AD 83–84 and again by Septimius Severus who reached beyond modern Aberdeen 208. Since the 18th century, the name has been revived as a romantic alternative for the whole of Scotland.

Callaghan (Leonard) James, Baron Callaghan 1912– . British Labour politician. As chancellor of the Exchequer 1964–67, he introduced corporation and capital-gains taxes, and resigned following devaluation. He was home secretary under Harold Wilson 1967–70. As foreign secretary 1974, Callaghan renegotiated Britain's membership of the European Community (now the European Union). he succeeded Harold Wilson as prime minister 1976 in a period of increasing economic stress and entered into a pact with the Liberals to maintain his government in office 1977. Strikes in the so-called 'winter of discontent' 1978–79 led to the government's losing a vote of no confidence in the Commons, forcing him to call an election, and his party was defeated at the polls May 1979.

He was the first prime minister since Ramsay MacDonald 1924 to be forced into an election by the will of the Commons.

Callaghan
British Labour politician James Callaghan, prime minister 1976–79. His premiership, which began when Harold Wilson unexpectedly resigned, was marked by currency crises and the collapse of any kind of working relationship between government and trades unions. His government was forced into a general election when it lost a vote of no confidence in the Commons.
United Nations

Calvert George, Baron Baltimore 1579–1632. English politician who founded the North American colony of Maryland 1632. As a supporter of colonization, he was granted land in Newfoundland 1628 but, finding the climate too harsh, obtained a royal charter for the more temperate Maryland 1632.

Calvinism Christian doctrine as interpreted by John Calvin and adopted in Scotland, parts of Switzerland, and the Netherlands; by the ◊Puritans in England and New England, USA; and by the subsequent Congregational and Presbyterian churches in the USA. Its central doctrine is predestination, under which certain souls (the elect) are predestined by God through the sacrifice of Jesus to salvation, and the rest to damnation. Although Calvinism is rarely accepted today in its strictest interpretation, the 20th century has seen a neo-Calvinist revival through the work of Karl Barth.

Cambridge University English university, one of the earliest in Europe, founded in the 12th century, though the earliest of the existing colleges, Peterhouse, was not founded until about 1284. The university was a centre of Renaissance learning and Reformation theology, and more recently has excelled in scientific research.

Famous students of the university include Rupert Brooke, Samuel Taylor Coleridge, Thomas Gray, Christopher Marlowe, John Milton, Samuel Pepys, and William Wordsworth. In 1990, there were 10,000 undergraduate and 3,000 postgraduate students. All colleges are now co-educational except for three single-sex colleges for women.

Camulodunum the Roman name for Colchester, Essex, the oldest recorded town in Britain, dating back to at least the time of ◊Cymbeline (*c.* AD 10–43). Coins dating from Cymbeline's reign have been found inscribed with the letters 'C A M V' for Camulodunum. The name derives from a Celtic word meaning 'fort of Camulos', the god of war.

Camelot legendary seat of King ◊Arthur. A possible site is the Iron Age hill fort of South Cadbury Castle in Somerset, where excavations from 1967 have revealed remains dating from 3000 BC to AD 1100, including those of a large 6th-century settlement, the time ascribed to Arthur.

Campaign for Nuclear Disarmament (CND) nonparty-political British organization advocating the abolition of nuclear weapons worldwide. Since its foundation 1958, CND has sought unilateral British initiatives to help start, and subsequently to accelerate, the multilateral process and end the arms race.

The movement was launched by the philosopher Bertrand Russell and Canon John Collins and grew out of the demonstration held outside the government's Atomic Weapons Research Establishment at Aldermaston, Berkshire, at Easter 1956. Its membership peaked in the early 1980s, during the campaign against the presence of US Pershing and cruise nuclear missiles on British soil.

Campbell family name of the dukes of Argyll; seated at Inveraray Castle, Argyll, Scotland.

There is nobody in politics I can remember, and no case I can think of in history, where a man combined such a powerful political personality with so little intelligence.

JAMES CALLAGHAN
Roy Jenkins, quoted in Richard Crossman's Diaries, 5 Sept 1969

Campbell Colin, 1st Baron Clyde 1792–1863. British field marshal. He served in the Peninsular War 1808–14 and in China 1842–46 then commanded the Highland Brigade at ◊Balaclava in the Crimean War. As commander in chief during the Indian Mutiny, he raised the siege of Lucknow and captured Cawnpore.

Campbell-Bannerman Henry 1836–1908. British Liberal politician, prime minister 1905–08. During his term of office, the South African colonies achieved self-government, and the Trades Disputes Act 1906, which protected unions from liability for the losses caused by industrial action, was passed.

Campbell-Bannerman, born in Glasgow, was chief secretary for Ireland 1884–85, war minister 1886 and again 1892–95, and leader of the Liberals in the House of Commons from 1899. He was to the left of his party and opposed the South African Wars. In 1905 he became prime minister and led the Liberals to an overwhelming electoral victory 1906. He began the conflict between Commons and Lords that led to the Parliament Act of 1911. He resigned 1908 due to ill-health.

Camperdown, Battle of (Dutch ***Kamperduin***) in the Revolutionary Wars, victory of a British fleet under Viscount Adam Duncan over Jan de Winter's Dutch fleet 11 Oct 1797 off the northwest coast of the Netherlands. The battle effectively marked the end of significant Dutch naval power.

Campion Edmund 1540–1581. English Jesuit and Roman Catholic martyr. A brilliant soldier, he became a Jesuit in Rome 1573 and in 1580 was sent to England as a missionary. He was imprisoned in the Tower of London 1581, accused of being a spy, and indicted on a false charge of treason. He was found guilty and executed.

Canada former British dominion in North America. The French took possession of it 1534 and founded Quebec 1608. Quebec was captured by British forces under Wolfe 1759 and the whole territory of Canada became a British possession by the Treaty of Paris 1763. The provinces of Ontario, Quebec, New Brunswick, and Nova Scotia were united as the Dominion of Canada by the British North America Act 1867, and the other provinces were admitted to the federation subsequently. The Statute of Westminster 1931 recognized Canada as an equal partner of Great Britain.

canals artificial waterways built for navigation. Several British canals were originally built for irrigation, such as the Roman Car Dyke, running from the River Nene at Peterborough to the Witham at Lincoln, and the Fossdyke, connecting the Witham with the Trent. The navigation canals of the 18th and early 19th centuries were the arteries of the Industrial Revolution. James Brindley and Thomas Telford were mainly responsible for the construction 1760–1840 of 6,800 km/4,250 mi of canals, including Brindley's Bridgewater Canal 1760, built to transport coal from the Duke of Bridgewater's mines at Worsley to Manchester, and Telford's great Caledonian Canal 1832, linking a chain of lochs from Inverness on the east coast of Scotland to Fort William in the west.

canals
View of the Paddington canal, a stretch of the Grand Junction Canal. The Grand Junction, which extended from Paddington to Uxbridge, opened 1801 at the height of the canal-building boom.
Philip Sauvain

The improvement in road-building did not seriously challenge the use of canals for transporting freight and troops but by the 1830s they were largely eclipsed by the expansion of the railways. Today, many of Britain's canals form part of an interconnecting system of waterways some 4,000 km/2,500 mi long. Several of these canals, long disused commercially, have recently been restored for recreation and the use of pleasure craft.

Canning Charles John, 1st Earl 1812–1862. British administrator, first viceroy of India from 1858. As governor general of India from 1856, he suppressed the Indian Mutiny with a fair but firm hand which earned him the nickname 'Clemency Canning'. He was the son of George Canning.

Canning George 1770–1827. British Tory politician, foreign secretary 1807–10 and 1822–27, and prime minister 1827 in coalition with the Whigs. He was largely responsible, during the Napoleonic Wars, for the seizure of the Danish fleet and British intervention in the Spanish peninsula.

Canning entered Parliament 1793. His verse, satires, and parodies for the *Anti-Jacobin* 1797–98 led to his advancement by Pitt the Younger. His disapproval of the ◊Walcheren expedition 1809 involved him in a duel with the war minister, ◊Castlereagh, and led to Canning's resignation as foreign secretary. He was president of the Board of Control 1816–20. On Castlereagh's death 1822, he again became foreign secretary, supported the independence movements in Greece and South America, and was made prime minister 1827. When Wellington, Peel, and other Tories refused to serve under him, he formed a coalition with the Whigs. He died in office.

Cantiaci British inhabitants of Cantium (Kent) who formed a *civitas* (area of local government) in Roman Britain. Their capital was at Durovernum (Canterbury), with a secondary centre at Durobrivae (Rochester). They were the only Romano-British people to adopted a geographical name instead of a tribal one.

Canterbury, archbishop of primate of all England, archbishop of the Church of England (Anglican), and first peer of the realm, ranking next to royalty. He crowns the sovereign, has a seat in the House of Lords, and is a member of the Privy Council. He is appointed by the prime minister.

Formerly selected by political consultation, since 1980 the new archbishops have been selected by a church group, the Crown Appointments Commission (formed 1977). The first holder of the office was St Augustine 601–04; his 20th-century successors have been Randall Davidson 1903, Cosmo Gordon Lang 1928, William Temple 1942, Geoffrey Fisher 1945, Michael Ramsey 1961, Donald Coggan 1974, Robert Runcie 1980, and George Carey 1991.

The archbishop's official residence is at Lambeth Palace, London, and second residence at the Old Palace, Canterbury.

Canute or *Cnut* c. 995–1035. King of England from 1016, Denmark from 1018, and Norway from 1028. Having invaded England 1013 with his father, Sweyn, king of Denmark, he was acclaimed king on his father's death 1014 by his ◊Viking army. Canute defeated ◊Edmund (II) Ironside at the Battle of ◊Ashingdon, Essex, 1016, and Canute and Edmund divided England between them, with Canute ruling Mercia and Northumbria until he inherited the whole

Canning
George Canning, British Tory politician and prime minister for four months during 1827. He resigned as foreign secretary 1809 after blaming his colleague Viscount Castlereagh, secretary of war, for two British defeats. The two men fought a duel on Wimbledon Common to settle the matter, during which Canning was wounded in the thigh.
Philip Sauvain

Archbishops of Canterbury from 1414

1414	Henry Chichele (1362–1414)	**1747**	Thomas Herring (1693–1757)
1443	John Stafford (?–1452)	**1758**	Matthew Hutton (1693–1758)
1452	John Kemp (c. 1380–1454)	**1758**	Thomas Secker (1693–1768)
1454	Thomas Bouchier (1410–1486)	**1768**	Hon. Frederick Cornwallis
1486	John Morton (c. 1429–1500)		(1713–1783)
1501	Henry Deane (?–1503)	**1783**	John Moore (1730–1805)
1503	William Warham (1450–1532)	**1805**	Charles Manners-Sutton (1755–1828)
1533	Thomas Cranmer (1489–1556)	**1828**	William Howley (1766–1848)
1556	Reginald Pole (1500–1558)	**1848**	John Bird Sumner (1780–1862)
1559	Matthew Parker (1504–1575)	**1862**	Charles Longley (1794–1868)
1576	Edmund Grindal (1519–1583)	**1868**	Archibald Campbell Tait (1811–1882)
1583	John Whitgift (1530–1604)	**1883**	Edward White Benson (1829–1896)
1604	Richard Bancroft (1544–1610)	**1896**	Frederick Temple (1821–1902)
1611	George Abbot (1562–1633)	**1903**	Randall Thomas Davidson
1633	William Laud (1573–1645)		(1848–1930)
1660	William Juxon (1582–1663)	**1928**	Cosmo Gordon Lanq (1864–1945)
1663	Gilbert Sheldon (1598–1677)	**1942**	William Temple (1881–1944)
1678	William Sancroft (1617–1693)	**1945**	Geoffrey Fisher (1887–1972)
1691	John Tillotson (1630–1694)	**1961**	Arthur Ramsey (1904–1988)
1695	Thomas Tenison (1636–1715)	**1974**	Donald Coggan (1909–)
1716	William Wake (1657–1737)	**1980**	Robert Runcie (1921–)
1737	John Potter (c.{tsp}1674–1747)	**1991**	George Carey (1935–)

Contemplating Spain as our ancestors had known her, I resolved that if France had Spain, it should not be Spain with the Indies. I called the New World into existence to redress the balance of the old.

GEORGE CANNING
speech in the House of Commons, 1826, explaining British intervention in Spain.

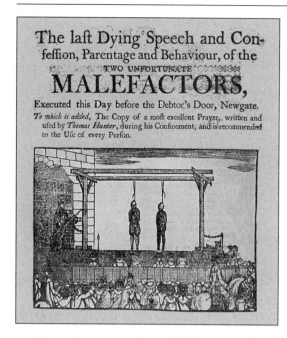

The last Dying Speech and Confession, Parentage and Behaviour, of the

TWO UNFORTUNATE

MALEFACTORS,

Executed this Day before the Debtor's Door, Newgate.

To which is added, The Copy of a most excellent Prayer, written and used by *Thomas Hunter*, during his Confinement, and is recommended to the Use of every Person.

capital punishment
Hanging was the most common form of capital punishment in Britain until its abolition 1969. Public executions were supposed to be a deterrent but more often became scenes of riotous entertainment and the practice was abandoned 1868.
Hulton Deutsch

kingdom on Edmund's death. Under Canute's rule English trade improved, and he gained favour with his English subjects by sending garrison troops back to Denmark. He married Emma, widow of Ethelred the Unready 1017, succeeded his brother Harold as king of Denmark 1018, compelled King Malcolm to pay homage by invading Scotland about 1027, and conquered Norway 1028. His empire collapsed on his death and he was succeeded by his illegitimate son Harold I. He was buried at Winchester.

The legend of Canute disenchanting his flattering courtiers by showing that the sea would not retreat at his command was first told by Henry of Huntingdon 1130.

Cape Colony former British colony in ◊South Africa.

capital punishment punishment by death. Capital punishment is retained in 92 countries and territories (1990), including the USA (37 states), China, and Islamic countries. It was abolished in the UK 1965 for all crimes except treason.

There were over 200 capital offences in Britain during the 18th century, but there was a great reduction in the number of these following campaigns from 1810 onward by Samuel Romilly (1757–1818) and others. Several acts were passed, each reducing the number of crimes liable to this penalty. From 1838 it was rarely used except for murder and it was formally abolished 1866 for all crimes except murder, treason, piracy, and certain arson attacks. Its use was subject to the royal prerogative of mercy. The punishment was carried out by hanging (in public until 1866). Capital punishment for murder was abolished 1965 but still exists for treason. In 1990, Ireland abolished the death penalty for all offences.

Caractacus British chieftain of the Catuvellauni who headed resistance to the Romans in southeast England AD 43–51, but was defeated on the Welsh border. Shown in Claudius's triumphal procession, he was released in tribute to his courage and died in Rome.

Caradon Baron. Title of Hugh ◊Foot, British Labour politician.

Cardwell Edward, Viscount Cardwell 1813–1886. British Liberal politician. He entered Parliament as a supporter of the Conservative prime minister ◊Peel 1842, and was secretary for war under Gladstone 1868–74, when he carried out many reforms, including the abolition of the purchase of military commissions and promotions and the abolition of flogging during peacetime.

Carolina former British colony in North America; see ◊Thirteen Colonies.

Caroline of Brunswick 1768–1821. Queen of George IV of Great Britain, who unsuccessfully attempted to divorce her on his accession to the throne 1820.

Second daughter of Karl Wilhelm, Duke of Brunswick, and Augusta, sister of George III, she married her first cousin, the Prince of Wales, 1795, but after the birth of Princess ◊Charlotte Augusta a separation was arranged. When her husband ascended the throne 1820 she was offered an annuity of £50,000 provided she agreed to renounce the title of queen and to continue to live abroad. She returned forthwith to London, where she assumed royal state. In July 1820 the government brought in a bill to dissolve the marriage, but Lord ◊Brougham's brilliant defence led to the bill's abandonment. On 19 July 1821 Caroline was prevented by royal order from entering Westminster Abbey for the coronation. Her funeral led to popular riots.

The King's party and mine are like two rival inns on the road, the George and the Angel.

CAROLINE OF
BRUNSWICK
remark made during her final attempt to be accepted as queen, 1821.

Carson Edward Henry, Baron Carson 1854–1935. Irish Unionist politician and lawyer who played a decisive part in the trial of the writer Oscar Wilde. In the years before World War I he led the movement in Ulster to resist Irish ◊Home Rule and organized the Ulster Volunteers.

Carteret Sir George *c.* 1599–1680. English Royalist politician, a supporter of Charles I and II during the period of parliamentarian rule. He was governor of Jersey 1643–51 and used his native island as a base for harrying parliamentarian ships. The growing maritime strength of parliament forced him into exile in France. At the Restoration he was appointed a Privy Councillor and was a close confidante of Charles II; he become a by-word for self-enrichment through public office. He acquired substantial amounts of territory in the new colonies of North America, in particular Carolina 1663 and New Jersey, which he named after his birth-place, 1664.

Carteret John, 1st Earl Granville 1690–1763. English diplomat and politician; chief adviser to George II 1742–44. Born the second Lord Carteret, a prodigious intellect and linguistic ability marked him out for a diplomatic career. As ambassador to Sweden he helped negoti-ate an end to the Great Northern War resulting in the Peace of Stockholm 1719. He was appointed one of two foreign secretaries in Robert ◊Walpole's ministry 1721 and attended the negotiations with France at the Congress of Cambrai but he proved a difficult colleague and Walpole moved him to Lord Lieutenant of Ireland 1724, only for him to be reinstated as secretary of state on Walpole's fall later in the year. He led the party opposed to Walpole in the House of Lords 1730–42, when he became the king's chief adviser. As secretary of state during the War of the Austrian Succession, he directed British foreign policy and was with George II at the Battle of Dettingen 1743. George tried to make him prime minister 1746 but he lacked the support necessary to form a ministry.

Carthusian order Roman Catholic order of monks and, later, nuns, founded by St Bruno 1084 at Chartreuse, near Grenoble, France. Living chiefly in unbroken silence, they ate one vegetar-ian meal a day and supported themselves by their own labours; the rule is still one of severe aus-terity. The order was introduced into England about 1178, when the first Charterhouse was founded at Witham in Essex. They were suppressed at the Reformation, but there is a Charter-house at Parkminster, Sussex, established 1833.

Casement Roger David 1864–1916. Irish nationalist. While in the British consular service, he exposed the ruthless exploitation of the people of the Belgian Congo and Peru, for which he was knighted 1911 (degraded 1916). He was hanged for treason by the British for his involve-ment in the Irish nationalist cause, specifically his role in helping organize the ◊Easter Rising.

In 1914 Casement went to Germany and attempted to induce Irish prisoners of war to form an Irish brigade to take part in a republican insurrection. He returned to Ireland in a submarine 1916 (actually to postpone, not start, the Easter Rising), was arrested, tried for treason, and hanged.

Cassino, Battles of in World War II, series of costly but ultimately successful Allied assaults Jan–May 1944 on heavily fortified German positions blocking the Allied advance to Rome. Both sides sustained heavy losses in the operation. Cassino is in southern Italy, 80 km/50 mi northwest of Naples, at the foot of Monte Cassino.

Cassivellaunus 1st century BC chieftain of the British tribe, the Catuvellauni, who led the British resistance to the Romans under Caesar 54 BC.

castles fortified buildings or group of buildings, characteristic of medieval Europe. The castle underwent many changes, its size, design, and construction being largely determined by changes in siege tactics and the development of artillery. The earliest castles in Britain were built following the Norman Conquest, and the art of castle building reached a peak in the 13th century, as at Caernarvon Castle, Wales. By the 15th century the need for cas-tles for domestic defence had largely disappeared, and the advent of gunpowder made them largely useless against attack.

Castle Barbara, Baroness Castle (born Betts) 1911– . British Labour politician, a cabinet minister in the Labour governments of the 1960s and 1970s. She led the Labour group in the European Parliament 1979–89.

Castle was minister of transport 1965–68, when she introduced breath tests for drivers suspected of drinking, employment 1968–70, when her White Paper on trade-union reform *In Place of*

Casement
Sir Roger Casement appearing at Bow Street magistrates' court charged with High Treason. A former British diplomat, Casement was an ardent supporter of Irish Home Rule; he was captured when he was dropped off the Irish coast by a German submarine at the start of the Easter Rising April 1916.
Philip Sauvain

castles
An aerial view of Pevensey Castle, Sussex. This medieval castle was built by William the Conqueror's half-brother, the Count of Mortrain, within the confines of an existing Roman fortress.
Aerofilms

Strife was abandoned because it suggested state intervention in industrial relations, and social services 1974–76, when she was dropped from the cabinet by Prime Minister James Callaghan.

Castlereagh Robert Stewart, Viscount Castlereagh 1769–1822. British Tory politician. As chief secretary for Ireland 1797–1801, he suppressed the rebellion of 1798 and helped the younger Pitt secure the union of England, Scotland, and Ireland 1801. As foreign secretary 1812–22, he coordinated European opposition to Napoleon and represented Britain at the Congress of Vienna 1814–15.

In Parliament Castlereagh was secretary for war and the colonies 1805–06 and 1807–09, when he had to resign after a duel with foreign secretary George ◊Canning. As foreign secretary from 1812, he devoted himself to the overthrow of Napoleon and subsequently to the Congress of Vienna and the congress system. Abroad, his policy favoured the development of material liberalism, but at home he repressed the Reform movement, and popular opinion held him responsible for the ◊Peterloo massacre of peaceful demonstrators 1819. He succeeded his father as Marquess of Londonderry 1821 but committed suicide the following year.

Cat and Mouse Act popular name for the *Prisoners, Temporary Discharge for Health, Act* 1913; an attempt by the UK Liberal government under Herbert Asquith to reduce embarrassment caused by the incarceration of ◊suffragettes accused of violent offences against property.

When the suffragettes embarked on hunger strikes, prison authorities introduced forced feeding, which proved humiliating and sometimes dangerous to the women. Following a public outcry, the hunger strikers were released on a licence that could be revoked without further trial. The government was accused of playing cat to suffragette mice by its adoption of powers of release and rearrest.

Catesby Robert 1573–1605. English Catholic conspirator and leader of the ◊Gunpowder Plot 1605. He took part in the uprising of the 2nd Earl of ◊Essex 1601 and was an accomplice in the ◊Rye House Plot 1603 to capture James I and force religious concessions from him. He was killed resisting arrest following the failure of the Gunpowder Plot to blow up parliament.

Catherine of Aragon 1485–1536. First queen of Henry VIII of England, 1509–33, and mother of Mary I. Catherine had married Henry's elder brother Prince Arthur 1501 and on his death 1502 was betrothed to Henry, marrying him on his accession. She failed to produce a male heir and Henry divorced her without papal approval, provoking the crisis which led to the English ◊Reformation.

Of their six children, only Mary lived. Wanting a male heir, Henry sought an annulment 1526 when Catherine was too old to bear children. When the pope demanded that the case be referred to him, Henry married Anne Boleyn, afterward receiving the desired decree of nullity from Cranmer, the archbishop of Canterbury, in 1533. The Reformation in England followed, and Catherine went into retirement until her death.

I met Murder on the way –
He had a mask like Castlereagh.

CASTLEREAGH
Percy Bysshe Shelley
'The Mask of Anarchy'

Catherine of Braganza 1638–1705. Queen of Charles II of England 1662–85. Her childlessness and practice of her Catholic faith were unpopular, but Charles resisted pressure for divorce. The daughter of John IV of Portugal (1604–1656), she brought the Portuguese possessions of Bombay and Tangier as her dowry and introduced tea drinking and citrus fruits to England. She was instrumental in Charles II's return to Catholicism on his deathbed; after his death she returned to Lisbon 1692.

Catherine of Valois 1401–1437. Queen of Henry V of England, whom she married 1420, as part of the Treaty of Troyes, and the mother of Henry VI. After the death of Henry V, she secretly married Owen Tudor (*c.* 1400–1461) about 1425, and their son Edmund Tudor became the father of Henry VII.

Catholic Emancipation acts of Parliament passed 1780–1829 to relieve Roman Catholics of civil and political restrictions imposed from the time of Henry VIII and the Reformation. Full emancipation was finally achieved 1829 in the wake of the election of the Irish Catholic Daniel ◊O'Connell as member of parliament for County Clare the previous year.

Cato Street conspiracy unsuccessful plot hatched in Cato Street, London, to murder the Tory foreign secretary Robert Castlereagh and cabinet 20 Feb 1820. The leader, the Radical Arthur Thistlewood (1770–1820), who intended to set up a provisional government, was hanged along with four others.

Catuvellauni leading southern British tribe of the time of the Roman invasions under Caesar and Claudius, with a fortified stronghold at what is now Wheathampstead, Hertfordshire. ◊Cassivellaunus, ◊Cymbeline, and his son ◊Caractacus were kings of the Catuvellauni.

cavalier horseman of noble birth, but mainly used as a derogatory nickname to describe a male supporter of Charles I in the Civil War (Cavalier), typically with courtly dress and long hair (as distinct from a Roundhead); also a supporter of Charles II after the Restoration. The Civil War nickname probably derives from the Spanish word for gentleman, *caballero*, a reference to the Cavaliers' pro-Catholic policies.

Cavell
English nurse Edith Cavell. Her execution by the Germans Oct 1915 for helping Allied prisoners of war to escape from Belgium caused a storm of anti-German outrage in Britain and the USA.
Image Select

Cavell Edith Louisa 1865–1915. English matron of a Red Cross hospital in Brussels, Belgium, in World War I, who helped Allied soldiers escape to the Dutch frontier. She was court-martialled by the Germans and condemned to death. The British government made much propaganda from her heroism and execution which was cited as an example of German atrocities.

Cavendish family name of dukes of Devonshire; the family seat is at Chatsworth, Derbyshire.

Cavendish Frederick Charles, Lord Cavendish 1836–1882. British administrator, second son of the 7th Duke of Devonshire. He was appointed chief secretary to the lord lieutenant of Ireland 1882 but on the evening of his arrival in Dublin he was murdered in Phoenix Park with Thomas Burke, the permanent Irish undersecretary, by members of the Irish Invincibles, a group of Irish Fenian extremists founded 1881.

Cavendish Spencer. See ◊Hartington, Spencer Compton Cavendish.

Caxton William *c.* 1422–1491. The first English printer. He learned the art of printing in Cologne, Germany, 1471 and set up a press in Bruges, Belgium, where he produced the first book printed in English, his own version of a French romance, *Recuyell of the Historyes of Troye* 1474. Returning to England 1476, he established himself in London, where he produced the first book printed in England, *Dictes or Sayengis of the Philosophres* 1477. The books from Caxton's press in Westminster included editions of the poets Geoffrey Chaucer, John Gower, and John Lydgate (*c.* 1370–1449). Altogether he printed about 100 books.

Cecil Robert, 1st Earl of Salisbury 1563–1612. Secretary of state to Elizabeth I of England, succeeding his father, Lord ◊Burghley; he was afterwards chief minister to James I (James VI of Scotland) whose accession to the English throne he secured. He negotiated peace with Spain 1604 and discovered the ◊Gunpowder Plot, the conspiracy to blow up the King and Parliament 1605. James I created him Earl of Salisbury 1605.

Celt (Greek *Keltoi*) member of an Indo-European people that originated in Alpine Europe and spread to the Iberian peninsula and beyond. They were mainly ironworkers and farmers. In

I realize that patriotism is not enough. I must have no hatred or bitterness towards any one.

EDITH CAVELL
last words, quoted in the Times, *23 October 1915*

the 1st century BC they were defeated by the Romans and by Germanic tribes and largely confined to Britain, Ireland, and northern France.

The main periods of Celtic emigration to Britain were between the 6th and 3rd centuries BC. Their Druids, or priests, performed ritualized magic ceremonies which survived in the forms of ordeal, augury and exorcism. The Celts were subdued when the Romans came to Britain, except in Ireland and those parts of Britain that the Romans did not reach. Some Celtic tribes re-established themselves, particularly in Wales, following the Roman withdrawal from Britain in the 5th century AD. The Celtic languages of Scotland (Gaelic), Ireland, Wales, Cornwall and the Isle of Man are a legacy of the Celts in Britain, while the modern Druids, associated with the Welsh Eisteddfodau, are a romantic and unhistoric revival of the original Celtic religion.

ceorl lowest class of ◊freeman in Anglo-Saxon England. A ceorl was a peasant farmer ranking between a serf and a noble who would either farm his own land or receive it from a lord in return for military service.

Cerdic Saxon king of Wessex. He is said to have come to Britain about AD 495, landing near Southampton. He defeated the British in Hampshire and founded Wessex about AD 500, conquering the Isle of Wight about AD 530.

Ceylon former British colony (now Sri Lanka), an island in the Indian Ocean south of India. It was settled by the Portuguese 1505, the Dutch 1658, and the British 1796, becoming a British crown colony 1802. It became a self-governing state as a member of the British Commonwealth 1948, and a republic 1972, when it adopted its present name.

Chadwick Edwin 1800–1890. English social reformer, author of the Poor Law Report 1834. He played a prominent part in the campaign that resulted in the ◊Public Health Act 1848. He was commissioner of the first Board of Health 1848–54.

A self-educated protégé of the philosopher Jeremy ◊Bentham and advocate of utilitarianism, Chadwick used his influence to implement measures to eradicate cholera, improve sanitation in urban areas, and clear slums in British cities.

Chain Home system of radar stations built around the east and south coasts of the UK 1938–39 to give early warning of German air attacks.

chamberlain financial official in Anglo-Saxon and Norman times. Originally a royal servant in the king's chamber with responsibility for the royal treasure, chamberlains 'left the household' as government became more bureaucratic, and became established as part of the royal exchequer. The office survives in the posts of lord chamberlain and lord great chamberlain.

Chamberlain, Lord chief officer of the royal household who engages staff and appoints retail suppliers. Until 1968 the Lord Chamberlain licensed and censored plays before their public performance. The office is temporary, and appointments are made by the government.

Chamberlain, Lord Great the only officer of state whose position survives from Norman times; responsibilities include the arrangements for the opening of Parliament, assisting with the regalia at coronations, and organizing the ceremony when bishops and peers are created.

Chamberlain (Joseph) Austen 1863–1937. British Conservative politician, elder son of Joseph Chamberlain; as foreign secretary 1924–29 he negotiated the Pact of ◊Locarno, for which he won the Nobel Peace Prize 1925, and signed the Kellogg–Briand pact to outlaw war 1928.

Chamberlain Joseph 1836–1914. British politician, reformist mayor of and member of Parliament for Birmingham; in 1886, he resigned from the cabinet over Gladstone's policy of home rule for Ireland, and led the revolt of the Liberal-Unionists.

By 1874 Chamberlain had made a sufficient fortune in the Birmingham screw-manufacturing business to devote himself entirely to politics. He adopted radical views, and took an active part in local affairs. Three times mayor of Birmingham, he carried through many schemes of municipal development. In 1876 he was elected to Parliament and joined the republican group led by Charles Dilke, the extreme left wing of the Liberal Party. In 1880 he entered Gladstone's cabinet as president of the Board of Trade. The climax of his radical

The day of small nations has long passed away. The day of Empires has come.

JOSEPH CHAMBERLAIN
speech in Birmingham,
12 May 1904

period was reached with the unauthorized programme, advocating, among other things, free education, graduated taxation, and smallholdings of 'three acres and a cow'.

Chamberlain (Arthur) Neville 1869–1940. British Conservative politician, son of Joseph Chamberlain. He was prime minister 1937–40; his policy of appeasement toward the fascist dictators Mussolini and Hitler (with whom he concluded the ◊Munich Agreement 1938) failed to prevent the outbreak of World War II. He resigned 1940 following the defeat of the British forces in Norway.

Younger son of Joseph Chamberlain and half-brother of Austen Chamberlain, he was born in Birmingham, of which he was lord mayor 1915. He was minister of health 1923 and 1924–29 and worked at slum clearance. In 1931 he was chancellor of the Exchequer in the national government, and succeeded Baldwin as prime minister 1937. He agreed to return to Eire those ports that had been occupied by the navy in an attempt to end the tension between Britain and Ireland.

He also attempted to appease the demands of the European dictators, particularly Mussolini. In 1938 he went to Munich and negotiated with Hitler the settlement of the Czechoslovak question. He was ecstatically received on his return, and claimed that the Munich Agreement brought 'peace in our time'. Within a year, however, Britain was at war with Germany.

Chancellor, Lord originally the monarch's chief secretary, today a member of the cabinet, who acts as Speaker of the House of Lords, may preside over the Court of Appeal, and is head of the judiciary. The Lord Chancellor's term of office ends with a change of government.

Until the 14th century the post was always held by an ecclesiastic, who also acted as royal chaplain and Keeper of the Great Seal. Under Edward III the Lord Chancellor became head of a permanent court to consider petitions to the king: the **Court of Chancery**. In order of precedence the Lord Chancellor comes after the archbishop of Canterbury.

Chancellor of the Duchy of Lancaster honorary post held by a cabinet minister who has other nondepartmental responsibilities; see ◊Lancaster, Chancellor of the Duchy of.

chancellor of the Exchequer senior cabinet minister responsible for the national economy. The office, established under Henry III, originally entailed keeping the Exchequer seal.

Chancery a division of the High Court that deals with such matters as the administration of the estates of deceased persons, the execution of trusts, the enforcement of sales of land, and ◊foreclosure of mortgages. Before reorganization of the court system 1875, it administered the rules of ◊equity as distinct from ◊common law.

The chancery originated in Anglo-Saxon times as the writing office of the royal chapel, under a chief clerk, the ◊Lord Chancellor. The office lost much of its political importance from the 13th century and instead gained judicial importance as the Lord Chancellor's court.

Channel Islands group of islands in the English Channel, off the northwest coast of France. They comprise the islands of Jersey, Guernsey, Alderney, Great and Little Sark, with the lesser Herm, Brechou, Jethou, and Lihou. They became a possession of the British crown after the Norman conquest 1066 and are the only part of the original duchy of Normandy still held by Britain. The islands came under the same rule as England 1066, and are dependent territories of the British crown. Germany occupied the islands June 1940–May 1945, the only British soil to be occupied by the Germans during World War II. The extent to which the authorities and inhabitants of the islands collaborated with the German occupation is still a matter of controversy.

The main islands have their own parliaments and laws, in particular they have different tax laws to the rest of the UK, making them an attractive 'tax haven' for those with sufficient amounts of money to invest. Unless specially signified, the Channel Islands are not bound by British acts of Parliament, though the British government is responsible for defence and external relations

Channel tunnel tunnel built beneath the English Channel, linking Britain with mainland Europe. It comprises twin rail tunnels, 50 km/31 mi long and 7.3 m/24 ft in diameter, located 40 m/130 ft beneath the seabed. It was begun 1986, and the French and English sections were linked Dec 1990. It was officially opened 6 May 1994. The shuttle train service for cars and

In war, whichever side may call itself the victor, there are no winners, but all are losers.

NEVILLE CHAMBERLAIN *speech at Kettering, 3 July 1938*

lorries, Le Shuttle, opened to commercial freight June 1994 and to fare-paying passengers Dec 1994. The tunnel's high-speed train service, Eurostar, opened Nov 1994.

In the 1880s British financier and railway promoter Edward Watkin started boring a tunnel near Dover, abandoning it 1894 because of governmental opposition after driving some 1.6 km/1 mile out to sea. In 1973 Britain and France agreed to back a tunnel, but a year later Britain pulled out following a change of government. The estimated cost of the tunnel has continually been revised upwards to a figure of £11 billion (1994).

charge of the Light Brigade disastrous attack by the British Light Brigade of cavalry against the Russian entrenched artillery 25 Oct 1854 during the Crimean War at the Battle of ◊Balaclava. Of the 673 soldiers who took part, there were 272 casualties.

Channel tunnel
A 7,6000 hp/5.6 MW locomotive heads a Eurotunnel shuttle, part of the service linking Britain and France beneath the English Channel. Proposals for a Channel tunnel were first advanced in 1802, but it was 192 years before the tunnel was built.
Channel Tunnel Group Ltd

The fiasco came about as a result of a badly phrased order from the commander-in-chief, Lord Raglan, to 'prevent the enemy carrying away the guns'. This seems to have been intended to refer to Turkish guns captured by Russian forces in the hills above the battlefield, but the Brigade's commander, Lord Lucan, assumed his target was the Russian guns about a mile away up the North Valley. He led the Brigade in a charge up the length of the valley between two rows of Russian artillery, sustaining heavy casualties. The Brigade was only saved from total destruction by French cavalry.

charity schools schools for the poor founded by the Society for the Promoting of Christian Knowledge from the late 17th century onward. They were criticized in the early 18th century for allegedly instilling High Church propaganda in their pupils and overeducating the poor. Until the 19th century, these locally run schools were often the only means for poor children to acquire basic numeracy and literacy.

Charles two kings of Britain:

Charles I 1600–1649. King of Great Britain and Ireland from 1625, son of James I of England (James VI of Scotland). He accepted the ◊Petition of Right 1628 but then dissolved Parliament

charge of the Light Brigade
The charge of the Light Brigade was a disastrous military blunder that acquired an air of heroism in the public mind largely due to Tennyson's famous poem. In military circles recriminations, especially over which officer should be held responsible for the fiasco, dragged on for years after.
Hulton Deutsch

Channel tunnel: chronology

1751	French farmer Nicolas Desmaret suggested a fixed link across the English Channel.
1802	French mining engineer Albert Mathieu-Favier proposed to Napoleon I a Channel tunnel through which horse-drawn carriages might travel. Discussions with British politicians ceased 1803 when war broke out between the two countries.
1834	Aim de Gamond of France suggested the construction of a submerged tube across the Channel.
1842	De la Haye of Liverpool designed an underwater tube, the sections of which would be bolted together underwater by workers without diving apparatus.
1851	Hector Horeau proposed a tunnel that would slope down towards the middle of the Channel and up thereafter, so that the carriages would be propelled downhill by their own weight and for a short distance uphill, after which compressed air would take over as the motive power.
1857	A joint committee of British and French scientists approved the aim of constructing a Channel tunnel.
1875	Channel-tunnel bills were passed by the British and French parliaments.
1876	An Anglo-French protocol was signed laying down the basis of a treaty governing construction of a tunnel.
1878	Borings began from the French and British sides of the Channel.
1882	British government forced abandonment of the project after public opinion, fearing invasion by the French, turned against the tunnel.
1904	Signing of the Entente Cordiale between France and the UK enabled plans to be reconsidered. Albert Sartiaux and Francis Fox proposed a twin-tunnel scheme.
1907	A new Channel-tunnel bill was defeated in the British parliament.
1930	A Channel-tunnel bill narrowly failed in British parliament.
1930–40	British prime minister Winston Churchill and the French government supported the digging of a tunnel.
1955	Defence objections to a tunnel were lifted in the UK by prime minister Harold Macmillan.
1957	Channel Tunnel Study Group established.
1961	Study Group plans for a double-bore tunnel presented to British government.
1964	Ernest Marples, Minister of Transport, and his French counterpart gave go-ahead for construction.
1967	British government invited tunnel-building proposals from private interests.
1973	Anglo-French treaty on trial borings signed.
1974	New tunnel bill introduced in British Parliament but was not passed before election called by Harold Wilson.
1975	British government cancelled project because of escalating costs.
1981	Anglo-French summit agreed to investigation of possible tunnel.
1982	Intergovernmental study group on tunnel established.
1984	Construction of tunnel agreed in principle at Anglo-French summit.
1986	Anglo-French treaty signed; design submitted by a consortium called the Channel Tunnel Group accepted.
1987	Legislation completed, Anglo-French treaty ratified; construction started in Nov.
1990	First breakthrough of service tunnel took place Dec.
1991	Breakthrough of first rail tunnel in May; the second rail tunnel was completed in June.
1994	*6 May* The Queen and President Mitterrand officially inaugurated the Channel Tunnel; train and shuttle services opened to fare-paying passengers during Nov and Dec.

and ruled without a parliament 1629–40. His advisers were ◊Strafford and ◊Laud, who persecuted the Puritans and provoked the Scots to revolt. The ◊Short Parliament, summoned 1640, refused funds, and the ◊Long Parliament later that year rebelled. Charles declared war on Parliament 1642 but surrendered 1646 and was beheaded 1649. He was the father of Charles II.

Charles was born at Dunfermline, and became heir to the throne on the death of his brother Henry 1612. He married Henrietta Maria, daughter of Henry IV of France. When he succeeded his father, friction with Parliament began at once. The Parliaments of 1625 and 1626 were dissolved, and that of 1628 refused supplies until Charles had accepted the Petition of Right. In 1629 it attacked Charles's illegal taxation and support of the ◊Arminians in the church, whereupon he dissolved Parliament and imprisoned its leaders. For 11 years he ruled without a parliament, the ◊Eleven Years' Tyranny, raising money by expedients, such as ◊ship money, that alienated the nation, while the ◊Star Chamber suppressed opposition by persecuting the Puritans. When Charles attempted 1637 to force a prayer book on the English model on Presbyterian Scotland he found himself confronted with a nation in arms. The Short Parliament, which

met April 1640, refused to grant money until grievances were redressed, and was speedily dissolved. The Scots then advanced into England and forced their own terms on Charles. The Long Parliament met 3 Nov 1640 and declared extraparliamentary taxation illegal, abolished the Star Chamber and other courts of royal prerogative, and voted that Parliament could not be dissolved without its own consent. Laud and other ministers were imprisoned, and Strafford condemned to death. After the failure of his attempt to arrest the parliamentary leaders 4 Jan 1642, Charles, confident that he had substantial support among those who felt that Parliament was becoming too radical and zealous, withdrew from London, and on 22 Aug declared war on Parliament by raising his standard at Nottingham (see English ◊Civil War). Charles's defeat at Naseby June 1645 ended all hopes of victory; in May 1646 he surrendered at Newark to the Scots, who handed him over to Parliament Jan 1647. In June the army seized him and carried him off to Hampton Court. While the army leaders strove to find a settlement, Charles secretly intrigued for a Scottish invasion. In Nov he escaped, but was recaptured and held at Carisbrooke Castle on the Isle of Wight; a Scottish invasion followed 1648, and was shattered by ◊Cromwell at Preston. In Jan 1649 the House of Commons set up a high court of justice, which tried Charles and condemned him to death. He was beheaded 30 Jan in front of the Banqueting House in Whitehall.

> *I die a Christian, according to the Profession of the Church of England, as I found it left to me by my Father.*
>
> CHARLES I
> *speech on the scaffold, 1649*

Charles II 1630–1685. King of Great Britain and Ireland from 1660, when Parliament accepted the restoration of the monarchy after the collapse of Cromwell's Commonwealth; son of Charles I. His chief minister Clarendon, who arranged his marriage 1662 with Catherine of Braganza, was replaced 1667 with the ◊Cabal of advisers. His plans to restore Catholicism in Britain led to war with the Netherlands 1672–74 in support of Louis XIV of France and a break with Parliament, which he dissolved 1681. He was succeeded by James II.

Charles was born in St James's Palace, London; during the Civil War he lived with his father at Oxford 1642–45, and after the victory of Cromwell's parliamentary forces withdrew to France. He accepted the ◊Covenanters' offer to make him king, landing in Scotland 1650, and was crowned at Scone 1 Jan 1651. He invaded England but was defeated by Cromwell at Worcester 3 Sept. Charles escaped, and travelled through Europe for nine years until the negotiations with parliament were started in 1660 by George Monk (1608–1670).

Charles issued the Declaration of Breda April 1660, promising a general amnesty and freedom of conscience, which parliament accepted and he was proclaimed king 8 May 1660. Charles wanted to make himself an absolute monarch, and hence tended toward Catholicism as more favourable to this system of government. The disasters of the Dutch war furnished an excuse for banishing Clarendon 1667, and he was replaced by the Cabal of Clifford and Arlington, both secret Catholics, and ◊Buckingham, Ashley (Lord ◊Shaftesbury), and ◊Lauderdale, who had links with the ◊Dissenters.

In 1670 Charles signed the secret Treaty of Dover, the full details of which were known only to Clifford and Arlington, under which he promised Louis XIV of France he would declare him-

> *This is very true: for my words are my own, and my actions are my ministers'.*
>
> CHARLES II
> *in reply to Lord Rochester's observation that the king 'never said a foolish thing, nor ever did a wise one.'*

self a Catholic, re-establish Catholicism in England, and support Louis's projected war against the Dutch; in return Louis was to finance Charles and in the event of resistance to supply him with troops. War with the Netherlands followed 1672, and at the same time Charles issued the Declaration of Indulgence, suspending all penal laws against Catholics and Dissenters. Parliament forced Charles to withdraw the Indulgence 1673 and accept a Test Act excluding all Catholics from office, and to end the Dutch war 1674. The Test Act broke up the Cabal, while Shaftesbury, who had learned the truth about the treaty, assumed the leadership of the opposition. ◊Danby, the new chief minister, built up a court party in the Commons by bribery, while subsidies from Louis relieved Charles from dependence on Parliament. In 1678 Titus ◊Oates's announcement of a 'popish   plot' started a general panic, which Shaftesbury exploited to introduce his Exclusion Bill, excluding James, Duke of York, from the succession as a Catholic; instead he hoped to substitute Charles's illegitimate son ◊Monmouth.

Charles II
Portrait of Charles II of England by Marcellus Laroon, Christ's Hospital, London. Despite the Civil War and the fate of his father, Charles I, he sought a return to absolutism and Catholicism, pursuing these aims with tact and political adroitness although in the end they led to war with the Netherlands 1672–74 and his dissolution of Parliament 1681.
   He proved a popular ruler and a keen patron of the arts and sciences, and is remembered for his flamboyant lifestyle.
E T Archive

In 1681 Parliament was summoned at Oxford, which had been the Royalist headquarters during the Civil War. The Whigs attended armed, but when Shaftesbury rejected a last compromise, Charles dissolved Parliament and the Whigs fled in terror. Charles now ruled without a parliament, financed by Louis XIV. When the Whigs plotted a revolt, their leaders were executed, while Shaftesbury and Monmouth fled to the Netherlands.

Charles Edward Stuart the *Young Pretender* or *Bonnie Prince Charlie* 1720–1788. British prince, grandson of James II and son of James, the Old Pretender. In the Jacobite rebellion 1745 Charles won the support of the Scottish Highlanders; his army invaded England to claim the throne but was beaten back by the Duke of ◊Cumberland and routed at ◊Culloden 1746. Charles went into exile.

charter open letter recording that a grant of land or privileges had been made on a specific date, as in the ◊Magna Carta. Witnesses either signed, made their mark, or affixed their seal. Based on the Roman *diploma*, the charter was re-introduced into Britain after the departure of the Romans to record donations of land to the Christian Church. These early charters were written in Latin, but from the 9th century charters were written in the vernacular; Latin again came into use after the Norman Conquest.

Chartism radical British democratic movement, mainly of the working classes, which flourished around 1838–48. It derived its name from the People's Charter, a six-point programme comprising universal male suffrage, equal electoral districts, secret ballot, annual parliaments, and abolition of the property qualification for, and payment of, members of Parliament.

   The radical MP, Thomas ◊Attwood, organized a National Convention 1839 and the following year a petition was presented to the House of Commons. Parliament refused even to consider the petition and a subsequent petition of May 1842 met the same fate. About 60 Chartists were transported to Australia after an abortive armed rising in response to these rejections. Under the leadership of Fergus ◊O'Connor, Chartism became a powerful expression of working class frustration and third Chartist petition was prepared 1848. The march and mass demonstration planned in its support caused the government great alarm and they threatened to use the military against any demonstration. The plans for a march were abandoned and Chartism declined thereafter, although its long-term demise is more probably due to greater prosperity among the populace as a whole, lack of organization, and rivalry among the leadership of the movement.

I am come home, sir, and I will entertain no notion at all of returning to that place whence I came, for I am persuaded my faithful Highlanders will stand by me.

CHARLES EDWARD STUART
on landing at Moidart, 1745 (attributed)

A feeling very generally exists that the condition and disposition of the Working Classes is a rather ominous matter at present; that something ought to be said, something ought to be done...

CHARTISM
Thomas Carlyle, Chartism, 1839

Château Gaillard castle and fortress above the Seine at Andelys, southeast of Rouen, France. It was built *c.* 1196 by Richard I the Lion-Heart, captured by Philip II of France 1204, and destroyed by Henry IV of France 1603, although several portions still stand. Its name means 'Cheeky Castle'.

Chesterfield Philip Dormer Stanhope, 4th Earl of Chesterfield 1694–1773. English politician and writer. He was the author of *Letters to his Son* 1774, which gave voluminous instruction on aristocratic manners and morals. A member of the literary circle of Swift, Pope, and Bolingbroke, he incurred the wrath of Dr Samuel Johnson by failing to carry out an offer of patronage. An opponent of Walpole, he was a Whig member of Parliament 1715–26, Lord Lieutenant of Ireland 1745–46, and secretary of state 1746–48.

Chevy Chase, Battle of alternative name for the Battle of ◊Otterburn 1388.

child labour the use of minors in place of adult workers. In the 19th century children and young people were used in factories in place of adult labour, often in harsh and dangerous conditions. There was little or no restriction on such labour until the Factory Act 1802 was introduced by Peel to provide for factory inspectors. The crusading zeal of politicians such as Lord Shaftesbury, writers such as Charles Kingsley and George Eliot, and artists such as George Cruikshank, shocked the complacency of Victorian England and did much to bring about the passing of further legislation to ameliorate the hardship of children forced to work in appalling conditions. The Mining Act 1842 forbade female and child labour in mines, and the Factory Act 1847 provided a 10-hour limit for women and children. Child labour is now restricted to light work such as delivering newspapers and is strictly regulated by both British and European legislation.

Childers (Robert) Erskine 1870–1922. British civil servant and, from 1921, Irish Sinn Féin politician, author of the spy novel *The Riddle of the Sands* 1903.

Before turning to Irish politics, Childers was a clerk in the House of Commons in London. In 1921 he was elected to the Irish Parliament as a supporter of the Sinn Féin leader de Valera, and took up arms against the Irish Free State 1922. Shortly afterwards he was captured, court-martialled, and shot as a Republican terrorist by the Irish Free State government of William T Cosgrave. His son, Erskine Hamilton Childers (1905–74) was president of the Irish Republic from 1973.

Chimney Sweepers Act law passed 1875 in Benjamin ◊Disraeli's second ministry forbidding the use of children to sweep chimneys, partly in response to public outcry at the practice. Earlier attempts by Lord Shaftesbury (in acts of 1840 and 1864) had failed to curb the use of children to clean chimneys. Employers were now forbidden from taking on apprentices under the age of 16 and no-one under the age of 21 was permitted to go up a chimney in order to clean it.

chivalry code of gallantry and honour that medieval knights were pledged to observe. Its principal virtues were piety, honour, valour, courtesy, chastity, and loyalty. The word originally meant the knightly class of the feudal Middle Ages.

Chivalry originated in feudal France and Spain, spreading rapidly to the rest of Europe and reaching its height in the 12th and 13th centuries. The earliest orders of chivalry were the Knights Hospitallers and Knights Templars, founded to serve pilgrims to the Holy Land, followed in England by orders such as those of the Garter and the Bath. A court of chivalry existed in England from Edward III's reign to 1737.

Christian Socialism 19th-century movement stressing the social principles of the Bible and opposed to the untrammelled workings of *laissez-faire* capitalism. Its founders, all members of the Church of England, were Frederick Denison Maurice (1805–1872), Charles Kingsley (1819–1875) and the novelist Thomas Hughes (1822–1896).

church, medieval The first Christians in Britain arrived with the Romans in the 1st century BC. This initial presence did not long survive the departure of the Romans. The lasting conversion of Britain to Christianity depended on two missionary endeavours: that of St Patrick in Ireland in the 5th century, influencing Scotland and northern England, and that of St Augustine in the late 6th century. The rival claims of the two strands of Christianity, respectively Celtic and Roman, were resolved at the Synod of Whitby 664, with the vote in favour of Rome. The new Anglo-Saxon church was centralized under Theodore of Tarsus, who was consecrated archbishop of Canterbury 668. The church subsequently flourished, fostering missionary activity (St Boniface) and learning (Bede) until the Danish raids and invasions of the 9th and 10th centuries brought disruption. Continuity was restored by Alfred the Great and his successors in Wessex, and Roman Catholicism remained the Christianity of Britain until the 16th century, when the Reformation resulted in the establishment of the Church of England.

Church in Wales the Welsh Anglican Church, independent from the ◊Church of England. The Welsh church became strongly Protestant in the 16th century, but in the 17th and 18th centuries declined from being led by a succession of English-appointed bishops. Disestablished by an act of Parliament 1920, with its endowments appropriated, the Church in Wales today comprises six dioceses (with bishops elected by an electoral college of clergy and lay people) with an archbishop elected from among the six bishops.

Church of England established form of Christianity in England. It was founded 1534 when Henry VIII dissociated from the Roman Catholic Church. Two archbishops head the provinces of Canterbury and York, which are divided into 44 dioceses. A General Synod, set up 1970 to replace the former Church Assembly, has three houses (bishops, other clergy, laity) to regulate church matters. A *Lambeth Conference*, first held 1867, is held every 10 years and is attended by bishops from all parts of the Anglican Communion. It is presided over in London by the Archbishop of Canterbury. Its decisions are not binding but are usually enacted. The *Church Commissioners*, established 1948, manage the considerable assets of the church. (It was revealed 1993 that the Commissioners had lost £800 million in property speculation.)

The main parties, all emerging in the 19th century, are: Low Church, or Evangelical, maintaining the Church's Protestant character; High Church, or Anglo-Catholic, stressing continuity with the pre-Reformation church and emphasizing the importance of sacraments, ritual, and religious communities of both sexes; and Modernist, or Liberal, concerned to reconcile the church with modern thought. The Pentecostal Charismatic movement, approving spontaneity of worship and glossolalia (speaking in tongues), is a recent development. The decision of the General Synod Nov 1992 to permit the ordination of women as priests has been the cause of much controversy both within the church and amongst the laity.

Church of Ireland form of the Church of England in the Irish Republic. The Church of England was established in Ireland in the 16th century, as in England. It failed to win the allegiance of most Irish, however, and was disestablished 1869. It is divided into the two provinces of Armagh and Dublin, each under an archbishop. The provinces are in turn subdivided into 12 dioceses. The legislative body is the General Synod, divided into the House of Bishops and House of Representatives. The Archbishop of Armagh is elected by the House of

The Church in Medieval England and Wales

The Church in Medieval England and Wales
The diocesan structure of the secular church in England and Wales remained virtually unchanged between the Norman reform of the Anglo-Saxon church and Henry VIII's Reformation nearly 500 years later.

Bishops, while other episcopal elections, including that of the Archbishop of Dublin, are made by an electoral college.

Church of Scotland established form of Christianity in Scotland. The national church in Scotland is Presbyterian in structure, unlike the episcopal Church of England. Scotland was influenced in the 16th century by the Protestant teachings of John Knox, but the Stuart kings later favoured an episcopal church. The episcopal cause was lost on the deposition of James II 1688, and by the Act of Settlement 1690 the Presbyterians were made the established church. Those who adhered to episcopacy after 1690 formed the Episcopal Church of Scotland, which is in full communion with the Church of England but is autonomous. Its governing authority is the General Synod, which meets once a year. The diocesan bishop who presides at its meetings is called the Primus and is elected by his fellow bishops.

A major rift took place in the Church of Scotland 1843, when about a third of its members left to form the Free Church of Scotland. Their protest was against the appointment of ministers by the patrons of livings rather than by their congregations. They were later joined by other groups that had seceded from the Church of Scotland, and together with them formed the United Free Church of Scotland 1900. This in turn caused some of their own members to secede. The seceders still called themselves the Free Church and became known as the 'Wee Frees' ('wee' in the sense of small in number). The larger secession ended 1929 when the United Free Church reunited with the Church of Scotland. The Church of Scotland is often generally referred to, especially in Scotland itself, as 'the Kirk'.

Churchill Randolph (Henry Spencer) 1849–1895. British Conservative politician, chancellor of the Exchequer and leader of the House of Commons 1886; father of Winston Churchill.

Born at Blenheim Palace, son of the 7th Duke of Marlborough, he entered Parliament 1874. In 1880 he formed a Conservative group known as the Fourth Party with Drummond Wolff (1830–1908), John Eldon Gorst, and Arthur Balfour, and in 1885 his policy of Tory democracy was widely accepted by the party. In 1886 he became chancellor of the Exchequer, but resigned within six months because he did not agree with the demands made on the Treasury by the War Office and the Admiralty. In 1874 he married Jennie Jerome (1854–1921), daughter of a wealthy New Yorker.

Churchill Lady Sarah, duchess of Marlborough 1660–1744. Whig wife of John Churchill, the 1st Duke of ◊Marlborough and confidante of Princess (later Queen) Anne. She was in the service of James II from 1673 and developed a long-standing friendship with his daughter, Anne. After the 'Glorious revolution' 1688 she initially tried to involve Anne in plots against the new king William III but then when Anne became queen, Churchill used her position to encourage the queen to favour Whig ministries. By 1707 her influence had been superseded by the Tory, Abigail Masham, and a Tory ministry was appointed 1710. Churchill finally broke with Anne 1711 and lost her positions at court.

Churchill Winston (Leonard Spencer) 1874–1965. British Conservative politician, prime minister 1940–45 and 1951–55. In Parliament from 1900, as a Liberal until 1923, he held a number of ministerial offices, including First Lord of the Admiralty 1911–15 and chancellor of the Exchequer 1924–29. Absent from the cabinet in the 1930s, he returned Sept 1939 to lead a coalition government 1940–45, negotiating with Allied leaders in World War II to achieve the unconditional surrender of Germany 1945; he led a Conservative government 1951–55. He received the Nobel Prize for Literature 1953.

He was born at Blenheim Palace, the elder son of Lord Randolph Churchill. During the Boer War he was a war correspondent and made a dramatic escape from imprisonment in Pretoria. In 1900 he was elected Conservative member of Parliament for Oldham, but he disagreed with Chamberlain's tariff-reform policy and joined the Liberals. Asquith made him president of the Board of Trade 1908, where he introduced legislation for the establishment of labour exchanges. He became home secretary 1910. In 1911 Asquith appointed him First Lord of the Admiralty but he was blamed for the failure of the Dardanelles campaign and 1915–16 served in the trenches in France. He returned to parliament as minister of munitions under Lloyd George 1917, and was involved with the development of the tank. After the armistice he was secretary for war 1918–21 and then as colonial secretary played a leading part in the establishment of the Irish Free State. During the postwar years he was active in support of the Whites (anti-Bolsheviks) in Russia.

In 1922–24 Churchill was out of Parliament. He left the Liberals 1923, and was returned for Epping as a Conservative 1924. Baldwin appointed him chancellor of the Exchequer, and he brought about Britain's return to the gold standard and was prominent in the defeat of the General Strike 1926. In 1929–39 he was out of office as he disagreed with the Conservatives on India, rearmament, and Chamberlain's policy of appeasement.

Churchill
British prime minister Winston Churchill inspecting the House of Commons Home Guard 1942. Many MPs were among the troops drawn up for inspection in the Speaker's Yard.
Hulton Deutsch

On the first day of World War II he went back to his old post at the Admiralty and was called to the premiership as head of an all-party administration May 1940; it was then that he made his much quoted 'blood, tears, toil, and sweat' speech to the House of Commons. He was a brilliant wartime leader, both as a strategist and as an inspirational speaker who did much to boost public morale. He had a close relationship with US president Roosevelt, and in Aug 1941 concluded the ♢Atlantic Charter with him. He travelled to Washington, Casablanca, Cairo, Moscow, and Tehran, meeting the other leaders of the Allied war effort. He met Stalin and Roosevelt in the Crimea Feb 1945 and agreed on the final plans for victory. He announced the unconditional surrender of Germany to the British people 8 May.

The coalition was dissolved 23 May 1945, and Churchill formed a caretaker government drawn mainly from the Conservatives. He was defeated after a Labour landslide in the general election July and became leader of the opposition. He won the next election Oct 1951 and again became prime minister, resigning April 1955. His home from 1922, Chartwell in Kent, is a museum. His books include a six-volume history of World War II (1948–54) and a four-volume *History of the English-Speaking Peoples* (1956–58). On his death Jan 1965, he was granted a state funeral 30 Jan which was watched on television by an estimated 350,000,000 people worldwide.

Cinque Ports group of Channel ports in southern England, which until the end of the 15th century supplied the ships and crew necessary to ward off invasion in return for certain privileges and tax exemptions. There were originally five, Sandwich, Dover, Hythe, Romney, and Hastings, which were joined by others later including Rye, Winchelsea, and others. Probably founded in Roman times, they rose to importance after the Norman conquest but declined in importance with the development of a standing navy in the 16th and 17th centuries, although the largely honorary office of lord warden still survives.

Cistercian order Roman Catholic monastic order established at Cîteaux 1098 by St Robert de Champagne, abbot of Molesme and other brethren, as a stricter form of the Benedictine order. The first foundation in England was at Waverley, Surrey 1128, followed soon after by Rievaulx *c.* 1131. The Cistercians were agricultural pioneers and played an important part in the development of English sheep farming.

Citizens' Advice Bureau (CAB) UK organization established 1939 to provide information and advice to the public on any subject, such as personal problems, financial, house purchase, or consumer rights. If required, the bureau will act on behalf of citizens, drawing on its own sources of legal and other experts. There are more than 900 bureaux located all over the UK.

civil list the annual sum provided from public funds to meet the official expenses of the sovereign and immediate dependents; private expenses are met by the ♢privy purse. Three-quarters of the civil list goes on wages for the royal household; the dependents it covers are the consort of a sovereign, children of a sovereign (except the Prince of Wales, who has the revenues from the Duchy of Cornwall), and widows of those children. Payments to other individual members of the royal family are covered by a contribution from the Queen.

Civil Wars: chronology

1625	James I died, succeeded by Charles I, whose first Parliament was dissolved after refusing to grant him tonnage and poundage (taxation revenues) for life.
1627	'Five Knights' case in which men who refused to pay a forced loan were imprisoned.
1628	Coke, Wentworth, and Eliot presented the Petition of Right, requesting the king not to tax without parliamentary consent, not to billet soldiers in private homes, and not to impose martial law on civilians. Charles accepted this as the price of parliamentary taxation to pay for war with Spain and France. Duke of Buckingham assassinated.
1629	Parliament dissolved following disagreement over religious policy, tonnage and poundage, beginning Charles's 'Eleven Years' Tyranny'. War with France ended.
1630	End of war with Spain.
1632	Strafford made lord deputy in Ireland.
1633	Laud became archibishop of Canterbury. Savage punishment of puritan William Prynne for his satirical pamphlet 'Histriomastix'.
1634	Ship money first collected in London.
1634–37	Laud attempted to enforce ecclesiastical discipline by metropolitan visits.
1637	Conviction of John Hampden for refusal to pay ship money infringed Petition of Right.
1638	Covenanters in Scotland protested at introduction of Laudian Prayer Book into the Kirk.
1639	First Bishops' War. Charles sent army to Scotland after its renunciation of episcopacy. Agreement reached without fighting.
1640	Short Parliament April–May voted taxes for the suppression of the Scots, but dissolved to forestall petition against Scottish war. Second Bishops' War ended in defeat for English at Newburn-on-Tyne. Scots received pension and held Northumberland and Durham in Treaty of Ripon. Long Parliament called, passing the Triennial Act and abolishing the Star Chamber. High Commission and Councils of the North and of Wales set up.
1641	Strafford executed. English and Scots massacred at Ulster. Grand Remonstrance passed appealing to mass opinion against episcopacy and the royal prerogative. Irish Catholic nobility massacred.
1642	*Jan* Charles left Westminster after an unsuccessful attempt to arrest five members of the Commons united both Houses of Parliament and the City against him. *Feb* Bishop's Exclusion Bill passed, barring clergy from secular office and the Lords. *May–June* Irish rebels established supreme council. Militia Ordinance passed, assuming sovereign powers for Parliament. Nineteen Propositions rejected by Charles. *Aug* Charles raised his standard at Nottingham. Outbreak of first Civil War. *Oct* General Assembly of the Confederate Catholics met at Kilkenny. Battle of Edgehill inconclusive.
1643	Irish truce left rebels in control of more of Ireland. Solemn League and Covenant, alliance between English Parliamentarians and Scots, pledged to establish Presbyterianism in England and Ireland, and to provide a Scottish army. Scots intervened in Civil War.
1643–49	Westminster Assembly attempted to draw up Calvinist religious settlement.
1644	Committee of Both Kingdoms to coordinate Scottish and Parliamentarians' military activities established. Royalists decisively defeated by Scots Covenanter army at Marston Moor, ending Royalist domination of N of England.
1644–45	Montrose's Royalist campaigns in Scotland seriusly weakened the Covenanters before his final defeat at Philliphaugh in 1645.
1645	Laud executed. New Model Army created. Charles pulled out of Uxbridge negotiations on a new constitutional position. Cromwell and the New Model Army destroyed Royalist forces at Naseby.
1646	Charles fled to Scotland. Oxford surrendered to Parliament. End of first Civil War.
1647	*May* Charles agreed with Parliament to accept Presbyterianism and to surrender control of the militia. *June–Aug* Army seized Charles and resolved not to disband without satisfactory terms. Army presented Heads of Proposals to Charles. *Oct–Dec* Army debated Levellers' Agreement of the People at Putney. Charles escaped to the Isle of Wight, and reached agreement with the Scots by Treaty of Newport.
1648	*Jan* Vote of No Addresses passed by Long Parliament declaring an end to negotiations with Charles. Scots under the Duke of Hamilton declared their support for Charles and invaded England. *Aug* Cromwell defeated Scots at Preston. Second Civil War began. *Nov–Dec* Army demanded trial of Charles I. Pride's Purge of Parliament transfered power to the Rump of independent MPs.
1649	*Jan–Feb* Charles tried and executed. Rump elected Council of State as its executive. Charles II was proclaimed king by Scots. *May* Rump declared England a Commonwealth. Cromwell landed in Dublin. *Sept–Oct* Massacres of garrisons at Drogheda and Wexford by Cromwell. Large numbers of native Irish were transplanted.
1650	*3 Sept* Cromwell defeated Scots under Leslie at Dunbar.
1651	Scots under Charles II invaded England, but were decisively defeated at Worcester (3 Sept) by Cromwell. Charles fled to the Continent and lived in exile for 9 years.

civil-list pension a pension paid to persons in need who have just claims on the royal beneficence, who have rendered personal service to the crown, or who have rendered service to the public by their discoveries in science and attainments in literature, art, or the like. The recipients are nominated by the prime minister, and the list is approved by Parliament. The pensions were originally paid out of the sovereign's civil list, but have been granted separately since the accession of Queen Victoria.

civil service body of administrative staff appointed to carry out the policy of a government. Members of the UK civil service may not take an active part in politics, and do not change with the government.

Civil servants were originally in the personal service of the sovereign. They were recruited by patronage, and many of them had only nominal duties. The great increase in public expenditure during the Napoleonic Wars led to a move in Parliament for reform of the civil service, but it was not until 1854 that two civil servants, Charles Trevelyan and Stafford Northcote, issued a report as a result of which recruitment by competitive examination, carried out under the Civil Service Commission 1855, came into force. Its recommendations only began to be effective when nomination to the competitive examination was abolished 1870. The two main divisions of the British civil service are the **Home** and **Diplomatic** services, the latter created 1965 by amalgamation of the Foreign, Commonwealth, and Trade Commission services. All employees are paid out of funds voted annually for the purpose by Parliament. Since 1968 the Civil Service Department has been controlled by the prime minister (as minister for the civil service), but everyday supervision is exercised by the Lord Privy Seal. In 1981 the secretary to the cabinet was also made head of the Home Civil Service. The present emphasis is on the professional specialist, and the **Civil Service College** (Sunningdale Park, Ascot, Berkshire) was established 1970 to develop training.

Civil War the conflict between King Charles I and the Royalists (Cavaliers) on one side and the Parliamentarians (also called Roundheads) on the other. Their differences centred on the king's unconstitutional acts but became a struggle over the relative powers of Crown and Parliament. The war continued until the final defeat of royalist forces at Worcester 1651. Oliver ◊Cromwell became Protector (ruler) from 1651 until his death 1658.

The crisis in relations between Crown and Parliament came to a head when Parliament issued the ◊Grand Remonstrance 1641, demanding the replacement of Charles's ministers and various reforms to the church. Charles responded with a disastrous attempt to arrest the ◊five members, five members of the House of Commons who he regarded as particular enemies, but succeeded only in uniting Parliament against him in widespread revulsion at his violation of its integrity.

Charles raised the royalist standard in Nottingham 22 Aug 1642 and the two sides first clashed at the Battle of ◊Edgehill two months later, with both sides claiming victory. The Royalists concentrated on taking London, a major parliamentary stronghold. Parliament's alliance with the Scots in the ◊Solemn League and Covenant 1643 led to victory against the Royalists at the Battle of ◊Marston Moor 1644 and the creation of the ◊New Model Army 1645 led to the decisive victory at ◊Naseby.

The war ceased 1646 when Charles I surrendered to the Scots, but attempts to negotiate a settlement with Parliament failed and Charles fled to the Isle of Wight 1647. From there he concluded a secret pact with the Scots, the ◊Engagement, agreeing to establish presbyterianism in England in return for their support. The second phase of the Civil War began March 1648 with a series of risings by royalist supporters in Wales, Kent, and Essex, but these were put down by Cromwell and Fairfax. The Scots invaded the north of England later in the year, but were defeated by parliamentary forces at the Battle of ◊Preston. The royalist cause was effectively over and Charles was captured, tried, and executed early 1649. England became a republic and was formally declared to be a ◊Commonwealth. The war continued with Cromwell campaigning in Ireland and Scotland and only ended when a revived royalist army under Charles II was defeated at the Battle of Worcester 1651.

civitas (Latin 'citizenship') in the Roman Empire, status conferred on provincial towns or communities granting the full privileges of citizenship to the members of that community. The privilege was much sought after as it gave tax benefits and enabled individuals to obtain political advancement within the imperial system.

As a Christian, I must tell you that God will not suffer Rebels and Traytors to prosper nor his Cause to be overthrown.

CIVIL WAR
Charles I, letter to Prince Rupert, 1645

Civil War battles, 1642–51

With the exception of Sir Ralph Hopton's successful Royalist campaign in the West Country in 1644 and Prince Rupert's disaster at Marston Moor, most action in the First Civil War took place in the Midlands and around Charles I's headquarters at Oxford. In Scotland, Montrose won a series of victories for the king until his defeat at Philiphaugh. Cromwell's campaigns of 1649–51 included victories at Worcester, Dunbar, and in Ireland.

Civil War battles, 1642–51

✘ battle, with date

✳ major siege

Auldearn 1645

North Sea

ATLANTIC OCEAN

Tippermuir 1644

Kilsyth 1645

Dunbar 1650

Philiphaugh 1645

Marston Moor 1644

Hull

Drogheda 1649

Irish Sea

Preston 1648

Preston

Limerick

Kilkenny

Chester

Nantwich 1644

Newark

Clonmel 1649

Carrick 1649

Wexford 1649

Worcester 1651

Cropredy Bridge 1644

Naseby 1645

Ross 1649

Edgehill 1642

Oxford

Gloucester

Chalgrove 1643

Reading

Bristol

Roundway Down 1648

Newbury 1643, 1644

Lansdown 1643

Portsmouth

Cheriton 1644

Stratton 1643

Langport 1645

Lostwithiel 1644

Plymouth

English Channel

0   100 mi

0   200 km

claim of right declaration by the Scottish estates 1689 accompanying their recognition of the new regime of William and Mary following the 'Glorious Revolution' 1688. The declaration asserted the right to depose any monarch who violated the law, listing grievances against James VII and II, as well as denouncing the ◊Lords of the Articles and episcopacy in Scotland.

clan (Gaelic *clann* 'children') social grouping based on kinship, such as the Highland clans of Scotland. Theoretically each clan is descended from a single ancestor from whom the name is derived – for example, clan MacGregor ('son of Gregor'). In reality many members of the clan were not blood relatives, but simply associated with the family in some way.

Clans developed an important role in Scotland as the monarchy became less stable toward the end of the 14th century. They played a large role in the Jacobite revolts of 1715 and 1745, after which their individual tartan Highland dress was banned 1746–82. Rivalry between them was often bitter.

THE WORLD TURNED UPSIDE DOWN

Civil War and Revolution

From 1640 to 1660 the British Isles witnessed some of the most dramatic events of their history. In this period, the English, Scottish, and Irish states all experienced major, and interconnected, internal convulsions.

Scotland
In the late 1630s the Scots rose in armed insurrection to defend their Calvinist, or presbyterian, church against a new 'popish' prayer book which Charles I was attempting to impose. In 1640 the Scots Covenanters defeated Charles's army at Newburn, precipitating the deep political crisis in England which led to civil war in 1642. In 1643 they entered into a military alliance with the English parliamentarians, and Scottish forces contributed much to the defeat of the Royalists. The Scots had assumed that Charles's defeat would be followed by the introduction of a Scottish-style church in England, but by 1649 the presbyterian English Parliament had lost power to the soldiers of the New Model Army, most of whom firmly rejected the concept of any national church.

The Scots then transferred their allegiance, backing the attempts of Charles I and then his son to win back the English crown. They were, however, defeated at Preston (1648), Dunbar (1650), and Worcester (1651) by Cromwell, who then brought all of Lowland Scotland under direct English rule for the first time in its history. In 1654 he forced Scotland into a union with England. While this union was overturned at the Restoration in 1660, the English hegemony it had established ensured that England entered the union of 1707 as much the dominant partner.

Ireland
In Ireland the mid-century crisis erupted with the Ulster Rising of 1641, during which several thousand native Catholics rose up against Protestant colonists planted on their lands earlier in the century. The rebellion quickly spread. A provisional Catholic government was set up at Kilkenny, and in 1643 Charles I recognized its authority in exchange for Irish military assistance in England. The recovery of Ireland was entrusted to Cromwell in 1649. Within nine months he broke the back of the rebellion with an efficiency and ruthlessness for which he has never been forgiven by the Irish people. This military reconquest was swiftly followed by the Cromwellian Land Settlement, which ejected most of the Catholic population from their lands and gave them the famous choice of going to 'Hell or Connaught'. These events laid the foundations for the English Protestant Ascendancy.

England
It was in England, however, that the revolutionary nature of the 1640s and 1650s was most apparent. Here a full-scale civil conflict resulted in the public trial and execution of a king who many still regarded as divinely appointed, the establishment of a republic, and the emergence of a military junta. In the religious sphere, the established national church was dismembered in favour of a large number of unorthodox radical sects, including the Ranters, who encouraged indulgence in alcohol, tobacco, and casual sex, and the Quakers, whose refusal to defer to social superiors made them especially subversive.

These 20 years were marked by an extraordinary intellectual ferment. Many English men and women began to espouse very radical solutions to a wide range of social and political problems. The Levellers advocated universal male suffrage. Gerrard Winstanley established a short-lived commune on St George's Hill near Weybridge, and argued in print for a communist solution to social inequalities. The poet John Milton sought liberal divorce laws, and other writers debated women's rights, polygamy, and vegetarianism.

England had fallen into civil war in 1642 for want of a peaceful solution to the serious differences between Charles I and some of his most influential subjects. Some of these differences had been political, but more important was a religious struggle manifested in the opposition of many English Calvinists to a clique of anti-Calvinists, or Arminians, who (under Charles's patronage) had gained control of the established church in the 1630s. Parliament's victory in the Civil War owed much to the organizational ability of its early leader John Pym, its access to the financial and demographic resources of London, and the creation of the New Model Army in 1645. After his defeat, Charles's own obstinate refusal to settle with his opponents finally drove the leaders of the army to the desperate expedient of regicide.

From 1649 to 1660, England remained a military state. Cromwell struggled to reconcile the country to his rule, but failed because of his association with the army in a nation now thoroughly fed up with the military. Moreover, Cromwell and his puritan colleagues considered it their duty to impose their own godly culture on the nation. Initiatives such as the introduction of the death penalty for adultery were met with widespread hostility. In restoring the Stuarts in 1660, the English were decisively rejecting this puritan culture in favour of a world once more turned right way up.

CHRISTOPHER DURSTON

Clapham sect early 19th-century evangelical group within the Church of England which advocated paternalist reforms for the underprivileged. Based on Rev. John Venn's church in Clapham between 1792 and 1830, the group consisted largely of liberal-minded wealthy families and had a profound influence on many of the most prominent social reformers of the time, including William ◊Wilberforce and the Earl of ◊Shaftesbury.

Clare Richard de, Earl of Pembroke and Striguil d. 1176. (known as 'Strongbow') English soldier. At the request of Dermot MacMurrough he invaded Ireland 1170 and captured Waterford and Dublin, beginning English intervention in Ireland. He was forced to hand over his conquests to Henry II but after helping him in Normandy was granted Wexford, Waterford, and Dublin, the first Anglo-Norman lordship. He is buried in Dublin Cathedral.

Clarence English ducal title, which has been conferred on a number of princes. The last was Albert Victor 1864–92, eldest son of Edward VII.

Clarendon Edward Hyde, 1st Earl of Clarendon 1609–1674. English politician and historian, chief adviser to Charles II 1651–67. A member of Parliament 1640, he joined the Royalist side 1641.

In the ◊Short and ◊Long Parliaments Clarendon attacked Charles I's unconstitutional actions and supported the impeachment of Charles's minister Strafford. In 1641 he broke with the revolutionary party and became one of the royal advisers. When civil war began he followed Charles to Oxford, and was knighted and made chancellor of the Exchequer. On the king's defeat 1646 he followed Prince Charles to Jersey, where he began his *History of the Rebellion*, published 1702–04, which provides memorable portraits of his contemporaries. In 1651 he became chief adviser to the exiled Charles II. At the Restoration he was created earl of Clarendon, while his influence was further increased by the marriage of his daughter Anne to James, Duke of York. His moderation earned the hatred of the extremists, however, and he lost Charles's support by openly expressing disapproval of the king's private life. After the disasters of the Dutch war 1667, he went into exile.

Clarendon, Constitutions of a series of resolutions agreed by a council summoned by Henry II at Clarendon in Wiltshire 1164. The Constitutions aimed at limiting the secular power of the clergy, particularly ecclesiastical courts, and were abandoned after the murder of Thomas à Becket. They form an early English legal document of great historical value.

Clarkson Thomas 1760–1846. British philanthropist. From 1785 he devoted himself to a campaign against slavery. He was one of the founders of the Anti-Slavery Society 1823 and was largely responsible for the abolition of slavery in British colonies 1833.

Clarendon Code a series of acts passed by the government 1661–65, directed at Nonconformists (or Dissenters) and designed to secure the supremacy of the Church of England. They were named after Charles II's chief minister, the 1st Earl of Clarendon, although he was a moderate who supported them only reluctantly.

The two most important acts were the **Corporation Act** 1661, which prevented Nonconformists from holding public office; and the **Act of Uniformity** 1662, which insisted on the use of a revised prayer book in the conduct of church services.

Claudius (Tiberius Claudius Drusus Nero Germanicus) 10 BC–AD 54. Roman emperor AD 41–54; a scholar, historian, and able administrator. During his reign the Roman empire was considerably extended, and he took advantage of tribal divisions in Britain to launch an invasion AD 43. He only stayed in Britain for the initial stages of the campaign and then left the conquest of the country to his commanders, although he was present at the capture of Colchester, ◊Caractacus' stronghold.

Claverhouse John Graham, Viscount Dundee 1649–1689. Scottish soldier. Appointed by Charles II to suppress the ◊Covenanters from 1677, he was routed at Drumclog 1679, but three weeks later won the battle of ◊Bothwell Bridge, by which the rebellion was crushed. Until 1688 he was engaged in continued persecution and became known as 'Bloody Clavers', regarded by the Scottish people as a figure of evil. His army then joined the first Jacobite rebellion and defeated the loyalist forces in the pass of Killiecrankie, where he was mortally wounded.

Clive Robert, Baron Clive of Plassey 1725–1774. British soldier and administrator who established British rule in India by victories over French troops at Arcot 1751 and over the nawab of Bengal at Plassey 1757. He was governor of Bengal 1757–60 and 1765–66. On his return to Britain 1766, his wealth led to allegations that he had abused his power. Although acquitted, he committed suicide.

Clive became a clerk in the East India Company's service in Madras 1743 and then joined the army. During a dispute over the succession to the Carnatic, an important trading centre, Clive marched from Madras with 500 troops, seized Arcot, the capital of the Carnatic, defended it for seven weeks against 10,000 French and Indian troops, and then sallied out and relieved the British forces besieged in Trichinopoli. He returned to Britain 1753 a national hero, hailed as 'Clive of India'. He returned to India 1755 as governor of Fort St David and after the incident of the Black Hole of Calcutta, when the city was seized by the nawab of Bengal, Clive defeated the nawab's 34,000-strong army with a force of only 1,900 troops outside Calcutta Feb 1757.

Meanwhile, the Seven Years' War had broken out in Europe, and Clive, discovering that Suraj-ud-Dowlah intended to assist the French, set out from Chandernagore and completely defeated the nawab's army at ◊Plassey 23 June. This victory all but secured Bengal for the East India Company and he was appointed governor of the province. Ill health forced Clive to return to Britain 1760, where he was made baron 1762. He went back to Bengal as governor 1765, only to be forced to return to Britain once more the following year, when he was accused of corruption and threatened with impeachment. A parliamentary enquiry held 1772–73 cleared him of the charges, but he remained obsessed by the charges and committed suicide.

Clontarf, Battle of victory of Irish high king Brian Boru over a Norse invasion force led by the Danish king of Dublin on 23 April (Good Friday) 1014 at Clontarf, northeast of Dublin. Although the Irish won a magnificent victory which completely lifted the Scandinavian threat to Ireland, Brian was reputedly slain in his tent by a fleeing Norseman.

close rolls rolls containing copies of private letters and documents of the Royal Court of Chancery. They included conveyances, writs of summons to Parliament and orders to royal officers. They were called 'close' as they were sealed, as opposed to 'letters patent', which were open and addressed 'to all and singular'.

Cluniac order Roman Catholic monastic order established at Cluny 910 by William of Aquitaine, as a revival movement based on the ◊Benedictine order. The first English Cluniac house was that of St Pancras at Lewes, founded 1077 by William de Warenne. Others followed at Wenlock c 1081, Bermondsey *c.* 1085, Castle Acre *c.* 1089, and Thetford 1104. As alien priories they were often sequestered by the Crown during the Hundred Years' War 1337–1453.

CND abbreviation for ◊*Campaign for Nuclear Disarmament*.

Cnut alternative spelling of ◊Canute.

coal mining coal was mined in Britain on a small scale from Roman times, but production expanded rapidly between 1550 and 1700. Coal was the main source of energy for the Industrial Revolution, and many industries were located near coalfields to cut transport costs. Competition from oil as a fuel, cheaper coal from overseas (USA, Australia), the decline of traditional users (town gas, railways), and the exhaustion of many underground workings resulted in the closure of mines (850 in 1955, 54 in 1992). Rises in the price of oil, greater pro-

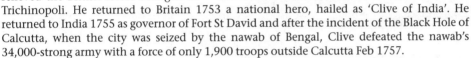

Clive
Robert Clive receiving the grant for the Clive Fund from the nawab of Bengal (1773) by E Penny, India Office Library, London. Clive defeated the nawab of Bengal 1757 after negotiations with his general Mir Jaffier, who was then installed as the new nawab. Mir Jaffier later made a large donation which was used to set up the Clive Fund for disabled officers.
E T Archive

A savage old Nabob, with an immense fortune, a tawny complexion, a bad liver and a worse heart.

ROBERT CLIVE
Historian Thomas Babington Macaulay, Historical Essays

Coalbrookdale
Coalbrookdale, Shropshire, is the site of the first bridge made entirely from cast iron. It was built by a local ironmaster, Abraham Darby III, and spans 30 m/100 ft across the river Severn.
Image Select

ductivity, and the discovery of new, deep coal seams suitable for mechanized extraction (for example, at Selby in Yorkshire) have improved the position of the British coal industry 1973–90, but it remains very dependent on the use of coal in electricity generation (74% of current use) and is now threatened by a trend toward using natural gas from the North Sea and Irish Sea gas fields for this purpose.

The British coal industry has never fully recovered from the effects of the miners' strike of 1984–85, a bitter and protracted dispute over pit closures, which ended in defeat for the miners and indicated a shifted balance of power away from the unions. In Oct 1992, the trade and industry secretary Michael Heseltine announced that 31 of the country's coal mines would be closed, putting some 30,000 miners out of work. After widespread protest from the public and from MPs from all parties, the government announced that 10 pits would close and the remaining 21 would be put under review. In March 1993 a revised closure programme reprieved 12 of the 21 collieries while they were assessed for economic viability. By August 1993, 18 collieries had closed.

Coalbrookdale (Ironbridge) town in the Severn Gorge, Shropshire, the so-called cradle of the Industrial revolution. It was here that Abraham Darby made the first successful attempt 1709 to use coke, rather than coal or charcoal, for smelting iron in a blast-furnace, thereby allowing for a massive increase in production.

Cobbett William 1763–1835. English Radical politician and journalist, who published the weekly *Political Register* 1802–35. He spent much time in North America. His crusading essays on the conditions of the rural poor were collected as *Rural Rides* 1830.

Born in Surrey, the self-taught son of a farmer, Cobbett enlisted in the army 1784 and served in Canada. He subsequently lived in the USA as a teacher of English, and became a vigorous pamphleteer, at this time supporting the Tories. In 1800 he returned to England. With increasing knowledge of the sufferings of the farm labourers, he became a Radical and leader of the working-class movement. He was imprisoned 1809–11 for criticizing the flogging of British troops by German mercenaries. He visited the USA again 1817–19. He became a strong advocate of parliamentary reform, and represented Oldham in the Reformed Parliament after 1832.

Cobden Richard 1804–1865. British Liberal politician and economist, co-founder with John Bright of the Anti-Corn Law League 1839. A member of Parliament from 1841, he opposed class and religious privileges and believed in disarmament and free trade.

A typical early Victorian radical, he believed in the abolition of privileges, a minimum of

Cobbett
Two pages from *The Life of William Cobbett – Written by Himself*. A British politician and journalist, William Cobbett also served in the army 1784–92. The left-hand page relates how he planned to disorganize the army before completely revolutionizing it; the right-hand page how, as a corporal, he found it impossible to teach officers their duty.
E T Archive

government interference, and the securing of international peace through free trade and by disarmament and arbitration. He opposed trade unionism and most of the factory legislation of his time, because he regarded them as opposed to liberty of contract. With other businessmen he founded the Anti-Corn Law League and began his lifelong association with John Bright, until 1845 devoting himself to the repeal of the ◊Corn Laws. His opposition to the Crimean War made him unpopular. He was largely responsible for the commercial treaty with France in 1860.

cockfighting the pitting of gamecocks against one another to make sport for onlookers and gamblers, now illegal in the UK but a popular sport in feudal England. Fighting cocks have steel spurs attached to their legs. They are between one and two years old when matched. A royal cockpit was built in Whitehall by Henry VIII, and royal patronage continued in the next century. During the Cromwellian period it was banned, but at the Restoration it was revived until it was banned in 1849. Cockfighting is still legal in some countries and continues secretly in others, including the UK.

Cockayne project scheme to manufacture cloth in England rather than export wool for this purpose to the Netherlands, named after its originator, Alderman Cockayne of London. A new company, the Merchant Adventurers was founded to exploit the idea, intended to transform England from being an exporter of primary material to a producer of value-added goods, and it was granted a monopoly over the export of cloth 1615. Despite James I's backing, the project had failed by 1617 due to underfunding and lack of expertise and its collapse caused a prolonged depression in the cloth trade.

coffee house alternative to ale-house as social meeting place, largely for the professional classes, popular in the 17th and 18th centuries. Christopher Bowman opened the first coffee house in London (later known as the 'Pasqua Rosee') in St Michael's Alley, Cornhill, 1652 and others soon followed in both London and Oxford so that by 1708 London alone boasted 3,000 coffee houses. Their popularity stemmed from their reputations as centres for the dissemination of news and ideas, making them good places to meet others of a like mind and also to conduct business. For this reason, coffee houses were often associated with radical readings and an attempt was made to suppress them by royal proclamation 1675 but coffee houses were too popular and the attempt was abandoned within a matter of days.

Many coffee houses attracted a particular group or profession and built their reputations and clientele around a certain business. For example, London underwriters specializing in marine insurance began to meet regularly in Edwin Lloyd's coffee house from about 1688 and the place was so heavily associated with that business that it gave its name to the Lloyds insurance market. The coffee houses declined in popularity toward the end of the 18th century as coffee itself was largely superseded by the new fashion for tea.

Coke Edward 1552–1634. Lord Chief Justice of England 1613–17. He was a defender of common law against royal prerogative; he drew up the ◊Petition of Right against Charles I 1628, which defines and protects Parliament's liberties.

Coke became a barrister 1578, and speaker of the House of Commons and solicitor-general 1592 . As attorney-general from 1594, he

Cobden
The British Liberal politician Richard Cobden, a cartoon by L Dickinson. Cobden's early struggles as a cloth merchant shaped his thinking on Free Trade and the increase of British commerce.
Hulton Deutsch

It is folly of too many to mistake the echo of a London coffee-house for the voice of the kingdom.

COFFEE HOUSE
Jonathan Swift, The Conduct of the Allies

coffee house
A contemporary picture of a coffee house from *c.* 1700. Coffee, chocolate, and tea were all introduced to England in the mid-17th century, and coffee houses rapidly became popular meeting places for the discussion of business affairs and literature.
Philip Sauvain

conducted the prosecution of Elizabeth I's former favourites Essex and Raleigh, and of the Gunpowder Plot conspirators. In 1606 he became Chief Justice of the Common Pleas, and began his struggle, as champion of the common law, against James I's attempts to exalt the royal prerogative. An attempt to silence him by promoting him to the dignity of Lord Chief Justice proved unsuccessful, and from 1620 he led the parliamentary opposition and the attack on Charles I's adviser Buckingham. Coke's *Institutes* are a legal classic.

Colenso, Battle of in the South African War, British defeat by Boer forces 15 Dec 1899 on the Tugela river about 32 km/20 mi south of Ladysmith. A British force under General Sir Redvers Buller attempting to relieve Ladysmith ran into a strong Boer defensive position on the Tulega river and was driven back with severe losses in troops and guns.

This loss, together with defeats at Magersfontein and Stormberg 10–11 Dec, became known as 'Black Week' for the British army, which suffered 7,000 casualties in the three battles. Buller was to make seven more attempts before succeeding in crossing the Tugela and relieving Ladysmith.

Collier Jeremy 1650–1726. British Anglican cleric, a ◊nonjuror, who was outlawed 1696 for granting absolution on the scaffold to two men who had tried to assassinate William III. His *Short View of the Immorality and Profaneness of the English Stage* 1698 was aimed at the dramatists William Congreve and John Vanbrugh.

Collingwood Cuthbert, Baron Collingwood 1748–1810. British admiral who served with Horatio Nelson in the West Indies against France and blockaded French ports 1803–05; he took command after Nelson's death at the Battle of ◊Trafalgar.

Collins Michael 1890–1922. Irish nationalist. He was a Sinn Féin leader, a founder and director of intelligence of the Irish Republican Army 1919, minister for finance in the provisional government of the Irish Free State 1922 (see ◊Ireland, Republic of), commander of the Free State forces in the civil war, and for ten days head of state before being killed by Irishmen opposed to the partition treaty with Britain.

Born in County Cork, Collins became an active member of the Irish Republican Brotherhood, and fought in the ◊Easter Rising 1916. In 1918 he was elected a Sinn Féin member to the Dáil, and became a minister in the Republican Provisional government. In 1921 he and Arthur Griffith (1872–1922) were mainly responsible for the treaty that established the Irish Free State. During the ensuing civil war, Collins took command and crushed the opposition in Dublin and the large towns within a few weeks. When Griffith died 12 Aug Collins became head of the state and the army, but he was ambushed near Cork by fellow Irishmen on 22 Aug and killed.

colonia (Latin, 'colony') Roman term for a settlement of Roman citizens. It consisted of a city and its dependent territory and often grew up around a legionary fortress, where retired soldiers might be granted plots of land in the town and in the surrounding countryside. The first British *colonia* was founded AD 49 at Camulodumum (Colchester). Others followed at Eboracum (York), Glevum (Gloucester), and Lindum (Lincoln).

Columba, St 521–597. Irish Christian abbot, missionary to Scotland. He was born in County Donegal of royal descent, and founded monasteries and churches in Ireland. In 563 he sailed with 12 companions to Iona, and built a monastery there that was to play a leading part in the conversion of Britain. Feast day 9 June. From his base on Iona St Columba made missionary journeys to the mainland. Legend has it that he drove a monster from the river Ness, and he crowned Aidan, an Irish king of Argyll.

That volley which we have just heard is the only speech which it is proper to make over the grave of a dead Fenian.

MICHAEL COLLINS
oration at the grave of Thomas Ashe, 1917

Combination Acts laws passed in Britain 1799 and 1800 making trade unionism illegal, introduced after the French Revolution for fear that the unions would become centres of political agitation. The unions continued to exist, but claimed to be friendly societies or went underground, until the acts were repealed 1824, largely owing to the Radical Francis Place.

Committee of Imperial Defence informal group established 1902 to coordinate planning of the British Empire's defence forces. Initially meeting on a temporary basis, it was established permanently 1904. Members were usually cabinet ministers concerned with defence, military leaders, and key civil servants. The committee had influence but no executive power. Its role was taken over by the War Council in wartime.

common law that part of the English law not embodied in legislation. It consists of rules of law based on common custom and usage and on judicial decisions. English common law became the basis of law in the USA and many other English-speaking countries.

Common law developed after the Norman Conquest 1066 as the law common to the whole of England, rather than local law. As the court system became established (under Henry II), and judges' decisions became recorded in law reports, the doctrine of **precedent** developed. This means that, in deciding a particular case, the court must have regard to the principles of law laid down in earlier reported cases on the same, or similar points, although the law may be extended or varied if the facts of the particular case are sufficiently different. Hence, common law (sometimes called 'case law' or 'judge-made law') keeps the law in harmony with the needs of the community where no legislation is applicable or where the legislation requires interpretation.

Common Market popular name for the **European Economic Community**; see ◊European Union.

common pleas, court of one of the courts into which the ◊Curia Regis (King's Court) was divided. It was originally the only superior court having jurisdiction in civil actions between subjects. It consisted of the Lord Chief Justice and five puisne judges. It was transferred to the High Court of Justice 1873 and is now represented by the Queen's Bench Division, one of the three divisions of the High Court.

Common Prayer, Book of the service book of the Church of England, based largely on the Roman breviary. The first service book in English was known as the *First Prayer Book of Edward VI*, published 1549, and is the basis of the *Book of Common Prayer* still, although not exclusively, in use. It was revised in a more Protestant light as the *Second Prayer Book of Edward VI* 1552, which omitted prayers for the dead in purgatory, and implied that Christ's body was not really present at communion, but was withdrawn 1553 on Mary's accession. In 1559 the *Revised Prayer Book* was issued, closely resembling that of 1549. This was suppressed by Parliament 1645, but its use was restored 1660 and a number of revisions were made. This is the officially authorized *Book of Common Prayer* but an act of 1968 legalized alternative services, and the Worship and Doctrine Measure 1974 gave the church control of its worship and teaching. The church's *Alternative Service Book* 1980, in contemporary language, is also in use.

Commons, House of the lower but more powerful of the two houses of ◊Parliament. It consists of 650 elected MPs (members of Parliament) each of whom represents a constituency. Its functions are to debate and legislate, and to scrutinize the activities of government.

Commonwealth, the republican rule of England by Parliament during the Interregnum 1649–60, more precisely the periods 1649–53 and 1659–60 – in the intervening years Oliver Cromwell ruled by direct personal government under the **Protectorate**. After the abolition of the monarchy 1649, the ◊Rump Parliament declared England to be a 'Commonwealth or Free State'. The House of Commons held supreme authority, with the former executive powers of the monarchy being vested in a 40-member Council of State. However, Parliament was not sufficiently radical for the army and was dissolved May 1653 by Cromwell. In Dec, the Barebones Parliament passed the Instrument of Government, placing supreme authority in the hands of Cromwell personally. Cromwell ruled under terms of the Protectorate until his death 1659 when he was succeeded briefly by his son Richard. Richard was unable to provide the strong leadership of his father and in May the army restored the Rump Parliament. However, Parliament and the army were unable to cooperate any better than in the first phase of the Commonwealth and the House of Commons began negotiations for the ◊Restoration of Charles II.

The term commonwealth or 'common weal' was used more generally by 17th-century writers such as Thomas Hobbes and John Locke to denote the concept of an organized political community. For them it meant much the same as the *res publica* (republic) did for the Romans, or as 'the state' means in modern times.

Commonwealth, the British voluntary association of 51 countries and their dependencies that once formed part of the British ◊Empire and are now independent sovereign states. They are all regarded as 'full members of the Commonwealth'. Additionally, there are some 20 territories that are not completely sovereign and remain dependencies of the UK or another of the fully sovereign members, and are regarded as 'Commonwealth countries'. Heads of gov-

Here out of the window it was a most pleasant sight to see the City from one end to the other with a glory about it, so high was the light of the bonfires, and so thick round the City, and the bells rang everywhere.

COMMONWEALTH
Samuel Pepys describing the celebrations marking the end of the Commonwealth/Diary, 21 February 1660.

The British Commonwealth today

country	capital	date joined	area in sq km	constitutional status
in Africa				
Botswana	Gaborone	1966	582,000	sovereign republic
British Indian Ocean Territory	Victoria	1965	60	British dependent territory
Gambia	Banjul	1965	10,700	sovereign republic
Ghana	Accra	1957	238,300	sovereign republic
Kenya	Nairobi	1963	582,600	sovereign republic
Lesotho	Maseru	1966	30,400	sovereign constitutional monarchy
Malawi	Zomba	1964	118,000	sovereign republic
Mauritius	Port Louis	1968	2,000	sovereign republic
Namibia	Windhoek	1990	824,000	sovereign republic
Nigeria	Lagos	1960	924,000	sovereign republic
St Helena	Jamestown	1931	100	British dependent territory
Seychelles	Victoria	1976	450	sovereign republic
Sierra Leone	Freetown	1961	73,000	sovereign republic
South Africa	Pretoria	1910†	1,221,000	sovereign republic
Swaziland	Mbabane	1968	17,400	sovereign republic
Tanzania	Dodoma	1961	945,000	sovereign republic
Uganda	Kampala	1962	236,900	sovereign republic
Zambia	Lusaka	1964	752,600	sovereign republic
Zimbabwe	Harare	1980	390,300	sovereign republic
in the Americas				
Anguilla	The Valley	1931	155	British dependent territory
Antigua and Barbuda	St John's	1981	400	sovereign constitutional monarchy*
Bahamas	Nassau	1973	13,900	sovereign constitutional monarchy*
Barbados	Bridgetown	1966	400	sovereign constitutional monarchy*
Belize	Belmopan	1982	23,000	sovereign constitutional monarchy*
Bermuda	Hamilton	1931	54	British dependent territory
British Virgin Islands	Road Town	1931	153	British dependent territory
Canada	Ottawa	1931	9,958,400	sovereign constitutional monarchy*
Cayman Islands	Georgetown	1931	300	British dependent territory
Dominica	Roseau	1978	700	sovereign republic
Falkland Islands	Port Stanley	1931	12,100	British dependent territory
Grenada	St George's	1974	300	sovereign constitutional monarchy*
Guyana	Georgetown	1966	215,000	sovereign republic
Jamaica	Kingston	1962	11,400	sovereign constitutional monarchy*
Montserrat	Plymouth	1931	100	British dependent territory
St Christopher–Nevis	Basseterre	1983	300	sovereign constitutional monarchy*
St Lucia	Castries	1979	600	sovereign constitutional monarchy*
St Vincent and the Grenadines	Kingstown	1979	400	sovereign constitutional monarchy*
Trinidad and Tobago	Port of Spain	1962	5,100	sovereign republic
Turks and Caicos Islands	Grand Turk	1931	400	British dependent territory
in the Antarctic				
Australian Antarctic Territory	uninhabited	1936	5,403,000	Australian external territory
British Antarctic Territory	uninhabited	1931	390,000	British dependent territory
Falkland Islands Dependencies	uninhabited	1931	1,600	British dependent territories
Ross Dependency	uninhabited	1931	453,000	New Zealand associated territory

The British Commonwealth today (continued)

country	capital	date joined	area in sq km	constitutional status
in Asia				
Bangladesh	Dhaka	1972	144,000	sovereign republic
Brunei	Bandar Seri Begawan	1984	5,800	sovereign monarchy
Hong Kong	Victoria	1931	1,100	British crown colony
India	Delhi	1947	3,166,800	sovereign republic
Malaysia	Kuala Lumpur	1957	329,800	sovereign constitutional monarchy
Maldives	Malé	1982	300	sovereign republic
Pakistan	Islamabad	1947††	803,900	sovereign republic
Singapore	Singapore	1965	600	sovereign republic
Sri Lanka	Colombo	1948	66,000	sovereign republic
in Australasia and the Pacific				
Australia	Canberra	1931	7,682,300	sovereign constitutional monarchy*
Cook Islands	Avarua	1931	300	New Zealand associated territory
Kiribati	Tawawa	1979	700	sovereign republic
Nauru	Yaren	1968	21	sovereign republic
New Zealand	Wellington	1931	268,000	sovereign constitutional monarchy*
Niue	Alofi	1931	300	New Zealand associated territory
Norfolk Island	Kingston	1931	34	Australian external territory
Papua New Guinea	Port Moresby	1975	462,800	sovereign constitutional monarchy*
Pitcairn Islands	Adamstown	1931	5	British dependent territory
Solomon Islands	Honiara	1978	27,600	sovereign constitutional monarchy*
Tokelau	Nukunonu	1931	10	New Zealand associated territory
Tonga	Nuku'alofa	1970	700	sovereign monarchy
Tuvalu	Funafuti	1978	24	sovereign constitutional monarchy*
Vanuatu	Villa	1980	15,000	sovereign republic
Western Samoa	Apia	1970	2,800	sovereign republic
in Europe				
Channel Islands		1931	200	UK crown dependencies
Guernsey	St Peter Port			
Jersey	St Helier			
Cyprus	Nicosia	1961	9,000	sovereign republic
Gibraltar	Gibraltar	1931	6	British dependent territory
Malta	Valletta	1964	300	sovereign republic
Isle of Man	Douglas	1931	600	UK crown dependency
United Kingdom	London	1931	244,100	sovereign constitutional monarchy*
England	London			
Northern Ireland	Belfast			
Scotland	Edinburgh			
Wales	Cardiff			
total			34,310,000	

* Queen Elizabeth II constitutional monarch and head of state
† withdrew from membership 1961 and readmitted 1994
†† left 1972 and rejoined 1989

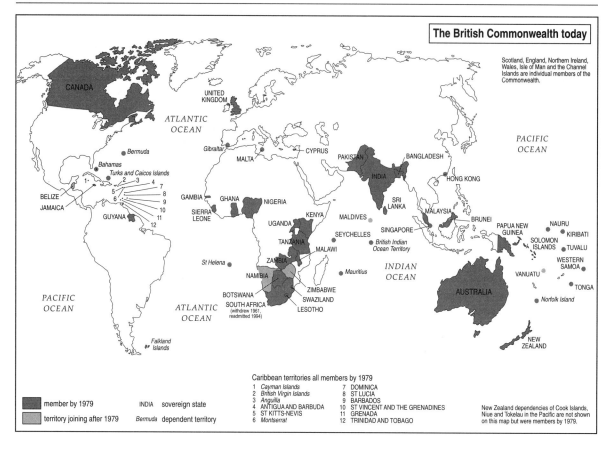

The British Commonwealth today

Scotland, England, Northern Ireland, Wales, Isle of Man and the Channel Islands are individual members of the Commonwealth.

Caribbean territories all members by 1979

1	*Cayman Islands*	7	DOMINICA
2	*British Virgin Islands*	8	ST LUCIA
3	*Anguilla*	9	BARBADOS
4	ANTIGUA AND BARBUDA	10	ST VINCENT AND THE GRENADINES
5	ST KITTS-NEVIS	11	GRENADA
6	*Montserrat*	12	TRINIDAD AND TOBAGO

member by 1979   INDIA   sovereign state

territory joining after 1979   *Bermuda*   dependent territory

New Zealand dependencies of Cook Islands, Niue and Tokelau in the Pacific are not shown on this map but were members by 1979.

The British Commonwealth today Though the period of British decolonialism in the 1960s and 1970s produced some indications that the hope of a coherent grouping of former colonies was misplaced, recent decades have seen some revival of the Commonwealth as a concept. The readmittance of South Africa, in particular, has prompted renewed interest in the Commonwealth as an alternative forum to the UN in a number of other former British colonies.

ernment meet every two years, apart from those of Nauru and Tuvalu; however, Nauru and Tuvalu have the right to participate in all functional activities. The Commonwealth has no charter or constitution, and is founded more on tradition and sentiment than on political or economic factors.

Queen Elizabeth II was the formal head but not the ruler of 16 member states in 1994; five member states had their own monarchs; and 30 were republics. The Commonwealth secretariat, headed from Oct 1989 by Nigerian Emeka Anyaoko (1933–   ) as secretary general, is based in London. The secretariat's staff come from a number of member countries, which also pay its operating costs.

Commonwealth Immigration Acts successive acts to regulate the entry into the UK of British subjects from the Commonwealth. The Commonwealth Immigration Act, passed by the Conservative government 1962, ruled that Commonwealth immigrants entering Britain must have employment or be able to offer required skills. Further restrictions have been added.

In 1968, many Asians fleeing from Kenya claimed British citizenship and the Labour government extended the controls of the 1962 Act by the 1968 Commonwealth Act. The 1971 Act introduced by the Conservative government set up a single system of entry and ended the quota of employment vouchers. There were concessions for 'patrials', who were defined as those who held British citizenship by birth or who had parents or grandparents born in the UK, or who had lived in the UK for five years. Subsequent legislation (the 1983 Nationality Act and the 1988 Immigration Act) tightened admission controls.

Communist Party of Great Britain (CPGB) British Marxist party founded 1920, largely inspired by the Russian Revolution 1917. It failed to affiliate with the Labour Party or to mobilize mass support, relying largely on Scottish or middle class voters. It enjoyed its greatest popularity in the 1930s and 1940s, particularly after Britain allied with the USSR during World War II. It had 18,000 members 1939 and had two MPs elected 1945, representing West Fife in Scotland and Mile End in London. The party was riven internally by the Soviet invasion of Hungary 1956 and its public image shattered by its refusal to condemn the invasion as other European communist parties did and by revelations of the brutal reality of Stalin's regime after his death. The party moved away from the USSR during the 1960s, particularly after the invasion of Czechoslovakia 1968, although it never fully embraced Euro-communism and remained one of the most pro-Soviet of the Western communist parties. The party was disbanded 1991 and relaunched as 'Democratic Left', although some splinter factions still lay claim to the old name.

Comyn John ('John the Black') d. *c.* 1303. Scottish nobleman. He was appointed ◊Guardian of Scotland 1286 and was one of the competitors for the throne after the death of Margaret, Maid of Norway 1290. He supported the claims of John Balliol instead and married his sister.

Comyn John ('John the Red') d. 1306. Scottish nobleman, son of John the Black. Like his father he supported the claim to the throne of John Balliol. He was murdered by Robert I the Bruce shortly before the latter declared himself king.

Congregation, Lords of the see ◊Lords of the Congregation.

Congregationalism form of church government adopted by those Protestant Christians known as Congregationalists, who let each congregation manage its own affairs. The first Congregationalists were the Brownists, named after Robert Browne, who defined the congregational principle 1580.

In the 17th century they were known as Independents – for example, the Puritan leader Cromwell and many of his Ironsides. Many emigrated to the American colonies until, during the Interregnum, they were accorded freedom of worship. Persecution resumed with the restoration of the established church 1662, when hundreds of ministers were driven from their churches and established separate congregations, but was finally ended with the Toleration Act 1689. The Congregational Union was formed 1832, renewing the fight for full civil rights. The Congregational church in England and Wales and the Presbyterian Church in England merged in 1972 to form the United Reformed Church. The latter, like its counterpart the Congregational Union of Scotland, has no control over individual churches but is simply consultative.

Connacht or ***Connaught*** one of the five ancient kingdoms of Ireland, in the west and northwest of the island. The original line of Connacht kings was displaced in the 4th century by the midland rulers, whose centre was at Tara. Two members of the Tara dynasty, Brion and Fiachra, founded septs (clans) to which all the rulers of Connacht belonged from the 5th to the 12th century. The English king Henry III granted Connacht 1227 to the Norman baron Richard de Burgh, whose descendants held the lordship of Connacht until the titles passed to the crown 1461. Connacht was divided 1576 into the present counties of Mayo, Sligo, Leitrim, Galway and Roscommon.

Connecticut former British colony in North America; see ◊Thirteen Colonies.

Connell James 1850–1929. Irish socialist who wrote the British Labour Party anthem 'The Red Flag' during the 1889 London strike.

Connolly James 1870–1916. Irish Socialist and patriot. As a young man he joined the British army in Dublin but deserted to marry an Irish girl in Scotland, where his father had taken his family 1880. He had a series of menial jobs in Scotland and joined the Social Democratic Federation, returning to Ireland as their emissary 1896. He founded the Irish Socialist Republican party, and then went on lecture tours in Great Britain and the USA where he helped found the syndicalist trade union, the Industrial Workers of the World (the 'Wobblies'). He returned to Ireland 1910 and together with James Larkin organized a strike of transport workers in Dublin 1913. He helped organize the ◊Easter Rising 1916 but was captured by the British and executed, although already fatally wounded.

conscription legislation for all able-bodied male citizens (and female in some countries, such as Israel) to serve with the armed forces. It originated in France 1792, and in the 19th and 20th centuries became the established practice in almost all European states.

In Britain conscription was introduced for single men between 18 and 41 in March 1916 and for married men two months later, but was abolished after World War I. It was introduced for the first time in peace April 1939, when all men aged 20 became liable to six months' military training. The National Service Act, passed Sept 1939, made all men between 18 and 41 liable to military service, and in 1941 women also became liable to be called up for the women's services as an alternative to industrial service. Men reaching the age of 18 continued to be called up until 1960.

Conservative Party UK political party, one of the two historic British parties; the name replaced *Tory* in general use from 1830 onwards. Traditionally the party of landed interests, it broadened its political base under Benjamin Disraeli's leadership in the 19th century. The present Conservative Party's free-market capitalism is supported by the world of finance and the management of industry.

Opposed to the *laissez-faire* of the Liberal manufacturers, the Conservative Party supported, to some extent, the struggle of the working class against the harsh conditions arising from the Industrial Revolution. The split of 1846 over Robert Peel's Corn Law policy led to 20 years out of office, or in office without power, until Disraeli 'educated' his party into accepting parliamentary and social change, extended the franchise to the artisan (winning considerable working-class support), launched imperial expansion, and established an alliance with industry and finance. The Irish Home Rule issue of 1886 drove Radical Imperialists and old-fashioned Whigs into alliance with the Conservatives, so that the party had nearly 20 years of office, but fear that Joseph Chamberlain's protectionism would mean higher prices led to a Liberal landslide in 1906. The Conservative Party fought a rearguard action against the sweeping reforms that followed and only the outbreak of World War I averted a major crisis. During 1915–45, except briefly in 1924 and 1929–31, the Conservatives were continually in office, whether alone or as part of a coalition, largely thanks to the break-up of the traditional two-party system by the rise of Labour.

Labour swept to power after World War II, but the Conservative Party formulated a new policy in their Industrial Charter of 1947, visualizing an economic and social system in which employers and employed, private enterprise and the state, work to mutual advantage. Antagonism to further nationalization and postwar austerity returned the Conservatives to power in 1951 with a small majority, and prosperity kept them in office throughout the 1950s and early 1960s. Narrowly defeated in 1964 under Alec Douglas-Home, the Conservative Party from 1965 elected its leaders, beginning with Edward Heath, who became prime minister 1970. The imposition of wage controls led to confrontation with the unions; when Heath sought a mandate Feb 1974, this resulted in a narrow defeat, repeated in a further election in Oct 1974.

Margaret Thatcher replaced Heath, and under her leadership the Conservative Party returned to power May 1979. Its economic policies increased the spending power of the majority, but also the gap between rich and poor; nationalized industries were sold off in a massive privatization programme; military spending and close alliance with the USA were favoured; and the funding of local government was overhauled with the introduction of the ◊poll tax. Margaret Thatcher was re-elected in 1983 and 1987, but resigned in Nov 1990. The Conservative government continued in office under John Major, re-elected in 1992, repudiating some of the extreme policies of Thatcherism. The party spent £11 million on the 1992 general election campaign, and received £7 million from undisclosed foreign sources. In 1993 the party had a deficit of nearly £20 million. John Major's administration has been dogged by splits in the party between those who favour closer ties with the European Union and the so-called 'Eurosceptics' who are hostile to the idea of any further integration with Europe. The row culminated in Major resigning and seeking re-election as party leader June 1995. He succeeded in defeating a right-wing challenger, John Redwood, and stayed on as leader and prime minister.

A Conservative government is an organized hypocrisy.

CONSERVATIVE PARTY
Benjamin Disraeli, speech,
17 March 1845

constable (Latin *comes stabuli* 'count of the stable') low-ranking British police officer. In medieval Europe, a constable was an officer of the king, originally responsible for army stores and stabling, and later responsible for the army in the king's absence. In England the constable subsequently became an official at a sheriff's court of law, leading to the title's current meaning.

Constantius I c. 250–306. Roman emperor, the father of Constantine the Great. He became Caesar 292 and was granted the provinces of Britain, Gaul, and Spain, with Augusta Treverorum (Trier) as his seat. After restoring Roman power in Britain and defeating the

Alemanni in Gaul, he was raised to the rank of Augustus 305 but died at Eboracum (York) the following year while on an expedition against the Picts and Scots.

Constantine the Great *c.* AD 280–337. First Christian emperor of Rome and founder of Constantinople. He defeated Maxentius, joint emperor of Rome AD 312, and in 313 formally recognized Christianity. As sole emperor of the west of the empire, he defeated Licinius, emperor of the east, to become ruler of the Roman world 324. He presided over the church's first council at Nicaea 325. Constantine moved his capital to Byzantium on the Bosporus 330, renaming it Constantinople (now Istanbul).

Constantine was born at Naissus (Niš, Yugoslavia), the son of Constantius I. He was already well known as a soldier when his father died in York in 306 and he was acclaimed by the troops there as joint emperor in his father's place. Constantine seems to have spent two years in Britain before leaving for Gaul to assert his claim as emperor 307. During the first three decades of the 4th century Britain enjoyed a period of great peace and prosperity under Constantine's reign, with many roads, cities, and villas being rebuilt and restored.

Conventicle Act statute of 1664 designed to suppress nonconformists, prohibiting five or more persons from holding religious meetings other than of the established Church. Similar to an Elizabethan statute 1593, this contentious measure expired 1667 but was then re-enacted in milder form 1670 before being repealed by the ◊Toleration Act 1689.

convoy system grouping of ships to sail together under naval escort in wartime. In World War I (1914–18) navy escort vessels were at first used only to accompany troopships, but the convoy system was adopted for merchant shipping when the unrestricted German submarine campaign began 1917. In World War II (1939–45) the convoy system was widely used by the Allies to keep the Atlantic sea lanes open.

Conway, Treaty of made in 1277, treaty in which Edward I of England extracted from Llewelyn II ap Gruffydd, Prince of Wales, an undertaking to ackowledge him as overlord and to surrender to him certain districts of North Wales. Edward subsequently established English rule over all Wales 1282–84.

Cook James 1728–1779. British naval explorer. After surveying the St Lawrence River in North America 1759, he made three voyages: 1768–71 to Tahiti, New Zealand, and Australia; 1772–75 to the South Pacific; and 1776–79 to the South and North Pacific, attempting to find the Northwest Passage and charting the Siberian coast. He was largely responsible for Britain's initial interest in acquiring colonies in Australasia. He was killed in Hawaii early 1779 in a scuffle with islanders.

Cooper Alfred Duff 1890–1954. Chancellor of the Duchy of Lancaster, sent to Singapore August 1941 to report on preparations for a Japanese attack. He had a notorious row with Shenton Thomas, Governor of the Straits Settlements in southeast Asia, and both Cooper and Thomas bear responsibility for the appalling lack of preparation for the Japanese invasion.

cooperative movement the banding together of groups of people for mutual assistance in trade, manufacture, the supply of credit, housing, or other services. The original principles of the cooperative movement were laid down 1844 by the Rochdale Pioneers, under the influence of Robert Owen, and by Charles Fourier in France.

Control is in the hands of a management committee elected by the members. Cooperative societies have several million members in the UK, especially the Cooperative Wholesale Society (CWS), a retail trading concern whose shops sell at current market prices, but return the bulk of their profits (less any sums placed to reserve) to their members as 'dividends' on

Cook
English explorer and mapmaker Capt James Cook. Cook made three major voyages between 1768 and 1797, visiting New Zealand, Easter Island, the South Sandwich Islands, and the E coast of Australia. He circumnavigated the Antarctic but searched in vain for a Pacific–Atlantic passage through North America. He was awarded the Royal Society's Copley Medal for work on scurvy.
E T Archive

At daylight in the morning we discovered a bay, which appeared to be tolerably well sheltered from all winds, into which I resolved to go with the ship.

JAMES COOK
referring to Botany Bay.
Journal, *28 April 1770*

the sums spent there. The 1970s and 1980s saw a growth in the number of workers' cooperatives, set up in factories otherwise threatened by closure due to economic depression.

Cooperative Party political party founded in Britain 1917 by the cooperative movement to maintain its principles in parliamentary and local government. A written constitution was adopted 1938. The party had strong links with the Labour Party; from 1946 Cooperative Party candidates stood in elections as Cooperative and Labour Candidates and, after the 1959 general election, agreement was reached to limit the party's candidates to 30.

Copenhagen, Battle of during the Napoleonic Wars, naval victory 2 April 1801 by a British fleet under Sir Hyde Parker (1739–1807) and ◊Nelson over the Danish fleet. Nelson put his telescope to his blind eye and refused to see Parker's signal for withdrawal, with the famous words 'I see no ships'. The victory effectively broke up the League of Armed Neutrality.

Corn Laws until 1846, laws used to regulate the export or import of cereals in order to maintain an adequate supply for consumers and a secure price for producers. For centuries the Corn Laws formed an integral part of the mercantile system in England; they were repealed because they became an unwarranted tax on food and a hindrance to British exports.

Although mentioned as early as the 12th century, the Corn Laws only became significant in the late 18th century. After the Napoleonic Wars, with mounting pressure from a growing urban population, the laws aroused strong opposition because of their tendency to drive up prices. A law passed by Lord Liverpool's government 1815 banned the import of foreign grain until the price of domestic produce reached 80 shillings a quarter. The law was modified with a sliding scale 1828 and again 1842. The Corn Laws became a hotly contested political issue as they were regarded by radicals as benefiting wealthy landowners at the expense of the ordinary consumer and the ◊Anti-Corn Law League was formed to campaign for their repeal 1838. Partly as a result of this pressure and partly because of the effects of the Irish potato famine, they were repealed by Conservative prime minister Robert ◊Peel 1846.

Cornwallis Charles, 1st Marquess 1738–1805. British general in the ◊American Revolution until 1781, when his defeat at Yorktown led to final surrender and ended the war. He then served twice as governor general of India where he introduced a series of reforms, the **Cornwallis code**, in Bengal. As Lord Lieutenant of Ireland he quashed the rebellion of 1798.

Corporation Act statute of 1661 which effectively excluded religious dissenters from public office. All magistrates in England and Wales were obliged to take sacrament according to the Church of England, to swear an oath of allegiance, to renounce the Covenant, and to declare it treason to carry arms against the King. The measure reflected the wishes of parliament rather than Charles II, though it was later circumvented prior to its repeal 1828.

corresponding society one of the first independent organizations for the working classes, advocating annual parliaments and universal male suffrage. The London Corresponding Society was founded 1792 by politicians Thomas Hardy (1752–1832) and John Horne Tooke (1736–1812). It later established branches in Scotland and the provinces. Many of its activities had to be held in secret and government fears about the spread of revolutionary doctrines led to its banning 1799.

Cosgrave William Thomas 1880–1965. Irish politician. He took part in the ◊Easter Rising 1916 and sat in the Sinn Féin cabinet of 1919–21. Head of the Free State government 1922–33, he founded and led the Fine Gael opposition 1933–44. His eldest son, Liam Cosgrave, was prime minister of Ireland 1973–77.

Council in the Marches royal court with jurisdiction over Wales and the English border counties; established as part of the process of imposing the King's rule over the semi-independent ◊Marcher Lords of the Welsh border regions. Edward IV empowered the council of his son Edward, Prince of Wales, to act as a court 1473. This power was revived to provide a role for Arthur, Prince of Wales, Henry VII's sickly elder son, who died prematurely at the council's headquarters in Ludlow 1502. The Council in the Marches was formally established Jan 1543 in the reign of Henry VIII and was abolished 1641. Though primarily a judicial court, it acted as a spearhead of Protestantism at the time of the Reformation.

Council of Estates executive committee, composed of members of Parliament and others, convened in the 17th century to govern Scotland during conflicts with the Crown, notably during the Civil War (1640–51), at the time of the Restoration (1660–61), and during the Glorious Revolution (1688–89). See also ◊remonstrant.

Council of the North royal council which supervised Yorkshire, Cumberland, Durham, Northumberland, and Westmoreland. Though its origins lay in the 15th century, it was reconstituted in 1537 after the Pilgrimage of Grace and was like the ◊Council in the Marches, imposing royal policies on the North, overseeing the introduction of Protestantism. It was abolished along with other regional councils 1641.

Country Party parliamentary opposition to the royal government in the 17th and 18th centuries. Although not a formal party as such, the term is used by many historians to identify a dissident strand of opinion consisting largely of landowners in the shires, generally associated with Protestantism and antipathy to the sophisticated manners and artistic tastes of the court.

county administrative unit of a country or state. It was the name given by the Normans to Anglo-Saxon 'shires', and the boundaries of many present-day English counties date back to Saxon times. The Local Government Act 1888 established a series of county councils across the country which were responsible for the government and administration of each county.

Under the Local Government Act 1972, which came into effect 1974, the existing English administrative counties were replaced by 45 new county areas of local government, and the 13 Welsh counties were reduced by amalgamation to eight. Under the Local Government (Scotland) Act 1973 the 33 counties of Scotland were amalgamated 1975 in nine new regions and three island areas. Northern Ireland has six geographical counties, but under the Local Government Act 1973 administration is through 26 district councils (single-tier authorities), each based on a main town or centre. Under the Local Government Act 1994 all county and county borough councils in Wales were abolished 1996, with many of the new authorities taking the names of the old counties. The regional and district councils in Scotland were similarly abolished.

county palatine in medieval England, a county whose lord held particular rights, in lieu of the king, such as pardoning treasons

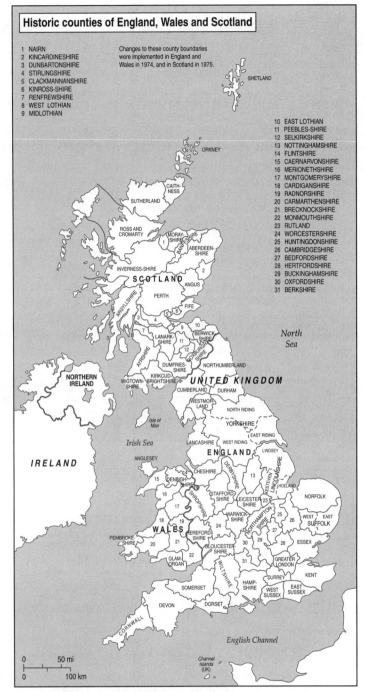

Historic counties of England, Wales and Scotland

1 NAIRN	10 EAST LOTHIAN
2 KINCARDINESHIRE	11 PEEBLES-SHIRE
3 DUNBARTONSHIRE	12 SELKIRKSHIRE
4 STIRLINGSHIRE	13 NOTTINGHAMSHIRE
5 CLACKMANNANSHIRE	14 FLINTSHIRE
6 KINROSS-SHIRE	15 CAERNARVONSHIRE
7 RENFREWSHIRE	16 MERIONETHSHIRE
8 WEST LOTHIAN	17 MONTGOMERYSHIRE
9 MIDLOTHIAN	18 CARDIGANSHIRE
	19 RADNORSHIRE
	20 CARMARTHENSHIRE
	21 BRECKNOCKSHIRE
	22 MONMOUTHSHIRE
	23 RUTLAND
	24 WORCESTERSHIRE
	25 HUNTINGDONSHIRE
	26 CAMBRIDGESHIRE
	27 BEDFORDSHIRE
	28 HERTFORDSHIRE
	29 BUCKINGHAMSHIRE
	30 OXFORDSHIRE
	31 BERKSHIRE

Changes to these county boundaries were implemented in England and Wales in 1974, and in Scotland in 1975.

Historic counties of England, Wales, and Scotland
The reorganization of local government in 1972–74 resulted in the disappearance of a number of county names familiar to most British citizens since the Middle Ages. Protests were understandably vigorous in some of the affected areas, but it seems unlikely that the ancient names and boundaries will be restored.

Counties of England after 1974

county	administrative headquarters	area in sq km
Avon	Bristol	1,340
Bedfordshire	Bedford	1,240
Berkshire	Reading	1,260
Buckinghamshire	Aylesbury	1,880
Cambridgeshire	Cambridge	3,410
Cheshire	Chester	2,320
Cleveland	Middlesbrough	580
Cornwall	Truro	3,550
Cumbria	Carlisle	6,810
Derbyshire	Matlock	2,630
Devon	Exeter	6,720
Dorset	Dorchester	2,650
Durham	Durham	2,440
East Sussex	Lewes	1,800
Essex	Chelmsford	3,670
Gloucestershire	Gloucester	2,640
Hampshire	Winchester	3,770
Hereford & Worcester	Worcester	3,930
Hertfordshire	Hertford	1,630
Humberside	Beverley	3,510
Isle of Wight	Newport	380
Kent	Maidstone	3,730
Lancashire	Preston	3,040
Leicestershire	Leicester	2,550
Lincolnshire	Lincoln	5,890
London, Greater*		1,580
Norfolk	Norwich	5,360
Northamptonshire	Northampton	2,370
Northumberland	Morpeth	5,030
North Yorkshire	Northallerton	8,320
Nottinghamshire	Nottingham	2,160
Oxfordshire	Oxford	2,610
Shropshire	Shrewsbury	3,490
Somerset	Taunton	3,460
Staffordshire	Stafford	2,720
Suffolk	Ipswich	3,800
Surrey	Kingston upon Thames	1,660
Warwickshire	Warwick	1,980
West Sussex	Chichester	2,020
Wiltshire	Trowbridge	3,480

metropolitan county**	area in sq km
Manchester, Greater	1,290
Merseyside	650
South Yorkshire	1,560
Tyne & Wear	540
West Midlands	900
West Yorkshire	2,040

* most administrative functions of the Greater London Council (GLC) reverted to individual boroughs from 1986

** most administrative functions of metropolitan counties reverted to metropolitan district councils from 1986

Historic counties of England

Bedfordshire	Norfolk
Berkshire	Northamptonshire
Buckinghamshire	Northumberland
Cambridgeshire and Isle of Ely	Nottinghamshire
Cheshire	Oxfordshire
Cornwall	Rutland
Cumberland	Shropshire
Derbyshire	Somerset
Devonshire	Staffordshire
Dorset	Suffolk
Durham	East Suffolk
Essex	West Suffolk
Gloucestershire	Surrey
Hampshire	Sussex
Herefordshire	East Sussex
Hertfordshire	West Sussex
Huntingdonshire and Peterborough	Warwickshire
Kent	Westmorland
Lancashire	Wight, Isle of
Leicestershire	Wiltshire
Lincolnshire	Worcestershire
Holland	Yorkshire
Kesteven	East Riding
Lindsey	North Riding
London, Greater	West Riding

Regions of Scotland after 1974

Borders	Lothian
Central	Orkney Islands
Dumfries and Galloway	Shetland Islands
Fife	Strathclyde
Grampian	Tayside
Highland	Western Isles

Historic Counties of Scotland

Aberdeen	Lanark
Angus (fomerly Forfar)	Midlothian
Argyll	Moray
Ayr	Nairn
Banff	Orkney
Berwick	Peebles
Bute	Perth
Caithness	Renfrew
Clackmannan	Ross and Cromarty
Dumfries	Roxburgh
Dunbarton	Selkirk
East Lothian	Stirling
Fife	Sutherland
Inverness	West Lothian
Kincardine	Wigtown
Kinross	Zetland
Kirkcudbright	

Counties of the Republic of Ireland

county	administrative headquarters	area in sq km
Ulster province		
Cavan	Cavan	1,890
Donegal	Lifford	4,830
Monaghan	Monaghan	1,290
Munster province		
Clare	Ennis	3,190
Cork	Cork	7,460
Kerry	Tralee	4,700
Limerick	Limerick	2,690
Tipperary (N)	Nenagh	2,000
Tipperary (S)	Clonmel	2,260
Waterford	Waterford	1,840
Leinster province		
Carlow	Carlow	900
Dublin	Dublin	920
Kildare	Naas	1,690
Kilkenny	Kilkenny	2,060
Laois	Port Laoise	1,720
Longford	Longford	1,040
Louth	Dundalk	820
Meath	Trim	2,340
Offaly	Tullamore	2,000
Westmeath	Mullingar	1,760
Wexford	Wexford	2,350
Wicklow	Wicklow	2,030
Connacht province		
Galway	Galway	5,940
Leitrim	Carrick-on-Shannon	1,530
Mayo	Castlebar	5,400
Roscommon	Roscommon	2,460
Sligo	Sligo	1,800

Counties of Wales after 1974

county	administrative headquarters	area in sq km
Clwyd	Mold	2,420
Dyfed	Carmarthen	5,770
Gwent	Cwmbran	1,380
Gwynedd	Caernarvon	3,870
Mid Glamorgan	Cardiff	1,020
Powys	Llandrindod Wells	5,080
South Glamorgan	Cardiff	420
West Glamorgan	Swansea	820

Historic Counties of Wales

Anglesey	Glamorgan
Brecknockshire	Merioneth
Caernarvonshire	Monmouthshire
Cardiganshire	Montgomeryshire
Carmarthenshire	Pembrokeshire
Denbighshire	Radnorshire
Flintshire	

Counties of Northern Ireland

county	administrative headquarters	area in sq km
Antrim	Belfast	2,830
Armagh	Armagh	1,250
Derry	Derry	2,070
Down	Downpatrick	2,470
Fermanagh	Enniskillen	1,680
Tyrone	Omagh	3,160

and murders. Under William I there were four counties palatine: Chester, Durham, Kent, and Shropshire.

Coupon Election British general election of 1918, named after the letter issued Nov 1918 by the ruling Liberal–Conservative coalition under Lloyd George and Bonar Law jointly endorsing their candidates. Asquith, who had been ousted as prime minister by Lloyd George in 1916, referred to this letter as a 'coupon', evoking the language of wartime rationing. The coalition won a massive victory 14 Dec 1918, securing a majority of 262, and Lloyd George remained in office.

Covenanters Scottish Presbyterian Christians who swore to uphold their forms of worship in a National Covenant, signed 28 Feb 1638, when Charles I attempted to introduce a liturgy on the English model into Scotland.

A general assembly abolished episcopacy, and the Covenanters signed with the English Parliament the Solemn League and Covenant 1643, promising military aid in return for the establishment of Presbyterianism in England. A Scottish army entered England and fought at Marston Moor 1644. At the Restoration Charles II revived episcopacy in Scotland, evicting resisting ministers, so that revolts followed 1666, 1679, and 1685. However, Presbyterianism was again restored 1688.

Craig James 1871–1940. Ulster Unionist politician, the first prime minister of Northern Ireland 1921–40. Craig became a member of Parliament 1906, and was a highly effective organizer of Unionist resistance to Home Rule. As prime minister he carried out systematic

discrimination against the Catholic minority, abolishing proportional representation 1929 and redrawing constituency boundaries to ensure Protestant majorities. He was created Viscount Craigavon 1927.

Cranmer Thomas 1489–1556. English cleric, archbishop of Canterbury from 1533. Cranmer suggested 1529 that the question of Henry VIII's marriage to Catherine of Aragon should be referred to the universities of Europe rather than to the pope, and in 1533 he declared it null and void. A Protestant convert, he helped to shape the doctrines of the Church of England under Edward VI. He was responsible for the issue of the Prayer Books of 1549 and 1552, and supported the succession of Lady Jane Grey 1553. Condemned for heresy under the Catholic Mary Tudor, he at first recanted, but when his life was not spared, resumed his position and was burned at the stake, first holding to the fire the hand which had signed his recantation.

Crécy, Battle of first major battle of the Hundred Years' War 26 Aug 1346 in which Philip VI of France was defeated by Edward III of England at Crécy-en-Ponthieu, now in Somme *département*, France, 18 km/11 mi northeast of Abbeville. The English victory reinforced the lesson of Courtrai – that infantry were well capable of dealing with cavalry.

cricket bat-and-ball game between two teams of 11 players each. It is played with a small solid ball and long flat-sided wooden bats, on a round or oval field, at the centre of which is a finely mown pitch, 20 m/22 yd long. At each end of the pitch is a wicket made up of three upright wooden sticks (stumps), surmounted by two smaller sticks (bails). The object of the game is to score more runs than the opposing team. A run is normally scored by the batsman striking the ball and exchanging ends with his or her partner until the ball is returned by a fielder, or by hitting the ball to the boundary line for an automatic four or six runs.

The exact origins of cricket are unknown, but it certainly dates back to the 16th century. The name is thought to have originated from the Anglo-Saxon word *cricc*, meaning a shepherd's staff. The first players were the shepherds of south-east England, who used their crooks as bats and the wicket gate and movable bail of the sheep pens as a target for the bowlers.

The games rules were codified with the formation of the Marylebone Cricket Club (MCC) 1797. It became the supreme authority on the rules and regulations of the game and its base,

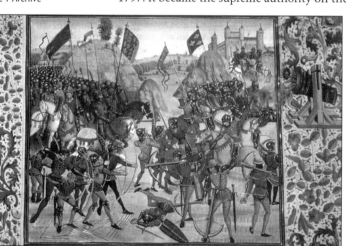

Lords (named after a founder member of the club, Thomas Lord), in St John's Wood, London, is still regarded by many as the spiritual home of the game.

In 1909 the Imperial Cricket Conference, renamed the International Cricket Conference 1965, was set up with England, Australia and South Africa as founder members; they were later joined by the West Indies, New Zealand, India, and Pakistan.

Crimean War war 1853–56 between Russia and the allied powers of England, France, Turkey, and Sardinia. The war arose from British and French mistrust of Russia's ambitions in the Balkans. When Russia occupied Moldavia and Wallachia 1853, then part of the Ottoman Empire, the Turks declared war.

They were soon joined by Britain and France and in 1854 an allied
Anglo-French expedition was sent to the Crimea to attack the
Russian Black Sea city of Sevastopol. The battles of the river Alma,
Balaclava (including the Charge of the Light Brigade), and Inkerman
1854 led to a siege which, owing to military mismanagement, lasted
for a year until Sept 1855. The war was ended by the Treaty of Paris
1856. The scandal surrounding French and British losses through
disease led to the fall of the government and the organization of
proper military nursing services by Florence ◊Nightingale.

1853 Russia invaded the Balkans (from which they were compelled to withdraw by Austrian intervention) and sank the Turkish
fleet at the Battle of Sinope 30 Nov.

1854 Britain and France declared war on Russia, invaded the
Crimea, and laid siege to Sevastopol (Sept 1854–Sept 1855). Battles of
◊Balaclava 25 Oct ◊Inkerman 5 Nov, and the Alma.

1855 Sardinia declared war on Russia.

1856 The Treaty of Paris in Feb ended the war.

Cripps (Richard) Stafford 1889–1952. British Labour politician,
expelled from the Labour Party 1939–45 for supporting a 'Popular
Front' against Chamberlain's appeasement policy. He was ambassador to Moscow 1940–42, minister of aircraft production 1942–45,
and as chancellor of the Exchequer 1947–50 introduced a policy of
economic austerity.

croft small farm in the Highlands of Scotland, traditionally farming
common land cooperatively; the 1886 Crofters Act gave security of
tenure to crofters. Today, although grazing land is still shared,
arable land is typically enclosed. Crofting is the only form of subsistence farming still found
in the UK.

Crompton's mule advanced spinning machine which made the production of fine yarns by
machine possible, developed 1779 in Bolton by Samuel Crompton. It was a cross between the
◊spinning jenny and a water-frame spinning machine. See also ◊hand-loom weavers.

Cromwell Oliver 1599–1658. English general and politician, leading Puritan figure of the Parliamentary side in the ◊Civil War. He raised cavalry forces (later called **Ironsides**) which aided
the victories at Edgehill 1642 and ◊Marston Moor 1644, and organized the New Model Army,
which he led (under General Fairfax) to victory at Naseby 1645. He declared Britain a republic

cricket
By the end of the 19th
century, cricket was
established as England's
premier summer sport.
Its popularity owed
much to the all-round
brilliance of W G Grace,
shown here, arguably
the greatest player of all
time.
Image Select

Crimean War
Typical conditions
during the winter
months of the Crimean
War. This photograph,
taken at the time, is
reputed to show the
journalist William Russell
at work (left) and
Florence Nightingale
(centre) awaiting
casualties from the front.
Hulton Deutsch

Cromwell
Thomas Cromwell succeeded his mentor, Cardinal Wolsey, as chief minister to Henry VIII. He fell from power after he arranged Henry's fourth marriage to Anne of Cleves, which Henry found less than satisfactory.
Philip Sauvain

('the Commonwealth') 1649, following the execution of Charles I. As Lord Protector (ruler) from 1653, Cromwell established religious toleration and raised Britain's prestige in Europe on the basis of an alliance with France against Spain.

Cromwell was born at Huntingdon, NW of Cambridge, son of a small landowner. He entered Parliament 1629 and became active in events leading to the Civil War. Failing to secure a constitutional settlement with Charles I 1646–48, he defeated the 1648 Scottish invasion at Preston. A special commission, of which Cromwell was a member, tried the king and condemned him to death, and a republic, known as 'the Commonwealth', was set up.

The ◊Levellers demanded radical reforms, but he executed their leaders 1649. He used terror to crush Irish clan resistance 1649–50, and defeated the Scots (who had acknowledged Charles II) at Dunbar 1650 and Worcester 1651. In 1653, having forcibly expelled the corrupt 'Rump' Parliament, he summoned a convention ('Barebone's Parliament'), soon dissolved as too radical, and under a constitution (Instrument of Government) drawn up by the army leaders, became Protector (king in all but name). The parliament of 1654–55 was dissolved as uncooperative, and after a period of military dictatorship, his last parliament offered him the crown; he refused because he feared the army's republicanism.

Cromwell Richard 1626–1712. Son of Oliver Cromwell, he succeeded his father as Lord Protector but resigned May 1659, having been forced to abdicate by the army. He lived in exile after the Restoration until 1680, when he returned.

Cromwell Thomas, Earl of Essex *c.* 1485–1540. English politician who drafted the legislation making the Church of England independent of Rome. Originally in Lord Chancellor Wolsey's service, he became secretary to Henry VIII 1534 and the real director of government policy. Cromwell had Henry divorced from Catherine of Aragon by a series of acts that proclaimed him head of the church. From 1536 to 1540 Cromwell suppressed the monasteries, ruthlessly crushed all opposition, and favoured Protestantism, which denied the divine right of the pope. His mistake in arranging Henry's marriage to Anne of Cleves (to cement an alliance with the German Protestant princes against France and the Holy Roman Empire) led to his being accused of treason and beheaded.

crown colony any British colony that is under the direct legislative control of the crown and does not possess its own system of representative government. Crown colonies are administered by a crown-appointed governor or by elected or nominated legislative and executive councils with an official majority. Usually the crown retains rights of veto and of direct legislation by orders in council.

Crown Estate title (from 1956) of land in UK formerly owned by the monarch but handed to Parliament by George III 1760 in exchange for an annual payment (called the ◊civil list). The Crown Estate owns valuable sites in central London, which, along with 268,400 acres in England and Scotland, are valued in excess of £1.2 billion. In 1992–3 the gross income from the Crown Estate totalled £119,924,000, and the sum paid to the Exchequer as surplus revenue was £70,500,000.

crown jewels or *regalia* symbols of royal authority. The British set (except for the Ampulla and the Anointing Spoon) were broken up at the time of Oliver Cromwell, and now date from the Restoration. In 1671 Colonel ◊Blood attempted to steal them, but was captured, then pardoned and pensioned by Charles II. They are kept in the Tower of London in the Crown Jewel House (1967).

Crystal Palace glass and iron building designed by Joseph Paxton (1801–1865), housing the Great Exhibition of 1851 in Hyde Park, London. It was later rebuilt in modified form at Sydenham Hill 1854 but burned down 1936.

I had rather have a plain russet-coated captain that knows what he fights for, and loves what he knows, than that which you call a gentleman and is nothing else.

OLIVER CROMWELL
letter to Sir William Spring, 1643

Culloden, Battle of defeat 1746 of the ◊Jacobite rebel army of the British prince ◊Charles Edward Stuart (the 'Young Pretender') by the Duke of Cumberland on a stretch of moorland in Inverness-shire, Scotland. This battle effectively ended the military challenge of the Jacobite rebellion.

Although the sides were numerically equal (about 8,000 strong), the Hanoverians were a drilled and disciplined force, while the Jacobites were a mixed force of French, Irish, and Scots, tired and lacking military cohesion. The Hanoverian army opened the battle with a canonade, after which the Jacobites charged. They retired in confusion, pursued by the Hanoverian cavalry which broke the Jacobite lines completely and shattered their force. About 1,000 were killed and a further 1,000 were captured, together with all their stores and cannon.

Cumberland William Augustus, Duke of Cumberland 1721–1765. British general who ended the Jacobite rising in Scotland with the Battle of Culloden 1746; his brutal repression of the Highlanders earned him the nickname of 'Butcher'.

Third son of George II, he was created Duke of Cumberland 1726. He fought in the War of the Austrian Succession at ◊Dettingen 1743 and Fontenoy 1745. In the Seven Years' War he surrendered with his army at Kloster-Zeven 1757.

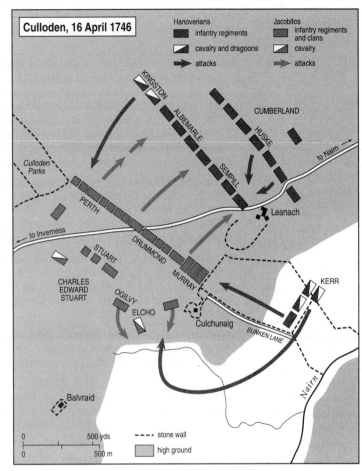

Culloden, 16 April 1746
The only possible Jacobite tactic against Cumberland's regulars at Culloden was a headlong frontal attack. But while Kerr's dragoons worked their way round the Jacobite right flank, disciplined Hanoverian musketry flailed the highlanders' charge across the boggy moor to a standstill. They were then ridden down by Kingston's horsemen. Charles Edward Stuart's army was destroyed in an action lasting only 40 minutes.

Cunedda early 5th century. British chieftain. He came with his sons and followers from Scotland to northwest Wales to defend Britain against barbarian invaders from Ireland. He laid the foundations of the kingdom of Gwynedd, which was named after him.

Cunningham Andrew Browne, 1st Viscount Cunningham of Hyndhope 1883–1963. British admiral in World War II, commander in chief in the Mediterranean 1939–42, maintaining British control; as commander in chief of the Allied Naval Forces in the Mediterranean Feb–Oct 1943 he received the surrender of the Italian fleet. He then became First Sea Lord and Chief of Naval Staff until 1946.

Cunobelin see ◊Cymbeline.

Curia Regis (the King's court) government by institutions of the royal court or household. In medieval times there was no separation of powers, and administrative and judicial powers were controlled by the court. Although some institutions such as the exchequer, which collected taxes, or the chancery, which drew up official government documents, eventually 'went out of court' to become fixed departments of state, they were often replaced by miniature versions of the original office which remained under direct royal supervision, such as the privy seal. The court only really ceased to be the main administrative centre of the country in the 18th century, but it retained considerable political influence into the 19th century. The most notable modern remnant of the court system is the ◊Privy Council.

Curragh 'Mutiny' demand March 1914 by the British general Hubert Gough and his officers, stationed at Curragh, Ireland, that they should not be asked to take part in forcing Protestant Ulster to participate in Home Rule. They were subsequently allowed to return to duty, and after World War I the solution of partition was adopted.

cursus neolithic earthworks composed of parallel banks of earth, possibly to form ritual sites for processions and other commemorations. They usually contain ◊barrows or other burial sites.

Curzon George Nathaniel, 1st Marquess Curzon of Kedleston 1859–1925. British Conservative politician, viceroy of India 1899–1905. During World War I, he was a member of the cabinet 1916–19. As foreign secretary 1919–24, he set up a British protectorate over Persia, contributed to the Treaty of Lausanne 1923, and proposed the ◊Curzon Line.

Curzon became a member of Parliament 1886 and travelled extensively in the East. As viceroy of India, he established the new province of Northwest Frontier 1901 and partitioned Bengal 1905. He resigned 1905 following a dispute with Horatio Kitchener, the commander of British forces in India, over who controlled the Indian army.

Curzon Line Polish-Soviet frontier proposed after World War I by the territorial commission of the Versailles conference 1919, based on the eastward limit of areas with a predominantly Polish population. It acquired its name after British foreign secretary Lord Curzon suggested in 1920 that the Poles, who had invaded the USSR, should retire to this line pending a Russo-Polish peace conference. The frontier established 1945 generally follows the Curzon Line.

Cuthbert, St d. 687. English monk and bishop of Lindisfarne. A shepherd in Northumbria, he entered the monastery of Melrose, Scotland, after receiving a vision. He travelled widely as a missionary before becoming prior of Lindisfarne 664, and retired 676 to Farne Island. In 684 he became bishop of Hexham and later of Lindisfarne. He is buried in Durham Cathedral. Feast day 20 March.

Cutty Sark British sailing ship, built 1869, one of the tea clippers that used to compete in the 19th century to bring their cargoes fastest from China to Britain. The ship is preserved in dry dock at Greenwich, London. The biennial Cutty Sark International Tall Ships Race is named after it.

Cymbeline or **Cunobelin** King of the Catuvellauni AD 5–40. His capital was at Colchester from which he ruled most of southeast England. Although he maintained reasonably friendly relations with the Romans, his son Caractacus who succeeded him led British resistance to the Roman invasion AD 43.

Cyprus former British colony, an island in the Mediterranean. Through a convention with Turkey, it was administered by Great Britain 1878–1914, and was annexed by Britain on the outbreak of the war with Turkey 1914. It was made a crown colony 1925. It became an independent republic 1960. There has been a British military presence in Cyprus since 1964 as part of the UN peace-keeping force.

I am now in a country so much our enemy that there is hardly any intelligence to be got, and whenever we do procure any it is the business of the country to have it contradicted.

DUKE OF
CUMBERLAND
letter from Scotland,
1746

Dalhousie James Andrew Broun Ramsay, 1st Marquess and 10th Earl of Dalhousie 1812–1860. British administrator, governor general of India 1848–56. In the second Sikh War he annexed the Punjab 1849, and, after the second Burmese War, Lower Burma 1853. He reformed the Indian army and civil service and furthered social and economic progress.

Dalriada Irish kingdom inhabited by Scots, in a region corresponding to modern Co Antrim, named after the family that founded it. They colonized the southwest Highlands of Scotland where *c.* 500 they established a kingdom of the same name.

Dalrymple John, 1st Earl of Stair 1648–1707. Scottish statesman, son of the lawyer James Dalrymple, 1st Viscount Stair. He was imprisoned 1682–83 after his father was forced to flee to Holland for opposing the ◊Test Act, but subsequently served James II in Scotland as Lord Advocate and Justice Clerk. He was again Lord Advocate 1689–92 under William III and joint Secretary of State 1691–95. He became very unpopular for his part in instigating the ◊Glencoe massacre 1692 but was rewarded for his loyalty when he was created earl 1703.

dame school former school for young children run singlehanded by an elderly woman. They dated from the 17th century, and were mainly in rural areas. The standard of instruction was generally very low. Such schools were often satirized in 18th- and 19th-century literature.

Danby Thomas Osborne, Earl of Danby 1631–1712. British Tory politician. He entered Parliament 1665, acted as Charles II's chief minister 1673–78 and was created Earl of Danby 1674, but was imprisoned in the Tower of London 1678–84. He signed the invitation to William of Orange to take the throne 1688 which led to the ◊Glorious Revolution. Danby was again chief minister 1690–95, and in 1694 was created Duke of Leeds.

danegeld in English history, a tax imposed from 991 by ◊Ethelred II 'the Unready' to pay tribute to the Vikings. After the Norman Conquest the tax continued to be levied until 1162, but the Normans used it to finance military operations.

Danelaw 11th-century name for the area of north and east England settled by the Vikings in the 9th century. It occupied about half of England, from the river Tees to the river Thames. Within its bounds, Danish law, customs, and language prevailed. Its linguistic influence is still apparent.

Reconquest of the Danelaw, 886–920
The Anglo-Saxon reconquest of the Danish territories was undertaken by Ethelflaed, 'Lady of the Mercians', and her brother Edward the Elder, king of Wessex. It was a slow war of attrition, and the English had also to contend with a renewed threat from the Norse kingdoms in the Irish Sea.

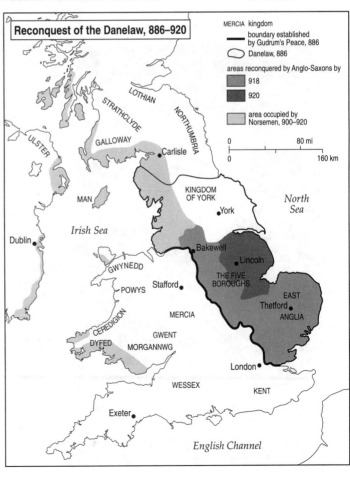

Reconquest of the Danelaw, 886–920

MERCIA kingdom
boundary established by Gudrum's Peace, 886
Danelaw, 886
areas reconquered by Anglo-Saxons by
918
920
area occupied by Norsemen, 900–920

0   80 mi
0   160 km

Darby Abraham 1677–1717. English iron manufacturer who developed a process for smelting iron ore using coke instead of the more expensive charcoal 1709. He employed the cheaper iron to cast strong thin pots for domestic use, and after his death it was used for the huge cylinders required by the new steam pumping-engines. In 1779 his grandson Abraham Darby (1750–1791) constructed the world's first iron bridge, over the river Severn at Coalbrookdale, Shropshire.

Dardanelles campaign in World War I, unsuccessful Allied naval operations 1915 against the Turkish-held Dardanelles, a narrow channel between Asiatic and European Turkey, forming a passage between the Mediterranean and the Sea of Marmora and thence to the Black Sea. After a series of unsuccessful naval attacks Jan–March 1915, in which much of the Anglo-French fleet was destroyed, the idea of a purely naval attack was abandoned, and instead planning began for a military action against the ◊Gallipoli peninsula. The only real impact of the naval attack was to alert the Turkish army so that they had time to reinforce and fortify the area before the Gallipoli landings.

Dardanelles Commission British Royal Commission appointed 1916 to enquire into the failure of the Dardanelles and Gallipoli expeditions in World War I. The Commission's final report 1919 concluded that planning had been poor, difficulties under-estimated, delays by the government after the first attack had wasted precious time, that there had been insufficient artillery and ammunition, and that there had been personality clashes among the commanders. Various people were mildly censured, but no careers were affected.

Darien scheme attempt by the Company of Scotland Trading to Africa and the Indies (founded 1695) to establish a Scottish colony on the Darien coast of the Isthmus of Panama 1698–1700. The scheme failed due to incompetence on the part of its promoters and opposition from the Spanish and also from the English who feared it would threaten the monopoly of the East India Company. The affair addded to Scotland's economic problems and caused considerable difficulties in relations with England for some years after.

Darwin
Charles Darwin, the founder of modern evolutionary theory, photographed by Elliott and Fry on the verandah of his home, Down House, Kent, *c.*1880.
Image Select

Darling Grace 1815–1842. British heroine. She was the daughter of a lighthouse keeper on the Farne Islands, off Northumberland. On 7 Sept 1838 the *Forfarshire* was wrecked, and Grace Darling and her father rowed through a storm to the wreck, saving nine lives. She was awarded a medal for her bravery.

Darnley Henry Stewart or Stuart, Lord Darnley 1545–1567. British aristocrat, second husband of Mary Queen of Scots from 1565, and father of James I of England (James VI of Scotland). On the advice of her secretary, David ◊Rizzio, Mary refused Darnley the crown matrimonial; in revenge, Darnley led a band of nobles who murdered Rizzio in Mary's presence. Darnley was assassinated 1567 in a plot formed by ◊Bothwell. Mary's part in his death remains a subject of controversy.

Darwin Charles (Robert) 1809–1882. English scientist who developed the modern theory of evolution and proposed, with Alfred Russel Wallace (1823–1913), the principle of natural selection. After research in South America and the Galápagos Islands as naturalist on HMS *Beagle* 1831–36, Darwin published *On the Origin of Species by Means of Natural Selection or the Preservation of Favoured Races in the Struggle for Life* 1859. This explained the evolutionary process through the principles of natural and sexual selection. It aroused bitter controversy because it disagreed with the literal interpretation of the Book of Genesis in the Bible.

David two kings of Scotland:

David I 1084–1153. King of Scotland from 1124. The youngest son of Malcolm III Canmore and St ◊Margaret, he was brought up in the English court of Henry I, and in 1113 married Maud, daughter of the Earl of Huntingdon. He invaded England 1138 in support of ◊Matilda, but was defeated at Northallerton in the Battle of the Standard. David strengthened the power of the throne in Scotland and eventually won recognition from Henry II of his territorial claims in northern England.

David II 1324–1371. King of Scotland from 1329, son of ◊Robert (I) the Bruce. David was married at the age of four to Joanna, daughter of Edward II of England. After the defeat of the Scots by Edward III at Halidon Hill 1333, the young David and Joanna were sent to France for safety. They returned 1341. In 1346 David invaded England, was captured at the Battle of Neville's Cross, and imprisoned for 11 years. He was succeeded by his nephew, Robert II.

David, St or **Dewi** d. c. 601. Patron saint of Wales, Christian abbot and bishop. According to legend he was the son of a prince of Dyfed and uncle of King Arthur. Tradition has it that David made a pilgrimage to Jerusalem, where he was consecrated bishop. He founded twelve monasteries in Wales, including one at Menevia (now St Davids), which he made his bishop's seat; he presided over a synod at Brefi and condemned the ideas of the British theologian Pelagius. He was responsible for the adoption of the leek as the national emblem of Wales, but his own emblem is a dove. Feast day 1 March.

Davitt Michael 1846–1906. Irish nationalist. He joined the Fenians (forerunners of the Irish Republican Army) 1865, and was imprisoned for treason 1870–77. After his release, he and the politician Charles Parnell founded the ◊Land League 1879. Davitt was jailed several times for land-reform agitation. He was a member of Parliament 1895–99, advocating the reconciliation of extreme and constitutional nationalism.

daylight saving attempt to increase daylight working hours by setting all clocks one hour ahead of Greenwich Mean Time in spring and summer. The system was first introduced in Britain 21 May 1916 to conserve fuel during World War I. The arrangement was made permanent in 1925, and was extended to 'Double Summer Time' 1941. Such alterations arouse controversy, as the latitudinal difference of Scotland and Northern Ireland from England and Wales means that some northerly areas may actually end up spending much of the working day in darkness.

D-day 6 June 1944, the day of the Allied invasion of Normandy under the command of General Eisenhower to commence Operation Overlord, the liberation of Western Europe from German occupation. The Anglo-US invasion fleet landed on the Normandy beaches on the stretch of coast between the Orne River and St Marcouf. Artificial harbours known as 'Mulberries' were constructed and towed across the Channel so that equipment and armaments could be unloaded on to the beaches. After overcoming fierce resistance the Allies broke through the German defences; Paris was liberated 25 Aug, and Brussels 2 Sept. Although the operation was a success, casualties were heavy: Allied losses during the day amounted to 2,500 killed and about 8,500 wounded. Allied air forces flew 14,000 sorties in support of the operation and lost 127 aircraft.

Dearham, Battle of victory 577 of Ceawlin of Wessex, ◊bretwalda (ruler) of southern England, over the Britons at Dearham (now Dyrham), north of Bath. Ceawlin's victory divided the western Britons from those of the southwest, and secured the capture of Gloucester, Cirencester, and Bath.

Declaration of Indulgence statement of government policy issued by order of the monarch with the aim of giving a lead to public opinion on religious tolerance.

There were four Declarations of Indulgence properly so called: (1) decree of Charles II 1662, proclaiming his intention to introduce a Bill suspending the penal laws against Dissenters in the Church of England. The bill was defeated in the Lords; (2) decree of Charles II 1672 guaranteeing freedom of worship and suspending all penal laws against Catholics and Protestant Dissenters. His attempt was blocked by Parliament 1673, obliging Charles to withdraw the Indulgence; (3) decree of James II 1687 allowing full freedom of worship. It suspended the operation of the penal laws and remitted all penalties for ecclesiastical offences, so endangering the Anglican monopoly in Church and State; (4) decree of James II 1688 reinforcing the earlier Indulgence and ordering it to be read in all Anglican churches. It provoked fierce opposition within the Church of England and led to the arrest and trial of seven bishops.

We must, however, acknowledge, as it seems to me, that man with all his noble qualities, still bears in his bodily frame the indelible stamp of his lowly origin.

CHARLES DARWIN
last words of
Descent of Man, *1871*

Declaration of Rights in Britain, the statement issued by the Convention Parliament Feb 1689, laying down the conditions under which the crown was to be offered to ◊William III and Mary. Its clauses were later incorporated in the ◊Bill of Rights.

Dee John 1527–1608. English alchemist, astrologer, and mathematician who claimed to have transmuted metals into gold, although he died in poverty. He long enjoyed the favour of Elizabeth I, and was employed by her as a secret diplomatic agent.

De Facto Act statute of 1495 protecting the property rights of those who served any current or 'de facto' monarch. The measure reassured both former Yorkist supporters of Richard III that they would be safe from political recriminations and those who supported Henry VII but had little certainty that his dynasty would survive that they would not suffer from backing the new regime.

Defence of the Realm Act granting emergency powers to the British government Aug 1914, the Act, popularly known as DORA, was revised several times in World War I and allowed the government to requisition raw materials, control labour, and censor cables and foreign correspondence. It was superseded by the Emergency Powers Act 1920.

Defender of the Faith (Latin *fidei defensor*) one of the titles of the English sovereign, conferred on Henry VIII 1521 by Pope Leo X in recognition of the king's treatise against the Protestant Martin Luther. It appears on coins in the abbreviated form ***F.D.***

de heretico comburendo ('on the necessity of burning heretics') statute of 1401 designed to suppress the ◊Lollards, banning unlicensed preachers and allowing heretics to be tried and imprisoned by the ecclesiastical authorities. If convicted heretics refused to abjure or denounce their beliefs, they were handed over to the secular authorities for burning. Many Lollards were burned under the terms of the act, the first being William Sawtry who was burnt at Smithfield 1401. The act was the principal means of suppressing heresy until it was repealed 1547 by Protector Somerset in order to facilitate the spread of Protestantism. It was briefly revived by Mary Tudor 1555 before being finally abolished 1559.

Deheubarth southern Welsh kingdom which resisted English domination until the reign of Edward I. Its name derives from the Latin *dextralis pars* ('the right-hand side') of Wales and it comprised most of southern Wales, apart from Monmouthshire and Glamorgan. The kingdom was consolidated during the 9th and 10th centuries by a series of strong and capable rulers such as Seisyll and Hywel Dda. It succeeded in holding off the Normans, although with some setbacks, until Henry II of England recognized the kingdom's independence under the leadership of Rhys ap Gruffydd (1155–97). Squabbling among his descendants left the kingdom open to subjugation and it was absorbed by 1277 when Edward I of England was accepted as overlord of Wales.

Deira 6th-century Anglo-Saxon kingdom in central and eastern Yorkshire, stretching from the Tees to the Humber. It was powerful enough for Pope Gregory I to know of its king Aelle *c*. 560. It was annexed by the kingdom of Bernicia to the north 588, but Aelle's exiled son Edwin returned and defeated the Bernician king to form the united kingdom of ◊Northumbria 616.

Delaware former British colony in North America; see ◊Thirteen Colonies.

demesne in the Middle Ages in Europe, land kept in the lord's possession, not leased out, but worked by villeins to supply the lord's household.

Depression, the (also known as the Great Depression) period of massive economic decline and high unemployment in the 1930s, the most severe depression ever experienced in the industrialized Western world. The depression began in the United States after the 'Wall Street Crash' 29 Oct 1929, when millions of dollars were wiped off US share values in a matter of hours, precipitating a world economic crisis. The consequences were widely felt in Europe, but especially in Germany and Britain, countries that were heavily indebted to the United States economically. Industrial and export sectors in Britain remained depressed until World War II, though growth was stimulated to some extent by rearmament programmes in the late 1930s.

The term is also used of the depression of 1873–96 which centred on falling growth rates in the British economy but also affected industrial activity in Germany and the USA. The crisis in the British economy is now thought to have lasted longer than these dates suggest.

Derby Edward (George Geoffrey Smith) Stanley, 14th Earl of Derby 1799–1869. British politician, prime minister 1852, 1858–59, and 1866–68. Originally a Whig, he became secretary for the colonies 1830, and introduced the bill for the abolition of slavery. He joined the Tories 1834, serving as secretary for war and the colonies in Peel's government. Derby was a protectionist and the split in the Tory Party over Robert Peel's free-trade policy gave him the leadership for 20 years. During his third administration, the second Reform Act 1867 was passed.

Dermot MacMurrough see ◊MacMurrough, Dermot.

Desmond revolt two Catholic rebellions against Protestant rule in Ireland 1569 and 1579, sparked by the proposed plantations of Munster and Connacht by Protestants. The Geraldine clan rose in protest, led by Sir James Fitzmaurice, a cousin of the Earl of Desmond. The revolt was suppressed 1573 and Fitzmaurice fled overseas. He settled in Lisbon but returned 1579 to lead another Geraldine rising, but was soon killed. Gerald ◊Fitzgerald, 15th Earl of Desmond took up arms, with some military assistance from Philip II of Spain and Pope Gregory XIII, but the revolt was crushed and the Earl killed 1583. In the aftermath of the revolt, plantations were undertaken all the more vigorously in Kerry and Limerick, further alienating the Irish from the royal administration.

Despard Plot in 1802, a plot led by Irish conspirator Edward M Despard (1751–1803) to seize the Tower of London and the Bank of England and assassinate King George III. The affair embarrassed the government not so much because of the seriousness of the plot itself, but because Admiral Nelson

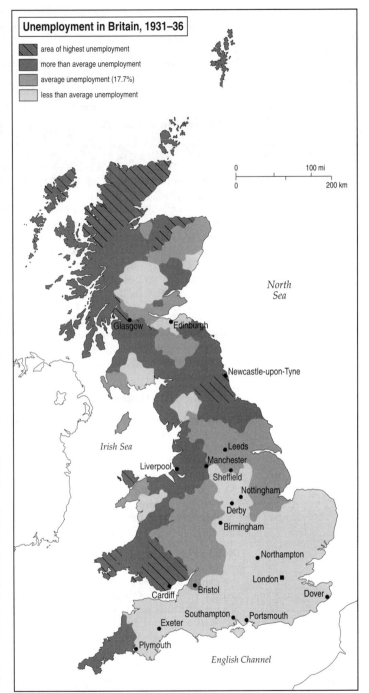

Unemployment in Britain, 1931–36

- area of highest unemployment
- more than average unemployment
- average unemployment (17.7%)
- less than average unemployment

Unemployment in Britain, 1931–36
The most severe unemployment in the Depression occurred in the Highlands and Islands and in the heavy industrial areas of the Clyde, the Northeast, and South Wales. It was the latter areas that provided most of the hunger marchers. The Midlands and the Southeast were much less severely affected.

spoke in defence of the conspirators. Despard was executed on 21 Feb 1803. He and his fellow conspirators were the last people in England to be sentenced to be hanged, drawn, and quartered.

Dettingen, Battle of in the War of the Austrian Succession, battle in the Bavarian village of that name where on 27 June 1743, an army of British, Hanoverians, and Austrians under George II defeated the French under Adrien-Maurice, duc de Noailles (1678–1766). This was the last battle in which a British sovereign led his troops in person.

de Valera Eámon 1882–1975. Irish nationalist politician, prime minister of the Irish Free State/Eire/Republic of Ireland 1932–48, 1951–54, and 1957–59, and president 1959–73. Repeatedly imprisoned, he participated in the Easter Rising 1916 and was leader of the nationalist ◊Sinn Féin party 1917–26, when he formed the republican ◊Fianna Fáil party; he directed negotiations with Britain 1921 but refused to accept the partition of Ireland until 1937.

De Valera was born in New York, sent to Ireland as a child, and became a teacher of mathematics. He was sentenced to death for his part in the Easter Rising, but was released under an amnesty 1917. In the same year he was elected member of Parliament for East Clare, and president of Sinn Féin. He was rearrested May 1918, but escaped to the USA 1919. He returned to Ireland 1920 and directed the struggle against the British government from a hiding place in Dublin. He authorized the negotiations of 1921, but refused to accept the ensuing treaty which divided Ireland into the Free State and the North.

Civil war followed. De Valera formed a new party, Fianna Fáil 1926, which secured a majority 1932. De Valera became prime minister and foreign minister of the Free State. Throughout World War II he maintained a strict neutrality, rejecting an offer by Churchill 1940 to recognize the principle of a united Ireland in return for Eire's entry into the war. He resigned after his defeat at the 1948 elections but was again prime minister in the 1950s and then president of the republic.

Devonshire, 8th Duke of see ◊Hartington, Spencer Compton Cavendish, British politician.

Diamond Jubilee celebration 1897 of the 60th year of Queen Victoria's rule. The jubilee was a celebration of both Crown and Empire at the peak of British colonial power. The scions of other royal houses, many related to Victoria, joined the celebrations and paid their respects to Victoria's rule, heightening Britain's sense of superiority over the continental powers. Ironically, even while the jubilee was being celebrated there was renewed tension between the Crown and the Boers in South Africa, which was to lead to the Boer War, a significant blow to British imperial prestige and morale. In retrospect, the jubilee celebrations neatly encapsulated both the splendour and the superficiality of Britain's achievements in the 19th century.

Dieppe Raid in World War II, disastrous Allied attack Aug 1942 on the German-held seaport on the English Channel about 305 km/190 mi northwest of Paris. The limited-objective raid was partly designed to obtain practical experience of amphibious landing techniques and German defences, but mostly to placate Stalin who was agitating for a Second Front in Europe. The raid was a dismal failure which cost the Allies heavily in casualties and strained relations between Canada and Britain for some time, although a number of valuable lessons about landing on hostile beaches were learned and applied in the ◊D-Day landings 1944.

Some 5,000 Canadian troops and 1,000 commandos took part in the landings 18–19 Aug. By 9 a.m. it was clear that the operation had failed and withdrawal was ordered, but it took three hours to remove the last of the survivors. The Canadians lost 215 officers and 3,164 troops, the commandos 24 officers and 223 troops, the Royal Navy 81 officers, 469 sailors, and 34 ships, and the RAF lost 107 aircraft. In contrast, the Germans lost only 345 killed and 268 wounded.

Digger or ***True Leveller*** member of an English 17th-century radical sect that attempted to seize and share out common land. The Diggers became prominent April 1649 when, headed by Gerrard Winstanley (*c.* 1609–1660), they set up communal colonies near Cobham, Surrey, and elsewhere. These colonies were attacked by mobs and, being pacifists, the Diggers made no resistance. The support they attracted alarmed the government and they were dispersed 1650. Their ideas influenced the early ◊Quakers.

Dilke Charles Wentworth 1843–1911. British Liberal politician, member of Parliament 1868–86 and 1892–1911. A Radical, he advocated a policy of imperial expansion and supported a minimum wage and legalization of trade unions. He was under-secretary at the Foreign Office 1880–82.

Dillon John 1851–1927. Irish nationalist. He initially supported ◊Parnell and the Land League and 1880 became a member of Parliament, where he was noted for the ferocity of his speeches. He turned against Parnell 1890 on well-intentioned political grounds and led the majority of the Irish party at Westminster until 1900, when he resigned in favour of ◊Redmond. He strongly supported home rule, and became leader of what remained of the Irish Nationalist party 1918 but lost his seat to de Valera, a member of Sinn Féin, 1919.

Diplock court in Northern Ireland, a type of court established 1972 by the British government under Lord Diplock (1907–1985) to try offences linked with terrorist violence. The right to jury trial was suspended and the court consisted of a single judge, because potential jurors were allegedly being intimidated and were unwilling to serve. Despite widespread criticism, the Diplock courts have remained in operation.

disestablishment the formal separation of a church from the State by ceasing to recognize it as the official church of a country or province. The special status of the Church of Ireland, created by Henry VIII 1541, was a major source of greivance to Irish Catholics in the 19th century and it was disestablished by Gladstone 1869, with its endowments converted to charitable ends. In 1920, after a bitter struggle lasting over 50 years, the Welsh Anglican Church was disestablished as the Church in Wales; it gained its own archbishop and was detached from the province of Canterbury. There have been several attempts to disestablish the Church of England which would involve the abolition of the Royal Supremacy over the Church and the concomitant right of the prime minister to advise the Crown on episcopal appointments.

Disinherited, the supporters of Simon de Montfort whose land was seized by Henry III after the Battle of ◊Evesham 1265. The Dictum of Kenilworth the following year imposed harsh financial conditions for the recovery of the confiscated lands. The name is also applied to the English lords who held land in Scotland which was confiscated by Robert the Bruce after his success at ◊Bannockburn 1314. In 1332, they landed in Fife under Edward Balliol, who was later crowned at Scone, and reigned as a client-king of Edward III of England until 1334.

Disraeli Benjamin, Earl of Beaconsfield 1804–1881. British Conservative politician and novelist. Elected to Parliament 1837, he was chancellor of the Exchequer under Lord ◊Derby 1852, 1858–59, and 1866–68, and prime minister 1868 and 1874–80. His imperialist policies brought India directly under the crown, and he was personally responsible for purchasing control of the Suez Canal. The central Conservative Party organization is his creation. His popular, political novels reflect an interest in social reform and include *Coningsby* 1844 and *Sybil* 1845.

After a period in a solicitor's office, Disraeli finally entered Parliament 1837 after four unsuccessful attempts. He was initially laughed at as a dandy, and when his maiden speech was shouted down, he angrily predicted 'The time will come when you will hear me.' Excluded from Peel's government of 1841–46, Disraeli formed his Young England group to keep a critical eye on Peel's Conservatism. Its ideas were expounded in the novel trilogy *Coningsby*, *Sybil*, and *Tancred* 1847.

When Peel decided to repeal the Corn Laws 1846, Disraeli opposed the measure in a series of witty and effective speeches; Peel's government fell soon after, and Disraeli gradually came to be recognized as the leader of the Conservative Party in the Commons. During the next 20

Disraeli
Cartoon from *Punch* depicting Disraeli (front) and Gladstone as two opposing lions making speeches in Lancashire 1872.
Philip Sauvain

years the Conservatives formed short-lived minority governments 1852, 1858–59, and 1866–68, with Lord Derby as prime minister and Disraeli as chancellor of the Exchequer and leader of the Commons. In 1852 Disraeli first proposed discrimination in income tax between earned and unearned income, but without success. The 1858–59 government legalized the admission of Jews to Parliament, and transferred the government of India from the East India Company to the crown. In 1866 the Conservatives took office after defeating a Liberal Reform Bill, and then attempted to secure the credit of widening the franchise by the Reform Bill of 1867. On Lord Derby's retirement in 1868 Disraeli became prime minister, but a few months later he was defeated by Gladstone in a general election. During the six years of opposition that followed he published another novel, *Lothair* 1870, and established Conservative Central Office, the prototype of modern party organizations.

Disraeli took office for the second time 1874, with a majority of 100. Some useful reform measures were carried, such as the Artisans' Dwelling Act, which empowered local authorities to undertake slum clearance, but the outstanding feature of the government's policy was its imperialism. It was Disraeli's personal initiative that purchased from the Khedive of Egypt a controlling interest in the Suez Canal, conferred on the Queen the title of Empress of India, and sent the Prince of Wales on the first royal tour of that country. Disraeli accepted an earldom 1876. The Bulgarian revolt of 1876 and the subsequent Russo-Turkish War of 1877–78 provoked one of many political duels between Disraeli and Gladstone, the Liberal leader, and was concluded by the Congress of Berlin 1878, where Disraeli was the principal British delegate and brought home 'peace with honour' and Cyprus. The government was defeated 1880, and a year later Disraeli died.

Dissenter former name for a Protestant refusing to conform to the established Christian church. For example, Baptists, Presbyterians, and Independents (now known as Congregationalists) were Dissenters.

dissenting academies schools founded in late 17th and 18th centuries for children of religious nonconformists who were otherwise banned from local schools and universities. They became a model of advanced education, with their emphasis on the sciences and modern languages. See also ◊charity schools.

dissolution of the monasteries closure of the monasteries of England and Wales 1536–40 and confiscation of their property by ◊Henry VIII. The operation was organized by Thomas ◊Cromwell and affected about 800 monastic houses with the aim of boosting royal income, which it did by about £90,000 a year. Most of the property was later sold off to the gentry.

divine right of kings principle of an absolute monarch, given a right to rule by God; see ◊absolutism.

The Continent will not suffer England to be the workshop of the world.

BENJAMIN DISRAELI
speech in House of Commons, 15 March 1838

dolmen prehistoric monument in the form of a chamber built of large stone slabs, roofed over by a flat stone which they support. Dolmens are grave chambers of the Neolithic period, found in Europe and Africa, and occasionally in Asia as far east as Japan. They are known in Wales as ***cromlechs***.

Domesday Book record of the survey of England carried out 1086 by officials of William the Conqueror in order to assess land tax and other dues, ascertain the value of the crown lands, and enable the king to estimate the power of his vassal barons. Every shire was investigated by a team of royal commissioners, but Northumberland and Durham were omitted, as were London, Winchester, and certain other towns. The survey caused great indignation, and in some places prolonged rioting. The name is derived from the belief that its judgement was as final as that of Doomsday. The Domesday Book is preserved in two volumes at the Public Record Office, London.

Dominican order Roman Catholic order of friars founded by St Dominic in France 1215. The Dominicans are also known as Friars Preachers, Black Friars, or Jacobins. The first Dominican house in England was established in Oxford 1221. The English Dominicans were suppressed 1559, but were restored to a corporate existence 1622. Dominicans have included Thomas Aquinas, Girolamo Savonarola, and Bartolome de las Casas. The order is worldwide and there is also an order of contemplative nuns; the habit is black and white.

domus conversorum house for converted Jews in Chancery Lane founded by Henry III 1232. Royal pensions and re-training were offered as incentives to conversion. After Jews were expelled from England en masse 1290, numbers dwindled and in 1377 the wardenship of the house was combined with the post of the Master of the Rolls, a senior judge and keeper of records. The house was demolished 1717 and the site was occupied by the Public Record Office.

Don Pacifico Affair incident in 1850 in which British foreign secretary Lord Palmerston was criticized in Parliament and elsewhere in Europe for using British naval superiority to impose his foreign policy. Palmerston sent gunboats to blockade the Greek coast in support of the claim of a Portuguese merchant, David Pacifico, who was born on Gibraltar (and thus a British subject), for compensation from the Greek government after his house was burned down in anti-Semitic riots.

Donald III Bane ('fair') *c.* 1031–*c.* 1100. King of Scotland. He came to the throne 1093 after seizing it on the death of his brother ◊Malcolm III. He was dethroned 1094 by Malcolm's eldest son, ◊Duncan II. He regained power 1094 but was defeated and captured 1097 by Malcolm's fourth son, Edgar, who had him blinded and imprisoned until his death.

Douglas Archibald, 3rd Earl of Douglas *c.* 1328–*c.* 1400. Scottish soldier and politician, the illegitimate son of Sir James Douglas. He became Constable of Edinburgh 1361 and was royal ambassador to France 1369, in which post he was largely responsible for the renewed Franco-Scottish alliance 1371. He became earl 1385 and continued to play an important role in Scottish politics. He led the invasion of England at ◊Otterburn 1388.

Douglas Archibald, 4th Earl of Douglas *c.* 1369–1424. Scottish soldier. He was captured at Homildon Hill 1402 by the Percys, whom he subsequently supported at the Battle of ◊Shrewsbury 1403, when he was again captured, this time by Henry IV. He went to France and was made Duke of Touraine by Charles VIII who he supported in the Hundred Years' War. He was killed by the English at Verneuil.

Douglas-Home Alec (Alexander Frederick), Baron Home of the Hirsel 1903–1995. British Conservative politician. He was foreign secretary 1960–63, and succeeded Harold Macmillan as prime minister 1963. He renounced his peerage (as 14th Earl of Home) to fight (and lose) the general election 1964, and resigned as party leader 1965. He was again foreign secretary 1970–74, when he received a life peerage. The playwright William Douglas-Home was his brother.

Dover, Treaty of secret treaty June 1670 between Charles II of England and Louis XIV of France in which Charles agreed to support Louis' plan to invade Holland in return for subsidies of £150,000, rising to £225,000 while the war with Holland lasted. He also agreed to declare himself a Roman Catholic in return for Catholic support in his attempts to remain independent of parliamentary scrutiny. The treaty led to the third ◊Anglo-Dutch War 1672–74.

Dover Patrol sub-unit of the British Navy based at Dover and Dunkirk throughout World War I. Its primary task was to close the English Channel to German vessels while escorting Allied ships safely through the area.

Dowding Hugh Caswall Tremenheere, 1st Baron Dowding 1882–1970. British air chief marshal. He was chief of Fighter Command at the outbreak of World War II in 1939, a post he held through the Battle of Britain 10 July–12 Oct 1940. A clear thinker, his refusal to commit more fighters to France in 1940 when he could see that the campaign was doomed proved to

There are two problems in my life. The political ones are insoluble and the economic ones are incomprehensible.

SIR ALEC DOUGLAS-HOME
speech, January 1964

I have singed the Spanish king's beard.

FRANCIS DRAKE
after his raid on Cadiz, 1587 (attributed)

be a vital factor in the later Battle of Britain, but his uncompromising attitude upset Churchill and other political leaders and he was replaced in Fighter Command Nov 1940. He retired 1942 and was created a baron 1943.

Drake Francis *c*. 1545–1596. English buccaneer and explorer. Having enriched himself as a pirate against Spanish interests in the Caribbean 1567–72, he was sponsored by Elizabeth I for an expedition to the Pacific, sailing round the world 1577–80 in the Golden Hind, robbing Spanish ships as he went. This was the second circumnavigation of the globe (the first was by the Portuguese explorer Ferdinand Magellan). Drake also helped to defeat the Spanish Armada 1588 as a vice admiral in the *Revenge*.

Drake suggested to Queen Elizabeth I the idea of an expedition to the Pacific, to which she gave her backing. He set sail Dec 1577 in the Pelican with four other ships and 166 crew toward South America. In Aug 1578 the fleet passed through the Straits of Magellan and was then blown south to Cape Horn. The ships became separated and returned to England, all but the *Pelican*, now renamed the *Golden Hind*. Drake sailed north along the coast of Chile and Peru, robbing Spanish ships as far north as California, and then, in July 1579, travelled southwest across the Pacific. He rounded the South African Cape June 1580, and reached England Sept 1580, thus completing the second voyage around the world. When the Spanish ambassador demanded Drake's punishment, the Queen knighted him on the deck of the *Golden Hind* in London. In a raid on Cádiz 1587 he burned 10,000 tons of shipping and delayed the ◊Spanish Armada for a year. Drake sailed on his last expedition to the West Indies 1595, and died on his ship Jan 1596.

Drake
Sir Francis Drake who led the second successful circumnavigation of the globe in the *Golden Hind* 1577–80.
Image Select

Dreadnought class of battleships built for the British navy after 1905 and far superior in speed and armaments to anything then afloat. The first modern battleship to be built, it was the basis of battleship design for more than 50 years. The first *Dreadnought* was launched 1906, with armaments consisting entirely of big guns. German plans to build similar craft led to the naval race that contributed to Anglo-German antagonism and the origins of World War I.

Drogheda, sack of seaport near the mouth of the river Boyne, County Louth, Republic of Ireland. In 1649 the town was held by Irish and English Royalists who refused to surrender to parliamentary forces under Oliver Cromwell. The town was taken by storm and Cromwell massacred 2,500 members of the garrison. In 1690 it surrendered to William III after the Battle of the Boyne.

drove roads trackways for cattle, maintained by constant usage. They were probably established in prehistoric times, when communities moved their livestock from one grazing area to another. They were in continual use until the first half of the 19th century, when enclosures and the advent of the railway made long-distance drove roads obsolete. Many former drove roads are now marked on Ordnance Survey maps as 'British trackways'.

Druidism religion of the Celtic peoples of the pre-Christian British Isles and Gaul. The word is derived from Greek *drus* 'oak'. The Druids regarded this tree as sacred; one of their chief rites was the cutting of mistletoe from it with a golden sickle. They taught the immortality of the soul and a reincarnation doctrine, and were expert in astronomy. The Druids are thought to have offered human sacrifices.

Druidism was stamped out in Gaul after the Roman conquest. In Britain their stronghold was Anglesey, Wales, until they were driven out by the Roman governor Agricola. They existed in Scotland and Ireland until the coming of the Christian missionaries. What are often termed Druidic monuments – cromlechs and stone circles – are of New Stone Age (Neolithic) origin, though they may later have been used for religious purposes by the Druids. A possible example of a human sacrifice by Druids is Lindow Man, whose body was found in a bog in Cheshire 1984.

Dudley Lord Guildford d. 1554. English nobleman, fourth son of the Duke of Northumberland. He was married by his father to Lady Jane ◊Grey 1553, against her wishes, in an attempt to prevent the succession of ◊Mary I to the throne. The plot failed, and he and his wife were executed.

Dumnonii tribe inhabiting a territory in modern Cornwall and part of Devon, with a capital at Isca Dumnoniorum (Exeter). They were overrun in the early years of the Roman invasion of AD 43 and were recognized as a tribal corporation or *civitas* c. AD 80. Their name is Celtic and means 'deep ones', either because they lived in valleys or worked mines.

Dunaverty, Massacre of slaughter by Scottish ◊Covenanters 1647 of 250 to 300 Highlanders who had unconditionally surrendered after holding Dunaverty Castle, Kintyre, against the besieging Convenanter forces.

Dunbar, Battles of two English victories over the Scots at Dunbar, now a port and resort in Lothian Region.

27 April 1296 defeat by John de Warenne, Earl of Surrey, of Scottish king John Balliol. The defeat all but ended Scottish resistance to Edward I. Edinburgh fell shortly after and in July John surrendered his throne to Edward and fled the country.

3 Sept 1650 crushing defeat by Oliver Cromwell of a Scottish army under David ◊Leslie supporting Charles II. Combined with Charles's defeat at Worcester the following year, it effectively ended Scotland's independence of action.

Duncan I King of Scotland 1034–40. He succeeded his grandfather, Malcolm II, as king 1034. In 1040 he attempted to extend his kingdom south but had to abandon the expedition after he failed to capture Durham. Later the same year, he was defeated and killed by ◊Macbeth. He is the Duncan in Shakespeare's play *Macbeth* 1605.

Duncan II King of Scotland, son of ◊Malcolm III and grandson of ◊Duncan I. He gained English and Norman help to drive out his uncle ◊Donald III 1094. He ruled for a few months before being killed by agents of Donald, who then regained power.

Duncan Adam, Viscount Duncan of Camperdown 1731–1804. British naval commander. As a lieutenant he was present at the blockade of Brest 1755. He commanded the *Valiant* in the sack of Havana 1762 and served at Cape St Vincent 1780. He became an admiral 1795 and was made commander in chief of the North Sea 1795–1801 to ward off the Dutch fleet. He blockaded the Texel and went on to defeat the Dutch admiral Jan de Winter off ◊Camperdown 1797, effectively breaking Dutch naval power and depriving the Irish rebellion of foreign support.

Dundalk, Battle of English victory over Scottish forces in Ireland 14 Oct 1318 at Dundalk, northeast Ireland. Edward Bruce, brother of Robert the Bruce, had been sent to Ireland by his brother 1315 and was proclaimed king of Ireland by the people of Ulster the following year. He failed to establish his authority and his forces were defeated by the English at Dundalk and where he was killed.

Dundas Henry, 1st Viscount Melville 1742–1811. Scottish Conservative politician. He became home secretary 1791 and, with revolution raging in France, carried through the prosecution of the English and Scottish radicals. After holding other high cabinet posts, he was impeached 1806 for corruption and, although acquitted on the main charge, held no further office.

Dunes, Battle of the victory of Cromwell's English forces and their French allies over a Spanish army 14 June 1658 on the dunes near Dunkirk, then in the Spanish Netherlands. The Spanish, backed by English royalists, came to relieve Dunkirk from a siege laid by the Marshal de Turenne and Sir William Lockhart. The Anglo-French force attacked the Spanish on the dunes outside the town and forced them to retreat.

Dunkeld, House of royal house of the kingdom of Scotland 1034–1290. Despite its origins in the struggle between Duncan I and his cousin Macbeth and almost constant pressure from Anglo-Norman and Plantagenet

Drogheda, sack of
The sack of Drogheda 1649. Oliver Cromwell, who had come to Ireland to suppress the Catholic rebellion which broke out 1641, ordered the massacre of the city's defenders when they refused to surrender to him. He described the slaughter as 'the righteous judgment of God upon these barbarous wretches'.
Hulton Deutsch

House of Dunkeld 1034–1290

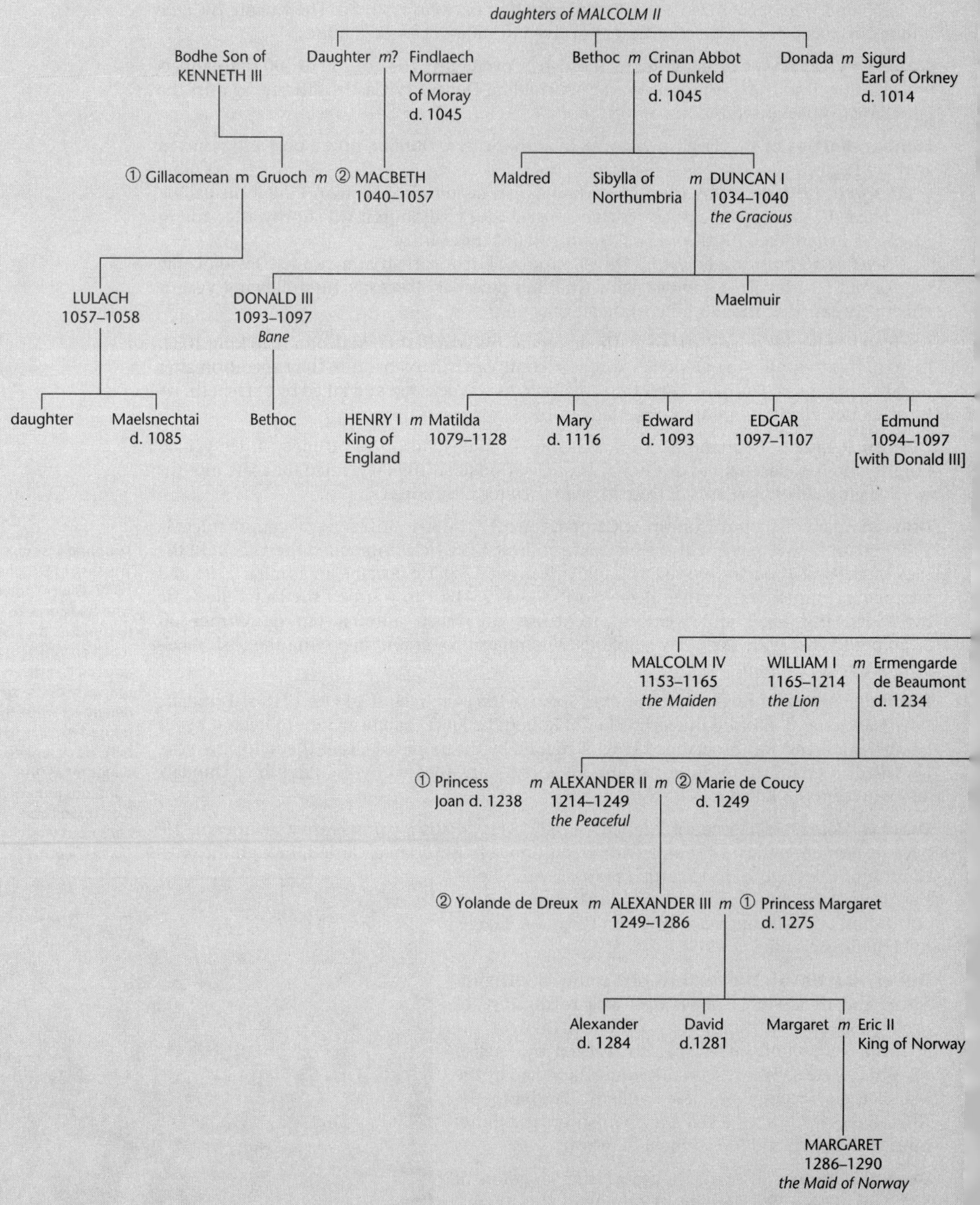

daughters of MALCOLM II

Bodhe Son of
KENNETH III

Daughter *m?* Findlaech
Mormaer
of Moray
d. 1045

Bethoc *m* Crinan Abbot
of Dunkeld
d. 1045

Donada *m* Sigurd
Earl of Orkney
d. 1014

① Gillacomean m Gruoch *m* ② MACBETH
1040–1057

Maldred   Sibylla of   *m* DUNCAN I
            Northumbria   1034–1040
                               the Gracious

LULACH
1057–1058

DONALD III
1093–1097
Bane

Maelmuir

daughter   Maelsnechtai
             d. 1085

Bethoc

HENRY I *m* Matilda
King of   1079–1128
England

Mary
d. 1116

Edward
d. 1093

EDGAR
1097–1107

Edmund
1094–1097
[with Donald III]

MALCOLM IV   WILLIAM I *m* Ermengarde
1153–1165   1165–1214   de Beaumont
the Maiden   *the Lion*   d. 1234

① Princess   *m* ALEXANDER II *m* ② Marie de Coucy
Joan d. 1238   1214–1249   d. 1249
                    the Peaceful

② Yolande de Dreux *m* ALEXANDER III *m* ① Princess Margaret
                       1249–1286   d. 1275

Alexander   David   Margaret *m* Eric II
d. 1284   d.1281   King of Norway

MARGARET
1286–1290
the Maid of Norway

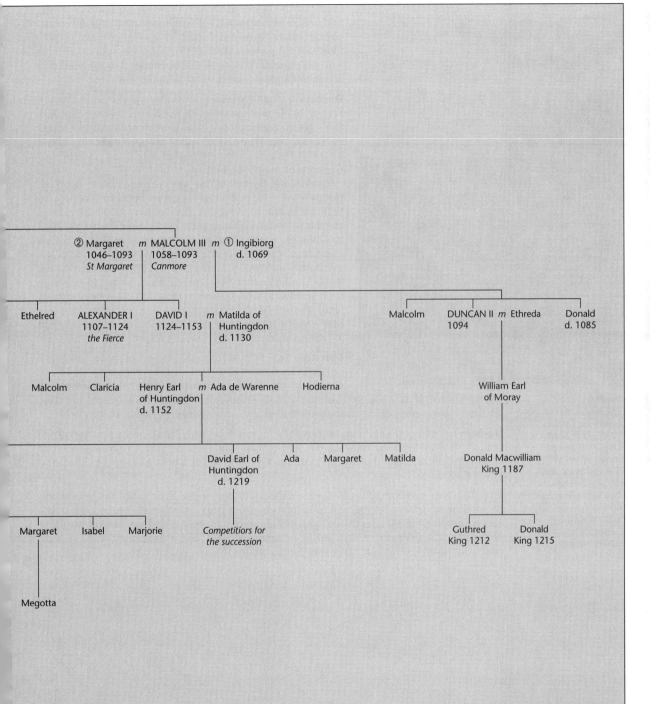

② Margaret *m* MALCOLM III *m* ① Ingibiorg
1046–1093   1058–1093   d. 1069
St Margaret   Canmore

Ethelred | ALEXANDER I | DAVID I | *m* Matilda of | Malcolm | DUNCAN II | *m* Ethreda | Donald
| 1107–1124 | 1124–1153 | Huntingdon | | 1094 | | d. 1085
| the Fierce | | d. 1130

Malcolm | Claricia | Henry Earl | *m* Ada de Warenne | Hodierna | William Earl
| | of Huntingdon | | | of Moray
| | d. 1152

David Earl of | Ada | Margaret | Matilda | Donald Macwilliam
Huntingdon | | | | King 1187
d. 1219

Margaret | Isabel | Marjorie | *Competitiors for* | Guthred | Donald
| | | *the succession* | King 1212 | King 1215

Megotta

*From 1058 the House of Dunkeld was also known as the
House of Canmore (after Malcolm III). The descendents
of David Earl of Huntingdon included both the House of
Balliol and the House of Bruce.*

England, the house of Dunkeld provided a series of strong and competent monarchs of Scotland. Among the more successful rulers were ◊Malcolm III Canmore (1058–1093), ◊William I the Lion (1165–1214), and ◊Alexander II and his son ◊Alexander III (1249–1286), under whom medieval Scotland enjoyed something of a Golden Age.

Dunkirk (French ***Dunkerque***) seaport on the north coast of France, in Nord *département*, on the Strait of Dover. Dunkirk was close to the front line during much of World War I, and in World War II, 337,131 Allied troops (including about 110,000 French) were evacuated from the beaches as German forces approached.

Operation Dynamo, the seaborne evacuation of Allied troops May 1940, was a much-needed boost to morale, particularly in Britain. A motley 'fleet' of over 1,000 ships, from warships down to private yachts, was assembled and sailed to Dunkirk. It was anticipated that perhaps 45,000 troops could be rescued before the Germans took the town. In the event, the Germans, thinking that the British troops penned inside Dunkirk could be safely left there, turned to complete their occupation of northern France. This leeway proved vital, giving the British sufficient time to evacuate some many more troops than had been believed possible and averting a potential disaster for the Allied effort.

Dunstan, St *c.* 909–988. English priest and politician, archbishop of Canterbury from 960. He was abbot of Glastonbury from 945, and made it a centre of learning. He was appointed archbishop of Canterbury under King Edgar and became one of his chief advisers. He was responsible for the reform of several monasteries. Feast day 19 May.

Durham John George Lambton, 1st Earl of Durham 1792–1840. British politician. Appointed Lord Privy Seal 1830, he drew up the first Reform Bill 1832, and as governor general of Canada briefly in 1838 drafted the Durham Report which led to the union of Upper and Lower Canada.

Dyfed ancient kingdom of Wales. It was in the southwest of the principality, in a region corresponding to Pembrokeshire, and took its name from the Celtic Demetae tribe, here in the 1st century. It emerged after the collapse of Roman rule in the 5th century AD and with four other political divisions (Gwynedd, Ceredigion, Gwent and Glamorgan) existed until medieval times. The historic name was resurrected for the new county formed 1974.

Dunkirk
British prisoners on the beaches at Dunkirk 1940. From 26 May to 4 June 1940 over 850 vessels, many of them small private boats, rescued thousands of British and French troops driven on to the beaches in Dunkirk by the German army.
Library of Congress

ealdorman Anglo-Saxon official; the office was gradually replaced by the hereditary title of ◊earl but was in part revived in the 19th century in the municipal office of ◊alderman. Originally a nobleman placed by the king in charge of a shire, much of their administrative role was gradually taken over by sheriffs. In the 10th and 11th century, they increasingly became governors and military leaders of a wider area, and by the time of King Canute the term earl was preferred. This term survived the Norman Conquest, and the position became a hereditary title rather than an office.

earl in the British peerage, the third title in order of rank, coming between marquess and viscount; it is the oldest of British titles, deriving from the Anglo-Saxon post of ealdorman. An earl's wife is a countess. The premier earldom is Arundel, now united with the dukedom of Norfolk.

East Africa Campaign in World War I, joint British–South African campaign to take German colony of East Africa (later Tanganyika, now Tanzania) 1914–18. The campaign made little headway until General Jan Smuts took charge 1916 and the Germans were steadily driven back from then until their final defeat Nov 1918.

East Anglia, kingdom of Anglo-Saxon kingdom of the East Angles, covering modern Norfolk, Suffolk, and parts of Essex and Cambridgeshire. The kingdom was founded c. 500 AD and prospered, as can be seen from the lavish treasures in the ◊Sutton Hoo ship burial. It was conquered by Mercia in the mid-7th century and again by the Danes in the 9th century. Finally, it was absorbed by Wessex 917.

East India Company (British) commercial company 1600–1858 chartered by Queen Elizabeth I and given a monopoly of trade between England and the Far East. In the 18th century, the company became, in effect, the ruler of a large part of India, partly through the military victories of Robert ◊Clive, and a form of dual control by the company and a committee responsible to Parliament in London was introduced by Pitt's India Act 1784. The end of the monopoly of China trade came 1834, and after the ◊Indian Mutiny 1857 the crown took complete control of the government of British India; the India Act 1858 abolished the company.

The East India Company set up factories in Masulipatam, near modern Madras, 1611; on the west coast of India in Surat 1612; on the east coast in Madras 1639; and near Calcutta on the Hooghly (one of the mouths of the Ganges) 1640. The company's trading ambitions in the Dutch East Indies were brought to an end when ten English merchants were tortured and murdered by the Dutch on the island of **Amboina** 1623. By 1652 there were some 23 English factories in India. Bombay came to the British crown 1662, and was granted to the East India Company for £10 a year. The British victory in the Battle of Plassey 1757 gave the company control of Bengal.

Easter Rising or **Easter Rebellion** in Irish history, a republican insurrection that began on Easter Monday, April 1916, in Dublin. It was inspired by the Irish Republican Brotherhood (IRB) in an unsuccessful attempt to overthrow British rule in Ireland. It was led by Patrick Pearce of the IRB and James Connolly of Sinn Féin.

Arms from Germany intended for the IRB were intercepted but the rising proceeded regardless with the seizure of the Post Office and other buildings in Dublin by 1,500 volunteers. The rebellion was crushed by the British army within five days, both sides suffering major losses: 220 civilians, 64 rebels, and 134 members of the crown forces were killed during the uprising. Pearce, Connolly, and about a dozen rebel leaders were subsequently

... establish such a politie of civil and military power and create and secure a large revenue ... as may be the foundation of a large, well-grounded sure English dominion in India for all time to come.

EAST INDIA COMPANY
letter from the Company in London to its agent in Surat, 1687

executed in Kilmainham Jail. Others, including Éamon de Valera, were spared due to US public opinion, to be given amnesty June 1917.

Eastland Company founded 1579 to challenge the ◊Hanseatic League's control of trade with the Baltic. An amalgamation of several smaller English associations, it imported grain and naval supplies, especially timber for masts, in return for woollen products, and succeeded in breaking the Hanseatic League's dominance of the trade. See also ◊Muscovy Company.

Eboracum Roman name of the English city of York. The Romans built a fortress here AD 71 and a *colonia* was subsequently established. The modern name of York derives ultimately from the Roman name, which itself is Celtic in origin. The archbishop of York still signs himself 'Ebor'.

Easter Rising
On the morning of Easter Monday 1916 a group of about 150 Irish nationalists took over the General Post Office in Sackville Street, Dublin, as part of a rebellion against British rule. The rebels were driven out when the building caught fire (as shown above) and almost all the survivors were executed.
Image Select

EC abbreviation for *European Community*, former name (to 1993) of the ◊European Union.

ecclesiastical law canon or church law. In England, the Church of England has special ecclesiastical courts to administer church law. Until the end of the 16th century, ecclesiastical courts dealt with all legal matters concerning the clergy and some concerning the laity that were deemed to come within the province of the church. Conflict often arose between the church and the crown over which had jurisdiction over certain cases or individuals, and ◊Henry II tried unsuccessfully to curb the power of the church courts.

Today their jurisdiction is extremely limited, they deal with the constitution of the Church of England, church property, the clergy, services, doctrine, and practice. Each diocese has a consistory court with a right of appeal to the Court of Arches (in the archbishop of Canterbury's jurisdiction) or the Chancery Court of York (in the archbishop of York's jurisdiction). These courts have no influence on churches of other denominations, which are governed by the usual laws of contract and trust.

Eden Anthony, 1st Earl of Avon 1897–1977. British Conservative politician, foreign secretary 1935–38, 1940–45, and 1951–55; prime minister 1955–57, when he resigned after the failure of the Anglo-French military intervention in the ◊Suez Crisis.

Eden resigned as foreign secretary Feb 1938 in protest at Neville Chamberlain's decision to open conversations with the Fascist dictator Mussolini. He was foreign secretary again in the wartime coalition, formed Dec 1940, and in the Conservative government, elected 1951. With the Soviets, he negotiated an interim peace in Vietnam 1954. In April 1955 he succeeded Churchill as prime minister. When Egypt nationalized the Suez Canal 1956, precipitating the ◊Suez Crisis, he authorized the use of force and a joint Anglo-French force was sent to Egypt. The force was forced to withdraw after pressure from the USA and the USSR and this led to his resignation Jan 1957. He was succeeded by Harold ◊MacMillan. He was created Earl of Avon 1961.

In the name of God, and of the dead generations from which she receives her old traditions of nationhood Ireland through us summons her children to her flag and strikes for freedom.

EASTER RISING
Patrick Pearse, proclamation at the General Post Office, Dublin, 1916

Edgar known as the *Atheling* ('of royal blood') *c.* 1050–*c.* 1130. English prince, born in Hungary. Grandson of Edmund Ironside, and great-nephew of Edward the Confessor. He possessed the best hereditary claim to the English throne on Edward's death 1066, but was passed over in favour of Harold II. He led two rebellions against William the Conqueror 1068 and 1069, but made peace 1074.

Edgar the Peaceful 944–975. King of Northumbria and Mercia 957–75 and of all England from 959. He was the younger son of Edmund I, and strove successfully to unite English and Danes as fellow subjects. He was a generous supporter of the monasteries and introduced a uniform English currency.

Edgehill, Battle of first battle of the Civil War 1642. It took place on a ridge in south Warwickshire, between Royalists led by Charles I and Prince Rupert and Parliamentarians led by the Earl of Essex. The result was indecisive, with both sides claiming victory.

Edington, Battle of defeat May 878 by Alfred the Great, King of Wessex, of the Danish forces of ◊Guthrum. The site is at Edington, 6km/4 mi east of Westbury, Wiltshire; the chalk white horse on the downs nearby is said to commemorate the victory. The battle was a decisive one for Alfred, and forced the Danes to retire from Wessex into East Anglia,

Edith d. 1075. Queen Consort of Edward the Confessor, and the daughter of Earl Godwin. Her father helped Edward the Confessor succeed Hardicanute to the throne 1042 and she married Edward 1045, strengthening her family's influence over the king. Following the Norman Conquest 1066, she submitted to William I and played no further part in public life.

Edmund I c. 921–46. King of England 939–46. The son of Edward the Elder, he succeeded his half-brother, Athelstan, as king 939. He succeeded in regaining control of Mercia, which on his accession had fallen to the Norse inhabitants of Northumbria, and of the ◊Five Boroughs, an independent confederation within the Danelaw. He then moved on to subdue the Norsemen in Cumbria and finally extended his rule as far as southern Scotland. As well as uniting England, he bolstered his authority by allowing St ◊Dunstan to reform the ◊Benedictine order. He was killed 946 at Pucklechurch, Gloucestershire, by an outlawed robber.

Edmund (II) Ironside c. 989–1016. King of England 1016, the son of Ethelred II 'the Unready'. He led the resistance to ◊Canute's invasion 1015, and on Ethelred's death 1016 was chosen king by the citizens of London, whereas the Witan (the king's council) elected Canute. In the struggle for the throne, Edmund was defeated by Canute at Assandun (Ashington), Essex, and they divided the kingdom between them; when Edmund died the same year, Canute ruled the whole kingdom.

Edmund, St c. 840–870. King of East Anglia from 855. In 870 he was defeated and captured by the Danes at Hoxne, Suffolk, and martyred on refusing to renounce Christianity. He was canonized and his shrine at Bury St Edmunds became a place of pilgrimage.

Edric the Forester or **Edric the Wild** English chieftain on the Welsh border who revolted against William the Conqueror 1067, around what is today Herefordshire, burning Shrewsbury. He was subsequently reconciled with William, and fought with him against the Scots 1072. Later writings describe him as a legendary figure.

Education Acts series of measures from the late 19th century onwards which provided for state education for all. The 1870 Education Act was the effective start of state-financed education in England and Wales. Existing grants to ◊charity schools were substantially increased and provision was made for local authorities to finance additional schools out of the rates. A series of subsequent acts made elementary education free and compulsory by 1891. Fisher's 1918 Education Act attempted to raise the school leaving age to 14, and some provision was intended for further training. Rab Butler's pioneering act of 1944 organized a Ministry of Education and intended that schooling be compulsory to the age of 16, though this took many years to achieve. The 1980s and 1990s saw a variety of Education Acts which restricted the ability of local authorities to determine the pattern of education by enforcing a National Curriculum and regular testing in all state schools.

Edward the Black Prince 1330–1376. Prince of Wales, eldest son of Edward III of England. The epithet (probably posthumous) may refer to his black armour. During the Hundred Years' War he fought at the Battle of Crécy 1346 and captured the French king at Poitiers 1356. He ruled

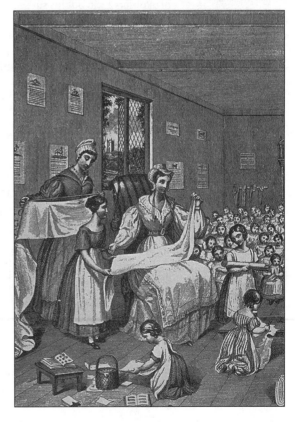

Education Acts
English schoolroom c. 1840. The state took over some elements of the provision of education with the Education Act 1870 which introduced universal elementary education in England and Wales.
Philip Sauvain

Aquitaine 1360–71; during the revolt that eventually ousted him, he caused the massacre of Limoges 1370.

Edward eight kings of England or Great Britain:

Edward I 1239–1307. King of England from 1272, son of Henry III. Edward led the royal forces against Simon de Montfort in the ◊Barons' War 1264–67, and was on a crusade when he succeeded to the throne. He established English rule over all Wales 1282–84, and secured recognition of his overlordship from the Scottish king, although the Scots (under William Wallace and Robert the Bruce) fiercely resisted actual conquest. He initiated many administrative reforms and Parliament took its approximate modern form during his reign with the ◊Model Parliament 1295. He was also reponsible for the expulsion of Jews from England 1290. He was succeeded by his son Edward II.

Edward II 1284–1327. King of England from 1307, son of Edward I. Born at Caernarvon Castle, he was created the first Prince of Wales 1301. Incompetent and frivolous, and unduly influenced by his favourite, Piers ◊Gaveston, Edward I struggled throughout his reign with discontented barons who attempted to restrict his power through the Ordinances 1311. His invasion of Scotland 1314 to suppress revolt resulted in defeat at ◊Bannockburn. When he fell under the influence of a new favourite, Hugh le Depenser, he was deposed 1327 by his wife Isabella (1292–1358), daughter of Philip IV of France, and her lover Roger de ◊Mortimer. Edward was murdered in Berkeley Castle, Gloucestershire. He was succeeded by his son Edward III.

Edward III 1312–1377. King of England from 1327, son of Edward II. He assumed the government 1330 from his mother, through whom in 1337 he laid claim to the French throne and thus began the ◊Hundred Years' War. He was succeeded by his grandson Richard II.

Edward improved the status of the monarchy after his father's chaotic reign. He began his reign by attempting to force his rule on Scotland, winning a victory at Halidon Hill 1333. During the first stage of the Hundred Years' War, English victories included the Battle of Crécy 1346 and the capture of Calais 1347. He captured the French king John II at the Battle of ◊Poitiers 1356 but his subsequent campaign failed and he was forced to abandon his claim to the French throne 1360, but the war resumed 1369. During his last years his son John of Gaunt acted as head of government.

Edward IV 1442–1483. King of England 1461–70 and from 1471. He was the son of Richard, Duke of York, and succeeded Henry VI in the Wars of the *Roses*, temporarily losing the throne to Henry when Edward fell out with his adviser ◊Warwick, but regaining it at the Battle of Barnet 1471. He was succeeded by his son Edward V.

Edward was known as Earl of March until his accession. After his father's death he occupied London 1461, and was proclaimed king in place of Henry VI by a council of peers. His position was secured by the defeat of the Lancastrians at Towton 1461 and by the capture of Henry. He quarrelled, however, with Warwick, his strongest supporter, who in 1470–71 temporarily restored Henry, until Edward recovered the throne by his victories at Barnet and Tewkesbury.

Edward V 1470–1483. King of England 1483. Son of Edward IV, he was deposed three months after his accession in favour of his uncle Richard, Duke of Gloucester, who became ◊Richard III. He is traditionally believed to have been murdered (with his brother) in the Tower of London on Richard's orders.

Edward VI 1537–1553. King of England from 1547, son of Henry VIII and Jane Seymour. The government was entrusted to his uncle the Duke of Somerset (who fell from power 1549), and then to the Earl of Warwick, later created Duke of Northumberland. He was succeeded by his sister, Mary I.

Edward was a staunch Protestant and the *Book of ◊Common Prayer* 1552 was introduced into the Church of England during his

Edward VI
King Edward VI's coronation medal. A brilliant scholar, deeply interested in theological speculation, Edward devoted his short reign to trying to secure the Protestant Reformation in England.
Philip Sauvain

1. The Battle of Agincourt 1415, a French 15th-century illustration. The remarkable triumph of Henry V's small army, mainly consisting of archers, over a large, powerful French royal army of knights, footsoldiers, and crossbowmen revived English claims to much of western France in the unsuccessful middle years of the Hundred Years' War.
E T Archive

2. Cardinal Thomas Wolsey, an oil painting by an unknown artist. Lord chancellor 1515–29, Wolsey was the last major figure in the long history of clerical domination of the English administration. He died, accused of treason after his failure to obtain papal dispensation for Henry VIII's divorce from Catherine of Aragon, on the eve of the English Reformation.
Image Select

3. King Henry VIII, an oil painting by Hans Holbein. Henry VIII dominates the transition of England from a medieval to a Renaissance state. His patronage of the arts and his diplomatic and military adventures ended a long period of relative English insignificance in European culture and politics after the Hundred Years' War. Above all, his seizure of control of the English church brought Reformation politics and social changes to Britain.
Image Select

4. The defeat of the Spanish Armada, a contemporary painting. The Spanish attempt to invade England in 1588 was defeated more by poor planning and violent weather than by English action, but the threat of invasion did much to ensure the unity of both Protestant and Catholic subjects of Elizabeth I behind their queen.
David Pratt

5. Oliver Cromwell, a painting attributed to Van Dyck. Lord Protector and virtual dictator of England after the execution of Charles I, Cromwell inherited a divided and war-weary nation, to which he forcibly united Scotland and Ireland for the first time in their histories. His rule became associated with an unpopular type of Puritan zeal, and the Stuart Charles II was welcomed back by most of Britain after Cromwell's death.
Philip Sauvain

6. Mary II, painted at the time of her engagement to William of Orange (autumn 1677), by Sir Peter Lely. Daughter of James II and Anne Hyde, Mary remained true to the Protestant faith despite her father's conversion to Catholicism. Her marriage to the Dutch William brought a major realignment in British politics, religion, and culture at the end of the 17th century.
E T Archive

7. Horatio Nelson, Britain's most celebrated naval hero, painted in about 1800 by F H Fuger. The inheritor of a long tradition of constant refinement in naval tactics, Nelson brought an unprecedented combination of intuition, daring, and control to the command of a sailing fleet in battle. His victory at Trafalgar (1805) finally ended the French naval challenge to Britain, and ensured the supremacy of the Royal Navy in the world's seas for the rest of the 19th century.
E T Archive

8. The Battle of Waterloo, by Felix Philipotteaux. The final defeat of Napoleon Bonaparte 18 June 1815 marks the end of some 750 years of intermittent warfare between England and France. After the collapse of the first British Empire in the French-supported American Revolution, Britain's victory at Waterloo removed the major obstacle to the creation of a new, world-wide Empire.
E T Archive

9. The First Anglo-Afghan War, an illustration published in 1850 showing British troops entering the Bolan Pass from Dadur. The creation of an empire based on territorial expansion rather than trading posts brought British troops to many parts of the world from the late 18th century to the mid-20th.
Image Select

10. Mary Robinson, president of the Republic of Ireland since 1990. Her surprise election marked a historic departure in modern Irish history. For the first time, a left-of-centre, socially-progressive candidate and a champion of women's rights had broken the conservative, male, religious, and republican hold on Irish politics.
Irish Embassy

THE HAMMER OF THE CELTS

Edward I and Wales

Edward I's conquest of Wales was achieved by the use of force on a scale that the Welsh could not hope to match, and by taking advantage of the divisions within the country. In the early and mid-13th century, the princes of Gwynedd, Llewelyn the Great and his grandson Llewelyn ap Gruffydd, had been remarkably successful in capitalizing on the political difficulties faced in England by King John and then by Henry III. Before he came to the throne, Edward himself had failed to maintain proper control of the lands in Wales granted to him in 1254. Llewelyn ap Gruffydd supported the Crown's opponent Simon de Montfort in the civil war of 1264–65. It was hardly surprising that, when he came to the throne, Edward should wish to take his revenge.

At the same time, Llewelyn's own position in Wales was not secure. His push to achieve dominance over members of his own family, notably his brother Dafydd and the other Welsh princes, had been successful, but left him with dangerous enemies. He overestimated the strength of his position, and his refusal to accept Edward's demands that he acknowledge English overlordship by performing homage left him fatally exposed.

The campaign of 1277

The conquest was achieved in three major campaigns. The first, in 1277, clearly demonstrated that the Welsh could not resist a substantial English army marching along the north Welsh coast; Llewelyn's support was limited, and he had to sue for peace on humiliating terms. Edward I, however, failed to reward those Welshmen, who even included Llewelyn's own brother Dafydd, who had supported him in 1277. Attempts to introduce English law in Welsh affairs were provocative, and there was widespread rebellion 1282–83. The English campaign to put down the rising was lengthy, and Edward's forces suffered a disaster when knights who had crossed to the mainland from Anglesey were ambushed and slaughtered. However, Llewelyn was slain at the battle of Irfon Bridge in December 1282, and Dafydd's attempts to carry on the fight ended in failure in the next year. He was handed over to Edward by men of his own nation. The Welsh ruling dynasties were ruined and Wales virtually became an English colony.

The 1294 rebellion

There was a minor rebellion in the south of the country in 1287, followed by a much more serious rising in 1294. The introduction of English methods of taxation, and general oppression by English officials led to the rebellion, which was timed to coincide with the English involvement in war with France. Edward was able to divert the troops intended for France to Wales and an expensive campaign ended in complete success for the English. Edward was capable of putting as many as 30,000 troops in the field against the Welsh. He had heavily armed cavalry in numbers which his opponents could never hope to match, and while he used the traditional feudal obligation as one means of recruitment, the majority of his troops were either paid, or were serving at their own expense. In 1282 he had hoped that the whole army would serve for wages, but this aroused hostility from the baronage, whose independence was threatened by such a move. Infantry were recruited in large numbers, many of them from south Wales, and the majority were armed with the longbow, a devastating weapon. In addition, during the second war he recruited a force of crossbowmen from his overseas dominion of Gascony. Every effort was made to ensure that food supplies for the armies were sufficient, while ships were brought from the south coast of England and Ireland to provide the naval support which was essential if the armies were to be properly provided for. Edward was able to keep his armies in being over the winter months of 1282–83 and 1294–95. The Welsh could not hold out for long against such unremitting pressure.

The great castles

Edward's campaigns were each marked by a programme of castle-building. New castles on a grand scale were designed to hold down the Welsh. Flint, Rhuddlan, Builth, and Aberystwyth were built after the first Welsh war; after the second Snowdonia was hemmed in much more closely by Conwy, Caernarfon, and Harlech, while after the rebellion of 1294 Beaumaris was founded to establish a secure hold on Anglesey. The castles were largely the work of a single man of genius, Master James of St George, a master mason recruited from Savoy. It was Savoyard, not English, masons who were responsible for much of the design and detail of the castles. Caernarfon was the exception. It was based on the walls of Constantinople, and was built as a grand imperial gesture by a king who wanted to express in stone not only his might, but also legendary connections with the Imperial past of ancient Rome.

MICHAEL PRESTWICH

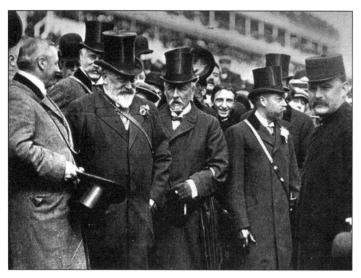

Edward VII
Edward VII (second left), a keen sportsman and gambler, at the 1909 Derby with the Prince of Wales (third from right). The race was won by Edward's horse Minoru. *Hulton Deutsch*

reign. He died from tuberculosis, having named Lady Jane ◊Grey as his successor.

Edward VII 1841–1910. King of Great Britain and Ireland from 1901. As Prince of Wales he was a prominent social figure, but his mother Queen Victoria considered him too frivolous to take part in political life. In 1860 he made the first tour of Canada and the USA ever undertaken by a British prince.

Edward was born at Buckingham Palace, the eldest son of Queen Victoria and Prince Albert. After his father's death 1861 he undertook many public duties, took a close interest in politics, and was on friendly terms with the party leaders. In 1863 he married Princess Alexandra of Denmark, and they had six children. He toured India 1875–76. He succeeded to the throne 1901 and was crowned 1902. Although he over-rated his political influence, he contributed to the Entente Cordiale 1904 with France and the Anglo-Russian agreement 1907.

Edward VIII 1894–1972. King of Great Britain and Northern Ireland Jan–Dec 1936, when he renounced the throne to marry Wallis Warfield Simpson (see ◊abdication crisis). He was created Duke of Windsor and was governor of the Bahamas 1940–45, subsequently settling in France.

Eldest son of George V, he received the title of Prince of Wales 1910 and succeeded to the throne 20 Jan 1936. In Nov 1936 a constitutional crisis arose when Edward wished to marry Mrs Simpson; it was felt that, as a divorcee, she would be unacceptable as queen. On 11 Dec Edward abdicated and left for France, where the couple were married 1937. He was succeeded by his brother, George VI.

Edward the Confessor *c.* 1003–1066. King of England from 1042, the son of Ethelred II. During the reign of ◊Canute he lived in Normandy until shortly before his accession. He married Edith, the daughter of Earl ◊Godwin 1045 who with his son ◊Harold was the dominant influence on Edward's reign. Edward largely devoted himself to religion, including the rebuilding of Westminster Abbey (consecrated 1065), where he is buried. His childlessness led ultimately to the Norman Conquest 1066. He was canonized 1161.

Edward the Elder *c.* 870–924. King of the West Saxons. He succeeded his father ◊Alfred the Great 899. He reconquered southeast England and the Midlands from the Danes, uniting Wessex and ◊Mercia with the help of his sister, Athelflad. By the time Edward died, his kingdom was the most powerful in the British Isles. He was succeeded by his son ◊Athelstan.

Edward the Martyr *c.* 963–978. King of England from 975. Son of King Edgar, he was murdered at Corfe Castle, Dorset, probably at his stepmother Aelfthryth's instigation as she wished to secure the crown for her son, Ethelred. He was canonized 1001.

Edwin *c.* 585–633. King of Northumbria from 617. He captured and fortified Edinburgh, which was named after him. He was defeated and killed in battle by Penda of Mercia 632.

Edwy King of England, son of Edmund I. He succeeded his uncle Edred as king 955 and drove Edred's chief adviser St ◊Dunstan, then virtually ruler, into exile 955. When the Mercians and Northumbrians revolted 957, and chose his brother ◊Edgar the Peaceful as king, he was left to rule Wessex and Kent 957–959.

Egbert d. 839. King of Wessex from 802, the son of Ealhmund, an under-king of Kent. He gained control over the whole of southern England in a succession of victories and was named ◊bretwalda, king of all England, 829. Mercia regained its independence the following year and Egbert was left with Wessex and its client kingdoms in the southeast.

Egypt former British protectorate in northeast Africa. Britain and France had dual control of it 1879–82, and Britain occupied it 1882. It was administered by Lord Cromer (Evelyn Baring)

Methinks I am in prison. Here be no galleries nor gardens to walk in.

EDWARD VI
aged 12, in Windsor after the fall of his uncle, the Duke of Somerset.

1883–1907 and declared a British protectorate 1914. It gained independence as a monarchy 1922, and became a republic 1953.

Eleanor of Aquitaine c. 1122–1204. Queen of France 1137–51 as wife of Louis VII until the marriage was annulled 1152. She then married Henry of Anjou, who became king of England as Henry II 1154, making her queen. Henry imprisoned her 1174–89 for supporting their sons, the future Richard I and King John, in a revolt against him. She had seven surviving children by Henry.

Eleanor of Castile c. 1245–1290. Queen of Edward I of England, the daughter of Ferdinand III of Castile. She married Prince Edward 1254, and accompanied him on his crusade 1270. She died at Harby, Nottinghamshire, and Edward erected stone crosses in towns where her body rested on the funeral journey to London. Several **Eleanor Crosses** are still standing, for example at Northampton.

Eleven Years' Tyranny pejorative contemporary term for the eleven years 1629–40 in which King Charles I ruled England without calling a parliament; now more usually termed the 'personal rule' to avoid the implication that he was acting illegally. There was little overt opposition to his imposition of direct rule in England, and only his efforts to impose the English *Book of* ◊*Common Prayer* on Scotland, and the resulting ◊Bishops' Wars, forced him to call a parliament April 1640.

Charles' rule had mixed success: he demonstrated concern for the poor by organizing more effective famine relief but squandered much of this goodwill by extending the traditional 'ship money' levy to include inland as well as maritime counties. Many regarded this as a tax in all but name which should have been sanctioned by Parliament. It was tested in the courts by John Hampden 1637 but, in an ambiguous ruling, the judges decided in favour of the Crown. Perhaps Charles' most serious political mistake was to continue to promote the ◊Arminians and High Church policies while persecuting Puritans, such as William Prynne, John Bastwick, and Robert Burton. In Ireland the harsh rule of Thomas Wentworth increased the Crown's revenues but at the cost of increasing discontent.

Eliot John 1592–1632. English politician, born in Cornwall. He became a member of Parliament 1614, and became a vice-admiral 1619 due to the Earl of Buckingham's patronage. In 1626 he was imprisoned in the Tower of London for demanding Buckingham's impeachment. He was a formidable supporter of the ◊Petition of Right opposing Charles I 1628, and with other parliamentary leaders was again imprisoned in the Tower of London 1629, where he died.

Elizabeth two queens of England or the UK:

Elizabeth I 1533–1603. Queen of England 1558–1603, the daughter of Henry VIII and Anne Boleyn. During her Roman Catholic half-sister Mary's reign, Elizabeth's Protestant sympathies brought her under suspicion, and she lived in seclusion at Hatfield, Hertfordshire, until on Mary's death she became queen. Her first task was her Religious Settlement of 1559 when she imposed the Protestant religion by law.

Parliament made many unsuccessful attempts to persuade Elizabeth to marry or settle the succession and she was courted by several European rulers. However, she found courtship a useful political weapon, and she used these bids to marry her to strengthen her position both at home and abroad. She maintained friendships with, among others, the courtiers ◊Leicester, Sir Walter ◊Raleigh, and ◊Essex. She never married and thanks to her machinations was known as the Virgin Queen.

The arrival in England 1568 of ◊Mary Queen of Scots and her imprisonment by Elizabeth caused a political crisis, and the feudal nobility of the north launched an unsuccessful rebellion 1569. Meanwhile, there was increased tension between England and Spain, and when the Dutch rebelled against Spanish rule Elizabeth secretly encouraged them; Philip II retaliated by aiding Catholic conspiracies against her. This undeclared war continued for many years, until the English invasion of the Netherlands in support of the Dutch 1585 and Mary's execution 1587. This brought the conflict into the open and Philip sent the ◊Spanish Armada to invade England 1588. The expedition met with total disaster, but the conflict with Spain continued until the end of her reign, while events at home foreshadowed the conflicts of the 17th century. Discontent with Elizabeth's religious settlement began to develop among the

Though God hath raised me high, yet this I count the glory of my crown: that I have reigned with your loves.

ELIZABETH I
The Golden Speech
1601, D'Ewes' Journal

Elizabeth II
Elizabeth II, queen of Great Britain and Northern Ireland. As a constitutional monarch, representing the supreme legal and political authority, she summons and dissolves Parliament, gives her official approval to acts of Parliament, sanctions government judicial appointments, and confers honours and awards. She is the head of the Commonwealth, and is queen of Canada, New Zealand, Australia, and several other countries.
Topham Picture Library

Puritans, and several were imprisoned or executed. Parliament showed a new independence, and forced Elizabeth to retreat on the question of the crown granting manufacturing and trading monopolies 1601. Despite this her authority remained intact until her death 1603, as was shown by the failure of Essex's rebellion 1601. The Elizabethan age was a successful period, with commercial expansion and geographical exploration, while the arts and literature flourished.

Elizabeth II 1926– . Queen of Great Britain and Northern Ireland from 1952, the elder daughter of George VI. She married her third cousin, Philip, the Duke of Edinburgh, 1947. They have four children: Charles, Anne, Andrew, and Edward. During World War II she served in the Auxiliary Territorial Service, and by an amendment to the Regency Act she became a state counsellor on her 18th birthday. She succeeded to the throne on the death of her father while she was in Kenya with her husband 1952 and was crowned 2 June 1953.

With an estimated wealth of £5 billion (1994), the Queen is the richest woman in Britain, and probably the world. In April 1993 she voluntarily began paying full rates of income tax and capital gains on her private income, which chiefly consists of the proceeds of a share portfolio and is estimated to be worth around £45 million.

Ellice Islands former British colony, an island group in the west Pacific. It was made part of the Gilbert and Ellice Islands Colony 1915, but was separated from the Gilbert Islands 1976 and made a territory of the British Commonwealth, changing its name to Tuvalu. It gained independence 1978.

Elmet Romano-British kingdom in the southern region of what is now North Yorkshire. When the English kingdoms of ◊Deira and ◊Berenicia merged to form Northumbria in the early 7th century, Elmet became absorbed as part of the new united kingdom. Its name survives in the village of Sherburn in Elmet, east of Leeds.

Emma of Normandy d. 1052. Daughter of Richard I of Normandy and the wife successively of Ethelred the Unready 1002–16 and Canute 1017–35. On the death of Canute she attempted to seize the throne for her son Hardicanute, but fled into exile in Normandy when the attempt failed. She returned to England when Hardicanute came to the throne 1040 but following his death two years later she came into conflict with his successor, Edward the Confessor, her son by Ethelred. She apparently became involved in plots against Edward and was made to forfeit her property 1043.

Emmet Robert 1778–1803. Irish nationalist leader. In 1803 he led an unsuccessful revolt in Dublin against British rule and was captured, tried, and hanged. His youth and courage made him an Irish hero.

Empire, the British various territories all over the world conquered or colonized by Britain from about 1600, most now independent or ruled by other powers; the British Empire was at its largest at the end of World War I, consisting of over 25% of the world's population and area. The ◊Commonwealth is composed of former and remaining territories of the British Empire.

The British Empire lasted more than three and a half centuries – almost as long as the Roman Empire. By the time the British began colonizing overseas, the Portuguese and Spaniards had already divided a considerable part of the earth's land surface between them.

The first successful British colony was Jamestown, Virginia, in North America, founded 1607, although there was an earlier settlement at Newfoundland 1583. The Empire grew

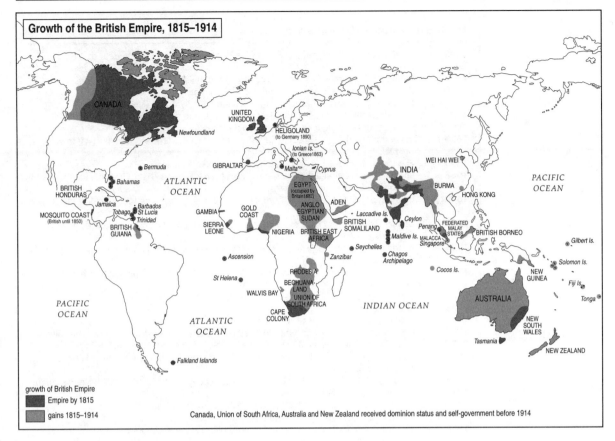

Growth of the British Empire, 1815–1914

growth of British Empire
- Empire by 1815
- gains 1815–1914

Canada, Union of South Africa, Australia and New Zealand received dominion status and self-government before 1914

comparatively quickly, initially with acquisitions in North America and India, as well as some marginal settlement in Africa, in the 17th and 18th centuries. The 19th century saw the largest expansion of the Empire as the British took many former French possessions in the West Indies and began to settle in numbers in Australia in the early part of the century and later competed fiercely with other European powers for territory in Africa. At the same time, there was serious expansion in Asia, notably the acquisition of Singapore (1824), Hong Kong (1841), and Burma (1886), and the South Pacific, particularly the settlement of New Zealand (1840). The only serious loss of territory was the loss of the 13 American colonies in the ◊American Revolution 1776.

The Empire faded gradually into the Commonwealth from the 1930s onward as one by one former British colonies and protectorates gained independence but retained this last link with the Crown.

The British showed little interest in Africa outside the Cape until the scramble for territory of the 1880s, although a few forts were kept in West Africa, where gold and ivory kept their importance after the slave trade was ended by Britain 1807. An early exception was the colony of Sierra Leone founded 1788 with the cession of a strip of land to provide a home for liberated slaves; a protectorate was established over the hinterland 1896. British influence in Nigeria began through the activities of the National Africa Company (the Royal Niger Company from 1886), which bought Lagos from an African chief 1861 and steadily extended its hold over the Niger Valley until it surrendered its charter 1899; in 1900 the two protectorates of North and South Nigeria were proclaimed. World War I ousted Germany from the African continent, and in 1921–22, under a League of Nations mandate, Tanganyika was transferred to British administration, southwest Africa to South Africa; Cameroons and Togoland, in West Africa, were divided between Britain and France.

The high ground of East Africa made it far more suitable for settlement by white colonists than the colonies in the west. Once again, private companies under charter from the British government pioneered the way, establishing their control over Kenya 1888 and Uganda

Growth of the British Empire, 1815–1914 Britain's imperial territories expanded enormously after the defeat of France in the Napoleonic Wars. In contrast to the earlier network of trading bases among which the American colonies were the only extensive possessions, the second British Empire represented territorial expansion on a world scale, particularly in Africa, South Asia, and the Pacific.

The British Empire: chronology

1600	Queen Elizabeth I granted a charter to the East India Company, for trade with the East Indies.
1607	England's first successful American colony was established at Jamestown (Virginia).
1620	*21 May* Puritans (later known as the Pilgrims), originally from England, reached Cape Cod, North America, on the *Mayflower* and then founded Plymouth (Massachusetts).
1623	An English colony was established on St Kitts, its first in the Caribbean; in 1625 Barbados was annexed and sugar cane introduced there 1640.
1638	In central America, shipwrecked English sailors established the settlement that is now Belize.
1655	English forces seized the Spanish Caribbean island of Jamaica.
1668	English traders claimed the Hudson Bay area (Canada); in 1670 the Hudson's Bay Company was granted a charter.
1672	Foundation of the Royal Africa Company, with a monopoly in the supply of slaves to English colonies.
1688–9	Unsuccessful attempt by Scotland to establish a colony at Darien on the coast of central America.
1713	By the peace of Utrecht, France ceded Acadia, Newfoundland, and the Hudson's Bay Territories in Canada to Britain.
1732	Foundation of Georgia, making 13 British colonies along the seaboard of North America between Spanish Florida and New France.
1763	In the Peace of Paris, France ceded the whole of Canada to Britain.
1765	The Treaty of Allahabad permitted the East India Company to levy taxes in northeast India, marking the start of British expansion in India.
1768–71	First voyage of James Cook, who explored the coasts of New Zealand and east Australia.
1775	Outbreak of war between Britain and the 13 colonies in North America, leading to the colonies' Declaration of Independence 1776 and their defeat of the British in 1781, ending the so-called First British Empire.
1788	*Jan* British expedition reached Botany Bay and Sydney, Australia, to establish a penal colony.
1799	Britain captured Malta.
1806	British conquered the Dutch colony at the Cape, South Africa.
1807	Abolition of the slave trade involving British subjects.
1808	The British Colonial Office accepted responsibility for the abolitionist settlement at Sierra Leone, west Africa.
1833	Britain abolished slavery within the Empire.
1840	Treaty of Waitangi with Maori chiefs established British sovereignty over New Zealand.
1840	Act of Union created a united Canada.
1841	China ceded Hong Kong island to Britain (confirmed by Treaty of Nanjing, 1842).
1843	Britain annexed the settlement at Natal, southeast Africa.
1857	*May–Sept* Indian Mutiny; in 1858, the British assumed the powers of the East India Company.
1867	British North America Act redivided Canada into provinces and made the country a dominion.
1869	Opening of the Suez Canal, shortening the sea route to India.
1880s	European powers joined the 'Scramble for Africa'; Britain acquired territories in south and east Africa.
1882	*July* Britain intervened in Egypt, leading to British rule.
1898	*Sept* Egyptian army led by General Kitchener invaded Sudan.
1901	*1 Jan* The Commonwealth of Australia came into existence.
1902	Following the South African War of 1899–1902, Britain acquired sovereignty over the Boer republics in South Africa.
1907	New Zealand became a Dominion.
1910	British territories in South Africa became a self-governing dominion.
1914–18	During World War I use of the term 'British Commonwealth of Nations' becomes common; in 1919 the Dominions and India are represented separately at the Peace Conference.
1947	*15 Aug* India was partitioned and became independent as India and Pakistan.
1949	The British Commonwealth is henceforth called the Commonwealth.
1957	The Gold Coast became independent as Ghana; most British territories in Africa became independent within 10 years.
1965	Rhodesia's white government made a unilateral declaration of independence (UDI).
1979	*11 Dec* White rebellion in Rhodesia ended, leading to independence as Zimbabwe (achieved 1 April 1980).
1984	*26 Sept* Britain and China signed a draft agreement on the future of Hong Kong after British leases lapse 1997.

The British Empire

current name	colonial names and history	colonized	independent
India	British East India Company	18th century–1858	1947
Pakistan	British East India Company	18th century–1858	1947
Myanmar	Burma	1866	1948
Sri Lanka	Portuguese, Dutch 1602–1796; Ceylon 1802–1972	16th century	1948
Ghana	Gold Coast; British Togoland integrated 1956	1618	1957
Nigeria		1861	1960
Cyprus	Turkish to 1878, then British rule	1878	1960
Sierra Leone	British protectorate	1788	1961
Tanzania	German E Africa to 1921; British mandate from League of Nations/UN as Tanganyika	19th century	1961
Jamaica	Spanish to 1655	16th century	1962
Trinidad & Tobago	Spanish 1532–1797; British 1797–1962	1532	1962
Uganda	British protectorate	1894	1962
Kenya	British colony from 1920	1895	1963
Malaysia	British interests from 1786; Federation of Malaya 1957–63	1874	1963
Malawi	British protectorate of Nyasaland 1907–53; Federation of Rhodesia & Nyasaland 1953–64	1891	1964
Malta	French 1798–1814	1798	1964
Zambia	N Rhodesia – British protectorate; Federation of Rhodesia & Nyasaland 1953–64	1924	1964
The Gambia		1888	1965
Singapore	Federation of Malaya 1963–65	1858	1965
Guyana	Dutch to 1796; British Guiana 1796–1966	1620	1966
Botswana	Bechuanaland – British protectorate	1885	1966
Lesotho	Basutoland	1868	1966
Bangladesh	British East India Company 18th century–1858; British India 1858–1947; E Pakistan 1947–71	18th century	1971
Zimbabwe	S Rhodesia from 1923; UDI under Ian Smith 1965–79	1895	1980
Belize	British Honduras	17th century	1981

1890. Northern Somalia came under direct control of the British government 1884 and in 1890 Germany, which had already relinquished its interests in Uganda, ceded Zanzibar to Britain in exchange for Heligoland, an island off the German coast.

The concept of self-government for some of the colonies was first formulated in Lord Durham's *Report on the Affairs of British North America* 1839 which recommended that responsible government (the acceptance by governors of the advice of local ministers) should be granted to Upper Canada (Ontario) and Lower Canada (Quebec). This pattern was subsequently applied to the other Canadian provinces and to the Australian colonies which attained responsible government by 1859, except for Western Australia (1890). New Zealand obtained responsible government 1856 and the Cape colony 1872, followed by Natal 1893. A further intermediate form of government, dominion status, was devised in the late 19th and early 20th century at a series of Colonial Conferences (renamed Imperial Conferences 1907). Canada became a dominion 1867, Australia 1901, New Zealand 1907, and South Africa by 1910. These four self-governing countries were known as Dominions within the British Empire. Their meetings with the British government were the basis for the idea of the Commonwealth of Nations. Dominion status was very inexactly defined until the ◊Statute of Westminster 1931 established it as synonymous with complete independence.

There were varying degrees of unrest throughout much of the Empire during the 1930s, although most notably in India, where Mahatma Gandhi led a campaign of 'civil disobedience' against British rule. World War II (1939–45) hastened the end of the former colonial empires, mainly because it destroyed the psychological basis upon which their existence depended. India gained complete independence 1947–48; Sudan, Ghana, and Malaya in the 1950s, and much of the rest of Africa in the 1960s. By 1970 the former British colonies in the West Indies were either independent or linked to Britain as associated states only by their

When we speak of Empire it is in no spirit of flag-wagging. We feel that in this great inheritance of ours, separated as it is by the seas, we have yet one home and one people.

BRITISH EMPIRE
*Stanley Baldwin, speech,
5 December 1924*

England and Great Britain: sovereigns from 901

reign	name	relationship	reign	name	relationship
West Saxon kings			**House of York**		
901–25	Edward the Elder	son of Alfred the Great	1461–70,	Edward IV	son of Richard, Duke of
925–40	Athelstan	son of Edward I	1471–83		York
940–46	Edmund	half-brother of Athelstan	1483	Edward V	son of Edward IV
946–55	Edred	brother of Edmund	1483–85	Richard III	brother of Edward IV
955–59	Edwy	son of Edmund			
959–75	Edgar	brother of Edwy	**House of Tudor**		
975–78	Edward the Martyr	son of Edgar	1485–1509	Henry VII	son of Edmund Tudor,
978–1016	Ethelred II	son of Edgar			Earl of Richmond
1016	Edmund Ironside	son of Ethelred	1509–47	Henry VIII	son of Henry VII
			1547–53	Edward VI	son of Henry VIII
Danish kings			1553–58	Mary I	daughter of Henry VIII
1016–35	Canute	son of Sweyn I of	1558–1603	Elizabeth I	daughter of Henry VIII
		Denmark, who			
		conquered England in	**House of Stuart**		
		1013	1603–25	James I	great-grandson of
1035–40	Harold I	son of Canute			Margaret (daughter of
1040–42	Hardicanute	son of Canute			Henry VII)
			1625–49	Charles I	son of James I
West Saxon kings (restored)			1649–60	*the Commonwealth*	
1042–66	Edward the Confessor	son of Ethelred II			
1066	Harold II	son of Godwin	**House of Stuart** (restored)		
			1660–85	Charles II	son of Charles I
Norman kings			1685–88	James II	son of Charles I
1066–87	William I	illegitimate son of Duke	1689–1702	William III and Mary	son of Mary (daughter of
		Robert the Devil			Charles I); daughter of
1087–1100	William II	son of William I			James II
1100–35	Henry I	son of William I	1702–14	Anne	daughter of James II
1135–54	Stephen	grandson of William II			
			House of Hanover		
House of Plantagenet			1714–27	George I	son of Sophia (grand-
1154–89	Henry II	son of Matilda (daughter			daughter of James 1)
		of Henry I)	1727–60	George II	son of George I
1189–99	Richard I	son of Henry II	1760–1820	George III	son of Frederick (son of
1199–1216	John	son of Henry II			George II)
1216–72	Henry III	son of John	1820–30	George IV	son of George III
1272–1307	Edward I	son of Henry III		(regent 1811–20)	
1307–27	Edward II	son of Edward I	1830–37	William IV	son of George III
1327–77	Edward III	son of Edward II	1837–1901	Victoria	daughter of Edward (son
1377–99	Richard II	son of Edward the Black			of George III)
		Prince			
			House of Saxe-Coburg		
			1901–10	Edward VII	son of Victoria
House of Lancaster			**House of Windsor**		
1399–1413	Henry IV	son of John of Gaunt	1910–36	George V	son of Edward VII
1413–22	Henry V	son of Henry IV	1936	Edward VIII	son of George V
1422–61,	Henry VI	son of Henry V	1936–52	George VI	son of George V
1470–71			1952–	Elizabeth II	daughter of George VI

own choice. Rhodesia declared itself independent 1965, but Britain declared its action illegal, and no other state recognized it.

By 1973, when Britain entered the EEC, only a few small possessions remained, most of which were proceeding toward independence. Some did not want to end their colonial status. Gibraltar and Hong Kong, for example, felt they risked absorption by Spain and China respectively if Britain withdrew. However, the British Empire as a whole largely faded away, to be replaced by the Commonwealth of Nations.

Employers and Workmen Act act of Parliament 1875 which limited to civil damages the penalty for a breach of contract of employment by a worker. Previously, employees who broke their contracts faced penalties imposed under criminal law.

THE LIGHT OF REASON

Britain and the Enlightenment

British participation in the 18th-century intellectual and political movement known as the Enlightenment is often ignored by historians. This is partly because of the difficulty of defining the term 'Enlightenment' itself. For many writers, the ideas encompassed are so diverse that the term can only be defined by reference to the key works of such French thinkers as Diderot, Montesquieu, Voltaire, and Rousseau.

But the Enlightenment was a Europe-wide phenomenon, and British intellectuals played a major role, from early Enlightenment heroes such as John Locke (1632–1704) and Isaac Newton (1642–1727) to later thinkers like Erasmus Darwin (1731–1802) and Thomas Paine (1737–1809). Moreover, the importance of Enlightenment thought in shaping early 19th-century politics and society in Britain was not much less than in France. In Britain, as in France, the Enlightenment saw the failure of the last attempt of an aristocratic intelligentsia to shape the wider society in which they lived. Quite apart from its intellectual legacy, this social dimension makes the Enlightenment in Britain well worthy of the historian's attention.

Enlightenment ideas

The Enlightenment can best be described as an age of critical, reasoned enquiry into all aspects of human experience. The novelty of such an approach can best be appreciated by reference to European history in the 17th century – which had not only seen Galileo forced by the Inquisition to recant his assertion that the Earth revolved around the Sun 1632, but also the continent-wide horrors of religious wars led by kings, popes, and popular religious leaders, all equally fervent in their belief in divine sanction for their actions. In Britain, the excesses of the Stuart kings on the one hand and their Puritan opponents on the other had convinced many thoughtful observers that the ordering of human society was as much in need of rational examination as was the wider, natural world: reason was thus a goal as well as a method of Enlightenment thinkers.

In France, the characteristic preoccupations of the Enlightenment were despotism, feudalism, and the Roman Catholic church: a reasoned critique led some commentators not only to social radicalism, but also to outright atheism. British thinkers tended to pursue an objective in which utilitarianism, religious faith, and the search for human happiness could combine. As early as 1695, Locke's *The Reasonableness of Christianity* had put the case for a faith stripped of its supernatural aspects, but not abandoned altogether. Most intellectuals and clegy alike shared Locke's view that a rational appreciation of the human situation would lead people to be Christians.

Experience and discovery

Experience, not received wisdom, was seen as the key to knowledge. A meticulous examination of human thought by the Scottish philosopher David Hume (1711–1776) resulted in his *A Treatise of Human Nature* (1739–40). The clearest statement to date of the empiricist view that all knowledge was ultimately derived from sense experience, Hume's *Treatise* exemplified the new, scientific approach. A firm belief that the sum total of empirical knowledge could be increased came to characterize the Enlightenment. Activities as diverse as James Cook's exploration of the Pacific and the historian Edward Gibbon's massively researched *Decline and Fall of the Roman Empire* (1776–88) were rooted in this belief. Some sense of the confidence of the age can be seen in Joseph Priestley's *History of the Present State of Electricity* 1767, in which he claimed that recent discoveries would 'extend the bounds of natural science ... New worlds may open to our view'. Evidence that interest in such discoveries reached far beyond the tiny minority actively involved can be seen in the 18th-century proliferation of scientific clubs and societies and scholarly journals, and even in that most obvious indicator of Britain's highly developed culture of print, the newspaper.

The perfection of society

Such confidence extended to the perfectibility of human society. Disciplines such as economics, jurisprudence, and public administration made great strides during the 18th century. In Britain, this was particularly evident in the so-called Scottish Enlightenment, where a distinctive legal system gave focus to the reconstruction of that country after the Jacobite revolt – but it also threw up politicians such as Edmund Burke (1729–1797) and Thomas Paine, and educationalists like Jeremy Bentham (1748–1832).

The turning point was the French Revolution, in which the opportunity to put into practice the theories of the Enlightenment in a major European society was presented. The ultimate failure of the Revolution, the excesses committed in its name, and the violent opposition it aroused in Britain all served to discredit the Enlightenment social theorists. Some, like Paine, were driven abroad, while others withdrew into literary or artistic activities largely ignored by the middle classes their ideas had once galvanized. At the popular level, the 19th century was to see a revival of evangelistic piety and the rise of social movements rooted in other social classes.

JEREMY BLACK

Employer's Liability Act Act of Parliament 1880, which obtained for workers or their families a right to compensation from employers whose negligence resulted in industrial injury or death at work.

enclosure appropriation of common land as private property, or the changing of open-field systems to enclosed fields (often used for grazing sheep). This process began in the 14th century and became widespread in the 15th and 16th centuries. It caused poverty, homelessness, and rural depopulation, and resulted in revolts 1536, 1569, and 1607.

Numerous government measures to prevent depopulation were introduced 1489–1640, including the first Enclosure Act 1603, but were sabotaged by landowning magistrates at local level. A new wave of enclosures by acts of Parliament 1760–1820 reduced the yeoman class of small landowning farmers to agricultural labourers, or forced them to leave the land. The Enclosure Acts applied to 4.5 million acres or a quarter of England. Some 17 million acres were enclosed without any parliamentary act. From 1876 the enclosure of common land in Britain was limited by statutes. Enclosures occurred throughout Europe on a large scale during the 19th century, often at the behest of governments. The last major Enclosure Act was 1903.

Engagement treaty between Charles I and an alliance of Scottish Royalists and moderate Presbyterians 26 Dec 1647 by which he agreed to abolish Episcopacy and restore Presbyterianism in return for their support against the parliamentarians who had overthrown him. The Scots agreed to control the militia, abolish the army, call a new Parliament, and restore the King by force if necessary. Oliver Cromwell's parliamentarian army smashed the Scottish army at Preston Aug 1648, and the more radical Kirk party gained the ascendancy in Scotland. See also ◊Heads of Proposals.

England largest division of the United Kingdom; the name derives from 'Angle-Land' after the early inhabitants (see ◊Anglo-Saxon).

English language member of the Germanic branch of the Indo-European language family. It is traditionally described as having passed through four major stages over about 1,500 years: *Old English* or *Anglo-Saxon* (*c*. 500–1050), rooted in the dialects of invading settlers (Jutes, Saxons, Angles, and Frisians); *Middle English* (*c*. 1050–1550), influenced by Norman French after the Conquest 1066 and by ecclesiastical Latin; *Early Modern English* (*c*. 1550–1700), including a standardization of the diverse influences of Middle English; and *Late Modern English* (*c*. 1700 onwards), including in particular the development and spread of current Standard English. Through extensive exploration, colonization, and trade, English spread worldwide from the 17th century onwards and remains the most important international language of trade and technology. It is used in many variations, for example, British, American, Canadian, West Indian, Indian, Singaporean, and Nigerian English, and many pidgins and creoles.

English Pale territory in Ireland where English rule operated after the English settlement of Ireland 1171. The area of the Pale varied, but in the mid-14th century it was comprised of the counties of Dublin, Louth, Meath, Trim, Kilkenny, and Kildare. It then gradually shrank until the ◊Plantation of Ireland 1556–1660.

Englishry legal term used to denote those not of Norman stock after the Norman conquest of England 1066. A person's ethnic status would determine, for example, how they were treated by courts: murder cases in which the victim was English were deemed to be less serious than those in which the victim was a Norman. The term also applied to those areas, especially the low-lying areas in the Marches of Wales, where 'English', meaning Anglo-Norman, customs prevailed over Welsh law.

Enlightenment European 18th-century movement towards secular, rational and human views of man and society. It arose in reaction to theological obscurantism, the political influence of the Church, religious intolerance, and harsh legal punishments. It was founded on the scientific discoveries of Isaac Newton and the philosophy of John Locke. Despite these pioneers, however, the Enlightenment played little part in Britain until the late 18th century.

The *Encyclopaedia Britannica* 1768–71 was partly a product of what came to be called the Scottish Enlightenment, as a distinctive intellectual movement. Writers or poets who developed the educational and political ideas of the Enlightenment include William Godwin, Percy

Byshe Shelley, Erasmus Darwin, Mark Akenside, and Maria Edgeworth. William Blake approved of the politics of the Enlightenment, but not its materialism. The American and French revolutions were justified by Enlightenment principles of human natural rights.

Entente Cordiale (French 'friendly understanding') agreement reached by Britain and France 1904 recognizing British interests in Egypt and French interests in Morocco. It formed the basis for Anglo-French cooperation before the outbreak of World War I 1914.

Episcopal Church of Scotland autonomous church in communion with the Church of England formed 1690 by those who refused to accept the victory of Presbyterianism in the Church of Scotland. Its first bishops were consecrated in secret 1705. The church was allowed to practice under the Toleration Act 1712, but only on condition that its adherents foreswore the Jacobite cause. The majority refused and Episcopalian involvement in the 1715 and 1745 Jacobite risings led to renewed persecution.

Eric Bloodaxe d. 954 King of Norway 942–54. He succeeded his father, Harald I Fairhair, 942 and killed seven of his eight half-brothers who had rebelled against him, hence his nickname. He was deposed by his youngest half-brother Haakon 947 and fled to England, where he became ruler of the Norse kingdom of Northumbria 948. He was expelled 954 and killed in battle at Stainmore, Yorkshire (now in Cumbria).

Ermine Street ancient road of Roman origin, or possibly earlier, running from London to York, and by extension to southern Scotland. The name is also applied to the Silchester to Gloucester route. Ermine Street, along with Watling Street, and the Icknield and Fosse Ways, were specially protected by the King's Peace at least from Norman times and probably earlier.

Erskine Thomas, 1st Baron Erskine 1750–1823. British barrister and lord chancellor. He was called to the Bar 1778 and defended a number of parliamentary reformers on charges of sedition. When the Whig Party returned to power 1806 he became lord chancellor and a baron. Among his speeches were those in defence of Lord George Gordon, Thomas Paine, and Queen Caroline.

escheat (Old French *escheir* 'to fall') in feudal society, the reversion of lands to the lord in the event of the tenant dying without heirs or being convicted for treason. By the late Middle Ages in Western Europe, tenants had insured against their lands escheating by granting them to trustees, or feoffees, who would pass them on to the grantor nominated in the will. Lands held directly by the king could not legally be disposed of in this way. In England, royal officials, called escheators, were appointed to safeguard the king's rights.

Essex, kingdom of the ancient kingdom of the East Saxons, hence the name, covering much the same area as the modern county of Essex. It reached its apogee in the 7th century, when it controlled Middlesex and had London as its principal town but by the middle of the 8th century it was dominated by Mercia. The kingdom came under the dominion of Wessex 825, along with Kent and other kingdoms south of London, but by the end of the century it was under Danish control and formed part of the kingdom of East Anglia. Little is known of the ruling family, sometimes not even their names, but they were the only Germanic royal family of this era which did not claim descent from the Norse god Woden

Essex Robert Devereux, 2nd Earl of Essex 1566–1601. English soldier and politician. He became a favourite with Queen Elizabeth I from 1587 after distinguishing himself in fighting in the Spanish Netherlands. He became Lieutenant of Ireland 1599 and led an army against Irish rebels under the Earl of Tyrone in Ulster, but failed to subude them. He made an unauthorized truce with Tyrone, and returned without permission to England. He was forbidden to return to court, and when he marched into the City of London at the head of a body of supporters 1601, he was promptly arrested, tried for treason, and beheaded on Tower Green.

Essex Robert Devereux, 3rd Earl of Essex 1591–1646. English soldier. Eldest son of the 2nd earl, he commanded the Parliamentary army at the inconclusive Civil War battle of Edgehill 1642. Following a disastrous campaign in Cornwall, he resigned his command 1645.

Ethelbert *c.* 552–616. King of Kent 560–616. He was defeated by the West Saxons 568 but later became ruler of all England south of the river Humber. Ethelbert received the Christian missionary Augustine 597 and later converted to become the first Christian ruler of Anglo-Saxon England. He issued the first written code of laws known in England.

I was never proud till you sought to make me too base. And now, since my destiny is no better, my despair shall be like my love was, without repentance.

ROBERT DEVEREAUX,
EARL OF ESSEX
letter to Elizabeth I, 1598

Ethelred I Anglo-Saxon king of Wessex 865–71, son of Ethelwulf and elder brother of ◊Alfred the Great. Together with his brother Alfred he resisted a large-scale invasion of East Anglia 865 by the Danes, defending Mercia and forcing them to abandon Nottingham 868. The Danes established a stronghold in Reading 870 and Ethelred drove them out then defeated them at Ashdown 871. He died of wounds sustained in this battle April 871. Despite some defeats shortly after, Ethelred had paved the way for Wessex to unite England in opposition to the Danes.

Ethelred (II) 'the Unready' *c.* 968–1016. King of England from 978. The son of King Edgar, Ethelred became king after the murder of his half-brother, Edward the Martyr by his mother Elfrida. He tried to buy off the Danish raiders by paying Danegeld. He ordered a massacre of the Danish settlers 1002, provoking an invasion by Sweyn I of Denmark. War with Sweyn and Sweyn's son, Canute, occupied the rest of Ethelred's reign. His nickname 'the Unready' is a corruption of the Old English 'unreed', meaning bad counsel or poorly advised.

Ethelwulf Anglo-Saxon king of Wessex 839–56 and father of Alfred the Great and Ethelred I. Before succeeding his father, Egbert, to the throne of Wessex, Ethelwulf had been sub-king of Kent, Surrey, Sussex, and ◊Essex. He had mixed success against the great Danish armies of the mid-9th century: at first he was defeated at sea 842, but recovered to rout the Danes at Aclea 851. In 855 he made a pilgrimage to Rome and on his return married a Frankish princess. Ethelred succeeded him on his death as Ethelwulf had succeeded his father, and this established the West Saxon tradition of succession from father to son.

European Community former name (to 1993) of the ◊European Union.

European Free Trade Association (EFTA) organization established 1960 consisting of Iceland, Norway, Switzerland, and (from 1991) Liechtenstein, previously a nonvoting associate member. There are no import duties between members. Of the original EFTA members, Britain and Denmark left (1972) to join the European Community (EC), as did Portugal (1985); Austria, Finland, and Sweden joined the EC's successor, the European Union, 1995.

European Parliament the parliament of the European Union, which meets in Strasbourg and Brussels to comment on the legislative proposals of the European Commission. Members are elected for a five-year term. The European Parliament has 626 seats, apportioned on the basis of population, of which Germany has 99; the UK, France, and Italy have 87 each; Spain 64; the Netherlands 31; Belgium, Greece, and Portugal 25 each; Sweden 22; Austria 21; Denmark and Finland 16 each; the Republic of Ireland 15; and Luxembourg 6.

Originally merely consultative, the European Parliament became directly elected 1979, and assumed increased powers. Though still not a true legislative body, it can dismiss the whole Commission and reject the Union budget in its entirety. Full sittings are in Strasbourg; most committees meet in Brussels, and the seat of the secretariat is in Luxembourg.

European Union (also known as the *EU*, *Common Market*, or *European Economic Community (EEC)*) association founded 1957 under the Treaty of Rome which now has 12 member countries – France, Germany, the Netherlands, Belgium, Luxembourg, Italy (the original 6 countries), the UK, Eire, Denmark, Spain, Portugal, and Greece.

On 1 Nov 1993 the ◊Maastricht Treaty on European union came into effect and the new designation European Union was adopted, embracing not only the various bodies of its predecessor, the European Community (EC), but also two intergovernmental 'pillars', covering common foreign and security policy (CFSP) and cooperation on justice and home affairs.

The aims of the EU include the expansion of trade, reduction of competition, the abolition of restrictive trading practices, encouragement of free movement of capital and labour within the alliance, and the establishment of a closer union among European people. A single market with free movement of goods and capital was established Jan 1993.

Britain tried to join the EU 1963 and 1967 but its application for membership was blocked, largely by France under General de Gaulle. Britain finally joined the EU after a fierce debate and a national referendum 1973 and the issue of the extent of involvement with Europe again became a highly charged controversy after the Maastricht Treaty committed the UK to yet closer ties with the EU in the future.

The EU is committed to creating a single community in Europe. This intially meant creating a single market with no tariffs or quotas between countries and since 1992 most remaining trade barriers have been dismantled. In the longer term, the EU is committed to full

This going into Europe will not turn out to be the thrilling mutual exchange supposed. It is more like nine middle-aged couples with failing marriages meeting in a darkened bedroom in a Brussels hotel for a Group Grope.

EUROPEAN
COMMUNITY
historian E P Thompson,
Sunday Times, *1975*

monetary union with a single currency. Much economic policy, particularly monetary policy and exchange rate policy will be decided at a European level. In the even longer term, there may be some sort of political union, with perhaps a European government and a single European army, although this remains a sensitive topic in many member states.

Evangelical Movement a 19th-century group that stressed basic Protestant beliefs and the message of the four Gospels. The movement was associated with the cleric Charles Simeon (1783–1836). It aimed to raise moral enthusiasm and ethical standards among Church of England clergy.

The religious education provided by the Bible Society and William ◊Wilberforce's campaign against the slave trade were both linked to the movement; it also attempted to improve the living conditions of the poor, and Evangelicals carried out missionary work in India.

Evesham, Battle of 4 Aug 1265, during the ◊Barons' Wars, battle in which Edward, Prince of Wales, defeated Simon de Montfort (who was killed). Henry III was subsequently released by the Barons.

excise duty indirect tax levied on certain goods produced within a country, such as petrol, alcohol, and tobacco. Excise duty was first levied in Britain 1643 to pay for the army during the Civil War. It is collected by the government's Customs and Excise department.

Exclusion Bills series of measures in the reigns of Charles I and II attempting to exclude Catholics from office. The first bill, proposed June 1641, aimed to exclude bishops from sitting in parliament in order to weaken Charles I's support in the House of Lords. The measure was initially rejected by the Lords, but after Charles's attempt to arrest the ◊five members it was re-introduced, becoming law Feb 1642.

From 1678–81 a series of measures were proposed during the Exclusion Crisis which were designed to bar Charles II's Catholic brother, James, Duke of York, from the throne. A bill was introduced in the aftermath of the Popish Plot to ensure the succession of Charles' illegitimate son, the Duke of Monmouth and Charles dissolved Parliament to prevent the bill's passage. A similar measure was introduced 1680 but was rejected by the House of Lords. Charles summoned the next parliament to Oxford, but another exclusion bill was put forward 1681 and Charles again dissolved Parliament.

eyre one of the travelling courts set up by Henry II 1176 to enforce conformity to the king's will; they continued into the 13th century. *Justices in eyre* were the judges who heard pleas at these courts. They were gradually superseded by ◊assizes.

If his Majesty come by any violent death, it shall be revenged to the utmost upon all Papists.

EXCLUSION BILLS
resolution of the House of Commons, 1679

Fabian Society socialist organization for research, discussion, and publication, founded in London 1884. Its name is derived from the Roman commander Fabius Maximus, and refers to the evolutionary methods by which it hopes to attain socialism by a succession of gradual reforms as opposed to revolution. Its membership largely consisted of middle class intellectuals and early members included the playwright George Bernard Shaw and Beatrice and Sidney Webb. The society helped to found the Labour Representation Committee 1900, which became the Labour Party 1906.

factory acts legislation such as the Health and Safety at Work Act 1974, which govern conditions of work, hours of labour, safety, and sanitary provision in factories and workshops.

In the 19th century legislation was progressively introduced to regulate conditions

Factory Acts
A series of Factory Acts passed in the 19th century established basic rights for workers primarily in the textile industry. Many of the great Lancashire cotton mills preferred to employ women and children because of their greater manual dexterity and the legislation provided the first legal protection for child workers.
Image Select

Factory Acts in the UK: chronology

1802	Health and Morals of Apprentices Act, a first attempt to regulate conditions for workhouse children in the textile industry.
1819	Factory Act prohibited children under nine working in cotton mills. Others were set an 11-hour maximum day.
1833	Althorp's Factory Act further limited working hours for children in textile factories. Four factory inspectors appointed.
1842	Mines Act prohibited employment of women and children under ten underground. Factory Act reduced hours for children and youths in textile factories.
1847	Factory Act imposed maximum ten-hour day for women and young people in textile factories. Subsequent 1850 Act specified hours as between 6 a.m. and 6 p.m.
1853	Shift work for children outlawed.
1864 and 1867	Factory Acts extended existing provisions to industries other than textiles and mines, and finally to all places employing over 50 people.
1878	Regulation of conditions in workshops, extended 1891.
1901	Minimum working age increased to 12. Trade Boards established to fix minimum wages, extended 1918.
1909	First Old Age Pensions Act gave five shillings per week to those over 70 with annual incomes less than 31 10 shillings.
1911	National Insurance Act covered sickness and unemployment in vulnerable trades.
1931	'Means-tested' unemployment benefit introduced.
1937	Factory Act limited workers under 16 to a 44-hour week and women to a 48-hour week. New safety regulations introduced.
1946	National Insurance Act provided comprehensive cover for industrial injuries.
1961	Factories Act extended safety regulations to all workplaces. Graduated pension scheme introduced.
1965	Graduated redundancy payments introduced.
1974	Health and Safety at Work legislation extended to cover all workers. Provisions applied to off-shore oil and gas workers from 1975.

of work, hours of labour, safety, and sanitary provisions in factories and workshops. The first legislation was the Health and Morals of Apprentices Act 1802 which restricted the employment of apprentices to 12 hours a day.

Lord ◊Shaftesbury's Factory Act 1833 prohibited the employment of children under the age of nine and introduced the first factory inspectors. The Mines Act 1842 prohibited the employment of women and boys under the age of thriteen in the mines. Legislation was extended to offices, shops, and railway premises 1963 and all employees are now covered by the 1974 Act, which is enforced by the Health and Safety Executive.

Fairfax Thomas, 3rd Baron Fairfax of Cameron 1612–1671. English general, commander in chief of the Parliamentary army in the Civil War. With Oliver Cromwell 1645 he formed the ◊New Model Army and defeated Charles I at Naseby. He opposed the king's execution, resigned in protest 1650 against the invasion of Scotland, and participated in the restoration of Charles II after Cromwell's death.

fairs in the middle ages, large scale gatherings combining trade with sideshows and other entertainment. Unlike markets which were usually weekly and local, fairs took place only once or twice a year and so attracted commercial buyers from great distances. Many now survive as civic festivals, such as Nottingham's Goose Fair or Oxford's St Giles' Fair, but modern trade fairs, such as the Farnborough Air Show, maintain the tradition.

Falaise, treaty of 1174 treatybetween King William I of Scotland and Henry II of England under which William became Henry's vassal. William had been captured at Alnwick during an invasion of England and was imprisoned in Normandy until he and the Scottish nobility agreed to swear loyalty to Henry.

Falkirk, Battle of 22 July 1298 battle at Falkirk, 37 km/23 mi west of Edinburgh at which ◊Edward I of England defeated the Scots. Sir William ◊Wallace faced the English in open battle, but his cavalry fled and his spearmen were outmatched by the English archers. The battle led to Wallace's fall from power.

Falkland Lucius Cary, 2nd Viscount *c.* 1610–1643. English soldier and politician. He was elected to the ◊Long Parliament 1640 and tried hard to secure a compromise peace between Royalists and Parliamentarians. He was Charles I's secretary of state from 1642 and was killed at the Battle of Newbury in the Civil War. The Falkland Islands are named after him.

Falkland Islands, Battle of the in World War I, British naval victory (under Admiral Sir Frederick Sturdee) over German forces under Admiral Maximilian von Spee 8 Dec 1914.

Von Spee intended to bombard the Falklands in passing before proceeding around the Cape of Good Hope to arouse the disaffected Boers of South Africa. However, there was already a British force stationed off the Falklands and when von Spee realised he had run into a trap he fled the area. The British gave chase and in the ensuing battle von Spee's squadron was entirely destroyed with a loss of 2,100 crew.

Falklands War dispute between Argentina and Britain over sovereignty of the Falkland Islands initiated when Argentina invaded and occupied the islands 2 April 1982. On the following day, the United Nations Security Council passed a resolution calling for Argentina to withdraw. A British task force was immediately dispatched and, after a fierce conflict in which more than 1,000 Argentine and British lives were lost, 12,000 Argentine troops surrendered and the islands were returned to British rule 14–15 June 1982. The Falklands War cost £1.6 billion and involved 15,000 British military personnel.

It has been argued that the war did much to restore prime minister Margaret ◊Thatcher's popularity, waning at the time due to the effects of the recession.

In April 1990 Argentina's congress declared the Falkland Islands and other British-held South Atlantic islands part of the new Argentine province of Tierra del Fuego.

Fairs
Fairs in medieval and early modern Britain combined the functions of today's trade fairs and popular holiday entertainments. This is a so-called frost fair, held on the frozen river Thames in the winter of 1683–84
Philip Sauvain

This has been a pimple on the ass of progress festering for two hundred years, and I guess someone decided to lance it.

FALKLANDS WAR
US general and politician Alexander Haig, referring to the outbreak of war.
Sunday Times, *1982*

family planning natural or artificial methods of controlling the numbers of children in a family became a matter of public discussion only in the late 19th and 20th centuries, although English philosopher Jeremy Bentham first put forward the idea of birth control 1797. Condoms became available in barbers shops from the 1890s and in 1910 the first contraceptive advertisement appeared in a chemist's trade journal. In 1918 Marie Stopes published *Married Love*, which was a landmark in the discussion of the issues. She opened a clinic in London 1921, which amalgamated with other clinics opened subsequently to form the charitable Family Planning Association 1930. In 1966 it ceased to distinguish between married and single clients, and in 1972 it was taken over by the National Health Service.

Faraday Michael 1791–1867. English chemist and physicist. In 1821 he began experimenting with electromagnetism, and ten years later discovered the induction of electric currents and made the first dynamo. He subsequently found that a magnetic field will rotate the plane of polarization of light. Faraday produced the basic laws of electrolysis 1834.

farthing formerly the smallest English coin, a quarter of a penny. It was introduced as a silver coin in Edward I's reign. The copper farthing became widespread in Charles II's reign, and the bronze 1860. It was dropped from use 1961.

Fashoda Incident dispute 1898 in the town of Fashoda (now Kodok) situated on the White Nile in southeast Sudan, in which a clash between French and British forces nearly led the two countries into war.

British troops under Lord Kitchener encountered a French force under Colonel Marchand which had reached the Nile after an 18-month expedition. The British were in the process of retaking the Sudan and refused to recognize any French claim to the region and for a time the incident came close to precipitating a full-scale war. However, the French were not prepared for war and Marchand's attitude allowed discussion to take place and a political solution to be found. The incident marked a turning point in Anglo-French relations which led ultimately to the ◊Entente Cordiale 1904.

Fastolf Sir John *c.* 1378–1459. English soldier who gave his name to Shakespeare's character Falstaff in *Henry IV Parts I–II* 1597 and *The Merry Wives of Windsor* 1600. In these plays he appears as a cowardly figure of fun, but the real Fastolf was a brave soldier. He fought with distinction at ◊Agincourt 1415 and in other battles of the Hundred Years' War. He apparently deserted Talbot, however, at the Battle of Patay 1429 but he seems subsequently to have retained his honours and it is possible the story has been exaggerated by a hostile source.

Faulkner Brian 1921–1977. Northern Ireland Unionist politician. He was the last prime minister of Northern Ireland 1971–72 before the Stormont Parliament was suspended.

Fawcett Millicent Garrett 1847–1929. English suffragette, younger sister of Elizabeth Garrett ◊Anderson. A non-militant, she rejected the violent acts of some of her contemporaries in the suffrage movement. She joined the first Women's Suffrage Committee 1867 and became president of the Women's Unionist Association 1889. She was also active in property reform and campaigned for the right of married women to own their own property.

Fawkes Guy 1570–1606. English conspirator in the ◊Gunpowder Plot to blow up King James I and the members of both Houses of Parliament. Fawkes, a Roman Catholic convert, was arrested in the cellar underneath the House 4 Nov 1605, tortured, and executed. The event is still commemorated in Britain and elsewhere every 5 Nov with bonfires, fireworks, and the burning of the 'guy', an effigy.

A desperate disease requires a desperate remedy.

GUY FAWKES
justification of the Gunpowder Plot. (attributed)

fealty in feudalism, the loyalty and duties owed by a vassal to his lord. In the 9th century fealty obliged the vassal not to take part in any action that would endanger the lord or his property, but by the 11th century the specific duties of fealty were established and included financial obligations and military service. Following an oath of fealty, an act of allegiance and respect (homage) was made by the vassal; when a ◊fief was granted by the lord, it was formalized in the process of investiture.

Federated Malay States former British protectorate, at the southern end of the Malay Peninsula. The four states Pahang, Perak, Selangor, and Negri Sembilan entered treaties from 1874 (Perak then, the others later) providing for their protection by the British government.

They were united as a federation 1895. They joined the Federation of Malaya 1948, and this became an independent country within the British Commonwealth 1957. Malaya was joined by Singapore, Sabah (formerly British North Borneo), and Sarawak to form the Federation of Malaysia 1963. (Singapore seceded 1965.)

Fenian movement Irish-American republican secret society, founded 1858 in New York and named after the ancient Irish legendary warrior band of the Fianna. The collapse of the movement began when an attempt to establish an independent Irish republic by an uprising in Ireland 1867 failed, as did raids into Canada 1866 and 1870. However, attacks on the English mainland 1867, on Chester and Clerkenwell jail, alerted Galdstone to the seriousness of the Irish problem.

Fens, the level, low-lying tracts of land in eastern England, west and south of the Wash, about 115 km/70 mi north–south and 55 km/34 mi east–west. They fall within the counties of Lincolnshire, Cambridgeshire, and Norfolk, consisting of a huge area, formerly a bay of the North Sea, but now crossed by numerous drainage canals and forming some of the most productive agricultural land in Britain. The peat portion of the Fens is known as the ***Bedford Level***.

The first attempts at drainage were made by the Romans. After the Norman conquest an earthwork 100 km/60 mi long was constructed as a barrage against the sea. In 1634 the 4th Earl of Bedford brought over the Dutch water-engineer Cornelius Vermuyden (*c.* 1596–1683) who introduced Dutch methods.

feorm in Anglo-Saxon times, food rent payable annually to a king and his retinue by a particular group of villages. It consisted of a supply of provisions sufficient for 24 hours, and typically comprised cattle, poultry, cheese, corn, loaves and ale. The Old English word *feorm* is a forerunner of the modern 'farm'.

Festival of Britain artistic and cultural festival held in London May–Sept 1951 both to commemorate the 100th anniversary of the Great Exhibition and to boost morale after years of postwar austerity. The South Bank of the Thames formed the focal point of the event and the Royal Festival Hall built specially for the festival is a reminder of the modernist style of architecture promoted at the time.

feudalism (Latin *feudem* 'fief', coined 1839) the main form of social organization in medieval Europe. A system based primarily on land, it involved a hierarchy of authority, rights, and power that extended from the monarch downwards. An intricate network of duties and obligations linked royalty, nobility, lesser gentry, free tenants, villeins, and serfs. Feudalism

We are the Fenian Brotherhood, /skilled in the arts of war, /And we're going to fight for Ireland, /the land that we adore.

FENIAN MOVEMENT
'Song of the Fenian Brotherhood'
anonymous, 19th century

was reinforced by a complex legal system and supported by the Christian church. With the growth of commerce and industry from the 13th century, feudalism gradually gave way to the class system as the dominant form of social ranking.

In return for military service the monarch allowed powerful vassals to hold land, and often also to administer justice and levy taxes. They in turn 'sublet' such rights. At the bottom of the system were the serfs, who worked on their lord's manor lands in return for being allowed to cultivate some for themselves, and so underpinned the system. They could not be sold as if they were slaves, but they could not leave the estate to live or work elsewhere without permission. The system declined from the 13th century, partly because of the growth of a money economy, with commerce, trade, and industry, and partly because of the many peasants' revolts 1350–1550. Serfdom ended in England in the 16th century, but lasted in France until 1789 and in the rest of Western Europe until the early 19th century. In Russia it continued until 1861.

Fianna Fáil (Gaelic 'Soldiers of Destiny') Republic of Ireland political party, founded by the Irish nationalist de Valera 1926. It was the governing party in the Republic of Ireland 1932–48, 1951–54, 1957–73, 1977–81, 1982, and 1987–94 (from 1993 in coalition with Labour). It aims at the establishment of a united and completely independent all-Ireland republic.

Fidei Defensor (Latin for ◊Defender of the Faith), one of the titles of the British sovereign, conferred by Pope Leo X on Henry VIII 1521 to reward his writing of a treatise against the Protestant Martin Luther.

fief or ***fiefdom*** state of lands granted to a ◊vassal by his lord after the former had sworn homage, or ◊fealty, promising to serve the lord. As a noble tenure, it carried with it rights of jurisdiction. In the later Middle Ages, it could also refer to a grant of money, given in return for service, as part of bastard feudalism.

Field of the Cloth of Gold site between Guînes and Ardres near Calais, France, where a meeting took place between Henry VIII of England and Francis I of France in June 1520, remarkable for the lavish clothes worn and tent pavilions erected. Francis hoped to gain England's support in opposing the Holy Roman emperor, Charles V, but failed.

Fifteen, the ◊Jacobite rebellion of 1715, led by the 'Old Pretender' ◊James Edward Stuart and the Earl of Mar, in order to place the former on the English throne. Mar was defeated at Sheriffmuir, Scotland, by a force of Loyalist Scots under the Duke of Argyll and the revolt collapsed.

Fifth Monarchy Men 17th century millenarian sect, particularly strong in Wales, which believed that the rule of Christ and his saints was imminent. The sect's name derives from a prophesy in the Book of Daniel that four ancient monarchies (Assyrian, Persian, Macedonian, and Roman) would precede Christ's return. The movement thrived during the ◊interregnum of the 1650s and originally supported Oliver Cromwell until his increasing role seemed at odds with their principals. Subsequently they were persecuted and, despite an abortive rising in London Jan 1661, they disappeared with the Restoration.

Fiji Islands former British colony, an island group in the southwest Pacific. The islands were discovered by Tasman 1643 and visited by Cook 1774. They were offered to Britain 1858 by their native ruler when he was pressed by the United States to grant them possession, and were annexed by Britain 1874. They gained independence 1970.

Finn Mac Cumhaill or ***Finn McCool*** legendary Irish hero, identified with a general who organized an Irish regular army in the 3rd century. The Scottish writer James Macpherson featured him (as Fingal) and his followers in the verse of his popular epics 1762–63, which were supposedly written by a 3rd-century bard called Ossian.

Fire of London 2–5 Sept 1666 fire that destroyed four fifths of the City of London. It broke out in a bakery in Pudding Lane and spread as far west as the Temple. It destroyed 87 churches, including St Paul's Cathedral, and 13,200 houses, although fewer than 20 people lost their lives.

In the aftermath of the fire, Sir Christopher Wren put forward a plan to rebuild the old city along more rational lines. This was not adopted but the new St Paul's Cathedral and 51 new churches were built.

Fire of London
The Fire of London 1666
– this contemporary
engraving shows the
devastation of the city as
viewed from the safety
of Southwark. Less than
20 people were killed in
the fire, but the
destruction of over
13,000 homes caused
widespread misery.
Philip Sauvain

first fruits and tenths a form of tax on clergy taking up a benefice. They had to pay a portion of their first year's income (known as annates) and a tenth of their revenue annually thereafter. Originally the money was paid to the papacy, but Henry VIII's Annates Act 1532 diverted the money to the Crown as part of his campaign to pressure the pope into granting him a divorce. Thomas Cromwell set up a special financial administration for these revenues and they later passed under the control of the ◊Exchequer. During the 18th century, these payments formed the basis of ◊Queen Anne's Bounty.

Fishbourne Palace a magnificent Romano-British villa, near Colchester in Essex, dating from the 1st century AD. It may have been built for the Roman client king, Tiberius Claudius Cogidubnus who ruled in that area. Originally a Roman supply centre, a palace was built with gardens and baths around AD 60 and about 15 years later, a larger complex was erected, extending well over 10 acres and centred on a large quadrangle with gardens. There were reception rooms, guest suites to the east and north, with the main living quarters looking south over the sea. It was destroyed by fire in the 3rd century.

Fisher John Arbuthnot, 1st Baron Fisher 1841–1920. British admiral, First Sea Lord 1904–10, when he carried out many radical reforms and innovations, including the introduction of destroyers 1893 and the dreadnought battleship 1906.

He served in the Crimean War 1855 and the China War 1859–60. He held various commands before becoming First Sea Lord, and returned to the post 1914, but resigned the following year, disagreeing with Winston Churchill over sending more ships to the Dardanelles, Turkey, in World War I.

Fisher John, St *c.* 1469–1535. English cleric, created bishop of Rochester 1504. He was an enthusiastic supporter of the revival in the study of Greek, and a friend of the humanists Thomas More and Desiderius Erasmus. In 1535 he was tried on a charge of denying the royal supremacy of Henry VIII and beheaded.

Fitzgerald Gerald, 8th Earl of Kildare d. 1513. Anglo-Irish nobleman. He was Lord Deputy of Ireland 1481–94, 1496–1513, and a supporter of the Yorkist cause in England. He was deprived of the deputyship 1494 for supporting the pretender Perkin Warbeck against Henry VII but was pardoned and reinstated two years later. He went on to prove his loyalty to Henry, defeating southern Irish chieftains at Knockdoe 1505, but died of wounds sustained during further campaigns against Gaelic chiefs.

Fitzgerald Gerald, 15th Earl of Desmond d. 1583. Anglo-Irish magnate. He resisted the extension of English authority over his territories in southwest Ireland in the ◊Desmond revolt 1579 but was defeated and killed 1583. After his death 1583 his vast estates went to English settlers.

Fitzgerald Thomas, Baron Offaly and 10th Earl of Kildare 1513–1537. Anglo-Irish nobleman, the son of Gerald Fitzgerald, 9th Earl of Kildare. On his father's imprisonment and death in England 1534 he rebelled against Henry VIII. He attacked Dublin Castle but was defeated, captured and executed, despite a guarantee of his personal safety from the English. His death ended the power of the house of Kildare.

FitzGerald Garret 1926– . Irish politician. As *Taoiseach* (prime minister) 1981–82 and again 1982–86, he was noted for his attempts to solve the Northern Ireland dispute, ultimately by

This fatal night about ten, began that deplorable fire near Fish Street in London... all the sky were of a fiery aspect, like the top of a burning oven, and the light seen above 40 miles round about for many nights.

FIRE OF LONDON
John Evelyn, Diary,
23 September 1666

participating in the Anglo-Irish agreement 1985. He tried to remove some of the overtly Catholic features of the constitution to make the Republic more attractive to Northern Protestants. He retired as leader of the Fine Gael Party 1987.

Fitzherbert Maria Anne 1756–1837. Wife of the Prince of Wales, later George IV. She became Mrs Fitzherbert by her second marriage 1778 and, after her husband's death 1781, entered London society. She secretly married the Prince of Wales 1785 and finally parted from him 1803.

five articles of Perth reforms imposed on the Kirk (Scottish church) 1618 by James VI in an attempt to bring it into line with the English church. The articles were ratified by the Scots Parliament 1621 despite vehement opposition from some Protestant elements who regarded them as an attempt to make the Scottish church more Catholic; they were rejected by the General Assembly of the Kirk 1638. The measures mainly concerned matters of order and reverence, such as kneeling when receiving communion, observance of Christmas and Easter, communion for the dying, and infant baptism and confirmation.

Five Boroughs five East Midlands towns of Leicester, Lincoln, Derby, Stamford, and Nottingham. They were settled by Danish soldiers in the 9th and 10th centuries, and formed an independent confederation within the ◊Danelaw. Their laws contained the first provision in England for a jury to find someone guilty by a majority verdict.

five members five prominent members of parliament who Charles I tried to have arrested 4 Jan 1642 for alleged treason. Charles tried to persuade the Lords to arrest the five – John Hampden, Sir Arthur Haselrig, Baron Holles, William Strode, and John Pym – on charges of treason for their negotiations with the Scots and a perceived threat to his Catholic queen, Henrietta Maria. When the Lords refused to comply, the king came to the Commons himself with 400 armed men but the members were forewarned and escaped by river to the City of London, where they were received as heroes rather than traitors. The whole affair increased the perception that Charles was not to be trusted and led to the exclusion of bishops from the House of Lords.

Five Mile Act act of 1665 forbidding dissenting clergy from coming within five miles of their former parishes or of any large towns, unless they swore an oath of nonresistance. The act, part of the post-Restoration attempt to entrench Anglicanism, also tried to prevent dissenters from becoming teachers. Most of the act's effects were repealed by 1689 but it was not formally abolished until 1812.

Flanders, Battle of in World War I, collective term for the series of actions as the British advanced into Belgium and northern France Sept–Nov 1918, driving the Germans out of the Benelux area and back into Germany itself. The battle is normally referred to as the battles of the Yser and ◊Ypres.

The overall plan conceived by the British commander Field Marshal Douglas Haig was to develop a series of attacks along the entire length of the British front from Dixmude to the Ypres salient. A massive Army Group consisting of French, Belgian, and British armies was assembled under the Belgian King Albert and the assault began 28 Sept 1918. By 1 Oct, the Allies had advanced 13 km/8 mi and taken the major German defensive lines. The Allies consolidated and reorganized for two weeks then continued their advance, reaching the Dutch frontier 20 Oct. They then began pushing the Germans east back into Germany itself and by 11 Nov had linked up with Haig's main group.

Fleet prison royal prison in the City of London dating from the 12th century. It originally received prisoners committed by the ◊Star Chamber, an off-shoot of the king's council,   and was later used to house debtors until it was closed 1842. It was pulled down two years later.

Fleet Street street in the City of London (named after the subterranean river Fleet), traditionally the centre of British journalism. It runs from Temple Bar eastwards to Ludgate Circus. With adjoining streets it contained the offices and printing works of many leading British newspapers until the mid-1980s, when most moved to sites farther from the centre of London. The last remaining major national news-gathering agency in the area, the Press Association, left Fleet Street for new offices in Vauxhall Aug 1995, and the street now has only historic connections with journalism.

Fleming Alexander 1881–1955. Scottish bacteriologist who discovered the first antibiotic drug, penicillin, 1928. In 1922 he had discovered lysozyme, an antibacterial enzyme present in saliva, nasal secretions, and tears. While studying this, he found an unusual mould growing on a neglected culture dish, which he isolated and grew into a pure culture; this led to his discovery of penicillin which first came into use 1941. In 1945 he won the Nobel Prize for Physiology or Medicine with Howard W Florey and Ernst B Chain, whose research had brought widespread realization of the value of penicillin.

Fletcher Andrew of Saltoun 1653–1716. Scottish patriot, the most outspoken critic of the Union of Scotland with England of 1707. He advocated an independent Scotland, and a republic or limited monarchy, and proposed 'limitations' to the treaty, such as annual Parliaments. After the Treaty of Union he retired to private life.

flight of the earls the voluntary exile in continental Europe 1607 of Hugh ◊O'Neill, Rory ◊O'Donnell, and more than 90 other Ulster chiefs following a failed attempt to expel the English from Ireland.

Flodden, Battle of defeat of an invading Scots army by the English under the Earl of Surrey 9 Sept 1513 on a site, 5 km/3 mi southeast of Coldstream, in Northumberland. The Scots had taken advantage of Henry VIII's absence campaiging in France to launch an invasion of England but were heavily defeated. The English lost 1,500 casualties, while the Scots lost 10,000, including King James IV.

florin old British coin worth two shillings. The florin was first struck 1849, initially of silver, and continued in use after decimalization as the equivalent of the ten-pence piece until 1992.

Many European countries have had coins of this name. The first florin was of gold, minted in Florence in 1252. The obverse bore the image of a lily, which led to the coin being called *fiorino* (from Italian *fiore*, flower).

foederati in the late Roman Empire, trusted native tribes which defended coasts or frontiers from further incursions as Imperial authority receded. *Foederati* were established in Britain in the 4th century AD, for example the Damnonii of southern Scotland who seem to have entered into an alliance with the Romans in the reign of Theodosius. Gildas and Bede record that in the mid-5th century AD Vortigern invited the Anglo-Saxons to settle in Kent to defend the coastline.

Foliot Gilbert d. 1187. English cleric. He was Bishop of Hereford 1147–63 and of London 1163–87. He was an enemy of Becket, who excommunicated him 1167, 1169, and again 1170 for officiating at the crowning of Henry II's young son, Henry (1155–1183). Following Becket's death 1170, Foliot was largely rehabilitated and continued to serve as an adviser to Henry II.

folly building with little or no practical purpose built as a curiosity or to catch the eye, popular in the 18th and 19th centuries. A sign of superfluous wealth, many examples take the form of ruined castles and were influenced by the Gothic revival.

food-rent in Anglo-Saxon England, the requirement of royal manors to provide provisions for the king's household. The system is recorded in Domesday as a form of payment in kind in the absence of any real system of economic exchange, but over the course of time these duties were transferred to nobles or commuted into a financial payment.

Foot Michael 1913– . British Labour politician and writer. A leader of the left-wing Tribune Group, he was secretary of state for employment 1974–76, Lord President of the Council and leader of the House 1976–79, and succeeded James Callaghan as Labour Party leader 1980–83. In 1995, he was wrongly accused by the *Sunday Times* of having been a KGB 'agent of influence' and he successfully sued both the paper and its editor.

football or *soccer* form of football originating in the UK, popular throughout Europe and Latin America.

The game is played by two teams of 11 players each with an inflated spherical ball. The object of the game is to knock the ball into the opposing teams' goal: players control the ball primarily with their feet, but also using their heads and occasionally the chest. Only one player on each side, the goalkeeper, is allowed to touch the ball with the hands and then only in an assigned penalty area.

The game has existed in many forms for centuries: a game resembling football, called *Tzu Chu*, was played in China as early as 500 BC and a simliar game was known to the ancient Greeks and Romans. In Britain, football was initially played largely according to local custom rather than any fixed set of rules, and could involve any number of players. Football was banned in England and Scotland at various times in the Middle Ages as the huge unstructured games, sometimes involving entire villages as opposing 'teams', became so unruly and violent as to be a serious threat to public order and, during the Hundred Years' War, because it was feared it would distract young men from archery practice.

The game's rules were first codified 1863 by the Football Association which is still the sport's ruling body in the UK. The FA Cup competition began 1872 and the FA allowed professional players from 1885. The Football League was founded 1888, at first consisting of 12 teams who played each other twice a season. In 1991, 22 of the top English clubs broke away from the Football League to form a new 'Premier League' which came into effect at the start of the 1992–93 season.

The first international football match was played between England and Scotland 1872 and the game quickly became popular across Europe in the latter half of the 19th century, leading to the formation of the world governing body, Fédération Internationale de Football Association (FIFA) 1904. FIFA organizes the competitions for the World Cup, held every four years since 1930. England won the World Cup 1966, the year they hosted the competition, beating Germany 4–2 in the final. The following year, Glasgow Celtic became the first British club to win the premier European club competition, the European Champions' Club.

forced loans the right of the Crown to demand money from its subjects without seeking the approval of Parliament, especially in times of war. These were technically loans to be repaid and guaranteed with a receipt under the Privy Seal, unlike a benevolence, which was ostensibly a free gift. The practice appears to have started under Henry VII who did repay the money, but from the time of Henry VIII subsequent parliaments were used to cancel the debt. The loans of 1522–23 were converted by statute into gifts, and the last loan made to Elizabeth I was never repaid by her successor, James I.

Opposition to the practice grew in the reign of the Stuarts, by which time it had become little better than legalized extortion. Charles I raised such a loan after Parliament refused to finance his foreign policy 1626 and several prominent nobles who refused to pay were arrested. The Five Knights' Case which resulted upheld the king's power to imprison at will. The uproar over Charles' behaviour led to the Petition of Right 1628, which demanded the king halt arbitrary arrests and not raise taxes without parliamentary consent. Forced loans were declared illegal 1689.

forest laws draconian legislation enacted mainly during the century following the Norman Conquest which prohibited common or agricultural use of land deemed to be royal hunting grounds and placed all game in such land under royal protection. Infringement of an order protecting royal forests was severely punished, with harsh penalties including mutilation and even death. It was not even necessary for the land to be wooded and so by the early 13th century almost one third of England was subject to such laws.

The laws became increasingly unpopular during the 12th century, and the Magna Carta 1215 mitigated some of the grievances. The scope of the laws was severely limited by a Charter of the Forest 1217 which specifically limited the areas designated as forest and replaced the harsher penalties with fines. The legislation continued to be enforced up until the time of the Glorious Revolution 1688: under Elizabeth and the first two Stuarts, technical infringements were used as a means to raise revenue. The laws were not finally abolished until 1817.

forfeiture confiscation of an outlaw's property, usually divided between the crown and the criminal's lord. In cases of treason all property went to the crown, but in most cases the crim-

Footeball... causeth fighting, brawling, contention, quarrel picking, murder, homicide and great effusion of bloode...

FOOTBALL
Puritan pamphleteer Philip Stubbes, Anatomie of Abuses, *1583*

inal's land would go to his lord and his chattels to the crown. In the case of great lords, however, a portion of the confiscated lands would usually be restored to the heirs to avoid creating a potentially dangerous resentful family. Forfeiture was much used by Parliament during the Civil War, and a special Commission for Forfeited Estates was set up after the Scottish rebellions of 1715 and 1745.

Forster William Edward 1818–1886. British Liberal reformer. In Gladstone's government 1868–74 he was vice president of the council, and secured the passing of the Education Act 1870, which made elementary education available to all children between the ages of 5 and 13 in England and Wales, and the Ballot Act 1872. He was chief secretary for Ireland 1880–82.

Forty-Five, the ◊Jacobite rebellion 1745, led by Prince ◊Charles Edward Stuart. With his army of Highlanders 'Bonnie Prince Charlie' occupied Edinburgh and advanced into England as far as Derby, but then turned back. The rising was crushed by the Duke of Cumberland at the Battle of ◊Culloden 1746.

Fosse Way Roman road running from Axmouth, Devon, to Lincoln, via Ilchester, Bath, and Cirencester. The road was probably constructed *c*. AD 47, when it marked the northern limit of Roman expansion and together with ◊Ermine Street was a crucial part of the Roman communication and transport system, enabling legions and goods to be transferred quickly across the country. Its name derives from the adjacent ditches, known as 'fosses'.

Fourth Party group of radical Tory activists within the Conservative Party 1880–85. Led by Lord Randolph ◊Churchill, they campaigned for 'Tory democracy': reform within the Conservative Party and stronger opposition to Gladstone's second administration. Arthur ◊Balfour was another prominent member of the group which applied the techniques of parliamentary disruption pioneered by Irish nationalists.

Fox Charles James 1749–1806. English Whig politician, son of the 1st Baron Holland. He entered Parliament 1769 as a supporter of the court, but went over to the opposition 1774. As secretary of state 1782, leader of the opposition to Pitt, and foreign secretary 1806, he welcomed the French Revolution and brought about the abolition of the slave trade.

He became secretary of state in Rockingham's government 1782, but resigned when Shelburne succeeded Rockingham. He allied with North 1783 to overthrow Shelburne, and formed a coalition ministry with himself as secretary of state. When the Lords threw out Fox's bill to reform the government of India, George III replaced him with Pitt. Fox now became leader of the opposition, although cooperating with Pitt in the impeachment of Warren Hastings, the governor general of India.

The 'Old Whigs' deserted to the government 1792 over the French Revolution, leaving Fox and a small group of 'New Whigs' to oppose Pitt's war of intervention and his persecution of the reformers. On Pitt's death 1806 Fox joined a new ministry as foreign secretary and was instrumental in bringing about the abolition of the slave trade. He opened peace negotiations with France, but died before their completion.

Fox George 1624–1691. English founder of the Society of ◊Friends. After developing his belief in a mystical 'inner light', he became a travelling preacher 1647, and in 1650 was imprisoned for blasphemy at Derby, where the term Quakers was first applied derogatorily to him and his followers, supposedly because he enjoined Judge Bennet to 'quake at the word of the Lord'.

franchise in politics, the eligibility, right, or privilege to vote at public elections, especially for the members of a legislative body, or parliament. The term derives from the medieval ◊frankpledge, the body of freemen in a manor and their rights and duties. The right to vote intially depended on how much property a freeman owned until the Reform Act 1832 extended the franchise to all householders rated at £10 a year or over. It was 1918 before all

Fox
Radical English Whig politician Charles James Fox. Among the many liberal causes he advocated were the extension of suffrage to 'educated' women and the abolition of slavery.
Image Select

O Oliver, hadst thou been faithful... the King of France should have bowed his neck under thee, the Pope should have withered as in winter, the Turk in all his fatness would have smoked.

GEORGE FOX
addressing Oliver Cromwell, 1675

British men had the right to vote, and 1928 before women were enfranchised; in New Zealand women were granted the right as early as 1893. In the UK today all adult citizens are eligible to vote from the age of 18, with the exclusion of peers, the insane, and criminals.

Franciscan order Catholic order of friars, **_Friars Minor_** or **_Grey Friars_**, founded 1209 by Francis of Assisi. Subdivisions were the strict Observants; the Conventuals, who were allowed to own property corporately; and the Capuchins, founded 1529.

The Franciscan order included such scholars as the English scientist Roger Bacon. A female order, the **_Poor Clares_**, was founded by St Clare 1215, and lay people who adopt a Franciscan regime without abandoning the world form a third order, **_Tertiaries_**.

frankpledge medieval legal term for a local unit based on the manor or groups of households which all freemen were required to join. The frankpledge was expected to keep its members of good behaviour and discover transgressors, although enforcement lay with the sheriff or the local lord's court. The frankpledge was established by the Normans in the 11th century to deal with lesser crimes and church tithes.

free companies in the Hundred Years' War, mercenary bodies of mixed nationality under professional captains who were employed by both the French and English. Their captains often became quite powerful and could dominate a region, but they often resorted to pillage during breaks in the fighting and caused widespread devastation. The French eventually recognized the scale of the problem and took measures to stamp out the free companies, but the English continued to employ them, causing great resentment of the English in the French countryside. The free companies were also used elsewhere, as in the Spanish civil wars of the 1360s.

free trade economic system where governments do not interfere in the movement of goods between countries; there are thus no taxes on imports. The case for free trade, first put forward in the 17th century, received its classic statement in Adam Smith's _Wealth of Nations_ 1776. The movement toward free trade began with Pitt's commercial treaty with France 1786, and triumphed with the repeal of the Corn Laws 1846. According to traditional economic theory, free trade allows nations to specialize in those commodities that can be produced most efficiently. In Britain, superiority to all rivals as a manufacturing country in the Victorian age made free trade an advantage, but when that superiority was lost the demand for protection was raised, notably by Joseph Chamberlain.

The Ottawa Agreements 1932 marked the end of free trade until in 1948 GATT came into operation. A series of resultant international tariff reductions was agreed in the Kennedy Round Conference 1964–67, and the Tokyo Round 1974–79 gave substantial incentives to developing countries. In the 1980s recession prompted by increased world oil prices and unemployment swung the pendulum back toward protectionism, which discourages foreign imports by heavy duties, thus protecting home products. Within the European Union, all protectionist tariffs were abolished 1993.

freemasonry the beliefs and practices of a group of linked national organizations open to men over the age of 21, united by a common code of morals and certain traditional 'secrets'. Modern freemasonry began in 18th-century Europe. Freemasons do much charitable work, but have been criticized in recent years for their secrecy, their male exclusivity, and their alleged use of influence within and between organizations (for example, the police or local government) to further each other's interests. There are approximately 6 million members.

Freemasonry is descended from a medieval guild of itinerant masons, which existed in the 14th century and by the 16th was admitting men unconnected with the building trade. The term 'freemason' may have meant a full member of the guild or one working in free-stone, that is, a mason of the highest class. There were some 25 lodges in 17th-century Scotland, of which 16 were in centres of masonic skills such as stonemasonry.

The present order of **_Free and Accepted Masons_** originated with the formation in London of the first Grand Lodge, or governing body, in 1717, and during the 18th century spread from Britain to the USA, continental Europe, and elsewhere. In France and other European countries, freemasonry assumed a political and anticlerical character; it has been condemned by the papacy, and in some countries was suppressed by the state.

French John Denton Pinkstone, 1st Earl of Ypres 1852–1925. British field marshal. In the second ◊South African War 1899–1902, he relieved Kimberley and took Bloemfontein; in World

War I he was commander in chief of the British Expeditionary Force in France 1914–15; he resigned after being criticized as indecisive and was replaced by ◊Haig. He was Lord Lieutenant of Ireland 1918–21.

French Revolutionary Wars series of wars 1791–1802 between France and the combined armies of England, Austria, Prussia, and others, during the period of the French Revolution and Napoleon's campaign to conquer Europe.

In 1793 Britain joined the alliance of Prussia and Austria, formed the previous year, to make up the First Coalition against France (along with Sardinia, Spain, and the Netherlands). Prussia, after initial successes in France, was crushingly defeated at the Battle of Valmy 1792. France occupied the Netherlands 1794–95 and Prussia and Spain then made peace. Bonaparte's Italian campaign of 1796–97 led to the Treaty of Campo-Formio and Austria's withdrawal from the war.

Britain, by now the only remaining member of the First Coalition, won a series of naval victories during 1797 against Spain, now France's ally, at Cape St Vincent and against the Dutch at Camperdown. Following the French defeat by Nelson at the naval battle of ◊Aboukir Bay 1798, British prime minister Pitt the Younger organized a new alliance against the French, the Second Coalition, composed of Britain, Russia, Turkey, Naples, Portugal, and Austria. The Coalition mounted its major campaign against the French in Italy under the Russian field marshal Suvorov, but dissent between Austria and Russia led to the Russian withdrawal from the alliance despite some initial successes.

Napoleon Bonaparte returned to France from his successful conquest of Egypt 1799 and as First Consul became virtual dictator of France. He set about reorganizing the French army and went on to defeat the Austrians at Marengo, northwest Italy, 1800 and again at Hohenlinden near Munich later the same year. Austria made peace with France under the Treaty of Luneville 1801 and the Portuguese were also forced to withdraw from the coalition after their defeat by Spain. Britain fought on, defeating the French at the Battle of Alexandria 1801, until the war was ended by the peace of ◊Amiens March 1802. The peace did not last and war broke out anew as the ◊Napoleonic Wars the following year.

friar a monk of any order, but originally the title of members of the mendicant (begging) orders, the chief of which were the Franciscans or Minors (Grey Friars), the Dominicans or Preachers (Black Friars), the Carmelites (White Friars), and Augustinians (Austin Friars).

friendly society association that makes provisions for the needs of sickness and old age by money payments. There are some 6,500 registered societies in the UK. Among the largest are the National Deposit, Odd Fellows, Foresters, and Hearts of Oak. In the USA similar 'fraternal insurance' bodies are known as **benefit societies**; they include the Modern Woodmen of America 1883 and the Fraternal Order of Eagles 1898.

In the UK the movement was the successor to the great medieval guilds, but the period of its greatest expansion was in the late 18th and early 19th centuries, after the passing 1797 of the first legislation providing for the registration of friendly societies.

Friends, Society of or **Quakers** Christian Protestant sect founded by George ◊Fox in England in the 17th century. They were persecuted for their nonviolent activism, and many emigrated to form communities elsewhere; for example, in Pennsylvania and New England. They now form a worldwide movement of about 200,000. Their worship stresses meditation and the freedom of all to take an active part in the service (called a meeting, held in a meeting house). They have no priests or ministers.

Frobisher Martin 1535–1594. English navigator. He made his first voyage to Guinea, West Africa, 1554. In 1576 he set out in search of the Northwest Passage, and visited Labrador, and Frobisher Bay, Baffin Island. Second and third expeditions sailed 1577 and 1578.

He was vice admiral in Drake's West Indian expedition 1585. In 1588, he was knighted for helping to defeat the Armada. He was mortally wounded 1594 fighting against the Spanish off the coast of France.

frost fairs medieval fairs held on rivers that had frozen over. Before bridges with many arches speeded up the flow of water, many English rivers, especially the Thames, were prone to freezing solid for days at a time in the winter and townspeople would take advantage by erecting stalls and holding entertainments on the water.

It is a solemn thought that at my signal all these fine young fellows go to their death.

SIR JOHN FRENCH
quoted in Brett, Journals and letters of Reginald, Viscount Esher

Fry
English Quaker and social reformer Elizabeth Fry reading to women prisoners in Newgate Prison. She first visited the prison 1813 and was so shocked by conditions that she devoted herself to prison reform.
Image Select

Fry Elizabeth (born Gurney) 1780–1845. English Quaker philanthropist and prison reformer. She formed an association for the improvement of conditions for female prisoners 1817, and worked with her brother, *Joseph Gurney* (1788–1847), on an 1819 report on prison reform. She was a pioneer for higher nursing standards and the education of working women.

fyrd Anglo-Saxon local militia in Britain. All freemen were obliged to defend their shire but, by the 11th century, a distinction was drawn between the *great fyrd*, for local defence, and the *select fyrd*, drawn from better-equipped and experienced warriors who could serve farther afield.

Gaelic language member of the Celtic branch of the Indo-European language family, spoken in Ireland, Scotland, and (until 1974) the Isle of Man. It is, along with English, one of the national languages of the Republic of Ireland, with over half a million speakers, and is known there as both Irish and Irish Gaelic. In Scotland, speakers of Gaelic number around 90,000 and are concentrated in the Western Isles, in parts of the northwest coast and in the city of Glasgow.

Gaelic has been in decline for several centuries, discouraged until recently within the British state. There is a small Gaelic-speaking community in Nova Scotia, Canada.

Gaitskell Hugh (Todd Naylor) 1906–1963. British Labour politician. In 1950 he became minister of economic affairs, and then chancellor of the Exchequer until Oct 1951. In 1955 he defeated Aneurin Bevan for the succession to Attlee as party leader, and tried to reconcile internal differences on nationalization and disarmament. He was re-elected leader 1960 and died suddenly while in office 1963.

Gale Richard 1896–1991. British general. In World War II, he raised and trained the 1st Parachute Brigade and during the D-Day landings led the small force which dropped ahead of the main invasion to capture the Orne bridges flanking the British beachhead. After the war he commanded the British Army of the Rhine and later became Chief of the General Staff.

Gallipoli port in European Turkey, giving its name to the peninsula (ancient name **Chersonesus**) on which it stands. In World War I, at the instigation of Winston Churchill, an unsuccessful attempt was made Feb 1915–Jan 1916 by Allied troops to force their way through the Dardanelles and link up with Russia. The campaign was fought mainly by Australian and New Zealand (ANZAC) forces, who suffered heavy losses. An estimated 36,000 Commonwealth troops died during the nine-month campaign.

gallowglass (Irish Gaelic *gallglach*, 'young foreign warrior-servant') armed mercenary soldier maintained by Irish and certain other Celtic chiefs from *c.* 1235 to the 16th century. Originally employed by the lords of Ulster to fight the English, they served the Anglo-Irish government until they were disbanded following the failure of Hugh ♭O'Neill's revolt 1603

Gambia former British colony, West Africa. The River Gambia was ascended by the agent of an English trading company 1618 and the British established Fort James on a small island some 32 km/20 mi from the river mouth 1664. The territory was captured by the French 1779, but British claims to it were recognized by the Treaty of Versailles 1783. It became a British colony 1843 and territory upstream was made a British protectorate 1894. The country achieved independence 1965.

game laws laws 1671–1831 restricting the taking of game to those of high social status. 'Game' itself was defined by the Games Act 1831 as hares, pheasants, partridges, grouse, heath or moor game, black game (the grouse *Lyrurus tetrix*) and bustards, though these last were deleted by the Protection of Birds Act 1954. It is necessary to have a game licence to take or pursue game.

Gandhi Mahatma (Sanskrit 'Great Soul'). Honorific name of Mohandas Karamchand Gandhi 1869–1948. Indian nationalist leader. A pacifist, he led the struggle for Indian independence from the UK by advocating nonviolent noncooperation (*satyagraha*, defence of and by truth) from 1915. He was imprisoned several times by the British authorities and was influential in the nationalist Congress Party and in the independence negotiations 1947. He was assassi-

All terrorists, at the invitation of the Government, end up with drinks at the Dorchester.

HUGH GAITSKELL
The Guardian,
23 August 1977

Perhaps as the years roll by we will be remembered as the expedition that was betrayed by jealousy, spite, indecision and treachery. The Turks did not beat us – we were beaten by our own High Command.

GALLIPOLI
Joseph Murray,
Diary, *1916*

Gandhi
Indian political leader
Mahatma Gandhi with
his granddaughters.
Leader of the nationalist
movement 1915–47,
Gandhi is regarded as
the founder of the Indian
state. His nonviolent
resistance to British rule
included such tactics as
his 1930 protest march
of 388 km/241 mi,
which inspired
widespread
demonstrations.
Topham Picture Library

nated by a Hindu nationalist in the violence that followed the partition of British India into India and Pakistan.

Gandhi was born in Porbandar and studied law in London, later practising as a barrister. He settled in South Africa where until 1914 he led the Indian community in opposition to racial discrimination. Returning to India, he emerged as leader of the Indian National Congress. He organized hunger strikes and events of civil disobedience, and campaigned for social reform, including religious tolerance and an end to discrimination against the so-called untouchable caste.

Gang of Four four members of the Labour Party who resigned 1981 to form the Social Democratic Party: Roy Jenkins, David Owen, Shirley Williams, and William Rodgers.

Gardiner Stephen *c.* 1493–1555. English priest and politician. After being secretary to Cardinal Wolsey, he became bishop of Winchester 1531. An opponent of Protestantism, he was imprisoned under Edward VI, and as Lord Chancellor 1553–55 under Queen Mary he tried to restore Roman Catholicism.

gas lighting the lighting of private or public premises by gas. Gas, derived from coal by distillation, was first used in Britain 1792 to light the office of the Scottish steam engineer William Murdock. Gas lighting was used 1805 in a Manchester factory, and Pall Mall, London, was the first public thoroughfare to be lit by gas 1807. The Chartered Gas Light and Coke Company, founded 1812, was the first of several private companies to produce and supply gas. By 1820 there were seven gasworks in London and the number of gaslights in London streets increased from 4,000 to 51,000 in only five years. By the 1840s gas lights were found in the streets, shops and homes of even small towns. By the end of the 19th century gas-producing companies were beginning to compete with electricity.

gavelkind system of land tenure mainly found in Kent. The tenant paid rent to the lord instead of carrying out services for him, as elsewhere. It came into force in Anglo-Saxon times and was only formally abolished 1926. The term comes from Old English *gafol*, 'tribute' and *gecynd*, 'kind'.

Gaveston Piers d. 1312. Gascon noble and favourite of Edward II. Gaveston was made Earl of Cornwall 1307 and when Edward went to France 1308, he left Gaveston as Keeper of the Realm. He aroused much jealousy among English barons who accused him of monopolizing royal patronage and they forced Edward to exile him 1306–07 and 1308–09. He was attacked in the ◊ordinances of 1311 and the following year he was seized by Edward's opponents and summarily executed on the orders of Thomas of Leicester, the king's cousin and bitter enemy.

General Belgrano Argentine cruiser torpedoed and sunk on 2 May 1982 by the British nuclear-powered submarine *Conqueror* during the ◊Falklands War while sailing away from the Falklands. Out of a ship's company of over 1,000, 368 were killed.

The *General Belgrano* was Argentina's second largest warship, weighing 13,645 tonnes and armed with Exocet missiles, Seacat anti-aircraft missiles, and Lynx helicopters. It had been purchased from the US Navy 1951, having survived the 1941 Japanese attack on Pearl Harbor.

General Strike, the nationwide strike called by the Trade Union Congress (TUC) 3 May 1926 in support of the miners' union. The immediate cause of the 1926 General Strike was the report of a royal commission on the coal-mining industry (Samuel Report 1926) which, among other things, recommended a cut in wages. The mine-owners wanted longer hours as well as lower wages. The miners' union, under the leadership of A J Cook, resisted with the slogan 'Not a penny off the pay, not a minute on the day'. A coal strike started early May 1926 and the miners asked the TUC to bring all major industries out on strike in support of the action; eventually it included more than 2 million workers. The Conservative government under Stanley Baldwin used troops, volunteers, and special constables to maintain food supplies and essential services, and had a monopoly on the information services, including BBC radio. After nine days the TUC ended the general strike, leaving the miners – who felt betrayed by the TUC – to remain on strike, unsuccessfully, until Nov 1926. The Trades Disputes Act of 1927 made general strikes illegal.

General Strike, the
The effectiveness of the 1926 General Strike was severely undermined by middle-class volunteers who came forward to run vital public services such as the buses. A police escort, as shown above, was often felt necessary.
Image Select

general warrants open writs for the arrest of unspecified persons suspected of committing a named offence. The warrants were issued by the Star Chamber and were mainly used under Charles II. They were abolished after their misuse against John Wilkes, who criticized King George III in his journal the *North Briton* April 1763. He and 49 others associated with the publication were arrested under general warrants against seditious libel and successfully challenged the legality of the procedure in the courts. Parliament concurred and they were abolished 1765, although they can still be issued to prevent sedition in the armed forces under the terms of an act of 1934.

Germanus, St *c.* 378–448. Bishop of Auxerre who was sent to Britain to restore Catholic orthodoxy in the face of Pelagianism 429. He led Christian Britons to a bloodless victory over a combined force of Picts and Saxons, in modern Powys, at which he taught the Britons the war cry 'Alleluia'.

gentry the lesser nobility, particularly in England and Wales, not entitled to sit in the House of Lords. By the later Middle Ages, it included knights, esquires, and gentlemen, and after the 17th century, baronets.

George six kings of Great Britain:

George I 1660–1727. King of Great Britain and Ireland from 1714. He was the son of the first elector of Hanover, Ernest Augustus (1629–1698), and his wife Sophia, and a great-grandson of James I. He succeeded to the electorate 1698, and became king on the death of Queen Anne. He attached himself to the Whigs, and spent most of his reign in Hanover, never having learned English.

The British Parliament, seeking to ensure a Protestant line of succession to oppose the claim of the Catholic ◊James Edward Stuart, made George third in line after Queen Anne and his mother. He was supported upon his succession by the Whigs, especially Stanhope, Townsend, and Walpole. The king grew more and more dependent upon his advisers as scandal surrounded him; his supporters turned against him, demanding freedom of action as the price of reconciliation.

George II 1683–1760. King of Great Britain and Ireland from 1727, when he succeeded his father, George I. His victory at Dettingen 1743, in the War of the Austrian Succession, was the last battle commanded by a British king. He married Caroline of Anspach 1705 and under her influence supported the policies of ◊Walpole. He was accused with his minister ◊Carteret of

His character would not afford subject for epic poetry, but will look well in the sober page of history.

GEORGE II
historian Elizabeth Montague

favouring Hanover at the expense of Britain's interests in the War of the Austrian Succession 1740–48. He was succeeded by his grandson George III.

George III 1738–1820. King of Great Britain and Ireland from 1760, when he succeeded his grandfather George II. Under the influence of his former tutor ◊Bute, he attempted to exercise his royal powers to the full and his rule was marked by intransigence resulting in the loss of the American colonies, for which he shared the blame with his chief minister Lord North. He effectively blocked moves for the emancipation of Catholics in England 1801 and 1807. Possibly suffering from porphyria, he had repeated attacks of insanity, permanent from 1811. He was succeeded by his son George IV.

George IV 1762–1830. King of Great Britain and Ireland from 1820, when he succeeded his father George III, for whom he had been regent during the king's period of insanity 1811–20. In 1785 he secretly married a Catholic widow, Maria ◊Fitzherbert, but the marriage was later declared invalid and in 1795 he married Princess ◊Caroline of Brunswick, in return for payment of his debts. He was a patron of the arts. His prestige was undermined by his treatment of Caroline (they separated 1796), his dissipation, and his extravagance. He was succeeded by his brother, the Duke of Clarence, who became William IV.

George III
Caricature by James Gillray depicting George III as the King of Brobdignag scrutinizing Napoleon as Gulliver, after a scene in Swift's *Gulliver's Travels*. This is an unusually favourable portrayal of the king.
Philip Sauvain

George V 1865–1936. King of Great Britain from 1910, when he succeeded his father Edward VII. He was the second son, and became heir 1892 on the death of his elder brother Albert, Duke of Clarence. In 1893, he married Princess Victoria Mary of Teck (Queen Mary), formerly engaged to his brother. During World War I he made several visits to the front and abandoned all German titles for himself and his family 1917. The name of the royal house was changed from Saxe-Coburg-Gotha (popularly known as Brunswick or Hanover) to Windsor.

George VI 1895–1952. King of Great Britain from 1936, when he succeeded after the abdication of his brother Edward VIII, who had succeeded their father George V. Created Duke of York 1920, he married in 1923 Lady Elizabeth Bowes-Lyon (1900–), and their children are Elizabeth II and Princess Margaret. During World War II, he visited the Normandy and Italian battlefields.

Gerald of Wales English name of ◊Giraldus Cambrensis, medieval Welsh bishop and historian.

Ghent, treaty of peace treaty signed 24 Dec 1814 ending the ◊War of 1812 between Britain and the United States. Each side agreed to restore conquered territory and Canada was confirmed as a British possession but commissions were appointed to determine the US frontier with Canada.

gibbeting the practice of exhibiting the bodies of executed felons in chains at public crossroads to deter others. Highwaymen, smugglers and rioters were most often punished in this way. The practice was at its height in the 17th century, but gibbets ceased to be used towards the end of the 18th century and gibbeting was formally abolished 1834.

George VI
George VI announcing the outbreak of World War II from Buckingham Palace Sept 1939. After his unexpected accession to the throne following his brother Edward VIII's abdication 1936, he overcame his natural shyness and a severe stammer to become a popular wartime leader.
Image Select

Gibraltar British colony, a peninsula in southern Spain. It was taken by the Spanish 1462 and captured by the British 1704 during the War of the Spanish Succession, being retained by Britain by the Treaty of Utrecht 1713. It became a British colony 1830. Britain has constantly rejected Spanish claims to the colony. Spain closed the border with Gibraltar 1969–85 and refused to engage in trade.

Gibson Guy Penrose 1918–1944. British bomber pilot of World War II. He became famous as leader of the 'dambuster raids' 16–17 May 1942; he formed 617 squadron specifically to bomb the Ruhr Dams, and as wing commander led the raid personally, dropping the first bomb on the Mohne Dam. He was awarded the Victoria Cross for his leadership in this action.

Gibson joined the RAF 1936 and by 1939 was an operational bomber pilot. Following the dambuster raid, he was relieved of operational duties and accompanied Churchill to Canada and the USA late 1944. On returning to Britain he obtained permission for 'one more operation', flying a De Havilland Mosquito on a raid on relatively unimportant targets in Bavaria. Tragically, on the return flight his plane crashed in Holland and he was killed.

Gilbert Islands former British colony, an island group in the west Pacific. The islands were visited by various British navigators 1767–1824 and were proclaimed a British protectorate 1892. They became part of the new Gilbert and Ellice Islands Colony 1915. They were set off as a separate territory 1976 and gained independence 1979 under the name Kiribati (a native form of 'Gilbert').

Gilbert of Sempringham, St. *c.* 1083–1189. English cleric and founder of the Gilbertines, the only purely British religious order. As incumbent of Sempringham, Lincolnshire, he encouraged seven women of his parish to adopt a rule of life similar to that of the Cistercians, later linking them with communities of lay brothers and sisters to help with the manual work. The order was approved by Rome 1148 but dissolved at the Reformation. By the end of his long life Gilbert had built 13 monasteries as well as orphanages and leper hospitals, mainly in eastern England. He was canonized 1202 and his feast day is 4 Feb.

Gilbert's Act statute passed 1762 allowing workhouse inmates to find outside work. Knatchbull's General Workhouse Act 1723 empowered parishes or groups of parishes to build workhouses, and by the mid-18th century there were about 2,000 workhouses in England. The inmates were generally confined to the limits of the workhouse, but Gilbert's Act allowed the able-bodied to obtain work outside, indoor relief being provided for those physically unable to work.

gin (Dutch *jenever* 'juniper') alcoholic drink made by distilling a mash of maize, malt, or rye, with juniper flavouring. The low price of corn led to a mania for gin during the 18th century, resulting in the Gin Acts of 1736 and 1751 which reduced gin consumption to a quarter of its previous level.

Giraldus Cambrensis (Welsh ***Geralt Gymro***) *c.* 1146–1220. Welsh historian, born in Pembrokeshire. He was elected bishop of St David's 1198. He wrote a history of the conquest of Ireland by Henry II, and *Itinerarium Cambriae/Journey through Wales* 1191.

We're not a family; we're a firm.

GEORGE VI
on modern British royalty

gin
Hogarth's *Gin Lane* 1751 showing how the availability of cheap spirits led to such social ills as maternal neglect, suicide, and starvation. The Gin Act of the same year prohibited the retail sale of gin by distillers. *Image Select*

Gladstone William Ewart 1809–1898. British Liberal politician, repeatedly prime minister. He entered Parliament as a Tory 1833 and held ministerial office, but left the party 1846 and after 1859 identified himself with the Liberals. He was chancellor of the Exchequer 1852–55 and 1859–66, and prime minister 1868–74, 1880–85, 1886, and 1892–94. He introduced elementary education 1870 and vote by secret ballot 1872 and many reforms in Ireland, although he failed in his efforts to get a Home Rule Bill passed.

Gladstone was born in Liverpool, the son of a rich merchant. In Peel's government he was president of the Board of Trade 1843–45, and colonial secretary 1845–46. He left the Tory Party with the Peelite group 1846. He was chancellor of the Exchequer in Aberdeen's government 1852–55 and in the Liberal governments of Palmerston and Russell 1859–66. In his first term as prime minister he carried through a series of reforms, including the disestablishment of the Church of Ireland, the Irish Land Act, and the abolition of the purchase of army commissions and of religious tests in the universities.

Gladstone strongly resisted Disraeli's imperialist and pro-Turkish policy during the latter's government of 1874–80, not least because of Turkish pogroms against subject Christians, and by his Midlothian campaign of 1879 helped to overthrow Disraeli. Gladstone's second government carried the second Irish Land Act and the Reform Act 1884 but was confronted with problems in Ireland, Egypt, and South Africa, and lost prestige through its failure to relieve General ◊Gordon. Returning to office in 1886, Gladstone introduced his first Home Rule Bill, which was defeated by the secession of the Liberal Unionists, and he thereupon resigned. After six years' opposition he formed his last government; his second Home Rule Bill was rejected by the Lords, and in 1894 he resigned. He led a final crusade against the massacre of Armenian Christians in 1896.

All the world over, I will back the masses against the classes.

WILLIAM GLADSTONE
speech in Liverpool, 28 June 1886

Glastonbury market town in Somerset, on the river Brue. Nearby are two excavated lake villages thought to have been occupied for about 150 years before the Romans came to Britain. *Glastonbury Tor*, a hill with a ruined church tower, rises to 159 m/522 ft.

The first church on the site was traditionally founded in the 1st century by Joseph of Arimathea. Legend has it that he brought the Holy Grail to Glastonbury. The ruins of the Benedictine abbey built in the 10th and 11th centuries by Dunstan and his followers were excavated 1963 and the site of the grave of King Arthur and Queen Guinevere was thought to have been identified. One of Europe's largest pop festivals is held outside Glastonbury most years in June.

glebe landed endowment of a parish church, designed to support the priest. It later became necessary to supplement this with taxation.

Like a second Assyrian, the rod of God's anger, he did deeds of unheard-of cruelty with fire and sword.

OWEN GLENDOWER
Adam of Usk, Chronicon Adae de Usk early 15th century.

Glencoe, massacre of slaughter of 37 members of the Macdonald clan 13 Feb 1692 at a glen in southern Scotland (modern Strathclyde Region). The massacre was carried out by troops quartered with the Macdonalds, led by Archibald Campbell, the 10th Earl of Argyll. The Macdonalds had refused to swear an oath of allegiance to the new king William III, but this was largely a pretext for the Campbells who had a long-standing feud with the Macdonalds. John Campbell, Earl of Breadalbane, was the chief instigator.

Glendower Owen *c.* 1359–*c.* 1416. (Welsh *Owain Glyndwr*) Welsh nationalist leader of a successful revolt against the English in North Wales, who defeated Henry IV in three campaigns 1400–02 and established an independent Welsh parliament. Wales was reconquered 1405–13 and Glendower disappeared 1416 after some years of guerrilla warfare.

Glorious Revolution: chronology

1669	James, Duke of York, heir to the English throne, was received into the Roman Catholic Church.
1678–81	Exclusion Crisis: following an alleged 'popish plot' to kill King Charles II and replace him with the Catholic James, three parliaments attempted to exclude James from the succession.
1685	*6 Feb* Death of Charles II; accession of James II.
June	*11–July 6* Monmouth's Rebellion: Charles II's illegitimate son invaded southeast England and attempted to overthrow James II.
1687	After dissolving parliament, James tried to organize the election of a compliant parliament that would permit Catholic monarchs and support the re-Catholicization of England.
1688	*4 May* The Privy Council required a revised Declaration of Indulgence (suspending laws against Catholic and Dissenters) to be read in Church of England churches.
	18 May Archbishop Sancroft and six bishops protested at the Privy Council's order; 8 June they were imprisoned, and then tried for seditious libel.
	10 June Queen Mary gave birth to a son, James Edward, giving England the prospect of a second Catholic king.
	30 June Archbishop Sancroft and the six bishops were acquitted. The same day, seven peers secretly invited the Protestant Prince William of Orange to invade England.
	5 Nov William of Orange landed at Torbay, southwest England, and advanced towards London, gaining popular support.
	10–11 Dec James fled to France, but was stopped at Faversham, Kent, and taken back to London.
	25 Dec James made a successful flight to France.
1689	*13 Feb* William of Orange and his wife Mary (daughter of James II) were proclaimed King and Queen.
	12 March James II landed in Ireland in a bid to regain the throne.
1690	*1 July* Battle of the Boyne: William defeated James; James returned to France.

Glevum Roman name for Gloucester, founded *c.* 97 AD. The foundation of St Peter's Abbey 681 by Osric, king of Northumbria, encouraged its growth and it became the capital of Mercia. The name is Celtic in origin and means 'bright place'.

Globe Theatre 17th-century London theatre, octagonal and open to the sky, near Bankside, Southwark, where many of Shakespeare's plays were performed by Richard Burbage and his company. Built 1599 by Cuthbert Burbage, it was burned down 1613 after a cannon, fired during a performance of Henry VIII, set light to the thatch. It was rebuilt 1614 but pulled down 1644. The site was rediscovered Oct 1989 near the remains of the contemporaneous Rose Theatre. Work begaon on recreating the theatre on the original site 1995.

Glorious Revolution events surrounding the removal of James II from the throne and his replacement by Mary (daughter of Charles I) and William of Orange as joint sovereigns 1689. James had become increasingly unpopular due to his unconstitutional behaviour and Catholicism. Various elements in England, including seven prominent politicians, plotted to invite the Protestant William to invade. Arriving at Torbay 5 Nov 1688, William rapidly gained support and James was allowed to flee to France after the army deserted him. William and Mary then accepted a new constitutional settlement, the ◊Bill of Rights 1689, which assured the ascendency of parliamentary power over sovereign rule.

Godiva Lady *c.* 1040–1080. Wife of Leofric, Earl of Mercia (d. 1057). Legend has it that her husband promised to reduce the heavy taxes on the people of Coventry if she rode naked through the streets at noon. The grateful citizens remained indoors as she did so, but 'Peeping Tom' bored a hole in his shutters and was struck blind.

Gododdin (or ***Wotadini***) tribe dominant in the Lothian region, Scotland, in the 4th century AD. Their capital was on Traprain Law, east of modern Edinburgh. They were apparently vanquished by invading Angles and had ceased to exist by the 9th century.

Godwin d. 1053. Earl of Wessex from 1020. He was a dominant political figure under Canute who made him the Earl of Wessex and in 1042 he secured the succession to the throne of ◊Edward the Confessor, to whom he married his daughter Edith. He became Edward's chief minister in opposition to the king's Norman favourites. He was exiled 1051 but returned the following year. King Harold II was his son.

A great king, with strong armies and mighty fleets, a great treasure and powerful allies, fell all at once, and his whole strength, like a spider's web, was... irrecoverably lost.

GLORIOUS
REVOLUTION
bishop and historian
Gilbert Burnet, History of
My Own Times *1688*

THE EMERGENCE OF A GREAT POWER

England after 1688

William III's seizure of power in England was opposed in both Scotland and Ireland, where supporters of James II (known as 'Jacobites' from *Jacobus*, Latin for James) fought a bitter war before finally being defeated in 1691. The Jacobites were to stage major risings in 1715 and 1745, but they were both defeated. The Glorious Revolution therefore led to English domination of the British Isles, albeit a domination supported by and identified with important sections of the Irish and Scottish population: Irish Anglicans and Scottish Presbyterians.

This process led to the Union of 1707 of England and Scotland: the Scottish Parliament was abolished and Scotland was thereafter represented in the Westminster Parliament. The Scottish Privy Council was also abolished 1708. Protestantism, war with France, and the benefits of empire helped to create a British consciousness alongside the still strong senses of English, Scottish, Irish, and Welsh identity. Parliamentary union with Ireland followed in 1800–01.

Wars with France

William III led England into war with Louis XIV of France, the War of the League of Augsburg (or Nine Years' War) of 1689–97, fought to stop France overrunning the Low Countries. Conflict resumed with the War of the Spanish Succession (1701–14) in which John Churchill, 1st Duke of Marlborough, heavily defeated the French in a number of battles, particularly Blenheim 1704. The Royal Navy also emerged during this period as the leading European navy.

Naval strength was crucial in seeing off the French threat during the War of the Austrian Succession (Britain's involvement lasted 1743–48) and the Seven Years' War 1756–63. The latter war ended with the Thirteen Colonies on the eastern seaboard of North America, and the British possessions in India, secure; with Canada, Florida, and many Caribbean islands acquired; and with Britain as the leading maritime power in the world, thus fulfilling what James Thomson had seen as the national destiny in his song *Rule Britannia* 1740:

'Rule, Britannia, rule the waves;
Britons never will be slaves.'

This was the achievement of the ministry of William Pitt the Elder and the Duke of Newcastle (1757–62), and of a number of able military leaders, including Wolfe, Clive, Hawke, and Boscawen. Robert Clive's victory at Plassey in 1757, over the vastly more numerous forces of the Indian Prince, Suraja Dowla, laid the basis for the virtual control of Bengal, Bihar, and Orissa by the East India Company (French forces in India were finally defeated in 1760–61, and Britain emerged as the leading European power in the subcontinent). A French attempt to invade Britain on behalf of the Jacobites was crushed by British naval victories at Lagos and Quiberon Bay in 1759. That year, British troops also defeated the French at Minden in Germany, while James Wolfe's troops scaled the Heights of Abraham near Québec to capture France's most important possession in Canada. The bell ringers at York Minster were paid four times between 21 August and 22 October that year for celebrating triumphs.

In 1762 British forces campaigned round the globe. They helped the Portuguese resist a Spanish invasion, fought the French in Germany, and captured Martinique from France and Havana and Manila from Spain, an extraordinary testimony to the global reach of British power, particularly naval power, and the strength of the British state.

The growth of empire

British control of the eastern seaboard of North America north of Florida had been expanded and consolidated with the gain of New York from the Dutch in 1664, the French recognition of Nova Scotia, Newfoundland, and Hudson Bay as British in 1713, and the foundation of colonies including Maryland 1634, Pennsylvania 1681, Carolina 1663 and Georgia 1732. Possibly 200,000 people emigrated from the British Isles to North America during the 17th century, far outnumbering the French settlers in Canada and Louisiana, and the settlements founded included Charleston 1672, Philadelphia 1682, Baltimore 1729, and Savannah 1733.

The English also made a major impact in their West Indian islands and developed there a sugar economy based on slave labour brought from West Africa, where British settlements included Accra (settled 1672). The East India Company, chartered in 1600, was the basis of British commercial activity, and later political power, in the Indian Ocean. Bombay was gained in 1661, followed by Calcutta in 1698. Trade outside Europe became increasingly important to the British economy, and played a major role in the growth of such ports as Bristol, Glasgow, Liverpool, and Whitehaven. The mercantile marine grew from 280,000 tonnes in 1695 to 609,000 in 1760.

By 1763 Britain was the leading maritime state in the world, unified at home and secure in the possession of a large trade-based empire. With France and Spain both vanquished, Britain's position as the world's leading power seemed beyond serious challenge.

JEREMY BLACK

Gold Coast former British colony, West Africa. The territory was a centre for the slave trade carried on in the 17th century by rival Dutch, English, French, and Danish companies. It was acquired by Britain through the purchase of Danish (1850) and Dutch (1871) settlements, and the original Gold Coast colony was set up in the coastal and southern areas 1874. The British trust territory of Togo voted for union with the Gold Coast 1956 and the new country achieved independence as Ghana 1957.

gold penny mainly in the 13th and 14th centuries, a ◊penny minted in gold instead of the more usual silver of the time, designed for prestige rather than everyday commercial use. They were occasionally produced in Anglo-Saxon times, including the reign of Edward the Confessor, but most were circulated between 1257 and 1270, although their face value was as high as two shillings by 1265. Edward III also minted gold coins, largely to increase his prestige in France.

gold standard system under which a country's currency is exchangeable for a fixed weight of gold on demand at the central bank. It was almost universally applied 1870–1914, but broke down during World War I and by 1937 no single country was on the full gold standard. Britain was the first country to go onto the gold standard 1816 and abandoned it 1931; the USA abandoned it 1971.

Golden Jubilee celebrations held throughout Britain and the Empire 1887 to mark the 50th year of Queen Victoria's rule. Colonial leaders gathered in London to attend the celebrations and this made possible the first Imperial Conference. A similar celebration, the ◊Diamond Jubilee, was held on the 60th anniversary.

goldsmith old commercial term for a dealer in bullion and foreign currency as opposed to one who works gold as an artisan. Goldsmiths existed from at least the 12th century and were granted a charter 1394. Their establishments were the precursors of modern banks, and by the 17th century their receipts or bonds were negotiable. Their influence was greatly diminished by the creation of the Bank of England, designed to halt the government's dependence on private credit.

Good Parliament the Parliament of April–July 1376 which attacked Edward III's government for excessive expenditure and the lack of success in the Hundred Years' War. The king was forced to change his ministers and to dismiss his mistress, Alice Perrers. The Commons denounced the corruption of many of the government's officials, including the chamberlain Lord Latimer, and indicted them before the House of Lords, the first instance of impeachment. It also created the office of Speaker by electing Sir Peter de la Mare to put the case of the Commons to Parliament as a whole. Most of its acts were repealed or annulled the following year.

Goose Green in the Falklands War, British victory over Argentina at Goose Green, south of San Carlos, 28 May 1982 during the advance on Port Stanley.

British troops landed at and around Port San Carlos on the western side of the West Falkland island 21 May and prepared to advance to Port Stanley, some 80 km/50 mi to the east. An Argentine force was known to be at Goose Green, to the south of San Carlos, and since this posed a threat to the flank of the British advance, troops of the Parachute Regiment, with a battery of 105 mm guns in support, were sent to deal with it. Due to a shortage of helicopters at a critical time, not all the battery of guns and its ammunition was able to get into position, and with this limited support the Parachute troops made an attack on foot. A brisk firefight resulted, in which the commanding officer of the Parachute troops was killed while leading a charge, for which he received a posthumous Victoria Cross. The Argentine garrison was overrun, the survivors taken prisoner, and the advance on Port Stanley was free to move.

Gordon George, 6th Earl and 1st Marquess of Huntly *c.* 1563–1636. Scottish nobleman. He led the intrigues of the northern earls in the Roman Catholic cause against James VI. He was imprisoned 1588–89, murdered the Earl of Moray 1592, and defeated the royal forces led by the Earl of Argyll at Glenlivet 1594. He subsequenty submitted to the king and was pardoned. James made Gordon a marquess 1599 but on succeeding to the English throne as James I 1603 curbed his power in the north.

Gordon Charles (George) 1833–1885. British general sent to Khartoum in the Sudan 1884 to rescue English garrisons that were under attack by the Mahdi, Muhammad Ahmed; he was himself besieged for ten months by the Mahdi's army. A relief expedition arrived 28 Jan 1885 to find that Khartoum had been captured and Gordon killed two days before.

Gordon served in the ◊Crimean War and in China 1864, where he earned his nickname 'Chinese' Gordon in ending the Taiping Rebellion. In 1874 he was employed by the Khedive of Egypt to open the country and 1877–80 was British governor of the Sudan.

Gordon George 1751–1793. British organizer of the so-called ◊*Gordon Riots* of 1778, a protest against removal of penalties imposed on Roman Catholics in the Catholic Relief Act of 1778; he was acquitted on a treason charge. Gordon and the 'No Popery' riots figure in Charles Dickens's novel *Barnaby Rudge*.

Gordon riots anti-Catholic riots in London 2–9 June 1780 led by Lord George ◊Gordon in protest at the Roman Catholic Relief Act 1778. Gordon led a mob of 50,000 Protestants in a march on Parliament to present a petition against the Act 2 June 1780. The mob set about detroying Catholic houses and other property and in the subsequent rioting about 300 people were killed and property worth over £180,000 was destroyed. After five days of uncontrolled rioting, the militia and the army were called in and even then it took another two days for order to be restored. Gordon was charged with (but later acquitted of) high treason.

Gorst J(ohn) E(ldon) 1835–1916. English Conservative Party administrator. A supporter of Disraeli, Gorst was largely responsible for extending the Victorian Conservative Party electoral base to include middle- and working-class support. Appointed Conservative Party agent in 1870, he established Conservative Central Office, and became secretary of the National Union in 1871. He was Solicitor-General 1885–86.

Grafton Augustus Henry, 3rd Duke of Grafton 1735–1811. British politician. Grandson of the first duke, who was the son of Charles II and Barbara Villiers (1641–1709), Duchess of Cleveland. He became First Lord of the Treasury in 1766 and an unsuccessful acting prime minister 1767–70 when his more conciliatory attitude to the American colonies was rejected by his colleagues.

Graham of Claverhouse John, 1st Viscount Dundee 1648–1689. Scottish soldier. After serving in the Dutch and French armies he joined the forces of Charles II against the Covenanters in southwest Scotland 1678. In the ◊Glorious Revolution 1688, he marched south in support of James II and was created Viscount Dundee. William III allowed him to withdraw unharmed and he set about organizing a Highland army in support of the Jacobites. He led the Highlanders in a rising 1689 and defeated a loyalist army at ◊Killiecrankie July, but was mortally wounded in the battle and died soon after.

grammar school secondary school catering for children of high academic ability, about 20% of the total, usually measured by the eleven-plus examination. Most grammar schools have now been replaced by comprehensive schools. By 1992 the proportion of English children in grammar schools was less than 3%.

Granby John Manners, Marquess of Granby 1721–1770. British soldier. He achieved popularity as a commander of the British forces fighting in Europe in the Seven Years' War, winning a notable victory over the French at Warburg 1760.

Grand National Consolidated Trades Union first large-scale British trade union founded 1834 by Robert Owen as a broad-based coalition of working people. Its aim of a general strike to force an eight-hour working day provoked harsh government reaction, including the sentencing of the Tolpuddle Martyrs to transportation, and the movement collapsed by Oct. Its main strength came from the support of the Lancashire cotton workers who had already been organized by John Doherty.

Grand Remonstrance petition passed by the English Parliament Nov 1641 listing the alleged misdeeds of Charles I and demanding Parliamentary approval for the king's ministers and the reform of the church. Charles refused to accept the Grand Remonstrance and countered by trying to arrest five leading members of the House of Commons (Pym, Hampden, Holles, Heselrig, and Strode). The worsening of relations between king and Parliament led to the outbreak of the Civil War in 1642.

Grattan Henry 1746–1820. Irish politician. He entered the Irish parliament 1775, led the patriot opposition, and obtained free trade and legislative independence for Ireland 1782. He failed to prevent the Act of Union of Ireland and England 1801, sat in the British Parliament from that year, and pressed for Catholic emancipation.

Great Britain official name for England, Scotland, and Wales, and the adjacent islands (except the Channel Islands and the Isle of Man) from 1603, when the English and Scottish crowns were united under James I of England (James VI of Scotland). With Northern Ireland it forms the United Kingdom.

Great Contract proposal of the Lord Treasurer Robert Cecil 1610 that the Crown's old feudal revenues be replaced with a fixed annual income of £200,000. The king's debts, a further £600,000, were also to be paid as part of the proposal which was intended to regularize government income. Although the scheme was initially accepted by the Commons, negotiations broke down as James feared that the sums may not be sufficient and was reluctant to surrender power while Parliament was concerned about granting the Crown too much financial independence.

Great Exhibition world fair held in Hyde Park, London, 1851, proclaimed by its originator Prince Albert as 'the Great Exhibition of the Industries of All Nations'. In practice, it glorified British manufacture: over half the 100,000 exhibits were from Britain or the British Empire. Over 6 million people attended the exhibition. The exhibition hall, popularly known as the ◊*Crystal Palace*, was constructed of glass with a cast-iron frame, and designed by Joseph Paxton (1801–1865).

Great Plague last major outbreak of bubonic plague in Britain 1665, mainly affecting London; about 100,000 of the 400,000 inhabitants died. The plague began late 1664 and reached its height in the autumn of 1665, dying down toward the end of the year. Samuel Pepys' diary contains graphic accounts of the devastation wrought by the plague, not just in terms of actual deaths, but also in the massive disruption of the life of the nation's capital.

Great Britain has lost an empire and has not yet found a role.

GREAT BRITAIN
US politician Dean Acheson, speech at the Military Academy, West Point, 5 December 1962

After the ◊Black Death in the 14th century, plague remained a problem for the next three centuries, but this was the most serious outbreak since then. Bubonic plague persists in many parts of the world – there were outbreaks in Latin America and India in the early 1990s.

great seal royal seal used to authenticate the monarch's assent to official documents, required for all the most important acts of state, such as dissolving parliaments and signing treaties. It was first used by Edward the Confessor in a period when monarchs were not expected to be able to write. The seal is kept by the Lord Chancellor who travelled with the monarch until the 13th century, when the court of chancery became established in Westminster. A lesser seal, the privy seal, was then devised to authorise the chancellor to move the great seal. The circular design of the great seal has remained fairly constant, showing the monarch enthroned on one side and on horseback on the other, although during the interregnum of the 1650s, an alternative design was created, with an image of the Speaker's Chair in the House of Commons representing sovereign authority.

Great War another name for ◊World War I.

Greater London Council (GLC) in the UK, local authority that governed London 1965–86. When the GLC was abolished 1986, its powers either devolved back to the borough councils or were transferred to certain non-elected bodies.

The GLC was established under the London Government Act 1963, and not only took over the administration of what was then the London County Council area, but also incorporated almost all of Middlesex and parts of Surrey, Kent, Essex, and Hertfordshire. It came into force on 1 April 1965. The existing 85 local authorities in the area covered by the new GLC were merged into 32 boroughs (excluding the City of London, which remained independent).

Green Cross Society corps of women motor drivers in World War I, officially known as the Women's Reserve Ambulance, established June 1915. They collected wounded soldiers from the main London railway stations and took them to various hospitals in the suburbs. They were also trained in first aid and ambulance duties. The corps also included several hundred part-time workers who staffed canteens, acted as guides for wounded soldiers, and rendered first aid during air raids. A company was sent as ambulance drivers to Romania and Russia.

Greenwich, Treaty of 1543 treaty between the Scots and Henry VIII under which the Prince of Wales, the future Edward VI, would marry ◊Mary Queen of Scots. The Scots reneged and Henry's attempts to enforce the treaty by a series of invasions over the next few years were known as the ◊rough wooing.

Grenville George 1712–1770. British Whig politician, prime minister, and chancellor of the Exchequer, whose introduction of the ◊Stamp Act 1765 to raise revenue from the colonies was one of the causes of the American Revolution. His government was also responsible for prosecuting the radical John ◊Wilkes. Grenville took other measures to reduce the military and civil costs in North America, including the Sugar Act and the Quartering Act. His inept management of the Regency Act 1765 damaged his relationship with George III and he was dismissed by the king.

Grenville Richard 1542–1591. English naval commander and adventurer who died heroically aboard his ship the *Revenge* when attacked by 15 Spanish warships off the Azores. Grenville fought in Hungary and Ireland 1566–69, and was knighted about 1577. In 1585 he commanded the expedition that founded Virginia, for his cousin Walter ◊Raleigh. From 1586 to 1588 he organized the defence of England against the Spanish Armada.

Grenville William Wyndham, Baron 1759–1834. British Whig politician, foreign secretary from 1791; he resigned along with Prime Minister Pitt the Younger 1801 over George III's refusal to assent to Catholic emancipation. He headed the ◊'All the Talents' coalition of 1806–07 that abolished the slave trade.

Grenville, son of George Grenville, entered the House of Commons 1782, held the secretaryship for Ireland, was home secretary 1791–94 and foreign secretary 1794–1801. He refused office in Pitt's government of 1804 because of the exclusion of Charles James ◊Fox.

Gresham Thomas c. 1519–1579. English merchant financier who founded and paid for the Royal Exchange. ***Gresham's law***: 'bad money tends to drive out good money from circulation' is attributed to him.

Thence I walked to the Tower; But Lord! how empty the streets are and how melancholy, so many poor sick people in the streets full of sores... in Westminster, there is never a physician and but one apothecary left, all being dead.

GREAT PLAGUE
Samuel Pepys, Diary, at the height of the plague 16 September 1665

Gretna Green village in Dumfries and Galloway region, Scotland, where runaway marriages remained legal after they were banned in England 1754; all that was necessary was the couple's declaration, before witnesses, of their willingness to marry. From 1856 Scottish law required at least one of the parties to be resident in Scotland for a minimum of 21 days before the marriage, and marriage by declaration was abolished 1940.

Grey Charles, 2nd Earl Grey 1764–1845. British Whig politician. He entered Parliament 1786, and in 1806 became First Lord of the Admiralty, and foreign secretary soon afterwards. As prime minister 1830–34, he carried the Great Reform Bill that reshaped the parliamentary representative system 1832 and the act abolishing slavery throughout the British Empire 1833. He resigned 1834 because of cabinet disagreements over the Irish question.

Grey Edward, 1st Viscount Grey of Fallodon 1862–1933. British Liberal politician, nephew of Charles Grey. As foreign secretary 1905–16 he negotiated an entente with Russia 1907, and backed France against Germany in the Agadir Incident of 1911. He took Britain into World War I in August 1914.

Grey Henry, 3rd Earl Grey 1802–1894. British politician, son of Charles Grey. He served under his father as undersecretary for the colonies 1830–33, resigning because the cabinet would not back the immediate emancipation of slaves; he was secretary of war 1835–39 and colonial secretary 1846–52.

He was unique among politicians of the period in maintaining that the colonies should be governed for their own benefit, not that of Britain, and in his policy of granting self-government wherever possible. Yet he advocated convict transportation and was opposed to Gladstone's Home Rule policy.

Grey Lady Jane 1537–1554. Queen of England for nine days, 10–19 July 1553, the great-granddaughter of Henry VII. She was married 1553 to Lord Guildford Dudley (d. 1554), son of the Duke of Northumberland. Edward VI was persuaded by Northumberland to set aside the claims to the throne of his sisters Mary and Elizabeth. When Edward died 6 July 1553, Jane reluctantly accepted the crown and was proclaimed queen four days later. Mary, although a Roman Catholic, had the support of the populace, and the Lord Mayor of London announced that she was queen 19 July. Grey was executed on Tower Green.

Griffith Arthur 1872–1922. Irish nationalist politician. He was active in nationalist politics from 1898 and united various nationalist parties to form Sinn Féin 1905. When the provisional Irish parliament declared a republic 1919, he was elected vice-president and signed the treaty which gave Eire its independence 1921. He was elected the country's first president 1922, dying in office later that year.

Grindal Edmund *c.* 1519–1583. English cleric and archbishop of Canterbury 1575–77. He served as a chaplain to Edward VI and during the reign of Mary I went into exile in Germany where he was influenced by Calvinist views. When Elizabeth I came to the throne 1558, he returned to England and became bishop of London 1559, archbishop of York 1570, and finally archbishop of Canterbury 1575. He antagonized the queen and her court with his Puritan ethic and was removed as archbishop of Canterbury 1577 after a dispute over 'prophesying', meetings of the clergy at which evangelical sermons were preached.

Grimond Jo(seph), Baron Grimond 1913–1993. British Liberal politician. As leader of the party 1956–67, he aimed at making it 'a new radical party to take the place of the Socialist Party as an alternative to Conservatism'. An old-style Whig and a man of considerable personal charm, he had a strong influence on post-war British politics, although he never held a major public position. During his term of office, the number of Liberal seats in Parliament doubled.

groat ('great penny') English coin worth four pennies. Although first minted 1279, the groat only became popular in the following century, when silver groats were produced. Half groats were introduced 1351.

groundnuts scheme unsuccessful attempt by Clement ◊Attlee's Labour government 1946 to grow groundnuts (peanuts) in East Africa. The scheme was intended partly to improve Britain's balance of payments and partly to stimulate economic activity in the colonies in preparation for eventual independence. By 1949 the scheme proved an expensive failure, and

The only way with newspapers is, as the Irish say, 'to keep never minding'. That has been my practice through life.

CHARLES, EARL GREY
attributed remark

The lamps are going out all over Europe; we shall not see them lit again in our lifetime.

EDWARD,
VISCOUNT GREY
on the impending war
3 Aug 1914
Twenty-five Years

the sheer improbability of the project, at huge cost to the taxpayer, made it a notorious fiasco.

Gruffydd ap Cynan c. 1054–1137. King of ◊Gwynedd 1081–1137. He was raised in Ireland, but came to claim the throne of Gwynedd 1075 and helped halt Norman penetration of Wales. Although defeated and exiled by the Normans 1098, he returned and was allowed to establish his kingdom after paying homage to Henry I. He led a rising against English dominance 1135 until his death two years later. He is traditionally regarded as a patron of music and the arts and helped codify much of the previously chaotic bardic tradition.

Gruffydd ap Llewellyn d.1063. King of ◊Gwynedd. He had gained control of Gwynedd and Powys by 1039, then ◊Deheubarth 1044 and extended his influence to Gwent 1055. By the middle of the 11th century, most of Wales was either under his direct control or subject to his wishes, but his successors were unable to retain this dominance after his death. He conducted a series of raids across the English border and formed alliances with elements in Mercia and other English border areas dissatisfied with King Harold's rule. Harold moved against him and defeated him at Rhuddlan 1063 and he was killed by his own supporters.

guardian in Scotland, title given to official regent appointed when there is no monarch or the monarch is deemed incapable of governing.

Guernsey second largest of the ◊Channel Islands; area 63 sq km/24.3 sq mi. The capital is St Peter Port. From 1975 it has been a major financial centre.

Guernsey has belonged to the English crown since 1066, but was occupied by German forces 1940–45. The island has no jury system; instead, it has a Royal Court with 12 jurats (full-time unpaid jurors appointed by an electoral college) with no legal training. This system dates from Norman times. Jurats cannot be challenged or replaced.

guild or *gild* medieval association, particularly of artisans or merchants, formed for mutual aid and protection and the pursuit of a common purpose, religious or economic. Guilds became politically powerful in Europe but after the 16th century their position was undermined by the growth of capitalism.

Guilds fulfilling charitable or religious functions (for example, the maintenance of schools, roads, or bridges, the assistance of members in misfortune, or the provision of masses for the souls of dead members) flourished in western Europe from the 9th century but were suppressed in Protestant countries at the Reformation.

The earliest form of economic guild, the *guild merchant*, arose during the 11th and 12th centuries; this was an organization of the traders of a town, who had been granted a practical monopoly of its trade by charter. As the merchants often strove to exclude craftworkers from the guild, and to monopolize control of local government, the *craft guilds* came into existence in the 12th and 13th centuries. These, which included journeymen (day workers) and apprentices as well as employers, regulated prices, wages, working conditions, and apprenticeship, prevented unfair practices, and maintained high standards of craft; they also fulfilled many social, religious, and charitable functions. By the 14th century they had taken control of local government, ousting the guild merchant.

guillotine in politics, a device used by UK governments to ensure the speedy passage of bills to receiving the royal assent (that is, to becoming law) by restricting the time allowed for debating it in the House of Commons. The tactic of guillotining was introduced during the 1880s to overcome attempts by Irish members of Parliament to obstruct the passing of legislation. The guillotine is also used as a parliamentary process in France.

guinea English gold coin, notionally worth 21 shillings (£1.05). It has not been minted since 1817, when it was superseded by the gold sovereign, but was used until 1971 in billing professional fees. Expensive items in shops were often priced in guineas.

Gujarat, Battle of final battle 21 Feb 1849 between the British and the Sikhs in the Sikh Wars 1845–49; the British subsequently annexed the Punjab.

The *Battle of Gujarat* was effectively a massacre of 50,000 Sikhs under Shir Singh by 25,000 British troops under Lord Gough. After the Battle of Chilianwala, Gough waited for reinforcements and then marched on the main Sikh army, estimated to be 60,000 strong. He found them drawn up outside Gujarat and opened his attack with an artillery bombardment lasting two and a half hours. The British infantry then advanced and the Sikh ranks broke and ran. They were pursued by cavalry for several miles and completely annihilated. The remainder of the Sikh armies surrendered at Rawalpindi 10 March and the war was ended. British casualties amounted to 96 killed and 700 wounded.

This battle was the first in which surgeons used anesthetics in the field to carry out amputations.

Gulf War 16 Jan–28 Feb 1991 war between Iraq and a coalition of 28 nations led by the USA. The invasion and annexation of Kuwait by Iraq 2 Aug 1990 provoked a build-up of US troops in Saudi Arabia, eventually totalling over 500,000. The UK subsequently deployed 42,000 troops, France 15,000, Egypt 20,000, and other nations smaller contingents. An air offensive lasting six weeks, in which 'smart' weapons came of age, destroyed about one-third of Iraqi equipment and inflicted massive casualties. A 100-hour ground war followed, which effectively destroyed the remnants of the 500,000-strong Iraqi army in or near Kuwait.

Gunpowder Plot Catholic conspiracy, led by Robert Catesby, to blow up James I and his parliament 5 Nov 1605. It was discovered through an anonymous letter from one of the

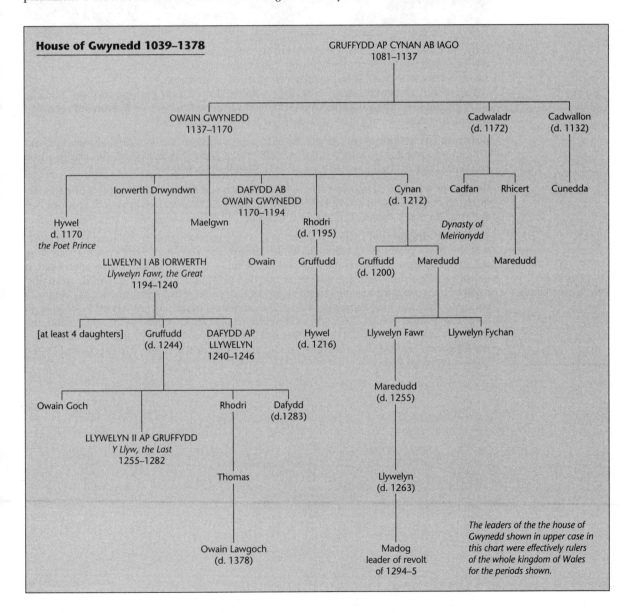

House of Gwynedd 1039–1378

The leaders of the the house of Gwynedd shown in upper case in this chart were effectively rulers of the whole kingdom of Wales for the periods shown.

conspirators, warning a Catholic MP not to attend parliament. Guy ◊Fawkes was found in the cellar beneath the Palace of Westminster, ready to fire a store of explosives. Several of the conspirators were killed, and Fawkes and seven others were executed.

The event is commemorated annually in England on 5 Nov by fireworks and burning 'guys' on bonfires. The searching of the vaults of Parliament before the opening of each new session, however, was not instituted until the 'Popish Plot' of 1678.

Guthrum Danish king of East Anglia. He led a large Danish invasion of Anglo-Saxon England 878 but was defeated by King ◊Alfred at the Battle of ◊Edington 878. Guthrum was baptized and settled in East Anglia where he reigned peacefully 880–890.

Gwyn (or *Gwynn*) Nell (Eleanor) 1651–1687. English comedy actress from 1665. She was formerly an orange-seller at Drury Lane Theatre, London. The poet Dryden wrote parts for her, and from 1669 she was the mistress of Charles II.

*Good people, let me
pass, I am the
Protestant whore.*

NELL GWYN
*to an angry crowd in
Oxford during the Popish
Terror, 1681 (attributed)*

Gwynedd, kingdom of medieval Welsh kingdom comprising north Wales and Anglesey. It was the most powerful kingdom in Wales during the 10th and 11th centuries: its king ◊Gruffydd ap Llewellyn dominated Wales in the mid-11th century and nearly succeeded in uniting the Welsh. When the Normans invaded England, Gwynedd led Welsh resistance against Norman efforts to extend their writ over the border, with mixed success. Llewellyn ap Gruffydd styled himself Prince of Wales 1258, and the English king Henry III was forced to acknowledge him as such 1267. Edward I rightly recognized Gwynedd as the key to subduing the Welsh and he launched a major offensive against Llewellyn 1277, ultimately destroying the kingdom. Gwynedd was broken up and the lands of the ruling dynasty passed to the English Prince of Wales.

H

habeas corpus (Latin, 'you may have the body') in law, a writ directed to someone who has custody of a person, ordering him or her to bring the person before the court issuing the writ and to justify why the person is detained in custody. Traditional rights to habeas corpus were embodied in the English Habeas Corpus Act 1679, mainly owing to the efforts of Lord ◊Shaftesbury. The main principles were adopted in the US Constitution. The Scottish equivalent is the Wrongous Imprisonment Act 1701.

Hadrian's Wall Roman fortification built AD 122–126 during the reign of the Emperor Hadrian to mark the northern boundary of Roman Britain. It runs 117 km/73 mi from Wallsend on the river Tyne to Maryport, West Cumbria. It was defended by 16 forts and smaller intermediate fortifications. It was breached by the Picts on several occasions and was finally abandoned about 383.

Haig Douglas, 1st Earl Haig 1861–1928. British army officer, commander in chief in World War I. His Somme offensive in France in the summer of 1916 made considerable advances only at enormous cost to human life, and his Passchendaele offensive in Belgium from July to Nov 1917 achieved little at a similar loss. He was created field marshal 1917 and, after retiring, became first president of the ◊British Legion 1921.

A national hero at the time of his funeral, Haig's reputation began to fall after Lloyd George's memoirs depicted him as treating soldiers' lives with disdain, while remaining far from battle himself.

Hailsham Quintin Hogg, Baron Hailsham of St Marylebone 1907– . British lawyer and Conservative politician. The 2nd Viscount Hailsham, he renounced the title in 1963 to re-enter the House of Commons, and was then able to contest the Conservative Party leadership elections, but took a life peerage 1970 on his appointment as Lord Chancellor 1970–74. He was Lord Chancellor again 1979–87.

Hakluyt Richard 1553–1616. English geographer whose chief work is *The Principal Navigations, Voyages and Discoveries of the English Nation* 1598–1600. He was assisted by Sir Walter Raleigh.

He lectured on cartography at Oxford, became geographical adviser to the East India Company, and was an original member of the Virginia Company.

Haldane Richard Burdon, Viscount Haldane 1856–1928. British Liberal politician. As secretary for war 1905–12, he sponsored the army reforms that established an expeditionary force, backed by a territorial army and under the unified control of an imperial general staff. He was Lord Chancellor 1912–15 and in the Labour government of 1924. His writings on German philosophy led to accusations of pro-German sympathies during World War I.

halfpenny (or 'ha'penny') originally round silver coins, first minted in the reign of Alfred the Great, and from 1672 the first English copper coin. From the 10th to the 13th centuries, the halfpenny was literally a full penny cut in half but it gradually became a coin in its own right. It was withdrawn with the advent of decimalization 1969, although it remained legal tender until the 1980s.

Halidon Hill, Battle of victory 19 July 1333 of Edward III of England and Edward Balliol over forces under Sir Archibald Douglas attempting to relieve the siege of Berwick. Douglas and five Scottish earls were killed and Berwick surrendered.

Halifax Charles Montagu, Earl of Halifax 1661–1715. British financier. Appointed commissioner of the Treasury 1692, he raised money for the French war by instituting the national

Houses of Hanover and Stuart 1603–1837

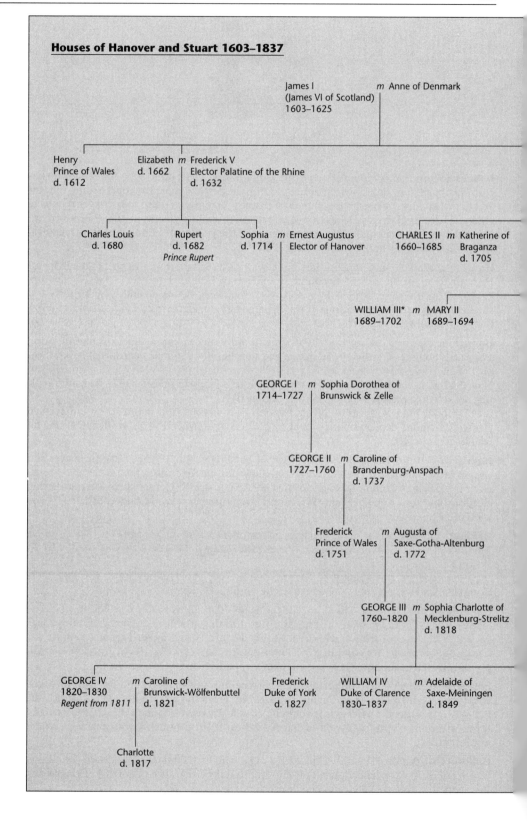

James I
(James VI of Scotland)
1603–1625
m Anne of Denmark

Henry
Prince of Wales
d. 1612

Elizabeth *m* Frederick V
d. 1662   Elector Palatine of the Rhine
            d. 1632

Charles Louis
d. 1680

Rupert
d. 1682
Prince Rupert

Sophia *m* Ernest Augustus
d. 1714   Elector of Hanover

CHARLES II *m* Katherine of
1660–1685   Braganza
            d. 1705

WILLIAM III* *m* MARY II
1689–1702   1689–1694

GEORGE I *m* Sophia Dorothea of
1714–1727   Brunswick & Zelle

GEORGE II *m* Caroline of
1727–1760   Brandenburg-Anspach
            d. 1737

Frederick *m* Augusta of
Prince of Wales   Saxe-Gotha-Altenburg
d. 1751   d. 1772

GEORGE III *m* Sophia Charlotte of
1760–1820   Mecklenburg-Strelitz
             d. 1818

GEORGE IV *m* Caroline of
1820–1830   Brunswick-Wölfenbuttel
Regent from 1811   d. 1821

Frederick
Duke of York
d. 1827

WILLIAM IV *m* Adelaide of
Duke of Clarence   Saxe-Meiningen
1830–1837   d. 1849

Charlotte
d. 1817

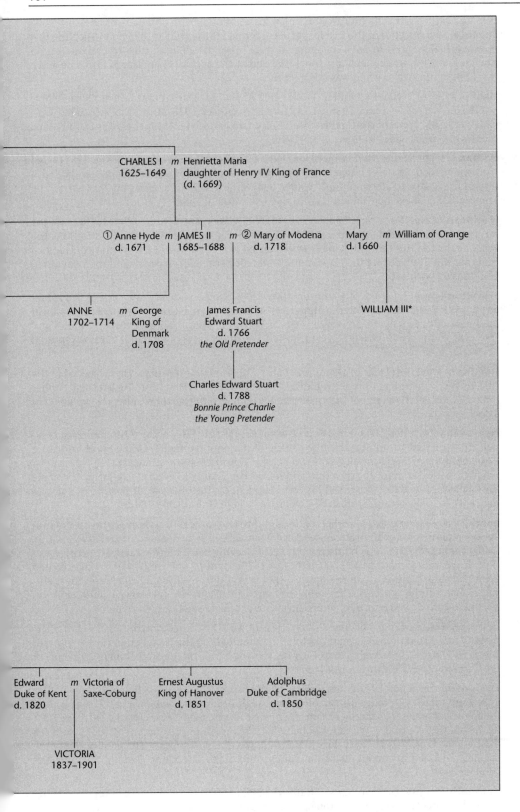

debt and carried out William Paterson's plan for a national bank (the Bank of England) 1694 and became chancellor of the Exchequer. He reformed the currency 1695 and issued the first 'Exchequer Bills', and in 1696 inaugurated the Consolidated Fund, used to pay interest on foreign loans. He was created a baron 1700, and at the accession of George I became again first Lord of the Treasury and was made an earl.

Halifax Edward Frederick Lindley Wood, Earl of Halifax 1881–1959. British Conservative politician, viceroy of India 1926–31. As foreign secretary 1938–40 he was associated with Chamberlain's 'appeasement' policy. He received an earldom 1944 for services to the Allied cause while ambassador to the USA 1941–46.

Halifax George Savile, 1st Marquess of Halifax 1633–1695. English politician. He entered Parliament 1660, and was raised to the peerage by Charles II, by whom he was also later dismissed. He strove to steer a middle course between extremists, and became known as 'the Trimmer'. He played a prominent part in the revolution of 1688.

Hamilton Emma (born Amy Lyon) 1765–1815. English courtesan. In 1782 she became the mistress of Charles Greville and in 1786 of his uncle Sir William Hamilton (1730–1803), the British envoy to the court of Naples, who married her 1791. After Admiral ◊Nelson's return from the Nile 1798 during the Napoleonic Wars, she became his mistress and their daughter, Horatia, was born 1801.

Hamilton James, 1st Duke of Hamilton 1606–1649. Scottish adviser to Charles I. He led an army against the ◊Covenanters (supporters of the National Covenant 1638 to establish Presbyterianism) 1639 and subsequently took part in the negotiations between Charles and the Scots. In the second Civil War he led the Scottish invasion of England, but was captured at Preston and executed.

Hamilton James, 4th Duke of Hamilton 1658–1712. Scottish nobleman. He succeeded to the title 1698 on the resignation of his mother Anne, Duchess of Hamilton. He led the Jacobites in the Scottish parliament but his inconsistency damaged the Jacobite cause. He was killed in a duel.

Hampden John 1594–1643. English politician. His refusal 1636 to pay ◊ship money, a compulsory tax levied to support the navy, made him a national figure. In the Short and Long Parliaments he proved himself a skilful debater and parliamentary strategist.

King Charles' attempt to arrest him and four other leading MPs (the ◊five members) made the Civil War inevitable. He raised his own regiment on the outbreak of hostilities, and was mortally wounded at the skirmish of Chalgrove Field in Oxfordshire 18 June 1643.

hand-loom weavers textile workers of the late 18th and early 19th centuries who used manually operated machines often as 'out-workers'. They were in great demand and relatively highly paid until the advent of mechanised methods of weaving made hand-weaving expensive and slow. There were as many as 200,000 in the late 1820s so the loss of work or cut in wages caused great hardship, particularly in the northwest of England where the trade had been the mainstay of many outlying villages. The problem caused great concern and a royal commission was established 1842, which recommended measures to find alternative employment.

Hanover, House of rulers of great Britain, Ireland, and the United Kingdom 1714–1901. The dynasty originated in the German Guelph (Welf) family, and the Hanoverian rulers of Britain were also Electors (hereditary rulers with the right of choosing the Holy Roman Emperor) of the German state of Hanover until 1837.

Hansard official report of the proceedings of the British Houses of Parliament, named after Luke Hansard (1752–1828), printer of the House of Commons *Journal* from 1774. It is published by Her Majesty's Stationery Office. The first official reports were published from 1803 by the political journalist William Cobbett who, during his imprisonment 1810–12, sold the business to his printer, Thomas Curson Hansard, son of Luke Hansard. The publication of the debates remained in the hands of the family until 1889. The name *Hansard* was officially adopted 1943.

Hanseatic League (German *Hanse* 'group, society') confederation of north European trading cities from the 12th century to 1669. At its height in the late 14th century the Hanseatic League included over 160 cities and towns, among them Lübeck, Hamburg, Cologne, Breslau, and Kraków. The basis of the league's power was its monopoly of the Baltic trade, especially in English cloths, and its relations with Flanders and England.

The League combined into a single company and established a major base at the Steelyard in London 1282, although it was present in provincial towns such as Ipswich and Great Yarmouth. The creation of the ◊Eastland Company 1579 undercut much of their importance, and they were expelled in 1597 as part of a trade war. The League declined from the 15th century due to trade routes moving or being closed and the development of nation states. The last general assembly 1669 marked the end of the league.

Hardicanute (or *Harthacnut*) *c.* 1019–1042. King of Denmark from 1028, and of England from 1040; the son of Canute and Emma, widow of Ethelred the Unready. He was unable to claim the English throne when his father died 1035 and his elder half-brother Harold I became regent and then King 1037. Hardicanute finally became King 1040 and his reign was marked by his violence against Harold's supporters, leading him to be considered a harsh ruler.

Hardie (James) Keir 1856–1915. Scottish socialist, member of Parliament 1892–95 and 1900–15. He worked in the mines as a boy and in 1886 became secretary of the Scottish Miners' Federation. In 1888 he was the first Labour candidate to stand for Parliament; he entered Parliament independently as a Labour member 1892 and was a chief founder of the ◊Independent Labour Party 1893. A pacifist, he strongly opposed the Boer War, and his idealism in his work for socialism and the unemployed made him a popular hero.

Harding (Allan Francis) John, 1st Baron Harding of Petherton 1896–1989. British field marshal. During World War II he was Chief of Staff in Egypt 1940 and Italy 1944. As governor of Cyprus 1955–57, during the period of political agitation prior to independence 1960, he was responsible for the deportation of Makarios III from Cyprus 1955.

Hardy Thomas Masterman 1769–1839. British sailor. At Trafalgar he was Nelson's flag captain in the *Victory*, attending him during his dying moments. He became First Sea Lord 1830.

Harfleur, siege of French siege of English-held port on the mouth of the Seine, late 1415. Henry V seized the port at great cost Aug–Sept 1415 and the French maintained vigorous efforts to recapture the town, even after their defeat at ◊Agincourt. Henry tried to promote Harfleur as a permanent English possession on French soil, like Calais, and went to great lengths to encourage English immigration. The English held until 1435 when it was retaken by the French for five years, before passing back into English possession 1440–49.

Hargreaves James *c.* 1720–1778. English inventor who co-invented a carding machine for combing wool 1760. About 1764 he invented his 'spinning jenny' (patented 1770), which enabled a number of threads to be spun simultaneously by one person. Hargreaves was born near Blackburn, and was initially a weaver, making the first spinning jenny for his family's use. When he began to sell the machines, spinners with the old-fashioned wheel became alarmed by the possibility of cheaper competition and in 1768 a mob from Blackburn gutted Hargreaves's house and destroyed his equipment. Hargreaves moved to Nottingham, where he formed a partnership and built a small cotton mill in which the jenny was used.

Harington Charles 1872–1940. British general. Harington served on the staff during the South African War 1899–1902, and in World War I became chief of the General Staff, British Forces Italy 1917. In 1918 he was appointed Deputy Chief of the Imperial General Staff, War Office.

Harley Robert, 1st Earl of Oxford 1661–1724. British Tory politician, chief minister to Queen Anne 1711–14, when he negotiated the Treaty of Utrecht 1713. Accused of treason as a ◊Jacobite after the accession of George I, he was imprisoned 1714–17.

Harold two kings of England:

Harold I King of England from 1035. The illegitimate son of Canute, known as *Harefoot*, he claimed the throne 1035 when the legitimate heir Hardicanute was in Denmark. He was elected king 1037. He died 1040 as Hardicanute was about to invade England.

Harold II *c.* 1020–1066. King of England from Jan 1066. He succeeded his father Earl Godwin 1053 as Earl of Wessex. In 1063 William of Normandy (◊William the Conqueror) tricked him into swearing to support his claim to the English throne, and when the Witan (a council of high-ranking religious and secular men) elected Harold to succeed Edward the Confessor,

William prepared to invade. Meanwhile, Harold's treacherous brother Tostig (d. 1066) joined the king of Norway, Harald Hardrada (1015–1066), in invading Northumbria. Harold routed and killed them at Stamford Bridge 25 Sept. Three days later William landed at Pevensey, Sussex, and Harold was killed at the Battle of ◊Hastings 14 Oct 1066.

harrying of the north ruthless Norman repression of Anglo-Saxon rebellion in the north of England 1069–70. After his victory at the Battle of ◊Hastings, William the Conqueror faced a series of revolts against Norman rule across England which he suppressed effectively but ruthlessly. One such rising, centred on York, was led by Edgar the Aetheling, an Anglo-Saxon prince, and Earl Waltheof, assisted by a Danish invasion. William first devastated the areas around York to isolate his enemies and the revolt was quickly suppressed and the Danes driven off. William continued his campaign around the north of England to deter further risings and in 1070 attacked parts of Mercia as well. The 'harrying' was effective in deterring further potential rebels but the Domesday Book records that large areas of the north were devastated.

Hartington Spencer Compton Cavendish 1833–1908. 8th Duke of Devonshire, Marquess of Hartington. British politician, first leader of the Liberal Unionists 1886–1903. As war minister he opposed devolution for Ireland in cabinet and later led the revolt of the Liberal Unionists that defeated Gladstone's Irish Home Rule bill 1886. Hartington refused the premiership three times, 1880, 1886, and 1887, and led the opposition to the Irish Home Rule bill in the House of Lords 1893.

Hartlepools, bombardment of in World War I, German attack on the north Yorkshire coast, specifically the seaports of Hartlepool, West Hartlepool, Whitby, and Scarborough 16 Dec 1914 by a German battle-cruiser squadron under the command of Admiral Hipper. The Germans fired 1,150 shells, killing 137 people and wounding 592.

Harvey William 1578–1657. English physician who discovered the circulation of blood. Harvey's discovery marked the beginning of the end of medicine as taught by Greek physician Galen, which had been accepted for 1,400 years. From 1618, he was court physician to James I and later to Charles I. He published his book *De motu cordis/On the Motion of the Heart and the Blood in Animals* 1618. He also explored the development of chick and deer embryos.

Hastings Henry, 3rd Earl of Huntingdon 1535–1595. English Puritan and heir presumptive to the crown. His claim was through his mother, a descendant of George, Duke of Clarence, the brother of Edward IV. He had charge of Mary Queen of Scots 1569–70 and from 1572 reimposed order after the northern rebellion.

Hastings John, 2nd Baron Hastings 1262–1313. Claimant to the Scottish throne. His claim 1290 was as grandson of Ada, third daughter of David, Earl of Huntingdon (later David I). He did not manage to assert his claim and subsequently served Edward I in Irish, Scottish, and Gascon campaigns and served as his lieutenant in Aquitaine 1302.

Hastings Warren 1732–1818. British colonial administrator. A protégé of Lord Clive, who established British rule in India, Hastings carried out major reforms, and became governor of Bengal 1772 and governor general of India 1774. Impeached for corruption on his return to England 1785, he was acquitted 1795.

Hastings, Battle of 14 Oct 1066 battle 14 Oct 1066 at which William, Duke of Normandy, ('the Conqueror') defeated and killed Harold, King of England and himself took the throne. The site is 10 km/6 mi inland from Hastings, at Senlac, Sussex; it is marked by Battle Abbey.

Having defeated an invasion by King Harald Hardrada of Norway at Stamford Bridge, Harold moved south with an army of 9,000 to counter the landing of William Duke of Normandy, who had laid a claim to the English throne, at Pevensey Bay, Kent. The Normans dominated the battle with archers supported by cavalry, breaking through ranks of infantry. Both sides suffered heavy losses but the decimation of the English army and Harold's death left England open to Norman rule.

Hatton Sir Christopher 1540–91. Lord Chancellor 1587–91 and favourite of Queen Elizabeth I. He first came to the queen's attention with his dancing and became an influential and conservative courtier. As a Privy Councillor from 1577, he acted as a government spokesman in the Commons and in Council supported the Earl of Leicester's hard-line anti-Spanish foreign policy. He took a conservative line on the religious status quo, playing a leading part in the trials of Catholic conspirators and ◊Mary Queen of Scots 1586, and as Lord Chancellor, working hard to suppress extreme Puritans and religious separatists.

Haughey Charles 1925–   . Irish Fianna Fáil politician of Ulster descent. Dismissed 1970 from Jack Lynch's cabinet for alleged complicity in IRA gun-running, he was afterward acquitted. He was prime minister 1979–81, March–Nov 1982, and 1986–92, when he was replaced by Albert Reynolds.

Hawkins John 1532–1595. English navigator and slave-trader, born in Plymouth. On his third slave-trading expedition 1567, his fleet was destroyed by the Spanish. Treasurer to the navy 1573–89, he was knighted for his services as a commander against the Spanish Armada 1588.

Hawkins Richard *c.* 1562–1622. English sailor, son of John Hawkins. He held a command against the Spanish Armada 1588, was captured in an expedition against Spanish possessions 1593–94 and released 1602. He was knighted 1603.

Heads of Proposals constitutional demands drawn up by senior Parliamentarian officers July 1647 as a basis for settlement with Charles I at the end of the Civil War. The proposals which were drafted by Henry Ireton, Cromwell's son-in-law, included demands for electoral reform, regular biennial parliaments, a mild form of episcopacy and some religious toleration, parliamentary control of the armed forces, and the right to nominate ministers for a ten-year period. Although the demands were relatively modest, Charles refused to accept the proposals and fled to the Isle of Wight from where he concluded an alternative ◊Engagement with the Scots.

hearth tax unpopular national tax introduced in 1662 at two shillings for every fire hearth, with exemptions for the poor. It was part of the government's attempt to replace feudal dues with a more regular source of revenue but proved highly unpopular and it had to be abandoned 1689 (1690 in Scotland) in favour of a ◊window tax.

Heath Edward (Richard George) 1916–   . British Conservative politician, party leader 1965–75. As prime minister 1970–74 he took the UK into the European Community but was brought down by economic and industrial relations crises at home. He was replaced as party leader by Margaret Thatcher 1975, and became increasingly critical of her policies and her opposition to the UK's full participation in the EC. In 1990 he undertook a mission to Iraq in an attempt to secure the release of British hostages. He returned 1993 to negotiate the release of three Britons held prisoner by Iraq.

Heath entered Parliament 1950, was minister of Labour 1959–60, and as Lord Privy Seal 1960–63 conducted abortive negotiations for Common Market membership. He succeeded Alec Douglas Home as Conservative leader 1965, the first elected leader of his party. Defeated in the general election 1966, he achieved a surprise victory 1970, but his confrontation with the striking miners as part of his campaign to control inflation led to Conservative defeats in the general elections of Feb 1974 and Oct 1974.

Hebrides group of more than 500 islands (fewer than 100 inhabited) off the West coast of Scotland; total area 2,900 sq km/1,120 sq mi. The Hebrides were settled by Scandinavians

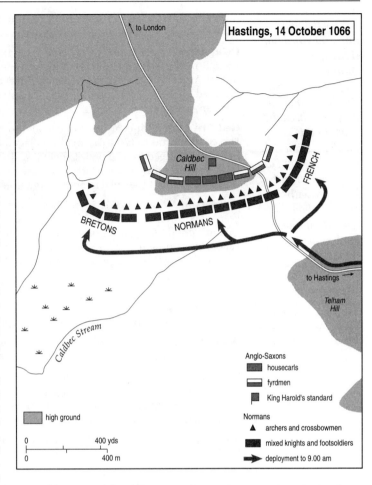

Hastings, 14 October 1066

Hastings, 14 October 1066
Caught off-balance by the immediate Norman acceptance of battle, Harold's housecarls and their supporting fyrdmen adopted a tightly-packed defensive formation on Caldbec Hill, near Hastings. The axe-wielding Anglo-Saxon heavy infantry held off repeated attacks, but steady attrition from Norman archery and combined attacks by knights and footsoldiers finally told, after fighting which lasted all day.

during the 6th to 9th centuries and passed under Norwegian rule from about 890 to 1266. They remained largely autonomous until the 17th century.

Heligoland former British possession, an island in the North Sea northwest of Germany. It was a British possession 1807–90 and was ceded to Germany 1890 in return for concessions in East Africa. Hitler's fortifications were destroyed by the Royal Navy 1947 and the island was used by the RAF for bombing practice until 1952, when it was formally returned to West Germany.

Hell-Fire Club 18th-century club devoted to hedonism and debauchery established by Sir Francis Dashwood (1708–81) in the village of Medmenham, Buckinghamshire. The club reputedly engaged in wild orgies, including devil worship, in caves under the village church. Most of these rumours were later proved to be untrue, but the club revelled in the notoriety they caused and it spawned a series of imitators.

Henderson Arthur 1863–1935. British Labour politician. Born in Glasgow, he worked for 20 years as an iron-moulder in Newcastle. He entered Parliament 1903, and contributed to Labour's political organization and its constitution 1918. He was home secretary in the first Labour government and foreign secretary 1929–31, when he accorded the Soviet government full recognition. He was awarded the Nobel Peace Prize 1934.

henge monument dug-out circular area, often with a surrounding bank, used for ritual purposes by megalithic religions *c.* 2000 BC. Many also contain stone circles, such as those at ◊Stonehenge and ◊Avebury in Wiltshire. Henge monuments are found all over Britain as well as northern France, but primarily in western England.

Hengist d. *c.* 488. Legendary leader, with his brother ***Horsa***, of the Jutes, who originated in Jutland and settled in Kent about 450, the first Anglo-Saxon settlers in Britain.

Henrietta Maria 1609–1669. Queen of England 1625–49. The daughter of Henry IV of France, she married Charles I of England 1625. By encouraging him to aid Roman Catholics and make himself an absolute ruler, she became highly unpopular and was exiled 1644–60. She returned to England at the Restoration but retired to France 1665.

Henry Frederick Prince of Wales 1594–1612. Eldest son of James I of England and Anne of Denmark; a keen patron of Italian art. On his death, his brother Charles became heir to the throne.

Henry eight kings of England:

Henry I 1068–1135. King of England from 1100 and Duke of Normandy from 1106. Youngest son of William the Conqueror, he succeeded his brother William II while his elder brother Robert was on crusade. Robert was compensated with the duchy of Normandy which William later seized, defeating Robert at the Battle of Twickenham 1006. He won the support of the Saxons by granting them a charter and marrying a Saxon princess. An able administrator, he established a professional bureaucracy and rationalized the legal system. In 1120, his only son, William, was drowned and Henry named his daughter Matilda as heir, but on his death the throne was seized by his nephew, Stephen.

Henry II 1133–1189. King of England from 1154, when he succeeded ◊Stephen. He was the son of ◊Matilda and Geoffrey of Anjou (1113–1151) and the first of the Angevin or ***Plantagenet*** kings. He brought order to England after the chaos of Stephen's reign, curbing the power of the barons and reforming the legal system; he introduced ◊assizes and the jury system. His attempt to bring the church courts under control had to be abandoned after the murder of Thomas à ◊Becket. The English conquest of Ireland began 1161 during his reign. He was succeeded by his son Richard I.

Henry III 1207–1272. King of England from 1216, when he succeeded John, but the royal powers were exercised by a regency until 1232 and by two French nobles, Peter des Roches and Peter des Rivaux, until the barons forced their expulsion 1234, marking the start of Henry's personal rule. His financial commitments to the papacy and his foreign favourites antagonized the barons who issued the Provisions of Oxford 1258, limiting the king's power. Henry's refusal to accept the provisions led to the second Barons' War 1264, a revolt of nobles led by his brother-in-law Simon de ◊Montfort. Henry was defeated at Lewes, Sussex, 1264 and imprisoned. He was restored to the throne after the royalist victory at ◊Evesham 1265. He was succeeded by his son Edward I.

Henry IV (Bolingbroke) 1367–1413. King of England from 1399, the son of ◊John of Gaunt and the first king of the House of Lancaster. In 1398 he was banished by ◊Richard II for political activity but returned 1399, forced Richard to abdicate and was accepted as king by Parliament. He had difficulty in keeping the support of Parliament and the clergy, and had to deal with baronial unrest and ◊Glendower's rising in Wales 1400–09. In order to win support he had to conciliate the church by a law for the burning of heretics, and to make many concessions to Parliament. He was succeeded by his son Henry V.

Henry V 1387–1422. King of England from 1413, son of Henry IV. He fought against ◊Glendower and the Welsh during the revolt of 1400–09. He claimed the French throne through his descent from Edward III and invaded Normandy 1415 (during the Hundred Years' War), captured Harfleur and defeated the French at ◊Agincourt. He invaded again 1417–19, capturing Rouen. His military victory forced the French into the Treaty of Troyes 1420, which gave Henry control of the French government. He married ◊Catherine of Valois 1420 and gained recognition as heir to the French throne by his father-in-law Charles VI, but died before him. He was succeeded by his son Henry VI.

Henry V
Henry V had a reputation as a stern but just ruler. Most of his reign was taken up by war with the French and such was his success that by 1420 he was recognized as the heir to the reigning French monarch, Charles VI, whose daughter he married.
Philip Sauvain

Henry VI 1421–1471. King of England from 1422, son of Henry V. He assumed royal power 1442 and sided with the party opposed to the continuation of the Hundred Years' War with France. Henry seems to have been badly suited to being a ruler and suffered from periodic bouts of insanity. After his marriage 1445, he was dominated by his wife, ◊Margaret of Anjou. The unpopularity of the government, especially after the loss of the English conquests in France, encouraged Richard, Duke of ◊York, to claim the throne, and though York was killed 1460, his son Edward IV proclaimed himself king 1461 and Henry fled to Scotland (see Wars of the ◊Roses). Henry was captured 1465, temporarily restored by the Earl of Warwick 1470, but was again imprisoned 1471 and then murdered.

Henry VII 1457–1509. King of England from 1485, son of Edmund Tudor, Earl of Richmond (c. 1430–1456), and a descendant of ◊John of Gaunt. He lived in Brittany until 1485, when he landed in Britain to lead the rebellion against Richard III which ended with Richard's defeat and death at the Battle of ◊Bosworth. By his marriage to Elizabeth of York 1486, he united the houses of York and Lancaster. Yorkist revolts continued until 1497, but Henry restored order after the Wars of the ◊Roses by the ◊Star Chamber and achieved independence from Parliament by amassing a private fortune through confiscations. He was succeeded by his son Henry VIII.

Henry VIII 1491–1547. King of England from 1509, when he succeeded his father Henry VII and married Catherine of Aragon, the widow of his brother.

During the period 1513–29 Henry pursued an active foreign policy, largely under the guidance of his Lord Chancellor, Cardinal Wolsey, who shared Henry's desire to make England stronger. Henry and Wolsey exploited the rivalry between Francis I of France and the Emperor Charles V by making England the arbiter between them, enhancing the prestige and influence of England. Both kings sought Henry's favour, Francis at the Field of the Cloth of Gold, and Charles, less ostentatiously, in Kent. The policy collapsed disastrously after Henry began supporting Charles 1522.

Wolsey was replaced by Thomas More 1529 for failing to persuade the pope to grant Henry a divorce from Catherine. Henry was becoming desperate for a male heir and was determined to marry Anne Boleyn. Henry acted through Parliament, and had the entire body of the

The kings, my predecessors, weakening their treasure, have made themselves servants to their subjects.

HENRY VII
to Henry Wyatt, one of his councillors.

clergy in England declared guilty of treason 1531. The clergy were suitably cowed and agreed to repudiate papal supremacy and recognize Henry as supreme head of the Church in England. He divorced Catherine 1533 and married Anne Boleyn, who was beheaded 1536, ostensibly for adultery.

Henry continued his attack on the church with the suppression of the monasteries 1536–39; their lands were confiscated and granted to his supporters. However, although he laid the ground for the English Reformation by the separation from Rome, he had little sympathy with Protestant dogmas. As early as 1521 a pamphlet which he had written against Lutheranism had won him the title of *Fidei Defensor* from the Pope, and Henry's own religious views are quite clearly expressed in the Statute of ◊Six Articles 1539 which instituted the orthodox Catholic tenets as necessary conditions for Christian belief. As a result Protestants were being burnt for heresy even while Catholics were being executed for refusing to take the oath of supremacy.

Henry's third wife, Jane Seymour, died 1537. He married Anne of Cleves 1540 in pursuance of Thomas Cromwell's policy of allying with the German Protestants, but rapidly abandoned this policy, divorced Anne, and beheaded Cromwell. His fifth wife, Catherine Howard, was beheaded 1542, and the following year he married Catherine Parr, who survived him. Henry never completely lost his popularity, but wars with France and Scotland toward the end of his reign sapped the economy, and in religion he not only executed Roman Catholics, including Thomas More, for refusing to acknowledge his supremacy in the church, but also Protestants who maintained his changes had not gone far enough.

Henry, the young king 1155–1183. Eldest son of Henry II, he was crowned 1170 as his father's successor and associate while his father was still king, in line with continental custom to avoid a disputed succession. However, it only succeeded in making the young Henry, incited by his mother Eleanor of Aquitaine, impatient for the power he regarded as rightfully his and he joined the baronial revolt against his father 1173–74. He was reconciled with his father 1174, but joined his brother Geoffrey in a subsequent rebellion during which he died.

Heptarchy the seven Saxon kingdoms thought to have existed in England before AD 800: Northumbria, Mercia, East Anglia, Essex, Kent, Sussex, and Wessex. The dominant king of the seven was called the 'bretwalda' and accepted fealty from the others.

heraldry insignia and symbols representing a person, family, or dynasty; the science of armorial bearings. Heraldry originated with simple symbols used on shields and banners for recognition in battle. By the 14th century, it had become a complex pictorial language with its own regulatory bodies (courts of chivalry), used by noble families, corporations, cities, and realms. The world's oldest heraldic court is the English College of Arms founded by Henry V; it was incorporated 1484 by Richard III.

The national flags (St George's cross for England, St Andrew's saltire for Scotland, St Patrick's cross for Ireland) indicate national identity. Similarly, the quartered Royal 'Standard', properly Banner, is the insignia of the ruling authority – the Crown – in Great Britain; the joined crosses, or Union Jack, the national flag, indicate British national identity.

Herbert William, 1st Earl of Pembroke d.1469. Welsh nobleman. He supported the Yorkists in the Wars of the Roses and became Edward IV's chief counsellor after 1461. He led a successful siege of Harlech Castle 1468 and was made earl. He was captured by the Lancastrians 1469 and executed.

Herbert of Lea Sidney Herbert, 1st Baron Herbert of Lea 1810–1861. British politician. He was secretary for war in Aberdeen's Liberal-Peelite coalition of 1852–55, and during the Crimean War was responsible for sending Florence Nightingale to the front.

Hereward the Wake English leader of a revolt against the Normans 1070. His stronghold in the Isle of Ely was captured by William the Conqueror 1071. Hereward escaped, but his fate is unknown.

Hexham, Battle of in the Wars of the Roses, Yorkist victory 15 May 1464 over the Lancastrian army of Henry Beaufort, 3rd Duke of Somerset. Somerset was caught in a trap near Hexham, Northumberland, and obliged to surrender to a Yorkist force under Lord Montague; he was executed.

hide or *hyde* Anglo-Saxon unit of measurement used to measure the extent of arable land; it varied from about 296 ha/120 acres in the east of England to as little as 99 ha/40 acres in

◊Wessex. One hide was regarded as sufficient to support a peasant and his household; it was the area that could be ploughed in a season by one plough and one team of oxen. The hide was the basic unit of assessment for taxation and military service; under Norman rule it became the basis for the feudal tax of hidage.

High Church group in the ◊Church of England that emphasizes aspects of Christianity usually associated with Catholics, such as ceremony and hierarchy. The term was first used in 1703 to describe those who opposed Dissenters, and later for groups such as the 19th-century ◊Oxford Movement.

High Commission ecclesiastical court established under the Royal Supremacy in the provinces of York and Canterbury following Henry VIII's break with Rome 1534. It dealt primarily with offences against the Acts of ◊Supremacy and ◊Uniformity and from the 1590s was used to root out extreme Puritanism and later to assist the ◊Arminians. Both Puritans and lawyers protested against its arbitrary abuse of procedure and the court became increasingly discredited until it was eventually abolished 1641 after the Stuarts had used it to enforce the royal prerogative.

Highland Clearances forced removal of tenants from Highland estates in Scotland starting in 1750. The clearances were carried out by landowners who sought to improve their estates by converting from arable to sheep farming. They caused much hardship and led to widespread immigration to North America, where thousands settled along the east coast of Canada. The major clearances were completed by the 1850s.

Highland Host force of highlanders brought into southwest Scotland 1678 to suppress Scottish Covenanters by the Earl of Lauderdale. For two months the host engaged in pillage and confiscation of lands until their brutality and their local unpopularity led to them being withdrawn. In some ways, they increased public sympathy for the Covenanters as many regarded them as Lowland Protestants being persecuted by Highlanders, even though up to a third of the Host were themselves Lowlanders. Lauderdale himself was a staunch supporter of Charles II, though he had himself been a Covenanter and had signed the ◊Engagement with Charles I.

highwayman in English history, a thief on horseback who robbed travellers on the highway (those who did so on foot were known as **footpads**). Highwaymen continued to flourish well into the 19th century. With the development of regular coach services in the 17th and 18th centuries, the highwaymen's activities became notorious, and the Bow Street runners (see ◊police) were organized to suppress them.

Among the best-known highwaymen were Jonathan ◊Wild, Claude Duval, John Nevison (1639–1684), the original hero of the 'ride to York', Dick ◊Turpin and his partner Tom King, and Jerry Abershaw (*c.* 1773–1795). Favourite haunts were Hounslow and Bagshot heaths and Epping Forest, around London.

hill figure any of a number of ancient figures, usually of animals, cut from downland turf to show the underlying chalk. Examples include the ◊White Horses, the Long Man of Wilmington, East Sussex, and the Cerne Abbas Giant, Dorset. Their origins are variously attributed to Celts, Romans, Saxons, Druids, or Benedictine monks.

hillfort European Iron Age site with massive banks and ditches for defence, used as both a military camp and a permanent settlement. An example is Maiden Castle, Dorset.

Hillsborough Agreement another name for the ◊Anglo-Irish Agreement 1985.

Hoare–Laval Pact plan for a peaceful settlement to the Italian invasion of Ethiopia Oct 1935. It was devised by Samuel Hoare (1880–1959), British foreign secretary, and

hill figure
The Uffington White Horse in Oxfordshire is one of Britain's most ancient hill figures. It is 374 foot high and is situated just below the ramparts of an Iron Age hill fort. It may have served as both a tribal deity and territorial boundary.
Aerofilms

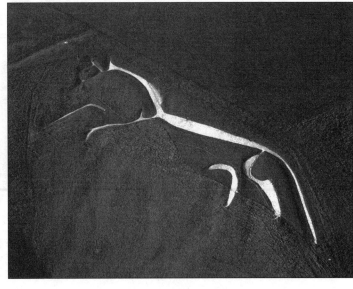

Pierre Laval, French premier, at the request of the League of Nations. Realizing no European country was willing to go to war over Ethiopia, Hoare and Laval proposed official recognition of Italian claims. Public outcry in Britain against the pact's seeming approval of Italian aggression was so great that the pact had to be disowned and Hoare was forced to resign.

Holland Henry Richard Vassall Fox, 3rd Baron Holland 1773–1840. British Whig politician. He was Lord Privy Seal 1806–07. His home, at Holland House, London, was for many years the centre of Whig political and literary society.

Hollis Roger 1905–1973. British civil servant, head of the secret intelligence service MI5 1956–65. He was alleged to have been a double agent together with Kim Philby, but this was denied by the KGB 1991.

Holy Island or *Lindisfarne* island in the North Sea, area 10 sq km/4 sq mi, 3 km/2 mi off Northumberland, with which it is connected by a causeway. St ♭Aidan founded a monastery here 635.

homage feudal ceremony symbolizing the submission of a tenant to his lord. The lord would take the clasped hands of a kneeling man, and kisses might be exchanged as a sign of friendship. The ceremony formed a mutual bond: while the man was bound to serve the lord, in return the lord guaranteed his protection. The ceremony could be used in a broader context, as for example, the Scottish king Malcolm III paying homage to Henry II of England to indicate his acceptance of Henry's rule.

home front the organized sectors of domestic activity in wartime, mainly associated with World Wars I and II. Features of the UK home front in World War II included the organization of the black-out, evacuation, air-raid shelters, the Home Guard, rationing, and distribution of gas masks. With many men on active military service, women were called upon to carry out jobs previously undertaken only by men.

Home Guard in World War II, unpaid force formed in Britain May 1940 to repel the expected German invasion, and known until July 1940 as the Local Defence Volunteers. It consisted of men aged 17–65 who had not been called up, formed part of the armed forces of the crown, and was subject to military law. Its members worked at their normal occupations and undertook military training in their spare time. In 1940 they were armed with a motley collection of shotguns and privately-owned weapons, but by 1942 they were a well-trained body liberally provided with automatic weapons and light artillery. Over 2 million strong by 1944, it was disbanded 31 Dec 1945, but revived 1951, then placed on a reserve basis 1955, and ceased activities 1957.

Home Rule, Irish movement to repeal the Act of ♭Union 1801 that joined Ireland to Britain and to establish an Irish parliament responsible for internal affairs. In 1870 Isaac Butt

Home Rule, Irish
Riots in support of Irish Home Rule, Glasgow 1880, the year Parnell took over as leader of the Home Rule movement. Gladstone introduced a Home Rule Bill six years later but it was defeated.
Hulton Deutsch

THE CONTINUING QUEST

Ireland and the Struggle for Home Rule

The Irish rebellion of 1798 demonstrated that the Protestant Ascendancy could not keep Ireland stable, and prompted British moves toward union. The Act of Union 1800 abolished the Irish Parliament in return for Irish representation at Westminster. However, Pitt the Younger's attempt to admit Catholics to public office was thwarted by George III; Catholics could not become MPs in the new Parliament until 1829, which created much resentment. The Union ensured that the politics of Ireland were more closely linked with those of Britain than ever before.

A brief survey of Ireland in this period might centre on hardship and discord: the potato famine of 1845–48 and the struggle for Irish political autonomy were both of great importance. Yet Ireland remained within the British Empire, there was no collapse into anarchy or civil war, and the Irish economy developed as part of the growing imperial economy, even while Ireland's Catholic areas became more socially and culturally distinct.

The closing decades of the century brought economic and social change, and reform as in mainland Britain. The (Anglican) Church of Ireland was disestablished 1869, and the position of the Catholic church markedly improved. By 1914 Ireland had gained a large share of economic independence. Legislation from 1860 to 1903 progressively broke the power of the landlords: farmers increasingly owned their holdings. Local government was also transferred to the control of the largely Catholic majority.

Irish nationalism

Nationalism was revived as a political issue by Daniel O'Connell, who campaigned in the 1830s and 1840s for the repeal of the Act of Union. The government responded by attempts at reform and by limiting extra-parliamentary agitation. Nonetheless, the potato famine led to allegations of government neglect as about 800,000 people died from starvation or diseases made more deadly by malnutrition.

The extension of the franchise in 1867 and 1884 greatly increased the number of Catholic voters; most supported Home Rule, which would have given an Irish Parliament control of all policy matters bar defence and foreign policy. The Home Government Association of 1870 was followed by the Home Rule League in 1873. Charles Stuart Parnell became leader of an organized and powerful parliamentary pro-Home Rule party 1879, with 61 MPs by 1880, 86 by 1885, and 85 by 1886.

Home Rule proposals introduced by Gladstone in 1886 and 1893 were defeated at Westminster. Conservatives led the resistance, renaming their party the Conservative and Unionist Party in 1886, but the defeat of the First Home Rule Bill in 1886 was due to the defection of 93 'Liberal Unionists' from Gladstone's government.

Nationalist agitation also had a violent dimension. In 1848 the Young Ireland movement attempted an insurrection. The Fenians, a secret organization founded in 1858, tried to launch a rebellion in Ireland in 1867 and were responsible for terrorist acts in Britain and an attempted invasion of Canada from the United States. Reconstituted as the Irish Republican Brotherhood in 1873, they continued to mount terrorist attacks, and in 1882 another secret society, the Invincibles, murdered Lord Frederick Cavendish, the Chief Secretary for Ireland, in Phoenix Park, Dublin. Some Irishmen served with the Boers during the South African War of 1899–1902.

The Easter Rising

Another Liberal government, dependent on Irish Nationalist support, introduced a Home Rule Bill in 1912. Twice rejected by the Conservative-dominated House of Lords, the Bill was passed in an amended form in 1914 with the proviso that it was not to be implemented until after the war. Protestant Ulster was determined to resist Home Rule. The formation of the Ulster Unionist Council in 1905 and the Ulster Volunteer Force in 1913 revealed an unwillingness of the Ulster Protestants to subordinate their identity to Irish nationalism. In 1914 the country came to the brink of civil war.

Half a million men of Irish descent, both Protestant and Catholic, volunteered to fight for Britain in 1914; fewer than 2,000 rose in the Easter Rising of 1916 in Dublin. The planned nationalist uprising failed to materialize outside Dublin. The British response, however, served to radicalize Irish public opinion. Martial law was declared and a series of trials, executions, and internments provided martyrs for the nationalist cause. In the 1918 general election 73 out of the 105 Irish parliamentary seats were won by Sinn Féin (Nationalists) under Eámon de Valera.

In Jan 1919 a unilateral Declaration of Independence was issued by a new national assembly (Dail Eireann) and the nationalist Irish Volunteers, soon to rename themselves the Irish Republican Army, staged their first fatal ambush. A brutal civil war ensued (1919–21), followed by the Anglo-Irish Treaty in December 1921, which brought partition and effective independence for the new Irish Free State. Six counties in Ulster opted out as Northern Ireland, which remained part of the United Kingdom.

JEREMY BLACK

Ireland 1801–1921: chronology	
1800	Act of Union established United Kingdom of Great Britain and Ireland. Effective 1801.
1823	Catholic Association founded by Daniel O'Connell to campaign for Catholic political rights.
1828	O'Connell elected for County Clare; forces granting of rights for Catholics to sit in Parliament.
1829	Catholic Emancipation Act.
1838	Tithe Act (abolishing payment) removed a major source of discontent.
1840	Franchise in Ireland reformed. 'Young Ireland' formed.
1846–51	Potato famine resulted in widespread death and emigration. Population reduced by 20%.
1850	Irish Franchise Act extended voters from 61,000 to 165,000.
1858	Fenian Brotherhood formed.
1867	Fenian insurrection failed.
1869	Church of Ireland disestablished.
1870	Land Act provided greater security for tenants but failed to halt agrarian disorders. Protestant Isaac Butt formed Home Government Association (Home Rule League).
1874	Home Rule League won 59 parliamentary seats and adopted a policy of obstruction.
1880	Charles Stuart Parnell became leader of Home Rulers, dominated by Catholic groups. 'Boycotts' against landlords unwilling to agree to fair rents.
1881	Land Act greeted with hostility. Parnell imprisoned. 'No Rent' movement began.
1882	'Kilmainham Treaty' between government and Parnell agreed conciliation. Chief Secretary Cavendish and Under Secretary Burke murdered in Phoenix Park, Dublin.
1885	Franchise Reform gave Home Rulers 85 seats in new parliament and balance between Liberals and Tories. Home Rule Bill rejected.
1886	Home Rule Bill rejected again.
1890	Parnell cited in divorce case, which split Home Rule movement.
1893	Second Home Rule Bill defeated in House of Lords; Gaelic League founded.
1900	Irish Nationalists reunited under Redmond. 82 MPs elected.
1902	Sinn Féin founded by Arthur Griffith.
1906	Bill for devolution of power to Ireland rejected by Nationalists.
1910	Sir Edward Carson led Unionist opposition to Home Rule.
1912	Home Rule Bill for whole of Ireland introduced. (Protestant) Ulster Volunteers formed to resist.
1913	Home Rule Bill defeated in House of Lords but overridden. (Catholic) Irish Volunteers founded in the South.
1914	Nationalists persuaded to exclude Ulster from Bill for six years but Carson rejected it. Curragh 'mutiny' cast doubt on reliability of British troops against Protestants. Extensive gun-running by both sides. World War I deferred implementation.
1916	Easter Rising by members of Irish Republican Brotherhood. Suppressed by troops and leaders executed.
1919	Irish Republican Army (IRA) formed.
1921	Partition of Ireland; creation of Irish Free State.

Before Irish Home Rule is conceded by the Imperial Parliament, England as the predominant member of the three kingdoms will have to be convinced of its justice and equality.

IRISH HOME RULE
speech by the Earl of Rosebery, House of Lords, 1894

(1813–1879) formed the Home Rule Association and the movement was led in Parliament from 1880 by Charles ◊Parnell. Gadstone's Home Rule bills 1886 and 1893 were both defeated. A third bill was introduced by the Liberals 1912, which aroused opposition in Ireland where the Protestant minority in Ulster feared domination by the Catholic majority. Ireland appeared on the brink of civil war but the outbreak of World War I rendered further consideration of Home Rule inopportune. After 1918 the demand for an independent Irish republic replaced that for home rule. In 1920 the Government of Ireland Act introduced separate parliaments in the North and South and led to the treaty 1921 that established the Irish Free State.

Homildon Hill, Battle of English victory in Northumberland 14 Sept 1402 over the Scots under Archibald ◊Douglas, 4th Earl of Douglas. The north of England had been troubled by Scots raids and Henry Percy, 1st Earl of Northumberland, and his son Sir Henry Percy (Hotspur) attacked Douglas and his allies, capturing him and 79 other Scottish nobles.

Hong Kong British crown colony, in southeast China. The island of Hong Kong was occupied by the British 1839 and ceded to Britain by the Chinese 1841. The Kowleen Peninsula was similarly ceded 1860 and the New Territories leased to Great Britain for 99 years 1898. Under a Sino-British agreement 1985, Hong Kong becomes a special administrative region (SAR) of the Chinese Republic 1997. Social and economic systems in the SAR, however, will remain unchanged for 50 years.

honour collection of feudal territories belonging to one lord. Originally a form of military control during the Norman conquest, in the next century many honours grew to encompass estates scattered throughout the kingdom or even over more than one country. The honorial court, comprising the major vassals of a great lord, was held at the head of the honour, usually a central castle from which the estate was administered. Most of the estates had gone by the 13th century, though royal honours and jurisdictions remained intact in the 16th and 17th centuries.

Hood Samuel, 1st Viscount Hood 1724–1816. British admiral. A masterly tactician, he defeated the French at Dominica in the West Indies 1783, and in the ◊French Revolutionary Wars captured Toulon 1793 and Corsica 1794.

Hooke Robert 1635–1703. English scientist and inventor, originator of ***Hooke's law***, and considered the foremost mechanic of his time. His inventions included a telegraph system, the spirit level, marine barometer, and sea gauge. He coined the term 'cell' in biology.

He studied elasticity, furthered the sciences of mechanics and microscopy, invented the hairspring regulator in timepieces, perfected the air pump, and helped improve such scientific instruments as microscopes, telescopes, and barometers.

Hopton Ralph, Baron Hopton 1596–1652. English Puritan and royalist commander. He intially supported Parliament against Charles I due to his Puritan beliefs, but changed his allegiance to the royalists when Parliament took control of the militia 1642. As Lieutenant General of western England he gained several royalist victories in the southwest, including Stratton May 1643 and Lansdown July 1643, where he was badly wounded. He was obliged to surrender to General Thomas Fairfax at Truro 1646 and retired into exile in Bruges where he died.

Hornby v Close court case 1867, in which it was decided that trade unions were illegal associations. The decision, overturned two years later by a special act of Parliament, indirectly led to the full legalization of trade unions under the Trade Union Acts 1871–76.

The case arose when the Boilermaker's Society attempted to recover funds held by the treasurer of its Bradford branch that the union thought were retrievable under the terms of the Friendly Societies Act of 1865. Local magistrates found against the Boilermakers on the grounds that ◊trade unions did not fall within the scope of the Act. The decision was upheld in a higher court where it was also held that although trade unions had ceased to be criminal organizations since the 1825 Act, they remained illegal associations because they acted in 'restraint of trade'. The implication of this was that union funds had no legal protection and could be embezzled with impunity.

Horsa Anglo-Saxon leader, brother of ◊Hengist.

Horton Max 1883–1951. British admiral and submarine specialist in World War II. In 1942 he became commander in chief on the Western Approaches, responsible for convoys crossing the Atlantic. He rapidly made his mark, adopting a variety of measures and tactics to neutralize the U-boat threat and eventually gained the upper hand. He remained in this post until the war ended.

houscarl 11th-century military fraternity used by the Danish kings of England as a form of bodyguard and standing army. The system was introduced by King Canute 1016 and was initially paid for by the *heregeld* ('army tax'), although from 1051 they no longer received direct payment but were instead given grants of land, in return for which they would fight when summoned.

House of Commons lower chamber of the UK ◊Parliament.

House of Lords upper chamber of the UK ◊Parliament. Its members are unelected and comprise the ***temporal peers***: all hereditary peers of England created to 1707, all

House of Lords
A contemporary illustration showing Edward I in the House of Lords, flanked by his vassals Alexander III, king of Scotland, and Llewelyn II, prince of Wales.
Philip Sauvain

hereditary peers of Great Britain created 1707–1800, and all hereditary peers of the UK from 1801 onwards; all hereditary Scottish peers (under the Peerage Act 1963); all peeresses in their own right (under the same act); all life peers (both the law lords and those created under the Life Peerages Act 1958); and the ***spiritual peers***: the two archbishops and 24 of the bishops (London, Durham, and Winchester by right, and the rest by seniority). Since the Parliament Act 1911 the powers of the Lords have been restricted in that they may delay a bill passed by the Commons but not reject it. The Lords are presided over by the Lord Chancellor.

Household, Royal see ◊royal household.

houses of correction early workhouses set up under the poor laws of 1576 and 1597 as a response to rising population and unemployment. A house of correction was set up in each county and major town, ostensibly to house the indigent and punish the work-shy but they soon became little more than prisons for petty criminals.

Howard Catherine *c.* 1520–1542. Queen consort of ◊Henry VIII of England from 1540. In 1541 the archbishop of Canterbury, Thomas Cranmer, accused her of being unchaste before marriage to Henry and she was beheaded 1542 after Cranmer made further charges of adultery.

Howard Charles, 2nd Baron Howard of Effingham and 1st Earl of Nottingham 1536–1624. English admiral, a cousin of Queen Elizabeth I. He commanded the fleet against the Spanish Armada while Lord High Admiral 1585–1618. and cooperated with the Earl of Essex in the attack on Cadiz 1596.

Howe Richard, Earl Howe 1726–1799. British admiral. He cooperated with his brother William against the colonists during the American Revolution and in the French Revolutionary Wars commanded the Channel fleets 1792–96. He won the victory of the Glorious First of June in 1794 off the island of Ushant, Brittany.

Howe William, 5th Viscount Howe 1729–1814. British general. During the American Revolution he won the Battle of Bunker Hill 1775, and as commander in chief in America 1776–78 captured New York and defeated Washington at Brandywine and Germantown. He resigned in protest at lack of home government support.

Hudson George 1800–1871. Conservative politician and industrialist. He started out as a draper in York until he inherited £30,000 1828 and invested heavily and successfully in the burgeoning railway system. By the late 1840s, he controlled up to a third of Britain's railways and had also begun a successful career in local politics. He was mayor of York three times and was elected as member of Parliament for Sunderland 1845. He was forced to flee the country briefly 1849 when financial difficulties led to allegations of fraud and his business empire all but collapsed.

Hudson's Bay Company chartered company founded by Prince ◊Rupert 1670 to trade in furs with North American Indians. In 1783 the rival North West Company was formed, but in 1851 this became amalgamated with the Hudson's Bay Company. It is still Canada's biggest fur company, but today also sells general merchandise through department stores and has oil and natural gas interests.

hue and cry alarm cry that inhabitants of a manor (or ◊frankpledge) were duty-bound to raise and respond to, in order to assist in the apprehension of criminals. All members of the manor were bound to join in the pursuit and apprehension of a suspected offender and hand them over to the sheriff for punishment and failure to do so was in itself punishable. The term has now come to refer to any form of general clamour or turmoil.

Huguenot French Protestant in the 16th century; the term referred mainly to Calvinists. Severely persecuted under Francis I and Henry II, the Huguenots survived both an attempt to exterminate them (the ***Massacre of St Bartholomew*** 24 Aug 1572) and the religious wars of the next 30 years. In 1598 Henry IV (himself formerly a Huguenot) granted them toleration under the ***Edict of Nantes***. Louis XIV revoked the edict 1685, attempting their forcible conversion, and 400,000 emigrated. Some 40,000 settled in Britain and a thriving community of silk weavers was established at Spitalfields, East London. Their descendants include the actor David Garrick and the textile manufacturer Samuel Courtauld.

The House of Lords is like a glass of champagne that has stood for five days.

HOUSE OF LORDS
Clement Attlee, attributed remark

Humble Petition and Advice constitutional proposal put to Oliver Cromwell by Parliament 25 May 1657 to moderate army rule under the major-generals. Although Cromwell refused the crown which the petition urged him to accept, he agreed to other clauses: he nominated a successor; created a second chamber of Parliament, consisting of up to 70 life peers; and curbed the powers of the Council of State. Parliament's power was greatly increased after the settlement, particularly in regard to taxation, and the petition formed the basis of the constitution until the disputes between Richard Cromwell and the ◊Rump Parliament 1659.

Hume John 1937– . Northern Ireland Catholic politician, leader of the Social Democratic Labour Party (SDLP) from 1979. Hume was a founder member of the Credit Union Party, which later became the SDLP. In 1993 he held talks with Sinn Féin leader, Gerry Adams, on

Hundred Years' War: chronology

1337	*24 May* Philip VI of France confiscated the duchy of Aquitaine in southwest France from Edward III of England. Edward responded by asserting his claim to the French throne.
1340	*Jan* Edward formally assumed the title 'king of France'. *24 June* Battle of Sluis: an English fleet defeated a larger French fleet off Sluys at the mouth of the River Zwyn. *25 Sept* Edward agreed the Treaty of Espléchin.
1346	*July* After negotiations failed, Edward landed in Normandy, north France, with a large army. *26 Aug* Battle of Crécy: the English defeated a French army at Crécy-en-Ponthieu.
1347	*4 Aug* After besieging Calais for a year, the English captured the town.
1356	After a pause in hostilities, the English defeated the French at the Battle of Poitiers and captured the French king, John II.
1360	*May* Following another English campaign in France, the Treaty of Brétigny was agreed: France ceded Aquitaine, Normandy and other territories to Edward. In the supplementary Treaty of Calais (Oct), Edward dropped his claim to the French throne.
1368	The new king of France, Charles V, agreed to intervene, as feudal superior, in a dispute in Aquitaine.
1369	*June* In retaliation for Charles's involvement in Aquitaine, Edward resumed the title 'king of France'. In Nov, Charles confiscated Aquitaine from Edward, thus restarting the conflict.
1370–6	The French conquered parts of Aquitaine. The English campaigned in French territory, but achieved little.
1393	The kings of England and France, Richard II and Charles VI, made an interim agreement. The king of England was to hold Calais and a defined part of Aquitaine.
1396	*March* The kings agreed a formal truce of 28 years. Richard II was to marry Isabella, a daughter of Charles VI.
1414	The new king of England, Henry V, renewed demands for territory in France. The French refused.
1415	*Aug–Sept* An English army landed in Normandy and captured Harfleur at the mouth of the River Seine. *25 Oct* Battle of Agincourt: English defeated the French.
1417–19	Henry V and the English returned to France and conquered Normandy.
1420	*May* Henry and Charles VI agreed the Treaty of Troyes; Henry V became regent of France and heir to the crown. On 2 June he married Charles's daughter Margaret.
1422	*31 Aug* Death of Henry V of England; succeeded by Henry VI, aged one. *21 Oct* Death of Charles VI of France; succeeded by Henry VI of England, but on 30 Oct Charles, son of Charles VI and dauphin (heir-apparent), assumed the title 'king of France' as Charles VII.
1424	*17 Aug* John Duke of Bedford, the English regent in France, defeated Charles VII at Verneuil. The English expanded their territory in northwest France and in Oct 1428 began the siege of Orléans.
1429	*Feb* A French peasant girl, Joan of Arc, persuaded Charles VII that she had been sent by God to save France from the English and was eventually allowed to lead attacks on the English at Orléans. On 8 May the English abandoned the siege. *17 July* Charles VII was crowned king in Reims Cathedral.
1430	*23 May* Joan of Arc was captured and handed to the English, who tried her and burnt her for heresy on 30 May 1431.
1444	*28 May* England and France agreed a truce with the Treaty of Tours.
1449–50	French invaded and conquered Normandy.
1451	French invaded and conquered most of Aquitaine.
1453	French captured the remaining English territory in southwest France, leaving Calais as the only English possession in France.

the possibility of securing peace in Northern Ireland. This prompted a joint Anglo-Irish peace initiative, which in turn led to a general cease-fire 1994.

Humphrey Duke of Gloucester 1391–1447. The youngest son of Henry IV, he was named as 'protector' for his nephew, the infant Henry VI, but in the regency council which ruled during Henry's minority 1422–37 he was in fact subordinate to his brother, John of Lancaster, Duke of Bedford. He was renowned as a patron of learning, and acquired the name the 'Good Duke Humphrey' as a result: he founded the library at Oxford University which was to become the Bodleian Library. He clashed with his uncle, Cardinal Henry Beaufort, over policy toward France, Humphrey favouring renewed war, and tried several times during the 1430s and 1440s to have Beaufort removed from office. His downfall came when he was accused of treason Feb 1447 and died in prison five days later, leading to suspicions that he had been murdered.

hundred subdivision of a shire in England, Ireland, and parts of the USA. The term was originally used by Germanic peoples to denote a group of 100 warriors, also the area occupied by 100 families or equalling 100 hides (one hide being the amount of land necessary to support a peasant family). When the Germanic peoples settled in England, the hundred remained the basic military and administrative division of England until its abolition 1867.

Hundred Years' War series of conflicts between England and France 1337–1453. Its origins lay with the English kings' possession of Gascony (southwest France), which the French kings claimed as their ◊fief, and with trade rivalries over Flanders. The two kingdoms had a long history of strife before 1337, and the Hundred Years' War has sometimes been interpreted as merely an intensification of these struggles. It was caused by fears of French intervention in Scotland, which the English were trying to subdue, and by the claim of England's ◊Edward III (through his mother Isabel, daughter of Charles IV) to the crown of France.

After the war, domestic problems, such as the War of the ◊Roses, prevented England (which kept Calais until 1558) from attempting to conquer France again. It gave up continental aspirations and began to develop as a sea power. France was ravaged by the Black Death, famine, and gangs of bandits, in addition to the devastation caused by the war. In both countries, the decline of the feudal nobility and the rise of the middle class allowed the monarchies gradually to become established.

hunger march procession of the unemployed, a feature of social protest in interwar Britain. The first took place from Glasgow to London in 1922 and another in 1929. In 1932 the

THE CENTURY OF STRIFE

England and the Hundred Years' War

The Hundred Years' War is a 19th-century term for a series of wars fought between 1337 and 1453. Complicated by the legal position of the English kings as vassals of the French for territories held in France, and by English counter-claims to the French throne, these wars saw the culmination of the long quest of the kings of France for territorial dominance in Western Europe.

Edward III's war

The end of the struggle between the Angevins and the French crown in 1259 had left the English monarchs only a narrow strip of territory in Aquitaine (Gascony). In the 1290s Edward I came into conflict with France over French support for Scotland; but it was not until the 1330s that war broke out. As a minor, Edward III (1327–77) had been unable to press his claim to the throne of France and had done homage to Philip VI (1328–50) for Gascony. When Philip used appeals to his law court as a pretext for reclaiming Gascony, Edward decided to fight.

His first campaigns were directed from Flanders, where the cloth towns of Ypres, Bruges, and Ghent were bound to England by the wool trade. In 1338–39 Edward could not draw the French into battle, and 1340 saw a crushing naval victory off Sluis; but no progress on land.

Edward's ambitions had bankrupted his government, and he now turned to cheaper expedients. First he intervened in the Breton succession dispute, which resulted in a war lasting from 1341 to 1364. Then he tried a *chevauchée* (a plundering raid) across Normandy, sacking Caen and challenging Philip VI

to battle outside Paris. His archers delivered him the brilliant victory of Crécy in 1346. Calais fell in 1347, to be held by England until 1558.

In 1356, another *chevauchée* by Edward, the Black Prince, led to the battle of Poitiers. This time King John of France (1350–64) was captured and held for an enormous ransom. In the Treaty of Bretigny (1359), John ceded a third of his kingdom in return for Edward's renunciation of his claim to the French throne. Prince Edward was made Duke of Aquitaine, but his harsh rule led the Gascon nobles to appeal to Charles V (1364–80). War resumed, and in 1369 King Edward revived his claim.

A change of strategy

The French now adopted a successful strategy of avoiding battle while harassing English *chevauchées*, as on John of Gaunt's expedition 1373. France was weakened by Charles VI's (1380–1422) attacks of insanity after 1392, but Richard II (1377–99) was eager for peace, and a 28-year truce was agreed in 1396.

Henry V (1413–22) came to the English throne determined to reassert his claim. Charles VI's illness had left France split between Armagnac and Burgundian factions. Their failure to combine in the face of Henry's invasion 1415 led to his crushing victory at Agincourt. Philip the Good, Duke of Burgundy, threw in his lot with the English after the murder of his father in 1419, substantially shifting the balance of power in Henry's favour. Henry was able to force the Treaty of Troyes in 1420, which declared him heir to the French throne. But he died before Charles, leaving only his baby son Henry VI (1422–61) to inherit.

The Dauphin, later Charles VII (1422–61), still ruled south of the Loire, in what was scornfully called the 'Kingdom of Bourges'. The Burgundian alliance seemed to give the English all the trump cards. They recorded victories at Cravant in 1423 and Verneuil in 1424 and in 1429 besieged Orléans. Here the death of the Earl of Salisbury and the arrival of Joan of Arc turned the tables. Although she was soon captured and executed by the English, Joan helped to inspire a French revival and saw Charles crowned at Rheims. When Philip of Burgundy reverted to the French allegiance 1435, the balance swung firmly against the English.

The triumph of Charles VII

Determined efforts to turn Normandy into an English colony proved unsustainable, and Henry VI was no war leader; a truce was agreed 1444. In 1449, Charles renewed the war and Normandy fell swiftly. Despite the vigorous leadership of John Talbot, Gascony too was threatened, and finally conquered in 1453 when Talbot was killed in battle at Castillon.

The loss of France led to a series of civil wars in England, known as the Wars of the Roses (1455–85, intermittently). Although Edward IV (1461–83) did invade France in 1474, he was bought off. When Charles the Bold of Burgundy (1467–77) was killed fighting the Swiss, the French king was left without a rival in his kingdom. Although there would be many later wars between France and England, the French crown was no longer at issue.

MATTHEW BENNETT

National Unemployed Workers' Movement organized the largest demonstration, with groups converging on London from all parts of the country, but the most emotive was probably the Jarrow Crusade of 1936, when 200 unemployed shipyard workers marched to the capital.

Hunne's case scandal when a London merchant, Richard Hunne was found hanging in his cell in the Bishop of London's prison 4 Dec 1514 while awaiting trial for heresy. The church claimed he had committed suicide out of guilt but it was widely believed that the charge of heterodoxy was only brought by Bishop Fitzjames because Hunne had challenged the church's right to levy a mortuary tax on the death of a parishioner. Hunne's corpse was burned by the church authorities, preventing its examination but a coroner's court charged the bishop's chancellor, Dr Horsey, with murder. The church protested that lay courts had no authority over the clergy and the case was taken up by the growing anti-clerical movement. It was brought before Henry VIII twice but ended in compromise: Horsey was fined and forbidden from living in London but was not formally prosecuted.

Hunt Henry ('Orator') 1773–1835. Radical politician who agitated for a wider franchise and the repeal of the Corn Laws. Born into an affluent farming family, he emerged as one of the best-known radical leaders in the agitation for parliamentary reform following the passage of the Corn Laws 1815, largely due to his inflammatory rhetoric. His speech at St Peter's Field in Manchester Nov 1819 caused the militia to intervene, charging the crowd in what became known as the ◊Peterloo Massacre, and Hunt was imprisoned for three years 1820–23. He was elected member of Parliament for Preston 1831–33.

husbandmen independent farmer below the rank of yeoman. Unlike yeomen, they did not usually own the land they farmed, but held tenancies of about 10–30 acres.

Huskisson William 1770–1830. British Conservative politician, financier, and advocate of free trade. He served as secretary to the Treasury 1807–09 and colonial agent for Ceylon (now Sri Lanka). He was active in the ◊Corn Law debates and supported their relaxation in 1821.

Huskisson
British politician William Huskisson, who entered Parliament as a supporter of William Pitt and held a succession of ministerial posts. His career was cut short by fatal injuries sustained at the opening of the Liverpool and Manchester Railway 1830.
Michael Nicholson

He was the first person to be killed by a train when he was hit at the opening of the Liverpool and Manchester Railway while crossing the tracks to greet Wellington.

Hyde Anne, duchess of York 1673–1701. Daughter of Edward Hyde, Duke of Clarendon, she married the future James II of England 1660 against the wishes of both their fathers. She bore James eight children, but only two survived – the future Mary II and Queen Anne.

Hywel Dda d. 950 (Hywel the Good) Welsh king. He succeeded his father Cadell as ruler of Seisyllwg (roughly former Cardiganshire and present Towy Valley), at first jointly with his brother Clydog *c.* 910–920 then alone 920–950. He extended his realm to Dyfed, Gwynedd, and Powys 942, creating a larger Welsh kingdom than any before. His reign was peaceful, mainly because he was subservient to English kings. He is said to have codified Welsh laws, but there is no contemporary record of this.

Iceni ancient people of East Anglia, who revolted against occupying Romans in AD 47 and again AD 60 under ◊Boudicca.

Icknield Way ancient pathway later developed by the Romans into a road running along high ground from the Wash, on the east coast of England, to Salisbury Plain in the southwest. It was an important route in Anglo-Saxon times, giving Mercia access to Wessex and the southwest. Parts of it still survive in the ◊Ridgeway which runs from Wiltshire to the Berkshire Downs.

impeachment judicial procedure by which government officials are accused of wrongdoing and brought to trial before a legislative body. From 1376 the House of Commons brought ministers and officers of state to trial before the House of Lords. The practice was revived in the 17th century in the struggles between the Crown and Parliament. Some notable examples include the impeachments of Bacon 1621, Strafford 1640, and Warren Hastings 1788.

imperial preference or ***colonial preference*** programme of tariff reform within the British Empire, advocated by Joseph ◊Chamberlain at the turn of the 20th century. Colonial products would receive preference in Britain's domestic market while duties would be levied on foreign foodstuffs and goods. Likewise, British industry would get favourable treatment in colonial markets at the expense of foreign competition. The revenue generated would pay for social welfare and defence measures. A limited programme was introduced with the ◊Ottawa Conferences 1932.

Imperial War Cabinet in World War I, inner circle of British cabinet ministers and officials directing both war matters and domestic affairs 1916–19. The idea of a war cabinet was devised by Sir Maurice Hankey largely to allow Lloyd George to govern without opposition. The Empire was represented only by the active participation of General Jan Smuts, the future South African prime minister.

impressment system of forced conscription, often of the poor or destitute, into the armed forces, particularly the Royal Navy, employed in the 18th and 19th centuries. In effect it was a form of kidnapping carried out by the services or their agents, often with the aid of armed men. This was similar to the practice of 'shanghaiing' sailors for duty in the merchant marine, especially in the Far East.

Until wages and conditions of service were of a level to attract recruits, a series of dubious 18th-century statutes permitted the use of 'press gangs', essentially gangs of thugs employed to force or cajole people to enlist. The army ceased to employ this method by 1815, but the navy continued to use press gangs until it was made to end the practice in the 1830s. Impressment was deeply unpopular and it was public hostility that forced the authorities to abandon the practice, but the legislation that permitted it is still in place and it is arguably still legal.

impropriation the transfer following the ◊dissolution of the monasteries 1536 of the tithes and ◊advowsons of parish churches to either the Crown or powerful lay persons. Tithes became a source of private wealth, as little tended to be passed on to the parochial curate, while advowsons were used by powerful patrons to nominate vicars of their own religious persuasion. In the 1620s the Feoffees for Impropriations attempted to divert these resources for the support of a Puritan ministry, while the ◊Arminians campaigned for institutional change to ensure that ecclesiastical rights were used for the benefit of the church, rather than private landowners.

Growth of British India, 1756–1805 British territorial expansion in India began with Clive's victory at Plassey in 1757, and continued under Hastings and Cornwallis. By the end of the 18th century, Mysore and the Maratha princes had replaced the French as the main obstacle to further expansion. The defeat of Mysore, British expansion up the Ganges valley, and the reduction of most Maratha territories to effective British control through subsidiary alliances had ensured by 1805 that Britain, not the Maratha Confederacy, would be the paramount power in India.

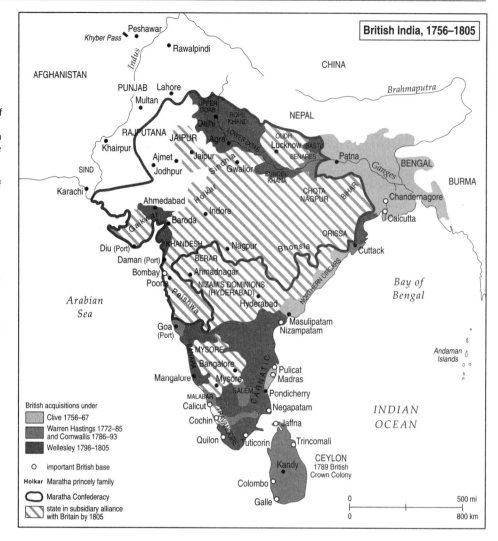

British India, 1756–1805

British acquisitions under
- Clive 1756–67
- Warren Hastings 1772–85 and Cornwallis 1786–93
- Wellesley 1798–1805

O   important British base

Holkar Maratha princely family

Maratha Confederacy

state in subsidiary alliance with Britain by 1805

Let us propose a Bill for the flaying alive, impalement or burning of the murderers of women and children at Delhi. The idea of simply hanging the perpetrators of such atrocities is maddening.

INDIAN MUTINY
British general John Nicholson, letter, 1857

Indemnity and Oblivion, Act of 1660 act of the Convention Parliament implementing the amnesty outlined in the Treaty of ◊Breda as a precursor to the Restoration of Charles II. Participants in the events of the previous 20 years were pardoned, with the exception of 50 named individuals, including 13 of the ◊regicides who had signed Charles I's death warrant.

indentured retainer in the later Middle Ages, a person bound in service to a lord on the basis of a contract rather than on the granting of land, as had been the case in the feudal system. The document of indenture was copied out twice on a single parchment, with a word or phrase between the two copies. Each party to the contract then retained one half of the document and its authenticity could be verified by matching the two halves of the phrase. Some indenture contracts were extremely long and complex, explaining in detail the precise nature of the services to be rendered and the recompense to be granted for it. For some time, indentured troops were the main source of recruitment to the army, particularly during the Hundred Years' War.

Independents in the 16th and 17th centuries, nonconformists who espoused total autonomy for local congregations from both the state and any established church. Independents rejected episcopacy outright and by the time of the Civil War the term meant those who even opposed a Presbyterian form of a national church. The main Independent groups were the ◊Congregationalists and the ◊Baptists though there were also smaller fringe groups such as the Anabaptists and the radical ◊Fifth Monarchy Men. Independents dominated the New Model Army.

Independent Labour Party (ILP) British socialist party, founded in Bradford 1893 by the Scottish member of Parliament Keir Hardie. In 1900 it joined with trades unions and Fabians in founding the Labour Representation Committee, the nucleus of the ◊Labour Party. Many members left the ILP to join the Communist Party 1921, and in 1932 all connections with the Labour Party were severed. After World War II the ILP dwindled, eventually becoming extinct. James Maxton (1885–1946) was its chair 1926–46.

India former British possession, southern Asia. Dynastic conflicts and declining Mogul power in India opened the way for European intervention in the early 18th century, when Britain and France set up rival trading posts. The rivalry led to war between Britain and France ending in defeat of the French at Plassey 1757 and the rise of the British East India Company. The first extensive British territorial acquisitions in India date from 1765, when Bengal and Bihar were claimed. A series of wars and further gains led to the British annexation of Burma 1826–86, Sind 1843, Punjab 1849, Berar 1853, Nagpur 1854, Oudh 1856, and Baluchistan 1887. Following the Indian Mutiny 1857–58 the Government of India Act 1858 transferred the responsibility for the administration of India from the East India Company to the Crown. By 1887 the parts of India not under direct British control (British India) were protected states, under native rulers. Following a bitter struggle between British rulers and Indian nationalists after World War I, British India was divided 1935 into 17 provinces, 11 with a governor and 6 under a chief commissioner responsible to the Governor General. British rule ended 1947 on the establishment of the sovereign states of India and Pakistan. India was regarded as the 'jewel in the crown' of Queen Victoria, Empress of India.

India Acts legislation which formed the basis of British rule in India until independence 1947. The 1858 Act abolished the administrative functions of the British ◊East India Company, replacing them with direct rule from London. The 1919 Act increased Indian participation at local and provincial levels but did not meet nationalist demands for complete internal self-government (Montagu-Chelmsford reforms). The 1939 Act outlined a federal structure but was never implemented.

India, Independence of (1947) the Indian Independence Act of July 1947, granting independence on the dissolution of the British Empire in India, set up two new independent dominions, India (predominantly Hindu), and East and West Pakistan (predominantly Muslim). The creation of Pakistan was followed by violent clashes (the Punjab massacres), and a war between the two countries over Kashmir which lasted until 1949.

Indian Mutiny or *Sepoy Rebellion* or *Mutiny* revolt 1857–58 of Indian soldiers (Sepoys) against the British in India. The uprising was caused by growing antagonism to Western innovations and was precipitated by British soldiers' alleged use of animal fat to grease rifle cartridges. The revolt was

Governors General and Viceroys of India 1858–1948	
1858–62	C J Canning, 1st Earl Canning
1862–63	J Bruce, 8th Earl of Elgin and Kincardine
1864–69	John L M Lawrence, 1st Earl Lawrence
1869–72	R S Bourke, 6th Earl of Mayo
1872–76	T G Baring, 1st Earl of Northbrook
1876–80	E R Bulwer-Lytton, 1st Earl of Lytton
1880–84	G F S Robinson, Earl and Marquess of Ripon
1884–88	F Hamilton-Temple-Blackwood, Earl and Marquess of Dufferin and Ava
1888–94	H C K Petty-Fitzmaurice, 5th Marquess of Lansdowne
1894–99	V A Bruce, 9th Earl of Elgin and Kincardine
1899–1905	G N Curzon, 1st Earl and Marquess Curzon of Kedleston
1905–10	G J Elliot-Murray-Kynynmond, Earl of Minto
1910–16	C Hardinge, 1st Baron Hardinge of Penhurst
1916–21	F J N Thesiger, 1st Viscount Chelmsford
1921–26	R D Isaacs, Marquess of Reading
1926–31	E F L Wood, Earl of Halifax
1931–36	F Freeman-Thomas, Earl and Marquess of Willingdon
1936–43	V A J Hope, 2nd Marquess of Linlithgow
1943–47	A P Wavell, Viscount and Earl Wavell
1947–48	Louis, 1st Earl Mountbatten of Burma

Indian Mutiny
British troops led by Sir Colin Campbell recapture Delhi from Indian rebels Sept 1857. The Siege of Delhi ended after three months when engineers blew up the Cashmere Gate and secured an entry point to the city.
Image Select

Industrial revolution
A *Punch* cartoon 1844 entitled *Capital and Labour* contrasts the luxurious life of a mineowner with the harsh working conditions in the pits.
Philip Sauvain

largely confined to the north, from Bengal to the Punjab, and central India. The majority of support for the mutiny came from the army and recently dethroned princes, but in some areas it developed into a peasant uprising and general revolt. It included the seizure of Delhi by the rebels, its siege and recapture by the British, and the defence of Lucknow by a British garrison. One of the rebel leaders was Nana Sahib. It led to the end of rule by the British ◊East India Company and its replacement by direct British crown administration.

Industrial revolution the sudden acceleration of technical and economic development that began in Britain in the second half of the 18th century. The traditional agrarian economy was replaced by one dominated by machinery and manufacturing, made possible through technical advances such as the steam engine. This transferred the balance of political power from the landowner to the industrial capitalist and created an urban working class. From 1830 to the early 20th century, the Industrial Revolution spread throughout Europe and the USA and to Japan and the various colonial empires.

Britain exhibited a combination of favourable circumstances for such a change: an increasing population creating a larger workforce; natural resources, especially plentiful and accessi-

Industrial revolution: chronology	
1708	Thomas Newcomen invented the self-acting steam pumping engine, which became widely used in coal-mines.
1709	Abraham Darby successfully produced quality pig iron by smelting with coke rather than charcoal.
1717	Thomas Lombe established an early large factory on the river Derwent, Derbyshire, which employed around 300 people in silk production.
1733	John Kay developed the 'flying shuttle', a mechanical device for throwing shuttles on weaving looms; it came into widespread use in the 1760s.
1738	Lewis Paul invented a method for the machine spinning of yarn.
1740s	Benjamin Huntsman invented a method for making high-quality steel in larger quantities.
1759–61	The Second Duke of Bridgewater built a canal from his mines at Worsley to Manchester, designed by James Brindley; 1762–72, extended to Runcorn on the River Mersey.
1764–7	James Hargreaves invented the spinning jenny, which enabled the simultaneous spinning of multiple weft threads.
1769	Richard Arkwright patented the water 'frame', a water-powered machine for spinning warp threads.
1769	Josiah Wedgwood established his Etruria porcelain works in Staffordshire.
1771	Arkwright established a water-powered carding factory at Cromford in Derbyshire.
1775	John Wilkinson developed a mill for boring cylinders to fine accuracy.
1777	First water-powered textile factory established in Lancashire; the county developed into the main centre of cotton production in Britain.
1777	Completion of the Grand Trunk Canal, linking the river Mersey with the river Trent.
c. 1779	Samuel Crompton produced his 'mule', a combination of the spinning jenny and the 'frame'; from 1790 steam engines are used to drive mules.
1783	Erection of the first rotative steam engine made by Matthew Boulton and James Watt.
1783	Thomas Bell devised a method of printing calico by rollers.
1783–4	Henry Cort patented his rolling and puddling method for converting pig iron into bar iron.
1784	Edmund Cartwright patented a powered weaving loom.
1790–94	Canal mania: a burst of speculative investment in canal-building.
1795	Matthew Boulton and James Watt establish the Soho Foundry in Birmingham for the manufacture of steam engines.
1825	Opening of the Stockton and Darlington Railway.
1856	Henry Bessemer invented a process for converting pig iron into steel.

DARK SATANIC MILLS

The Industrial Revolution in Britain

The British economy changed dramatically in the late 18th and early 19th centuries. Technological innovation, agricultural development, communications improvements, growing trade, and the increased consumer demand and labour supply afforded by a rising population took Britain to the forefront of economic progress. These changes had a profound impact on the lives and the mental outlook of contemporaries.

Technological development

Though the rate of industrialization in Britain in the late 18th century was less impressive than used to be believed, and was restricted to only a few sectors (notably cotton textiles and metallurgy), a sense of economic change and the possibilities of progress was powerfully obvious to many contemporary observers. A popular metaphor was that of Prometheus Unbound, of extraordinary opportunities offered by technological innovation.

John Kay's flying shuttle of 1733, which was in general use in Yorkshire by the 1780s, increased the productivity of hand-loom weavers. James Hargreaves' spinning jenny *c.* 1764, Richard Arkwright's 'spinning frame' 1768, and Samuel Crompton's mule 1779 revolutionized textile spinning. Arkwright and his partners built a number of cotton mills in Lancashire and the Midlands with all the characteristic features of factory system, including the precise division of labour and the co-operation of workers in different manufacturing processes. Cotton production grew by nearly 13% in the 1780s.

In 1769 James Watt patented a more energy-efficient use of steam engines. Steam pumps removed water from deep coal mines, and steam-powered winding engines were introduced in the early 1790s. Coal production increased rapidly, allowing a similar increase in the production of iron and lead. Canals and waggon-ways built to move coal prompted a wider revolution in transportation: for example, the 4th Duke of Portland built a new harbour at Troon on the west coast of Scotland 1808, linked to his coal pits at Kilmarnock by a waggon-way which during 1839 carried over 130,000 tons of coal.

The coalfields attracted new, heavy industry, particularly in South Wales, Strathclyde, Northeast England, West Yorkshire, South Lancashire, the Vale of Trent, and the West Midlands. The smelting of iron and steel using coke, rather than charcoal, freed a major industry from dependence on wood supplies, while technological development spurred by Britain's wars and the demands of an Empire revolutionized the secondary metallurgical industries, especially gun founding. The percentage of the male labour force employed in industry rose from 19 in 1700 to 30 in 1800.

The social dimension

The strains of industrialization in the early 19th century caused much social and political tension. Improvements in working conditions brought about by technological changes were very gradual, with the result that general living standards only began to rise noticeably after mid-century. The social – and indeed biological – pressure placed on the bulk of the population by the emergence of industrial work methods and economics is indicated by a marked decline in the height of army recruits in the second quarter of the century. Working conditions were often unpleasant and hazardous with, for example, numerous fatalities in mining accidents. The Factory Acts regulating conditions of employment in the textile industry still left work there both long and arduous. The 1833 Act established a factory inspectorate and prevented the employment of under-9s, but 9–13 year olds could still work 8-hour days, and 13–17 year olds 12 hours. The 1844 Act cut that of under-13s to 6 and a half hours, and of 18-year olds and all women to 12; those of 1847 and 1850 reduced the hours of women and under-18s to 10 hours. Despite such legislation, there were still about 5,000 half-timers under 13 in the Bradford worsted industry in 1907.

If the bulk of the working population faced difficult circumstances, the situation was even worse for those more marginal to the new economy.

'Hell is a city much like London –
A populous and a smoky city;'

The poet Shelley's comment in *Peter Bell the Third* 1819 seemed increasingly appropriate. Fast-expanding towns became crowded and polluted, a breeding ground for disease. In 1852, 8,032 of the 9,453 houses in Newcastle lacked toilets.

Britain the world leader

The Industrial Revolution gave Britain a distinctive economy. It became the world leader in industrial production and foreign trade. The annual averages of coal and lignite production, in million metric tons, for 1820–24 were 18 for Britain, compared with 2 for France, Germany, Belgium, and Russia combined. The comparable figures for 1855–59 were 68 and 32, and for 1880–84 159 and 108. The annual production of pig-iron in million metric tons in 1820 was 0.4 for Britain and the same for the rest of Europe, in 1850 2.3 and 0.9, and in 1880 7.9 and 5.4. Raw cotton consumption in thousand metric tons in 1850 was 267 for Britain and 162 for the rest of Europe. Britain was the workshop of the world.

JEREMY BLACK

ble coal; raw materials from its colonies; expanding markets in its increasing population and its colonies; a strong middle class and comparatively stable political system; a sound monetary system and cheap capital as a result of low interest rates, essential for the high levels of investment required in the new technology.

The invention of the steam engine provided the spur for much of the innovation and development in this period. Originally developed for draining mines (by Thomas ◊Newcomen), it was rapidly adapted for use in factories and on the railways (by James ◊Watt, Richard ◊Arkwright, Samuel ◊Crompton, and Richard ◊Trevithick). This led to the concentration of industrial centres around coalfields, with the result that huge industrial conurbations developed around Manchester, Leeds, Birmingham, and Newcastle.

Inkerman, Battle of in the Crimean War, British and French victory 5 Nov 1854 over Russians attacking the Inkerman Ridge, which was occupied by the British army besieging Sevastopol. The fighting lasted about seven hours, during which time the British lost about 2,400 troops, the French about 1,000 and the Russians an estimated 11,000.

INLA abbreviation for ◊*Irish National Liberation Army*.

Inns of Court four private legal societies in London: Lincoln's Inn, Gray's Inn, Inner Temple, and Middle Temple. All barristers (advocates in the English legal system) must belong to one of the Inns of Court. The main function of each Inn is the education, government, and protection of its members. Each is under the administration of a body of Benchers (judges and senior barristers).

Instrument of Government, the English constitution of 1653–57 which established a Protectorate, with Oliver Cromwell at its head, assisted by a Council of State, and established a single-chamber Parliament, consisting of 460 members. When Parliament was not sitting the Lord Protector was empowered to issue legislation along with the Council of State. Protestants were also granted toleration under the new constitution. The settlement was imposed by the army and was widely perceived as being weighted too heavily in favour of the army, so that it was soon superseded by the ◊Humble Petition May 1657.

interdict in the Christian church, a punishment that excludes an individual, community, or realm from participation in spiritual activities except for communion. It was usually employed against heretics or realms whose ruler was an excommunicant. Interdicts were placed on Scotland by Pope Alexander III 1181, on England under King John by Pope Innocent III 1208, and on England by Pope Paul III following Henry VIII's break with Rome 1535.

interregnum two periods in British history when the nation was temporarily without a monarch. The first interregnum covers both the Commonwealth and the Protectorate, starting with the execution of Charles I 30 Jan 1649 until the Restoration of the monarchy 8 May 1660, although Charles II always dated his reign from 1649. The second interregnum occurred at the time of the ◊Glorious Revolution, in the period between the flight of James II 22 Dec 1688 and the accession of William and Mary to the English throne 23 Feb 1689.

intelligence services British intelligence services consist of M(ilitary) I(ntelligence) 6, the secret intelligence service, which operates mainly under Foreign Office control; the counter-intelligence service, M(ilitary) I(ntelligence) 5, which is responsible directly to the prime minister for internal security and has Scotland Yard's ◊Special Branch as its executive arm; and Government Communications Headquarters (GCHQ), which carries out electronic surveillance for the other two branches. The chief of MI6 from 1994 is David Spedding; the director-general of MI5 from 1992 is Stella Rimington. The overall head of intelligence in the UK is the chair of the Joint Intelligence Committee (Pauline Neville-Jones from 1994).

From 1991, in a government move to reduce secrecy and increase the accountability of the British intelligence services, information was gradually released into the public domain. The names of those in charge, and the whereabouts, of MI5 and MI6 were made public (until 1992, MI6 did not officially exist in peacetime). GCHQ's base in Cheltenham, Gloucestershire, was already public knowledge. It was also announced that, in future, the accounts of all three branches of the service would be audited by the National Audit Office, serving the controller and auditor general, and the House of Commons. In addition, legislation was expected to be passed giving powers to a House of Commons select committee to scrutinize the work of the services.

MI5 was found in breach of the European Convention on Human Rights 1990 in having carried out secret surveillance of civil-liberties campaigners and covert vetting of applicants for jobs with military contractors.

Invergordon Mutiny incident in the British Atlantic Fleet, Cromarty Firth, Scotland, 15 Sept 1931. Ratings refused to prepare the ships for sea following the government's cuts in their pay; the cuts were consequently modified.

Inverlochy, Battles of two battles 1431 and 1645 northeast of the present site of Fort William, Scotland. In the first battle royal forces under the Earls of Mar and Caithness were routed by Highlanders supporting the imprisoned Earl of Ross, the self-styled Lord of the ◊Isles. The second battle 2 Feb 1645 was a major victory for a royalist army composed of Highlanders and Irish under the Marquess of Montrose over the Duke of Argyll's Covenanter army composed of Campbells and some Lowland forces.

Iona island in the Inner Hebrides; area 850 hectares/2,100 acres. A centre of early Christianity, it is the site of a monastery founded 563 by St ◊Columba. Monks from Iona were invited by King Oswald to convert the people of Northumbria to Christianity 634. It later became a burial ground for Irish, Scottish, and Norwegian kings. It has a 13th-century abbey.

Ionian Islands former British protectorate, an island group in the Ionian Sea. Following possession by France 1797 and Russia 1799, the islands became a British protectorate 1815. They were annexed to Greece 1864.

IRA abbreviation for ◊*Irish Republican Army*.

Iraq former British mandate, in southwest Asia. The kingdom of Iraq was established 1921 out of former Turkish territory. It passed to Britain as mandate territory 1920 but following an intermediate period as a semi-independent state in alliance with Great Britain from 1922 and as a limited monarchy from 1924 became fully independent under King Faisal 1932.

Ireland one of the British Isles, lying to the west of Great Britain, from which it is separated by the Irish Sea. It comprises the provinces of Ulster, Leinster, Munster, and Connacht, and is divided into the Republic of ◊Ireland and Northern ◊Ireland which is part of the United Kingdom.

Ireland, early history Gaelic Ireland was divided into kingdoms, nominally subject to an *Ardri* or High King; the chiefs were elected under the tribal or Brehon law, and were usually at war with one another. Ireland was known to the Romans as Hibernia, but no invasion was ever attempted. Christianity was introduced by St ◊Patrick about 432, and during the 5th and 6th centuries Ireland became the home of a civilization which sent out missionaries to Britain and Europe. From

High Kings and Queens of Ireland	
445–452	Niall of the Nine Hostages (king of Tara; traditional ancestor of claimants to the high kingship)
452–463	Lóegaire (son)
463–482	Ailill Molt (grandnephew of Niall)
482–507	Lugaid (son of Lóegaire)
507–534	Muirchertach I (great-grandson of Niall)
534–544	Tuathal Máelgarb (great-grandson of Niall)
544–565	Diarmait I (great-grandson of Niall)
565–566	Domnall Ilchelgach (brother; co-regent)
566–569	Ainmire (fourth in descent from Niall)
569–572	Bétán I (son of Muirchertach I)
569–572	Eochaid (son of Domnall Ilchelgach; co- regent)
572–586	Báetán II (fourth in descent from Niall)
586–598	Áed (son of Ainmire)
598–604	Áed Sláine (son of Diarmait I)
598–604	Colmán Rímid (son of Báetán I; co-regent)
604–612	Áed Uaridnach (son of Domnall Ilchelgach)
612–615	Máel Cobo (son of Áed)
615–628	Suibne Menn (grandnephew of Muirchertach I)
628–642	Domnall (son of Áed)
642–654	Conall Cáel (son of Máel Cobo)
642–658	Cellach (brother; co-regent)
658–665	Diarmait II (son of Áed Sláine)
658–665	Blathmac (brother; co-regent)
665–671	Sechnussach (son)
671–675	Cennfáelad (brother)
675–695	Fínsnechta Fledach (grandson of Áed Sláine)
695–704	Loingsech (grandson of Domnall)
704–710	Congal Cennmagair (grandson of Domnall)
710–722	Fergal (great-grandson of Áed Uaridnach)
722–724	Fogartach (great-grandson of Diarmait II)
724–728	Cináed (fourth in descent from Áed Sláine)
728–734	Flaithbertach (son of Loingsech; deposed, d. 765)
734–743	Áed allán (son of Fergal)
743–763	Domnall Midi (seventh in descent from Diarmait I)
763–770	Niall Frossach (son of Fergal; abdicated, d. 778)
770–797	Donnchad Midi (son of Domnall Midi)
797–819	Áed Oirdnide (son of Niall Frossach)
819–833	Conchobar (son of Donnchad Midi)
833–846	Niall Caille (son of Áed Oirdnide)
846–862	Máel Sechnaill I (nephew of Conchobar)
862–879	Áed Findliath (son of Niall Caille)
879–916	Flann Sinna (son of Máel SechnailI)
916–919	Niall Glúndub (son of Áed Findliath)
919–944	Donnchad Donn (son of Flann Sinna)
944–956	Congalach Cnogba (tenth in descent from Áed Sláine)
956–980	Domnall ua Néill (grandson of Niall Glúundub)
980–1002	Máel Sechnaill II (grandson of Donnchad Donn; deposed)
1002–1014	Brian Bóruma (Dál Cais; king of Munster)
1014–1022	Máel Sechnaill II (restored; interregnum 1022–72)
1072–1086	Tairrdelbach I (grandson of Brian Bóruma; king of Munster)
1086–1119	Muirchertach II (son)
1119–1121	Domnall ua Lochlainn (fourth in descent from Domnall ua Néill?; king of Ailech)
1121–1156	Tairrdelbach II (Ua Conchobair; king of Connacht)
1156–1166	Muirchertach III (grandson of Domnall ua Lochlainn)
1166–1186	Ruaidrí (son of Tairrdelbach II; deposed, d.1198; regional kingships under English domination)

A UNITY IMPOSED

Ireland under the Stuarts

From the accession of James I 1603 to the death of Anne 1714, Ireland witnessed a significant expansion of the authority of the Dublin administration in both political and religious life, at a time of conflict and dramatic economic growth.

The New English

Sixteenth-century Ireland had been a fragmented polity, dominated by individual native and Anglo-Irish lords. The defeat in the Nine Years War (1594–1603) of a coalition of native lords under Hugh O'Neill, Earl of Tyrone, ensured that royal authority and the common law were finally extended throughout the whole country. The aim in Dublin was an English style 'commonwealth', promoted by unplanned settlement from England and Scotland in areas such as East Ulster, and more regulated plantation, notably in Ulster after the flight of O'Neill and other lords in 1607. The emerging New English settler group, mainly protestant in religion, challenged the traditional political elite, the Old English Catholic community, just as their identity was being reinforced by the European Counter-Reformation.

Despite increasing economic influence through a trade boom, the Old English were losing political power. They responded with appeals to Charles I as king of Ireland. In the late 1620s a political compromise, the Graces, was devised but not implemented.

Formal plantation and informal New English settlement, along with the growth in Old English landowning power, resulted in the replacement of the 16-century lords by a new overmighty group of mixed New and Old English lords by the 1630s. The arrival of Thomas Wentworth, Earl of Strafford, as Lord Deputy, intent on re-establishing royal power, upset the precarious political balance. All groups in Ireland combined with allies in the English parliament to impeach Strafford, who was impeached 1640 and executed. However, the Irish parliament failed to agree on a new polity, and some Irish Catholics, many now well integrated into the new order, feared that they would suffer under an increasingly vociferous Protestant parliament in England. This, combined with a downturn in economic fortunes, drove a number of the most prominent of the Irish Catholics into a 'loyal rebellion' in October 1641 to protect the king's interests against parliament.

The Cromwellian intervention

The Catholic camp operated under the umbrella of the Confederation of Kilkenny. In practice there were political divisions within this group, notably between Old English and native Irish Catholics. As the war continued it became more radical and the issue of religion more divisive. The papacy became involved, providing both funds for the war and a nuncio to ensure its own rights were protected.

The war quickly became inextricably linked with the civil war in England. By 1649 the Confederation had been dissolved and both religious groups formed a united royalist front, forcing the Cromwellian intervention. Ten years of Cromwellian government saw a transfer of land and power from royalist losers, both Protestant and Catholic, to parliamentary winners, as well as punitive taxation. The abolition of the Irish parliament also undermined the existing political framework. This, together with the economic effects of war in the 1640s, effectively resolved the problem of overmighty lords. It introduced other problems, however, notably the emergence of dissent in the form of Quaker, Presbyterian, Baptist, and Independent congregations in a society in which Protestantism had hitherto been the exclusive preserve of the Established Church.

The Anglo-Irish

From the 1660s the political and social life of Ireland was rebuilt, in favourable economic conditions generated by diversification and increased specialization of the economy. Protestant settlers monopolized parliament and were the main beneficiaries of the Acts of Settlement 1663 and Explanation 1665.

The result was a growing identification of the settlers with Ireland and the emergence of an Anglo-Irish identity, manifested in opposition to the London administration in the parliament of 1692, and in the early 18-century ideology of 'colonial nationalism'. Irish Protestants were prepared to support James II as king of Ireland after his deposition from the English throne in 1688 despite the Catholicization of corporations and the army after 1685. It was James's attempt to undermine the land settlement in the Jacobite parliament of 1689 which finally drove his Protestant supporters into the William of Orange's camp and made inevitable a reconquest of Ireland.

After 1692 the Ascendancy, fearful of another judgement of God (as they interpreted the events of 1688–91), attempted reform by establishing religious societies and enacting a number of bills against Catholicism, culminating in a comprehensive act in 1704 to reduce Catholic landownership. But other problems loomed: prolonged economic recession after 1700 was attributed by many to the English parliament's prohibition of Irish wool exports. Such grievances, ironically, led the Anglo-Irish to adopt in the 18th century the ideas and tactics of the Old English whom they had ousted in the early 17th.

RAYMOND GILLESPIE

about 800 the Danes began to raid Ireland, and later founded Dublin and other coastal towns, until they were defeated by Brian Boru (king from 976) at the Battle of ◊Clontarf 1014. Anglo-Norman adventurers invaded Ireland 1167, but by the end of the medieval period English rule was still confined to the Pale, the territory around Dublin. The Tudors adopted a policy of conquest, confiscation of Irish land, and the ◊Plantation of Ireland by English settlers, and further imposed the ◊Reformation and English law on Ireland.

Ireland, English conquest of The Norman invasion of Ireland began 1169 and Henry II established English rule 1171 over a strip of coast around Dublin. This became known as the Pale, though its extent varied. The Irish parliament confirmed Henry VIII as king of Ireland 1541 and it was then that the first English ◊plantations were set up, as the forerunners of American colonies. Cromwell subdued all Ireland after the Rebellion 1641, and the island was colonized, especially in the north, by Scots, Welsh, and English. After the victory of William III at the Battle of the Boyne 1690, Ireland united legislatively with Great Britain, forming the United Kingdom of Great Britain and Ireland 1801.

Ireland, Northern The creation of Northern Ireland dates from 1921 when the Irish Free State (subsequently the Republic of Ireland) was established separately from the mainly Protestant counties of Ulster (six out of nine), which were given limited self-government but continued to send members to the House of Commons. Spasmodic outbreaks of violence by the ◊Irish Republican Army (IRA) continued, but only in 1968–69 were there serious disturbances arising from Protestant political dominance and discrimination against the Roman Catholic minority in employment and housing. British troops were sent 1969 to restore peace and protect Catholics, but disturbances continued and in 1972 the parliament at Stormont was prorogued and superseded by direct rule from Westminster. Under the ◊Anglo-Irish Agreement 1985, the Republic of Ireland was given a consultative role (via an Anglo-Irish conference) in the government of Northern Ireland, but agreed that there should be no change in its status except by majority consent. The agreement was approved by Parliament, but all 12 Ulster members gave up their seats, so that by-elections could be fought as a form of 'referendum' on the views of the province itself. A similar boycotting of the Northern Ireland Assembly led to its dissolution 1986 by the UK government.

The question of Northern Ireland's political future was debated in talks held in Belfast April–Sept 1991 – the first direct negotiations between the political parties for 16 years. Follow-up talks between the British government and the main Northern Ireland parties Sept–Nov 1992 made little progress. In Sept

Anglo–Norman conquest of Ireland: chronology	
1152	Dermot MacMurrough, king of Leinster, abducted Dervorguilla, wife of Tiernan O'Rourke, prince of Breffny (she returned the following year).
1155	Pope Adrian IV, in bull *Laudabiliter*, granted the lordship of Ireland to Henry II.
1166	Tiernan O'Rourke, High King Rory O'Rourke, and supporters forced Dermot MacMurrough to flee Ireland.
1167	Dermot MacMurrough sought help to regain his throne from Henry II (in southwest France); Henry authorized him to recruit in England and Wales. He obtained the support of Richard de Clare (called 'Strongbow'), who would marry MacMurrough's daughter and succeed him as king.
1167, 1169	First contingents of Anglo–Normans arrived in Ireland.
1170	Main Anglo–Norman force arrived in Ireland, followed 23 Aug by Strongbow; on 21 Sept they captured Dublin.
1171	*April* Death of Dermot MacMurrough, leaving Strongbow as his successor. Henry II ordered Strongbow to return home. *17 Oct* (to 17 April 1172) visit of Henry II to Ireland, where he received the submission of Irish kings except Rory O'Rourke, the high king. Henry granted the overlordship of Leinster to Strongbow and the overlordship of Meath to Hugh de Lacy, retaining Dublin, Waterford, Wexford and other lands.
1171–72	2nd Synod of Cashel, which legislated for the payment of tithes (leading to the establishment of parishes) and adopted the liturgy of the Church of England.
1175	*Oct* Rory O'Connor, high king of Ireland outside Leinster, Meath, and Waterford, visited England and swore allegiance to Henry II.
1176	*20 April* Death of Strongbow; succeeded by his son, a minor. John de Courcy, an associate of the regent, organized a force of knights and troops which then conquered part of Ulster.
1177	*May* Henry II made his son John Lord of Ireland.
1185	Prince John visited Ireland with 300 knights, amid continuing expansion of Anglo–Norman rule in central Ireland, the creation of knight's fees, and the founding of castles and towns.
1199– 1216	Reign of King John of England, during which period the English administrative and legal pattern of shires, sheriffs, county courts, and itinerant justices was introduced to Ireland.
1201	*May* Hugh de Lacy defeated John de Courcy; King John made Lacy Earl of Ulster and gave him Courcy's lands.
1210	King John visited Ireland, receiving the homage of Irish kings.
1235	Richard de Burgh completed the Anglo–Norman conquest of Connaught (west Ireland).
1246	Henry III sent details of English writs to Ireland, thereby extending use of English common law in Ireland.
1248	Permanent court of king's bench established in Dublin.
1307	Twelve counties and four liberties now established in Ireland under the English crown, leaving only the west and northwest unshired.

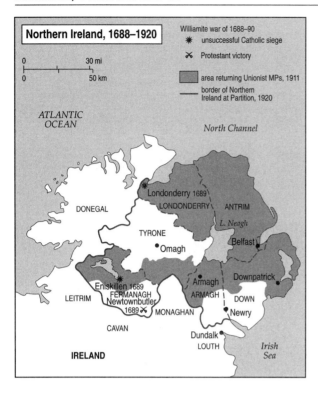

Northern Ireland, 1688–1920

Williamite war of 1688–90
* unsuccessful Catholic siege
✗ Protestant victory

█ area returning Unionist MPs, 1911
— border of Northern Ireland at Partition, 1920

0   30 mi
0   50 km

ATLANTIC OCEAN

North Channel

Londonderry 1689
LONDONDERRY   ANTRIM
DONEGAL   L. Neagh
TYRONE   Belfast
●Omagh

Eniskillen 1689   Armagh   Downpatrick
LEITRIM FERMANAGH ARMAGH DOWN
Newtownbutler
1689 ✗ MONAGHAN   ●Newry
CAVAN
Dundalk●
LOUTH   Irish Sea
IRELAND

1993 it emerged that the Catholic nationalist Social Democratic Labour Party (SDLP) and Sinn Fein (political wing of the outlawed IRA) had held talks aimed at achieving a political settlement. This revelation prompted the British government to engage in bilateral talks with the main Northern Ireland parties, and in Dec 1993 London and Dublin issued a joint peace proposal, the Downing Street Declaration, for consideration by all parties. In Aug 1994 the Provisional IRA announced a unilateral cease-fire in an attempt to reach a non-violent solution to the conflict in the province, followed two months later by a similar declaration by the Loyalist paramilitaries. By the time of the cease-fire's first anniversary in Aug 1995, it still held but the 'peace process' had made little further progress.

Job discrimination was outlawed under the Fair Employment Act 1975, but in 1987 Catholics in Northern Ireland were two and a half times more likely to be unemployed than their Protestant counterparts – a differential that had not improved since 1971. In 1993, unemployment was running at 14.2%, and 75% of the unemployed were Catholic. Residential integration was still sparse in 1993: 650,000 people lived in areas that were 90% Catholic or Protestant.

Ireland, Plantation of see ◊Plantation of Ireland.

Northern Ireland 1688–1920
The successful defence of Enniskillen and Londonderry and the defeat of Jacobite Catholic forces at Newtownbutler during the 1688 war between William III and James II marked a defining point in Irish Protestant history. By 1911, as pressure grew for Irish independence, the Protestant majority was voting openly for Unionist candidates, and the border of the Irish Free State was drawn to reflect their views in 1920.

Ireland, Republic of In 1921 a treaty gave Southern Ireland dominion status within the ◊Commonwealth, while six out of the nine counties of Ulster remained part of the UK, with limited self-government. The Irish Free State, as Southern Ireland was formally called 1921, was accepted by Irish Republican Army (IRA) leader Michael Collins but not by many of his colleagues, who shifted their allegiance to the Fianna Fáil party leader Éamon ◊de Valera. A civil war ensued, in which Collins was killed. The partition was eventually acknowledged 1937 when a new constitution established the country as a sovereign state under the name of Eire.

The IRA continued its fight for an independent, unified Ireland through a campaign of violence, mainly in Northern Ireland but also on the British mainland and, to a lesser extent, in the Irish republic. Eire remained part of the Commonwealth until 1949, when it left, declaring itself the Republic of Ireland, while Northern Ireland remained a constituent part of the UK.

In 1983 all the main Irish and Northern Irish political parties initiated the New Ireland Forum as a vehicle for discussion. Its report was rejected by Margaret Thatcher's Conservative government in the UK, but discussions between London and Dublin resulted in the signing of the Anglo-Irish Agreement 1985, providing for regular consultation and exchange of information on political, legal, security, and cross-border matters. The agreement also stated that the status of Northern Ireland would not be changed without the consent of a majority of the people. The agreement was criticized by the Unionist parties of Northern Ireland, who asked that it be rescinded.

In Jan 1993, after prolonged negotiations, Albert Reynolds succeeded in forming a Fianna Fáil–Labour coalition, with Dick Spring as deputy to Reynolds in the post of minister for foreign affairs. The new coalition began working closely with the UK government in seeking an end to the violence in Northern Ireland, culminating in the Downing Street Declaration Dec 1993, in which both Reynolds and UK prime minister John Major offered constitutional talks with all parties if violence was renounced. After lengthy, behind-the-scenes negotiations on both sides of the Irish border, the IRA formally ended its 'military operations' Aug 1994 and in Oct Protestant paramilitaries announced an end to their campaign of violence as long as the IRA cessation held.

In Nov 1994 Labour leader Dick Spring withdrew his support from the governing coalition in protest over a controversial judicial appointment made by Reynolds. Having lost his par-

Northern Ireland 1967–95: chronology

1967   Northern Ireland Civil Rights Association set up to press for equal treatment for Catholics in the province.

1968   Series of civil rights marches sparked off rioting and violence, especially in Londonderry.

1969   Election results weakened Terence O'Neil's Unionist government. Further rioting led to call-up of (Protestant-based) B-Specials to Royal Ulster Constabulary.
Chichester-Clark replaced O'Neil. Irish Republican Army (IRA) split into 'official' and more radical 'provisional' wings. Resumption of IRA activities: urban guerrilla warfare in North and kidnap and murder in South. RUC disarmed and B-Specials replaced by Ulster Defence Regiment (UDR). British Army deployed in Belfast and Londonderry.

1971   First British soldier killed. Brian Faulkner replaced Chichester-Clark. IRA stepped up bombing campaign. Internment of people suspected of IRA membership introduced.

1972   'Bloody Sunday' in Londonderry when British troops fired on demonstrators: 13 killed. Direct rule from Westminster introduced. Constitution suspended. IRA extended bombing campaign to mainland England. Seven soldiers killed in bomb attack in Aldershot.

1973   Sunningdale Agreement, to establish Council of Ireland with representatives from north and south.

1974   'Power sharing' between Protestant and Catholic groups tried but failed. Bombs in Guildford and Birmingham caused a substantial number of fatalities.

1976   British Ambassador in Dublin, Christopher Ewart Biggs, assassinated. Ulster Peace Movement founded by Betty Williams and Mairead Corrigan, later awarded Nobel Prize for Peace.

1979   British MP Airey Neave assassinated by Irish National Liberation Army (INLA) at the House of Commons. Earl Mountbatten and three others killed by IRA bomb.

1980   Meeting of British Prime Minister Margaret Thatcher and Irish premier Charles Haughey on a peaceful settlement to the Irish question. Hunger strikes and 'dirty protests' started by Republican prisoners in pursuit of political status.

1981   Hunger strikes by detainees of Maze Prison led to deaths of Bobby Sands and nine other hunger strikers; Anglo-Irish Intergovernmental Council formed.

1982   Northern Ireland Assembly created to devolve legislative and executive powers back to the province. Social Democratic Labour Party (19%) and Sinn Féin (10%) boycotted the assembly.

1983   Six killed in IRA bomb attack outside Harrods, London.

1984   Series of reports from various groups on the future of the province. IRA bomb at Conservative Party conference in Brighton killed five people. Second Anglo-Irish Intergovernmental Council summit meeting agreed to oppose violence and cooperate on security; Britain rejected ideas of confederation or joint sovereignty.

1985   Meeting of Margaret Thatcher and Irish premier Garrett Fitzgerald at Hillsborough produced Anglo-Irish agreement on the future of Ulster; regarded as a sell-out by Unionists.

1986   Unionist opposition to Anglo-Irish agreement included protests and strikes. Loyalist violence against police; Unionist MPs boycotted Westminster.

1987   IRA bombed British Army base in West Germany. Unionist boycott of Westminster ended. Extradition clauses of Anglo-Irish Agreement approved in Eire. IRA bombed Remembrance Day service at Enniskillen, killing 11 people – later admitted it to be a 'mistake'.

1988   Three IRA bombers killed by security forces on Gibraltar.

1989   After serving 14 years in prison, the 'Guildford Four' were released when their convictions were ruled unsound by the Court of Appeal.

1990   Anglo-Irish Agreement threatened when Eire refused extraditions. Convictions of 'Birmingham Six' also called into question and sent to the Court of Appeal. Murder of Ian Gow, MP.

1991   IRA renewed bombing campaign on British mainland, targetting a meeting of the cabinet in Downing Street and mainline railway stations. Formal talks on political future of Northern Ireland initiated by Peter Brooke, Secretary of State for Northern Ireland.

1992   *June:* leaders of four main political parties as well as British and Irish government ministers held round-table talks for first time in 70 years.
Aug: UDA officially proscribed as an illegal organization.
Nov: round-table talks on future of province ended without agreement.

1993   *May:* Northern Ireland Secretary, Sir Patrick Mayhew, denied secret talks with IRA, but it emerged that there had been clandestine contact between the government and Sinn Féin/IRA representatives on possible end to conflict.
Dec: John Major and the Irish prime minister Albert Reynolds issued joint Anglo-Irish peace proposal for Northern Ireland, the Downing Street Declaration.

1994   *Aug:* Sinn Féin announced IRA Army Council had declared ceasefire and demanded British troops begin withdrawal as reciprocal act in province's 'demilitarization'.
Oct: Loyalist paramilitaries responded to IRA ceasefire by declaring their own. Both sides refused to define how 'permanent' the ceasefires would be.

1995   *Feb:* Framework document forming a basis for peace negotiations issued.
May: Sinn Féin engaged in the first public talks with British government officials since 1973. Talks stalled over the issues of the decommissioning of arms and release of prisoners.

liamentary majority, Reynolds resigned as premier and as leader of Fianna Fáil. Spring announced the formation of a new coalition of Fine Gael, Labour, and the Democratic Left Party Dec 1994. Fine Gael leader John Bruton, as the new premier, stressed his commitment to the Northern Ireland peace process and, with Dick Spring retaining the post of deputy and foreign minister, Anglo-Irish negotiations on a framework peace document resumed. The document, published in Feb, contained the Republic's agreement to renounce its claim to Northern Ireland and a proposal for joint Ulster–Ireland administrative bodies with limited powers.

Ireton Henry 1611–1651. Civil War general. He joined the Parliamentary forces and fought at ◊Edgehill 1642, Gainsborough 1643, and ◊Naseby 1645. After the Battle of Naseby, Ireton, who was opposed to both the extreme republicans and ◊Levellers, strove for a compromise with Charles I, but then played a leading role in his trial and execution. He married his leader Cromwell's daughter in 1646. Lord Deputy in Ireland from 1650, he died after the capture of Limerick.

Irish Free State former name (1922–37) of Southern Ireland, now the Republic of ◊Ireland.

Irish National Liberation Army (INLA) terrorist organization committed to the end of British rule in Northern Ireland and the incorporation of Ulster into the Irish Republic. The INLA was a 1974 offshoot of the Irish Republican Army (IRA), adopting a more hard-line Marxist political position than the IRA. The INLA was responsible for actions such as the killing of British politician Airey Neave in 1979. It declared a cease-fire 1994, following similar action by the IRA.

Irish nationalism political movement objecting to British rule of Ireland (which had no elected government of its own but sent members to the British Parliament in Westminster) and campaigned for ◊Home Rule.

Irish Republican Army
Eamon de Valera taking the salute of the IRA's mid-Clare brigade 1922. Following the Anglo-Irish Treaty of 1921, the split in the IRA between those who supported the treaty and those who wished to fight on for a united independent Ireland resulted in civil war in the newly formed Free State.
Image Select

Irish Republican Army (IRA) militant Irish nationalist organization whose aim is to create a united Irish socialist republic including Ulster. The paramilitary wing of ◊Sinn Féin, it was founded 1919 by Michael ◊Collins and fought a successful war against Britain 1919–21. It came to the fore again 1939 with a bombing campaign in Britain, having been declared illegal 1936. Its activities intensified from 1968 onwards, as the civil-rights disorders ('the Troubles') in Northern Ireland developed. In 1969 a group in the north broke away to become the *Provisional IRA*, its objective being the expulsion of the British from Northern Ireland and it is this group that is most often referred to today by the term IRA. The 'Official IRA' is largely quiescent. The left-wing Irish Republican Socialist Party, with its paramilitary wing, the Irish National Liberation Army, split from the IRA 1974.

Committed to the use of force in trying to achieve its objectives, the IRA regularly carried out bombings and shootings prior to the cease-fire of Sept 1994. In 1979 it murdered Louis ◊Mountbatten, and its bomb attacks in Britain included an attempt to kill members of the UK cabinet during the Conservative Party conference in Brighton, Sussex, 1984. Several attacks were also carried out against British military personnel serving outside the UK, especially in Germany. The peace process was set in motion Sept 1993 when talks aimed at achieving a 'lasting peace' were held between Social Democratic Labour Party leader, John ◊Hume, and Sinn Féin leader, Gerry ◊Adams. The process led to the IRA Council's announcement Aug 1994 of a cessation of its military activities in response to the UK–Irish peace initiative.

Between 1969 and the 1994 cease-fire, the IRA caused the deaths of over 3,000 people, both military and civilian. At the beginning of 1994 there were 18,000 troops in Northern Ireland. The total cost of the emergency in Northern Ireland was calculated 1993 by the House of Commons research department at £14.5 billion at current prices.

Ironsides nickname of a cavalry regiment raised by ◊Cromwell 1643 during the ◊Civil War. It was noted for its discipline and religious fanaticism, and first won fame at the Battle of ◊Marston Moor 1644. The nickname came from that of 'Ironside' given Cromwell by Prince ◊Rupert.

Isabella of Angoulême d. 1246. Queen of England 1200–16, as the second wife of King John. His loss of Normandy was popularly blamed on his infatuation with her, but this did not last. She was imprisoned in Gloucester 1214 until his death 1216 when she returned to France and married a former lover. She inherited Angoulême in her own right, and persuaded her son, Henry III to wage an abortive war in France 1241. They were defeated and Isabella was forced to flee to an abbey 1244 where she remained until her death.

Isabella of France 1292–1358. Daughter of King Philip IV of France, she married King Edward II of England 1308, but he slighted and neglected her for his favourites, first Piers Gaveston (died 1312) and later the Despenser family. Supported by her lover, Roger Mortimer, Isabella conspired to have Edward deposed and murdered and from 1327 she and Mortimer effectively ruled the country on behalf of her son Edward III. Mortimer was executed by Edward 1330 and Isabella sent into retirement.

Isandhlwana, Battle of in the Anglo-Zulu War, Zulu victory over British forces 22 Jan 1879 about 160 km/100 mi north of Durban. Only about 350 troops of the original contingent of 1,800 escaped and the invasion of Zululand was temporarily halted until reinforcements were received from Britain.

Isca Roman fortress near the River Usk at Caerleon, south Wales. The name represents that of the river itself, and is Celtic in origin.

Isle of Man see ◊Man, Isle of.

Isle of Wight see ◊Wight, Isle of.

Isles, Lord of the title adopted by successive heads of the MacDonald clan to assert their dominance over the Scottish highlands and the Western Isles and independence from the king of Scots. James IV acquired their rights 1493 and today the title is held by the Prince of Wales as heir to the monarch in Scotland.

Jack the Ripper popular name for the unidentified mutilator and murderer of at least five women prostitutes in the Whitechapel area of London 1888. The murders understandably provoked public outrage; the police were heavily criticized, which later led to a reassessment of police procedures. Jack the Ripper's identity has never been discovered, although several suspects have been proposed, including members of the royal household.

Jacobite supporter of the royal house of Stuart after the deposition of James II 1688. They include the Scottish Highlanders, who rose unsuccessfully under ◊Claverhouse 1689; and those who rose in Scotland and northern England under the leadership of ◊James Edward Stuart, the Old Pretender, 1715, and followed his son ◊Charles Edward Stuart in an invasion of England that reached Derby 1745–46. After the defeat at ◊Culloden, Jacobitism disappeared as a political force.

Jamaica former British colony, an island in the West Indies. Jamaica was discovered by Columbus 1494 and became a Spanish possession 1509. It was captured by the English 1655 and remained a British colony until 1958, when it became a territory of the West Indies Federation. It achieved full independence 1962.

James two kings of Britain; seven kings of Scotland:

James I 1566–1625. The first Stuart king of England from 1603 and Scotland (as **James VI**) from 1567. The son of Mary Queen of Scots and Lord Darnley, he succeeded on his mother's abdication from the Scottish throne, assumed power 1583, established a strong centralized authority, and in 1589 married Anne of Denmark (1574–1619).

James I
James I of England was already king of Scotland, as James VI, when he acceded to the English throne 1603. Although a physically weak man, he was extremely learned and wrote two books advocating the 'divine right of kings'.
Philip Sauvain

Jacobite revolts: chronology

1688　The Glorious Revolution: following the Protestant William of Orange's invasion from Holland (Nov), James II, the Catholic king of England, Wales, Scotland, and Ireland, fled to France (Dec).

1689　*27 July* Battle of Killiekrankie: supporters of James II (the Jacobites) under Viscount Dundee defeated a Protestant Covenanter army.
　　　　　21 Aug Jacobites attempted a rising at Dunkeld in Ireland.

1690　*1 July* William of Orange defeated James II and supporters at the Battle of the Boyne in Ireland.

1691　*12 July* Irish Jacobites were defeated at the Battle of Aughrim.
　　　　　Aug William of Orange offered a pardon to all Jacobites in the Scottish Highlands who swore allegiance by year-end.

1692　*Jan* King William III issued an order for the disciplining of Jacobites in the Highlands.
　　　　　13 Feb The Glencoe Massacre: members of the Campbell clan and supporters killed 38 members of the MacDonald clan at Glencoe, Scotland, after the MacDonald chief was late taking his oath to King William.

1696　*Feb* A Jacobite plot to murder King William III was discovered.
　　　　　March Jacobite invasion scare.

1701　*12 June* Act of Succession provided for the continuation of Protestant monarchy in England after the death of Princess Anne by settling succession on the Electress Sophia of Hanover and her descendants.
　　　　　6 Sept Death of the former James II; Louis XIV recognized his son as King James III (later known as the 'Old Pretender').

1708　*23–4 March* A French naval squadron attempted to land the Old Pretender on the Firth of Forth, but withdrew.

1715　*6 Sept* Start of 'the Fifteen': following the accession of King George I 1714, a Jacobite rebellion started at Braemar in Scotland.
　　　　　13 Nov The Scottish Jacobites were defeated at the Battle of Sheriffmuir. The following day, a Scottish and English Jacobite force was defeated at Preston, northwest England.
　　　　　22 Dec The Old Pretender landed at Peterhead, northeast Scotland, and joined Jacobites at Perth; he returned to France on 4 Feb 1716.

1722　*24 Sept* The Atterbury Plot: Francis Atterbury, bishop of Rochester and Jacobite leader was arrested; he was sent into exile May 1723.

1745　*23 July* Start of the 'Forty-five': Prince Charles Edward, son of James and known as the Young Pretender, landed on Eriskay Island off the west coast of Scotland.
　　　　　11 Sept Jacobites captured Edinburgh; on 21 Sept they defeated British forces at Prestonpans and then moved south.
　　　　　4 Dec Jacobites reached Derby, but withdrew for want of support.

1746　*16 April* Battle of Culloden, northeast Scotland: the Jacobite army was defeated.
　　　　　20 Sept Charles Edward escaped to France.

1766　*1 Jan* Death of the Old Pretender.

1788　*31 Jan* Death of the Young Pretender.

1807　*13 July* Death of Henry Stuart, Cardinal York, younger brother of the Young Pretender and the last Stuart in the male line. (The Jacobite claim then passed through various European royal families.)

As successor to Elizabeth I in England, he alienated the Puritans by his High Church views and Parliament by his assertion of the 'divine right of kings', and was generally unpopular because of his favourites, such as ◊Buckingham, and his schemes for an alliance with Spain. He was succeeded by his son Charles I.

James I 1394–1437. King of Scotland 1406–37. The second son of Robert III, he was captured by the English 1406 and did not assume power until 1424. He was a cultured and strong monarch whose improvements in the administration of justice brought him popularity among the common people. However he ruthlessly persecuted his enemies among the nobility and was assassinated by a group of conspirators led by the Earl of Atholl.

James II 1633–1701. King of England and Scotland (as *James VII*) from 1685, second son of Charles I. He succeeded his brother Charles II. He was appointed Lord High Admiral at the Restoration, and was successful both as an administrator and as a commander in the Anglo-Dutch wars. James married Anne Hyde 1659 (1637–1671, mother of Mary II and Anne) and ◊Mary of Modena 1673 (mother of James Edward Stuart). He became a Catholic 1671, which led first to attempts to exclude him from the succession, then to the rebellions of ◊Monmouth and ◊Argyll, and finally to the Whig and Tory leaders' invitation to William of

... it is now become like a little World within itself, being entrenched and fortified round about with a natural and yet admirably strong pond or ditch, whereby all the former fears are now quite cut off.

JAMES I
first speech to Parliament, referring to the uniting of England and Scotland, March 1603

Orange to take the throne 1688. James fled to France, then led an uprising in Ireland 1689, but after defeat at the Battle of the ◊Boyne 1690 remained in exile in France.

James II 1430–1460. King of Scotland from 1437. He assumed power 1449 with the help of the powerful Douglas family, with whom he later quarrelled, murdering the 8th earl 1452, and seizing the estates of his heirs. The only surviving son of James I, he was supported by most of the nobles and Parliament. He sympathized with the Lancastrians during the Wars of the ◊Roses, and attacked English possessions in southern Scotland. He was killed while besieging Roxburgh Castle.

James III 1451–1488. King of Scotland from 1460, who assumed power 1469. His reign was marked by rebellions by the nobles, including his brother Alexander, Duke of Albany, who the English recognized as king of Scotland. He was defeated and killed at Sauchieburn during a rebellion supported by his son, who then ascended the throne as James IV.

James IV 1473–1513. King of Scotland from 1488. He came to the throne after his followers murdered his father, James III, at Sauchieburn. He married Margaret Tudor (1489–1541, daughter of Henry VII and sister of Hnery VIII) 1503. His reign was internally peaceful, but an alliance with the French obliged him to attack England after the English invaded France 1513. He was defeated and killed at the Battle of ◊Flodden. James IV was a patron of poets and architects as well as a military leader.

James V 1512–1542. King of Scotland from 1513, who assumed power 1528. During the long period of his minority, he was caught in a struggle between pro-French and pro-English factions. When he assumed power, he allied himself with France and upheld Catholicism against the Protestants. Following an attack on Scottish territory by Henry VIII's forces, he was defeated near the border at Solway Moss 1542 and died shortly after. He was succeeded by his daughter, Mary Queen of Scots.

James VI of Scotland. See ◊James I of England.

James VII of Scotland. See ◊James II of England.

James Edward Stuart 1688–1766. British prince, known as the ***Old Pretender*** (for the ◊Jacobites, he was James III). Son of James II and Mary of Modena, he was born at St James's Palace and after the revolution of 1688 was taken to France. He landed in Scotland 1715 to head a Jacobite rebellion but withdrew through lack of support. He later settled in Rome.

Jamestown first permanent British settlement in North America, established by Captain John Smith 1607. It was capital of Virginia 1624–99.

Jarrow Crusade march in 1936 from Jarrow to London, protesting at the high level of unemployment following the closure of Palmer's shipyard in the town. The march was led by Labour MP Ellen Wilkinson, and it proved a landmark event of the 1930s ◊Depression. A similar march was held 1986, on the fiftieth anniversary of the event, to protest at the high levels of unemployment in the 1980s.

Jeffreys George, 1st Baron 1648–1689. Welsh judge, popularly known as the hanging judge. He became Chief Justice of the King's Bench 1683, and presided over many political trials, notably those of Philip Sidney, Titus Oates, and Richard Baxter, becoming notorious for his brutality.

In 1685 he was made a peer and Lord Chancellor and, after ◊Monmouth's rebellion, conducted the 'bloody assizes' during which 320 rebels were executed and hundreds more flogged, imprisoned, or transported.

Jellicoe John Rushworth, 1st Earl 1859–1935. British admiral who commanded the Grand Fleet 1914–16 during World War I; the only action he fought was the inconclusive battle of ◊Jutland. He was First Sea Lord 1916–17, when he failed to push the introduction of the convoy system to combat U-boat attacks. Created 1st Earl 1925.

Jenkins's Ear, War of in 1739 war between Britain and Spain, arising from Britain's illicit trade in Spanish America; it merged into the War of the ◊Austrian Succession 1740–48. The name derives from the claim of Robert Jenkins, a merchant captain, that his ear had been cut off by Spanish coastguards near Jamaica. The incident was seized on by opponents of Robert ◊Walpole who wanted to embarrass his government's antiwar policy and force war with Spain.

Jenner Edward 1749–1823. English physician who pioneered vaccination. In Jenner's day, smallpox was a major killer. His discovery 1796 that inoculation with cowpox gives immunity to smallpox was a great medical breakthrough.

Jervis John, Earl of St Vincent 1735–1823. English admiral who secured the blockage of Toulon, France, 1795 in the Revolutionary Wars, and the defeat of the Spanish fleet off Cape St Vincent 1797, in which Admiral ◊Nelson played a key part. Jervis was a rigid disciplinarian.

Jews in Britain England was the last of the major European countries to be reached by the Jews, and it was also the first to expel them. Many Jews came to England with William the Conqueror 1066 and settled in the large towns. There was a disturbance in Norwich 1144 when Jews there were accused of killing a Christian boy. Similar accusations followed elsewhere, notably at Lincoln, where the Jews were said to have killed a Christian boy subsequently venerated as St Hugh of Lincoln. Protestations by Jews of oppression were frequent, and when a deputation of leading Jews appeared at Westminster for the coronation of Richard I 1189 they were attacked by the mob. A report spread that Richard had ordered a general massacre. The Jews were expelled from England by Edward I 1290 and did not return until 1656.

In modern times Jews have generally integrated well in British public life. Nathan Meyer Rothschild opened an important branch of his famous bank in London 1804 and his son Lionel Nathan took a seat in the House of Commons 1858, when the restriction on the holding of public office by Jews was lifted. By the mid-1990s there were about 300,000 Jews in Britain. Many Jews have made important contributions to business and the arts.

jingoism blinkered, war-mongering patriotism. The term originated 1878, when the British prime minister Disraeli developed a pro-Turkish policy, which nearly involved the UK in war with Russia. His supporters' war song included the line 'We don't want to fight, but by jingo if we do...'.

Joan of Kent 1328–1385. Countess of Kent. She married ◊Edward the Black Prince 1361 and their younger son became ◊Richard II. ◊John of Gaunt took refuge at her home in Kennington when his palace was besieged by Londoners 1376. Her beauty and gentleness earned her the nickname 'Fair Maid of Kent'.

John (I) Lackland 1167–1216. King of England from 1199 and acting king from 1189 during his brother Richard the Lion-Heart's absence on the third Crusade. He lost Normandy and almost all the other English possessions in France to Philip II of France by 1205. His repressive policies and excessive taxation brought him into conflict with his barons, and he was forced to seal the ◊Magna Carta 1215. Later repudiation of it led to the first Barons' War 1215–17, during which he died.

John's subsequent bad reputation was only partially deserved. It resulted from his intrigues against his brother Richard I, his complicity in the death of his nephew Prince Arthur of Brittany, a rival for the English throne, and the effectiveness of his ruthless taxation policy, as well as his provoking Pope Innocent III to excommunicate England 1208–13. John's attempt to limit the papacy's right of interference in episcopal elections, which traditionally were the preserve of English kings, was resented by monastic sources, and these provided much of the evidence upon which his reign was later judged.

John of Gaunt 1340–1399. English nobleman and politician, born in Ghent, fourth son of Edward III, Duke of Lancaster from 1362. He distinguished himself during the Hundred Years' War. During Edward's last years, and the years before Richard II attained the age of majority, he acted as head of government, and Parliament protested against his corrupt rule. He was the father of Edward IV who was later to usurp Richard II.

Jews in Britain
Aaron the Jew of Colchester, a medieval cartoon. Jews were initially encouraged to settle in England but by the 13th century they had become victims of high taxation and persecution. They were expelled from England by Edward I 1290 and did not return in numbers until the mid-17th century.
Philip Sauvain

My brother John is not the man to conquer a country if there is anyone to offer even the feeblest resistance.

JOHN LACKLAND
Richard I (attributed)

John of Lancaster Duke of Bedford 1389–1435. English prince, third son of Henry IV. He was regent of France 1422–31 during the minority of Henry VI, his nephew, and protector of England 1422–35. He mostly left English affairs to his brother, Humphrey, duke of Gloucester. He allowed Joan of Arc to be burnt as a witch 1431 and had Henry VI crowned king of France 1431.

Johnson Amy 1903–1941. English aviator. She made a solo flight from England to Australia 1930, in 9$^1/_2$ days, and in 1932 made the fastest ever solo flight from England to Cape Town, South Africa. Her plane disappeared over the English Channel in World War II while she was serving with the Air Transport Auxiliary.

jointure a means by which a groom's family prescribed a certain amount of land or possessions for his widow. It prevented her from claiming a third of whatever the husband owned at his death.

Joyce William 1906–1946. Born in New York, son of a naturalized Irish-born American, he carried on fascist activity in the UK as a 'British subject'. During World War II he made propaganda broadcasts from Germany to the UK, his upper-class accent earning him the nickname *Lord Haw Haw*. He was hanged for treason.

Junius, Letters of series of letters published in the English *Public Advertiser* 1769–72, under the pseudonym Junius. Written in a pungent, epigrammatic style, they attacked the 'king's friends' in the interests of the opposition Whigs. They are generally believed to have been written by Sir Philip Francis (1740–1818).

Junto pejorative name (from the Spanish, *junta*) given to a group of Whig ministers who held power under William III 1696–97 and Queen Anne 1708–10. The group included Lords Somers, Sunderland, Wharton, Ormond, and Earl ◊Halifax, all Whigs who favoured an aggressive foreign policy against the French in support of British commercial interests.

jury body of lay people (usually 12) sworn to decide the facts of a case and reach a verdict in a court of law. Juries, used mainly in English-speaking countries, are implemented primarily in criminal cases, but also sometimes in civil cases; for example, inquests and libel trials.

The British jury derived from Germanic custom. It was introduced into England by the Normans. Originally it was a body of neighbours who gave their opinion on the basis of being familiar with the protagonists and background of a case. Eventually it developed into an impartial panel, giving a verdict based solely on evidence heard in court. The jury's duty is to decide the facts of a case: the judge directs them on matters of law. Jurors are selected at random from the electoral roll. Certain people are ineligible for jury service (such as lawyers and clerics), and others can be excused (such as members of Parliament and doctors). If the jury cannot reach a unanimous verdict it can give a majority verdict (at least 10 of the 12).

justice of the peace (JP) in England, an unpaid magistrate appointed from 1361 by the Lord Chancellor after consultation with local advisory committees. Two or more sit to dispose of minor charges (formerly their jurisdiction was much wider), to commit more serious cases for trial by a higher court, and to grant licences for the sale of alcohol.

justiciar the chief justice minister of Norman and early Angevin kings, second in power only to the king. By 1265, the government had been divided into various departments, such as the Exchequer and Chancery, which meant that it was no longer desirable to have one official in charge of all. The last justiciar, Hugh Despenser, was killed fighting for the baronial opposition to Henry II at the Battle of Evesham 1265.

Jute member of a Germanic people who originated in Jutland but later settled in Frankish territory. They occupied Kent, southeast England, about 450, according to tradition under Hengist and Horsa, and conquered the Isle of Wight and the opposite coast of Hampshire in the early 6th century.

Jutland, Battle of World War I naval battle between British and German forces 31 May 1916, off the west coast of Jutland. Its outcome was indecisive, with both sides claiming victory, but the German fleet remained in port for the rest of the war.

Early on 31 May the German High Seas Fleet under Admiral Reinhard Scheer entered the North Sea from the Baltic, intending to entice British battle cruisers in the area to the Norwegian coast and there destroy them. The two sides' scouts saw each other in the after-

There's something wrong with our bloody ships today, Chatfield.

JUTLAND
Admiral David Beatty commenting to an aide during the battle.

noon of 31 May and the German battle cruiser force, leading their fleet, promptly turned away to draw the British battle cruisers towards the waiting German fleet. The British took the bait and a long-range gunnery duel took place in which the British squadron lost two battle cruisers and sustained damage to Admiral David Beatty's flagship. The British force then themselves turned away to draw the Germans north towards Admiral John Jellicoe's Grand Fleet. The fleets met, and a general melée ensued during which another British battle cruiser was sunk. However, Scheer realized he was outgunned and turned for home. Jellicoe, fearful of torpedoes in the failing light of evening, decided not to follow.

Kandahar, Battle of British victory 1880 over Afghan forces besieging a fort 160 km/100 mi northwest of Quetta and 440 km/275 mi southwest of Kabul. In March 1880 a British force of about 4,000 troops was besieged in the fort at Kandahar; about the same time another British force was annihilated at Maiwand. A relief column under General Frederick ◊Roberts set out from Kabul 9 Aug and the Afghans raised the siege. He then marched after the Afghans and routed Ayub Khan 1 Sept, capturing the Afghan camp and supplies. Roberts became famous for what was in fact a relatively minor engagement and was later ennobled as Lord Roberts of Kandahar and Waterford.

Keble John 1792–1866. Anglican priest and religious poet. His sermon on the decline of religious faith in Britain, preached 1833, heralded the start of the ◊Oxford Movement, a Catholic revival in the Church of England. Keble College, Oxford, was founded 1870 in his memory.

Keeler Christine 1942– . British prostitute of the 1960s. She became notorious in 1963 after revelations of affairs with both a Soviet attaché and the war minister John ◊Profumo, who resigned after admitting lying to the House of Commons about their relationship. Her patron, the osteopath Stephen Ward, convicted of living on immoral earnings, committed suicide and Keeler was subsequently imprisoned for related offences.

Keeper of the Great Seal an officer who had charge of the ◊great seal of England (the official seal authenticating state documents). During the Middle Ages the great seal was entrusted to the chancellor. Later, a special Lord Keeper was appointed to take charge of it, but since 1761 the posts of chancellor and keeper have been combined.

Kells, Book of 8th-century illuminated manuscript of the Gospels produced at the monastery of Kells in County Meath, Ireland. It is now in Trinity College library, Dublin.

Kenilworth, siege of July 1265–Dec 1266 siege of Simon de Montfort and his supporters in Kenilworth castle by forces loyal to Henry III following the defeat of the barons at the Battle of ◊Evesham. Henry offered peace terms in the Dictum of Kenilworth Oct 1266 but the barons held out until Dec when de Montfort fled to the Isle of Ely. The terms of the dictum offered the barons a chance of reconciliation with the crown and an opportunity for the ◊Dispossesed to recover the lands seized from them after Evesham.

Kenneth two kings of Scotland:

Kenneth I (called *MacAlpin*) d. 858. King of Scotland from about 844. Traditionally, he is regarded as the founder of the Scottish kingdom (Alba) by virtue of his final defeat of the Picts about 844. He invaded Northumbria six times, and drove the Angles and the Britons over the river Tweed.

Kenneth II d. 995. King of Scotland from 971, son of Malcolm I. He invaded Northumbria several times, and his chiefs were in constant conflict with Sigurd the Norwegian over the area of Scotland north of the river Spey. He is believed to have been murdered in a feud, possibly by Constantine III who succeeded him.

Kent, kingdom of Anglo-Saxon kingdom in southeast England, founded by the Jutes when they arrived in Britain as ◊*foederati* under Hengest and Horsa in the 5th century. Kent was the first English kingdom to convert to Christianity 597 under its king, Ethelbert, although when he died 616 much of the kingdom reverted to paganism. Kent was divided from 686–90 and then came under the control of Mercia *c.* 762 before being absorbed by Wessex 825.

Kent and Strathearn Edward, Duke of Kent and Strathearn 1767–1820. British general. The fourth son of George III, he married Victoria Mary Louisa (1786–1861), widow of the Prince of Leiningen, in 1818, and had one child, the future Queen Victoria.

Kenya former British colony, East Africa. The coastal territory was visited by British traders from the 19th century. It belonged to the ruler of Zanzibar, who leased it 1887 to the British East Africa Company, which soon extended its holdings into the interior. It was organized as the British East Africa Protectorate 1895 except for a narrow coastal strip which with its islands was named the Kenya Protectorate. The whole territory became a British colony 1920. It gained independence 1963.

Ketch Jack d. 1686. English executioner who included ◊Monmouth 1685 among his victims; his name was once a common nickname for an executioner.

Kett's Rebellion popular rebellion 1549 in Norfolk led by Robert Kett against enclosures of common land. It was suppressed by the Earl of Warwick and Kett was hanged.

Keys, House of elected assembly of the Isle of Man; see ◊Tynwald.

khaki election snap election Oct 1900 called by the Conservative prime minister, the Earl of Salisbury, in the wake of British successes in the 2nd Boer War. Salisbury hoped to build on the public euphoria at the victories in South Africa to restore his government, but although he won a slightly increased majority he did not manage to make good the losses in his majority since 1895. It is called the 'khaki' election after the colour of the army's uniform in South Africa.

Kidd 'Captain' (William) c. 1645–1701. Scottish pirate. He spent his youth privateering for the British against the French off the North American coast, and was given a royal commission to suppress piracy in the Indian Ocean 1695. Instead, he joined a group of pirates in Madagascar. On his way to Boston, Massachusetts, he was arrested 1699, taken to England, and hanged.

Kilkenny, Statutes of legislation passed 1366 by the parliament of Ireland at Kilkenny. The 35 statutes were designed to halt the assimilation of Anglo-Normans into Irish society and included a ban on their intermarriage with the Irish and on the adoption of the Irish language, dress, or legal system. The laws proved unenforceable and were eventually repealed 1613.

Killiecrankie, Battle of during the first ◊Jacobite uprising, defeat 7 May 1689 of General Mackay (for William of Orange) by John Graham of ◊Claverhouse, a supporter of James II, at Killiecrankie, Scotland. Despite the victory, Claverhouse was killed and the revolt soon petered out; the remaining forces were routed on 21 Aug.

Kilmainham Treaty informal secret agreement April 1882 that secured the release of the nationalist Charles ◊Parnell from Kilmainham jail, Dublin, where he had been imprisoned for six months for supporting Irish tenant farmers who had joined the Land League's campaign for agricultural reform. The British government realized that Parnell could quell violence more easily out of prison than in it and in return for his release, Parnell agreed to accept the Land Act of 1861. The Kilmainham Treaty marked a change in British policy in Ireland from confrontation to cooperation, with the government attempting to conciliate landowners and their tenants, who were refusing to pay rent. This strategy was subsequently threatened by the ◊Phoenix Park Murders.

Kilsyth, Battle of final victory of ◊Montrose's royalist forces over the Covenanters 15 Aug 1645 in Stirling, the last of his six successive victories over them. No Covenanters' army remained active in Scotland after this defeat and their cause temporarily collapsed. Montrose was himself defeated in a suprise attack at Philliphaugh Sept 1645.

'King and Country' debate controversial debate Feb 1933 in which the Oxford Union, the university's debating society, passed the motion 'this House will in no circumstances fight for its King and its Country'. The debate sent shockwaves throughout the country as many saw it as signalling that Britain's young elite had lost their sense of patriotism, although it probably more accurately reflected a commitment to disarmament after the horrors of World War I.

Can't row; won't fight.

'KING AND COUNTRY' DEBATE
Winston Churchill, following Oxford's defeat in the Boat Race, 1933

King's Champion or *Queen's Champion* ceremonial office held by virtue of possessing the lordship of Scrivelsby, Lincolnshire. A document of 1332/33 described the champion as 'an armed knight on horseback to prove by his body, if necessary, against whomsoever, the King who is crowned that day is the true and right heir of the kingdom'. Sir John Dymoke established his right to champion the monarch on coronation day 1377 and it is still held by his descendant. This office was last performed on the coronation of King George IV in 1821, at a banquet in Westminster Hall. The gold cup from which the king drank at the banquet was the champion's fee.

King's Council in medieval England, a court that carried out much of the monarch's daily administration. It was first established in the reign of Edward I, and became the Privy Council 1534–36.

king's evil another name for the skin condition scrofula. In medieval England and France, it was thought that the touch of an anointed king could cure the condition.

King's Friends in the 1760s and 80s, those politicians, mainly Tories, who supported George III's view that the monarch had the right to choose his own ministers. The king presented this as a preference for good government over an administration riven by parties, but many Whigs regarded it as an attack on constitutional rule. The term was later also applied to an inchoate group of politicians, including Winston Churchill, who supported Edward VIII's wish to marry Wallace Simpson and remain on the throne in the ◊abdication crisis of 1936.

King's Peace form of jurisdiction of the former King's Court. In medieval times criminal matters and offences against public order were within the jurisdiction of local lords and local courts, while the King's Court had jurisdiction over offences committed within the vicinity of the king himself. Such offences were said to have been committed *contra pacem Domini*, 'against the peace of our Lord (the king)'. The King's Peace was fictitiously extended to the highways and ultimately to the whole realm, so that the King's Court finally acquired a comprehensive jurisdiction. The modern successor of the King's Court, which was held in the presence of the sovereign, is the Queen's Bench Division of the High Court.

Kinnock Neil 1942– . British Labour politician, party leader 1983–92. Born and educated in Wales, he was elected to represent a Welsh constituency in Parliament 1970 (Islwyn from 1983). He was further left than prime ministers Wilson and Callaghan, but as party leader (in succession to Michael Foot) adopted a moderate position, initiating a major policy review 1988–89 and expelling members of the left-wing Militant Tendency. He resigned as party leader after Labour's defeat in the 1992 general election. In 1994 he left Parliament to become a European commissioner.

Kitchener Horatio Herbert, Earl Kitchener of Khartoum 1850–1916. British soldier and administrator. Kitchener was commissioned 1871, and transferred to the Egyptian army 1882. Promoted to commander in chief 1892, he forced a French expedition to withdraw in the ◊Fashoda Incident. He defeated the Sudanese dervishes at Omdurman 1898 and reoccupied Khartoum. During the South African War he conducted war by a scorched-earth policy and created the earliest concentration camps for civilians. Subsequently he commanded the forces in India 1902–09 and acted as British agent in Egypt, and in 1914 received an earldom. As British secretary of state for war from 1914, he modernized the British forces. He was one of the first to appreciate that the war would not be 'over by Christmas' and planned for a three-year war for which he began raising new armies. He bears some responsibility for the failure of the ◊Gallipoli campaign, having initially refused any troops for the venture, and from then on his influence declined. He drowned when his ship was sunk on the way to Russia.

Those who prate on about Blimpish patriotism in the mode of Margaret Thatcher are also the ones who will take millions off the caring services of this country.

NEIL KINNOCK
speech at the Labour Party Conference, 1983

Kitchener armies British volunteer armies raised at the outbreak of World War I at the urging of Lord ◊Kitchener; also known as 'New Armies'. Kitchener issued a call for 100,000 troops 7 Aug 1914 and further calls followed. Within a year over 2 million men had volunteered and three new armies had been created but by early 1916 volunteers dwindled and conscription was introduced.

knight member of a medieval elite recognized as having the right to bear arms in return for a duty of mounted military service to the Crown, a system first known from Norman times. Often this was associated with a specific grant of land, the ◊knight's fee, and at times it was held that a knight might be required to serve for 40 days each year. Although initially relatively humble professional fighters, the rising costs of maintaining the equipment and trappings necessary meant that knights needed to be relatively wealthy. At the same time, military expeditions began to involve lengthy periods of absence abroad and the techniques of warfare changed, so that kings began to require a standing army rather than bands of knights. As knights lost their military importance, they were increasingly involved in government and knighthood became a mark more of social eminence than military competence.

Knights were initially 'dubbed' with a set of arms by their lords and until the early 17th century, knighthood could be conferred by a general on the battlefield, but today knighthood is conferred solely by the monarch. Some knighthoods are awarded within the various orders of chivalry, but most, known as knights bachelor, are independent creations. Knights have the right to prefix their first name with the title 'Sir', though this title is not hereditary. Their wives are titled 'Lady', but before the surname, e.g., Sir Richard and Lady Webb. The equivalent rank to knight for a woman is that of dame.

knight's fee in the 150 years after the Norman Conquest, a grant of land by the Crown which was held by a lord on condition that a knight would perform strict duties as required, such as 40 days' military service or castle duty. Though the fee could be the estate of one man, it was usually granted out in multiples, and it is sometimes said that the most common formula was that for every 5 hides of land granted to a lord, one knight was required by the king. Heirs to a knight's fee who were minors became wards of the Crown, which took control of the land, or granted it to another, until they were of age. This feudal system of tenure ended with the Civil War.

knighthood, order of fraternity carrying with it the rank of knight, admission to which is granted as a mark of royal favour or as a reward for public services. During the Middle Ages in Europe such fraternities fell into two classes, religious and secular. A knight **bachelor** belongs to the lowest stage of knighthood, not being a member of any specially named order.

The **Order of the Garter**, founded about 1347, is the oldest now in existence; there are eight other British orders: the **Thistle** founded 1687, the **Bath** 1725, the **St Patrick** 1788, the **St Michael and St George** 1818, the **Star of India** 1861, the **Indian Empire** 1878, the **Royal Victorian Order** 1896, and the **Order of the British Empire** (OBE) 1917. The **Order of Merit** (OM), founded 1902, comprises the sovereign and no more than 24 prominent individuals.

Knox John c. 1505–1572. Scottish Protestant reformer, founder of the Church of Scotland. He spent several years in exile for his beliefs, including a period in Geneva where he met John ◊Calvin. Originally a Roman Catholic priest, Knox is thought to have been converted by the reformer George Wishart. When Wishart was burned for heresy, Knox went into hiding, but later preached the reformed doctrines. Captured by French troops in Scotland 1547, he was imprisoned in France, sentenced to the gallows, and released only by the intercession of the British government 1549. In England he assisted in compiling the Prayer Book, as a royal chaplain from 1551. On Mary's accession 1553 he fled the country and in 1557 was, in his absence, condemned to be burned. He returned to Scotland 1559 to promote Presbyterianism. He was tried for treason but acquitted 1563. His books include *First Blast of the Trumpet Against the Monstrous Regiment of Women* 1558 and a *History of the Reformation in Scotland* 1586.

Korean War war 1950–53 between North Korea, supported by China, and South Korea, supported by the United Nations. The war was a direct consequence of World War II. The UN sent out a multinational force to repel the North Korean invaders. About half the army was from the United States, with the rest mainly from Australia, Britain, Canada and Turkey. 22 Ships of the Royal Navy in the Far East, including two aircraft carriers, were placed under the command of the UN Supreme Commander, US General Douglas McArthur, while some 4,000 troops of the British Army were also sent to the war zone. At one stage over 1,000 British prisoners were held incommunicado in South Korea.

Kruger telegram message sent by Kaiser Wilhelm II of Germany to President Kruger of the Transvaal 3 Jan 1896 congratulating him on defeating the 'Jameson' raid of 1895. The text of the telegram provoked indignation in Britain and elsewhere, and represented a worsening of Anglo-German relations, in spite of a German government retraction.

He is rather like one of those revolving lighthouses which radiate momentary gleams of revealing light far out into the surrounding gloom, and then relapse into complete darkness.

Lord Kitchener
*David Lloyd George
(attributed)*

Kūt-al-Imāra, Siege of in World War I, siege by Turkish forces of a town in Iraq Dec 1915–April 1916, when the joint British and Indian garrison surrendered. They were harshly treated by the Turks: two-thirds of the British and half the Indian troops died during a forced march to captivity of some 1,900 km/1,200 mi. The town was eventually recaptured 23 Feb 1917, remaining in British hands for the rest of the war.

Kuwait former British protectorate, on the northwest shore of the Persian Gulf. Lasting links were formed with the British in the 1770s when the East India Company moved its operations from Basra to Kuwait. An 'exclusive agreement' (treaty) 1899, allowing Britain to control Kuwait's foreign policy, was formally abrogated 1961 when Kuwait achieved independence.

Labour Party political party based on socialist principles, originally formed to represent workers. It was founded 1900 and first held office 1924. The first majority Labour government 1945–51 introduced ◊nationalization and the National Health Service, and expanded social security. Labour was again in power 1964–70 and 1974–79. The party leader (Tony Blair from 1994) is elected by an electoral college, with a weighted representation of the Parliamentary Labour Party (30%), constituency parties (30%), and trade unions (40%).

The Labour Party, the Trades Union Congress, and the cooperative movement together form the National Council of Labour, whose aims are to coordinate political activities and take joint action on specific issues.

Although the Scottish socialist Keir Hardie and John Burns, a workers' leader, entered Parliament independently as Labour members 1892, it was not until 1900 that a conference representing the trade unions, the Independent Labour Party (ILP), and the ◊Fabian Society, founded the Labour Party, known until 1906, when 29 seats were gained, as the Labour Representation Committee. All but a pacifist minority of the Labour Party supported World War I, and a socialist programme was first adopted 1918, with local branches of the party set up to which individual members were admitted. By 1922 the Labour Party was recognized as the official opposition, and in 1924 formed a minority government (with Liberal support) for a few months under the party's first secretary Ramsay MacDonald. A second minority government 1929 followed a conservative policy, and in 1931 MacDonald and other leaders, faced with a financial crisis, left the party to support the national government. The ILP seceded 1932.

In 1936–39 there was internal dissension on foreign policy; the leadership's support of non-intervention in Spain was strongly criticized and Stafford Cripps, Aneurin Bevan, and others were expelled for advocating an alliance of all left-wing parties against the government of Neville Chamberlain. The Labour Party supported Winston Churchill's wartime coalition, but then withdrew and took office for the first time as a majority government under Clement Attlee, party leader from 1935, after the 1945 elections. The welfare state was developed by nationalization of essential services and industries, a system of national insurance was established 1946, and the National Health Service was founded 1948. Defeated in 1951, Labour was split by disagreements on further nationalization, and unilateral or multilateral disarmament, but achieved unity under Hugh Gaitskell's leadership 1955–63.

Under Harold Wilson the party returned to power 1964–70 and, with a very slender majority, 1974–79. James Callaghan, who had succeeded Wilson in 1976, was forced to a general election 1979 and lost. Michael Foot was elected to the leadership in 1980; Neil Kinnock succeeded him in 1983 after Labour had lost another general election. The party adopted a policy of unilateral nuclear disarmament in 1986 and expelled the left-wing faction Militant Tendency, but rifts remained. Labour lost the 1987 general election, a major reason being its non-nuclear policy. In spite of the Conservative government's declining popularity, Labour was defeated in the 1992 general election, following which Neil Kinnock stepped down as party leader; John Smith succeeded him July 1992 but died suddenly May 1994. Tony Blair was elected to succeed him July 1994, in the first fully democratic elections to the post, and began an attempt to revise the party's constitution by scrapping Clause 4, concerning common ownership of the means of production.

Labour Representation Committee forerunner 1900–1906 of the Labour Party. The committee was founded in Feb 1900 after a resolution drafted by Ramsay ◊MacDonald and moved by the Amalgamated Society of Railway Workers (now the National Union of Railwaymen) was carried at the 1899 Trades Union Congress (TUC). The resolution called for

> *We are not here just to manage capitalism but to change society and to define its finer values.*
>
> Labour Party
> *Tony Benn,
> speech to the Labour
> Party Conference, 1975*

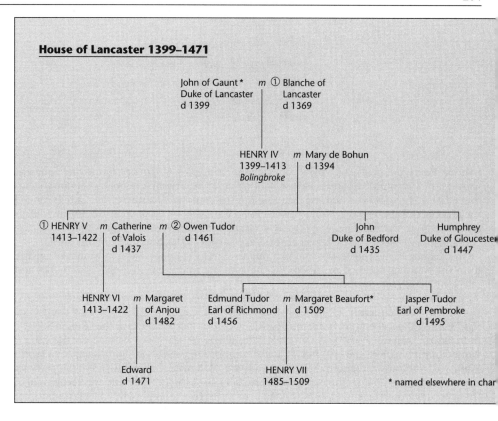

House of Lancaster 1399–1471

John of Gaunt *   *m* ① Blanche of
Duke of Lancaster   Lancaster
d 1399   d 1369

HENRY IV   *m* Mary de Bohun
1399–1413   d 1394
Bolingbroke

① HENRY V   *m* Catherine   *m* ② Owen Tudor   John   Humphrey
1413–1422   of Valois   d 1461   Duke of Bedford   Duke of Gloucester
        d 1437   d 1435   d 1447

HENRY VI   *m* Margaret   Edmund Tudor   *m* Margaret Beaufort*   Jasper Tudor
1413–1422   of Anjou   Earl of Richmond   d 1509   Earl of Pembroke
        d 1482   d 1456   d 1495

Edward   HENRY VII
d 1471   1485–1509   * named elsewhere in char

a special congress of the TUC parliamentary committee to campaign for more Labour members of Parliament. Ramsay MacDonald became its secretary. Following his efforts, 29 Labour members of Parliament were elected in the 1906 general election, and the Labour Representation Committee was renamed the Labour Party.

Labourers, Statute of legislation 1351 designed to prevent costs in wages and feudal services from growing out of control in the labour shortage caused by the Black Death as labourers demanded higher wages from lords. The act was widely unpopular and was one of the causes of the Peasants' Revolt.

Ladysmith town in Natal, South Africa, 185 km/115 mi northwest of Durban, near the Klip. It was besieged by the Boers, 2 Nov 1899–28 Feb 1900, in the South African War. Ladysmith was named in honour of the wife of Henry Smith, a British soldier and colonial administrator.

Lambert John 1619–1683. English general, a cavalry commander in the Civil War under Cromwell (at the battles of Marston Moor, Preston, Dunbar, and Worcester). Lambert broke with Cromwell over the proposal to award him the royal title. After the Restoration he was imprisoned for life.

Lancaster, Chancellor of the Duchy of public office created 1351 and attached to the Crown since 1399. The Chancellor of the Duchy of Lancaster was originally the monarch's representative controlling the royal lands and courts within the duchy. The office is now a sinecure without any responsibilities, usually held by a member of the cabinet with a special role outside that of the regular ministries; for example, Harold Lever as financial adviser to the Wilson–Callaghan governments from 1974.

Lancaster, House of English royal house, a branch of the Plantagenets. It originated in 1267 when Edmund (d. 1296), the younger son of Henry III, was granted the earldom of Lancaster. Converted to a duchy for Henry of Grosmont (d. 1361), it passed to John of Gaunt in 1362 by his marriage to Blanche, Henry's daughter. John's son, Henry IV, established the royal dynasty of Lancaster in 1399, and he was followed by two more Lancastrian kings, Henry V

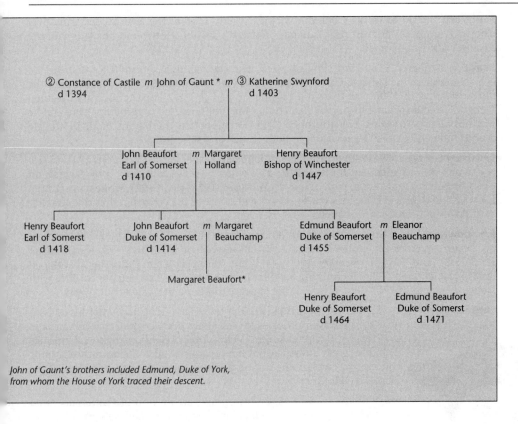

② Constance of Castile *m* John of Gaunt * *m* ③ Katherine Swynford
d 1394   d 1403

John Beaufort   *m* Margaret   Henry Beaufort
Earl of Somerset   Holland   Bishop of Winchester
d 1410   d 1447

Henry Beaufort   John Beaufort   *m* Margaret   Edmund Beaufort *m* Eleanor
Earl of Somerst   Duke of Somerset Beauchamp   Duke of Somerset Beauchamp
d 1418   d 1414   d 1455

Margaret Beaufort*

Henry Beaufort   Edmund Beaufort
Duke of Somerset   Duke of Somerst
d 1464   d 1471

John of Gaunt's brothers included Edmund, Duke of York, from whom the House of York traced their descent.

and Henry VI. Lancastrian succession was disputed by the House of York in the Wars of the ◊Roses 1455–85.

Lancaster House Agreement accord reached at a conference held in Sept 1979 at Lancaster House, London, between Britain and representative groups of Rhodesia, including the Rhodesian government under Ian Smith and black nationalist groups. The agreement enabled a smooth transition to the independent state of Zimbabwe in 1980.

Land Acts, Irish a series of 19th-century laws designed to improve the lot of the Irish peasantry. The first act 1870 awarded tenants compensation for improvements they had made to land, but offered no protection against increased rents or eviction. The second act 1881 introduced the 'three f's' – fair rents, fixity of tenure, and freedom of sale. The third act 1885, part of ◊Gladstone's abortive plans for Home Rule, provided £5 million for tenants to buy out their landlords. This scheme was further strengthened by the Wyndham Act 1903 which offered inducements to landlords to sell. Before the end of the Union with Britain, some 11 million acres were purchased with government assistance.

Land League Irish peasant-rights organization, formed 1879 by Michael ◊Davitt and Charles ◊Parnell to fight against tenant evictions. Through its skilful use of the boycott against anyone who took a farm from which another had been evicted, it forced Gladstone's government to introduce a law 1881 restricting rents and granting tenants security of tenure.

land tax a tax on land, based on an assessment of 1692, which became the principal source of crown revenue in the 18th century. It averaged around 20% of rental income, although this could be increased in war time. It was largely superseded by Income Tax.

Lanfranc *c.* 1010–1089. Italian archbishop of Canterbury from 1070; he rebuilt the cathedral, replaced English clergy by Normans, enforced clerical celibacy, and separated the ecclesiastical from the secular courts. His skill in theological controversy did much to secure the church's adoption of the doctrine of transubstantiation. He came over to England as an adviser to William the Conqueror.

Langport, Battle of in the Civil War, victory 10 July 1645 of the New Model Army over Charles I's army of the west near Langport, Somerset. Bristol fell two months later and the royalist cause was doomed.

Langton Stephen *c.* 1150–1228. English priest who was mainly responsible for drafting the charter of rights, the ♦Magna Carta. He studied in Paris, where he became chancellor of the university, and in 1206 was created a cardinal. When in 1207 Pope Innocent III secured Langton's election as archbishop of Canterbury, King John refused to recognize him, and he was not allowed to enter England until 1213. He supported the barons in their struggle against John and worked for revisions to both church and state policies.

Lansbury George 1859–1940. British Labour politician, leader in the Commons 1931–35. He was a member of Parliament for Bow 1910–12 – when he resigned to force a by-election on the issue of votes for women, which he lost – and again 1922–40. In 1921, while mayor of the London borough of Poplar, he went to prison with most of the council rather than modify their policy of more generous unemployment relief.

Lansdowne Henry Charles, 5th Marquis of Lansdowne 1845–1927. British Liberal Unionist politician, governor-general of Canada 1883–88, viceroy of India 1888–93, war minister 1895–1900, and foreign secretary 1900–06. While at the Foreign Office he abandoned Britain's isolationist policy by forming an alliance with Japan and an entente cordiale with France. His letter of 1917 suggesting an offer of peace to Germany created controversy.

Latimer Hugh 1490–1555. English Christian church reformer and bishop. After his conversion to Protestantism 1524 he was imprisoned several times but was protected by Cardinal Wolsey and Henry VIII. Under Edward VI his sermons denouncing social injustice won him great influence, but he was arrested in 1553, once the Catholic queen Mary was on the throne, and two years later he was burned at the stake in Oxford.

Laud William 1573–1645. English priest; archbishop of Canterbury from 1633. Laud's High Church policy, support for Charles I's unparliamentary rule, censorship of the press, and persecution of the Puritans all aroused bitter opposition, while his strict enforcement of the statutes against enclosures and of laws regulating wages and prices alienated the propertied classes. His attempt to impose the use of the *Prayer Book* on the Scots precipitated the ♦Bishops' Wars. Impeached by Parliament 1640, he was imprisoned in the Tower of London, summarily condemned to death, and beheaded.

Lauderdale John Maitland, Duke of Lauderdale 1616–1682. Scottish politician. Formerly a zealous ♦Covenanter, he joined the Royalists 1647, and as high commissioner for Scotland 1667–79 persecuted the Covenanters. He was created Duke of Lauderdale 1672, and was a member of the ♦Cabal ministry 1667–73.

Law Andrew Bonar 1858–1923. British Conservative politician. Elected leader of the opposition 1911, he became colonial secretary in Asquith's coalition government 1915–16, chancellor of the Exchequer 1916–19, and Lord Privy Seal 1919–21 in Lloyd George's coalition. He formed a Conservative Cabinet 1922, but resigned on health grounds the following year.

Law John 1671–1729. Scottish economist. He persuaded the French to set up a Bank of France 1716 and to invest heavily in the colonization of the Mississippi delta before the collapse of the project 1720.

law courts bodies that adjudicate in legal disputes. Civil and criminal cases are usually dealt with by separate courts. In England and Wales the court system was reorganized under the Courts Act 1971. The higher courts are: the **House of Lords** (the highest court for the whole of Britain), which deals with both civil and criminal appeals; the **Court of Appeal**, which is divided between criminal and civil appeal courts; the **High Court of Justice** dealing with important civil cases; **crown courts**, which handle criminal cases; and **county courts**, which deal with civil matters. **Magistrates' courts** deal with minor criminal cases and are

Laud
Portrait of Archbishop William Laud. He took an uncompromising stance on imposing uniformity of religious worship. His antipathy to the Puritans and support for his patron Charles I contributed to the outbreak of the English Civil War and led to his execution in 1645.
Michael Nicholson

served by ◊justices of the peace or stipendiary (paid) magistrates; and *juvenile courts* are presided over by specially qualified justices. There are also special courts, such as the Restrictive Practices Court and the Employment Appeal Tribunal.

In Scotland, the supreme civil court is the **Court of Session**, with appeal to the House of Lords; the highest criminal court is the **High Court of Justiciary**, with no appeal to the House of Lords.

The courts are organized in six circuits. The towns of each circuit are first-tier (High Court and circuit judges dealing with both criminal and civil cases), second-tier (High Court and circuit judges dealing with criminal cases only), or third-tier (circuit judges dealing with criminal cases only). Cases are allotted according to gravity among High Court and circuit judges and recorders (part-time judges with the same jurisdiction as circuit judges). In 1971 solicitors were allowed for the first time to appear in and conduct cases at the level of the crown courts, and solicitors as well as barristers of ten years' standing became eligible for appointment as recorders, who after five years become eligible as circuit judges. In the UK in 1989 there were 5,500 barristers and 47,000 solicitors.

Lawrence T(homas) E(dward), known as **Lawrence of Arabia** 1888–1935. British soldier, scholar, and translator. Appointed to the military intelligence department in Cairo, Egypt, during World War I, he took part in negotiations for an Arab revolt against the Ottoman Turks, and in 1916 attached himself to the emir Faisal. He became a guerrilla leader of genius, combining raids on Turkish communications with the organization of a joint Arab revolt, described in *The Seven Pillars of Wisdom* 1926.

Law
Canadian-born Andrew Bonar Law led the Conservative party from 1911 to 1923, and was prime minister 1921–23. He helped bring about the end of Llyd George's domination of British politics.
Hulton Deutsch

League of Nations international organization formed after World War I to solve international disputes by arbitration. Established in Geneva, Switzerland, 1920, the league included representatives from states throughout the world, but was severely weakened by the US decision not to become a member, and had no power to enforce its decisions. It was dissolved 1946. Its subsidiaries included the **International Labour Organization** and the **Permanent Court of International Justice** in The Hague, Netherlands, both now under the auspices of the United Nations (UN).

The League of Nations was suggested in US president Woodrow Wilson's 'Fourteen Points' 1917 as part of the peace settlement for World War I. The league covenant was drawn up by the Paris peace conference in 1919 and incorporated into the Versailles and other peace treaties. The member states undertook to preserve the territorial integrity of all, and to submit international disputes to the league.

Lee Jennie, Baroness Lee 1904–1988. British socialist politician. She became a member of Parliament for the Independent Labour Party at the age of 24, and in 1934 married Aneurin ◊Bevan. On the left wing of the Labour Party, she was on its National Executive Committee 1958–70 and was minister of education 1967–70, during which time she was responsible for founding the Open University 1969.

leet in medieval East Anglia, administrative subdivision of a hundred for the purposes of collecting tax, roughly corresponding to a ◊hide.

Left Book Club book club founded by publisher Victor Gollancz 1936 to circulate to its members political books intended to counter the upsurge of fascism. It produced mainly non-fiction, such as George Orwell's *The Road to Wigan Pier* 1937. It was disbanded 1948.

Leicester Robert Dudley, Earl of Leicester *c.* 1532–1588. English courtier. Son of the Duke of Northumberland, he was created Earl of Leicester 1564. Queen Elizabeth I gave him command of the army sent to the Netherlands 1585–87 and of the forces prepared to resist the threat of Spanish invasion 1588. His lack of military success led to his recall, but he retained Elizabeth's favour until his death.

It's the most amateurish, Buffalo-Billy sort of performance, and the only people who do it well are the Bedouin.

LAWRENCE OF ARABIA
describing an attack on a Turkish train, letter, 1917

Leicester's good looks attracted Queen Elizabeth, who made him Master of the Horse 1558 and a privy councillor 1559. But his poor performance in the army ended any chance of marrying the queen. He was a staunch supporter of the Protestant cause.

Leinster, kingdom of ancient Irish kingdom, in the southeast of the present Republic. Its northern part, Meath, was made a separate kingdom in the 2nd century AD. The MacMurroughs were kings over the remainder until the early 12th century, when it became independent. Their descendants continued in Wexford and Carlow until the 16th century. Richard Strongbow accepted Leinster from Henry II 1171 as a fief of the Crown. The present province of Leinster comprises the counties of Dublin, Kildare, Carlow, Kilkenny, Laois, Offaly, Longford, Louth, Meath, Westmeath, Wicklow and Wexford.

lend-lease US act of Congress passed March 1941 giving the president power to order 'any defense article for the government of any country whose defense the president deemed vital to the defense of the USA'. During World War II, the USA negotiated many lend-lease agreements, notably with Britain and the Soviet Union. Lend-lease was officially ended Aug 1945, by which time goods and services to the value of $42 billion had been supplied in this way, of which the British Empire had received 65% and the Soviet Union 23%.

Lennox Matthew Stewart, 4th Earl of Lennox 1516–1571. Scottish magnate. He forfeited his title 1545 after acting as an agent for the English, but it was restored 1564. The following year his son, Lord Darnley, married Mary Queen of Scots. After Darnley was murdered 1567 Lennox retired to England. He was appointed regent for Scotland for James VI 1570 but was killed soon after in a skirmish with supporters of Mary.

Leofric Earl of Mercia d. 1057. English nobleman. He was created earl c. 1034 by King ◊Canute, and was a rival of ◊Godwin, Earl of Wessex, supporting ◊Edward the Confessor against him 1051. His wife was Lady ◊Godiva.

Leslie Alexander, 1st Earl of Leven c. 1580–1661. Scottish military commander. After 30 years in the army of Gustavus Adolphus of Sweden, he returned to lead the Scots in the ◊Bishops' Wars, defeating the English at Newburn 1640. During the Civil War he commanded the Scots army that invaded England and fought at Marston Moor 1644. He accepted the surrender of Charles I at Newark 1646 and later handed the king over to Parliament. He fought for the Scottish Royalists at Dunbar 1650 and was imprisoned by the Parliamentarians 1651–54.

Leslie David, 1st Baron Newark d. 1682. Scottish military commander. He led the cavalry at Marston Moor 1644 and defeated Montrose at Philiphaugh 1645. He was himself defeated by Cromwell at Dunbar 1650 and Worcester 1651 and was held prisoner in England 1651–60.

Levant Company Established 1592 to trade English cloth and tin for oriental silk or Turkish carpets in the eastern Mediterranean, the company was formed by the merger of the Turkey Company (1581) and the Venice Company (1583).

Levellers democratic party in the Civil War. The Levellers, led by John ◊Lilburne, found wide support among Cromwell's New Model Army and the yeoman farmers, artisans, and small traders, and proved a powerful political force 1647–49. Their programme included the establishment of a republic, government by a parliament of one house elected by male suffrage, religious toleration, and sweeping social reforms. Cromwell's refusal to implement this programme led to mutinies by Levellers in the army, which were suppressed by Cromwell 1649, ending the movement.

Leven Alexander Leslie, 1st Earl of Leven c. 1580–1661. Scottish general in the ◊Civil War. He led the ◊Covenanters' army which invaded England 1640, commanded the Scottish army sent to aid the English Puritans 1643–46, and shared in the Parliamentarians' victory over the Royalists in the Battle of Marston Moor.

Leveson-Gower Granville George, 2nd Earl Granville 1815–1891. English politician. He held several cabinet posts 1851–86, including that of foreign secretary 1870–74 and 1880–85 under ◊Gladstone. He supported Gladstone's ◊Home Rule policy and played a leading part in the decision to send General ◊Gordon to Khartoum 1884.

Lewes, Battle of defeat and capture 1264 of English King Henry III by rebel barons, led by Simon de Montfort, Earl of Leicester (1208–65). The barons objected to Henry's patronage of

French nobles in the English court, his weak foreign policy, and his support for the papacy against the Holy Roman Empire. In 1258, they forced him to issue the ◊Provisions of Oxford, and when he later refused to implement them, they revolted. They defeated and captured the king at Lewes in Sussex. Their revolt was broken by de Montfort's death and defeat at ◊Evesham 1265.

Liberal Democrats common name for the ◊Social and Liberal Democrats.

Liberal Party British political party, the successor to the ◊Whig Party, with an ideology of liberalism. In the 19th century, it represented the interests of commerce and industry. Its outstanding leaders were Palmerston, Gladstone, and Lloyd George. From 1914 it declined, and the rise of the Labour Party pushed the Liberals into the middle ground. The Liberals joined forces with the Social Democratic Party (SDP) as the Alliance for the 1983 and 1987 elections. In 1988, a majority of the SDP voted to merge with the Liberals to form the ◊Social and Liberal Democrats.

The term 'Liberal', used officially from about 1840 and unofficially from about 1815, marked a shift of support for the party from aristocrats to include also progressive industrialists, backed by supporters of the utilitarian reformer Jeremy ◊Bentham, Nonconformists (especially in Welsh and Scottish constituencies), and the middle classes. During the Liberals' first period of power, 1830–41, they promoted parliamentary and municipal government reform and the abolition of slavery, but their laissez-faire theories led to the harsh Poor Law of 1834. Except for two short periods, the Liberals were in power 1846–66, but the only major change was the general adoption of free trade. Liberal pressure forced Peel to repeal the Corn Laws 1846, splitting the Tory party.

The extension of the franchise 1867 and Gladstone's emergence as leader began a new phase, dominated by the 'Manchester school' with a programme of 'peace, retrenchment, and reform'. Gladstone's 1868–74 government introduced many important reforms, including elementary education and vote by ballot. The party's left, mainly composed of working-class Radicals led by Charles ◊Bradlaugh (a lawyer's clerk) and Joseph ◊Chamberlain (a wealthy manufacturer), repudiated laissez-faire and inclined toward republicanism, but in 1886 the Liberals were split over the policy of Home Rule for Ireland, and many became Liberal Unionists or joined the Conservatives.

Except for 1892–95, the Liberals remained out of power until 1906, when, reinforced by Labour and Irish support, they returned with a huge majority. Old-age pensions, National Insurance, limitation of the powers of the Lords, and the Irish Home Rule Bill followed. Lloyd George's alliance with the Conservatives 1916–22 divided the Liberal Party between him and his predecessor Asquith, and although reunited 1923 the Liberals continued to lose votes. They briefly joined the National Government 1931–32. After World War II they were reduced to a handful of members of Parliament.

A revival began under the leadership 1956–67 of Jo Grimond and continued under Jeremy Thorpe, who resigned after controversy within the party 1976. After a caretaker return by Grimond, David Steel became the first party leader in British politics to be elected by party members who were not MPs. In 1977–78 Steel entered into an agreement to support Labour in any vote of confidence in return for consultation on measures undertaken. He resigned 1988 and was replaced by Paddy Ashdown who became leader of the newly merged Social and Liberal Democratic Party.

Liberator, the title given to Daniel ◊O'Connell, Irish political leader.

liberties in the Middle Ages, freedom from direct royal jurisdiction, usually granted to border territories in return for protecting the border area from raiders. The privilege was granted in cases such as the ◊Marcher Lords on the Welsh border, or in the Palatinate of Durham where the bishop was granted special privileges as a bulwark against the Scots.

More restricted liberties provided freedom from prosecution in the king's courts. The most famous of these was that of Westminster Abbey, where sanctuary extended beyond its buildings to much of the city of Westminster, but boroughs or even smaller towns, such as Bewdley, also enjoyed such privileges.

As monarchs grew stronger, they resented liberties which served no purpose, as in the case of Wales, but despite efforts by Edward I in particular to subjugate these lordships their privileges remained largely intact until the 16th century.

licensing laws laws governing the sale of alcoholic drinks. In Britain, sales can only be made by pubs, restaurants, shops, and clubs which hold licences obtained from licensing justices. The hours during which alcoholic drinks can be sold are restricted, but they have been recently extended in England and Wales in line with Scotland. Current laws allow licensed premises to sell alcohol between 11am and 11pm Monday to Saturday, and the same on Sundays. These hours may be extended for special occasions, by application to the licensing justices.

From the late 19th century, temperance and nonconformist movements lobbied for tighter restrictions on the consumption of alcohol. In Wales, Sunday closing was enforced from 1881 and in 1913 Scotland was permitted to hold local referenda on licensing issues. Restrictions on pub hours in England were initially introduced as a temporary war measure in World War I, not as a morality act, but to improve efficiency on the home front, but the regulations were retained after the war.

Light Brigade, Charge of the see ◊Charge of the Light Brigade.

Lilburne John 1614–1657. English republican agitator. He was imprisoned 1638–40 for circulating Puritan pamphlets, fought in the Parliamentary army in the Civil War, and became leader of the ◊Levellers by his advocacy of a democratic republic. He was put in the Tower of London for accusations against Cromwell 1647, banished 1652, and arrested again on his return 1653. He was acquitted, but still imprisoned until 1655 for 'the peace of the nation'.

Limerick, Treaty of signed 3 Oct 1691 in Limerick, Ireland, treaty dictating the terms of surrender of the ◊Jacobites who had resisted the invading armies of William III. The Jacobites were granted amnesty or allowed to go into exile, and religious tolerance, in particular of Catholics, was guaranteed. This latter promise was broken by the penal code introduced from 1695 by the Protestant MPs of the Dublin parliament.

Lincoln, Battles of two battles near the town of Lincoln:

2 Feb 1141 King Stephen was defeated and captured by supporters of ◊Matilda and taken to Bristol. The victory temporarily put Matilda ahead in the battle for the crown, but Stephen was soon exchanged for the Earl of Gloucester and she was defeated at the Battle of ◊Winchester in Sept.

20 May 1217 in the first Barons War, defeat of Prince Louis of France (the future King Louis VIII) and the barons by William Marshall, Earl of Pembroke. The victory led to Louis being expelled from his stronghold in southeast England.

Lindisfarne site of a monastery off the coast of Northumberland; see ◊Holy Island.

Lindsey small Anglo-Saxon kingdom northwest of the Wash in Eastern England. It was overshadowed by its neighbours and was ruled by Northumbria in the 7th century until it passed into Mercian control 678. It was finally overrun by Danish invaders 841. It survived as the *Parts of Lindsey*, an administrative subdivision of the county of Lincolnshire, until the reorganization of local government 1974.

Lindsey, Parts of former administrative county within Lincolnshire. It was the largest of the three administrative divisions (or 'parts') of the county, with its headquarters at Lincoln. When county councils were reorganized 1974 Lindsey was divided between the new county of Humberside and a reduced Lincolnshire.

Lindum Roman name for Lincoln, where the first permanent fortress of the IXth Legion was established *c.* AD 60. The name is Celtic in origin, meaning 'pool'. The modern name Lincoln derives from the combination of 'Lindum' and the title ◊*colonia*, a status the fortress acquired *c.* AD 96.

linkman person employed to show the way through city streets with lighted torches. They were employed in most cities until the advent of street lighting made them unnecessary.

Lister Joseph, 1st Baron Lister 1827–1912. English surgeon and founder of antiseptic surgery, influenced by Louis Pasteur's work on bacteria. He introduced dressings soaked in carbolic acid and strict rules of hygiene to combat wound sepsis in hospitals.

Liverpool Robert Banks Jenkinson, 2nd Earl Liverpool 1770–1825. British Tory politician. He entered Parliament 1790 and was foreign secretary 1801–03, home secretary 1804–06 and

1807–09, war minister 1809–12, and prime minister 1812–27. His government conducted the Napoleonic Wars to a successful conclusion, but its ruthless suppression of freedom of speech and of the press aroused such opposition that there was serious unrest during 1815–20 and revolution frequently seemed imminent.

livery and maintenance the traditional marks of a man's relation to his lord; *livery* being the uniform of the lord and *maintenance* the help a lord would give his followers in legal cases, often by illegal means or coercion of the courts. The practice led to widespread corruption and abuses of the legal system and Henry VII passed a series of acts against it but these largely amounted to little more than a system of licences. Until the advent of a standing army in the 17th century kings depended on their lords having strong retinues, and so could do little to act against their followers.

Livingstone David 1813–1873. Scottish missionary explorer. In 1841 he went to Africa, reached Lake Ngami 1849, followed the Zambezi to its mouth, saw the Victoria Falls 1855, and went to East and Central Africa 1858–64, reaching Lakes Shirwa and Malawi. From 1866, he tried to find the source of the river Nile, and reached Ujiji in Tanganyika in Nov 1871. British explorer Henry Stanley joined Livingstone in Ujiji. He died in Old Chitambo (now in Zambia) and was buried in Westminster Abbey, London.

Llewelyn two princes of Wales:

Llewelyn I 1173–1240. Prince of Wales from 1194 who extended his rule to all Wales not in Norman hands, driving the English from North Wales 1212, and taking Shrewsbury 1215. During the early part of Henry III's reign, he was several times attacked by English armies. He was married to Joanna, illegitimate daughter of King John.

Llewelyn II ap Gruffydd *c.* 1225–1282. Prince of Wales from 1246, grandson of Llewelyn I. In 1277 Edward I of England compelled Llewelyn to acknowledge him as overlord and to surrender South Wales. He died while leading a national uprising, ending Welsh independence.

Lloyd John, known as *John Scolvus*, 'the skilful'. Welsh sailor who carried on an illegal trade with Greenland and is claimed to have reached North America, sailing as far south as Maryland, in 1477 (15 years before the voyage of Columbus).

Lloyd George David 1863–1945. Welsh Liberal politician, prime minister of Britain 1916–22. A pioneer of social reform, as chancellor of the Exchequer 1908–15 he introduced old-age pensions 1908 and health and unemployment insurance 1911. High unemployment, intervention in the Russian Civil War, and use of the military police force, the ◊Black and Tans, in Ireland eroded his support as prime minister, and the creation of the Irish Free State 1921 and his pro-Greek policy against the Turks caused the collapse of his coalition government.

Lloyd George was born in Manchester, became a solicitor, and was member of Parliament for Caernarvon Boroughs from 1890. During the Boer War, he was a prominent member of the pro-Boer faction in Parliament. His 1909 budget (with graduated direct taxes and taxing land values) provoked the Lords to reject it, and resulted in the Act of 1911 limiting their powers. He held ministerial posts during World War I until 1916 when there was an open breach between him and Prime Minister ◊Asquith, and he became prime minister of a coalition government. He secured a unified Allied command which enabled the Allies to withstand the last German offensive and achieve victory. After World War I he had a major role in

Livingstone
The Scottish missionary and explorer David Livingstone. Although regarded as a hero by the Victorians, he failed to achieve his greatest ambition – to find the source of the Nile – and only ever made one convert.
Image Select

Lloyd George
David Lloyd George (centre), Liberal Chancellor, on his way to present the budget to the House of Commons 1914. In the first budget of World War I, he doubled the rate of income tax from 1s 3d (6.25 p) in the pound to 2s 6d (12.5p).
Hulton Deutsch

the Versailles peace treaty. In the 1918 elections, he achieved a huge majority over Labour and Asquith's followers. He had become largely distrusted within his own party by 1922, and never regained power.

local government that part of government dealing mainly with matters concerning the inhabitants of a particular area or town, usually financed at least in part by local taxes. England and Wales are divided into counties (Scotland into regions) and these are subdivided into districts.

The system of local government in England developed haphazardly; in the 18th century it varied in the towns between democratic survivals of the ◊guild system and the narrow rule of small oligarchies. The Municipal Reform Act 1835 established the rule of elected councils, although their actual powers remained small. In country areas local government remained in the hands of the justices of the peace (JPs) assembled in quarter sessions, until the Local Government Act 1888 established county councils. These were given a measure of control over the internal local authorities, except the major bodies, which were constituted as county boroughs. The Local Government Act 1894 set up urban and rural district councils and, in the rural districts only, parish councils.

Four spectres haunt the poor – old age, accident, sickness and unemployment. We are going to exorcise them. We are going to drive hunger from the hearth. We mean to banish the workhouse from the horizon of every workman in the land.

DAVID LLOYD GEORGE
speech, 1910

Under the Local Government Act 1972 the upper range of local government for England and Wales was established on a two-tier basis, with 46 counties in England and eight in Wales. London and six other English cities were created metropolitan areas (their metropolitan county councils were abolished 1986, and their already limited functions redistributed to **metropolitan district councils**), and the counties had **county councils**. The counties were subdivided into districts (of which there are 300, each with a **district council**, replacing the former county borough, borough, and urban and rural district councils) and then, in rural areas, into parishes and, in Wales, into 'communities' across the country, each again with its own council dealing with local matters.

Under the Local Government Act 1974 a Commission for Local Administration for England and Wales was set up, creating an **ombudsman** for complaints about local government. Under the Local Government (Scotland) Act 1973 **Scotland** was divided into nine regions and three island areas, rather than counties; these are subdivided into districts, which may in turn have subsidiary community councils, but the latter are not statutory bodies with claims on public funds as of right. **Northern Ireland** has a single-tier system of 26 district councils.

The activities of local government are financed largely by the council tax, a local tax based on property values but taking into account the number of inhabitants in a property. This tax

. Stonehenge, Britain's finest surviving monument to the history of these islands from the late Neolithic to the Bronze ages. Begun in about 2000
: and attaining approximately its present form in about 1400 BC, Stonehenge belongs to a period well after the establishment of a the first, farm-
g-based civilization in Britain. It was a major ceremonial centre.
ilip Sauvain

12. Maiden Castle, Dorset, a major Iron Age hill fort. From about 1300 BC onwards, there is evidence of a decline of the former civilization base around ceremonial sites, and the emergence of a society based on mixed-farming, trade with the Continent, and hill forts. Maiden Castle, a larg and elaborate example, remained in use until the Roman conquest of Britain.
Aerofilms

3. The Great Bath, part of the temple and baths complex in the Roman town of Aquae Sulis (Bath), one of the most important Roman settlements
า Britain. At the end of the 4th century, drainage problems caused serious flooding and the baths were abandoned. In reflection perhaps of their
nistrust of Roman town-based culture as much as of the curative properties of Bath water, the Anglo-Saxon inheritors of Aquae Sulis called the
own Akemanceaster, or Sick Man's Town.
& L Adkins

. Ruins of Fountains Abbey, Yorkshire, one of the largest and best-known Cistercian monastic houses in England. The arrival of the Cistercian
der in the 12th century, with its policy of settlement in waste land and creed of physical labour as holy work, had a great impact on the British
ıdscape. Houses such as Fountains included extensive drainage and engineering works, and brought large-scale commercial sheep farming to
eviously underpopulated areas.
rofilms

15. Medieval pilgrims on their way to the shrine of St Thomas à Becket at Canterbury. Pilgrimage, immortalized by Geoffrey Chaucer, was a remarkably common activity throughout medieval Europe, at all social levels. Canterbury was the most important English pilgrimage site, attracting pilgrims from elsewhere in Europe too.
Philip Sauvain

16. Harlech castle, built during Edward I's conquest of Welsh Wales in the late 13th century, ranks among the finest castles anywhere in Europe. Edward's Welsh castles were built by the Savoyard master mason James of St George, for a king who was among the richest in Europe at the beginning of his reign. They represent the apogee of medieval military architecture in the British Isles.
Aerofilms

7. The Ranelagh Gardens, Chelsea, London, showing the rotunda and the Chinese pavilion, from an engraving of 1751. Opened as public pleasure gardens in 1742, the Ranelagh Gardens confirmed the existence of a whole class of Londoners in the 18th century with disposable income to spend in the innumerable booths for eating, drinking, and socializing that the Gardens provided.
Image Select

18. Blenheim Palace, designed by John Vanbrugh and Nicholas Hawksmoor and partly paid for by the nation, was begun in 1705 at Woodstock, Oxfordshire, for the Duke of Marlborough, in honour of his victories over Louis XIV. Its size and sumptuous decoration make it one of the relatively few outstanding British examples of Baroque architecture.
Aerofilms

19. Cyrus McCormick's reaping machine of 1831 (patented 1834), as exhibited at the Crystal Palace Exhibition of 1851. The first widely adopted reaping machine, McCormick's invention typified the mechanization that transformed British agriculture from the end of the 18th century.
Image Select

20. The Pitman, from George Walker's *The Costume of Yorkshire*, published in Leeds in 1814. Though the the changes brought by the industrial revolution in Britain were initially more gradual and less widespread than is often assumed, the mining industry was one of the first to be transformed by industrialization. To the left is a steam locomotive built by Matthew Murray for John Blenkinsop, and used to haul coal from Middleton Colliery from 1812 onwards.
Image Select

21. The cover of the Beatles' album *Sgt Pepper's Lonely Hearts Club Band* 1967. The 1960s saw a transformation of the social attitudes of British society after the hardships of the war years and the conservative 1950s. Despite continuing economic problems and a shrinking world role for Britain, many Britons embraced a more hedonistic, relaxed image of society; the influence of psychedelic drugs on art, music, and fashions, promoted by the Beatles and others, went far beyond the small numbers of people who actually used such drugs.
David Pratt

22. Anti-Poll Tax demonstration in London in the early 1990s. The collapse in the 1980s of the postwar concensus between the major British political parties on social and economic policy led to a number of incidents of widespread public opposition to Conservative government policies. Demonstrations larger than any since the 1960s, and considerable disorder, ultimately led to a government change of policy on taxation plans for local government.
Rex Features

superseded in 1993 the community charge, popularly known as the poll tax, which itself had replaced in England and Wales in 1990 (Scotland 1989) a system of local property taxes known as rates.

Locarno, Pact of series of diplomatic documents initialled in Locarno, Switzerland, 16 Oct 1925 and formally signed in London 1 Dec 1925. The pact settled the question of French security, and the signatories – Britain, France, Belgium, Italy, and Germany – guaranteed Germany's existing frontiers with France and Belgium. Following the signing of the pact, Germany was admitted to the League of Nations. British foreign secretary Austen Chamberlain was the prime mover in the pact.

Lollard follower of the English religious reformer John ◊Wycliffe in the 14th century. The Lollards condemned the doctrine of the transubstantiation of the bread and wine of the Eucharist, advocated the diversion of ecclesiastical property to charitable uses, and denounced war and capital punishment. They were active from about 1377; after the passing of the statute ◊*De heretico comburendo* ('The Necessity of Burning Heretics') 1401 many Lollards were burned, and in 1414 they raised an unsuccessful revolt in London, known as Oldcastle's rebellion.

The name is derived from the Dutch *lollaert* (mumbler), applied to earlier European groups accused of combining pious pretensions with heretical belief. Lollardy lingered on in London and East Anglia, and in the 16th century became absorbed into the Protestant movement.

Londinium Roman name for London, where a settlement was established soon after the Roman invasion AD 43. This was burnt down by Boadicea AD 61, after which the Romans built a new settlement that extended as far as modern Ludgate Hill and established a fort in the Cripplegate area. The name is Celtic or pre-Celtic but of uncertain meaning.

London capital of England and the United Kingdom, on the river Thames; its metropolitan area, **Greater London**, has an area of 1,580 sq km/610 sq mi. The **City of London**, known as the 'square mile', area 274 hectares/677 acres, is the financial and commercial centre of the UK. Greater London from 1965 comprises the City of London and 32 boroughs. Popular tourist attractions include the Tower of London, St Paul's Cathedral, Buckingham Palace, and Westminster Abbey.

Roman **Londinium** was established soon after the Roman invasion AD 43; in the 2nd century London became a walled city; by the 11th century, it was the main city of England and gradually extended beyond the walls to link with the originally separate Westminster. Throughout the 19th century London was the largest city in the world (in population).

Since 1986 there has been no central authority for Greater London; responsibility is divided between individual boroughs and central government. The City of London has been governed by a corporation from the 12th century. Its structure and the electoral procedures for its common councillors and aldermen are medievally complex, and it is headed by the lord mayor (who is, broadly speaking, nominated by the former and elected annually by the latter). After being sworn in at the Guildhall, he or she is presented the next day to the lord chief justice at the Royal Courts of Justice in Westminster, and the **Lord Mayor's Show** is a ceremonial procession there in November.

London, Treaty of any of several peace treaties signed in London; they include:

1827 treaty in which Britain, France, and Russia agreed to use force against Turkey unless it accepted mediation in the war against Greece. This led to the naval Battle of Navarino 1827 where the three powers' fleets destroyed those of Turkey and Egypt, ensuring Greek independence.

1839 treaty confirming the independence of Belgium from the kingdom of the Netherlands. Signed by the five major powers (Britain, France, Austria, Russia, and Prussia), it guaranteed the new state's neutrality.

1852 an unsuccessful attempt by the five major European powers to settle the secession for the Duchies of Schleswig and Holstein. It was effectively overturned by the bids of the Danish king Christian IX to incorporate the two states 1863.

1913 treaty which ended the first Balkan War, but whose terms were ignored by the signatories, leading to the second Balkan War.

1915 treaty bringing Italy into World War I on the side of the Triple Entente against the Central Powers, in return for territorial concessions.

London Bridge
London Bridge *c.* 1635. The first record of houses along the bridge is from 1201 and the bridge continued to have houses until the mid-18th century, some as high as seven storeys.
Image Select

London Bridge bridge over the river Thames in the centre of London, from the City of London to Southwark. A bridge was first built near the current site by the Romans c. AD 80, and several wooden bridges were built on the site until replaced with a stone bridge at the end of the 12th century. In the middle ages, the bridge was crowded with houses and shops. A new bridge was built by John Rennie 1824–34 which lasted until 1968 when it was bought by a US oil company, disassembled, and reconstructed as a tourist attraction in Arizona 1971. The current bridge dates from then.

London County Council (LCC) former administrative authority for London created 1888 by the Local Government Act; it incorporated parts of Kent, Surrey, and Middlesex in the metropolis. It was replaced by the Greater London Council 1964–86. Relations between the LCC and the government of the day were frequently discordant, in part because more often than not the two were in the hands of opposing parties.

London Working Men's Association (LWMA) campaigning organization for political reform, founded June 1836 by William Lovett and others, who in 1837 drew up the first version of the People's Charter (see ◊Chartism). It was founded in the belief that popular education, achieved through discussion and access to a cheap and honest press, was a means of obtaining political reform. By 1837 the LWMA had 100 members.

Londonderry, Siege of 17 April–30 July 1689, siege of some 20,000 Protestants in Londonderry, Ulster, by the Jacobite forces of James II. After holding out for 105 days, the Protestants were relieved and the Jacobites driven off.

Long Parliament English Parliament 1640–53 and 1659–60, which continued through the Civil War. It was first called by Charles I 1640 following his defeat by the Scots in the second ◊Bishops' War. It attacked the king's abuses of power and impeached his ministers ◊Stafford and ◊Laud. It abolished the ◊Star Chamber and the court of High Commission and the Councils of the North and of Wales. After the Royalists withdrew 1642 and the Presbyterian right was excluded 1648 by Colonel ◊Pride, the remaining ◊Rump Parliament ruled England until expelled by Oliver Cromwell 1653. Reassembled 1659–60, the Long Parliament initiated the negotiations for the restoration of the monarchy.

Long Range Desert Group highly mobile British penetration force formed July 1940 to carry out reconnaissance and raids deep in the desert of North Africa. After the successful conclusion of the North African campaign 1942, the group was redeployed to carry out operations in Greece, Italy, and Yugoslavia. It was disbanded Aug 1945.

longbow longer than standard bow, made of yew, introduced in the 12th century. They were favoured by English archers in preference to the cross bow, as the longer bow allowed arrows of greater weight to be fired further and more accurately. They were highly effective in the ◊Hundred Years' War, to the extent that the French took to removing the first two fingers of prisoners so that they would never again be able to draw a bow.

Longchamp William d. 1197. Bishop of Ely from 1189, when he was also appointed Chancellor of England. He became papal legate 1190 and administered England in the absence of Richard I until Prince John brought about his fall from power 1191. He continued to serve the king abroad, helping to secure Richard's release from captivity in Germany 1193. He was reinstated as Chancellor but left England with Richard 1194 and never returned.

Lords, House of upper house of the UK ◊Parliament; see ◊House of Lords.

Lords Appellant five English nobles who made an 'appeal of treason' 14 Nov 1387, impeaching several of Richard II's ministers for exercising undue influence over the king. The affair was part of baronial attack on the powers of the monarchy, as represented by the king's favourites, headed by Robert de Vere the Earl of Oxford. The attack was initiated by the king's uncle, Thomas of Woodstock, Duke of Gloucester, Richard, Earl of Arundel, and Thomas, Earl of Warwick, and they were later joined by Henry Bolingbroke, Earl of Derby, and Thomas Mowbray, Earl of Nottingham. After the Earl of Derby defeated the Earl of Oxford at the Battle of Radcot Bridge Dec 1387, the king was forced to refer the charges to the ◊Merciless Parliament Feb 1388. The Earls of Oxford and Suffolk, the archbishop of York, Chief Justice Tresilian, and Nicholas Brembre were condemned by the Lords in Parliament. All escaped overseas, except Tresilian and Brembre who were executed. Richard later turned Parliament against the principal Appellants 1398: Arundel was executed, Warwick exiled, and Thomas of Gloucester was almost certainly murdered in Calais.

Lords of the Articles Scottish parliamentary committee which supervised all legislation to be presented to the full Parliament, which could not debate what the Lords proposed, only reject or amend. Though of 15th century origin, the committee became a vital instrument of royal control in the early 17th century, as James VI's revival of episcopacy allowed him to use crown-appointed bishops to dominate the committee. The ◊Covenanters abolished the system, but with the restoration of the Stuart monarchy the Lords re-appeared. They were finally abolished 1690.

Lords of the Congregation association of Scottish noblemen formed 1557 to further Protestantism by ousting the French-backed Catholic regent, Mary of Guise. When Mary attempted to supress Protestant preachers 1559, they rose in outright rebellion against Mary and the French. The lords of the Congregation concluded the first Treaty of ◊Berwick with Queen Elizabeth I Jan 1560, securing English intervention and the withdrawal of the French. The Congregation was left in control of Scotland and the Reformation Parliament banned the saying of Mass, rejected papal authority, and introduced an essentially Calvinist religious system.

Lostwithiel, Battle of in the Civil War, battle 2 Sept 1644 at Lostwithiel, Cornwall, in which the Royalists, commanded in person by Charles I, surrounded and defeated the Parliamentarian army of Lord Essex. This and later victories that year enabled Charles to launch a direct attack on London.

Loudun Hill, Battle of May 1307 battle in which Robert the Bruce defeated the forces of Edward II of England at Loudon Hill, east of Kilmarnock, Scotland. The victory marked the turning point in Bruce's campaign to recover Scotland.

Lovat Simon Fraser, 12th Baron Lovat c. 1667–1747. Scottish ◊Jacobite. Throughout a political career lasting 50 years he constantly intrigued with both Jacobites and Whigs, and was beheaded for supporting the 1745 rebellion.

Lovett William 1800–1877. Moderate chartist who drafted the ◊Peoples' Charter of 1838. Originally a cabinet maker, along with a number of other skilled craftsmen he helped found the London Working Men's Association 1836. He believed that democratic reform could be achieved peacefully and that technological innovation might be of benefit to working men's conditions.

Low David 1891–1963. New Zealand-born British political cartoonist, creator (in newspapers such as the London *Evening Standard*) of such characters as the reactionary military man Colonel Blimp and the 'TUC carthorse'.

Loyalist member of approximately 30% of the US population remaining loyal to Britain in the ◊American Revolution. Many Loyalists went to East Ontario, Canada, after 1783. Known as Tories, most were crown officials, Anglican clergy, and economically advantaged, although they were represented in every segment of colonial society.

The term also refers to people in Northern Ireland who wish to remain part of the United Kingdom rather than becoming citizens of a unified Republic of Ireland.

Lucan George Charles Bingham, 3rd Earl 1800–1888. British soldier who mistakenly ordered the the ◊Charge of the Light Brigade at the Battle of Balaclava 1854. He was commander of the light cavalry division but misinterpreted ambigous orders from Lord ◊Raglan, the British commander in chief, and led a charge on a heavily defended Russian gun position, with heavy casualties. He was later promoted to field marshal.

Luddite one of a group of people involved in machine-wrecking riots in northern England 1811–16. The organizer of the Luddites was referred to as General Ludd, but may not have existed. Many Luddites were hanged or transported to penal colonies, such as Australia.

The movement, which began in Nottinghamshire and spread to Lancashire, Cheshire, Derbyshire, Leicestershire, and Yorkshire, was primarily a revolt against the unemployment caused by the introduction of machines in the Industrial Revolution. The term has subsequently been applied to anybody who resists new technology.

Ludford Bridge, Rout of or *Ludlow Bridge* in the Wars of the Roses, Lancastrian victory over Yorkist forces 12–13 Oct 1459 at Ludford, Shropshire. Richard, Duke of York, had joined forces with the Earl of Salisbury in a retreat to his home at Ludlow Castle. They were confronted by a larger Lancastrian army across the River Teme at Ludford Bridge and Richard's army disintegrated. The Lancastrians sacked Ludlow Castle, and he fled to Ireland with his supporters and his son, Edward.

Lugard Frederick John Dealtry, 1st Baron Lugard 1858–1945. British colonial administrator. He served in the army 1878–89 and then worked for the British East Africa Company, for whom he took possession of Uganda in 1890. He was high commissioner for North Nigeria 1900–07, governor of Hong Kong 1907–12, and governor general of Nigeria 1914–19.

Lusitania ocean liner sunk by a German submarine 7 May 1915 with the loss of 1,200 lives, including some US citizens; its destruction helped to bring the USA into World War I.

Lutine British bullion ship that sank in the North Sea 1799. Its bell, salvaged 1859, is at the headquarters in London of Lloyd's, the insurance organization. It is sounded once when a ship is missing and twice for good news.

Lynch 'Jack' (John) 1917–   . Irish politician, prime minister 1966–73 and 1977–79. A Gaelic footballer and a barrister, he entered the parliament of the republic as a Fianna Fáil member 1948.

Lytton Edward Robert Bulwer-Lytton, 1st Earl of Lytton 1831–1891. British diplomat, viceroy of India 1876–80, where he pursued a controversial 'Forward' policy. Only son of the novelist Edward George Earle-Bulwer-Lytton, 1st Baron Lytton of Knebworth (1803–1873), he was himself a poet under the pseudonym *Owen Meredith*, writing *King Poppy* 1892 and other poems.

Never under the most despotic of infidel governments did I behold such squalid wretchedness as I have seen since my return in the very heart of a Christian country.

LUDDITE
speech by Lord Byron in the House of Lords against the death penalty for machine wrecking.

Maastricht Treaty European union treaty which took effect 1 Nov 1993, from which date the European Community (EC) became known as the ◊European Union (EU). Issues covered by the treaty included the EU's decision-making process and the establishment of closer links on foreign and military policy. A European Charter of Social Rights was approved by all member states except the UK.

The treaty was signed 10 Dec 1991 by leaders of EC nations in Maastricht, the Netherlands. Ratification by the parliaments of member states was preceded by a national referendum in France, Spain, Ireland, and two in Denmark.

McAdam John Loudon 1756–1836. Scottish road engineer, inventor of the *macadam* road surface, the first to be largely impervious to wear. He was appointed surveyor-general of Bristol roads 1815, and of all the roads in Britain 1827. It originally consisted of broken granite bound together with slag or gravel, raised for drainage. Today, it is bound with tar or asphalt.

Macaulay Thomas Babington, Baron Macaulay 1800–1859. English historian, essayist, poet, and politician, secretary of war 1839–41. His *History of England* in five volumes 1849–61 celebrates the Glorious Revolution of 1688 as the crowning achievement of the Whig party.

He entered Parliament as a liberal Whig 1830. In India 1834–38, he redrafted the Indian penal code. He sat again in Parliament 1839–47 and 1852–56, and in 1857 accepted a peerage.

Macbeth King of Scotland from 1040. The son of Findlaech, hereditary ruler of Moray, he was commander of the forces of Duncan I, King of Scotia, whom he killed in battle 1040. Macbeth was a generous benefactor of the church and made a pilgrimage to Rome 1050. His reign was prosperous until Duncan's son Malcolm III led an invasion and killed him at Lumphanan.

MacDonald Alexander 1866–1881. The first working man to become a member of Parliament. A Lanarkshire miner and trades unionist, he gained a law degree from Glasgow University, and was elected Liberal MP for Stafford 1874.

Macdonald Flora 1722–1790. Scottish heroine who rescued Prince Charles Edward Stuart, the Young Pretender, after his defeat at Culloden 1746. Disguising him as her maid, she escorted him from her home in the Hebrides to France. She was arrested, but released 1747.

MacDonald (James) Ramsay 1866–1937. British politician, first Labour prime minister Jan–Oct 1924 and 1929–31. Failing to deal with worsening economic conditions, he left the party to form a coalition government 1931, which was increasingly dominated by Conservatives, until he was replaced by Stanley Baldwin 1935.

MacDonald joined the ◊Independent Labour Party 1894, and became first secretary of the new Labour Party 1900. He was elected to Parliament 1906, and led the party until 1914, when his opposition to World War I lost him the leadership. He was re-elected leader 1922, and in Jan 1924 he formed a government dependent on the support of the Liberal Party. When this was withdrawn in Oct the same year, he was forced to resign. He returned to office 1929, again as leader of a minority government, which collapsed 1931 as a result of the economic crisis. MacDonald left the Labour Party to form a national government with backing from both Liberal and Conservative parties. He resigned the premiership 1935.

Machine Gun Corps British regiment in World War I, formed 1915 and disbanded after the war. The unit was a consolidation of infantry machine gun companies into a separate, specialist unit, reflecting the growing importance of the machine gun.

Macmillan (Maurice) Harold, 1st Earl of Stockton 1894–1986. British Conservative politician, prime minister 1957–63; foreign secretary 1955 and chancellor of the Exchequer 1955–57. In 1963 he attempted to negotiate British entry into the European Economic Community, but was blocked by French president de Gaulle. Much of his career as prime minister was spent defending the retention of a UK nuclear weapon, and he was responsible for the purchase of US Polaris missiles 1962.

Macmillan was MP for Stockton 1924–29 and 1931–45, and for Bromley 1945–64. As minister of housing 1951–54 he achieved the construction of 300,000 new houses a year. He became prime minister on the resignation of Anthony ◊Eden after the Suez crisis, and led the Conservative Party to victory in the 1959 elections on the slogan 'You've never had it so good' (the phrase was borrowed from a US election campaign). Internationally, his realization of the 'wind of change' in Africa advanced the independence of former colonies. Macmillan's nickname 'Supermac' was coined by the cartoonist Vicky.

MacMurrough Dermot (or *Diarmid MacMurchada*) *c.* 1110–1171. Irish king of Leinster. He succeeded his father as king 1126 but proved a fierce and cruel ruler, and he was driven out of Ireland by the high king, Rory O'Connor, 1166. He appealed to Henry II and was allowed to recruit help in Wales. His allies led by Richard de Clare (Strongbow) helped him regain Leinster 1170. Strongbow married his daughter and succeeded him on the throne of Leinster on his death the following year.

Macmillan
British Conservative prime minister Harold MacMillan's political opportunism and enthusiasm enabled him to win a remarkable election victory in 1959, gaining him the title 'Supermac'.
Hulton Deutsch

Madog ap Maredudd died 1160, king of Powys. He was the last ruler of a united kingdom of Powys, and was defeated by Owain Gwynedd at the Battle of Coleshill 1150. Some of the territory surrendered to Owain was recovered 1157 when Madog supported the expedition led by Henry II against Owain.

Mafeking, Siege of Boer siege during the South African War of British-held town (now Mafikeng) 12 Oct 1899–17 May 1900. The British commander Col Robert Baden-Powell held the Boers off and kept morale high until a relief column arrived and relieved the town. The raising of the siege was a great boost to morale in Britain. The announcement of the town's relief led to wild scenes of celebration in London and across Britain, far out of proportion to the actual strategic value of the operation, and even led to the coining of a new verb – 'to maffick', meaning to celebrate intemperately.

Magersfontein, Battle of during the South African War, Boer victory over the British 11 Dec 1899 at a crossing of the Modder river 65 km/40 mi south of Kimberley, South Africa. British defeats at Colenso and Stormberg in the same week led to the nickname 'Black Week'.

Mafeking, Siege of
A one-pound note issued during the siege of Mafeking. During the seven-month siege, the British commander, Col Baden-Powell, authorized the issue of a temporary currency for the duration of the siege.
Hulton Deutsch

Magna Carta (Latin 'great charter') in English history, the charter granted by King John 1215, traditionally seen as guaranteeing human rights against the excessive use of royal power. As a reply to the king's demands for excessive feudal dues and attacks on the privileges of the church, Archbishop ◊Langton proposed to the barons the drawing-up of a binding document 1213. John was forced to accept this at Runnymede (now in Surrey) 15 June 1215.

Magna Carta begins by reaffirming the rights of the church. Certain clauses guard against infringements of feudal custom: for example, the king was prevented from making excessive demands for money from his barons without their consent. Others are designed to check extortions by officials or maladministration of justice: for example, no freeman to be arrested, imprisoned, or punished except by the judgement of his peers or the law of the land. The privileges of London and the cities were also guaranteed.

As feudalism declined Magna Carta lost its significance, and under the Tudors was almost forgotten. It was revived in the 17th century when it was rediscovered and reinterpreted by the Parliamentary party as a democratic document. Four original copies exist, one each in Salisbury and Lincoln cathedrals and two in the British Library.

Maiden Castle prehistoric hillfort and later earthworks near Dorchester, Dorset, England. The site was inhabited from Neolithic times (about 2000 BC) and was stormed by the Romans AD 43.

THE GREAT CHARTER.
British Museum.

Magna Carta
The Magna Carta of 1215. The name was given to distinguish the charter from smaller-sized reissues, not for political reasons.
Image Select

Main Plot conspiracy 1603 to replace James I on the English throne with Lady Arabella Stuart, the English-born daughter of the Earl of Lennox. The Spanish were involved, but the plot failed and its leader Henry Brooke (d. 1619) was imprisoned, although Arabella remained at liberty until 1610. Sir Walter Raleigh was also implicated but was later reprieved. The plot was investigated at the same time together with a second, but unrelated conspiracy, the so-called Bye Plot, an attempt to kidnap the king.

Maine former British colony in North America; see ◊Thirteen Colonies.

mainprise early form of bail, under which a 'mainpernor' would give an undertaking to guarantee a felon's appearance in court.

Major John 1943– . British Conservative politician, prime minister from Nov 1990. Formerly a banker, he became MP for Huntingdonshire 1979 and deputy to Chancellor Nigel Lawson 1987. Major was appointed foreign secretary 1989 and, after Lawson's resignation, chancellor, within the space of six months. As chancellor he led Britain into the European Exchange Rate Mechanism (ERM) Oct 1990. The following month he became prime minister on winning the Conservative Party leadership election in a contest with Michael Heseltine and Douglas Hurd, after the resignation of Margaret Thatcher.

His initial positive approach to European Community matters was hindered from 1991 by divisions within the Conservative Party. Despite continuing public dissatisfaction with the poll tax, the National Health Service, and the recession, Major was returned to power in the April 1992 general election. He subsequently faced mounting public criticism over a range of issues, including the sudden withdrawal of the

Major
British prime minister John Major, who succeeded Margaret Thatcher 1990 and was re-elected 1992. Features of his premiership include Britain's participation in the Gulf War, a greater committment to the European Union, replacement of the poll tax with the council tax, worsening unemployment and recession, and the highly criticized management policy of the National Health Service and the coal industry.
United Nations

pound from the ERM, a drastic pit-closure programme, and past sales of arms to Iraq. In addition, Major had to deal with 'Euro-sceptics' within his own party who fiercely opposed any moves which they saw as ceding national sovereignty to Brussels. His ability to govern either the party or country effectively was called into question by his handling of a series of domestic crises and scandals besetting his party, but his success in negotiating a Northern Ireland cease-fire 1994 did much to improve his standing. His postion was destablizied by crushing defeats in European and local elections 1994 and his critics within the Conservative Party renewed their attacks on him as a result. In June 1995 Major reasserted his leadership of the party by resigning to force a party leadership election, in which he beat the sole contender, John Redwood, the following month.

major-general after the Civil War, an office created by Oliver Cromwell 1655 to oversee the 12 military districts into which England had been divided. Their powers included organizing the militia, local government, and the collection of some taxes.

Malacca former British colony, part of the ◊Federated Malay States.

Malcolm four kings of Scotland, including:

Malcolm III called ***Canmore*** c. 1031–1093. King of Scotland from 1058, the son of Duncan I (murdered by ◊Macbeth 1040). He fled to England when the throne was usurped by Macbeth, but recovered south Scotland and killed Macbeth in battle 1057. He attempted five invasions of England and was killed at Alnwick, Northumberland, on the last of these expeditions.

Maldon English market town in Essex, at the mouth of the river Chelmer. It was the scene of a battle commemorated in a 325-line fragment of an Anglo-Saxon poem *The Battle of Maldon*, describing the defeat and death of Ealdorman Byrhtnoth by the Vikings 991.

Malplaquet, Battle of during the War of the ◊Spanish Succession, victory of the British, Dutch, and Austrian forces over the French forces 11 Sept 1709 at Malplaquet, in Nord *département*, France. No other battle during this war approached Malplaquet for ferocity and losses sustained by both sides – the joint Imperial force lost over 20,000 troops and the French 12,000, both having begun with about 90,000.

The Imperial army was under the command of the Duke of Marlborough and Prince Eugène of Savoy while the French were under Marshal Claude de Villars.

malt tax tax, first imposed 1697, on the use of malt in brewing. It supplemented the existing beer duty when a hop duty was imposed between 1711 and 1862. The malt tax was abolished 1880 when replaced by a tax on drinking beer.

Malta former British crown colony, in the Mediterranean. The three islands were held by Napoleon 1798–1800, then captured by the British 1800. The Maltese requested the protection of the British crown 1802 on condition that their rights and privileges be respected. Malta became a British crown colony 1814 and an independent state within the British Commonwealth 1964.

Man, Isle of island in the Irish Sea, a dependency of the British crown, but not part of the UK. The island was Norwegian until 1266, when it was ceded to Scotland; it came under UK administration 1765.

It is governed by a crown-appointed lieutenant-governor, a legislative council, and the representative House of Keys, which together make up the Court of Tynwald, passing laws subject to the royal assent. Laws passed at Westminster only affect the island if specifically so provided.

Manning Henry Edward 1808–1892. English priest, one of the leaders of the Oxford Movement. In 1851 he was converted from the Church of England to Roman Catholicism, and in 1865 became archbishop of Westminster. He was created a cardinal 1875 and the same year held an ardent dispute with the Liberal leader William Gladstone on the question of papal infallibility.

manor basic economic unit in ◊feudalism in Europe, established in England under the Norman conquest. It consisted of the lord's house and cultivated land, land rented by free tenants, land held by villagers, common land, woodland, and waste land.

Mansfield judgment or ***Somersett's Case*** legal ruling 1772 delivered by the Lord Chief Justice, the Earl of Mansfield, which effectively abolished slavery in England and Wales.

Mansfield ruled that the runaway slave James Somersett was free, on the grounds that the only type of slavery recognized in English law was ◊serfdom.

manumission in medieval England, the act of freeing a villein or serf from his or her bondage. The process took place in a county court and freedom could either be bought or granted as a reward for services rendered.

Mappa Mundi 13th-century symbolic map of the world. It is circular and shows Asia at the top, with Europe and Africa below and Jerusalem at the centre (reflecting Christian religious rather than geographical belief). It was drawn by David de Bello, a canon at Hereford Cathedral, England, who left the map to the cathedral, where it was used as an altarpiece.

Mar John Erskine, 11th Earl of Mar 1672–1732. Scottish noble and leader of the ◊Jacobite rising of 1715. He raised an army of episcopalian and Catholic highlanders in support of ◊James Edward Stuart, the Old Pretender, after being dismissed from office by George I. He was forced to retreat after an indecisive battle at ◊Sherriffmuir and went into exile in France. He was known as 'Bobbing John' because of his changes of political allegiance.

Marcher Lords semi-independent nobles on the Welsh–English border, granted special privileges in return for protecting the border area. In William the Conqueror's reign, strong lords were placed in Chester, Shrewsbury and Hereford to protect England from Celtic or Saxon incursions. They began to usurp power in their own right, making wars of their own, particularly in the valleys of South Wales, and claiming rights of conquest. After Edward I subjugated Wales, the Marcher Lords no longer played a vital role in the protection of the realm and Edward sought to restrict their independence. They increasingly lost influence during the 12th and 13th centuries but remained important in moments of crisis for the Crown, such as the ◊Marshall Rebellion or the Wars of the Roses. By the end of the 15th century most of the lordships had come into the possession of the Crown and the last independent lordship, Brecon, was taken by the Crown 1521. They were formally united with England 1536.

Marches boundary areas of England with Wales, and England with Scotland. In the Middle Ages these troubled frontier regions were held by lords of the Marches, sometimes called *marchiones* and later earls of March. The 1st Earl of March of the Welsh Marches was Roger de Mortimer (*c.* 1286–1330); of the Scottish Marches, Patrick Dunbar (d. 1285).

Marconi Scandal in 1912 scandal in which UK chancellor Lloyd George and two other government ministers were found by a French newspaper to have dealt in shares of the US Marconi company shortly before it was announced that the Post Office had accepted the British Marconi company's bid to construct an imperial wireless chain.

A parliamentary select committee, biased toward the Liberal government's interests, found that the other four wireless systems were technically inadequate and therefore the decision to adopt Marconi's tender was not the result of ministerial corruption. The scandal did irreparable harm to Lloyd George's reputation.

Margaret, the Maid of Norway 1282–1290. Queen of Scotland from 1285, the daughter of Eric II, King of Norway, and Princess Margaret of Scotland. When only two years old she became queen of Scotland on the death of her grandfather, Alexander III, but died in the Orkneys on the voyage from Norway to her kingdom.

Her great-uncle Edward I of England arranged her marriage to his son Edward, later Edward II. Edward declared himself overlord of Scotland by virtue of the marriage treaty, and 20 years of civil war and foreign intervention in Scotland followed.

Margaret of Anjou 1430–1482. Queen of England from 1445, wife of ◊Henry VI of England. After the outbreak of the Wars of the ◊Roses 1455, she acted as the leader of the Lancastrians, but was defeated and captured at the battle of Tewkesbury 1471 by Edward IV.

Her one object had been to secure the succession of her son, Edward (born 1453), who was killed at Tewkesbury. After five years' imprisonment Margaret was allowed in 1476 to return to her native France, where she died in poverty.

Margaret, St 1045–1093. Queen of Scotland, the granddaughter of King Edmund Ironside of England. She went to Scotland after the Norman Conquest, and soon after married Malcolm III. The marriage of her daughter Matilda to Henry I united the Norman and English royal houses. Through her influence, the Lowlands, until then purely Celtic, became largely anglicized. She introduced the Benedictines to Scotland and was canonized 1251 in recognition of her benefactions to the church.

Markievicz Constance Georgina, Countess Markievicz (born Gore Booth) 1868–1927. Irish nationalist who married the Polish count Markievicz 1900. Her death sentence for taking part in the Easter Rising of 1916 was commuted, and after her release from prison 1917 she was elected to the Westminster Parliament as a Sinn Féin candidate 1918 (technically the first British woman member of Parliament), but did not take her seat.

Marlborough John Churchill, 1st Duke of Marlborough 1650–1722. English soldier, one of the greatest military strategists in British history. He was created a duke 1702 by Queen Anne and was granted the Blenheim mansion in Oxfordshire in recognition of his services, which included defeating the French army outside Vienna in the Battle of ◊Blenheim 1704, during the War of the ◊Spanish Succession.

In 1688 he deserted his patron, James II, for William of Orange, but in 1692 fell into disfavour for Jacobite intrigue. He had married Sarah Jennings (1660–1744), confidante of the future Queen Anne, who created him a duke on her accession. As commander in chief of the Allied forces, he achieved further victories in Belgium at the battles of ◊Ramillies 1706 and ◊Oudenaarde 1708, and in France at ◊Malplaquet 1709. However, the return of the Tories to power and his wife's quarrel with the queen led to his dismissal 1711 and his flight to Holland to avoid charges of corruption. He returned 1714 after the accession of George I and was restored to his former positions.

Marne, Battles of the in World War I, two unsuccessful German offensives in northern France. In the ***First Battle*** 6–9 Sept 1914 German advance was halted by French and British troops under the overall command of the French general Joseph Joffre; in the ***Second Battle*** 15 July–4 Aug 1918, the German advance was defeated by British, French, and US troops under the French general Henri Pétain, and German morale crumbled.

Marprelate controversy pamphleteering attack on the clergy of the Church of England 1588 and 1589 made by a Puritan writer or writers, who took the pseudonym of ***Martin Marprelate***. The pamphlets were printed by John Penry, a Welsh Puritan. His press was seized, and he was charged with inciting rebellion and hanged 1593.

Married Women's Property Acts two acts passed 1870 and 1882 granting women basic rights in the division of property between husband and wife. Until 1870 common law decreed that a wife's property, including money and shares, passed to her husband. The first act allowed women to retain their earnings and the second act allowed women to retain the property they owned at the time of their marriage.

Marshall rebellion 1233–34 rebellion against Henry III led by Richard Marshall, Earl of Pembroke, in alliance with some of the Marcher lords and the Welsh kingdom of ◊Gwynedd. The rebellion was sparked by the king's employment of French advisers, the ***poitevins***. It was widely supported in Wales but in Ireland the royalists predominated, and Marshall was captured and killed by Irish royalists. English bishops procured a settlement under which Henry dismissed the poitevins and replaced them with Marshall's brother, Gilbert.

Marshalsea court presided over by the marshall and steward of the royal household to deal with offences committed within the bounds of the royal court, wherever it might be. It was renamed the Palace Court 1630 and abolished 1849. Those convicted at the court were held in Marshalsea prison in Southwark, which largely held debtors from the 17th century until it was abolished 1842.

Marston Moor, Battle of 2 July 1644 battle fought in the Civil War on Marston Moor, 11 km/7 mi west of York. The Royalists were conclusively defeated by the Parliamentarians and Scots.

The Royalist forces were commanded by Prince Rupert and the Duke of Newcastle; their opponents by Oliver Cromwell and Lord Leven. Lord Fairfax, on the right of the Parliamentarians, was routed, but Cromwell's cavalry charges were decisive. The battle virtually ended Charles I's support in the north.

Martello tower circular tower for coastal defence. Formerly much used in Europe, many were built along the English coast, especially in Sussex and Kent, in 1804, as a defence against the threatened French invasion. The name is derived from a tower on Cape

Mortella, Corsica, which was captured by the British with great difficulty 1794, and was taken as a model. They are round towers of solid masonry, sometimes moated, with a flat roof for mounted guns.

Mary two queens of England:

Mary I (called **Bloody Mary**) 1516–1558. Queen of England from 1553. She was the eldest daughter of Henry VIII by Catherine of Aragon. When Edward VI died, Mary secured the crown without difficulty in spite of the conspiracy to substitute Lady Jane ◊Grey. In 1554 Mary married Philip II of Spain, and as a devout Roman Catholic obtained the restoration of papal supremacy and sanctioned the persecution of Protestants. Some 300 Protestants were killed during her reign, earning her the nickname 'Bloody Mary'. There were three unsuccessful rebellions against her religious policies, the first led by Sir Thomas Wyatt (◊Wyatt's rebellion) 1554. She was succeeded by her Protestant half-sister Elizabeth I who introduced a religious settlement which finally introduced some stability.

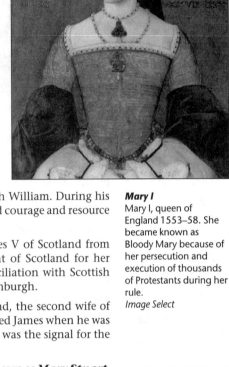

Mary I
Mary I, queen of England 1553–58. She became known as Bloody Mary because of her persecution and execution of thousands of Protestants during her rule.
Image Select

Mary II 1662–1694. Queen of England, Scotland, and Ireland from 1688. She was the Protestant elder daughter of the Catholic ◊James II and Anne Hyde, and in 1677 was married to her cousin ◊William of Orange. After the 1688 revolution she accepted the crown jointly with William. During his absences from England she took charge of the government, and showed courage and resource when invasion seemed possible 1690 and 1692.

Mary of Guise, or Mary of Lorraine 1515–1560. French wife of James V of Scotland from 1538. In 1554 she succeeded the pro-English Earl of Arran as regent of Scotland for her daughter ◊Mary Queen of Scots. A Catholic, she moved from reconciliation with Scottish Protestants to repression, and died during a Protestant rebellion in Edinburgh.

Mary of Modena 1658–1718. Queen consort of England and Scotland, the second wife of James II. She was the daughter of the Duke of Modena, Italy, and married James when he was Duke of York 1673. The birth of their son James Francis Edward Stuart was the signal for the revolution of 1688 that overthrew James II. Mary fled to France.

Mary Queen of Scots 1542–1587. Queen of Scotland 1542–67. Also known as **Mary Stuart**, she was the daughter of James V and Mary of Guise. Mary's connection with the English royal line from Henry VII made her a threat to Elizabeth I's hold on the English throne, especially as she represented a champion of the Catholic cause. Mary was sent to France, where she married the dauphin, later Francis II. After his death she returned to Scotland 1561, which, during her absence, had become Protestant. She married her cousin, the Earl of ◊Darnley, 1565, but they soon quarrelled, and Darnley took part in the murder of Mary's secretary, ◊Rizzio. Darnley was assassinated 1567 in a conspiracy led by the Earl of ◊Bothwell, and she married Bothwell shortly after. A rebellion followed; defeated at Carberry Hill, Mary abdicated and was imprisoned. She escaped 1568, raised an army, and after its defeat at Langside fled to England. She was the constant focus of plots by dissatisfied English Catholics, and Elizabeth I kept her incarcerated. Anthony Babington's plot against Elizabeth led to her trial and execution at Fotheringay Castle 1587. Her son by the Earl of Darnley became James VI of Scotland and James I of England.

No more tears now; I will think upon revenge.

Mary Queen of Scots
on hearing of David Rizzio's murder by Lord Darnley (attributed)

Mary Rose greatest warship of Henry VIII of England, which sank off Southsea, Hampshire, 19 July 1545. The wreck was located 1971, and raised for preservation in dry dock in Portsmouth harbour 1982.

Mary Queen of Scots
Mary Queen of Scots' life has intrigued historians who continue to debate her actions and motives, as well as the quality of the evidence of her connivance with conspirators that led to her execution. Her son James became king of Scotland after she was forced to abdicate.
Michael Nicholson

Maryland former British colony in North America; see ◊Thirteen Colonies.

Massachusetts Bay former British colony in North America; see ◊Thirteen Colonies.

Matilda *the Empress Maud* 1102–1167. Claimant to the throne of England. Daughter of Henry I, Matilda was recognized during the reign of Henry I as his heir but on his death, 1135, the barons elected her cousin Stephen to be king. Matilda invaded England 1139, and was crowned by her supporters 1141. Civil war ensued until Stephen was finally recognized as king 1153, with Henry II (Matilda's son) as his successor.

She married first the Holy Roman emperor Henry V and, after his death, Geoffrey Plantagenet, Count of Anjou (1113–1151).

Maundy Thursday in the Christian church, the Thursday before Easter. The ceremony of washing the feet of pilgrims on that day was instituted in commemoration of Jesus' washing of the apostles' feet and observed from the 4th century to 1754. In Britain it was performed by the English sovereigns until the time of William III, and ***Maundy money*** is still presented by the sovereign to poor people each year.

Maximus Magnus d. 388. Spanish-born Roman emperor. He commanded the Roman troops in Britain against the Picts and Scots and his British troops proclaimed him emperor 383. He then immediately crossed to Gaul to attack Gratian. The latter was defeated, and Gaul, Spain and Britain acknowledged Maximus as emperor. He invaded Italy 387 where he was defeated by Theodosius and subsequently captured and executed 388.

Maynooth Grant parliamentary subsidy 1795 to finance a Catholic seminary in Maynooth, Co. Kildare, some 12 miles from Dublin. The grant was introduced by Pitt the younger both to mollify Catholics and avoid priests having to go to seminaries in France with whom Britain was at war. The grant aroused much opposition, and was not increased from 1813 until 1845, when Sir Robert Peel was forced to rely on Whig support to push through an increase. Although he was successful, the tactic exacerbated the splits in the Tory party and led to Gladstone's resignation from the board of trade.

Meal Tub Plot non-existent conspiracy to prevent the accession of the Duke of York, the future James II, invented by Thomas Dangerfield 1679 during the attempts to pass the ◊Exclusion Bills. Dangerfield was initially believed in the atmosphere of panic arising from the Popish Plot, but he was soon discredited and then claimed the plot was a false trail laid by Catholics to conceal a real conspiracy. The name came from the meal tub under which Dangerfield claimed to have found evidence of the plot.

Meath, Kingdom of or ***Midhe*** one of the five ancient kingdoms of Ireland. It replaced Ulster as the dominant kingdom in the 6th century and controlled most of Ireland from its capital at Tara, northwest of Dublin. It was subsequently absorbed as a county of the province of Leinster.

Medway, Battle of the Roman victory AD 43 over the Britons, led by Caractacus and Togodumnus on the River Medway in Kent. The Romans, led by Aulus Plautius, crossed the River Medway and surprised the Britons, who scattered and fled after two days of heavy fighting. Togodumnus was killed but Caractacus survived to continue the struggle against the invaders.

megalith prehistoric stone monument of the late Neolithic or early Bronze Age. Most common in Europe, megaliths include single, large uprights (***menhirs***, for example, the Five Kings, Northumberland, England); ***rows*** (for example, Carnac, Brittany, France); ***circles***, generally with a central 'altar stone'; and the remains of burial chambers with the covering earth removed, looking like a hut (***dolmens***, for example Kits Coty, Kent, England).

Melbourne William Lamb, 2nd Viscount 1779–1848. British Whig politician. Home secretary 1830–34, he was briefly prime minister in 1834 and again 1835–41. He was accused of seducing Caroline Norton 1836 and lost the favour of William IV.

Melbourne was married 1805–25 to Lady Caroline Ponsonby (novelist Lady Caroline Lamb, 1785–1828). He was an adviser to the young Queen Victoria.

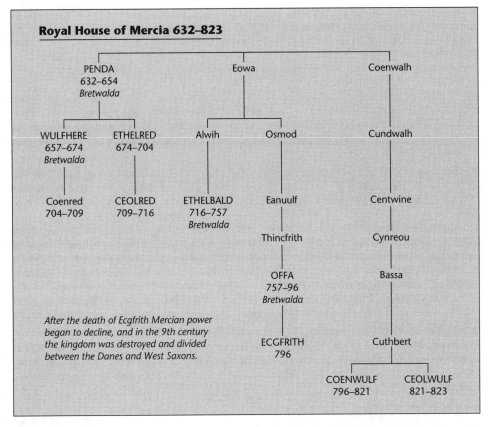

Royal House of Mercia 632–823

PENDA
632–654
Bretwalda

Eowa

Coenwalh

WULFHERE
657–674
Bretwalda

ETHELRED
674–704

Alwih

Osmod

Cundwalh

Coenred
704–709

CEOLRED
709–716

ETHELBALD
716–757
Bretwalda

Eanuulf

Centwine

Thincfrith

Cynreou

OFFA
757–96
Bretwalda

Bassa

After the death of Ecgfrith Mercian power began to decline, and in the 9th century the kingdom was destroyed and divided between the Danes and West Saxons.

ECGFRITH
796

Cuthbert

COENWULF
796–821

CEOLWULF
821–823

Melville Henry Dundas, Viscount Melville 1742–1811. British Tory politician, born in Edinburgh. He entered Parliament 1774, and as home secretary 1791–94 persecuted the parliamentary reformers. His impeachment for malversation (misconduct) 1806 was the last in English history.

Merchants Adventurers English trading company founded 1407, which controlled the export of cloth to continental Europe. It comprised guilds and traders in many north European ports. In direct opposition to the Hanseatic League, it came to control 75% of English overseas trade by 1550. In 1689 it lost its charter for furthering the traders' own interests at the expense of the English economy. The company was finally dissolved 1806.

merchet in medieval England, payment made by a villein to his lord as compensation if his daughter married outside the manor, if his son was educated, or if he sold some of his livestock. Payment of merchet was an important proof of serfdom.

Mercia, kingdom of Anglo-Saxon kingdom that emerged in the 6th century. By the late 8th century it dominated all England south of the Humber, but from about 825 came under the power of ◊Wessex. Mercia eventually came to denote an area bounded by the Welsh border, the river Humber, East Anglia, and the river Thames.

Merciless Parliament parliament summoned by the ◊Lords Appellant 1388, Parliament called 'merciless' after it imposed the death penalty for treason on five supporters of Richard II. Three escaped abroad, but Sir Robert Tresilian, Chief Justice of the King's Bench, and Sir Nicholas Brembre, Lord Mayor of London, were executed.

Merthyr rising revolt of miners and ironworkers 1831 in Merthyr Tydfil, Wales. They took possession of the town for three days until the military were brought in to suppress the rising and in the ensuing confrontation about 16 were killed. One of the leaders of the revolt, Richard Lewis (known as Dic Penderyn), was condemned to death. The rising was caused by poverty and falling wages, but the intial spark was the uproar caused by the parliamentary reform bill.

Mesopotamian Campaign in World War I, British campaign to secure the oil installations along the Tigris and the Euphrates and safeguard the route to India. A small force from the Indian Army was sent to the area Nov 1914 and quickly took Basra in modern-day Iraq but then made slow progress. In the aftermath of the disastrous ◊Dardanelles Campaign 1915, a counter-attack was authorized on Baghdad but this failed and the army retreated to ◊Kūt-al-Imāra, where 10,000 prisoners were taken. The War Office in London took charge of the campaign directly, and a further force of 120,000 troops was sent. The British made steady progress, taking Baghdad March 1917 and then moved swiftly through the rest of the region until the Turks in Mesopotamia surrendered Oct 1918. The cost to Britain and India was about 16,000 dead, and almost 100,000 casualties and it was criticized as having little military basis or control.

Methodism evangelical Protestant Christian movement that was founded by John ◊Wesley 1739 within the Church of England, but became a separate body 1795. The Methodist Episcopal Church was founded in the USA 1784. There are over 50 million Methodists worldwide.

The itinerant, open-air preaching of John and Charles Wesley and George Whitefield drew immense crowds and led to a revival of faith among members of the English working and agricultural classes who were alienated from the formalism and conservatism of the Church of England. Methodist doctrines are contained in Wesley's sermons and *Notes on the New Testament*. A series of doctrinal divisions in the early 19th century were reconciled by a conference in London 1932 that brought Wesleyan methodists, primitive methodists, and United methodists into the Methodist Church. The church government is presbyterian in Britain and episcopal in the USA.

Methven, Battle of 19 June 1306 battle at Methven, west of Perth, in which the English under Aylmer de Valence decisively defeated a Scots force under Robert I the Bruce. Bruce attempted to rally his men but was obliged to flee. Many of his followers were imprisoned or executed.

metropolitan county in England, a group of six counties established under the Local Government Act 1972 in the largest urban areas outside London: Tyne and Wear, South Yorkshire, Merseyside, West Midlands, Greater Manchester, and West Yorkshire. Their elected assemblies (county councils) were abolished 1986 when most of their responsibilities reverted to the metropolitan district councils.

MI5 abbreviation for ***Military Intelligence, section five***, the counter-intelligence agency of the British ◊intelligence services.

MI6 abbreviation for ***Military Intelligence, section six***, the secret intelligence agency of the British ◊intelligence services which operates largely under Foreign Office control.

Middle Anglia Anglo-Saxon province between Mercia and East Anglia, corresponding to parts of present Leicestershire, Cambridgeshire, Lincolnshire, and Northamptonshire. By the 6th century, it had come under Mercian control. Christianity was introduced in the mid-7th century by Peada, the son of Penda, king of Mercia, who became earldorman 653.

Midhe ancient name for ◊Meath; one of the five ancient kingdoms of Ireland.

Mildenhall treasure hoard of 4th century Romano-British silverware discovered at Mildenhall, Suffolk, 1942. The hoard consisted of 34 pieces of silver kitchenware, some with Christian motifs. It was probably buried by a wealthy family as protection against the Saxon raids.

Militant Tendency left-wing faction originally within the Labour Party, aligned with the publication *Militant*. It became active in the 1970s, with radical socialist policies based on Trotskyism, and gained some success in local government, for example in the inner-city areas of Liverpool. In the mid-1980s the Labour Party considered it to be a separate organization within the party and banned it.

millenary petition presented to James I by moderate Puritans 1603, a petition requesting reform of the Church of England. The petition, presented as James travelled to London after his accession to the throne, disclaimed any desire to abolish episcopacy or abandon a national church, but sought the removal of certain ceremonies and ecclesiastical vestments.

At the Hampton Court Conference 1604, James rejected most of the petition but arranged for a new translation of the Bible and made some small alterations to the liturgy.

Milner Alfred, Viscount Milner 1854–1925. British colonial administrator. As governor of Cape Colony 1897–1901, he negotiated with ◊Kruger but did little to prevent the second ◊South African War; and as governor of the Transvaal and Orange River colonies 1902–05 after their annexation, he reorganized their administration. In 1916 he became a member of Lloyd George's war cabinet.

Minden, Battle of during the Seven Years' War, French defeat by a combined British-Hanoverian army 1 Aug 1759 at Minden, 70 km/44 mi west of Hanover, Germany. Due to mismanagement of the Allied cavalry, the French were able to withdraw in good order, but at a loss of over 7,000 casualties and 43 guns. Allied losses were some 2,700; over half of these were in the six English battalions, the descendants of which still wear a rose in their caps on the anniversary of the battle.

Mines Act legislation regulating working conditions and safety standards for coalminers from 1842. The first act prohibited the employment of females and boys below the age of 10. Inspection of mines was introduced 1850 and a Royal School of Mines was established the following year to train inspectors. In 1860 the lower limit for the ages of boys working in the mines was raised to 12. Various safety measures were introduced 1872, including a requirement that managers of mines be correctly trained and certified. The working day was limited to eight hours 1908, reduced further to seven and a half hours 1930.

After the nationalization of the coal industry 1946, the National Coal Board was responsible for ensuring adequate safety standards and proper working conditions for miners. In the coal strikes of the 1970s and 1980s, the withdrawal of a certification of safety was often as crucial as the withdrawal of labour.

minster a church formerly attached to a monastery: for example, York Minster. Originally the term meant a monastery, and in this sense it is often preserved in place names, such as Westminster.

miracle play popular medieval dramatized biblical story.

missionary societies religious societies established to organize and finance Christian evangelization in the former British Empire. The Anglican Society for Promoting Christian Knowledge (SPCK) was founded 1698 followed by the Society for the Propagation of the Gospel (SPG) 1701.

As the Empire grew, so did the number of societies. The London Missionary Society (LMS) was founded 1795, followed by the Church Missionary Society (CMS) 1799, and the British and Foreign Bible Society (BFBS) 1804. The Anglo-Catholic Universities Mission to Central Africa (UMCA) was founded 1859 in response to the challenge sent out by David Livingstone. In 1965 it joined with the SPG to become the United Society for the Propagation of the Gospel (USPG). Outside the Church of England, the Methodist Missionary Society dates from 1786 and the Baptist Missionary Society from 1792.

Model Parliament English Parliament set up 1295 by Edward I; it was the first to include representatives from outside the clergy and aristocracy, and was established because Edward needed the support of the whole country against his opponents: Wales, France, and Scotland. His sole aim was to raise money for military purposes, and the Parliament did not pass any legislation.

The Parliament comprised archbishops, bishops, abbots, earls, and barons (all summoned by special writ, and later forming the basis of the House of Lords); also present were the lower clergy (heads of chapters, archdeacons, two clerics from each diocese, and one from each cathedral) and representatives of the shires, cities, and boroughs (two knights from every shire, two representatives from each city, and two burghers from each borough).

Monck or **Monk** George, 1st Duke of Albemarle 1608–1669. English soldier. During the Civil War he fought for King Charles I, but after being captured changed sides and took command of the Parliamentary forces in Ireland. Under Oliver ◊Cromwell he became commander in chief in Scotland. In 1660 he led his army into England, reinstated the MPs expelled from the ◊Long Parliament, and brought about the restoration of Charles II.

Monmouth James Scott, Duke of Monmouth 1649–1685. Claimant to the English crown, the illegitimate son of Charles II and Lucy Walter. When ◊James II converted to Catholicism, the Whig opposition attempted unsuccessfully to secure Monmouth the succession to the crown by the Exclusion Bill, and having become implicated in a Whig conspiracy, the ◊Rye House Plot 1683, he fled to Holland. After James II's accession 1685, Monmouth landed in England at Lyme Regis, Dorset, claimed the crown, and raised a rebellion, which was crushed at ◊Sedgemoor in Somerset. He was executed with 320 of his accomplices.

monopoly the domination of a market for a particular product or service by a single company, which can therefore restrict competition and keep prices high. In the middle ages, the Crown granted trading or manufacturing privileges to specific companies or individuals in order to raise revenue or allow new industries to grow, such as the grant of privileges to develop new techniques in glass-making. By the 16th century, the system was open to widespread abuse and was being used as a form of patronage to favour individuals who used the monopoly solely for financial gain, as when playing cards became the subject of a monopoly. Elizabeth I was forced to annul many of her grants after campaigns in Parliament 1597, 1598, and 1601 but monopolies were revived under James I and Charles I. The system was extended to include the administrative powers of the Crown, such as licensing alehouses. Monopolies were restricted to fostering economic innovation 1624 and the Long Parliament abolished industrial monopolies, although they continued in the commercial field until after the Glorious Revolution of 1688. The Monopolies Commission, now the Monopolies and Mergers Commission, was established 1948 to regulate monopolies and investigate whether they operate against the public interest.

Mons, Battle of in World War I, German victory over the ◊British Expeditionary Force Aug 1914. A planned attack on the German armies invading Belgium fell apart when French troops did not arrive, leaving the British to extricate themselves as best they could.

Mons Badonicus (or Badon Hill) battle *c.* 493–516, probably in southwest England, in which indigenous Britons defeated the Anglo-Saxons and other settlers from the continent. Little else is definitely known, but this battle appears to have been the culmination of some 12 battles fought to drive the Saxons back and it apparently halted further incursions into the west of England for the next two generations. According to Gildas, a 6th-century Welsh monk, the encounter took the form of a siege, with the Britons probably led by a Roman, Ambrosius Aurelianus, against an enemy sent by God to punish them for their moral laxity. Some sources identify the victorious leader as 'Arturus, Dux Bellorum', the legendary King Arthur. The fortifications at ◊Wansdyke may also have formed part of this campaign.

Mons Graupius, Battle of battle fought against the Caledonians (Scots) AD 84 by the Roman general ◊Agricola at an unidentified site. Agricola's victory pushed the Roman frontier northward as far as the Firth of Forth.

Montagu Edward, 2nd Earl of Manchester 1602–1671. Civil War commander. He led the Parliamentary forces at Marston Moor 1644 but was accused by Cromwell of incompetence at Newbury 1644 and resigned 1645. He opposed the trial of Charles I 1648 and subsequently retired from public life until the Restoration 1660.

Montfort Simon de Montfort, Earl of Leicester *c.* 1208–1265. English politician and soldier. Born in Normandy, the son of ***Simon de Montfort*** (about 1160–1218) who led a crusade against the Albigenses, he arrived in England in 1230, married Henry III's sister, Eleanor, and was granted the earldom of Leicester. From 1258 he led the baronial opposition to Henry III's misrule during the second ◊Barons' War and in 1264 defeated and captured the king at Lewes, Sussex. In 1265, as head of government, he summoned the first Parliament in which the towns were represented; he was killed at the Battle of Evesham during the last of the Barons' Wars.

Montgomery, Treaty of 25 Sept 1267 treaty in which Henry III recognized Llewellyn ap Gruffydd, king of Gwynedd as 'Prince of Wales'. The treaty acknowledged his unique position in uniting the principality and marked the high point of his power until Edward finally overran Wales 1282.

Montgomery Bernard Law, 1st Viscount Montgomery of Alamein 1887–1976. British field marshal. In World War II he commanded the 8th Army in N Africa in the Second Battle of El

Montgomery
British general Bernard
Montgomery in Nov
1942, after he had taken
command of the British
8th Army in N Africa. A
month later the 8th
Army defeated Rommel's
army at El Alamein.
Library of Congress

◊Alamein 1942. As commander of British troops in N Europe from 1944, he received the German surrender at his 21st Army Group headquarters on Lüneberg Heath 3 May 1945. He was in command of the British occupation force in Germany until Feb 1946, when he was appointed Chief of the Imperial General Staff.

Montrose James Graham, 1st Marquess of Montrose 1612–1650. Scottish soldier, son of the 4th Earl of Montrose. He supported the ◊Covenanters against Charles I, but after 1640 changed sides. In 1644 Charles created him a marquess and lieutenant-general in Scotland, whereupon he rallied the Highlanders and won a succession of victories against the Covenanters.

Defeated in 1645 at Philiphaugh, Montrose escaped to Norway. Returning in 1650 to raise a revolt, he survived shipwreck only to have his weakened forces defeated, and (having been betrayed to the Covenanters) was hanged in Edinburgh.

Moore (John) Jeremy 1928–   . British major general of the Commando Forces, Royal Marines, 1979–82. He commanded the land forces in the UK's conflict with Argentina over the Falklands 1982. He was made Knight Commander of the Bath 1982.

Moore John 1761–1809. Scottish-born British general. He entered the army in 1776, serving in the American and French Revolutionary Wars and against the Irish rebellion of 1798. In 1808 he commanded the British army sent to Portugal in the ◊Peninsular War. After advancing into Spain he had to retreat to Corunna in the northwest, and was killed in the battle fought to cover the embarkation.

moot legal and administrative assembly found in nearly every community in medieval England.

Moray another spelling of ◊Murray, regent of Scotland 1567–70.

Moray risings series of revolts in Moray, northeast Scotland, during the 12th century. Moray was a former Pictish kingdom ruled by an independent *mormaer* (great steward). The *mormaer* Angus led a rebellion against David I 1130 in an attempt to halt the expansion of Scottish rule. He was defeated and killed, but rebellions against royal authority continued throughout the century.

More Hannah 1745–1833. Religious writer and educationalist. A friend of Dr Johnson, she wrote moralistic dramas as an alternative to the more lurid writing then popular with young people. She founded schools for the poor, although she believed they should have a very pre-scribed education befitting their station.

More (St) Thomas 1478–1535. English politician and author. From 1509 he was favoured by ◊Henry VIII and employed on foreign embassies. He was a member of the privy council from 1518 and Lord Chancellor from 1529 but resigned 1532 because he could not agree with the

The commands of my sovereign were to defend his safety in his deep distress against wicked rebels... It was my duty to obey.

MARQUESS OF
MONTROSE
*last words before being
hanged, 1650
(attributed)*

king on his ecclesiastical policy and marriage with Anne Boleyn. In 1534 he refused to take the oath of supremacy to Henry VIII as head of the church, and after a year's imprisonment in the Tower of London he was executed. The title of his political book *Utopia* 1516 has come to mean any supposedly perfect society.

Morgan Frederick 1894–1967. British general in World War II. He was appointed Chief of Staff to plan the future invasion of Europe Jan 1943. His plan was accepted in July and with some modifications became the plan for Operation ◊Overlord. He and his staff spent the following year working out the plan in minute detail.

Morgan Henry *c.* 1635–1688. Welsh buccaneer in the Caribbean. He made war against Spain, capturing and sacking Panama 1671. After the Peace of Madrid between England and Spain 1670, he was tried for piracy but acquitted. In 1674 he was knighted and appointed lieutenant governor of Jamaica.

Morley John, 1st Viscount Morley of Blackburn 1838–1923. British Liberal politician and writer. He entered Parliament in 1883, and was secretary for Ireland in 1886 and 1892–95.

As secretary for India 1905–10, he was co-author (with Viceroy Gilbert Minto) of the Morley-Minto reforms 1909 which prepared the way for more representative government. He was Lord President of the Council 1910–14, but resigned in protest against the declaration of war. He published lives of the philosophers Voltaire and Rousseau and the politicians Burke and Gladstone. He received a peerage 1908.

Morrison Herbert Stanley, Baron Morrison of Lambeth 1888–1965. British Labour politician. He was a founder member and later secretary of the London Labour Party 1915–45, and a member of the London County Council 1922–45. He entered Parliament in 1923, and organized the Labour Party's general election victory in 1945. He was twice defeated in the contest for leadership of the party, once to Clement Attlee in 1932, and then to Hugh Gaitskell 1955. A skilful organizer, he lacked the ability to unite the party.

He was minister of transport 1929–31, home secretary 1940–45, Lord President of the Council and leader of the House of Commons 1945–51, and foreign secretary March–Oct 1951.

Mortimer Roger de, 8th Baron of Wigmore and 1st Earl of March *c.* 1287–1330. English politician and adventurer. He opposed Edward II and with Edward's queen, Isabella, led a rebellion against him 1326, bringing about his abdication. From 1327 Mortimer ruled England as the queen's lover, until Edward III had him executed.

Mortimer's Cross, Battle of in Wars of the Roses, victory of Edward, eldest son of Richard, Duke of York, over a Lancastrian army 2 Feb 1461 at Mortimer's Cross. Herefordshire. Richard had been killed in the Battle of Wakefield Dec 1460 and the Yorkist position was at a low ebb. Edward attacked and defeated a Lancastrian army under the Earls of Pembrokeshire and Wiltshire which was heading for London to meet up with the army of Margaret of Anjou. Owen Tudor was captured and executed and Edward marched on London, where he was crowned little over a month later.

mortmain lands held by a corporate body, such as the church, in perpetual or inalienable tenure. In the Middle Ages, alienation in mortmain, usually to a church in return for a chantry foundation, deprived the feudal lord of his future incidents (payments due to him when the land changed ownership) and rights of wardship, and so attempts were often made to regulate the practice.

Morton James Douglas, 4th Earl of 1516–81. Scottosh noble and regent for James VI 1572–78. He headed the Protestant anti-French party under ◊Mary Queen of Scots and was her Lord Chancellor 1563–66 but was instrumental in the murder of her favourite, Rizzio, 1566. He may also have been involved in the murder of her husband, Lord Darnley, the following year. He joined the rebelion against Mary 1567–68 and defeated royalist forces at the battles of Carberry Hill and Langside. From 1572–78 he was a successful regent for the young James VI, but his moderate episcopalianism alienated many and he was subsequently executed by the king for his alleged part in the murder of Darnley, the king's father.

Mosley Oswald (Ernald) 1896–1980. British politician, founder of the British Union of Fascists (BUF) 1932, also known as the 'blackshirts' from their distinctive uniforms. He was a member of Parliament 1918–31, first as a Conservative, then an Independent, and finally as a member of the Labour Party. He then led the BUF until his internment 1940–43 during World War II. In 1946 Mosley was denounced when it became known that Italy had funded his pre-war efforts to establish fascism in Britain, but in 1948 he resumed fascist propaganda with his Union Movement, the revived BUF.

Mosquito Coast former British protectorate, on the east coast of Nicaragua. The English established a protectorate over the Miskito Indians 1655 (hence the name). The British claim was disputed by Spain, Nicaragua, and the United States until the Clayton Bulwer treaty of 1850 between the United States and Great Britain, when the territory passed to Nicaragua.

motte fortified mound within a castle or other fortification. At the Norman conquest, it was necessary to garrison the country at speed, and mottes, often surrounded only by ditches or wooden walls, were the obvious solution.

Mountbatten Louis, 1st Earl Mountbatten of Burma 1900–1979. British admiral and administrator. In World War II he became chief of combined operations 1942 and commander in chief in SE Asia 1943. As last viceroy of India 1947 and first governor general of India until 1948, he oversaw that country's transition to independence. He was killed by an Irish Republican Army bomb aboard his yacht in the Republic of Ireland.

Mowbray Thomas, 12th Baron Mowbray and 1st Duke of Norfolk d. 1399. English noble-man. He took part in the defeat of Robert de Vere, 9th Earl of Oxford, at Radcot Bridge 1388. He was subsequently reconciled to Richard II and was appointed Governor of Calais 1391, where he probably connived in the murder 1397 of Thomas of Woodstock, Duke of Gloucester. He was accused of treason by the Duke of Hereford (later Henry IV) and was ban-ished from England for life 1398.

Munich Agreement pact signed 29 Sept 1938 by the leaders of the UK (Neville ◊Chamberlain), France (Edouard Daladier), Germany (Hitler), and Italy (Mussolini), under which Czechoslovakia was compelled to surrender its Sudeten-German districts (the *Sudetenland*) to Germany. Chamberlain claimed it would guarantee 'peace in our time', but it did not prevent Hitler from seizing the rest of Czechoslovakia in March 1939.

Municipal Corporations Act English act of Parliament 1835 that laid the foundations of modern local government. The act made local government responsible to a wider electorate of ratepayers through elected councils. Boroughs incorporated in this way were empowered to take on responsibility for policing, public health, and education, and were also subject to regulation and auditing which served to reduce corruption. Similar acts were passed for Scotland (1833) and Ireland (1840).

municipia official Roman status, below the rank of ◊*colonia*, granted to a provincial town as the first stage of full romanization. Its members were not full Roman citizens, unless they had been a magistrate or other high official. Verulamium (St. Albans) is the only municipium known of in Britain, though there may have been others.

Munster, Kingdom of ancient Irish kingdom, in the southwest of the present Republic. The kingship alternated between the O'Briens and the MacCarthys. In the 11th century its king, Brian Boru of the O'Briens, became the first effective high king of Ireland. The Normans con-quered most of Munster in the 13th century, but never subdued the extreme southwest, which remained independent. Today the province comprises the counties of Cork, Waterford, Kerry, Limerick, Tipperary and Clare.

murage medieval tax for the upkeep of a town's defensive walls and gates. The name comes from the French *mur*, 'wall'.

Murdock William 1754–1839. Scottish inventor and technician. Employed by James ◊Watt and Matthew Boulton to build steam engines, he was the first to develop gas lighting on a commercial scale, holding the gas in gasometers, from the 1790s.

Murray family name of dukes of Atholl; seated at Blair Castle, Perthshire, Scotland.

Murray Archibald 1860–1945. British general. At the start of World War I, he went to France as Chief of Staff but returned to Britain Oct 1915 to become Chief of the Imperial General Staff. He was appointed to command the Mediterranean Expeditionary Force and went to

Egypt where he organized the country's defences. He led the British advance into Palestine but failed to capture Gaza.

Murray Lord George 1694–1760. Jacobite commander. He was one of the leading generals of Charles Edward Stuart and contributed much to the important Jacobite victories at Prestonpans 1745 and Falkirk 1746. He commanded the right wing at Culloden 1746, then escaped abroad and died in exile.

Murray James Stuart, Earl of Murray, or Moray 1531–1570. Regent of Scotland from 1567, an illegitimate son of James V. He was one of the leaders of the Scottish Reformation, and after the deposition of his half-sister ◊Mary Queen of Scots, he became regent. He was assassinated by one of her supporters.

Muscat and Oman independent sultanate, on the southeast Arabian Peninsula. When the territory's importance decreased in the 19th century, it became politically and economically dependent on the British government of India. It entered into close ties with Britain by a treaty of 1939. This was renewed 1951 and extended by a 'memorandum of understanding' 1982. A rebellion against the sultan 1954–57 was suppressed with the aid of British forces. Muscat and Oman became simply Oman 1970.

Muscovy Company company founded 1555 to foster trade with Russia via the Arctic seas, after attempts to find a northerly route to China 1553 opened the way for trade with Russia. Furs, timber, and naval supplies were traded for cloth and weapons. The first voyage after Queen Mary granted a charter was financed by the sale of 250 shares at £25 each. The Company lost its monopoly 1698, but extended its trade overland through Muscovy to Persia. It survived until the Russian Revolution 1917.

Mutiny Act in Britain, an act of Parliament, passed 1689 and re-enacted annually since then (since 1882 as part of the Army Acts), for the establishment and payment of a standing army. The act is intended to prevent an army from existing in peacetime without Parliament's consent.

Myton, Battle of victory of a Scottish army under Sir James Douglas over an army hastily raised by the archbishop of York, William Melton, 20 Sept 1319 at Myton-in-Swaledale, Yorkshire. The victory forced Edward II to lift his siege of Berwick, which had fallen to Robert the Bruce the year before. The archbishop's force was virtually wiped out as it was composed mainly of untrained clerics, giving rise to the nickname 'the Chapter of Myton'.

nabob 18th- and 19th-century nickname for those who made their fortune in India, a corruption of the Mogul royal title *nawab*. The name became widespread when many 'nabobs' returned to England and frustrated attempts to limit the privileges of the East India Company.

Naoroji Dadhabai 1825–1917. Indian-born British politician. A founder-member of the Indian National Congress, he left India 1886 to seek a seat in Parliament, which he achieved as Liberal for Finsbury Central 1892, the first black British MP.

Napier Charles James 1782–1853. British general. He conquered Sind in India (now a province of Pakistan) 1841–43 with a very small force and governed it until 1847. He was the first commander to mention men from the ranks in his dispatches.

Napier Robert Cornelis, 1st Baron Napier of Magdala 1810–1890. British field marshal. Knighted for his services in relieving Lucknow during the ◊Indian Mutiny, he took part in capturing Peking (Beijing) 1860 during the war against China. He was commander in chief in India 1870–76 and governor of Gibraltar 1876–82.

Napoleonic Wars series of European wars (1803–15) conducted by Napoleon I following the ◊French Revolutionary Wars, aiming for French conquest of Europe.

Britain rejoined the war with France fourteen months after the peace of ◊Amiens 1802, following continued French aggression in Europe and rumours of a fresh campaign in Egypt and a projected invasion of Britain. When ◊Pitt the Younger resumed the premiership 1805 he negotiated a new alliance, the Third Coalition, with Russia, Austria, Sweden, and Naples. In the same year Napoleon won convincing victories over the Austrians at Ulm and over a combined Austrian–Russian force at Austerlitz. The allies maintained their naval supremacy when Nelson halted Napoleon's planned invasion of Britain from Boulogne with a decisive victory at ◊Trafalgar. Prussia replaced Austria in the coalition 1806 but suffered heavy defeats at Jena and Auerstadt.

Napoleon then initiated the **Continental System**, a form of economic warfare designed to isolate Britain from Europe, in which continental ports were closed to British commerce. Russia was defeated at Eylau and Friedland and made peace with Napoleon under the **Treaty of Tilsit** 1807. Russia then changed sides, agreeing to attack Sweden, but was forced to retreat.

Napoleon's invasion of Portugal and Spain 1808 in support of tenuous claims of his relatives as puppet kings in the region led to the ◊**Peninsular War** in which the British army under ◊Wellington combined with Portuguese and Spanish guerillas against the French.

Following the failure of Napoleon's disastrous invasion of Russia 1812, the British foreign secretary Castlereagh set up the fourth coalition 1813 with Russia, Austria, Prussia, and Sweden. The new coalition defeated Napoleon at the **Battle of the Nations**, Leipzig, 1813 and he was forced to abdicate and exiled to Elba 1814. He returned to France for his 'hundred days' campaign 1815 but was finally defeated at the Battle of ◊Waterloo 18 June 1815. The post-war European settlement was worked out at the Congress of Vienna 1814–15.

The annual cost of the British army during the Napoleonic Wars was between 60% and 90% of total government income.

Naseby, Battle of decisive battle of the Civil War 14 June 1645, when the Royalists, led by Prince Rupert, were defeated by the Parliamentarians ('Roundheads') under Oliver Cromwell and General Fairfax. It is named after the nearby village of Naseby, 32 km/20 mi south of Leicester.

Roll up that map [of Europe]: it will not be wanted these ten years.

NAPOLEONIC WARS
Pitt the Younger, on hearing of Napoleon's victory at Austerlitz, 1805 (attributed)

French Revolutionary and Napoleonic wars: chronology

1789	Outbreak of the French Revolution.
1793	*1 Feb* French government declared war on Britain.
1794	*1 June* The 'Glorious First': A British fleet commanded by Lord Howe captured six French ships in the north Atlantic.
1797	*14 Feb* A British fleet commanded by Sir John Jervis and Horatio Nelson defeated the Spanish off Cape St Vincent, southwest Portugal.
1798	*1 Aug* Battle of the Nile: A British fleet commanded by Nelson inflicted a crushing defeat on the French navy in Aboukir Bay of northwest Egypt.
1799	Income tax introduced in Britain, to pay for the war.
	9 Nov In France, in a coup d'état, Napoleon Bonaparte overthrew the Directory.
1801	*2 April* Battle of Copenhagen: Nelson's fleet attacked the Danish fleet.
	In French-occupied Egypt, British forces captured Cairo and Alexandria.
1802	*27 March* Britain and France agreed the Peace of Amiens.
1803	*18 May* War between France and Britain recommenced.
1805	*21 Oct* Battle of Trafalgar: a British fleet commanded by Nelson defeated a Franco–Spanish fleet off southwest Spain; during the battle a French sharpshooter shot Nelson.
1806	*21 Nov* Napoleon issued the Berlin Decree, declaring Britain to be under blockade and forbidding neutral countries to trade with the country.
1807	*Oct–March 1808* French forces crossed Spain to stop Portugal's trade with Britain.
1808	*10 May* King Charles IV of Spain and his son surrendered the Spanish throne, which Napoleon granted to his brother Joseph.
	1 July Start of the Peninsular War: British land forces established a base at Corunna, northwest Spain.
	1 Aug A British army commanded by Sir Arthur Wellesley (later Duke of Wellington) landed in Portugal and defeated the French at Vimeiro 21 Aug. By the Convention of Cintra 30 Aug the French agreed to withdraw to Spain.
	Oct–Jan 1809 The British army, commanded by John Moore, campaigned in northwest and central Spain but withdrew to Corunna where Moore died 11 Jan. The army was then evacuated.
1809	*22 April* A British army under Wellesley returned to Portugal, defeated the French at Talavera 27 July, but then withdrew to defend Portugal.
1811	British forces advanced from Portugal into Spain.
1812	*24 June–14 Dec* Napoleon's invasion of Russia.
	>July Battle of Salamanca: the British army defeated the French forces in Spain.
	12 Aug Wellington entered Madrid.
1813	*21 June* Battle of Vitoria: the British victory forced the French to evacuate Spain.
	7 Oct British forces invaded southwest France.
	16–19 Oct In Eastern Europe, Britain's allies defeated the French at the Battle of Leipzig.
1814	*March* The British army commanded by the Duke of Wellington entered Toulouse in southwest France, ending the Peninsular War.
	11 April Napoleon abdicated and was exiled to the island of Elba.
1815	*1 March* Having escaped from Elba, Napoleon landed in France and raised a new army.
	18 June Battle of Waterloo: Britain and its allies defeated France.
	20 Nov Treaty of Vienna was signed, providing for the future containment of France.

The whole booty of the Field fell to the soldiers, which was very rich and considerable, there being amongst it, beside the riches of court and officers, the rich plunder of Leicester.

NASEBY

Joshua Sprigge on the aftermath of the battle.
Anglia Rediviva, *1647*

Both armies drew up in similar formation, infantry in the centre, cavalry on the flanks, and reserves behind. The Royalists opened the battle by dashing downhill, across the intervening valley, and up the facing hill to where the Roundheads were massed. Prince Rupert's cavalry broke the Parliamentary right wing and then recklessly pursued them toward the village of Naseby. On the other wing, however, Cromwell's cavalry routed the force opposing them and then turned inward to take the Royalist infantry in the flank. King Charles I ordered his last reserves to charge, but the Earl of Carnwath, seeing this to be a futile move, turned his horse away and led his troops off the field; the Parliamentarians took heart from this, rallied, and completed the victory. Prince Rupert, returning from his chase, found the battle over and could do nothing but follow the king to Leicester. The Royalists lost about 1,000 killed and 5,000 were taken prisoner, together with all their artillery.

Nassau agreement treaty signed 18 Dec 1962 under which the USA provided Britain with Polaris missiles, marking a strengthening in Anglo-American relations.

Natal former British colony in ◊South Africa. The region was part of the British Cape Colony 1843–1856, when it was made into a separate colony. Zululand was annexed to Natal 1897, and the districts of Vrijheid, Utrecht, and part of Wakkerstroom were transferred from the

Transvaal to Natal 1903; the colony became a part of the Union of South Africa 1910.

National Front extreme right-wing political party founded 1967. The NF was formed from a merger of the League of Empire Loyalists and the British National Party (the latter broke off again 1982 and has now largely eclipsed the NF). Some of its members had links with the National Socialist Movement of the 1960s. It reached its high point in the late 1970s but by 1980 dissension arose and splinter groups formed. Electoral support in the 1983 and 1987 general elections was minimal. In 1991, the party claimed 3,000 members.

National Government (1931) a government of Labour, Liberal and Conservative MPs formed 1931, following a rapidly declining financial situation which had led to a split in the Labour government.

The Labour leader, Ramsay ◊MacDonald, was prime minister of the National Government but the majority of his own party refused to support him. Thus the National Government was mainly Conservative, and Macdonald (who resigned in 1935) was succeeded as prime minister by the Conservative leader Stanley ◊Baldwin who was in turn succeeded by Neville ◊Chamberlain. The national government was replaced by a wartime coalition government led by Winston Churchill 1940.

Naseby, 14 June 1645
Charles I's only battle against the numerically superior New Model Army opened with Prince Rupert's rout of Ireton's Parliamentary cavalry and the resolute advance of the veteran Royalist infantry against Skippon. However, while Rupert's men plundered the Parliamentary baggage train, Cromwell and Rossiter scattered Sir Marmaduke Langdale's cavalry and attacked the Royalist footsoldiers from the rear. Charles escaped from the field, but his army was destroyed.

National Health Service (NHS) government medical scheme founded 1948 to provide free medical, dental, and optical treatment for all. The National Health Service Act 1946 was largely the work of Aneurin ◊Bevan, Labour minister of health.

Successive governments, both Labour and Conservative, have introduced charges for some services. The NHS now includes hospital care, but limited fees are made for ordinary doctors' prescriptions, eye tests and spectacles, and dental treatment, except for children and people on very low incomes. A White Paper published Jan 1989 by the Conservative government proposed legislation for decentralizing the control of hospitals and changes in general practice giving greater responsibilities to doctors to manage their practices. Private health schemes such as BUPA are increasingly used in the UK.

Since 1990 there have been changes in the way doctors run their practices. Doctors with 7,000 patients or more can apply to manage part of their NHS budgets. This improves services for patients and enables doctors to explore more innovative methods of treatment. From 1994 certain district nurses and health visitors have been able to prescribe drugs and medical appliances, so reducing the time that patients have to wait for treatment.

national insurance state social-security scheme that provides child allowances, maternity benefits, and payments to the unemployed, sick, and retired, and also covers medical treatment. It is paid for by weekly or monthly contributions from employees and employers.

National Insurance Act 1911, act of Parliament introduced by Lloyd George, Liberal chancellor, which first provided insurance for workers against ill health and unemployment. It was superseded by another act providing a more comprehensive system July 1946.

Part I of the act introduced compulsory health insurance for all manual workers aged between 16 and 70 and nonmanual workers with incomes below £250 a year who did not claim exemption. Part II of the act provided insurance against unemployment for 2 million workers but excluded domestic servants, agricultural workers, and nonmanual workers exempt from Part I. The schemes were contributory, with employer, employee, and the state making regular contributions. The act provided for medical assistance and maternity benefits and supplemented recently introduced welfare provisions for disabilities and pensions.

National Liberal Foundation central organization of the British ◊Liberal Party, established 1877 in Birmingham. The first president was Joseph Chamberlain.

national schools schools founded from 1811 by the National Society for the Education of the Poor as an Anglican alternative to the nonconformist schools or ◊dissenting academies. The schools used older pupils, known as 'monitors' to supervise the younger children.

national service ◊conscription into the armed services in peacetime, introduced in Britain shortly before the start of World War II and reintroduced 1947–62.

nationalization policy of bringing a country's essential services and industries under public ownership, notably pursued by the Labour government of 1945–51. Acts were passed nationalizing the Bank of England, coal, and most hospitals 1946; transport and electricity 1947; gas 1948; and iron and steel 1949. In 1953 the succeeding Conservative government provided for the return of road haulage to private enterprise and for decentralization of the railways. It also denationalized iron and steel in 1953, but these were renationalized by the next Labour government in 1967. In 1977 Callaghan's Labour government nationalized the aircraft and shipbuilding industries. With the advent of a Conservative government 1979, the process was reversed in the form of ◊privatization.

NATO abbreviation for ◊*North Atlantic Treaty Organization*.

Navigation Acts series of acts of Parliament passed from 1381 to protect English shipping from foreign competition and to ensure monopoly trading between Britain and its colonies. The last was repealed 1849 (coastal trade exempt until 1853). The Navigation Acts helped to establish England as a major sea power, although they led to higher prices. They ruined the Dutch merchant fleet in the 17th century, and were one of the causes of the ◊American Revolution.

1650 'Commonwealth Ordinance' forbade foreign ships to trade in English colonies.

1651 Forbade the importation of goods except in English vessels or in vessels of the country of origin of the goods. This act led to the Anglo-Dutch War 1652–54.

1660 All colonial produce was required to be exported in English vessels.

1663 Colonies were prohibited from receiving goods in foreign (rather than English) vessels.

Nelson Horatio, Viscount Nelson 1758–1805. English admiral. He joined the navy in 1770. In the Revolutionary Wars against France he lost the sight in his right eye 1794 and lost his right arm 1797. He became a national hero, and rear admiral, after the victory off Cape St Vincent, Portugal. In 1798 he tracked the French fleet to Aboukir Bay where he almost entirely destroyed it. In 1801 he won a decisive victory over Denmark at the Battle of ◊Copenhagen, and in 1805, after two years of blockading Toulon, another over the Franco-Spanish fleet at the Battle of ◊Trafalgar, near Gibraltar, at which he was mortally wounded.

New Armies alternative name for the ◊Kitchener Armies of World War I.

New Guinea former British colony in the SW Pacific, N of Australia. The western half of New Guinea was annexed by the Dutch 1828. In 1884 the area of Papua on the southeast coast was proclaimed a protectorate by the British, and in the same year Germany took possession of the northeast quarter of New Guinea. Under Australian control 1914–21, German New Guinea was administered as a British mandate and then united with Papua 1945. Papua and New Guinea jointly gained full independence as Papua New Guinea 1975. The Dutch retained control over the western half of the island (West Irian) after Indonesia gained its independence 1949, but were eventually forced to transfer administrative responsibility to Indonesia 1963.

New Ireland Forum meeting between politicians of the Irish Republic and Northern Ireland May 1983. It offered three potential solutions to the Northern Irish problem, but all were rejected by the UK the following year.

I have only one eye, – I have a right to be blind sometimes:... I really do not see the signal!

HORATIO NELSON
at the battle of Copenhagen, 1801

New Jersey former British colony in North America; see ◊Thirteen Colonies.

New Model Army army created 1645 by Oliver Cromwell to support the cause of Parliament during the English ◊Civil War by the merger of the armies of Sir Thomas Walter and the Earl of Essex. It was characterized by organization and discipline. Thomas Fairfax was its first commander.

New Orleans, Battle of in the Anglo-American War of 1812, inconclusive battle between British and American forces Dec 1814–Jan 1815, at New Orleans; the war was already over by the time the battle was fought – peace had been signed 24 Dec 1814 – but neither of the two forces in the area had received the news.

new town centrally planned urban area. New towns such as Milton Keynes and Stevenage were built after World War II to accommodate the overspill from cities and large towns, at a time when the population was rapidly expanding and inner-city centres had either decayed or been destroyed. In 1976 the policy, which had been criticized for disrupting family groupings and local communities, destroying small shops and specialist industries, and furthering the decay of city centres, was abandoned.

New York former British colony in North America; see ◊Thirteen colonies.

New Zealand former British crown colony, southwest Pacific. The islands were circumnavigated by Cook 1769 and soon settled by European whalers and missionaries. Native leaders ceded the territory to Britain by the Treaty of Waitangi 1840 and it was proclaimed a crown colony under British sovereignty 1841. The colonial status of New Zealand was formally terminated 1907, when it was designated a dominion.

Newbury, Battles of two battles of the Civil War:
  20 Sept 1643 victory of the Earl of Essex with the London militia over royalist forces. The Royalists retreated to Oxford and Essex succeeded in capturing Reading.
  27 Oct 1644 indecisive battle in which parliamentary forces failed to capture a small force under Charles I and he was able to escape to Oxford.

Newcastle Thomas Pelham-Holles, Duke of Newcastle 1693–1768. British Whig politician, prime minster 1754–56 and 1757–62. He served as secretary of state for 30 years from 1724, then succeeded his younger brother, Henry Pelham, as prime minister 1754. In 1756 he resigned as a result of setbacks in the Seven Years' War, but returned to office 1757 with ◊Pitt the Elder (1st Earl of Chatham) taking responsibility for the conduct of the war.

Newcastle Propositions humiliating demands presented by the Scots and ◊Independents to Charles I 14 July 1646. They included demands that Charles abolish bishops, sacrifice his supporters, and allow Parliament to monitor both the army and foreign affairs for 20 years. Charles was reluctant to give an answer as he could not afford to reject the Scots outright, but equally could not accept a climbdown of this scale. The Scots grew impatient, and handed over the king to Parliament before withdrawing over the border.

Newfoundland former British colony, an island off the east coast of Canada. English ownership of the island was formally proclaimed 1583 by Sir Humphry Gilbert, who established the first colony at St John's. Following a territorial claim by the French, Newfoundland became English by the Treaty of Utrecht 1713, but with fishing rights retained by France. It became a British colony 1934, but passed to Canada together with Labrador 1949.

Newgate prison in London, which stood on the site of the Old Bailey central criminal court. Originally a gatehouse (hence the name), it was established in the 12th century, rebuilt after the Great Fire of London 1666 and again in 1780, and was demolished 1903. Public executions were held outside it 1783–1868. One of the cells is preserved in the Museum of London.

Newman John Henry 1801–1890. English Roman Catholic theologian. While still an Anglican, he wrote a series of *Tracts for the Times*, which gave their name to the Tractarian Movement (subsequently called the ◊Oxford Movement) for the revival of Catholicism. He became a Catholic 1845 and was made a cardinal 1879. His autobiography, *Apologia pro vita sua*, was published 1864.

Nightingale
Although nursing was thought to be totally unsuitable work for a woman of the Victorian middle classes, Florence Nightingale (seen in this 1859 photograph) was unwavering in her determination to transform both the standard of care that nurses provided and their professional status. The publicity surrounding her work in the Crimean War as 'the Lady with the Lamp' allowed her to achieve both aims.
St Thomas's Library

It may seem a strange principle to enunciate as the very first requirement in a Hospital that it should do the sick no harm.

Florence
Nightingale
Notes on Hospitals

Newport Riots violent demonstrations by the ◊Chartists 1839 in Newport, Wales, in support of the Peoples' Charter. They were suppressed with the loss of 20 lives.

NHS abbreviation for the ◊*National Health Service.*

Nigeria former British colony, West Africa. The first land acquired by Britain here was Lagos, ceded by the native king 1861. The territory was administered by Sierra Leone 1861–74 and by the Gold Coast Colony 1874–86, when it was reconstituted as the Colony and Protectorate of Lagos. The Oil Rivers Protectorate, formed 1885, became the two Protectorates of Northern and Southern Nigeria 1914. Administration was granted to the British mandate of the Cameroons 1922. The Federation of Nigeria was established 1954, comprising Lagos, the Eastern, Northern, and Western regions, and part of the British Cameroons mandate. Independence was achieved 1960.

Nightingale Florence 1820–1910. English nurse, the founder of nursing as a profession. She took a team of nurses to Scutari (now Üsküdar, Turkey) in 1854 and reduced the ◊Crimean War hospital death rate from 42% to 2%. She quickly improved the standard of hygiene on the wards and improved working conditions and standards of professionalism of nurses. She earned the nickname 'Lady with the Lamp' because of her habit of touring the wards with an oil lamp, checking on patients. She returned from the Crimea already a heroine and was received by Queen Victoria. Her subsequent evidence to a royal commission led to the founding of the Army Medical School 1857. She founded the Nightingale School and Home for Nurses in London 1856. She was awarded the Order of Merit 1907.

Nile, Battle of the alternative name for the Battle of ◊Aboukir Bay.

Nineteen Propositions demands presented by the Long Parliament to Charles I 1642. The demands, which were designed to limit the powers of the crown, included parliamentary approval for dismissal and appointment of all officers of state; strict enforcement of anti-Catholic legislation and ecclesiastical reform; and parliamentary control of the militia. Charles rejected the demands, marking the beginning of the Civil War.

Ninian, St *c.* 360–432. First Christian missionary to Scotland. He appears to have been the son of a Cumbrian chief, but was educated in Rome. He was made a bishop by the pope 394 and sent to convert Britain. According to Bede, he converted the Picts of southern Scotland, and founded the monastery at Whithorn *c.* 397.

Nithsdale William Maxwell, 5th Earl of Nithsdale 1676–1744. English ◊Jacobite leader who was captured at Preston, brought to trial in Westminster Hall, London, and condemned to death 1716. With his wife's assistance he escaped from the Tower of London in women's dress, and fled to Rome.

noble coin to the value of 6s. 8d. (one half of a mark) issued by Edward III 1344, along with half-nobles and quarter-nobles. They served as currency for just over 100 years.

nonconformist originally a member of the Puritan section of the Church of England clergy who, in the Elizabethan age, refused to conform to certain practices, for example the wearing of the surplice and kneeling to receive Holy Communion. After 1662 the term was confined to those who left the church rather than conform to the Act of Uniformity requiring the use of the *Prayer Book* in all churches. Though subject to the ◊Penal Laws (along with Catholics), after the Restoration they were allowed to worship and came to exercise influence through the Whig party. The term is now applied mainly to members of the Free churches.

nonjuror any of the priests of the Church of England who, after the revolution of 1688, refused to take the oaths of allegiance to William and Mary. They continued to exist as a rival church for over a century, and consecrated their own bishops, the last of whom died 1805.

Nore mutiny naval mutiny May 1797, caused by low pay and bad conditions. It took place at an anchorage by the Nore in the Thames. The mutineers held out for four weeks before surrendering; their leader, Richard Parker, was hanged.

Norfolk Thomas Howard, 3rd Duke of Norfolk 1473–1554. Brother-in-law of Henry VII and a leading Catholic politician under Henry VIII and Mary Tudor. He was appointed Lord High Admiral 1531 and served at the Battle of ◊Flodden. He led various campaigns against the French in the 1520s and returned to England to oppose Wolsey. He subsequently saw two nieces, Anne Boleyn and Katherine Howard marry Henry VIII. His willingness to preside over his nieces' trials and executions proved his loyalty to the king, even though he remained conservative in religion and opposed Thomas Cromwell's reforms. He was arrested 1546 when his son and heir, Henry Howard, Earl of Surrey, claimed during Henry's last illness that his father should be protector for the young Edward VI. Though his son was beheaded, the duke was saved by Henry's own death, and he was released from the Tower by Queen Mary I.

Norfolk Thomas Howard, 4th Duke of Norfolk 1536–1572. Catholic peer who hoped to marry ◊Mary Queen of Scots and have her declared heir to Elizabeth. Through his opposition to Secretary Cecil he was implicated in the ◊Northern Rebellion of 1569 but released. He was arrested after the failure of the Ridolfi Plot and executed.

Norman any of the descendants of the Norsemen (to whose chief, Rollo, Normandy was granted by Charles III of France 911) who adopted French language and culture. During the 11th and 12th centuries they conquered England 1066 (under William the Conqueror), Scotland 1072, parts of Wales and Ireland, southern Italy, Sicily, and Malta, and took a prominent part in the Crusades.

They introduced feudalism, Latin as the language of government, and Norman French as the language of literature. Church architecture and organization were also influenced by the Normans, although they ceased to exist as a distinct people after the 13th century.

Norman Conquest invasion and settlement of England by the ◊Normans, following the victory of ◊William the Conqueror at the Battle of ◊Hastings 1066.

The opening years of William's English rule were insecure as he depended on the co-operation of men who had previously served Harold. However, by about 1072 the Norman hold on the kingdom was finally established and the affairs of Church and state were completely in Norman hands. The Domesday Book shows the huge extent of Norman landholdings within only 20 years of the Battle of Hastings. The break with the past was not complete, for William continued, or adopted, many established Anglo-Saxon institutions for the greater stability of his own system.

The Conquest turned England away from Scandinavia and toward France. England was brought more closely into the European stream of political

Norman Conquest: chronology

1066 *5 Jan* Death of Edward the Confessor, king of England. He was succeeded the next day by his brother-in-law Harold Godwinson (Harold II).
25 Sept Battle of Stamford Bridge: Harold II defeated the invading army of Harold Hardrada, king of Norway.
28 Sept Normans and others, led by Duke William of Normandy, landed at Pevensey, Kent.
14 Oct Battle of Hastings: Normans defeated the English, killing Harold II. They later abandoned an attempt to cross London Bridge and crossed the Thames at Wallingford, Berkshire. At Berkhamstead, leading Englishmen and Londoners submitted to William.
25 Dec Archbishop Ealdred of York crowned William as king of England.

1067 *Dec* William suppressed a major rebellion in Exeter.

1068 William ordered the building of castles across the Midlands and in York.

1069 In the autumn, rebellions erupted in Yorkshire (supported by Scandinavians), Cornwall and Devon, Somerset and Dorset, and the Welsh Marches. The Normans suppressed the rebellions and laid waste the rebellious areas, especially Yorkshire (the 'harrying of the North').

1070 King Sweyn of Denmark supported an English rebellion in the Isle of Ely, but in spring 1070 was persuaded by William to withdraw. The English rebellion continued until suppressed 1071.

1071 William appointed Hugh d'Avranches as Earl of Chester. Together with his cousin Robert of Rhuddlan, Hugh extended Norman lordship into north Wales and made Gwynedd a tributary province.

1072 William invaded Scotland and received the submission of Malcolm III, king of Scots, at Abernethy on Tay.

c. 1075 William created the earldom of Shrewsbury for Roger, Lord of Arundel. Roger took land in north Wales and pushed into central Wales, establishing the castle of Montgomery.

1075 Waltheof, Earl of Northumbria, Ralph, Earl of East Anglia, and Roger de Breteuil, Earl of Hereford, rebelled against William, but were checked. (Ralph went into exile, Roger was imprisoned, and Waltheof was executed.)

1080 Walcher, bishop of Durham and Earl of Northumbria, and household members were murdered by Northumbrians at Gateshead. In response, Bishop Odo, Earl of Kent, harried the area around Durham.
Autumn Robert (Curthose), eldest son of King William, led a Norman expedition into Scotland, to Falkirk. He also founded Newcastle-upon-Tyne.

1081 William led a military expedition across south Wales, to St David's.

1082 William ordered the imprisonment of his half-brother, Bishop Odo, for recruiting knights to support a bid for the papacy.

1085 *25 Dec* William ordered a survey to be made of land-holders' estates and their resources in England, resulting in the Domesday Book.

1086 *1 Aug* William required major land-holders in England to do homage to him at Salisbury.

1087 *9 Sept* William died while in Normandy, after falling from his horse. He was succeeded as Duke of Normandy by his eldest son Robert and as king of England by his third son William (the second son, Richard, had died in 1075).

THE NEW ORDER

The Impact of the Normans

Of all dates, 1066 is probably the best remembered in English history. But exactly what impact the Norman Conquest really had has always been controversial. Did it represent a clear break in the history of Anglo-Saxon England, or were the Normans quickly assimilated, simply hastening developments already underway, and even learning from them?

In a more nationalistic age than ours, many English historians felt instinctively that the virtues and institutions long thought to be characteristically English ought somehow to be traceable to a purely English past – a past that predated the arrival of the 'French' Normans. Detailed research into the survival of pre-Conquest institutions such as shire- and hundred-based local government, the common law, an efficient royal administration, and a national taxation system (Danegeld), led to the argument that the Norman Conquest did little to change an already highly sophisticated society. A less nationalistic view, however, reveals the Norman Conquest as a manifestation of wider changes in Western Europe as a whole, in social and cultural terms, in military terms, and in religious terms.

Society and culture

Changes already taking place in Anglo-Saxon society by 1066 made it less 'English' than was previously thought. As recently as 1042, England had been ruled by a Danish king. The Danes had brought new types of landholding (and therefore social status) to parts of England, and the Anglo-Saxon term 'thane' had been replaced by the Scandinavian 'housecarl' for the warrior class, perhaps also reflecting a social change. Scandinavian influence in the east and north of the country contributed to the lukewarm support which some chroniclers noted in those

regions for Harold II, the former Earl of Wessex. A surviving legal case from the reign of William I features a landowner dispossessed in the Conquest who argues that his land should be returned as he is a Dane, and was therefore neutral in the struggle between Normans and Anglo-Saxons.

The Norman Conquest brought the wholesale replacement of the Anglo-Saxon nobility, but it also brought changes in the way English society was conceived. Above all, the ancient Germanic concept of the free peasant owing personal military service to his king was finally brought to an end: after the Conquest, the Anglo-Scandinavian free peasants were reduced to the status of feudal villeins, bound to the land and excluded from military service. Elsewhere in western Europe this new conception of society, central to what we call feudalism, had developed since the 10th century; in England, the older conceptions were only swept away by the Normans.

Military change

The events of 1066 can be seen as part of a wider colonization of the borderlands of Europe by a military elite from Western Europe. The Battle of Hastings was one of the key points of conflict between two of the three distinct military systems of 11th-century Europe. In Scandinavia and Anglo-Scandinavian England the heavy infantryman had dominated the battlefield, armed with the two-handed axe. On the Celtic fringe, mobile light infantrymen, expert with bows, were characteristic. And in feudal Western Europe the warrior par excellence was the heavy horseman, the knight. The knight's charge, with his lance held firm (couched) so as to focus the whole weight of man and charging horse at its point, was the classic tactical device of medieval warfare. Its use at Hastings can be seen in the Bayeux

Tapestry. The *Anglo-Saxon Chronicle* confirms the novelty in post-Conquest England of both knights and castles, the two defining features of feudal warfare.

Religious change

Some of the most obvious changes in post-Conquest England were in the church. Most notably, church lands exempt from taxation or military service to the Anglo-Saxon kings were brought within the feudal system of knight-service. Under Lanfranc, appointed archbishop of Canterbury in 1070, the English church itself was thoroughly reorganized. He enforced unity and discipline within the church and the monasteries under the authority of Canterbury, established regular councils and synods, and introduced a whole system of canonical law and separate courts for the church. Above all, the bishops and abbots brought in to replace Anglo-Saxon prelates re-integrated England into the cultural and intellectual mainstream of Northern France.

The ideological importance of these changes cannot be stressed enough. The late Anglo-Saxon church, despite significant reform, had become moribund in a way that was obvious to many of its members; the Norman church in post-Conquest England was perceived even by those nostalgic for the old ways as a positive, dynamic influence. Changes in the church impressed contemporaries as much as the spread of castles or the organization of the Domesday survey.

In many respects, then, it is possible to view the Norman Conquest as a reintegration of the kingdom of England into the cultural, intellectual, military, and religious world of Western Europe, itself on the verge of great changes in the 12th century.

SIMON HALL

Norman Conquest of England, 1066–70
Despite the drama of Hastings, Duke William's advance on Anglo-Saxon London in 1066 was circumspect, and preceded by the securing of a firm base in Kent in case withdrawal should be necessary. Rebellions in the north and west of England in the following three years, and short-lived Danish and Scottish invasions, had to be overcome before the Norman Conquest was complete.

Norman Conquest of England, 1066–70

thought, but at the cost of the obliteration of a society which, for all its many weaknesses, had a cultural tradition without parallel in Normandy.

Normandy, House of royal house of England 1066–1154, from the conquest of England by ◊William I the Conqueror, Duke of Normandy, to the accession of ◊Henry II, son of Geoffrey Plantagenet, Count of Anjou, in 1154. During this period the County of Normandy, in France, remained an integral part of the lands of the kings of England.

Normandy landings alternative name for ◊D-day.

North Frederick, 8th Lord North 1732–1792. British Tory politician. He entered Parliament 1754, became chancellor of the Exchequer 1767, and was prime minister in a government of Tories and 'king's friends' from 1770. His hard line against the American colonies was supported by George III, but in 1782 he was forced to resign by the failure of his policy. In 1783 he returned to office in a coalition with Charles ◊Fox. After its defeat, he retired from politics.

North Atlantic Treaty Organization (NATO) association set up 1949 to provide for the collective defence of the major W European and North American states against the perceived threat from the USSR. The collapse of communism in eastern Europe from 1990 prompted the most radical review of its policy and defence strategy since its inception. After the East European Warsaw Pact was disbanded 1991, an adjunct to NATO, the **North Atlantic Cooperation Council**, was established, including all the former Soviet republics, with the aim of building greater security in Europe. In July 1992 it was agreed that the Conference on Security and Cooperation in Europe would in future authorize all NATO's military responses within Europe.

At the 1994 Brussels summit a 'partnership for peace' programme was formally launched, inviting former members of the Warsaw Pact and ex-Soviet republics to take part in a wide range of military cooperation arrangements, without the implications of imminent NATO membership. Romania was the first to join, in Jan, followed by Estonia, Lithuania, and Poland; Russia joined in June. By July 1994 the partnership included 12 of the 15 former Soviet republics (Armenia, Belarus, and Tajikistan declined to join), plus Hungary, the Slovak Republic, Bulgaria, Albania, the Czech Republic, Finland, and Sweden.

The original signatories of the North Atlantic Treaty 1949 were Belgium, Canada, Denmark, France, Iceland, Italy, Luxembourg, Netherlands, Norway, Portugal, the UK, and the USA. Greece and Turkey were admitted as parties to the treaty 1952, West Germany 1955, and Spain 1982.

North Briton weekly periodical June 1762–April 1763, published by the radical John ◊Wilkes. It achieved notoriety when issue 45 accused George III of lying in a speech to Parliament. Wilkes and the magazine were prosecuted under a ◊general warrant for seditious libel. In the ensuing case, Wilkes was acquitted and general warrants were declared illegal.

It is the habitation of strangers and the dominion of foreigners. There is today no Englishman who is either earl, bishop or abbot. The newcomers devour the riches and entrails of England, and there is no hope of the misery coming to an end.

NORMAN CONQUEST
William of Malmesbury, on England after the Conquest.

Royal Genealogy in 11th-century England

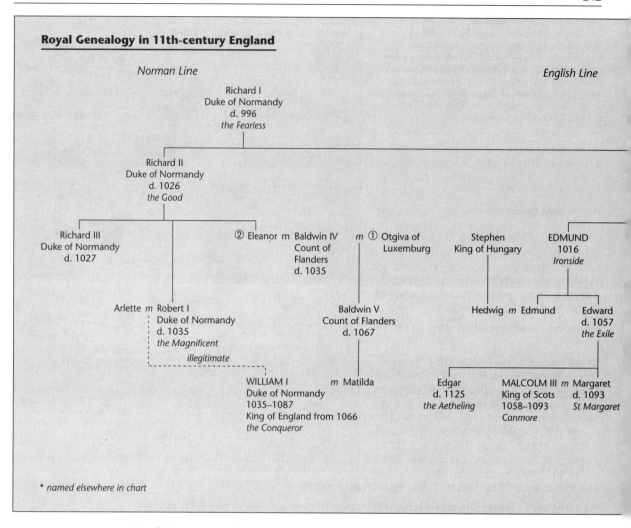

Norman Line   *English Line*

Richard I
Duke of Normandy
d. 996
the Fearless

Richard II
Duke of Normandy
d. 1026
the Good

Richard III
Duke of Normandy
d. 1027

② Eleanor m Baldwin IV
Count of
Flanders
d. 1035

m ① Otgiva of
Luxemburg

Stephen
King of Hungary

EDMUND
1016
Ironside

Arlette *m* Robert I
Duke of Normandy
d. 1035
the Magnificent
illegitimate

Baldwin V
Count of Flanders
d. 1067

Hedwig *m* Edmund

Edward
d. 1057
the Exile

WILLIAM I
Duke of Normandy
1035–1087
King of England from 1066
the Conqueror

m Matilda

Edgar
d. 1125
the Aetheling

MALCOLM III *m* Margaret
King of Scots   d. 1093
1058–1093   *St Margaret*
Canmore

* *named elsewhere in chart*

Northampton, Battle of in the Wars of the Roses, defeat and capture of Henry VI in an early attack by the Yorkists under Richard Neville, Duke of Warwick, 10 July 1460. The Lancastrian Duke of Buckingham was killed in the battle which paved the way for Richard of York to be recognized as successor to Henry.

Northcliffe Alfred Charles William Harmsworth, 1st Viscount Northcliffe 1865–1922. British newspaper proprietor, born in Dublin. Founding the *Daily Mail* 1896, he revolutionized popular journalism, and with the *Daily Mirror* 1903 originated the picture paper. In 1908 he also obtained control of *The Times*. His brother Harold Sidney Harmsworth, 1st Viscount Rothermere (1868–1940), was associated with him in many of his newspapers.

Northern rebellion or *Rebellion of the Earls* rising 1569–70 led by the earls of Northumberland and Westmoreland in support of the Catholic ◊Mary Queen of Scots. They demanded Mary be declared Elizabeth's successor and the restoration of Catholicism. The bishop of Durham was seized and the mass was restored, but promised Spanish support did not arrive and the rising was suppressed. The earls were forced to flee to Scotland and 400 rebels were executed.

Northern Rhodesia former British colony in southern Africa; see ◊Rhodesia.

Northumberland Earls of; title of the ◊Percy family.

Northumberland John Dudley, Duke of Northumberland *c.* 1502–1553. English politician, son of the privy councillor Edmund Dudley (beheaded 1510), and chief minister until

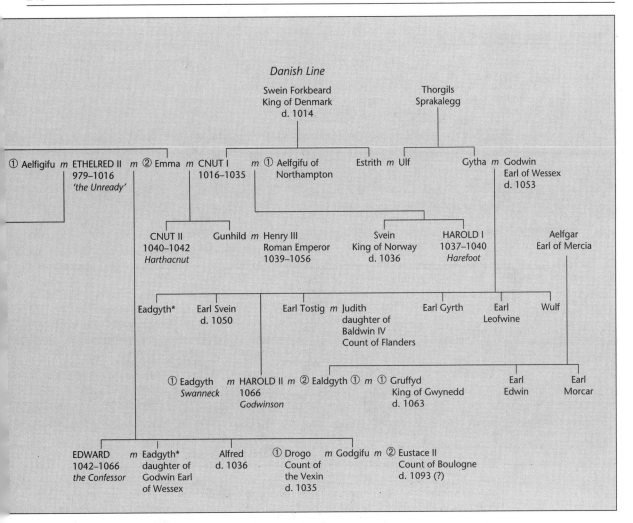

Edward VI's death 1553. He tried to place his daughter-in-law Lady Jane ◊Grey on the throne, and was executed on Mary I's accession.

Northumbria Anglo-Saxon kingdom that covered northeast England and southeast Scotland, comprising the 6th-century kingdoms of Bernicia (Forth–Tees) and Deira (Tees–Humber), united in the 7th century. It accepted the supremacy of Wessex 827 and was conquered by the Danes in the late 9th century. Under the influenced of Irish missionaries, it became a cultural and religious centre until the 8th century with priests such as Bede, Cuthbert, and Wilfrid.

Notting Hill Riots racial fighting in the Notting Hill area of London Aug and Sept 1958 involving up to 2,000 youths. The riots were the culmination of constant attacks by whites against blacks common in the area in the late 1950s. Along with a similar riot in Nottingham 1958, the riots brought racial issues to prominence and were cited as arguments for restricting further immigration. They influenced the development of the Commonwealth Immigrants Act (1962) which restricted immigration of non-whites.

Nova Scotia former British colony in North America; see ◊Canada.

nuclear deterrent Research into nuclear weapons began in Britain 1940 but was transferred to the USA after it entered World War II. Since the 1960s Britain's nuclear deterrent has consisted of nuclear-powered submarines armed with United States rockets (Polaris and Trident) carrying British nuclear warheads. Four Polaris submarines were built in the 1960s and were updated in the 1970s. In 1980 the government announced a plan to build a replacement fleet

Surely the right course is to test the Russians, not the bomb.

NUCLEAR DETERRENT
Hugh Gaitskell, Observer
1957

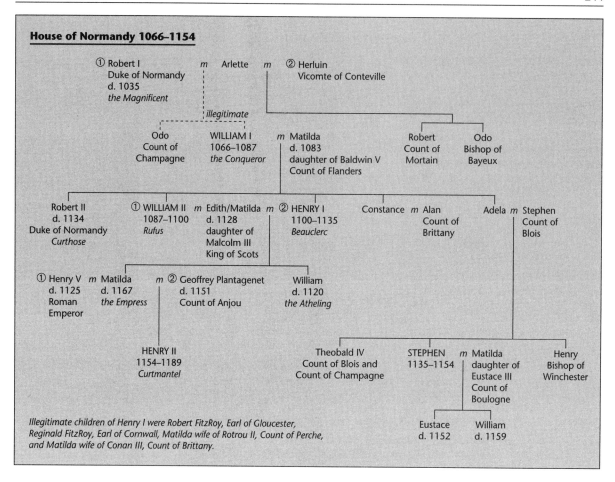

House of Normandy 1066–1154

Illegitimate children of Henry I were Robert FitzRoy, Earl of Gloucester,
Reginald FitzRoy, Earl of Cornwall, Matilda wife of Rotrou II, Count of Perche,
and Matilda wife of Conan III, Count of Brittany.

of four submarines, carrying the latest Trident missiles, to serve as Britain's independent deterrent in the 1990s. The first such submarine, HMS *Vanguard*, was launched 1992 and the second, HMS *Victorious*, underwent trials 1994. The total of four ensures that one submarine will always be at sea, and so be invulnerable to a pre-emptive attack.

Nuffield William Richard Morris, Viscount Nuffield 1877–1963. English manufacturer and philanthropist. Starting with a small cycle-repairing business, in 1910 he designed a car that could be produced cheaply, and built up Morris Motors Ltd at Cowley, Oxford. He endowed Nuffield College, Oxford, 1937 and the Nuffield Foundation 1943.

Nyasaland former British protectorate (now Malawi), in southeast Africa. The region was visited by Livingstone 1859 and became a British protectorate 1891, bearing the name British Central Africa Protectorate 1893–1907, then Nyasaland. It was part of the federation of Rhodesia and Nyasaland 1953–63, and achieved independence under its present name 1964.

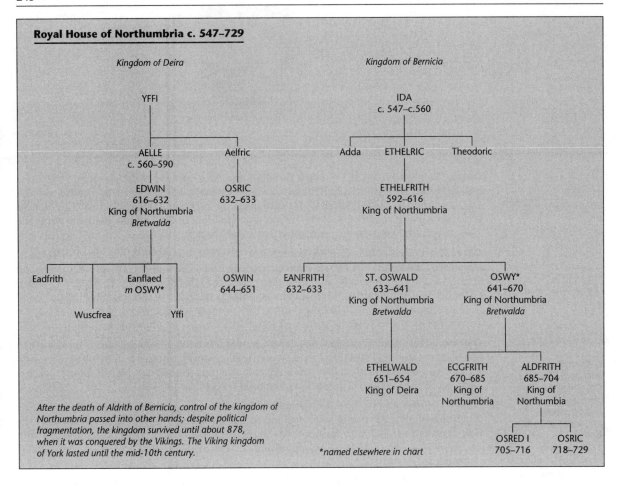

Royal House of Northumbria c. 547–729

Kingdom of Deira

YFFI

AELLE
c. 560–590

Aelfric

EDWIN
616–632
King of Northumbria
Bretwalda

OSRIC
632–633

Eadfrith

Eanflaed
m OSWY*

OSWIN
644–651

Wuscfrea

Yffi

Kingdom of Bernicia

IDA
c. 547–c.560

Adda

ETHELRIC

Theodoric

ETHELFRITH
592–616
King of Northumbria

EANFRITH
632–633

ST. OSWALD
633–641
King of Northumbria
Bretwalda

OSWY*
641–670
King of Northumbria
Bretwalda

ETHELWALD
651–654
King of Deira

ECGFRITH
670–685
King of
Northumbria

ALDFRITH
685–704
King of
Northumbia

OSRED I
705–716

OSRIC
718–729

After the death of Aldrith of Bernicia, control of the kingdom of Northumbria passed into other hands; despite political fragmentation, the kingdom survived until about 878, when it was conquered by the Vikings. The Viking kingdom of York lasted until the mid-10th century.

*named elsewhere in chart

Oastler Richard 1789–1861. English social reformer. He opposed child labour and the ◊poor law 1834, which restricted relief, and was largely responsible for securing the Factory Act 1833 and the Ten Hours Act 1847. He was given the nickname of the 'Factory King' for his achievements on behalf of workers. He was jailed for debt in Fleet prison 1840 and wrote the *Fleet Papers*, attacking the government policy of laissez-faire.

Oates Titus 1649–1705. English conspirator. A priest, he entered the Jesuit colleges at Valladolid, Spain, and St Omer, France, as a spy 1677–78, and on his return to England announced he had discovered a 'Popish Plot' to murder Charles II and re-establish Catholicism. Although this story was almost entirely false, many innocent Roman Catholics were executed during 1678–80 on Oates's evidence. He was flogged, pilloried, and imprisoned for perjury 1685. He was pardoned and granted a pension after the revolution of 1688.

O'Brien James Bronterre 1805–1864. Irish Chartist. He moved from Ireland to London 1829 where he became leader of the Chartist working class movement (see ◊Chartism). He was editor of the *Poor Man's Guardian* 1831–35 and was imprisoned for his seditious speeches 1840–41. He helped found the socialist National Reform League 1850.

O'Brien Murrough, 1st Earl of Inchiquin 1614–1674. Irish general. Raised a Protestant, he fought for the English in the Irish rebellion of 1641, earning the nickname Murrough of the Burnings. In the Civil War he submitted to the parliamentarians 1644 but later sided with Charles I 1648. After Cromwell's suppression of the Irish, he went to France 1650, finally returning to Ireland 1663.

Occam or **Ockham** William of *c.* 1300–1349. English philosopher and scholastic logician who revived the fundamentals of nominalism. As a Franciscan monk he defended evangelical poverty against Pope John XXII, becoming known as the Invincible Doctor. He was imprisoned in Avignon, France, on charges of heresy 1328 but escaped to Munich, Germany, where he died. The principle of reducing assumptions to the absolute minimum is known as **Occam's razor**.

O'Connell
Irish politician Daniel O'Connell, an ardent advocate of Catholic emancipation. O'Connell set up the Catholic Association in 1823, and was important for a time as a focus for nascent Irish unity.
Michael Nicholson

O'Connell Daniel 1775–1847. Irish politician, called 'the Liberator'. O'Connell founded the Catholic Association to press Roman Catholic claims 1823. His reserved and vacillating leadership and conservative outlook on social questions alienated his most active supporters, who broke away and formed the nationalist ◊Young Ireland movement. Although ineligible, as a Roman Catholic, to take his seat, he was elected member of Parliament for County Clare 1828 and so forced the government to grant Catholic emancipation. He cooperated with the Whigs in Parliament in the hope of obtaining concessions until 1841, when he launched his campaign for repeal of the union.

O'Connor Feargus 1794–1855. Irish parliamentarian, a follower of Daniel ◊O'Connell. He sat in Parliament 1832–35, and as editor of the *Northern Star* became an influential figure of the radical working-class Chartist movement (see ◊Chartism).

Odo *c.* 1030–1097. Bishop of Bayeux. Half-brother of William the Conqueror and Earl of Kent, Odo gave unswerving support to the Norman Conquest, governing England during the king's absences. In return, he became the country's greatest landowner, but fell out of favour with

William for reasons that are not clear and was imprisoned 1082–87. He led baronial opposition to William II (Rufus) and was forced to return to Normandy 1088. He is generally believed to have commissioned the Bayeux Tapestry, almost certainly in England.

O'Donnell Hugh Roe *c.* 1571–1602. Lord of Tyrconnell. He was imprisoned by the English administration but escaped 1591 and joined O'Neill's revolt 1594. After their defeat at Kinsale 1601, he fled to Spain to seek support, but was poisoned by an English agent 1602.

O'Donnell Rory, 1st Earl of Tyrconnell 1575–1608. Irish chief, the brother of Hugh Roe O'Donnell. He waged guerrilla warfare in Connaught 1602 until Dec, when his brother fled to Spain and left him chief of the clan. He submitted to the English and James I made him Earl of Tyrconnell 1603, but he continued to resist English authority over his territory. He plotted with O'Neill to seize Dublin Castle 1607 but the plot was discovered and they fled to Rome where he died. Their departure (the 'Flight of the Earls') left Ulster open to British colonization.

Offa King of Mercia, England, from 757. He conquered Essex, Kent, Sussex, and Surrey; defeated the Welsh and the West Saxons; and established Mercian supremacy over all England south of the river Humber. He was recognized by the pope as king of the English and was treated as an equal by the emperor Charlemagne.

Offa's Dyke defensive earthwork along the Welsh border, of which there are remains from the mouth of the river Dee to that of the river Severn. It represents the boundary secured by ◊Offa's wars with Wales. The dyke covered a distance of 240 km/149 mi, of which 130 km/ 81 mi are still standing.

Official Secrets Act 1989 act of Parliament, prohibiting the disclosure of confidential material from government sources by employees. The 1989 act replaced Section 2 of an act of 1911, which had long been accused of being too wide-ranging. It remains an absolute offence for a member or former member of the security and intelligence services (or those working closely with them) to disclose information about their work. There is no public-interest defence, and disclosure of information already in the public domain is still a crime. Journalists who repeat disclosures may also be prosecuted.

Ogham early Celtic alphabet, comprising in its basic form 20 letters made up of straight lines at a right angle or an oblique angle to a base line. It has been found in Cornwall, Wales and Scotland, and dates from the 4th century.

O'Higgins Kevin (Christopher) 1892–1927. Irish nationalist. He was elected a Sinn Féin MP 1918 and sided with Arthur Griffith in supporting the Anglo-Irish Treaty that set up the Irish Free State 1921. He was appointed minister of justice 1923 but was assassinated 1927.

O'Kelly Sean (Thomas) 1883–1966. President of Ireland 1945–59. He joined Sinn Féin as a young man and followed de Valera in repudiating the Anglo-Irish Treaty 1921. He served in successive Fianna Fáil governments 1932–45 before becoming president 1945. He was succeeded 1959 by de Valera.

Old Bailey popular name for the Central Criminal Court in London, situated in a street of that name in the City of London, off Ludgate Hill. It was established 1834 on the site of ◊Newgate prison.

'Old Contemptibles' name adopted by British soldiers who survived the retreat from Mons 1914 and other early battles of World War I. The name came from Kaiser Wilhelm's angry outburst at his forces in Belgium being held up by 'Sir John French's contemptible little army'. The troops seized on this with delight and named their post-war veterans' association 'The Old Contemptibles'.

Old Pretender nickname of ◊James Edward Stuart, the son of James II of England.

Omdurman, Battle of victory 2 Sept 1898 of British and Egyptian troops under General Horatio Kitchener over Sudanese tribesmen (Dervishes) led by the Khalifa Abdullah el Taashi. The Khalifa escaped, to be pursued and later brought to battle and killed.

The Khalifa was the successor to the Mahdi Mahomet Ahmed, who had fomented a revolt of Sudanese tribes against Egyptian rule, and had gradually become the unofficial ruler of the southern Sudan. The British force sent to deal with him advanced slowly up the Nile, to a position in a crescent north of Omdurman, the Khalifa's base (now Umm Durman, about

I think we've given them a good dusting, gentlemen.

OMDURMAN
Horatio Kitchener, after the battle, 1898

1,600 km/1,000 mi south of Cairo). The British were attacked 2 Sept by about 50,000 Dervishes, few of whom got within 500 yds of the British lines before being shot down, and an estimated 10,000 were killed. Kitchener ordered a march on to Omdurman, not realizing the main Dervish army had not yet moved and he was about to march into it. As the column moved off a force of 20,000 Dervishes fell upon the rearguard, under the command of General Hector 'Fighting Mac' MacDonald, who wheeled his troops and stopped the Dervishes, killing most and scattering the remainder. When the battle ended it was found that MacDonald's force had an average of two bullets each left in their pouches.

O'Neill Daniel *c.* 1612–1664. Irish Royalist. He was impeached and imprisoned 1642 for involvement in army plots, but escaped and fought with Prince Rupert in the Civil War at Newbury 1643 and 1644, Marston Moor 1644, and Naseby 1645. He gained command of the Ulster army temporarily 1649 and later worked for Charles II in exile.

O'Neill Hugh, 3rd Baron of Dungannon and 2nd Earl of Tyrone *c.* 1540–1616. Irish rebel chief known as *the Great O'Neill*. He was made earl on submitting to Henry VIII 1542 and lived in England in the 1560s, then returned to Ireland as a rival to the chief of the O'Neills. He served the government in the 1580s but became engaged in several intrigues against Elizabeth I and rebelled 1594. He was defeated by Mountjoy at Kinsale 1602 while supporting Spanish forces who had landed there. He made his peace with James I but resented the increasing English administration in Ulster and again plotted with the Spanish against James. He fled to the Continent 1607 with Rory O' Donnell, 1st Earl of Tyrconnell (the 'Flight of the Earls').

O'Neill Owen Roe *c.* 1590–1649. Irish soldier, the nephew of Hugh O'Neill. He served in the Spanish forces for 30 years but returned to Ireland 1642 and led the Irish Catholic forces until his death.

O'Neill Sir Phelim 1604–1653. Irish rebel. He was expelled from the Irish parliament 1641 and played a key role in the Irish rebellion that year. He was the rebels' military commander until ousted by the arrival of Owen Roe O'Neill 1642. He was captured and executed by English parliamentary forces 1653.

O'Neill Shane, 2nd Earl of Tyrone *c.* 1530–67. Irish chief known as *the proud earl*. After a dispute over the succession to the title he expelled his father and seized the chieftainship. After initial support from Elizabeth I he launched attacks on both Ulster and the Pale, but was stopped by Sir Henry Sidney and the opposition of his rivals, the O'Donnells. He was virtually independent of English rule in Ulster.

O'Neill Terence, Baron O'Neill of the Maine 1914–1990. Northern Irish Unionist politician. In the Ulster government he was minister of finance 1956–63, then prime minister 1963–69. He resigned when opposed by his party on measures to extend rights to Roman Catholics, including a universal franchise.

open-field system agricultural system in lowland areas of England during the Middle Ages. A village would normally have three large fields throughout which each farmer's land was distributed in scattered strips, while another area was set aside for common grazing. By the early 19th century, ◊enclosure meant that most farmland had been consolidated into individual holdings.

Opium Wars two wars waged by Britain against China to enforce the opening of Chinese ports to trade in opium. Opium from British India paid for Britain's imports from China, such as porcelain, silk, and, above all, tea.

First Opium War 1839–42, between Britain and China, resulted in the cession of Hong Kong to Britain and the opening of five treaty ports. Other European states were also subsequently given concessions.

Second Opium War 1856–60, followed between Britain and France in alliance against China, when there was further Chinese resistance to the opium trade. China was forced to give the European states greater trading privileges, at the expense of its people.

Orange, House of royal family of the Netherlands. The title is derived from the small principality of Orange in southern France, held by the family from the 8th century to 1713. King ◊William III of the House of Orange was offered the English throne 1688 by parliamentary elements opposed to the Catholic James II in the ◊Glorious Revolution.

The ***Orange Order*** is a sectarian lodge in Northern Ireland named after William, pledged to maintain Protestant ascendancy in the province. It was established 1795 in opposition to the United Irishmen and the Roman Catholic secret societies. It was a revival of the Orange Institution 1688, formed in support of William of Orange, whose victory over the Catholic James II at the Battle of the Boyne 1690 is commemorated annually by Protestants in parades on 12 July. Since 1920, the lodge has been a bastion of Ulster Unionism, with most senior Unionist politicians as members.

ordeal, trial by medieval method of testing the guilt of an accused person based on the belief in heaven's protection of the innocent. In Europe the practice originated with the Franks in the 8th century, and survived until the 13th century. Ordeals took many forms including walking barefoot over heated iron, dipping the hand into boiling water, and swallowing consecrated bread (causing the guilty to choke). A notorious ordeal, used particulalry for those accused of witchcraft, involved the accused being bound and thrown into cold water; if he or she sank, it would prove innocence, but remaining afloat showed guilt.

Ordinances, the demands made by the baronial opponents of Edward II 1311. The 41 demands were designed to weaken the powers of the monarchy and strengthen the role of the barons in government. They included the expulsion of the king's favourite Piers ◊Gaveston, control over the king's officers, preservation of the royal demesne, and annual parliaments. The demands were initially met but were repealed 1322 by the Statute of York.

Ordovices Celtic tribe in central and northwest Wales which resisted Roman occupation AD 43–78. They supported Caratacus and he died in their territory AD 51. Their frequent revolts eventually subsided AD 78, but they remained under a form of military occupation and were never really romanized.

Orkney Islands island group off the northeast coast of Scotland, comprising about 90 islands and islets. The population is of Scandinavian descent. Harald I (Fairhair) of Norway conquered the islands 876; they were pledged to James III of Scotland 1468 for the dowry of Margaret of Denmark and annexed by Scotland (the dowry unpaid) 1472. Scapa Flow, between Mainland and Hoy, was a naval base in both world wars, and the German fleet scuttled itself here 21 June 1919.

Orléans, Siege of during the Hundred Years' War, English defeat by the French Oct 1428 – May 1429. The English were rapidly conquering France at this stage of the war until this victory turned the tide of French fortunes; thereafter a string of French successes gradually brought the war to an end.

A force of about 5,000 troops under the Earl of Salisbury attempted to take Orléans 12 Oct 1428. The attempt failed, the Earl was killed, and the English laid siege to the city. They were not present in sufficient strength to seal off the city completely, so that there was no chance of starving out the French, and the siege lingered on until April 1429 when Joan of Arc arrived in Orléans. She took charge of the garrison and led them in a series of attacks on different English positions, taking them one after another until the remaining English, seeing the futility of their enterprise, raised the siege 4 May 1429 and departed.

Ormonde James Butler, 1st Duke of Ormonde 1610–1688. Irish general. He commanded the Royalist troops in Ireland 1641–50 during the Irish rebellion and the Civil War, and was lord lieutenant 1644–47, 1661–69, and 1677–84. He was created a marquess 1642 and a duke 1661. Colonel ◊Blood made an attempt on his life 1670.

Ormonde James Butler, 2nd Duke of Ormonde 1665–1745. English Jacobite. He supported William of Orange 1688 and served under him in Ireland and Europe. Queen Anne made him Lord Lieutenant of Ireland 1703–05 and 1710–11, and after the recall of Marlborough 1711, commander in chief. As a Tory, he opposed the accession of George I 1714 and was impeached. He took part in the Jacobite uprising 1715 and led a Spanish invasion fleet 1719 in an abortive attempt to restore the Stuarts. He lived the rest of his life in exile abroad.

Ormonde Thomas Butler, 10th Earl of Ormonde 1532–1614. Anglo-Irish noble. Raised as a Protestant, he won the favour of Elizabeth I and was a lifelong supporter of the crown. He established his power in southwest Ireland after the defeat 1583 of his rival, Gerald Fitzgerald, 15th Earl of Desmond, in the abortive ◊Desmond revolt.

O'Rourke's revolt rising 1590–91 of the O'Rourkes, an Irish tribe in Leitrim. They opposed the imposition of English authority in the late 16th century and rebelled when they were attacked by government troops following Sir Brian O'Rourke's aid to survivors of the Spanish Armada 1588. The revolt was suppressed, and Sir Brian fled to Scotland. He sought support from James VI but was handed over to the English and executed 1591.

Osborne Judgement legal ruling 1909 that prevented ◊trade unions from using membership subscriptions to finance the Labour Party. The judgement was negated by the Trade Union Act 1913, which permitted them to raise political levies and provide financial support to the Labour Party. Individual trade unionists could 'contract out' of the political levy by signing a form saying they did not wish to pay.

The case is named after W V Osborne, the secretary of the Walthamstow branch of the Amalgamated Society of Railway Servants and a member of the Liberal Party, who took legal action to restrain the union and prohibit financial support for political parties. He won on an appeal judgement that was upheld in the House of Lords.

Ossory ancient kingdom, lasting until 1110, in Leinster, Ireland; the name is preserved in some Church of Ireland and Roman Catholic bishoprics.

Oswald, St *c.* 605–642. King of Northumbria from 634, after killing the Welsh king Cadwallon. He became a Christian convert during his time in exile on the Scottish island of Iona. With the help of St Aidan he furthered the spread of Christianity in northern England. Oswald was defeated and killed by King Penda of Mercia. His feast day is 9 Aug.

Oswin d. 651. King of Deira 642–51. He became king on the death of his cousin Oswald. He was assassinated 651 at Gilling, Yorkshire, on the order of Oswy, Oswald's brother.

Oswy d. 671. Anglo-Saxon king. He became king of ◊Bernicia, one of the two divisions of Northumbria, on the death of his brother Oswald 641 and defeated and killed King ◊Penda of Mercia 655. As King of Northumbria 655–70 he gained supremacy over all Mercia, the South Angles, East Angles, and East Saxons, as well as many Britons and Scots. He presided at the Synod of ◊Whitby 664.

Ottawa Conferences two Imperial conferences held in Ottawa, Canada, 1894 and 1932. The earlier meeting of leaders from the British Empire discussed improved communications between the dominions and Britain. The later meeting took place during the Depression, but instead of an empire-wide trading agreement, Imperial preference was negotiated through 12 separate agreements, ending any hopes of a self-sufficient Commonwealth.

Otterburn, Battle of or ***Chevy Chase*** battle 15 Aug 1388 in which an inferior Scottish army heavily defeated an English army under Henry 'Hotspur' ◊Percy, who was himself taken prisoner. The Scottish commander, the 3rd Earl of Douglas, was killed in the battle.

Oudenaarde, Battle of during the War of the Spanish Succession, French defeat by an Allied army of British, Hanoverian, Prussian, and Dutch troops under the Duke of Marlborough and Prince Eugène of Savoy 11 July 1708. Oudenaarde is a town of East Flanders, Belgium, on the River Scheldt. The French suffered a crushing defeat and the allies were able to take the campaign into northern France.

outlawry in medieval England, a declaration that a criminal was outside the protection of the law, with his or her lands and goods forfeited to the Crown, and all civil rights being set aside. It was a lucrative royal 'privilege'; ◊Magna Carta restricted its use, and under Edward III it was further modified. Some outlaws, such as ◊Robin Hood, became popular heroes.

Outram James 1803–1863. British general, born in Derbyshire. He entered the Indian Army 1819, served in the Afghan and Sikh wars, and commanded in the Persian campaign of 1857. On the outbreak of the ◊Indian Mutiny, he cooperated with General Henry Havelock (1795–1857) to raise the siege of Lucknow, and held the city until relieved by Sir Colin Campbell.

Overlord, Operation during World War II, codename for the Allied invasion of Normandy 6 June 1944 (◊D-day) and the subsequent operation to liberate occupied Europe.

Owain ap Gruffydd or ***Owain Gwynedd*** *c.* 1100–1170. Ruler of Gwynedd 1137–70. He succeeded his father Gruffydd ap Cynan 1137, and made his principality the most powerful in

Wales, acquiring more lands in northeast Wales following his defeat of Madog ap Maredudd 1150. Although he submitted to Henry II 1157, he retained his dominance in Wales and helped to defeat Henry's invasion of South Wales 1165. He was frequently supported by ◊Rhys ap Gruffydd.

Owen Robert 1771–1858. British socialist, born in Wales. In 1800 he became manager of a mill at New Lanark, Scotland, where by improving working and housing conditions and providing schools he created a model community. His ideas stimulated the ◊cooperative movement (the pooling of resources for joint economic benefit).

From 1817 Owen proposed that 'villages of cooperation', self-supporting communities run on socialist lines, should be founded; these, he believed, would ultimately replace private ownership. His later attempt to run such a community in the USA (called New Harmony) failed. He organized the Grand National Consolidated Trades Union 1834, in order that the unions might take over industry and run it cooperatively, but the scheme collapsed by the end of the year.

Oxford and Asquith, Earl of title of British Liberal politician Herbert Henry ◊Asquith.

Oxford Movement also known as *Tractarian Movement* or *Catholic Revival* movement that attempted to revive Catholic practices in the Church of England. John Henry ◊Newman dated the movement from ◊Keble's sermon in Oxford 1833 which criticized the proposed suppression of ten Irish bishoprics. The Oxford Movement advocated greater liturgical ritual and ceremony, the establishment of religious communities, and a more active social role for the church. By the turn of the century it had transformed the Anglican communion, and survives today as Anglo-Catholicism.

Oxford University oldest British university, established during the 12th century, the earliest existing college being founded 1249. After suffering from land confiscation during the Reformation, it was reorganized by Elizabeth I 1571.

Besides the colleges, notable academic buildings include the Bodleian Library (including the New Bodleian, opened 1946, with a capacity of 5 million books), the Divinity School, the Radcliffe Camera, and the Sheldonian Theatre. The university is governed by the Congregation of the University; Convocation, composed of masters and doctors, has a delaying power. Normal business is conducted by the Hebdomadal Council.

oyer and terminer ('hear and determine') judicial circuit established in the 13th century and convening more frequently than the existing ◊eyre. They were established specifically to hear pleas of the crown (cases involving a serious breach of the king's peace), and were often presided over by junior judges or serjeants. They were assimilated into the courts of ◊assizes.

P

Palmerston
British Tory politician Lord Palmerston, a Tory MP for 58 years, 9 of them as prime minister. As foreign secretary, his abrasive style of diplomacy and his arrogance with colleagues earned him the nickname 'Lord Pumice-stone'.
Image Select

page an apprentice ◊knight.

Paine Thomas 1737–1809. English left-wing political writer and revolutionary. He was active in the American and French revolutions. His pamphlet *Common Sense* 1776 ignited passions in the American Revolution; others include *The Rights of Man* 1791 and *The Age of Reason* 1793. He advocated republicanism, deism, the abolition of slavery, and the emancipation of women.

Paine fought for the colonists in the revolution and was indicted for treason 1792. He escaped to France, to represent Calais in the National Convention. Narrowly escaping the guillotine, he regained his seat after the fall of Robespierre. Paine returned to the USA 1802 and died in New York.

Paisley Ian (Richard Kyle) 1926–   . Northern Ireland politician and cleric, leader of the Democratic Unionist Party from 1972. A member of the Northern Ireland parliament from 1969 and the European Parliament since 1979, he has represented North Antrim in the House of Commons since 1974. An almost fanatical loyalist, he resigned his Commons seat 1985 in protest against the ◊Anglo-Irish Agreement, but returned 1986 to continue his opposition to closer co-operation with the South. His blunt and forthright manner, stentorian voice, and pugnaciousness are hallmarks of his political career.

Pale see ◊English Pale.

Palestine former British mandate, southwest Asia. The territory was conquered by the British under Allenby 1917 and assigned as a British mandate 1920, becoming effective 1923. It received many Jewish immigrants as a result of the Balfour Declaration 1917, expressing British support for the setting up of a national home for Jews in Palestine. Following the reversal of British policy 1939 and an increase in Jewish immigrants before and after World War II, it became the scene of conflicts between Jews and Arabs. The British mandate was abolished 1948, when the territory was divided into the State of Israel and the western part of the Kingdom of Jordan.

Palmerston Henry John Temple, 3rd Viscount Palmerston 1784–1865. British politician. He was prime minister 1855–58 (when he rectified Aberdeen's mismanagement of the Crimean War, suppressed the ◊Indian Mutiny, and carried through the Second Opium War) and 1859–65 (when he almost involved Britain in the American Civil War on the side of the South). Initially a Tory, in Parliament from 1807, he was secretary-at-war 1809–28. He broke with the Tories 1830 and sat in the Whig cabinets of 1830–34, 1835–41, and 1846–51 as foreign secretary.

Pankhurst Emmeline (born Goulden) 1858–1928. English suffragette. Founder of the Women's Social and Political Union 1903, she launched the militant suffragette campaign 1905. She joined the Conservative Party 1926 and was a prospective Parliamentary candidate.

She was supported by her daughters **Christabel Pankhurst** (1880–1958), political leader of the movement, and **Sylvia Pankhurst** (1882–1960). The latter was imprisoned nine times under the 'Cat and Mouse Act', and was a pacifist in World War I.

Paris Matthew *c.* 1200–1259. English chronicler. He entered St Albans Abbey 1217, and wrote a valuable history of England up to 1259.

parish subdivision of a county often coinciding with an original territorial subdivision in Christian church administration, served by a parish church. The origins of the parish lie in early medieval Italian cities, and by the 12th century, most of Christian Europe was divided into parishes. The parish has frequently been the centre of community life, especially in rural areas.

Parish registers were instituted in England by Thomas Cromwell 1538, as a record of christenings, burials, and marriages in each parish. Similar orders were made for baptisms from 1552, and for burials 1565. The orders reflect the desire of both Catholic and Protestant churches to monitor the life and behaviour of their parishioners.

Parisii British tribe in Yorkshire. They were conquered by the Romans *c.* AD 70 and probably became a ◊*civitas*, with their capital at Petuaria, possibly modern Brough on Humber. They are known for their cart-burials.

Park Mungo 1771–1806. Scottish explorer who traced the course of the Niger River 1795–97. He published *Travels in the Interior of Africa* 1799. He disappeared and probably drowned during a second African expedition 1805–06. Even though he did not achieve his goal of reaching Timbuktu, he proved that it was feasible to travel through the interior of Africa.

Parker Matthew 1504–1575. English cleric. He was converted to Protestantism at Cambridge University. He received high preferment under Henry VIII and Edward VI, and as archbishop of Canterbury from 1559 was largely responsible for the Elizabethan religious settlement (the formal establishment of the Church of England).

parliament (French 'speaking') legislative body of a country. Parliament is the supreme British legislative body, comprising the ◊*House of Commons* and the ◊*House of Lords*. The origins of Parliament are in the 13th century, usually dated from 1265, but its powers were not established until the late 17th century. The powers of the Lords were curtailed 1911, and the duration of parliaments was fixed at five years, but any parliament may extend its own life, as happened during both world wars. The UK Parliament meets in the Palace of Westminster, London.

Parliament originated under the Norman kings as the Great Council of royal tenants-in-chief, to which in the 13th century representatives of the shires were sometimes summoned. The Parliament summoned by Simon de Montfort 1265 (as head of government in the Barons' War) set a precedent by including representatives of the boroughs as well as the shires. Under Edward III the burgesses and knights of the shires began to meet separately from the barons, thus forming the House of Commons.

By the 15th century Parliament had acquired the right to legislate, vote, and appropriate supplies, examine public accounts, and impeach royal ministers. The powers of Parliament were much diminished under the Yorkists and Tudors but under Elizabeth I a new spirit of independence appeared. The revolutions of 1640 and 1688 established parliamentary control over the executive and judiciary, and finally abolished all royal claim to tax or legislate without parliamentary consent. During these struggles the two great parties (Whig and Tory) emerged, and after 1688 it became customary for the sovereign to choose ministers from the party dominant in the Commons. The English Parliament was united with the Scottish 1707, and with the Irish 1801–1922. The ◊franchise was extended to the middle classes 1832, to the urban working classes 1867, to agricultural labourers 1884, and to women 1918 and 1928. The duration of parliaments was fixed at three years 1694, at seven 1716, and at five 1911. Payment of MPs was introduced 1911. A *public bill* that has been passed is an ◊act of Parliament.

Parliament, European governing body of the European Union (formerly the European Community); see ◊European Parliament.

Parliament, Houses of building where the UK legislative assembly meets. The present Houses of Parliament in London, designed in Gothic Revival style by the architects Charles Barry and Augustus Pugin, were built 1840–60, the previous building having burned down 1834. It incorporates portions of the medieval Palace of Westminster.

The Commons debating chamber was destroyed by incendiary bombs 1941: the rebuilt chamber (opened 1950) is the work of architect Giles Gilbert Scott and preserves its former character.

Parliament Act 1911 statute severely curtailing the power of the the House of Lords and asserting the primacy of the House of Commons. The law, introduced after the Lords rejected

As the Roman, in the days of old, held himself free from indignity when he could say Civis Romanus sum, so also a British subject in whatever land he may be, shall feel confident that the watchful eye and the strong arm of England will protect him against injustice and wrong.

VISCOUNT PALMERSTON
speech, June 1850

Is not a woman's life, is not her health, are not her limbs more valuable than panes of glass? There is no doubt of that, but most important of all, does not the breaking of glass produce more effect upon the Government?

EMMELINE PANKHURST
speech, 16 February 1912

The British, being brought up on team games, enter the House of Commons in the spirit of those who would rather be doing something else.

PARLIAMENT
Cyril Northcote Parkinson, Parkinson's Law

Lloyd George's radical ◊People's Budget 1909, prohibited the Lords from interfering with financial legislation and abolished their power to reject other types of legislation passed by the Commons, restricting them to delaying it for up to 2 years. The law also reduced the maximum life of a parliament from 7 years to 5.

The act was fiercely resisted and only received the Lords' assent when George V agreed to create sufficient Liberal peers to force it through. A second Parliament Act 1949, further limiting the period the Lords could delay legislation to a year, was also strongly opposed and was eventually passed without the Lords' assent under the terms of the 1911 act.

parliamentary reform acts 1918, 1928, and 1971 acts of Parliament. The 19th century witnessed the gradual reform of the voting system in Britain and suffrage was extended in the 20th century. In 1918 the Representation of the People Act gave the vote in the UK to men over 21 years and to women over 30. In 1928 a further act gave women the vote from the age of 21. In 1971 the voting age for men and women was lowered to the age of 18.

Parnell Charles Stewart 1846–1891. Irish nationalist politician. Parnell, born in County Wicklow, was elected member of Parliament for Meath 1875. He supported a policy of obstruction and violence to attain ◊Home Rule, and became the president of the Nationalist Party 1877. In 1879 he approved the ◊Land League, and his attitude led to his imprisonment 1881. He welcomed Gladstone's Home Rule Bill, and continued his agitation after its defeat 1886. In 1887 his reputation suffered from an unfounded accusation by *The Times* of complicity in the murder of Lord Frederick ◊Cavendish, chief secretary to the Lord-lieutenant of Ireland. His career was ruined 1890 when he was cited as co-respondent in a divorce case.

Parr Catherine 1512–1548. Sixth wife of Henry VIII of England. She had already lost two husbands when she married Henry VIII 1543. She survived him, and in 1547 married Lord Seymour of Sudeley (1508–1549).

Parsons Charles Algernon 1854–1931. English engineer who invented the Parsons steam turbine 1884, a landmark in marine engineering and later universally used in electricity generation to drive an alternator.

Passchendaele, Battle of in World War I, successful but costly British operation to capture the Passchendaele ridge in western Flanders, part of the third battle of ◊Ypres Oct–Nov 1917; British casualties numbered nearly 400,000. The name is often erroneously applied to the whole of the battle of Ypres, but Passchendaele was in fact just part of that battle.

The ridge, some 60 m/200 ft high, had been captured and fortified by the Germans Oct 1914. It was a vital strategic gain as it gave them command of the Allied lines. Hence, its capture was an important target of the British strategy during the third battle of Ypres, despite the strong resistance offered by the German defenders. It was re-taken by the Germans March 1918 and recovered again by the Belgians Oct 1918.

Paston family a family of Norfolk, England, whose correspondence and documents (known as the Paston letters) for 1422–1509 throw valuable light on the period.

Patay, Battle of during the Hundred Years' War, French victory led by Joan of Arc over the English 19 June 1429 at the village of Patay, 21 km/13 mi northwest of Orléans.

Joan of Arc was continuing her determined resistance, forcing the English to send an army to reinforce their siege of ◊Orléans. Led by Sir John Talbot, Earl of Shrewsbury, they reached Patay to discover that the English army mounting the siege had been driven off and their commander, the Earl of Suffolk, taken prisoner. The French fell on the English before they could disperse into a fighting formation and Talbot was taken prisoner. The English advance guard scattered, but the main body were able to make an orderly retreat back toward Paris.

patent rolls records of royal grants of privileges or office made under the ◊Great Seal from 1201. Most important administrative acts were recorded in this way, but by the later Middle Ages patent rolls were used only for more formal decisions, such as the creation of peerages or royal appointments. They are still maintained but patents for inventions are held by the Post Office.

Pathfinder Force in World War II, special RAF force of highly experienced and skilled bomber crews carrying the best navigational equipment and used to find and mark targets for the main bombing forces.

Patrick, St 389–*c.* 461. Patron saint of Ireland. Born in Britain, probably in South Wales, he was carried off by pirates to six years' slavery in Antrim, Ireland, before escaping either to Britain or Gaul – his poor Latin suggests the former – to train as a missionary. He is variously said to have landed again in Ireland 432 or 456, and his work was a vital factor in the spread of Christian influence there. His symbols are snakes and shamrocks; feast day 17 March.

patronage the power to give a favoured appointment to an office or position in politics, business, or the church. Patronage was for centuries bestowed mainly by individuals (in Europe often royal or noble) or by the church.

In Britain, where it was nicknamed 'Old Corruption', patronage existed in the 16th century, but was most common from the Restoration of 1660 to the 19th century, when it was used to manage elections and ensure party support. Patronage was used not only for the preferment of friends, but

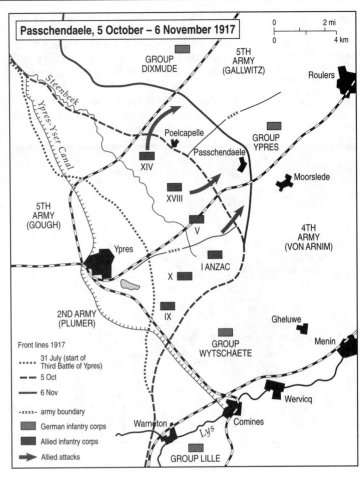

also as a means of social justice, often favouring, for example, the families of those in adversity. Political patronage has largely been replaced by a system of meritocracy (in which selection is by open competition rather than by personal recommendation).

Patronage survives today in the political honours system (awards granted to party supporters) and the appointment of university professors, leaders of national corporations, and government bodies or quangos, which is often by invitation rather than by formal application.

Paulinus d. 644. Roman missionary to Britain who joined St ◊Augustine in Kent 601. He was made a bishop 625 and went to Northumbria where he succeeded in converting King Edwin and his court 627. He became the first archbishop of York 633 but following Edwin's death later in the year fled back to Kent where he was made bishop of Rochester. Excavations 1978 revealed a church he built in Lincoln.

Peace Pledge Union pacifist movement founded 1936 by Canon Dick Sheppard (1880–1937). It grew rapidly in the late 1930s, attracting support from Bertrand Russell and the pacifist writer Vera Brittain, and by 1940 had a membership of about 140,000. Support rapidly fell away after the German invasion of the Low Countries and France.

Pearse Patrick Henry 1879–1916. Irish poet and nationalist. He was prominent in the Gaelic revival, a leader of the ◊Easter Rising 1916. Proclaimed president of the provisional government, he was court-martialled and shot after its suppression.

Peasants' Revolt the rising of the English peasantry in June 1381, the result of economic, social, and political disillusionment. Following the plague of the Black Death, a shortage of agricultural workers led to higher wages. The ◊Statute of Labourers, enacted 1351, attempted to return wages to pre-plague levels. The immediate course of the revolt was the imposition of a new poll tax, three times the rates of those imposed in 1377 and 1379. When this tax was

Passchendaele,
5 October –
6 November 1917
In a year of disasters for the Allies, Sir Hubert Gough's failure to break the German lines around Ypres was one of the bitterest British disappointments of World War I. Plumer's dramatic preliminary capture of Messines Ridge, south of Warneton, had suggested that the right tactics had at last been found, but around Ypres the British attack bogged down in the Flanders mud. The capture of Passchendaele only brought home the truth that the strategic horizon had again closed in to a few miles of bloodsoaked ground.

enforced 1381, riots broke out all over England, especially in Essex and Kent. Led by Wat ◊Tyler and John ◊Ball the rebels went on to London, where they continued plundering, burning John of Gaunt's palace at the Savoy, and taking the prisons at Newgate and Fleet. The young king Richard II attempted to appease the mob, who demanded an end to serfdom and feudalism. The rebels then took the Tower of London and murdered Archbishop Sudbury and Robert Hales. Again the king attempted to make peace at Smithfield, but Tyler was stabbed to death by William Walworth, the Lord Mayor of London. The king made concessions to the rebels, and they dispersed, but the concessions were revoked immediately and the remaining rebels were dealt with by force.

Peel Robert 1788–1850. British Conservative politician. Peel, born in Lancashire, entered Parliament as a Tory 1809. As home secretary 1822–27 and 1828–30, he founded the modern police force and in 1829 introduced Roman Catholic emancipation. He was prime minister 1834–35 and 1841–46, when his repeal of the ◊Corn Laws caused him and his followers to break with the party.

After the passing of the Reform Bill of 1832, which he had resisted, he reformed the Tories under the name of the Conservative Party, on a basis of accepting necessary changes and seeking middle-class support. He fell from prime ministerial office because his repeal of the Corn Laws 1846 was opposed by the majority of his party. He and his followers then formed a third party standing between the Liberals and Conservatives; the majority of the Peelites, including Gladstone, subsequently joined the Liberals.

peel tower or ***tower house*** Scottish fortified building comprising a main tower surrounded by an enclosure for livestock ('peel'), designed as protection against cross-border cattle raids.

> *[Peel's smile is] like the silver plate on a coffin.*
>
> ROBERT PEEL
> *Daniel O'Connell*
> *(attributed)*

Pelagius 360–420. British theologian. He taught that each person possesses free will (and hence the possibility of salvation), denying Augustine's doctrines of predestination and original sin. The Roman Catholic Church officially banned the teaching, which denied original sin and granted salvation to unbaptized infants. Pelagianism is optimistic about human nature and opposed to Manichaeism, which encouraged moral pessimism. Cleared of heresy by a synod in Jerusalem 415, was later condemned by the pope and the emperor.

penal code series of anti-Catholic laws introduced by the Dublin parliament 1695–1727 in defiance of the Treaty of ◊Limerick. Catholics were deprived of the franchise, barred from sitting in parliament or holding office, prevented from buying land from Protestants, and excluded from entry to higher education and the professions. The measures were gradually repealed in the late 18th century, although Catholics were not allowed to sit in parliament until the ◊Catholic emancipation of 1829.

Penda c. 577–654. King of Mercia, an Anglo-Saxon kingdom in England, from about 632. He raised Mercia to a powerful kingdom, and defeated and killed two Northumbrian kings, ◊Edwin 632 and ◊Oswald 642. He was killed in battle by ◊Oswy, king of Northumbria.

> *They are fine people. The roads swarmed with armed peasants; every man would be a soldier. If Spain is subdued it will not be the fault of her people.*
>
> PENINSULAR WAR
> *George Jackson, a veteran of the war, Diary 1880*

Peninsular War 1808–14 war caused by the French emperor Napoleon's invasion of Portugal and Spain (the Iberian Peninsula). The Spanish rebelled against Napoleon's installation of his brother Joseph as a puppet king of Spain and a British expeditionary force under Sir Arthur Wellesley (Duke of ◊Wellington), combined with Spanish and Portuguese resistance, succeeded in defeating the French at Vimeiro 1808, Talavera 1809, Salamanca 1812, and Vittoria 1813. The results were inconclusive, and the war was ended by Napoleon's abdication.

Penn William 1644–1718. English member of the Society of Friends (Quakers), born in London. He joined the Society 1667, and in 1681 obtained a grant of land in America (in settlement of a debt owed by the king to his father) on which he established the colony of Pennsylvania as a refuge for persecuted Quakers.

Penn made religious tolerance a cornerstone of his administration of the colony. He maintained good relations with neighbouring colonies and with the Indians in the area, but his utopian ideals were not successful for the most part. In 1697 he presented a plan, never acted upon, for a union among the colonies. In 1701 he established, with his Charter of Privileges, a bicameral legislature as the government for Pennsylvania.

Pennsylvania former British colony in North America; see ◊Thirteen Colonies.

penny basic coin of English currency from about the 6th century, apparently named after Penda, king of Mercia. The penny was the only coin in general circulation until the 13th century and was defined in terms of a pound (libra) of silver, the equivalent of 240 pennies. One side showed the king's head, the other displayed the mark of the mint. See also ◊gold penny.

penny post first pre-paid postal service, introduced 1840. Until then, postage was paid by the recipient according to the distance travelled. Rowland Hill of Shrewsbury suggested a new service which would be paid for by the sender of the letter or package according to its weight. The *Penny Black* stamp was introduced May 1840, and bore the sovereign's portrait in the manner of coins.

Penruddock's Rising failed royalist rising in Wiltshire March 1655, led by Col Penruddock who, with 200 followers, entered Salisbury and seized members of the judiciary. The revolt was swiftly crushed, its leaders executed, and martial law under the ◊major-generals imposed throughout the country.

People's Budget the Liberal government's budget of 1909 to finance social reforms and naval rearmament. The chancellor of the Exchequer David Lloyd George proposed graded and increased income tax and a 'supertax' on high incomes. The budget aroused great debate and precipitated a constitutional crisis.

The People's Budget was passed in the House of Commons but rejected by the House of Lords. The prime minister Herbert Henry Asquith denounced the House of Lords for a breach of the constitution over the finance bill and obtained the dissolution of Parliament. The Liberals were returned to power in the general election of 1910 and passed the 1911 ◊Parliament Act, greatly reducing the power of the House of Lords.

People's Charter the key document of ◊Chartism, a movement for reform of the British political system in the 1830s. It was used to mobilize working-class support following the restricted extension of the franchise specified by the 1832 Reform Act. It was drawn up in Feb 1837. The campaign failed but within 70 years four of its six objectives, universal male suffrage, abolition of property qualifications for members of Parliament, payment of MPs, and voting by secret ballot had been realized.

Pepys Samuel 1633–1703. English diarist. His diary 1659–69 was a unique record of both the daily life of the period and his own intimate feelings. Written in shorthand, it was not deciphered until 1825.

Born in London, he entered the navy office 1660, and was secretary to the Admiralty 1672–79. Pepys was imprisoned 1679 in the Tower of London on suspicion of being connected with the ◊Popish Plot. He was reinstated 1684 but finally deprived of his post after the 1688 Revolution, for suspected disaffection. He published *Memoires of the Navy* 1690.

Perceval Spencer 1762–1812. British Tory politician. He became chancellor of the Exchequer 1807 and prime minister 1809. He was shot in the lobby of the House of Commons 1812 by a merchant who blamed government measures for his bankruptcy.

Percy family name of dukes of Northumberland; seated at Alnwick Castle, Northumberland, England.

Percy Henry, 1st Earl of Northumberland 1342–1408. Warden of the Scottish marches. He captured Berwick 1378 and was victorious at Homildon Hill 1402. He led a rebellion 1403 against Henry IV, in which his son, the 4th Earl of Northumberland, was killed, and joined an alliance 1405 with Edmund de Mortimer and Owen Glendower against the king. He was obliged to flee to Scotland, but later invaded England and died on the field at Bramham Moor 1408.

It is a reproach to religion and government to suffer so much poverty and excess.

WILLIAM PENN
Reflexions and Maxims
part 1, no. 52

Percy Henry 'Hotspur', 4th Earl of Northumberland 1364–1403. English soldier, son of the 1st Earl of Northumberland. He made his name as a soldier in France and was nicknamed Hotspur for his bravery and impetuousness. In repelling a border raid, he defeated the Scots at ◊Homildon Hill in Durham 1402. He supported Henry Bolingbroke's claim to the throne 1399 but joined his father's rebellion against the king (Henry IV) 1403. He was killed at Shrewsbury 1403.

Peter's pence in the Roman Catholic Church, a voluntary annual contribution to papal administrative costs; during the 10th–16th centuries it was a compulsory levy of one penny per household.

Peterborough Charles Mordaunt, 3rd Earl of Peterborough 1658–1735. English military commander and diplomat. He was a leading supporter of William II and was made First Lord of the Treasury 1689. He commanded an Anglo-Dutch force in the War of the Spanish Succession and won an impressive series of victories in Spain 1705–07, including the capture of Barcelona 1705.

Peterloo massacre the events in St Peter's Fields, Manchester, 16 Aug 1819, when an open-air meeting in support of parliamentary reform was charged by yeomanry and hussars. Eleven people were killed and 500 wounded. The name was given in ironic reference to the Battle of Waterloo.

Petillius Cerialis Quintus d. *c.* AD 74. Roman governor of Britain AD 71–74. After defeating the Brigantes, he established the IX Legion at ◊Eboracum (York) as the chief Roman garrison in the north of England.

petition of right the procedure under which a subject petitioned for legal relief against the Crown, for example for money due under a contract, or for property of which the Crown had taken possession. Parliament presented a petition of right to Charles I 1628 which he accepted, declaring illegal taxation without parliamentary consent, imprisonment without trial, billeting of soldiers on private persons, and use of martial law. The procedure was abolished by the Crown Proceedings Act 1947.

petitioners supporters of the 1st Earl of Shaftesbury, who petitioned Charles II to call the parliament elected Aug 1679 but suspended until Oct 1680. They supported the proposed ◊Exclusion Bill to prevent a Catholic succession to the throne The petitioners were eventually to become the Whigs, and their opponents, the Abhorrers, so called because they objected to interference with the king's prerogative to summon a parliament, were to became known as the Tories.

Peterloo massacre
Hussars charged the pro-reform crowd at St Peter's Fields, Manchester, 16 August 1819. The image of official violence against British citizens (11 were killed and hundreds injured) was particularly damaging in a society which prided itself on its avoidance of the horrors of Revolutionary France.
E T Archive

petty schools type of school existing in the 16th and 17th centuries to give a basic education in reading, writing and arithmetic to children before they entered grammar school. The pupils were called 'petties'. The first part of Charles Hoole's *New Discovery of the Old Art of Teaching Schools*, published 1660, is entitled *The Petty School* and deals with the education of children aged five to eight. The schools themselves were usually of a low standard.

Philby Kim (Harold) 1912–1988. British intelligence officer from 1940 and Soviet agent from 1933. He was liaison officer in Washington 1949–51, when he was confirmed to be a double agent and asked to resign. Named in 1963 as having warned Guy Burgess and Donald Maclean (similarly double agents) that their activities were known, he fled to the USSR and became a Soviet citizen and general in the KGB. A fourth member of the ring was Anthony ◊Blunt.

Philip II 1527–1598. King of Spain from 1556. He was born at Valladolid, the son of the Habsburg emperor Charles V, and in 1554 married Queen Mary of England. On his father's abdication 1556 he inherited Spain, the Netherlands, and the Spanish possessions in Italy and the Americas, and in 1580 he annexed Portugal. His intolerance and lack of understanding of the Netherlanders drove them into revolt. Political and religious differences combined to involve him in war with England and, after 1589, with France. The defeat of the ◊Spanish Armada (the fleet sent to invade England in 1588) marked the beginning of the decline of Spanish power.

Phoenix Park Murders the murder of several prominent members of the British government in Phoenix Park, Dublin 6 May 1882. The murders threatened the cooperation between the Liberal government and the Irish nationalist members at Westminster which had been secured by the ◊Kilmainham Treaty.

The murders began with the stabbing of Thomas Burke, the permanent under-secretary for Ireland and Lord Frederick Cavendish, chief secretary to the viceroy. A murderous campaign was continued by the Irish National Invincibles until some members turned 'Queen's evidence'.

phoney war the period in World War II between Sept 1939, when the Germans had occupied Poland, and April 1940, when the invasions of Denmark and Norway took place. During this time there were few signs of hostilities in Western Europe; indeed, Hitler made some attempts to arrange a peace settlement with Britain and France.

Picquigny, Treaty of signed 29 Aug 1475, treaty between Edward IV of England and Louis XI of France, in which Edward agreed to withdraw his troops in return for payment of a lump sum at the time and a regular annual pension thereafter. Edward had landed at Calais to mount an invasion of France, but discovered he would not receive the support he had expected from his Burgundian allies. The payment of the pension in the 16th century was the last trace of the English Crown's claim to France.

Pict Roman term for a member of the peoples of north Scotland, possibly meaning 'painted' (tattooed). Of pre-Celtic origin, and speaking a Celtic language which died out in about the 10th century, the Picts are thought to have inhabited much of England before the arrival of the Celtic Britons. They were united with the Celtic Scots under the rule of Kenneth MacAlpin 844. Their greatest monument is a series of carved stones, whose symbols remain undeciphered.

piepowder courts (French pieds poudré, 'dusty feet') medieval courts which regulated fairs, markets, or seaports. The name is most likely a reference to the dusty feet of travellers coming to these venues.

pilgrimage journey to sacred places inspired by religious devotion. The three major centres of pilgrimage in medieval England were Canterbury, Bury (the shrine of St Edmund), and Walsingham, Norfolk. Walsingham is still a site of pilgrimage each Easter.

Pilgrimage of Grace rebellion against Henry VIII of England 1536–37, originating in Yorkshire and Lincolnshire. The uprising was directed against the policies of the monarch (such as the dissolution of the monasteries and the effects of the enclosure of common land).

At the height of the rebellion, the rebels controlled York and included the archbishop there among their number. A truce was arranged Dec 1536 and the rebels dispersed, but their demands were not met, and a further revolt broke out 1537, which was severely suppressed, with the execution of over 200 of the rebels, including the leader, Robert Aske.

Pilgrims' Way track running from Winchester to Canterbury, England, which was the route taken by medieval pilgrims visiting the shrine of St Thomas à Becket. Some 195 km/120 mi long, the Pilgrims' Way can still be traced for most of its length.

pillory former instrument of punishment consisting of a wooden frame set on a post, with holes in which the prisoner's head and hands were secured, similar to the stocks. Bystanders threw whatever was available at the miscreant. Its use was abolished in England 1837.

Pinkie, Battle of 10 Sept 1547, battle near Musselburgh, Lothian, Scotland, in which the Scots under the Earl of Arran were defeated by the English under the Duke of Somerset, protector of England.

pipe rolls records of the Exchequer 1130–1832, which record the sheriff's annual accounts for each county. They form the longest series of public records in England. The term was also used by important ecclesiastics, such as the bishop of Winchester, for estate records.

There is something behind the throne greater than the King himself.

Pitt the Elder
speech, January 1770

Pitt
British Tory politician William Pitt the Younger. He died from overwork while still in office, having served two terms as prime minister for a total period of almost 20 years. His last words were reputedly 'I could just do with one of Bellamy's meat pies'.
Michael Nicholson

Necessity is the plea for every infringement of human freedom. It is the argument of tyrants; it is the creed of slaves.

PITT THE YOUNGER
*speech in the House of Commons,
18 November 1783*

Pitt William, ***the Elder***, 1st Earl of Chatham 1708–1778. British Whig politician, 'the Great Commoner'. Entering Parliament 1735, Pitt led the Patriot faction opposed to the Whig prime minister Robert Walpole and attacked Walpole's successor, Carteret, for his conduct of the War of the Austrian Succession. As paymaster of the forces 1746–55, he broke with tradition by refusing to enrich himself; he was dismissed for attacking the Duke of Newcastle, the prime minister. Recalled by popular demand to form a government on the outbreak of the Seven Years' War 1756, he was forced to form a coalition with Newcastle 1757. A 'year of victories' ensued 1759, and the French were expelled from India and Canada. In 1761 Pitt wished to escalate the war by a declaration of war on Spain, George III disagreed and Pitt resigned, but was again recalled to form an all-party government 1766. He championed the Americans against the king, though rejecting independence, and collapsed during his last speech in the House of Lords – opposing the withdrawal of British troops – and died a month later.

Pitt William, ***the Younger*** 1759–1806. British Tory prime minister 1783–1801 and 1804–06. He raised the importance of the House of Commons, clamped down on corruption, carried

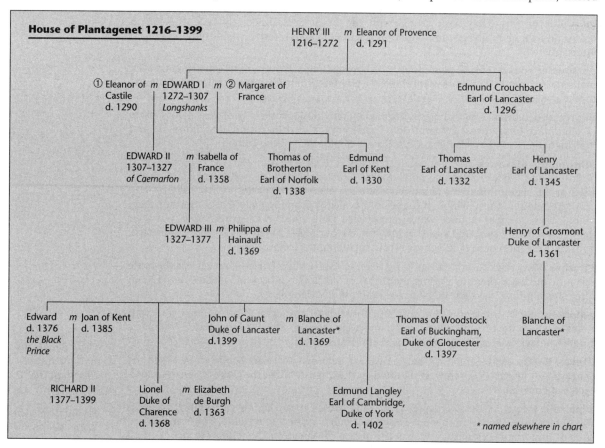

House of Plantagenet 1216–1399

HENRY III
1216–1272 *m* Eleanor of Provence
d. 1291

① Eleanor of *m* EDWARD I *m* ② Margaret of
Castile   1272–1307   France
d. 1290   *Longshanks*

Edmund Crouchback
Earl of Lancaster
d. 1296

EDWARD II *m* Isabella of
1307–1327   France
of Caernarfon d. 1358

Thomas of
Brotherton
Earl of Norfolk
d. 1338

Edmund
Earl of Kent
d. 1330

Thomas
Earl of Lancaster
d. 1332

Henry
Earl of Lancaster
d. 1345

EDWARD III *m* Philippa of
1327–1377   Hainault
d. 1369

Henry of Grosmont
Duke of Lancaster
d. 1361

Edward *m* Joan of Kent
d. 1376   d. 1385
*the Black
Prince*

John of Gaunt *m* Blanche of
Duke of Lancaster   Lancaster*
d.1399   d. 1369

Thomas of Woodstock
Earl of Buckingham,
Duke of Gloucester
d. 1397

Blanche of
Lancaster*

RICHARD II
1377–1399

Lionel *m* Elizabeth
Duke of   de Burgh
Charence   d. 1363
d. 1368

Edmund Langley
Earl of Cambridge,
Duke of York
d. 1402

* named elsewhere in chart

out fiscal reforms, and effected the union with Ireland. He attempted to keep Britain at peace but underestimated the importance of the French Revolution and became embroiled in wars with France from 1793; he died on hearing of Napoleon's victory at Austerlitz.

Son of William Pitt the Elder, he entered Cambridge University at 14 and Parliament at 22. He was the Whig Shelburne's chancellor of the Exchequer 1782–83, and with the support of the Tories and king's friends became Britain's youngest prime minister 1783. He reorganized the country's finances and negotiated reciprocal tariff reduction with France. In 1793, however, the new French republic declared war and England fared badly. Pitt's policy in Ireland led to the 1798 revolt, and he tried to solve the Irish question by the Act of Union 1800, but George III rejected the Catholic emancipation Pitt had promised as a condition, and Pitt resigned 1801. On his return to office 1804, he organized an alliance with Austria, Russia, and Sweden against Napoleon, which was shattered at Austerlitz. In declining health, he died on hearing the news, saying. His last words were reputedly 'I could just do with one of Bellamy's meat pies.'

Place Francis 1771–1854. English Radical. He showed great powers as a political organizer, and made Westminster a centre of pro-labour union Radicalism. He secured the repeal of the anti-union Combination Acts 1824 and campaigned in favour of the Reform Act 1832.

placemen members of Parliament who also held royal office, often sinecures, or were granted royal pensions in return for supporting the Crown. Placemen were a feature of parliamentary life from the reigns of James II and William III but increased greatly with the expansion of Crown patronage in the late 17th century. Acts to prevent the placing of MPs invariably failed.

Plaid Cymru (Welsh 'Party of Wales') Welsh nationalist political party established 1925, dedicated to an independent Wales. In 1966 the first Plaid Cymru member of Parliament was elected.

Plantagenet English royal house, reigning 1154–1399, whose name comes from the nickname of Geoffrey, Count of Anjou (1113–1151), father of Henry II, who often wore in his hat a sprig of broom, *planta genista*. In the 1450s, Richard, Duke of York, took 'Plantagenet' as a surname to emphasize his superior claim to the throne over Henry VI's.

Plantation of Ireland colonization and conquest of Ireland by mainly Presbyterian English and Scottish settlers 1556–1660. There were several rebellions against the plantation by the Irish and the Anglo-Irish aristocracy. The final stages of the conquest took place under Oliver ◊Cromwell.

Plassey, Battle of British victory under Robert ◊Clive over the Nawab of Bengal, Suraj Dowla, 23 June 1757 which brought Bengal under the effective control of the East India Company and hence under British rule. The battle took place at the former

With the loss of twenty-two soldiers killed and fifty wounded, Clive had scattered an army of nearly sixty thousand men, and subdued an empire larger and more populous than Great Britain.

PLASSEY
historian Thomas Babington Macaulay,
Life and Works, *1897*

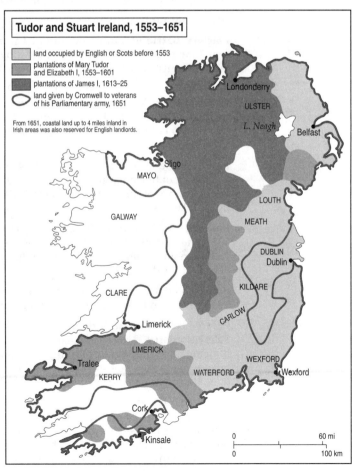

Tudor and Stuart Ireland, 1553–1651

land occupied by English or Scots before 1553
plantations of Mary Tudor and Elizabeth I, 1553–1601
plantations of James I, 1613–25
land given by Cromwell to veterans of his Parliamentary army, 1651

From 1651, coastal land up to 4 miles inland in Irish areas was also reserved for English landlords.

Londonderry
ULSTER
L. Neagh
Belfast
Sligo
MAYO
LOUTH
GALWAY
MEATH
DUBLIN
Dublin
KILDARE
CLARE
CARLOW
Limerick
LIMERICK
WEXFORD
Tralee
WATERFORD
Wexford
KERRY
Cork
Kinsale

0   60 mi
0   100 km

Tudor and Stuart Ireland, 1553–1651
English and Scottish colonization of Ireland increased dramatically under the Tudors and early Stuarts, in parallel with colonization of the New World. It was under Cromwell, however, that the whole of Ireland was finally brought under English control. Irish landholding was restricted to Galway and Clare after 1651, and Irish and royalist Old English landlords alike were dispossessed throughout the remainder of the island.

village of Plassey, about 150 km/95 mi north of Calcutta. Suraj had taken Calcutta 1756 and carried out the notorious atrocity of the Black Hole of Calcutta.

Although outnumbered, Clive won the battle with minimal losses through Suraj's impetuous squandering of his advantage in an all-out bombardment which exhausted his ammunition. Clive used the support of his Indian banker allies to buy the defection of Suraj's general Mir Jafar, who he then installed as nawab.

Plumer Hubert Charles Onslow, 1st Baron 1857–1932. British major-general in World War I. Plumer spent much of the war on the Western Front around the Ypres area, scene of much heavy fighting. He was responsible for the planning and execution of the attack on Messines 1917, generally considered to be one of the best organized British operations of the war.

He was highly popular with his troops (who referred to him as 'Daddy') as he planned carefully, organized meticulously, and generally executed his plans at far less cost in lives than any of his contemporaries could have managed. After the Armistice he marched his army to the Rhine as part of the forces of occupation. He was made a field-marshal and created a baron 1919, and was appointed governor of Malta.

Plunket St Oliver 1629–1681. Catholic archbishop of Armagh and Primate of Ireland. He was executed, along with 30 or more other victims, in panic surrounding the fictitious Popish Plot to murder Charles II, burn London, and put the Catholic James II on the throne. He was canonized 1976.

Plunket William Conyngham Plunket, 1st Baron Plunket 1764–1854. Irish politician. He became an MP in the Irish parliament 1798 and opposed the union with Britain. Despite this, he accepted the post of Solicitor General 1803 and that of Attorney General 1805. He became an MP at Westminster 1807 and from 1812 made impassioned speeches urging Catholic emancipation. He was Lord Chancellor of Ireland 1830–41.

pocket borough alternative name for a ◊rotten borough.

Poitiers, Battle of during the Hundred Years' War, victory for Edward the Black Prince 13 Sept 1356 over King John II of France. King John, his son Philip, and 2,000 knights were taken prisoner, and about 3,000 French were killed.

Pole Edmund de la, Earl of Suffolk *c.* 1472–1513. English Yorkist. He lived at court in the favour of Henry VII until 1499 when he fled abroad following an indictment for murder. He was persauded to return but fled again to the Continent 1501. He was handed over to Henry VII 1506 by Philip, Archduke of Burgundy, imprisoned in the Tower, and executed by Henry VIII 1513.

Pole John de la, Earl of Lincoln *c.* 1464–1487. English heir to the throne. He was Lord Lieutenant of Ireland from 1484 and named as heir to Richard III. He supported the conspiracy of Lambert Simnel following Henry VII's seizure of the crown 1485 and was killed in battle at Stoke 1487.

Pole Michael de la, 1st Earl of Suffolk d. 1389. Adviser to Richard II. He became Chancellor 1383 and Earl of Suffolk 1385. He was impeached 1386 for corruption and imprisoned. Richard restored him to power but the threat of a treason charge 1387 forced him to flee to France. He died in exile.

Pole Richard de la d. 1525. Yorkist pretender to the English throne. He was forced into exile by Henry VII and died fighting for Francis I of France at the battle of Pavia 1525.

Pole William de la, 4th Earl and 1st Duke of Suffolk 1396–1450. Grandson of Michael de la Pole. He negotiated Henry VI's marriage with Margaret of Anjou 1445 and was instrumental in bringing about the disgrace of Humphrey, Duke of Gloucester 1447. He was created duke 1448 but was impeached 1450 after ceding Anjou and Maine to France and banished from the kingdom. His ship was seized by his enemies off Dover and he was assassinated at sea 1450.

police civil law-and-order force. In the UK it is responsible to the Home Office, with 56 autonomous police forces, generally organized on a county basis; mutual aid is given in circumstances such as mass picketing in the 1984–85 miners' strike, but there is no national police force or police riot unit (such as the French CRS riot squad). The predecessors of these forces were the ineffective medieval watch and London's ◊Bow Street Runners, introduced

1749 by Henry Fielding which formed a model for the London police force established by Robert ◊Peel's government 1829 (hence 'peelers' or 'bobbies'); the system was introduced throughout the country from 1856.

Landmarks include: ***Criminal Investigation Department*** (CID) detective branch of the London Metropolitan Police (New Scotland Yard) 1878, recruited from the uniformed branch (such departments now exist in all UK forces); women police 1919; motorcycle patrols 1921; two-way radio cars 1927; personal radio on the beat 1965; and ***Special Patrol Groups*** (SPG) 1970, squads of experienced officers concentrating on a specific problem (New York has the similar Tactical Patrol Force). Unlike most other police forces, the British are armed only on special occasions, but the arms are issued to officers increasingly frequently.

poll tax form of tax levied on every individual, without reference to income or property. Being simple to administer, it was among the earliest sorts of tax (introduced in England 1379), but because of its indiscriminate nature (it is a regressive tax, in that it falls proportionately more on poorer people) it has often proved unpopular. The poll tax of 1379 contributed to the ◊Peasants' Revolt of 1381 and was abolished in England 1698.

The ***community charge***, a type of poll tax, was introduced in Scotland by the British government April 1989, and in England and Wales 1990, replacing the property-based local taxation (the rates). Its unpopularity led to its replacement 1993–94 by a council tax, based both on property values and on the size of households.

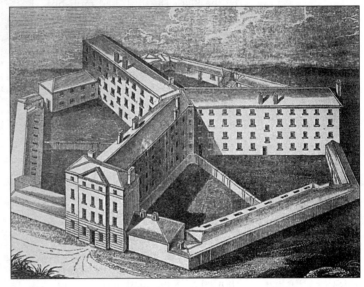

poor laws
Design for a model workhouse 1834, the year workhouses were introduced under the Poor Law Amendment Act. The prison-like conditions were meant to induce a sense of shame in the inmates and deter all but the most needy.
Image Select

poor laws English system for poor relief, established by the Poor Relief Act 1601. Each parish was responsible for its own poor, paid for by a parish tax. The care of the poor was transferred to the Ministry of Health 1918, but the poor law remained in force until 1930.

Poor law was reformed in the 19th century. After the Royal Commission on the Poor Law 1834, 'outdoor' relief for able-bodied paupers was abolished and replaced by ◊workhouses run by unions of parishes. Conditions in such workhouses were designed to act as a deterrent for all but the genuinely destitute, but the Andover workhouse scandal 1847 removed some of the greatest corruptions and evils of the system.

The various poor laws included:

Poor Law Act 1601 codified earlier Tudor legislation, for example, the powers of job creation and chastisement within some 15,000 parishes given to Overseers of the Poor 1598 were extended. By this time, it was gradually accepted that there were other causes of vagrancy (or unemployment) than personal idleness. The measure remained a backbone of social legislation till the 19th century.

Poor Law Act 1723 established workhouses to provide for commercial exploitation of the poor. Those who refused to enter could be punished, even if it meant breaking up families.

Poor Law Amendment Act 1834 required inmates of workhouses to be paid below the lowest market rates; curtailed outdoor relief; and replaced the parochial system with 600 Poor Law Boards. The measures were in response to the findings of a royal commission created after complaints from ratepayers about the increasing cost of poor law relief. The commission also found that individual acts of charity increased dependence.

Popish Plot supposed plot to murder Charles II; see under Titus ◊Oates.

Poplarism attempt in 1921 by the London borough of Poplar to force the richer boroughs to assist with poor relief in the East End. George Lansbury, later leader of the Labour Party, was imprisoned for supporting a rates strike but a shared system was eventually introduced.

population the number of people inhabiting a particular country or region. Population figures for Britain before the 19th century are at best approximate. The population of England at the time of the Domesday Book survey 1086 is believed to have been just over 1 million. It may have grown to about 4 million by 1300, but was greatly reduced in the 1340s by the Black Death. It had probably recovered to 4 million by the mid-16th century, thereafter reaching 5 million by 1600 and 6 million by 1700.

The first nationwide census was taken in 1801. It showed a figure of almost 9 million for England and Wales, with 1.6 million in Scotland. By 1851 the population had doubled, with 18 million people in England and Wales and almost 3 million in Scotland. Northern Ireland, not included earlier, had a population of almost 1.5 million, giving a total for the whole UK of over 22 million. This figure had almost doubled again by 1901, with a UK total of 38 million. Population growth since then has been much slower. The 1991 census showed a UK population of 56.5 million. A census is held every 10 years.

United Kingdom Population from 1801 (millions)

year	United Kingdom	England and Wales	Scotland	Northern Ireland
1801	—	8.893	1.608	—
1811	13.368	10.165	1.806	—
1821	15.472	12.000	2.092	—
1831	17.835	13.897	2.364	—
1841	20.183	15.914	2.620	1.649
1851	22.259	17.928	2.889	1.443
1861	24.525	20.066	3.062	1.569
1871	27.431	22.712	3.360	1.359
1881	31.015	25.974	3.736	1.305
1891	34.264	29.003	4.026	1.236
1901	38.237	32.528	4.472	1.237
1911	42.082	36.070	4.761	1.251
1921	44.027	37.887	4.882	1.258
1931	46.038	39.952	4.843	1.243
1951	50.225	43.578	5.096	1.371
1961	52.709	46.105	5.179	1.425
1971	55.515	48.750	5.229	1.536
1981	55.848	49.155	5.131	1.533
1991	56.487	49.890	4.999	1.578

estimated population of England only in earlier years

year	population (millions)
1570	4.160
1600	4.811
1630	5.600
1670	5.773
1700	6.045
1750	6.517

Port Sunlight
Workers' cottages in the garden village of Port Sunlight, the Wirral, NW England. The entire village, with a church, hospital, civil hall, and library, was built by the soap manufacturer and philanthropist William Hesketh Lever and named after Sunlight soap. Lever based his philanthropy on what he called 'enlightened self-interest'.
Unilever

Port Sunlight model village built 1888 by William Lever (1851–1925) for workers at the Lever Brothers (now Unilever) soap factory on the Wirral Peninsula at Birkenhead, near Liverpool, northwest England. Designed for a population of 3,000, and covering an area of 353 ha/130 acres, it includes an art gallery, church, library, and social hall. It is now a part of Bebington, Merseyside.

Porteous riots in Edinburgh 1736 riots after Lieutenant John Porteous, captain of the Edinburgh militia, ordered his men 14 April to open fire on a crowd rioting in protest at the execution of smugglers. Six members of the crowd were killed and Porteous was sentenced to death but was later reprieved. The prison in which Porteous was being held was stormed 8 Sept by an angry mob which dragged him out and lynched him. The city was fined £2,000 and the Lord Provost was dismissed. Walpole lost the crucial support of the Duke of Argyll, who led Scottish peers in the House of Lords, as a result of the affair.

Portland William Bentinck, 1st Earl of Portland 1649–1709. Dutch politician who accompanied William of Orange to England 1688, and was created an earl 1689. He served in several of William's campaigns.

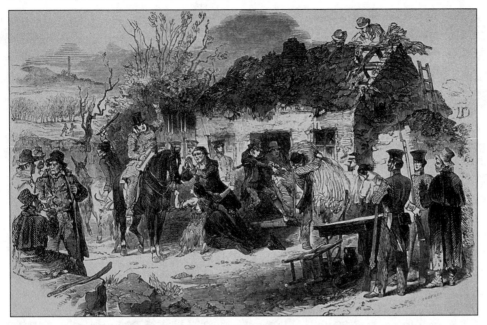

potato famine
Irish peasants being evicted from their cottage at the height of the potato famine. The British government offered minimal relief to the starving, not wishing to interfere in the 'operation of natural causes'.
Image Select

Portland William Henry Cavendish Bentinck, 3rd Duke of Portland 1738–1809. British politician, originally a Whig, who in 1783 became nominal prime minister in the Fox–North coalition government. Initially in opposition to Pitt, during the French Revolution he joined the coalition government, and was prime minister 1807–09.

potato famine in Ireland 1845–48 famine caused by the failure of the potato crop, the staple of the Irish diet. Nearly a million people died from malnutrition-related diseases such as cholera, dysentery and typhus and at least the same number again emigrated, mainly to America. The former Irish population of 8 million had thus fallen by at least 2 million. The famine devastated Ireland for many years after. The British government was slow to provide relief and provoked Irish hostility in consequence.

Potsdam Conference conference held in Potsdam, Germany, 17 July–2 Aug 1945, between representatives of the USA, the UK, and the USSR. They established the political and economic principles governing the treatment of Germany in the initial period of Allied control at the end of World War II, and sent an ultimatum to Japan demanding unconditional surrender on pain of utter destruction.

Pound (Alfred) Dudley Pickman Rogers 1877–1943. British Admiral of the Fleet. As First Sea Lord and chief of the British naval staff 1939–43, he was responsible for the effective measures taken against the German submarine U-boats in World War II.

Powell (John) Enoch 1912– . British Conservative politician. He was an MP for Wolverhampton from 1950 and subsequently a member of the cabinet. He was minister of health 1960–63, and contested the party leadership 1965. In 1968 he made an inflammatory speech against immigration that led to his dismissal from the shadow cabinet. Declining to stand in the Feb 1974 election, he attacked the Heath government and resigned from the Conservative Party. He was Official Unionist Party member for South Down, Northern Ireland 1974–87.

Powys, kingdom of ancient kingdom in Wales, bordering England in the east. It was frequently threatened from the east, and lands in the present English counties of Hereford and Worcester and Shropshire were lost following the incursion of the Mercians in the period leading up to the construction in the late 8th century of Offa's dyke between the two countries. The rulers of Powys often fought those of neighbouring Gwynedd. The last ruler of Powys as an intact kingdom was Madog ap Maredudd. His successors ruled over a Powys divided into north and south. The name was restored for the present county of Powys, formed 1974 from the counties of Breconshire, Montgomeryshire and Radnorshire.

As I look ahead, I am filled with foreboding. Like the Roman, I seem to see 'the River Tiber foaming with much blood'.

ENOCH POWELL
speech at Conservative Political Centre, Birmingham, 20 April 1968

House of Powys 1075–1309

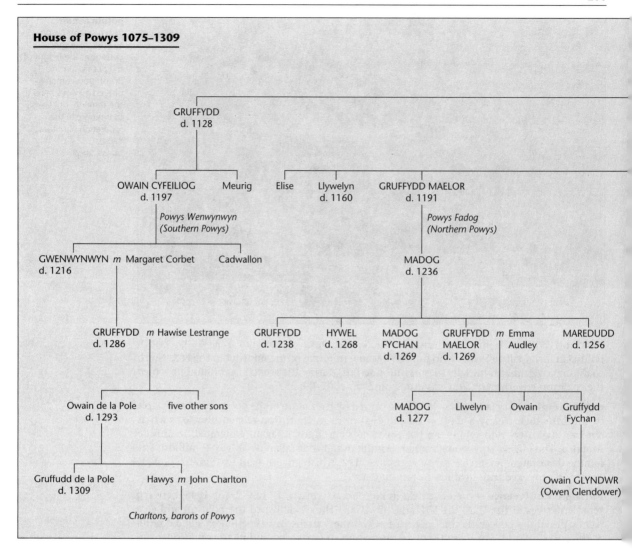

praemunire three English acts of Parliament passed 1353, 1365, and 1393, aimed to prevent appeal to the pope against the power of the king; an early demonstration of independence from Rome. The statutes were opposed by English bishops.

Presbyterianism system of Christian Protestant church government, expounded during the Reformation by John Calvin, which gives its name to the established Church of Scotland, and is also practised in England, Wales, Ireland, Switzerland, North America, and elsewhere. There is no compulsory form of worship and each congregation is governed by presbyters or elders (clerical or lay), who are of equal rank. Congregations are grouped in presbyteries, synods, and general assemblies.

press gang body of men used to recruit soldiers and sailors into the British armed forces in the 18th and early 19th centuries; see ◊impressment.

Preston, Battle of in the Civil War, battle 17–19 Aug 1648 at Preston, Lancashire, in which the English defeated the Scottish supporters of Charles I. The Scots invaded England under the Duke of ◊Hamilton, but were cut off from Scotland by ◊Cromwell and fled in a series of running fights. Hamilton was captured and executed.

Prestonpans, Battle of 1745 battle in which Prince ◊Charles Edward Stuart's Jacobite forces defeated the English in the ◊Forty-Five rebellion. It took place near the town of Prestonpans in

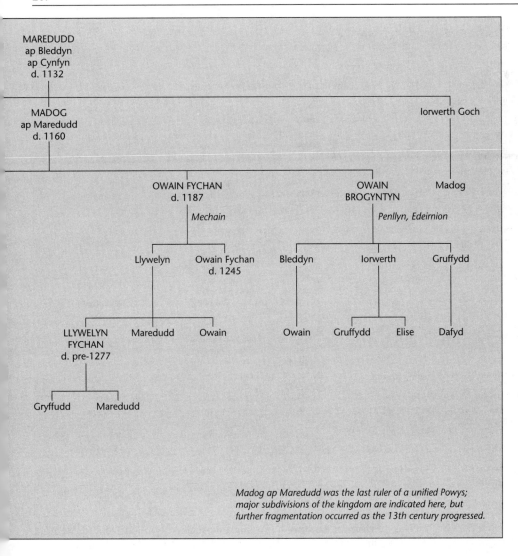

MAREDUDD
ap Bleddyn
ap Cynfyn
d. 1132

MADOG
ap Maredudd
d. 1160

Iorwerth Goch

OWAIN FYCHAN
d. 1187

Mechain

OWAIN
BROGYNTYN

Penllyn, Edeirnion

Madog

Llywelyn

Owain Fychan
d. 1245

Bleddyn

Iorwerth

Gruffydd

LLYWELYN
FYCHAN
d. pre-1277

Maredudd

Owain

Owain

Gruffydd

Elise

Dafyd

Gryffudd

Maredudd

Madog ap Maredudd was the last ruler of a unified Powys; major subdivisions of the kingdom are indicated here, but further fragmentation occurred as the 13th century progressed.

Lothian region, eastern Scotland. Charles' success encouraged him to march south toward London, but he turned back at Derby and was eventually defeated at the Battle of Culloden 1746.

pretender claimant to a throne. The term is widely used to describe the Old Pretender (◊James Edward Stuart) and the Young Pretender (◊Charles Edward Stuart).

Pride's purge the removal of about 100 Royalists and Presbyterians of the English House of Commons from Parliament by a detachment of soldiers led by Col Thomas Pride (d. 1658) in 1648. They were accused of negotiating with Charles I and were seen as unreliable by the army. The remaining members were termed the ◊Rump and voted in favour of the king's trial.

Pride (a former London drayman or brewer who rose to be a colonel in the Parliamentary army) acted as one of the judges at the trial and also signed the king's death warrant. He opposed the plan to make Cromwell king.

priest's hole hiding place, in private homes, for Catholic priests in the 16th–17th centuries when the penal laws against Catholics were in place. Many still exist, for example at Speke Hall, near Liverpool.

prime minister or **_premier_** head of a parliamentary government, usually the leader of the largest party. The first prime minister of Britain is usually considered to have been Robert ◊Walpole, but the office was not officially recognized until 1905.

Once, when a British Prime Minister sneezed, men half a world away would blow their noses. Now when a British Prime Minister sneezes nobody else will even say 'Bless You'.

PRIME MINISTER
journalist Bernard Levin,
The Times *1976*

Prime Ministers of the United Kingdom from 1721

term	name	party	term	name	party
1721–42	Sir Robert Walpole	Whig	1866–68	Earl of Derby	Conservative
1742–43	Earl of Wilmington	Whig	1868	Benjamin Disraeli	Conservative
1743–54	Henry Pelham	Whig	1868–74	W E Gladstone	Liberal
1754–56	Duke of Newcastle	Whig	1874–80	Benjamin Disraeli	Conservative
1756–57	Duke of Devonshire	Whig	1880–85	W E Gladstone	Liberal
1757–62	Duke of Newcastle	Whig	1885–86	Marquess of Salisbury	Conservative
1762–63	Earl of Bute	Tory	1886	W E Gladstone	Liberal
1763–65	George Grenville	Whig	1886–92	Marquess of Salisbury	Conservative
1765–66	Marquess of Rockingham	Whig	1892–94	W E Gladstone	Liberal
1767–70	Duke of Grafton	Whig	1894–95	Earl of Rosebery	Liberal
1770–82	Lord North	Tory	1895–1902	Marquess of Salisbury	Conservative
1782	Marquess of Rockingham	Whig	1902–05	Arthur James Balfour	Conservative
1782–83	Earl of Shelburne	Whig	1905–08	Sir H Campbell-Bannerman	Liberal
1783	Duke of Portland	coalition	1908–15	H H Asquith	Liberal
1783–1801	William Pitt the Younger	Tory	1915–16	H H Asquith	coalition
1801–04	Henry Addington	Tory	1916–22	David Lloyd George	coalition
1804–06	William Pitt the Younger	Tory	1922–23	Andrew Bonar Law	Conservative
1806–07	Lord Grenville	coalition	1923–24	Stanley Baldwin	Conservative
1807–09	Duke of Portland	Tory	1924	Ramsay MacDonald	Labour
1809–12	Spencer Perceval	Tory	1924–29	Stanley Baldwin	Conservative
1812–27	Earl of Liverpool	Tory	1929–31	Ramsay MacDonald	Labour
1827	George Canning	coalition	1931–35	Ramsay MacDonald	national coalition
1827–28	Viscount Goderich	Tory	1935–37	Stanley Baldwin	national coalition
1828–30	Duke of Wellington	Tory	1937–40	Neville Chamberlain	national coalition
1830–34	Earl Grey	Tory	1940–45	Sir Winston Churchill	coalition
1834	Viscount Melbourne	Whig	1945–51	Clement Attlee	Labour
1834–35	Sir Robert Peel	Whig	1951–55	Sir Winston Churchill	Conservative
1835–41	Viscount Melbourne	Whig	1955–57	Sir Anthony Eden	Conservative
1841–46	Sir Robert Peel	Conservative	1957–63	Harold Macmillan	Conservative
1846–52	Lord Russell	Liberal	1963–64	Sir Alec Douglas-Home	Conservative
1852	Earl of Derby	Conservative	1964–70	Harold Wilson	Labour
1852–55	Lord Aberdeen	Peelite	1970–74	Edward Heath	Conservative
1855–58	Viscount Palmerston	Liberal	1974–76	Harold Wilson	Labour
1858–59	Earl of Derby	Conservative	1976–79	James Callaghan	Labour
1859–65	Viscount Palmerston	Liberal	1979–90	Margaret Thatcher	Conservative
1865–66	Lord Russell	Liberal	1990–	John Major	Conservative

Prime Ministers of Ireland from 1922

term	name	party
1922	Michael Collins	Sinn Féin
1922–32	William T Cosgrave	Fine Gael
1932–48	Eamonn de Valera	Fianna Fáil
1948–51	John A Costello	Fine Gael
1951–54	Eamonn de Valera	Fianna Fáil
1954–57	John A Costello	Fine Gael
1957–59	Eamonn de Valera	Fianna Fáil
1959–66	Sean Lemass	Fianna Fáil
1966–73	Jack Lynch	Fianna Fáil
1973–77	Liam Cosgrave	Fine Gael
1977–79	Jack Lynch	Fianna Fáil
1979–81	Charles Haughey	Fianna Fáil
1981–82	Garrett Fitzgerald	Fine Gael
1982	Charles Haughey	Fianna Fáil
1982–87	Garrett Fitzgerald	Fine Gael
1987–92	Charles Haughey	Fianna Fáil
1992–94	Albert Reynolds	Fianna Fáil
1994–	John Bruton	Fine Gael

Primrose League quasi-masonic society founded 1883 to promote the Tory democracy of the ◊Fourth Party among working class voters. It particularly opposed Home Rule for Ireland, and promoted the values of church, hierarchy, and empire. By 1910 it had attracted some 2 million members. It was supposedly named after Disraeli's favourite flower.

Prince Consort title awarded to Prince ◊Albert, husband of Queen Victoria 1857, in recognition of his great contribution to her reign. The title became closely associated with Albert personally, and has not been awarded since.

Prince Regent prince who carries out the duties of a sovereign during the sovereign's minority, incapacity, or prolonged absence from the country. The title is applied specifically to Prince George, Prince of Wales, who acted as regent 1811–20 for his father George III during the latter's mental illness until he succeeded him as George IV. Earlier, during the minorities of Henry III 1216–27, Richard II 1377–89, and Henry VI 1422–37, the general practice was for a council of advisers or a protector to be appointed. On each occasion there was much unseemly wrangling for power among the nobles.

The earliest regency resting upon a particular statute was that of the Protector Somerset 1547–49, after the accession of the nine-year-

Princesses Royal

1642	Mary (eldest daughter of Charles I)
1727	Anne (eldest daughter of George II)
1766	Charlotte (eldest daughter of George III)
1840	Victoria (eldest daughter of Queen Victoria)
1905	Louise (eldest daughter of Edward VII)
1932	Mary (only daughter of George V)
1987	Anne (only daughter of Elizabeth II)

old Edward VI. English law first made provision for a regency by the Regency Act 1937. The law resulted from the wish of George VI, who acceded 1936, to make provision for his two daughters, who were then both minors. Regent means 'ruling'.

Princes in the Tower popular name for King ◊Edward V and his younger brother Richard, Duke of York (1472–1483). They are said to have been murdered in the Tower of London by order of their uncle, the Duke of Gloucester, so that he could succeed to the throne as ◊Richard III but it is equally likely that Henry VII was responsible. Two child skeletons were discovered in the tower 1674 and were later interred in Westminster Abbey.

Princess Royal title borne only by the eldest daughter of the British sovereign, granted by royal declaration. It was first borne by Mary, eldest daughter of Charles I, probably in imitation of the French court, where the eldest daughter of the king was styled 'Madame Royale'. The title is currently held by Princess Anne.

printing printed matter was largely unknown in Europe until the 15th century when movable type was reinvented, traditionally by Johannes Gutenberg (1400–1468) in Germany. From there printing spread to Italy, France, and England, where it was introduced by William ◊Caxton. The first known English book to bear a date was the *Dictes or Sayengis of the Philosophers*, issued by Caxton from his press at Westminster 1477, although it is probable that it was not the first work printed there. Other notable British printers are William Caslon (1692–1766), considered the greatest English typefounder of the 18th century, and John Baskerville (1706–1765). William Morris's designs for new types and decorated pages, produced at his Kelmscott Press from 1890, greatly influenced the work of other private presses.

Prior Matthew 1664–1721. British poet and diplomat. He was associated under the Whigs with the negotiation of the Treaty of Ryswick 1697 ending the war with France and under the Tories with that of Utrecht 1714 ('Matt's Peace') ending the War of the Spanish Succession, but on the Whigs' return to power he was imprisoned by Walpole 1715–17. His gift as a poet was for light occasional verses.

Prince Consort
Much of the energy of Albert, the Prince Consort, was devoted to artistic and social causes. He organized the Great Exhibition 1851, and also drew up designs for improving working class housing.
Hulton Deutsch

And certaynly our langage now used varyeth ferre from that which was used and spoken when I was borne.

PRINTING
William Caxton, the first English printer, 1490

printing
William Caxton produced both the first printed book in English, *Recuyell of the Historyes of Troy* 1475, and also the first book to be printed in England, *Dictes or Sayengis of the Philosophers* 1477.
Philip Sauvain

privateer privately owned and armed ship commissioned by a state to attack enemy vessels. The crews of such ships were, in effect, legalized pirates; they were not paid but received a share of the spoils. Sir Francis Drake and Sir John Hawkins were both privateers; the practice continued until the 19th century, when it was declared illegal by the Declaration of Paris 1856.

privatization policy or process of selling or transferring state-owned or public assets and services (notably nationalized industries) to private investors, in Britain particularly associated with the Conservative administration of Margaret ◊Thatcher. Privatization of services involves the government contracting private firms to supply services previously supplied by public authorities. In many cases the trend toward privatization has been prompted by dissatisfaction with the high level of subsidies being given to often inefficient state enterprise. The term 'privatization' is used even when the state retains a majority share of an enterprise.

Many major public utilities and industries have been privatized since 1979 including British Telecom, the British Gas Corporation, Water Supply, and the electricity industry. In the period 1980–93 the UK government paid consultants more than £258 million for advice on how to sell off nationalized industries and government services. In Nov 1994, approval of a 75% pay increase for the chief executive of British Gas led to a public outcry and calls for regulation of the salaries of executives of recently privatized companies.

industries in the UK privatized since 1979:

British Telecom	British Transport Docks Board
British Gas Corporation	British Water Board
British National Oil Corporation	National Freight Company
British Airways	Enterprise Oil
British Airports Authority	Jaguar
British Aerospace	National Freight Company
British Shipbuilders	Rover Group
British Steel	Water Supply

Privy Council composed originally of the chief royal officials of the Norman kings in Britain, the Privy Council under the Tudors and early Stuarts became the chief governing body. It was replaced from 1688 by the ◊cabinet, originally a committee of the council, and the council itself now retains only formal powers in issuing royal proclamations and orders in council. Cabinet ministers are automatically members, and it is presided over by the Lord President of the Council.

The **Judicial Committee of the Privy Council**, established 1833, still acts as a final court of appeal for some members of the Commonwealth. It is now almost completely obsolete.

privy purse personal expenditure of the British sovereign, which derives from his/her own resources (as distinct from the ◊civil list, which now finances only expenses incurred in pursuance of official functions and duties). The office that deals with this expenditure is also known as the Privy Purse.

Privy Seal, Lord until 1884, the UK officer of state in charge of the royal seal to prevent its misuse. The honorary title is now held by a senior cabinet minister who has special non-departmental duties.

Profumo John (Dennis) 1915– . British Conservative politician, secretary of state for war from 1960 to June 1963, when he resigned on the disclosure of his involvement with Christine Keeler, who was also the mistress of a Soviet naval attaché. The scandal caused immense damage to the MacMillan government, ultimately causing its downfall. In 1982 Profumo became administrator of the social and educational settlement Toynbee Hall in London.

protectorate formerly in international law, a small state under the direct or indirect control of a larger one. The 20th-century equivalent was a trust territory. In English history the rule of Oliver and Richard ◊Cromwell 1653–59 is referred to as **the Protectorate**.

Provisional IRA breakaway group of the ◊Irish Republican Army in Northern Ireland which has been responsible for most of the Republican terrorism in the province since the 1970s.

Provisions of Oxford provisions issued by Henry III of England 1258 under pressure from Simon de Montfort and the baronial opposition. They provided for the establishment of a baronial council to run the government, carry out reforms, and keep a check on royal power.

The members of our secret service have apparently spent so much time looking under the beds for Communists, they haven't had time to look in the bed.

PROFUMO
Michael Foot, referring to the Profumo Affair, 1963 (attributed)

They were supplemented the following year by the Provisions of Westminster.

Provisions of Westminster reforms issued by the parliament that met at Westminster 13 Oct 1259. They were forced on ◊Henry III by his rebellious barons, and forbade the king to grant lands, castles, or offices of state to foreigners. These provisions were a further step following the more radical ◊Provisions of Oxford 1258.

Provisors, Statutes of two acts 1351 and 1390 limiting the papacy's right to appoint clergy to church benefices over the heads of local patrons. The first gave the Crown the power to overrule papal provisions to benefices in England; the second prohibited individual clergy from accepting papal nominations.

Prynne William 1600–1669. English Puritan. He published *Histriomastix* 1632, a work attacking stage plays; it contained aspersions on the Queen, Henrietta Maria, for which he was pilloried and lost his ears. In 1637 he was again pilloried and branded for an attack on the bishops. He opposed the execution of Charles I, and actively supported the Restoration.

Public Health Acts legislation enacted by Parliament 1848, 1872, and 1875 to deal with squalor and disease and to establish a code of sanitary law. The first act, in 1848, established a central board of health with three members who were responsible to Parliament to impose local boards of health in districts where the death rate was above the national average and to make provision for other local boards of health to be established by petition. The 1872 act made it obligatory for every local authority to appoint a medical officer of health. The 1875 act consolidated previous acts and provided a comprehensive code for public health.

Puritan from 1564, a member of the Church of England who wished to eliminate Roman Catholic survivals in church ritual, or substitute a presbyterian for an episcopal form of church government. The Puritan theological position was essentially Calvinist and was associated with strict observance of the Sabbath, moral inflexibility, and abstinence from pleasure. The term also covers the various separatist groups who withdrew from the church altogether. The Puritans were identified with the parliamentary opposition under James I and Charles I. After the Restoration they were driven from the church, and more usually known as ◊Dissenters or ◊Nonconformists.

Putney debates discussions held in Putney church Oct–Nov 1647 among representatives of the New Model Army to consider the radical proposals of the ◊Levellers. Two officers and two representatives of the radicals from each regiment debated 'the Agreement of the People', proposals for a radical republic based on near universal male suffrage. Oliver Cromwell and his generals opposed the proposals, but there was strong support for them among the rank and file. No consensus was reached and the debate served to highlight rather than resolve the differences within the Parliamentarian army.

Pym John 1584–1643. English Parliamentarian, largely responsible for the ◊petition of right 1628. As leader of the Puritan opposition in the ◊Long Parliament from 1640, he moved the impeachment of Charles I's advisers the Earl of Strafford and William Laud, drew up the ◊Grand Remonstrance, and was the chief of the ◊five members of Parliament Charles I wanted arrested 1642. The five hid themselves and then emerged triumphant when the king left London.

Puritan
The term puritan is usually applied to those Protestants who wished to remain in the Church of England but wanted it to be further reformed after the break with Rome. It is often applied perjoratively to describe someone as sanctimonious and mean-spirited.
Philip Sauvain

A Parliament is that to the Commonwealth which the soul is to the body.... It behoves us therefore to keep the facility of that soul from distemper.

JOHN PYM
speech in the House of Commons, April 1640

Qatar independent emirate, southwest Persian Gulf. The emirate formerly had special treaty relations with Britain 1868–1971.

Quadruple Alliance three military alliances of four nations:

1718 Austria, Britain, France, and the United Provinces (Netherlands) joined forces to prevent Spain from annexing Sardinia and Sicily. Following hostilities, in which Spain supported an unsuccessful Jacobite invasion of England, Spain complied with the demands of the alliance 1720;

1813 Austria, Britain, Prussia, and Russia allied to defeat the French emperor Napoleon; renewed 1815 and 1818. See Congress of ◊Vienna.

1834 Alliance negotiated by British foreign secretary ◊Palmerston, in which Britain, France, Portugal, and Spain guaranteed the constitutional monarchies of Spain and Portugal against rebels in the Carlist War.

Quaker popular name, originally derogatory, for a member of the Society of ◊Friends.

quarter session former English local criminal court, consisting of the justices of the peace of a shire meeting four times a year to administer criminal justice and laws relating to local government. The quarter sessions were held from 1363 until they were replaced 1972 by crown courts (see also ◊law courts).

Quatre Bras, Battle of during the Napoleonic Wars, victory of the Allied coalition under the British commander Wellington over French forces under Marshal Ney 16 June 1815 near a hamlet in Brabant, Belgium, 32 km/20 mi southeast of Brussels. Napoleon was finally defeated two days later at the Battle of ◊Waterloo.

Québec, Battle of British victory in the Seven Years' War; see ◊Abraham, Plains of.

Québec Conference two conferences of Allied leaders in the city of Québec during World War II.

The *first conference* 1943 approved British admiral Mountbatten as supreme Allied commander in southeast Asia and made plans for the invasion of France, for which US general Eisenhower was to be supreme commander.

The *second conference* Sept 1944 adopted plans for intensified air attacks on Germany, created a unified strategy against Japan, and established a postwar policy for a defeated Germany.

Queen Alexandra's Imperial Military Nursing Service (QAIMNS) British military nursing organization, founded 1902 from the Army Nursing Service. They provided staff nurses, sisters, and matrons for military hospitals throughout the world.

Queen Anne's Bounty fund established by Queen Anne 1704 to support Church of England clergy whose annual income was less than £10. The Crown's income from ◊first fruits and tenths was set aside to pay for the fund. The income limit was later raised to £35 and from 1777 loans were made to improve parsonages. The revenue has been administered by the Church Commissioners since 1948.

Queensberry John Sholto Douglas, 8th Marquess of Queensberry 1844–1900. British patron of boxing. In 1867 he formulated the *Queensberry Rules*, which form the basis of today's boxing rules. He was the father of Lord Alfred Douglas and it was his misspelled insult to Oscar Wilde that set in motion the events leading to the playwright's imprisonment.

quia emptores (Latin, 'because purchasers') statute July 1290 stipulating that purchasers of land owed feudal rights to services and payments to the lord who ultimately held the land, rather than to the subtenant from whom the land had been bought.

Quiberon Bay, Battle of during the Seven Years' War, victory of the British admiral Edward Hawke (1705–1781) over a French fleet (under the Marquis de Conflans) in Quiberon Bay, off northwest France, 1759. The victory wrecked French plans for an invasion of England and reasserted British command of the sea.

quo warranto (Latin, 'by what authority') writ issued by the Court of the King's Bench from mid-13th century demanding proof of ◊liberty holders rights to enjoy such privileges. The measure was first used by Edward I to challenge the power of the ◊Marcher Lords. A modification 1290 allowed long established use of such privileges as proof of right to hold them in addition to the established defence of a royal grant. The measure was revived by Charles II after the Restoration to investigate corporations and James II used it to remodel borough charters.

race-relations acts 1965, 1968, and 1976 acts of Parliament to combat discrimination. The Race Relations Act 1976 prohibits discrimination on the grounds of colour, race, nationality, or ethnic origin. Indirect as well as direct discrimination is prohibited in the provision of goods, services, facilities, employment, accommodation, and advertisements. The Commission for Racial Equality was set up under the act to investigate complaints of discrimination.

Radcot Bridge, Battle of 19 Dec 1387 battle north of Faringdon, Oxfordshire, in which a force under Robert de Vere, Earl of Oxford, favourite of Richard II, was defeated by the ◊Lords Appellant, Henry Bolingbroke, Earl of Derby, and Thomas, Duke of Gloucester. The victory deprived Richard of any chance of defeating his enemies by force.

Radical supporter of parliamentary reform before the Reform Bill 1832. As a group the Radicals later became the progressive wing of the Liberal Party. During the 1860s (led by Richard Cobden, John Bright, and John Stuart Mill) they campaigned for extension of the franchise, free trade, and laissez faire policies, but after 1870, under the leadership of Joseph Chamberlain and Charles Dilke, they adopted a republican and semi-socialist programme. With the growth of socialism in the later 19th century, Radicalism ceased to exist as an organized movement.

Raedwald d. 627. Early 7th-century king of East Anglia. He was the only East Anglian king to be accepted as ◊Bretwalda, following a long period of Northumbrian hegemony. He was baptized by missionaries from Kent, but his conversion may well have been more symbolic than deep-felt and he later kept Christian and pagan symbols in one temple. It has been suggested that the ◊Sutton Hoo ship burial, found near Colchester, commemorated him.

Raffles Thomas Stamford 1781–1826. British colonial administrator, born in Jamaica. He served in the British ◊East India Company, took part in the capture of Java from the Dutch 1811, and while governor of Sumatra 1818–23 was responsible for the acquisition and founding of Singapore 1819.

ragged schools founded by John Pounds (1766–1839), schools dedicated to the education of poor and delinquent children in industrial areas.

Raglan FitzRoy James Henry Somerset, 1st Baron Raglan 1788–1855. English general. He took part in the Peninsular War under Wellington, and lost his right arm at Waterloo. He commanded the British forces in the Crimean War from 1854 and issued the ambiguous order that led to the disastrous ◊Charge of the Light Brigade. He was created field marshal after the Battle of Inkerman Nov 1854, but his failure to take Sevastopol and the privations of his troops are said to have accelerated his death from dysentery. The ***raglan sleeve***, cut right up to the neckline with no shoulder seam, is named after him.

Rahere d. 1144. Minstrel and favourite of Henry I of England. In 1123, having recovered from malaria while on a pilgrimage to Rome, he founded St Bartholomew's priory and St Bartholomew's hospital in London.

railways method of transport in which trains convey passengers and goods along a twin rail track. Following the work of English steam pioneers such as Scottish engineer James ◊Watt,

English engineer George ◊Stephenson built the first public steam railway, from Stockton to Darlington, in 1825. This heralded extensive railway building in Britain, continental Europe, and North America, providing a fast and economical means of transport and communication. After World War II, steam engines were replaced by electric and diesel engines. At the same time, the growth of road building, air services, and car ownership destroyed the supremacy of the railways.

growth years Four years after building the first steam railway, Stephenson opened the first steam passenger line, inaugurating it with his locomotive *Rocket*, which achieved speeds of 50 kph/30 mph. The railway construction that followed resulted in 250 separate companies in Britain, which resolved into four systems 1921 and became the nationalized British Railways 1948, known as British Rail from 1965.

decline of railways With the increasing use of private cars and government-encouraged road haulage after World War II, and the demise of steam, rising costs on the railways meant higher fares, fewer passengers, and declining freight traffic. In the UK many rural rail services closed down on the recommendations of the ◊Beeching Report 1963, reducing the size of the network by more than 20% between 1965 and 1970, from a peak of 24,102 km/14,977 mi. In the 1970s, national railway companies began investing in faster intercity services: in the UK, the diesel high-speed train (HST) was introduced.

Raleigh or **Ralegh** Walter *c.* 1552–1618. English adventurer, writer, and courtier to Queen Elizabeth I. He organized expeditions to colonize North America 1584–87, all unsuccessful, and made exploratory voyages to South America 1595 and 1616. His aggressive actions against Spanish interests, including attacks on Spanish ports, brought him into conflict with the pacific James I. He was imprisoned for treason 1603–16 and executed on his return from an unsuccessful final expedition to South America. He is traditionally credited with introducing the potato to Europe and popularizing the use of tobacco. He was knighted 1584.

Ramillies, Battle of during the War of the ◊Spanish Succession, English and Dutch victory under the Duke of Marlborough over the French 23 May 1706, near Ramillies, 19 km/12 mi north of Namur, Belgium. The French lost all their artillery and some 15,000 casualties; English and Dutch losses were fewer than 4,000.

Railways in Britain, 1852
In the 20 years from 1866, railway construction revolutionized British inland transport and trade. The railways brought social changes as profound as their impact on the British landscape.

railways
The Liverpool and Manchester railway as it crosses the peat bog at Chat Moss near Manchester. The railway, engineered by George Stephenson, was opened 1830.
Image Select

Railways in Britain, 1852

— railways built by 1836 (1000 miles)
— railways built by 1852 (7000 miles)

0   80 mi
0   160 km

Ramsay Bertram 1883–1945. British admiral in World War II. He was responsible for organizing Operation Dynamo, the evacuation of about 350,000 British and Allied troops from ◊Dunkirk in the face of the German army 1940. He was killed in an aircraft accident Jan 1945.

rationing restricted allowance of provisions or other supplies in time of war or shortage. Food rationing was introduced in Germany and Britain during World War I. During World War II food rationing, organized by the government, began in Britain in 1940. Each person was issued with a ration book of coupons. Bacon, butter, and sugar were restricted, followed by other goods, including sweets, petrol, clothing, soap, and furniture. Some people tried to buy extra on the black market. In 1946 the world wheat shortage led to bread rationing. All food rationing finally ended in Britain 1954, although petrol rationing was reintroduced during the Suez Crisis of 1956.

Rawlinson Henry Seymour, 1st Baron of Trent 1864–1925. British soldier in World War I. Commanding the 4th Army, he was responsible for the main attack on the Somme 1916 and played a decisive part in stemming the German Spring Offensive and then the Allied offensive which ended the war.

Rebecca Riots
Punch cartoon 1846 drawing a parallel between the 'Rebecca Riots' which had recently afflicted southwest Wales and the risks to prime minister Robert Peel in adopting reformist policies.
Philip Sauvain

Rebecca Riots disturbances in southwest Wales 1842–44. They were primarily a protest against toll charges on public roads, but were also a symptom of general unrest following the ◊Poor Law Amendment Act 1834, which made obtaining poor relief much harder. The rioters, many disguised as women, destroyed the tollhouses and gates. Each leader was known as 'Rebecca' and followers were 'her daughters'. They took their name from the biblical prophecy that the seed of Rebekah would 'possess the gate of those which hate them' (Genesis 24,60).

recusant those who refused to attend Anglican church services, especially applied to Catholics. The Acts of Uniformity 1552 and 1559 imposed fines on those who refused to attend, and it was not until the reign of Elizabeth I that the idea of a large and permanent Catholic minority gradually began to be accepted. Even then, an act of 1587 provided for the seizure of up to two-thirds of a recusant's property, although this was only enforced in times of crisis. The fines later became a means of raising revenue rather than a matter of religious policy. Recusants were often associated with the houses of gentry in certain parts of the country, such as the West Midlands which had a strong Catholic community.

Redmond John Edward 1856–1918. Irish politician, Charles Parnell's successor as leader of the Nationalist Party 1890–1916. The 1910 elections saw him holding the balance of power in the House of Commons, and he secured the introduction of a ◊Home Rule bill, which was opposed by Protestant Ulster.

Redmond supported the British cause on the outbreak of World War I, and the bill was passed although its implementation was suspended until the war ended. The growth of the nationalist party Sinn Féin (the political wing of the Irish Republican Army) and the 1916 Easter Rising brought his influence to an end.

reeve Anglo-Saxon official charged with the administration of a shire or burgh, fulfilling functions similar to those of the later sheriff. After the Norman Conquest, the term tended to be restricted to the person elected by the villeins to oversee the work of the manor and to communicate with the manorial lord.

Reform acts 1832, 1867, and 1884 acts of Parliament that extended voting rights and redistributed parliamentary seats; also known as ◊Representation of the People Acts.

THE AGE OF REFORM

Politics and Social Change in 19th-Century Britain

Reform was the leading political issue of 19th-century Britain – reform of the protectionist system, reform of the franchise, and reform of society. It was an issue which politicized British society, and increased middle class social awareness, to a level not seen since the 1640s.

The repeal of the protectionist Corn Laws (which had controlled movements of grain in order to keep domestic prices high) by Sir Robert Peel 1846 split the governing Tories, but reflected the extent to which the interests of an increasingly urbanized and literate society set the political agenda.

The Reform Acts

Successive extensions of the franchise (right to vote) created a mass electorate, though it was still all-male until the following century. The First Reform Act of 1832, described by its authors as final, fixed a more uniform right to vote that brought the franchise to the middle class, and reorganized the distribution of seats in order to reward growing towns, such as Birmingham, Bradford, and Manchester, and counties, at the expense of 'rotten' boroughs, seats with a small population that were open to corruption. The electorate increased greatly, to about one-fifth of all English adult males.

The Second Reform Act 1867 nearly doubled the existing electorate and, by offering household suffrage, gave the right to vote to about 60% of adult males in boroughs. The Third Reform Act of 1884 extended this franchise to the counties.

Changes in the franchise led naturally to further changes: to Liberal election victories in 1868 and 1886, and to changes in the nature of the political system itself. A growing democratization of society led to a far greater emphasis in government on the conditions and attitudes of the people.

Society and environment

A society influenced by both religious evangelism and the teachings of Charles Darwin (whose *Origin of the Species* appeared in 1859) was increasingly aware of the importance of environment, and thus living standards. At the same time, a belief in progress and perfectibility was widespread. It was taken up by both politicians and commentators, such as novelists. Charles Dickens (1812–70) was a supporter of reform in fields such as capital punishment, prisons, housing, and prostitution. His novel *Bleak House* of 1852–53 was an indictment of the coldness of law and church; *Little Dorrit* 1855–57 was an attack on snobbery, imprisonment for debt, business fraud, and bureaucracy. The novels of Wilkie Collins (1824–89) dealt with divorce, vivisection, and the impact of heredity and environment. Moral campaigns, against slavery, alcohol, and cruelty to animals, aroused widespread support, fuelling a major expansion in the voluntary societies that characterized Victorian Britain. Though compromise and the search for short-term advantage played a major role in political reform, idealism was also genuine and important.

Reform was in part a desire to control the new, more dangerous, society and environment of Victorian Britain. Peel's Metropolitan Police Act 1829 created a uniformed and paid force for London. The County and Borough Police Act 1856 made the formation of paid forces obligatory. The Poor Law Amendment Act 1834 sought to control the poor, introducing a national system of workhouses. Cholera and typhoid led to the public health movement of the 1840s. The Health of Towns Act 1848 created a Great Board of Health and an administrative structure to improve sanitation, especially water supply.

An interventionist state

The pace of reform accelerated after the Liberal victory of 1868. The first government of William Gladstone pushed through the disestablishment of the Irish Church in 1869, the introduction of open competition in the Civil Service in 1870, and the secret ballot in 1872. The 1870 Education Act set a minimum level of educational provision, introducing school district authorities where existing parish provision was inadequate. In 1872 the powers of turnpike trusts were ended and road maintenance was placed totally under public control.

The Tories, or Conservatives, came to power under Benjamin Disraeli in 1874 and maintained the pace of reform. Legislation on factories in 1874, and Public Health, Artisans' Dwellings, and Pure Food and Drugs Acts in 1875, systematized and extended the regulation of important aspects of public health and social welfare. Building on the Factory Acts of 1833, 1844, 1847, and 1850, those of 1874 and 1878 limited work hours for women and children in industry. The Prison Act 1877 established central government control of prisons.

A collectivist state was developing, and in some respects it looked toward the later Welfare State. State intervention in education helped to reduce illiteracy. Greater social intervention by the new, more formal and responsive, mechanisms of local government established under the Local Government Act 1888 (which created directly elected county councils and county boroughs) encouraged, by the end of the century, a general expectation of state intervention in the life of the people, in health, education, and housing.

JEREMY BLACK

Parliamentary Reform in the UK: chronology

1822	Lord John Russell proposed a redistribution of seats. Whig Party espoused cause of reform.
1830	Duke of Wellington resigned as prime minister, bringing in Whig ministry under Lord Grey, committed to reform. (Electorate 516,000 = 2% of population.)
1832	Reform Act involved redistribution of parliamentary seats from 'rotten boroughs' to urban constituencies. Franchise extended to householders paying £10 per year rent in towns and 40-shilling freeholders in counties. (Electorate 813,000 = 3% of population.)
1867	Reform Act involved further redistribution of seats and extension of franchise to all ratepayers in boroughs. (Electorate 2,500,000 = 8% of population.)
1872	Ballot Act introduced secret ballots for elections.
1883	Corrupt and Illegal Practices Act set limits to election expenses.
1884	Reform Act again involved redistribution of seats and equalization of franchise for boroughs and counties, to include all householders and ratepayers. (Electorate 5,600,000 = 16% of population.)
1885	Further redistribution of parliamentary seats.
1918	Representation of the People Act gave the vote to all men over 21 and all women ratepayers (or wives of ratepayers) over 30.
1928	Representation of the People (Equal Franchise) Act gave the vote to all women over 21.
1948	Plural voting abolished. Permanent Boundary Commission established.
1970	Voting age reduced to 18.
1979	Constituencies established for direct election to European Parliament in Strasbourg.
1983	Number of parliamentary seats raised from 635 to 650.
1985	Representation of the People Act gave the vote to British citizens living abroad for a period of five years after they have left Britain.
1989	Representation of the People Act extended the period during which British citizens abroad may vote to 20 years after leaving Britain. Live televising of House of Commons proceedings approved.
1992	Number of parliamentary seats raised from 650 to 651.
1994	Number of UK seats in European parliament raised from 81 to 87.

Reform Acts
A political cartoon entitled *The Reformers' Attack on the Old Rotten Tree* 1832. The majority of Tory MPs were opposed to the Reform Act of 1832 since over 200 of their seats were gained in so-called rotten or pocket boroughs. The act provoked a series of riots and marches, and a general election took place before it was finally passed 15 months after its first proposal.
E T Archive

The 1832 act abolished pocket and ◊rotten boroughs, which had formed unrepresentative constituencies, redistributed seats on a more equitable basis in the counties, and formed some new boroughs. The franchise was extended to male householders in property worth £10 a year or more in the boroughs and to owners of freehold property worth £2 a year, £10 copyholders, or £50 leaseholders in the counties. The 1867 act redistributed seats from corrupt and small boroughs to the counties and large urban areas. It also extended the franchise in boroughs to adult male heads of households, and in counties to males who owned, or held on long leases, land worth £5 a year, or who occupied land worth £12 on which they paid poor rates. The 1884 act extended the franchise to male agricultural labourers.

Reformation religious and political movement in 16th-century Europe to reform the Roman Catholic Church, which led to the establishment of Protestant churches. Anticipated from the 12th century by the Waldenses, Lollards, and Hussites, it was set off by German priest Martin Luther 1517, and became effective when the absolute monarchies gave it support by challenging the political power of the papacy and confiscating church wealth.

causes In the early 16th century the Roman Catholic Church was in need of reform. The papacy had become an Italian political power, many of the higher clergy were concerned with worldly authority, and moral standards were low. With such an example, the parochial clergy showed little spirituality, and outside the universities clerical learning was meagre and misdirected.

England In about 1520 a group of Cambridge theologians began to meet to study Luther's writings. ◊Tyndale's transla-

SOVEREIGNS AND PURITANS

The British Reformation

The conventional history of the British Reformation, written by the victorious Protestants, is a tale of how a decaying, corrupt, and unpopular medieval Church was bowled over by an irresistible movement of reform and renewal. Recent research has destroyed this picture completely. Historians are now certain that in 1520 the Church in Britain was a thriving, dynamic, and well-loved institution. Parish churches were the foci of intense local devotion, ecclesiastical courts were respected and much in demand, and there were more applicants for the priesthood than there were jobs. To be sure, there were also problems: too many religious houses, clashes with the growing numbers of common lawyers, and the persistence of small groups of people in southern England, collectively called Lollards, who privately rejected aspects of the official religion. None of these, however, represented a serious weakness.

Royal involvement

The real issue after 1520 was not that the old Church was going wrong, but that an increasing number of people started to think that it had never been right. It depended upon the doctrine that Christians could best get to heaven by performing ritual works: by joining in ceremonies, by beautifying churches, and by revering saints as personal divine patrons. Over the centuries this behaviour had become ever more elaborate, intense, and expensive. The argument of Protestantism, as first preached by Martin Luther in Germany in 1517, was that it was all a confidence trick, for the Bible suggested that none of it was necessary. Indeed, to Protestants it was actually evil, for it diverted attention from direct concern with God and Scripture.

Nonetheless, popular Protestantism was so weak in Britain before 1550 that it would have made little impact had not the English Crown embraced the new ideas. All over Europe in this period monarchs were increasing their control over the Church within their realms. This could be accomplished perfectly well by allying with it against Protestantism, and such a line was taken by Henry VIII of England during the 1520s. In 1529, however, he quarrelled with the Pope over the latter's refusal to grant him a divorce, and resolved to take over the Church in England himself. His avowed aim was to reform it within a Catholic tradition, but he came increasingly to rely upon Protestant advisers and the latter took control when Henry died, on behalf of his young son Edward VI.

Counter-Reformation

Under Henry the monasteries were dissolved and the cult of the saints destroyed, while Edward's regime removed the old ornaments and rituals altogether. Both encountered fierce resistance, Henry provoking the huge northern rising known as the Pilgrimage of Grace and Edward's ministers facing the Western Rebellion in 1549. The first was defeated by trickery and the second in pitched battles. By early 1550 a majority of the English, especially in the southeast, had probably ceased to believe in the old Church, but only a minority had acquired any active commitment to the new faith. In Scotland, the association of Protestantism with England, the old enemy, had kept the traditional religion in power even though a growing number of Scots were turning against it.

There was therefore a real potential for the Reformation to be reversed, and so it was when Edward died in 1553 and was succeeded by

his Catholic sister Mary. She restored her Church, with more streamlining and central control than before, and persecuted Protestants with a savagery unique in British religious history, burning about 300. It seems likely that had she lived for a further 20 years then Britain would be Catholic to this day, but she died after only 5 years and left her Protestant sister, Elizabeth, to take over.

The Elizabethan compromise

The English Catholics were demoralized by the lack of any alternative heir and comforted by promises of good treatment. The Scottish Protestants now chose their moment to rebel and Elizabeth sent an English army to help them into power. Another English expeditionary force in 1573 secured their position, and the young king of the Scots, James VI, was brought up in the Protestant tradition and inherited England when Elizabeth died in 1603.

It was the sheer length of Elizabeth's reign which allowed the Reformation to triumph in Britain, so that by the 1580s the majority of its people had been so thoroughly re-educated in the new faith that they genuinely identified with it. It never, however, achieved the unity of the old one. The Church of England reflected Elizabeth's wish for compromise, yoking Protestant doctrine to a Catholic structure of bishops, cathedrals, and festivals. Many Protestants remained deeply unhappy with it. The Church of Scotland, formed in revolution, made a more radical departure, to a presbyterian structure and a complete abolition of the old festivals and vestments. The defeat of Catholicism in Britain made certain a future struggle between the different strands of Protestantism.

RONALD HUTTON

The British Reformation: chronology

1509	*11 June* By papal dispensation, Henry VIII of England married Catherine of Aragon, widow of his late brother Arthur.
1516	*8 Feb* Catherine gave birth to Princess Mary.
mid-1520s	Henry became infatuated with Anne Boleyn.
1527	*24 Jan* Henry, seeking a divorce, sent two bishops to Rome to request acceleration of the proceedings. Under pressure from Emperor Charles V, uncle of Catherine of Aragon, Pope Clement VII could not grant the divorce and played for time.
1531	*11 Feb* Convocation recognized Henry as 'Supreme Head' of the English Church.
1533	*25 Jan* Henry secretly married Anne Boleyn.
	30 March Thomas Cranmer was consecrated archbishop of Canterbury. On 23 May he pronounced that Henry's marriage to Catherine of Aragon was void.
	11 July Pope Clement VII excommunicated Henry.
1534	*16 March* acts of Parliament completed the legal severance of the English church from Rome.
1535	Opponents of the break with Rome were executed: members of the London Charterhouse 4 May, Bishop John Fisher 22 June, and former chancellor Thomas More 6 July.
1536	*14 April* Parliament passed an act dissolving the smaller monasteries.
	19 May Execution of Anne Boleyn for treasonable adultery. On 30 May Henry married Jane Seymour, who gave birth to a son, Edward, on 12 Oct 1537.
1539	*April 1539–March 1540* The larger religious houses were dissolved.
1540	*May* Passage of act of Parliament imposing the neo-Catholic Six Articles of Religion (July, two Protestant-inclined bishops resigned).
1541	The Irish parliament acknowledged Henry as king of Ireland and head of the Irish Church.
1546	*1 March* In Scotland, the proponent of Church reform George Wishart was burnt for heresy in St Andrew's.
	29 May Church reformers seized St Andrew's and murdered Cardinal David Beaton, archbishop of St Andrew's.
1547	*28 Jan* Death of Henry VIII; succeeded by Edward VI, aged nine.
1548	*Nov* English Parliament passed an act to dissolve chantries.
1549	*15 Jan* Parliament passed the Act of Uniformity, imposing the *Book of Common Prayer* (in English) – used from 9 June.
1552	*Jan* Parliament met and passed another Act of Uniformity, imposing the revised, more Protestant, second *Book of Common Prayer*.
1553	*6 July* Edward VI died; succession of Lady Jane Grey was proclaimed on 10, but she was deposed 19 May and Mary was proclaimed Queen.
1554	*30 Nov* Formal reconciliation made between England and the papacy.
1556	*21 March* The deposed Archbishop Cranmer was burned in Oxford for heresy.
1557	*3 Dec* Four Scottish nobles signed the 'First Band' or covenant, pledging themselves to work for a reformed Church. (They became known as the 'lords of the congregation'.)
1558	*17 Nov* Death of Queen Mary; succeeded by Elizabeth I.
1559	*8 May* New Act of Supremacy passed, which restored anti-papal laws of Henry VIII and the royal supremacy over the Church of England. The Act of Uniformity imposed a revised *Book of Common Prayer*.
	10 May effective start of the Reformation in Scotland, when reformer John Knox preached in St John's Church, Perth, against idolatry, resulting in the sacking of many religious houses.
1560	*1 Aug* start of the Reformation Parliament in Scotland, which adopted a Calvinist Confession of Faith and abolished papal authority in Scotland and the mass.
1562	Convocation of the Church of England approved the 39 Articles of Religion.
1603	*24 March* Death of Elizabeth I; succeeded by James VI of Scotland as James I.
1604	*14–16 Jan* Hampton Court Conference held, at which puritans demanded further reforms in the Church of England. James I rejected proposals apart from the request for a new translation of the Bible. It appeared in 1611 as the Authorized Version.

tion of the *New Testament* (first edition 1526), with Luther's own notes, spread these views to a wider audience. Reform was helped when Henry VIII made England independent of the pope in order to divorce Catherine of Aragon, and the new views became prominent when the reformer Thomas ◊Cranmer was made archbishop of Canterbury (1533). Though Henry introduced certain reforms, he later took a more conservative view, but two facts show his essential support for reformed views – his reliance on Cranmer, and his choice of a Protestant education for his son Edward. At Edward's succession in 1547 Cranmer was able to go further in reform, with *The First Book of Homilies* 1547, Sternhold's metrical psalms of 1547 and 1549,

The Book of Common Prayer 1549, revised 1552, the Forty-two Articles, precursors of the Thirty-nine 1553, and a projected reform of canon law. When Edward died in 1553, his Roman Catholic sister Mary succeeded, and many reformers fled abroad. Some leaders, including Cranmer, stayed at their posts, and were arrested. Retribution followed, and over 300 Protestants from all walks of life were burned, including Cranmer, ◊Ridley, and ◊Latimer, but Mary's attempt to return papal supremacy failed, and when her sister Elizabeth succeeded her in 1558, the restoration of Protestantism was welcomed. The resulting church settlement followed lines that Cranmer would have approved. Those returning exiles who wanted to imitate Genevan discipline and practice found themselves in opposition. It is partly to this that Puritanism owes its growth.

Scotland Lutheran writings reached Scotland through the east coast ports, where they began to arrive in the early 1520s. This stage is summed up in the life and death of Patrick Hamilton. He studied at Wittenberg under Luther, and his theses *Patrick's Places* contain the pith of Luther's views. In 1527 he returned home, and in 1528 was burned at St Andrews. His death showed that Protestant opinions were worth dying for, and gave an impetus to the new movement. Attempts at reform from within the Church were made in the 1540s and 1550s, notably by Archbishop Hamilton (1512–71), culminating in the councils of 1549 and 1550, but these failed to improve the state of the Kirk. Reform had to come from a more dynamic quarter. George Wishart was the first Scot to come into contact with the Swiss reformers, who increasingly became the dominant influence, supplanting the earlier Lutheranism. The government's fixed policy of repression was dependent on the 'auld alliance' with France, and when this collapsed in 1559 the reformers, led by John ◊Knox, were able to have their beliefs legalized. This was done in three documents of 1560 – *The Scots Confession*, *The Book of Common Order*, and *The First Book of Discipline* – but in spite of acts of Parliament, the mass did not disappear. The total reform of the Kirk was perhaps not fully effected until 1690; only the foundation was laid in 1560.

Reformation Parliament Nov 1529–April 1536 Parliament which passed Thomas Cromwell's anti-papal legislation. It acknowledged the sovereign as head of the Church in place of the pope, empowered Henry to abolish payments to Rome of the first year's income of all newly installed bishops, as had hitherto been the practice, sanctioned the installation of Thomas Cranmer as primate of the English church, and enabled Henry to divorce Catherine of Aragon and have Anne Boleyn executed, so that he at last had a male heir (Edward) 1537 by Jane Seymour. The dissolution of the monasteries followed 1636–40. The Parliament lasted an unprecedented seven years and altogether enacted 137 statutes, 32 of which were of vital importance.

In Ireland, the Dublin parliament largely shadowed the measures passed in Westminster, although it acknowledged Henry as king (not just lord) of Ireland and Supreme Head of the Irish Church 1541. In Scotland, a pro-English parliament met 1560, while Queen Mary was still in France, and abolished papal supremacy and adopted a mild form of Calvinism, including predestination, for the Kirk.

Regency the years 1811–20 during which ◊George IV (then Prince of Wales) acted as regent for his father ◊George III during the king's final period of incapacity (see ◊Prince Regent).

Regicides the forty-nine signatories on the instrument of execution for Charles I of England 1649, together with the two executioners (who were anonymous). After the Restoration 1660, 29 of these men were put on trial and ten were sentenced to death.

Regicides
Two contemporary illustrations of the execution of the Regicides 1660. The diarist Samuel Pepys records Oct 1660 having seen 'the limbs of some of our new traitors set upon Aldersgate, which was a sad sight to see ... ' In fact only 10 of the 51 men directly responsible for the death of Charles I were ever executed.
Hulton Deutsch

Dante without the poetry, Irving without the mystery, Mephistopheles without the fun.

LORD REITH

writer Alan Dent, on Reith's character; quoted in James Agate's Ego, 1939

Reith John Charles Walsham, 1st Baron 1889–1971. First general manager 1922–27 and director general 1927–38 of the ◊British Broadcasting Corporation. He was enormously influential in the early development of the BBC and established its high-minded principles of public service broadcasting. He held several ministerial posts in government during World War II including minister of information 1940, transport 1940, and minister of works 1940–42.

revers or ***moss troopers*** families living on the Anglo-Scottish border who supplemented farming by cross-border cattle raids.

remonstrant one of a group of radical Scottish Calvinists who called 1650 for Charles II's removal from the throne until he accepted Calvinism. They were opposed in the Committee of Estates by Resolutioners.

Renaissance revival of European culture that began in Italy around 1400 and lasted there until the end of the 16th century; elsewhere in Europe it flourished later, and lasted until the 17th century. Characteristic of the Renaissance is the discovery of the world and of the individual, and the rediscovery of pagan classical antiquity (led by Boccaccio and Petrarch). Central to the Renaissance was humanism, the belief in the active, rather than the contemplative life, and a faith in the republican ideal. The greatest expression of the Renaissance was in the arts and learning.

In the 15th century, English scholars studied at Italian universities, or were pupils of such famous teachers as Guarino and Vittorino. William Grocyn (*c.* 1446–1519) introduced the study of Greek to Oxford in 1491, others collected manuscripts for Duke Humphrey of Gloucester (to be incorporated in the Bodleian Library), while round Thomas More in London a circle of scholars welcomed Dutch intellectual Erasmus (1466–1536) to England. In architecture a feeling of symmetry, with Italianate detail, appeared surprisingly at Longleat House, Wiltshire, in 1568, well before the pure doctrine was proclaimed by Inigo Jones (1573–1652) in the Banqueting House in Whitehall and the Queen's House at Greenwich. After the Baroque architecture of Christopher Wren (1632–1723) (itself derived from Italy) the era of Palladianism pervaded the English country house in the 18th century, and was felt as far afield as Russia, and the colonies of North America.

Representation of the People Acts
Nomination process for the Lambeth election 1865. Two years later the Representation of the People Act doubled the electorate to 2 million.
Hulton Deutsch

Representation of the People Acts series of UK acts of Parliament from 1867 that extended voting rights, finally creating universal suffrage 1928. The 1867 and 1884 acts are known as the second and third ◊Reform Acts.

The 1918 act gave the vote to men over the age of 21 and women over the age of 30, and the 1928 act extended the vote to women over the age of 21. Certain people had the right to more than one vote; this was abolished by the 1948 act. The 1969 act reduced the minimum age of voting to 18.

Requests, Court of or ***Court of Poor Men's Causes*** court of equity offering redress for those too poor to apply to the regular civil courts. Originally a 14th-century offshoot of the king's council, it was granted offical recognition as a separate institution 1497 and was reorganized by Thomas Cromwell. It survived until 1642 when it was abolished after increasingly encroaching on common law courts.

Restoration the period when the monarchy, in the person of Charles II, was re-established after the English Civil War and the fall of the ◊Protectorate 1660.

retainer servant of a lord who owed loyalty in return for a payment, rather than the holding of land. Retainers formed the personal retinue of medieval lords, originally in a primarily military capacity but later in administrative and judicial roles, and they became increasingly

CHANGE AND DIVERSITY
English Renaissance Literature and Art

H istorians have found the term 'renaissance' (the 'rebirth' of art and letters, influenced by classical models) difficult to apply to 16th-century England. Certainly it was a time of unprecedented change in English literary and artistic culture, with a growing concern in humanist scholarship and the 'new' learning of classical philosophy, literature, history, and art. But England was geographically and culturally isolated from continental Europe where many of these interests originated; nor did Tudors use the term 'renaissance' to describe their own culture. Sixteenth-century English literature and art is perhaps best characterized by its increasing diversity: writers and artists produced an extraordinary range of works in the period, for different audiences in new and developing markets.

Literature for the elite
Much 16th-century literature is in Latin: plays, poems, letters, tracts, and original works, such as Thomas More's *Utopia* of 1516. But Latin only reached a small audience of gentlemen (few women were taught the language) – thus translations and adaptations of the classics became widely popular (Shakespeare, for instance, probably used Thomas North's 1579 translation of Plutarch's *Lives* in writing *Julius Caesar*). Many poetic forms proliferated in the Elizabethan era – epic romances such as Spenser's *The Faerie Queene* of 1590–96, narrative poems, short lyrics (often intended to be sung), and sonnets. Imitation – the skilled or witty reproduction of a literary style – was a popular mode of writing, and numerous poems were modelled on the love sonnets of Petrarch (1304–74): the Earl of Surrey (*c.* 1517–47) and Sir Thomas Wyatt (*c.* 1503–42) circulated sonnets in manuscript at Henry VIII's court, and in 1591 Sir Philip Sidney's influential sonnet sequence *Astrophel and Stella* was

published. Their poems are not simple 'copies': like many Tudor authors, Surrey, Wyatt, Sidney, and Spenser were not writers by profession but politicians and civil servants. In their hands literature could be used to explore not only literary subjects, but wider concerns, from the state of society to the rule of the monarch.

Popular audiences
By the late 16th century, new markets in more popular forms of literature were well established. Ballads could be bought for a penny; pamphlets, tracts, and sermons were cheaply available, as were books of narrative verse and prose fiction. But only a small percentage of the population in 16th-century England could read or had the leisure to do so; drama, however, could reach a more diverse audience. There were two types of theatre in Elizabethan London: private theatres (such as Blackfriars) that generally offered scholarly or sophisticated plays with elaborate settings, and cheaper public theatres (such as The Globe). The establishment of permanent theatre companies in the late 16th century led to an increased demand for plays – ranging from tragedies and comedies modelled on the classical writers Seneca and Terence, to drama combining elements of popular song, farce, or moralistic fable. Shakespeare was only one of many contemporary dramatists: Christopher Marlowe, Thomas Middleton, and Ben Jonson, among others, produced a remarkable variety of plays addressing topics as diverse as British history, classical mythology, city manners, and domestic violence.

For women, a writing career was out of the question: it was considered a breach of feminine modesty for a woman to promote herself through publication. Nevertheless, some gentlewomen not only published their own prose and poetry (such as Lady

Mary Wroth), but promoted literature in their role as patrons. As the canon of English Renaissance literature is currently revised by modern editors, their work is once again being published.

Tudor art
English Renaissance art has been criticized for its insularity. But English 16th-century visual culture was surprisingly rich: Tudor churches were dense with images, from wall-paintings of the Annunciation and alabaster sculptures of saints to secular subjects (particularly funeral monuments) following the Reformation. Henry VIII was a prolific patron of the arts, commissioning artists such as Hans Holbein (1497/8–1543), and employing a team of painters to decorate temporary structures at court entertainments and the royal palaces. Although there were no public galleries, great houses were sumptuously decorated with wall-paintings and hangings, embroideries, tapestries (often imported from the Low Countries), sculptures, and carving. All manner of interior surfaces were ornamented with elaborate designs – many of which were reproduced for patrons and craftsmen in continental 'pattern books'. Most of the paintings that survive today are portraits, ranging from lavish full-length paintings of Henry VIII and Elizabeth I used to promote their image as sovereigns, to jewel-like miniature portraits (such as those by Nicholas Hilliard, *c.* 1547–1619), which offered a far more intimate 'souvenir' of loved ones. Much work remains anonymous: above all, English patrons were concerned with the symbolic and allegorical messages that a work of art could communicate to others – often through emblems, mottoes, and a wealth of surface detail.

SASHA ROBERTS

important throughout the Middle Ages. Retainers were often identified by a uniform (◊livery and maintenance) and formal agreements were sometimes drawn up stating the exact nature of the obligations of both lord and retainer (see ◊indentured retainer).

Reynolds Albert 1933– . Irish politician, prime minister 1992–94. He joined Fianna Faíl 1977, and held various government posts including minister for industry and commerce 1987–88 and minister of finance 1989–92. He became prime minister when Charles ◊Haughey was forced to resign Jan 1992, but his government was defeated on a vote of confidence Nov 1992. He succeeded in forming a Fianna Faíl–Labour coalition but resigned as premier and party leader Nov 1994 after Labour disputed a judicial appointment he had made and withdrew from the coalition.

He fostered closer relations with Britain and in Dec 1993 he and UK prime minister John Major issued a joint peace initiative for Northern Ireland, the 'Downing Street Declaration', which led to a general cease-fire the following year.

RFC abbreviation for ◊***Royal Flying Corps***, a forerunner of the Royal Air Force.

Rheged Romano-British kingdom in a region approximating to present Dumfries and Galloway, southwest Scotland. It was overrun by the Angles in the 7th century and became part of Northumbria.

Rhode Island former British colony in North America; see ◊Thirteen Colonies.

Rhodes Cecil (John) 1853–1902. South African politician, born in the UK, prime minister of Cape Colony 1890–96. Aiming at the formation of a South African federation and the creation of a block of British territory from the Cape to Cairo, he was responsible for the annexation of Bechuanaland (now Botswana) in 1885. He formed the British South Africa Company 1889, which occupied Mashonaland and Matabeleland, thus forming ***Rhodesia*** (now Zambia and Zimbabwe).

Rhodes went to Natal 1870 and amassed a large fortune as head of De Beers Consolidated Mines and Goldfields of South Africa Ltd. He entered the Cape legislature 1881, and became prime minister 1890, but the discovery of his complicity in the Jameson Raid forced him to resign 1896. Advocating Anglo-Afrikaner cooperation, he was less concerned with the rights of black Africans, despite the final 1898 wording of his dictum: 'Equal rights for every civilized man south of the Zambezi.'

The ***Rhodes scholarships*** were founded at Oxford University, UK, under his will, for students from the Commonwealth, the USA, and Germany.

Rhodesia former name of Zambia and Zimbabwe in southern Africa. It was governed from 1889 by Cecil ◊Rhodes' British South Africa Company. The territory was divided into ◊Northern Rhodesia and ◊Southern Rhodesia 1911. The two were reunited in the Central African Federation 1953 but when the Federation was dissolved 1963, the northern territory became Zambia and Southern Rhodesia reverted to the name of Rhodesia.

Rhodri Mawr d. 878. King of Gwynedd, Powys and Seisyllwg. He gained the kingdoms through his own marriage and that of his father, Marfyn Frych. He was harassed by both Vikings and Saxons; he defeated a Viking force and killed their leader, Gorm, 856 but was himself killed in battle 878 by the Saxons.

Rhuddlan, Robert of d. 1088. Norman noble. He built a castle and set up a small borough at Rhuddlan, North Wales, and at first supported Gruffydd ap Cynan, king of Gwynedd. He later captured him and for a brief period won control of Gwynedd west of the River Conway.

Rhuddlan, Statute of legal and administrative arrangements made 1284 at Rhuddlan, North Wales, by Edward I for the conquered territories of Llewelyn ap Gruffydd. New regional centres were established at Caernarfon and Carmathen, and five new counties were formed (Anglesey, Caernarfon, Merioneth, Cardigan, Carmarthen) in addition to Flint. English criminal law was made compulsory, but Welsh civil law was allowed to continue until its abolition 1536–43.

Rhys ap Gruffydd 1132–1197 known as ***Yr Arglwydd Rhys***, 'Rhys the lord'. Lord of Deheubarth and son of Gruffydd ap Rhys. He established himself as sole ruler of Deheubarth by 1155 and although he submitted to Henry II 1158 he established himself as the chief

Welsh ruler. After the death of Owen Gwynedd 1170, his dominance of Wales was secured and Henry appointed him justice of South Wales 1172. He presided over an eisteddfod at Cardigan 1176.

Rhys ap Tewdwr d. 1093. Lord of Deheubarth. He gained control of Deheubarth 1073 and consolidated his hold over this territory at the battle of Mynydd Carn 1081. He probably formed an alliance with William I 1081. He was killed near Brecon 1093 while resisting the Norman advance into the region under Bernard de Newmarch.

Rice-Davies Mandy (Marilyn) 1944–   . English model. She achieved notoriety 1963 following the revelations of the affair between her friend Christine ◊Keeler and war minister John ◊Profumo, and his subsequent resignation.

Richard three kings of England:

Richard (I) the Lion-Heart (French *Coeur-de-Lion*) 1157–1199. King of England from 1189, who spent all but six months of his reign abroad. He was the third son of Henry II, against whom he twice rebelled. In the third Crusade 1191–92 he won victories at Cyprus, Acre, and Arsuf (against Saladin), but failed to recover Jerusalem. While returning overland he was captured by the Duke of Austria, who handed him over to the emperor Henry VI, and he was held prisoner until a large ransom was raised. He then returned briefly to England, where his brother John I had been ruling in his stead. His later years were spent in warfare against Philip II of France, and he was killed besieging Châlus.

Richard (I) the Lion-Heart
The great seal of King Richard I who spent most of his reign away from England. He was a notable soldier who fought in the third Crusade 1191–92, defeating the Muslim leader Saladin and capturing Acre.
Philip Sauvain

Richard II 1367–1400. King of England from 1377, effectively from 1389, son of Edward the Black Prince. He reigned in conflict with Parliament; they executed some of his associates 1388, and he executed some of the opposing barons 1397, whereupon he made himself absolute. Two years later, forced to abdicate in favour of ◊Henry IV, he was jailed and probably assassinated.

Richard was born in Bordeaux. He succeeded his grandfather Edward III when only 10, the government being in the hands of a council of regency. His fondness for favourites resulted in conflicts with Parliament, and in 1388 the baronial party headed by the Duke of Gloucester had many of his friends executed. Richard recovered control 1389, and ruled moderately until 1397, when he had Gloucester murdered and his other leading opponents executed or banished, and assumed absolute power. In 1399 his cousin Henry Bolingbroke, Duke of Hereford (later Henry IV), returned from exile to lead a revolt; Richard II was deposed by Parliament and imprisoned in Pontefract Castle, where he died mysteriously.

Richard III 1452–1485. King of England from 1483. The son of Richard, Duke of York, he was created Duke of Gloucester by his brother Edward IV, and distinguished himself in the Wars of the ◊Roses. On Edward's death 1483 he became protector to his nephew Edward V, and soon secured the crown for himself on the plea that Edward IV's sons were illegitimate. He proved a capable ruler, but the suspicion that he had murdered Edward V and his brother undermined his popularity. In 1485 Henry, Earl of Richmond (later ◊Henry VII), raised a rebellion, and Richard III was defeated and killed at ◊Bosworth.

Scholars now tend to minimize the evidence for his crimes as Tudor propaganda and there is no historical evidence that he was a hunchback, despite the popular literary image fostered of him.

Richard III
Richard III was portrayed by Shakespeare as an evil, scheming hunchback. In fact this depiction was based on Tudor propaganda and has no basis in historical fact.
Hulton Deutsch

Richard Earl of Cornwall 1209–1272. Second son of King John. Following service in France he supported the barons in opposition to the foreign influence at court of his brother Henry III. He was reconciled with Henry 1239 and regent 1253–54 during the king's absence abroad. He was elected king of the Romans in the Holy Roman Empire 1257 but never gained complete authority. During the second Barons' War he fought for Henry. He was captured at Lewes 1264 and held until 1265.

Richard 3rd Duke of York 1411–1460. Protector of England and Yorkist leader. He was lieutenant in France 1436–37 and 1440–45 and married Cicily, daughter of Ralph Neville, 1st Earl of Westmorland 1438. An enemy of Edmund Beaufort, Duke of Somerset, he was sent to be lieutenant in Ireland 1447. In 1452 he led a force to London with the aim of ousting Somerset, which he achieved 1453. He held the protectorship during the illness of Henry VI 1454–55, but Somerset was reinstated. As a result, York and the Nevilles took up arms in the Wars of the Roses and defeated the royal forces at St Albans, where Somerset was killed 1455. York was again named protector 1455 but his position was undermined by Queen Margaret. Following the Yorkist victory at Northampton 1460 he was granted the succession. Soon after, however, he was killed by Queen Margaret's forces at Wakefield. Two of his sons were kings of England: Edward IV and Richard III.

Ridgeway, the grassy track dating from prehistoric times that runs along the Berkshire Downs in southern England from Avebury, Wiltshire.

riding (Old English *thriding*, 'third part') administrative division used in Yorkshire (East, West, and North Riding) and Lincolnshire (◊Lindsey) until the reorganization of local government 1974. Originally, the third part of a shire in the ◊Danelaw.

Ridley Nicholas *c.* 1500–1555. English Protestant bishop. He became chaplain to Henry VIII 1541, and bishop of London 1550. He took an active part in the Reformation and supported Lady Jane Grey's claim to the throne. After Mary's accession he was arrested and burned as a heretic.

Ridolfi Plot conspiracy 1571 led by the Italian banker Roberto Ridolfi with Spanish and papal backing to replace Elizabeth I with ◊Mary Queen of Scots. Spanish troops in the Netherlands were to invade England and lead a Catholic uprising against Elizabeth. The plot was discovered before it became a serious threat. Ridolfi was overseas at the time but another conspirator, Thomas Howard, Duke of Norfolk, was executed the following year. Mary was placed in stricter confinement as a result of the plot.

Rimington Stella 1935– . British public servant and director-general of the counter-intelligence security service (MI5) from 1992. She was the first head of MI5 to be named publicly, and in July 1993 published a booklet containing hitherto undisclosed details on the service, including its history, organization, and constitutional role.

riot disturbance caused by a potentially violent mob. In the UK, riots formerly suppressed under the Riot Act are now governed by the Public Order Act 1986. Methods of riot control include plastic bullets, stun bags (soft canvas pouches filled with buckshot which spread out in flight), water cannon, and CS gas (tear gas).

Riots in Britain include the Spitalfields weavers' riot 1736, the ◊Gordon riots 1780, the Newport riots 1839, and riots over the Reform Bill in Hyde Park, London, 1866; in the 1980s inner-city riots occurred in Toxteth, Liverpool; St Paul's, Bristol; Broadwater Farm, Tottenham, and Brixton, London; and in 1990 rioting took place in London and several other cities after demonstrations against the ◊poll tax.

Riot Act 1714 act of Parliament passed to suppress the ◊Jacobite disorders. If twelve or more persons assembled unlawfully to the

Riot Act
Engraving by George Cruikshank showing a justice of the peace attempting to read the Riot Act to an unruly mob. The Act could be read out if 12 or more persons were 'unlawfully, riotously, or tumultuously assembled together' and the rioters then had an hour to disperse before force was used to break up the crowd. As the engraving shows, the simple reading of the Act was not always effective. *Hulton Deutsch*

disturbance of the public peace, a magistrate could read a proclamation ordering them to disperse ('reading the Riot Act'), after which they might be dispersed by force. It was superseded by the Public Order Act 1986, which was instituted in response to several inner-city riots in the early 1980s, and greatly extends police powers to control marches and demonstrations by re-routing them, restricting their size and duration, or by making arrests. Under the act a person is guilty of riot if in a crowd of twelve or more, threatening violence; the maximum sentence is ten years' imprisonment.

Ripon, treaty of signed 26 Oct 1640, treaty ending the second ◊Bishops' War between Charles I and his Scottish subjects. The treaty was a profound humiliation for Charles – the Scots were to retain Northumberland and Durham and he agreed to pay the Scots £850 a day until the issues were resolved. Charles was obliged to summon the ◊Long Parliament to ratify the treaty.

Rivaux Peter des d. 1258. French favourite of Henry III. The king was forced to dismiss him from the post of treasurer following the Marshal rebellion 1234.

River Plate, Battle of the World War II naval battle in the South Atlantic between a British cruiser squadron of three ships and the German 'pocket battleship' *Admiral Graf Spee* Dec 1939. The British damaged the *Graf Spee* and pursued it as it sought refuge in Montevideo, Uruguay. The ship's captain was ordered to scuttle his vessel rather than risk it falling to the British.

Rizzio David 1533–1566. Italian adventurer at the court of Mary Queen of Scots. After her marriage to ◊Darnley, Rizzio's influence over her incited her husband's jealousy, and he was murdered by Darnley and his friends at Holyrood Palace.

RNAS abbreviation for ◊*Royal Naval Air Service*.

Roanoke site of the first English settlement in North America, an island near the southern entrance to Albermarle Sound, North Carolina. The settlement was established by Raleigh 1585 but remained only ten months. A second colony was established 1587 with Captain John White appointed as governor by Raleigh. White's granddaughter, Virginia Dare, was born here 1587 as the first child born in America to English parents. All colonists had vanished by 1591.

Rob Roy nickname of Robert MacGregor 1671–1734. Scottish Highland ◊Jacobite outlaw. After losing his estates, he lived by cattle theft and extortion. Captured, he was sentenced to transportation but pardoned 1727. He is a central character in Walter Scott's historical novel *Rob Roy* 1817.

Robert three kings of Scotland:

Robert (I) the Bruce 1274–1329. King of Scotland from 1306, and grandson of Robert de Bruce. He shared in the national uprising led by William ◊Wallace, and, after Wallace's execution 1305, rose once more against Edward I of England, and was crowned at Scone 1306. He defeated Edward II at ◊Bannockburn 1314. In 1328 the Treaty of Northampton recognized Scotland's independence and Robert as king. He was succeeded by his son David II.

Robert II 1316–1390. King of Scotland from 1371. He was the son of Walter (1293–1326), steward of Scotland, who married Marjory, daughter of Robert the Bruce. He was the first king of the house of Stewart. He proved to be a weak and indecisive ruler.

Robert III *c.* 1340–1406. King of Scotland from 1390, son of Robert II. He was unable to control the nobles, and the government fell largely into the hands of his brother, Robert, Duke of ◊Albany.

Roberts Bartholomew 1682–1722. British merchant-navy captain who joined his captors when taken by pirates 1718. He became the most financially successful of all the sea rovers until surprised and killed in battle by the British navy.

Roberts Frederick Sleigh ('Bobs'), 1st Earl Roberts 1832–1914. British field marshal. During the Afghan War of 1878–80 he occupied Kabul, and during the Second South African War 1899–1902 he made possible the annexation of the Transvaal and Orange Free State.

Robin Hood legendary outlaw and champion of the poor against the rich, said to have lived in Sherwood Forest, Nottinghamshire, during the reign of Richard I (1189–99). He feuded

He, that his people and heritage might be delivered out of the hands of our enemies, met toil and fatigue, hunger and peril... and bore them cheerfully.

ROBERT THE BRUCE
Bernard de Linton, letter to Pope John XXII, 1320

THE EDGE OF THE WORLD

Britain and the Coming of Rome

The expeditions of Julius Caesar and the conquest under Claudius brought most of Britain (but not Ireland) within the political, cultural, and economic system of the Mediterranean-based empire of Rome. But the Roman conquest of Britain was a long process, and cultural domination, at first no more than superficial, was established only slowly.

Britain before the conquest

The *Cassiterides* or 'Tin Islands' known to Greek writers are generally identified with southwest Britain. During his conquest of Gaul, Julius Caesar crossed to Britain in 55 and 54 BC. This was more for the propaganda effect at Rome of invading the mysterious island in the Ocean than with any serious intent to conquer the island. For the next hundred years the peoples of the southeast of Britain were increasingly influenced by the Romans, and native kings such as Cunobelin (Shakespeare's Cymbeline) maintained diplomatic relations with them. In AD 43 the new emperor Claudius rewarded the army which had placed him on the throne by taking up the work of his ancestor Caesar and invading Britain with a view to conquest.

Conquest, resistance, and domination

The initial invasion of AD 43 under its commander Aulus Plautius soon overran the southeast of Britain, taking Camulodunum (Colchester) the centre for the most powerful tribe. Its leader, Caractacus, escaped to the Silures of south Wales, where he stirred up resistance until his defeat and capture in AD 51, when he was sent to Rome. Resistance continued in Wales, particularly inspired by the Druids, the priests and law-givers of the Celtic peoples.

The Romans depict them as practising barbarous rites such as human sacrifice, but this may be more of an attempt to blacken the image of leaders of resistance than the truth.

The next serious resistance to Rome came from the Iceni of East Anglia. When their king Prasutagus died in 60 or 61, their territory was forcibly annexed to the province of Britannia and Prasutagus' widow Boudicca (Boadicea) and her daughters abused. The Iceni and their southern neighbours the Trinovantes of Essex rose in revolt and sacked the now Roman-style towns at Colchester, London, and Verulamium (St Albans) before being slaughtered in battle by Roman troops under the governor Suetonius Paullinus. This was the last concerted effort to shake off Roman rule, though it was not until the 70s that the Romans completed the conquest of what are now England and Wales.

Scotland and the walls

In the early 80s Roman power was advanced into Scotland under the governor Gnaeus Julius Agricola, the best-known governor of Britain as the biography by his son-in-law the historian Tacitus has survived. Agricola defeated the Caledonian tribes under their leader Calgacus at the battle of Mons Graupius in north-eastern Scotland, but over the next forty years the Romans gradually gave up their conquests in Scotland. In AD 122 the emperor Hadrian visited Britain and commanded the construction of a wall from sea to sea. Hadrian's Wall ran from Newcastle to west of Carlisle. With a gate (milecastle) every mile as well as watch-towers and forts, it was designed to control movement across the frontier, supervise the tribes to the north, and stand as a great monument to the might of

Hadrian and Rome. At Hadrian's death in AD 138, his successor Antoninus Pius abandoned the newly completed Wall and advanced to a new line from the Forth to the Clyde, the Antonine Wall. But with the death of its originator in AD 161 the Antonine Wall was abandoned, and thereafter Hadrian's Wall marked the northern boundary of Rome in Britain.

The development of Britannia

The initial conquest was long drawn out and occasionally bloody, and the Romans never succeeded in subduing all the island. Thus there was always a substantial military garrison in Britain and resistance by unconquered tribes. But the great majority of the people of Britain soon settled down to Roman rule and adapted to the style of their conquerors. Under Roman influence towns appear in Britain, including colonies for military veterans such as Colchester, Gloucester, and Lincoln, the great port of London and other towns which have remained important to the present such as Canterbury and York. Roman fashions can also be seen in the introduction of temples, altars, and sculpture for the worship of native gods, new burial practices, the construction of Roman-style country residences (villas), and the importation of luxuries such as spices or glass from elsewhere in the empire. This 'Romanization' of Britain principally affected the aristocracy, who used Roman manners to please their overlords and to impress the rest of the populace. But the great majority of the people continued to live on the land and eke out a living as peasants, relatively little touched by the forms of Roman civilization.

SIMON ESMONDE CLEARY

with the sheriff of Nottingham, accompanied by Maid Marian and a band of followers known as his 'merry men'. He appears in ballads from the 13th century, but his first datable appearance is in Langland's *Piers Plowman* in the late 14th century.

Robinson Mary 1944– . Irish Labour politician, president of Ireland from 1990. She became a professor of law at 25. A strong supporter of women's rights, she has campaigned for the liberalization of Ireland's laws prohibiting divorce and abortion.

Robinson William Leefe 1895–1919. British fighter pilot. During an air-raid Sept 1916, he shot down the first German airship to be brought down over the UK, for which he was awarded the Victoria Cross.

Robsart Amy *c.* 1532–1560. wife of Robert Dudley, the Earl of ◊Leicester. She died in mysterious circumstances and it was widely believed she had been murdered so that her husband could marry Elizabeth I.

Rochdale Pioneers the founders of the ◊cooperative movement; a group of Lancashire workers who opened a cooperative shop in Rochdale 1844 inspired by the ideas of Robert ◊Owen. The profits were divided among all the members of the cooperative rather than among a restricted group of shareholders.

Roches Peter des d. 1238. Bishop of Winchester and French favourite of King John. He was consecrated bishop 1205 but was very unpopular with the English. Henry III restricted him to purely spiritual duties 1234 after pressure from the barons.

Rockingham Charles Watson Wentworth, 2nd Marquess of Rockingham 1730–1782. British Whig politician, prime minister 1765–66 and 1782 (when he died in office); he supported the American claim to independence and initiated peace negotiations after the loss of the American colonies.

Rodney George Brydges Rodney, Baron Rodney 1718–1792. British admiral. In 1762 he captured Martinique, St Lucia, and Grenada from the French. He relieved Gibraltar 1780 by defeating a Spanish squadron off Cape St Vincent. In 1782 he crushed the French fleet under Count de Grasse off Dominica, for which he was raised to the peerage.

Roger of Salisbury d. 1139 English cleric and politician. He was appointed chancellor under ◊Henry II 1100 and bishop of Salisbury 1101. He was next in power to the king and ruled in his absence, introducing many reforms. On Henry's death 1135 he went over to ◊Stephen. His greed and acquisition of castles angered the barons, who removed him from office and forced him to surrender the castles 1139.

Roman Britain period in British history from the mid-1st century BC to the mid-4th century AD. England was rapidly Romanized, but north of York fewer remains of Roman civilization have been found. Roman towns include London, York, Chester, St Albans, Colchester, Lincoln, Gloucester, and Bath. The most enduring mark of the occupation was the system of military roads radiating from London such as ◊Watling Street.

Roman contact with Britain began with ◊Caesar's invasions of 55 and 54 BC, but the

Roman Britain (Britannia)
Roman Britain was a civilization based around towns, which were usually built on the sites of pre-Roman settlements, and with a population which may not have been reached again in Britain until the 18th century. The major military roads were given their familiar names by the Anglo-Saxon successors to Roman Britain.

Roman Britain (Britannia)

▲ important town or fort
— major Roman road
⌐⌐⌐ Roman wall
Iceni people

0   80 mi
0   160 km

Inchtuthil
ANTONINE WALL
Votadini
Dumnonii
Selgovae
Novantae
HADRIAN'S WALL
Carlisle
Carvetii
Brigantes
Textoverdi
Lopocares
North Sea
Gabrantovices
Parisi
Brough-on-Humber
Setantii
York
Irish Sea
Manchester
Lincoln
Deceangli
Chester
Cornovii
Coritani
ERMINE STREET
Iceni
Ordovices
Wroxeter
Caistor-by-Norwich
WATLING STREET
Godmanchester
Trinovantes
Demetae
Carmarthen
Gloucester
Catuvellauni
Colchester
Silures
Caerwent
St Albans
Canterbury
FOSSE WAY
Dobunni
London
Caerleon
Atrebates
Cantiaci
Bath
Silchester
Dover
Belgae
Winchester
Regnenses
Durotriges
Chichester
Dorchester
Exeter
Dumnonii
English Channel

Roman Britain: chronology

55 BC	*Aug* A small Roman force under Julius Caesar landed in Kent. Ships bringing cavalry rein-forcements across the Channel were scattered four days later, so Caesar withdrew.
54 BC	*July–Sept* Caesar and a large army landed again in Kent, marched inland and attacked the stronghold of the Catuvellauni in Hertfordshire. Their leader, Cassivellaunus, agreed terms and the Romans withdrew to Gaul.
AD 43	Start of Roman conquest of Britain, ordered by Emperor Claudius. The Romans send 40,000 troops to Britain, probably landing at Richborough. Crossing the Thames near Westminster, they captured the capital of the Catuvellauni near modern Colchester. Eleven British kings surrendered.
43–47	Roman legions advanced north through Lincolnshire to the river Humber, into the east Midlands, and across the south into the southwest. A frontier was established along the Fosse Way.
49	Foundation of Camulodunum.
by 50	Foundation of Londinium (London) and Verulamium (St Albans).
57–60	Roman forces campaigned in Wales; Anglesey was captured in 60.
60	Revolt of the Iceni tribe, led by Boudicca. Iceni tribesmen captured Camulodunum, Verulamium, and Londinium, but were then defeated by the Romans somewhere in the Midlands. The Romans laid waste Iceni territory.
71–72	After anti-Roman elements became dominant among the Brigantes of north England, Roman troops established control of the north, founding Eboracum (York) in 71.
74–84	Six campaigns under Agricola into Scotland took Roman power to the far northeast. In 84, the Romans defeated Caledonian tribesmen at Mons Graupius, in the area of modern Aberdeen.
87	Following the withdrawal of army units to the Continent, Roman troops were withdrawn from northeast Scotland and the Clyde–Forth isthmus adopted as the northern border.
90	*Coloniae* were founded at Lindum (Lincoln) and Glevum (Gloucester) by 96–8. By *c.* 100 most of the major Roman towns had been founded.
c. 105	Roman forces in Scotland were pulled back and a new border established somewhere across north England.
122	Start of construction of Hadrian's Wall across north England, dividing the Brigantes from their allies in Scotland.
c. 139–42	Romans recaptured the Scottish lowlands and constructed the turf Antonine Wall across the Clyde–Forth isthmus.
c. 154–58	Roman troops withdrew from the Antonine Wall. They may have been required to crush rebellion in north England.
158 or 159	Romans reoccupied the Antonine Wall.
163 or 164	Roman forces made their final withdrawal from the Antonine Wall, and reestablished Hadrian's Wall as the northern frontier of Roman Britain.
197	Possible date when Britain was divided into two provinces, *Britannia Superior* or Upper Britain, probably governed from Londinium, and *Britannia Inferior* or Lower Britain, gov-erned from Eboracum.
c. 208–09	Martyrdom of St Alban.
208, 209	Emperor Severus led campaigns in northeast Scotland against the Caledonians.
210	Revolt of the Maeatae in Scotland; put down by a punitive expedition.
259–74	Britain, along with Spain, adhered to the Gallic Empire formed by the usurper Postumus.
268–82	Probable period of attacks along east coast of England by Saxon sea-raiders.
276–82	Forts built along east coast of England – the Saxon shore.
286–96	Period of the British Empire, established by Carausius in Britain and north Gaul; Carausius was murdered in 293 by Allectus, who became Emperor. In 296 Emperor Constantius killed Allectus in battle near Silchester, restoring Britain to the Empire.
c. 296–314	Britain was divided into four provinces: *Maxima Caesariensis* based on Londinium; *Britannia Prima* based on Corinium (Cirencester); *Flavia Caesariensis* based on Lindum; *Britannia Secunda* based on Eboracum.
360s	Picts, Scots, and Saxons attacked Britain, including a concerted attack in 367, leading to major disruption; in 368 Count Theodosius succeeded in restoring order.
369	A fifth province was created in Britain, *Valentia*, which may have been in the northwest and based on Luguvalium (Carlisle).
383	Rebellion of Magnus Maximus, a Roman commander in Britain who withdrew troops to Gaul (killed by Emperor Theodosius in 388).
401	Stilicho, guardian of Emperor Honorius, withdrew troops from Britain for the defence of Italy.
406	The army in Britain established Marcus as Emperor; soon killed.
407	The army elevated Gratian as Emperor; he lasted for four months. The army then made Constantine III Emperor, who withdrew troops to Gaul.
408	Severe raid on Britain by Saxons.
409	British leaders may have expelled Roman officials and then raised their own forces to deal with Saxon invaders.

THE SAXON SHORE

The End of Roman Britain

In the 3rd century AD the European provinces of the Roman empire suffered greatly from barbarian invasion and political turmoil. Though Britain was relatively immune, these events set in motion the longer-term dissolution of the western Roman empire.

The Sea Wolves

The 3rd century AD was a time of peace on the northern frontier of Roman Britain. Treaties and the garrisons of Hadrian's Wall held the northern tribes in check, but at the same time Gaul and Germany were afflicted by invasions, and the fringes of the storm reached. Britain. From across the North Sea came Saxon raiders, threatening the villas and settlements of the southeastern coasts. To fend them off a series of strong, new forts, the forts of the Saxon Shore, were built in the late 3rd century around the coasts of East Anglia and the southeast, from Brancaster in Norfolk via the Straits of Dover to Portchester in Hampshire. They show the high walls and towers of late Roman defences and were associated with both land and sea forces to intercept and repel invaders.

By the 4th century the northern frontier was again giving concern, with the Picts and powerful new peoples such as the Scots menacing Hadrian's Wall., which was refurbished to meet the threat. Occasionally the defensive system based on the Wall failed, most notably in the great 'Barbarian Conspiracy' of AD 367. In this year the Picts, Scots, and Saxons combined to attack Britain from all sides and the army in Britain temporarily collapsed, having to be restored by the general Theodosius (father of the emperor of the same name).

Britain in the 4th century

A 4th-century writer refers to Britain as 'a very wealthy island' and its importance to the politics and economy of the late Roman west are clear. The island spawned a succession of claimants to the imperial throne, starting successfully with Constantine I, the first Christian emperor, proclaimed at York in AD 306. Less successful were Magnentius (350–53) and Magnus Maximus (383–88), both of whom may have removed troops to the continent, and whose suppression brought reprisals upon Britain.

Nonetheless, excavations on the towns and villas of Britain have shown that the first half of the 4th century was their heyday and the time of greatest prosperity and stability for Roman Britain. The villas in particular were at their most numerous and elaborate, with palatial residences such as Bignor (Sussex) or Woodchester (Gloucestershire). Both villas and town-houses were embellished with mosaics whose designs drew on themes from Greco-Roman mythology or the newly fashionable Christianity. The well-to-do proprietors of these villas enjoyed a Roman lifestyle comparable with their peers in Gaul, Spain, or Italy. Finds of silver plate such as that from Corbridge (Northumberland) and Mildenhall (Suffolk) or of jewellery from Hoxne and Thetford (both Suffolk) attest to the wealth and the artistic and religious tastes of British aristocrats.

Decline and fall

By the late 4th century the archaeological evidence shows that the glory days of Roman Britain were passing. Villas were becoming dilapidated or were abandoned, damaged mosaics went unpatched, and the streets and services of the towns fell into decay. The critical moment came early in the 5th century. In AD 406 the army in Britain proclaimed another claimant to the imperial purple, Constantine III. He took part of the army with him to Gaul, where he was defeated and killed AD 411. At the time Gaul was in turmoil through barbarian invasions, and the central Roman authorities were unable to re-establish control or re-garrison Britain.

Though the Romans never formally abandoned Britain (the famous 410 letter of the Emperor Honorius urging the British to look to their own defences may actually refer to Bruttium in southern Italy), it slipped from their grasp in the early 5th century and was never recovered. Despite the level of success of Roman civilization among the British upper classes, the removal of military protection and the imperial system dealt this way of life a body-blow which it could not withstand, and the decay and dilapidation of the late 4th century hastened the final collapse of Roman-style living in the early 5th century.

The Dark Ages

There is an almost total lack of contemporary historical sources for the mid and late 5th centuries. Yet it is in this time that the Anglo-Saxons became established in Britain. One story has it that some were brought over by a post-Roman ruler in Kent, Vortigern, to protect his kingdom against other raiders. Because of Vortigern's treachery they turned against him and took the kingdom for themselves. This has also been seen as the time of the 'historical' King Arthur, a post-Roman war-leader rallying the Britons against the Anglo-Saxon invaders, the last standard-bearer of Rome in Britain.

SIMON ESMONDE CLEARY

actual conquest was not begun until AD 43 by the emperor ◊Claudius. After several unsuccessful attempts to conquer Scotland, the northern frontier was fixed at ◊Hadrian's Wall. During the 4th century Britain was raided by the Saxons, Picts, and Scots. The Roman armies were withdrawn 407 as the Roman Empire came under increasing pressure from barbarian tribes on its northern and eastern borders from the late 4th century but there were partial reoccupations 417–*c.* 427 and *c.* 450.

Roman roads network of well-built roads constructed across Britain by the Romans, to facilitate rapid troop movements and communications, as well as trade. The best known are Ermine Street, Watling Street, and Fosse Way. Many Roman roads were constructed afresh, others, such as the ◊Icknield Way, were based on ancient routes. The roads were usually as straight as possible to aid speed of travel, and were built from large kerb stones between smaller stones covered with river gravel, often accompanied by drainage ditches. Many of the roads continued in use throughout the Middle Ages.

Room 40 in World War I, room in the British Admiralty building for the cryptanalysis staff who deciphered German naval signals, including the Zimmermann Telegram.

Root and Branch Petition presented to the Long Parliament 11 Dec 1640, petition calling for the abolition 'root and branch' of episcopacy. The petition was supported by 15,000 Londoners and a bill was introduced in the House of Commons the following May. However, Charles I would not countenance the loss of bishops and the issue was dropped. Many moderate members of Parliament rallied to support both the king and the church.

Rorke's Drift, Battle of during the Anglo-Zulu War, British victory over a Zulu army 22 Jan 1879 at Rorke's Drift, a farm about 170 km/105 mi north of Durban, Natal. A small British force on the farm, which was little more than a field hospital, held off 4,000 Zulus who had just defeated a much larger British force at Isandhlwana. Eleven Victoria Crosses were awarded to the defenders, the most ever given for a single battle, and nine Distinguished Conduct Medals. British casualties were 17 killed and 10 wounded while the Zulus left 400 dead on the field.

Rosebery Archibald Philip Primrose, 5th Earl of Rosebery 1847–1929. British Liberal politician. He was foreign secretary 1886 and 1892–94, when he succeeded Gladstone as prime minister, but his government survived less than a year. After 1896 his imperialist views gradually placed him further from the mainstream of the Liberal Party.

Roses, Wars of the civil wars in England 1455–85 between the houses of Lancaster (badge, red rose) and York (badge, white rose), both of whom claimed the throne through descent from the sons of Edward III. As a result of ◊Henry VI's lapse into insanity 1453, Richard, Duke of York, was installed as protector of the realm. Upon his recovery, Henry forced York to take up arms in self-defence. The wars lasted intermittently for the next 30 years. Behind the dynastic struggle between the houses of York and Lancaster, lay a complex series of rivalries and jealousies between powerful aristocratic families, such as the Beauforts and the Nevilles, who took the opportunity to settle old scores and strengthen their own positions.

The name Wars of the Roses was first used in the 19th century by novelist Walter Scott.

Wars of the Roses, 1455–85
A series of intermittent conflicts between rival dynasties over a 30-year period, the Wars of the Roses were characterized by shifting baronial allegiances to the rival Yorkist and Lancastrian claimants to the throne. The extensive landholdings of the major families ensured that skirmishing and disorder occurred over large parts of England.

Wars of the Roses, 1455–85

The Wars of the Roses: chronology

1447   *23 Feb* Death of Humphrey, Duke of Gloucester; Richard, Duke of York, became heir to his cousin King Henry VI.

1453   *Aug* Henry VI became insane. Leading magnates assumed responsibility for government and admitted York to the council.
13 Oct Birth of Edward, son of King Henry VI and Queen Margaret, providing a direct heir.
23 Nov Duke of Somerset, rival of Richard of York, was imprisoned in the Tower of London.

1454   *27 March* The council appointed Richard of York as protector and defender of the realm.
Dec King Henry VI recovered his sanity. York was dismissed as protector and on 4 Feb 1455 Somerset was released from the Tower.

1455   *22 May* Battle of St Alban's: armies led by York and Somerset clashed. Somerset was killed. On 19 Nov, York was again appointed protector.

1456–59 On 25 Feb 1456 York was removed as protector, but remained on the council. During the next few years, Queen Margaret built up an anti-Yorkist court party.

1459   *June* Richard of York and followers were excluded from a meeting of the royal council.
23 Sept Battle of Blore Heath: Richard Neville, Earl of Warwick and Yorkist, defeated a royalist (Lancastrian) force in Staffordshire.
12 Oct Battle of Ludford Bridge: Lancastrians defeated the Yorkists in Shropshire. Richard of York fled to Ireland, while his son and the Earl of Warwick went to Calais. On 20 Nov the 'parliament of devils' attainted the Yorkists.

1460   *10 July* Battle of Northampton: Yorkists defeated the Lancastrian army and captured King Henry VI. On 10 Oct, the Duke of York returned from Ireland to London and was made heir. In response Queen Margaret raised a new army.
30 Dec Battle of Wakefield: Lancastrians defeated the Yorkists in Yorkshire. Casualties included Richard of York, who was succeeded by his son Edward.

1461   *2 Feb* Battle of Mortimer's Cross: the Yorkists defeated Welsh Lancastrians in Herefordshire.
17 Feb 2nd Battle of St Albans: Queen Margaret's Lancastrian army defeated the Yorkists and rescued King Henry VI.
4 March Edward of York, now in London, was proclaimed king.
29 March Battle of Towton: Yorkists defeated Lancastrians in Yorkshire, killing many Lancastrian leaders. King Henry, Queen Margaret, and the prince of Wales fled to Scotland.

1461–68 Yorkists eliminated opposition in Wales and the north of England. On 24 June 1465, King Henry VI was captured in Lancashire and imprisoned in the Tower of London.

1470   *1 May* Richard, Earl of Warwick, who had been implicated in a revolt against King Edward IV, fled to France where he became reconciled with Margaret, wife of the deposed Henry VI (22 July).
13 Sept The Earl of Warwick landed in southwest England. In Oct King Edward was deserted by his supporters and fled to Burgundy. On 13 Oct, Warwick restored Henry VI as king.

1471   *14 March* King Edward landed in Yorkshire with a small army.
14 April Battle of Barnet: Edward's Yorkist army defeated Warwick's Lancastrian army north of London. Warwick was killed.
4 May Battle of Tewkesbury: Lancastrians led by Queen Margaret and the prince of Wales were defeated in Gloucestershire. The prince was killed and Margaret captured.
21–22 May Henry VI killed in the Tower of London.
Sept Henry Tudor, Earl of Richmond, the Lancastrian claimant to the throne, escaped to Brittany.

1483   *9 April* Death of King Edward IV, who was succeeded by his son Edward V, a minor. On 23 June, Parliament declared him and his brother illegitimate and asked the Duke of Gloucester to become king (as Richard III).

1485   *7 Aug* Henry Tudor landed in south Wales.
22 Aug Battle of Bosworth: Henry Tudor and supporters defeated and killed Richard III. Henry was proclaimed king as Henry VII.

Rothschild European family active in the financial world for two centuries. **Mayer Anselm** (1744–1812) set up as a moneylender in Frankfurt-am-Main, Germany, and business houses were established throughout Europe by his ten children.

Nathan Mayer (1777–1836) settled in England, and his grandson **Nathaniel** (1840–1915) was created a baron in 1885. **Lionel Walter** (1868–1937) succeeded his father as 2nd Baron Rothschild and was an eminent naturalist. His daughter **Miriam** (1908–   ) is an entomologist, renowned for her studies of fleas. The 2nd baron's nephew, **Nathaniel** (1910–1990), 3rd Baron Rothschild, was a scientist. During World War II he worked in British military intelligence. He was head of the central policy-review staff in the Cabinet Office (the

The slaughter of men was immense: for besides the dukes, earls, barons and distinguished warriors who were cruelly slain, multitudes almost innumerable of common people died of their wounds.

WARS OF THE ROSES
described in the
Historiae Croylandensis
Continuatio, *second half 15th century.*

'think tank' set up by Edward Heath) 1970–74. James de Rothschild (1878–1957), originally a member of the French branch, but who became a naturalized Briton, bequeathed to the nation Waddesdon Manor, near Aylesbury.

rotten borough or ***pocket borough*** English parliamentary constituency, before the Great Reform Act 1832, that returned members to Parliament in spite of having small numbers of electors. Such a borough could easily be manipulated by those with sufficient money or influence and MPs were often returned at the whim of local landowners. A borough became rotten when the population had shrunk dramatically since the later Middle Ages but the borough's right to return MPs had not been reviewed accordingly, as at Old Sarum or Winchelsea. The alternative name pocket borough arose because the dominant local landowner had the seat 'in his pocket'.

rough wooing English invasions of Scotland 1543–1549 in a vain attempt to enforce the Treaty of ◊Greenwich 1543. Henry VIII sent Edward Seymour, Earl of Hertford, to harry the Scottish borders. Seymour extended the policy while Lord Protector for the underage Edward VI and established English garrisons in Scotland.

Round Table conferences discussions on the future of India held in London 1930–32 between representatives of British India, the Princely States, and the British government. The Indian princes agreed to join a united India (including Pakistan) at the first conference 1930–31, but there was little progress in the second conference 1931 as Mahatma Gandhi demanded a wider franchise. After the third conference 1932, the British passed the Government of India Act 1935. See ◊India Acts, ◊India, Independence of.

Roundhead member of the Parliamentary party during the English Civil War 1640–60, opposing the royalist Cavaliers. The term referred to the short hair then worn only by men of the lower classes.

Roundway Down, Battle of 13 July 1643, battle at Roundway Down, 3 km/2 mi north of Devizes, Wiltshire, between Royalist troops under Lord Wilmot and Parliamentarians under Sir William Waller. The Parliamentarians were defeated, losing all their cannon and much ammunition.

Rowntree Benjamin Seebohm 1871–1954. English entrepreneur and philanthropist. Much of the money he acquired as chair (1925–41) of the family firm of confectioners, H I Rowntree, he used to fund investigations into social conditions. His writings include *Poverty, A Study of Town Life* 1900. The three ***Rowntree Trusts***, which were founded by his father ***Joseph Rowntree*** (1836–1925) in 1904, fund research into housing, social care, and social policy, support projects relating to social justice, and give grants to pressure groups working in these areas.

Royal Air Force the air force of Britain. The first British air force was the Royal Flying Corps (RFC), founded 1912 as a joint army and navy organization. In World War I the naval side separated as the Royal Naval Air Service (RNAS, later the Fleet Air Arm), and in the final months of the war the two merged as the Royal Air Force 1918. In World War II the RAF proved Britain's main defence against invasion, so assuming a role that the navy had formerly exercised for centuries.

Royal Flying Corps (RFC) forerunner of the ◊Royal Air Force, created 1912 from the Air Battalion, Royal Engineers, as the air arm of the British army.

The RFC was organized in squadrons, each of three flights of four aircraft; at first these were mixed, but during World War I separate squadrons dedicated to fighter, bomber, reconnaissance, training, or other roles were formed. It was merged into the Royal Air Force 1 April 1918.

royal household personal staff of a sovereign. In Britain the chief officers are the Lord Chamberlain, the Lord Steward, and the Master of the Horse. The other principal members of the royal family also maintain their own households.

Royal Naval Air Service (RNAS) air arm of the Royal Navy during World War I, formed July 1914 from naval officers and elements of the ◊Royal Flying Corps.

The RNAS performed patrol duties over the North Sea, pioneered the use of aircraft carriers, and was also responsible for the air defence of Britain until 1916. It pioneered strategic bombing, attacking German airship bases as early as 1914.

The Royal Navy of England has ever been its greatest defence and ornament; it is its ancient and natural strength, the floating bulwark of the island.

ROYAL NAVY
jurist Sir William Blackstone,
Commentaries on the Laws of England
1765–69

Royal Navy the navy of Britain. Alfred the Great established a navy in the 9th century, and by the 13th century there was already an official styled 'keeper of the king's ships'. This office grew to become the Navy Board 1546, the body responsible for administering the fleet of Henry VIII, some 80 ships, with the *Great Harry* as his flagship. The Navy Board administered the navy until 1832, when the Board of Admiralty was instituted. The government head of the Admiralty was the First Lord of the Admiralty, while the senior serving officer in command of the navy was the First Sea Lord (now known as Chief of Naval Staff and First Sea Lord). The Admiralty was abolished 1964 and replaced by the naval department of the Ministry of Defence.

It was only in the reign of Elizabeth I 1558–1603 that the navy grew from Henry's private fleet to become a national defensive force. It gained the title Royal Navy in the reign of Charles II 1660–85. During the 18th century the Royal Navy successfully vied for maritime supremacy with the French navy, leading Britain to victory in four separate wars between 1688 and 1763. It played a key role in Britain's stand against Napoleon and was never again challenged by the French after Trafalgar 1805. Meanwhile the navy had been the means by which the British Empire extended round the world from the 17th century. The Royal Navy continued to be the world's most powerful navy well into the 20th century. In World War I its main task was to protect shipping from submarine attack. After World War II the Royal Navy was second in size only to the US Navy and continued to be a world leader, especially in submarine warfare. By the 1980s, however, as a result of defence cuts, the Royal Navy had declined to third in world size, after the USA and USSR. Despite this smaller presence, the Royal Navy has been responsible for Britain's nuclear deterrence from 1969 and in 1995 had a fleet of four nuclear submarines. As a fighting force in recent times the Royal Navy played a vital national role in the Falklands War 1982 and also formed part of an international force in the Korean War 1950–3, Gulf War 1990–1 and Balkans War 1992–5.

Royal Pavilion or ***Brighton Pavilion*** palace in Brighton, built 1784 and bought in the early 19th century for the Prince Regent (the future George IV) who had it extensively rebuilt in a mix of classical and Indian styles. Queen Victoria was the last monarch to use it and it is now municipal property.

Royal Pavilion
The Royal Pavilion, Brighton, rebuilt between 1815 and 1821 for the pleasure-loving Prince of Wales (later George IV). The Prince's favourite architect, John Nash, employed an exotic hybrid style that has been dubbed 'Hindoo-Gothic'.
Philip Sauvain

Royal Society oldest and premier scientific society in Britain, originating 1645 and chartered 1662; Robert Boyle, Christopher Wren, and Isaac Newton were prominent early members. Its Scottish equivalent is the *Royal Society of Edinburgh* 1783.

Royalist in the Civil War, a supporter of Charles I and later Charles II, as opposed to the parliamentarians. Royalists supported episcopacy and the established church, as well as the king himself. The majority of peers were Royalists and there was strong popular support in the north and west, and in Wales. Many Royalists were Catholics.

Rump, the English Parliament formed between Dec 1648 and Nov 1653 after ◊Pride's purge of the ◊Long Parliament to ensure a majority in favour of trying Charles I. It was dismissed 1653 by Cromwell, who replaced it with the ◊Barebones Parliament.

Reinstated after the Protectorate ended 1659 and the full membership of the Long Parliament restored 1660, the Rump dissolved itself shortly afterwards and was replaced by the Convention Parliament, which brought about the restoration of the monarchy.

Russell
Whig (Liberal) MP John Russell, prime minister 1846–52 and 1865–66, was a major force behind Liberal achievements of the early 19th century, including Catholic emancipation and the 1831 Reform Bill.
Michael Nicholson

rune character in the oldest Germanic script, chiefly adapted from the Latin alphabet, the earliest examples being from the 3rd century, and found in Denmark. Runes were scratched on wood, metal, stone, or bone. Examples of runes in England include those on the Bewcastle and Ruthwell crosses.

Runnymede meadow on the south bank of the river Thames near Egham, Surrey, England, where on 15 June 1215 King John put his seal to the ◊Magna Carta.

Rupert Prince 1619–1682. English Royalist general and admiral, born in Prague, son of the Elector Palatine Frederick V and James I's daughter Elizabeth. He was renowned as a cavalry leader and led the royalist forces at Edgehill. Defeated by Cromwell at ◊Marston Moor and ◊Naseby in the Civil War, he commanded a privateering fleet 1649–52, until routed by Admiral Robert Blake, and, returning after the Restoration, was a distinguished admiral in the Dutch Wars. He founded the ◊Hudson's Bay Company.

Rupert's Land former British colony in northern ◊Canada, of which Prince ◊Rupert was the first governor. Granted to the ◊Hudson's Bay Company 1670, it was later split among Québec, Ontario, Manitoba, and the Northwest Territories.

Russell John, 1st Earl Russell 1792–1878. British Liberal politician, son of the 6th Duke of Bedford. He entered the House of Commons 1813 and supported Catholic emancipation and helped draft the 1831 Reform Bill. He held cabinet posts 1830–41, became prime minister 1846–52, and was again a cabinet minister until becoming prime minister again 1865–66. He retired after the defeat of his Reform Bill 1866.

As foreign secretary in Aberdeen's coalition 1852 and in Palmerston's second government 1859–65, Russell assisted Italy's struggle for unity, although his indecisive policies on Poland, Denmark, and the American Civil War provoked much criticism. He had a strained relationship with Palmerston.

Russell Lord William 1639–1683. British Whig politician. Son of the 1st Duke of Bedford, he was among the founders of the Whig Party, and actively supported attempts in Parliament to exclude the Roman Catholic James II from succeeding to the throne. In 1683 he was accused, on dubious evidence, of complicity in the ◊Rye House Plot to murder Charles II, and was executed.

Rye House Plot conspiracy 1683 by English Whig extremists against Charles II because of his Roman Catholic leanings. They intended to murder Charles and his brother James, Duke of York, at Rye House, Hoddesdon, Hertfordshire, as they returned to London from the Newmarket races but the plot was betrayed. The Duke of ◊Monmouth was involved, and alleged conspirators, including Lord William ◊Russell and Algernon Sidney (1622–1683), were executed for complicity.

Sacheverell Case prosecution of Dr Henry Sacheverell (*c*. 1674–1724) for preaching a High Anglican sermon 1709 attacking the Glorious Revolution. He was impeached by the Whig government and convicted the following year in the Lords, although only by a small majority. He was barred from preaching for the next three years. His case aroused much public sympathy and helped pave the way for the Tories' resumption of office.

Sackville Thomas, 1st Earl of Dorset 1536–1608. English poet and politician. He was charged with telling Mary Queen of Scots that she was to be executed and succeeded Lord ◊Burghley as Lord High Treasurer. He collaborated with Thomas Norton on *Gorboduc* 1561, written in blank verse, one of the earliest English tragedies.

St Brice's Day massacre mass killing 13 Nov (St Brice's Day) 1002 of Danes resident in England. The slaughter was ordered by Ethelred 'the Unready', who feared Danish plots against him. The massacre provoked the Danish invasion of 1003.

St Ffagan, Battle of in the Civil War, battle 8 May 1648 at St Ffagan, west of Cardiff, in which an army led by rebel parliamentarians planned to capture Cardiff but was heavily defeated by Cromwell's troops under General Thomas Horton. It was the only major battle of the Civil War fought in Wales.

St Germain, Treaty of 1919 peace treaty between Austria and the Allies after World War I, signed at St Germain-en-Laye, a town 21 km/13 mi west of Paris. The treaty confirmed the break-up of the Austro-Hungarian Empire and prohibited any future union between Austria and Germany. The USA made a separate peace with Austria in 1921.

St Helena British island territory, South Atlantic. Discovered by the Portuguese 1502, St Helena was annexed by the Dutch 1633. They never occupied it, however, and the English East India Company seized it 1659. It was ceded to the British Crown 1834. The British lent the island to the French 1815–21 as a place of exile for Napoleon, who died there 1821.

St Paul's Cathedral
One of Sir Christopher Wren's unexecuted designs for St Paul's Cathedral, London. The cathedral was to have been the centrepiece of a new urban plan, designed by Wren, for the City of London following the Great Fire. The scheme was rejected as it would felt it would interfere with the city's commercial life.
Philip Sauvain

St Lucia former British island territory, West Indies. The second largest island in the Windward group was first settled by the English 1603. Its possession was fiercely challenged by the French, to whom it passed many times in the wars of the late 19th century and the Napoleonic Wars. It finally became British 1814. It gained independence within the British Commonwealth 1979.

St Paul's Cathedral cathedral church of the City of London, the largest Protestant church in England. A Norman building, which had replaced the original Saxon church, was burned down in the Great Fire 1666; the present cathedral, designed by Christopher Wren, was built 1675–1710.

Saints, Battle of the during the ◊American Revolution, British naval victory over the French 12 April 1782, off the islands of Les Saintes in the channel separating Dominica

from Guadeloupe in the Windward Islands. The British achieved their short-term aim of preventing a French convoy from sailing, but more importantly this battle also had the effect of reasserting British naval supremacy in the western hemisphere.

Salamanca, Battle of during the ◊Peninsular War, victory 22 July 1812 of the British led by the Duke of Wellington over the French under Marshal Auguste Marmont. Marmont was able to collect his forces and made a fighting retreat to Valladolid, while the British entered Salamanca. French casualties came to 15,000, and Marmont himself was forced to return to France to recover from a wound sustained in the operation; British losses were 6,000. The battle took place to the south of Salamanca, 170 km/105 mi northwest of Madrid.

Salisbury Robert Cecil, 1st Earl of Salisbury. Title conferred on Robert ◊Cecil, secretary of state to Elizabeth I of England.

Salisbury Robert Arthur Talbot Gascoyne-Cecil, 3rd Marquess of Salisbury 1830–1903. British Conservative politician. He entered the Commons 1853 and succeeded to his title 1868. He was secretary for India 1866–67 but resigned in protest at the second Reform Act. As foreign secretary 1878–80, he took part in the Congress of Berlin which helped settle the Eastern question. As prime minister 1885–86, 1886–92, and 1895–1902 he gave his main attention to foreign policy, especially British expansion in Africa, and he also retained the post of foreign secretary for most of this time.

Salisbury Robert Arthur James Gascoyne-Cecil, 5th Marquess of Salisbury 1893–1972. British Conservative politician. He was Dominions secretary 1940–42 and 1943–45, colonial secretary 1942, Lord Privy Seal 1942–43 and 1951–52, and Lord President of the Council 1952–57.

Salvation Army Christian evangelical, social-service, and social-reform organization, established 1865 in London with the work of William ◊Booth. Originally called the Christian Revival Association, it was renamed the East London Christian Mission 1870 and from 1878 has been known as the Salvation Army, now a worldwide organization. It has military titles for its officials, is renowned for its brass bands, and its weekly journal is the *War Cry*.

San Francisco conference conference attended by representatives from 50 nations who had declared war on Germany before March 1945; held in San Francisco, California, USA. The conference drew up the United Nations Charter, which was signed 26 June 1945.

Sandwich John Montagu, 4th Earl of Sandwich 1718–1792. British politician. He was an inept First Lord of the Admiralty 1771–82 during the American Revolution, and his corrupt practices were blamed for the British navy's inadequacies.

The Sandwich Islands (Hawaii) were named after him, as are sandwiches, which he invented so that he could eat without leaving the gaming table.

Saratoga, Battle of during the ◊American Revolution, British defeat by the Americans Sept–Oct 1777 near Saratoga Springs, about 240 km/150 mi north of New York. The defeat was a humiliation for the British and a substantial victory for the American general Horatio Gates.

A British force, under General John Burgoyne, was cut off by Gates and eventually forced to surrender 17 Oct. Under the terms of the surrender, known as the Convention of Saratoga, the British were to be allowed to march to Boston and there embark for England, but Congress refused to ratify it and Burgoyne and his force became prisoners of war until peace was signed.

Saxe-Coburg-Gotha Saxon duchy. Albert, the Prince Consort of Britain's Queen Victoria, was a son of the 1st Duke, Ernest I (1784–1844), who was succeeded by Albert's elder brother, Ernest II (1818–1893). It remained the name of the British royal house until 1917, when it was changed to Windsor.

Saxon member of a Germanic tribe inhabiting the Danish peninsula and northern Germany. The Saxons migrated from their homelands, under pressure from the Franks, and spread into various parts of Europe, including Britain (see ◊Anglo-Saxon) in the 5th century. They also undertook piracy in the North Sea and English Channel.

Saxon language or *Anglo-Saxon* another term for Old English. Many basic English words derive from the Angles (who gave the language its name) and the Saxons, two invading peoples in the 5th century AD. The Saxons came first, and the Angles' language was so similar that both were called Saxon.

The suffixes *ton* and *ham* are Saxon words ('town' and 'home') that have left their mark on the language – in Preston, Northampton, Nottingham, and other place names.

Saxon Shore Roman coastal defences constructed in the 3rd and 4th centuries from the Wash to the Solent to prevent incursions by the 'barbarian' tribes of the Continent, especially the Saxons. Strategic harbours and estuaries were fortified to withstand sieges and a fleet of ships (*classis Britanniae*) was established.

Scapa Flow expanse of sea in the Orkney Islands, Scotland, between Mainland and Hoy, until 1957 a base of the Royal Navy. It was the main base of the Grand Fleet during World War I·and in 1919 was the scene of the scuttling of 71 surrendered German warships. It was abandoned as the main base for the fleet 1919 and operations transferred to Rosyth, but was reactivated as a base in World War II.

Scilly, Isles of or **Scilly Isles/Islands**, or **Scillies** group of islands and islets lying 40 km/ 25 mi southwest of Land's End, England; administered by the Duchy of Cornwall; area 16 sq km/6.3 sq mi. The five inhabited islands are **St Mary's**, the largest, on which is Hugh Town, capital of the Scillies; **Tresco**, the second largest, with subtropical gardens; **St Martin's**, noted for beautiful shells; **St Agnes**; and **Bryher**.

The islands are crowded with remains of Bronze Age settlements. In the 16th century they were fortified against raids by Spain and marauding pirates, and Star Castle was built on St Mary's. They were leased at this time to the Godolphin family, who were required to keep a garrison. The Scillies were the last stronghold of the Royalists in the Civil War, and were subdued by the Cromwellians 1651 when Admiral Blake took Tresco and controlled the approach to St Mary's. There have been many shipwrecks on the islands, including that of Sir Cloudesley Shovell's fleet 1707. His flagship, HMS *Association*, was located on the Gilstone Ledge 1967.

Scone site of ancient palace where most of the Scottish kings were crowned on the Stone of Destiny, seized by Edward I 1296 and now in the Coronation Chair at Westminster, London. The village of Scone is in Tayside, Scotland, north of Perth.

Scot inhabitant of Scotland, or person of Scottish descent. Originally the Scots were a Celtic (Gaelic) people of Northern Ireland who migrated to Scotland in the 5th century.

scot and lot medieval municipal tax which brought with it the right to take part in town government and voting. The name comes from the terms 'scot', meaning payment, and 'lot', meaning a share. The modern expression 'Scot free' derives from this tax.

Scotland the northernmost part of the United Kingdom, formerly an independent country, now part of the UK, although there is a movement for an independent or devolved Scottish assembly. Scotland sends 72 members to the UK Parliament at Westminster. Local government is on similar lines to that of England, but there is a different legal system.

Scott Robert Falcon 1868–1912 known as **Scott of the Antarctic**. English explorer who commanded two Antarctic expeditions, 1901–04 and 1910–12. Born at Devonport, he entered the navy in 1882. He reached the South Pole 18 Jan 1912, accompanied by Wilson, Laurence Oates, Bowers, and Evans. They reached the pole shortly after Norwegian Roald Amundsen, but on the return journey they died in a blizzard only a few miles from their base camp. His journal was recovered and published in 1913.

Sovereigns of Scotland 1005–1603

from the unification of Scotland to the union of the crowns of Scotland and England

reign	name
Celtic kings	
1005	Malcolm II
1034	Duncan I
1040	Macbeth
1057	Malcolm III Canmore
1093	Donald III Donalbane
1094	Duncan II
1094	Donald III (restored)
1097	Edgar
1107	Alexander I
1124	David I
1153	Malcolm IV
1165	William the Lion
1214	Alexander II
1249	Alexander III
1286–90	Margaret of Norway
English domination	
1292–96	John Baliol
1296–1306	annexed to England
House of Bruce	
1306	Robert I the Bruce
1329	David II
House of Stuart	
1371	Robert II
1390	Robert III
1406	James I
1437	James II
1460	James III
1488	James IV
1513	James V
1542	Mary
1567	James VI
1603	union of crowns

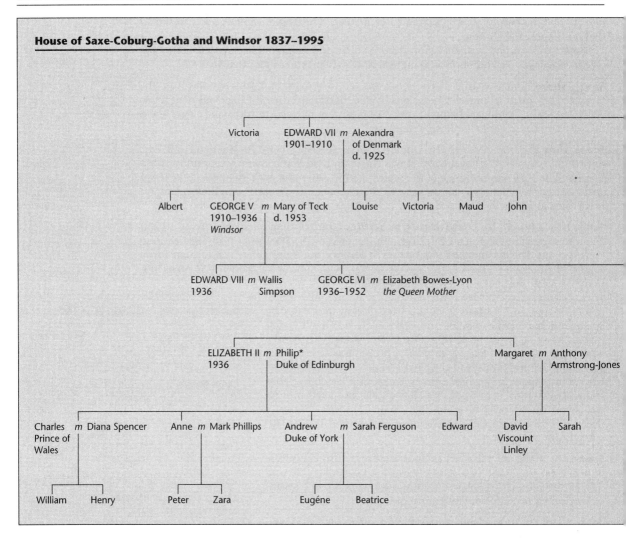

House of Saxe-Coburg-Gotha and Windsor 1837–1995

Scottish National Party (SNP) nationalist party, advocating the separation of Scotland from the UK as an independent state within the European Union. It was formed by the amalgamation of several early nationalist parties 1934 and at first advocated only autonomy within the UK. It gained its first parliamentary victory 1945 but did not make serious headway in Parliament until the 1970s when it became an influential bloc at Westminster, and its support was crucial to James ◊Callaghan's Labour government. It is now second only to the Labour Party in Scotland, having forced the Conservatives into third place.

scutage feudal tax imposed on knights as a substitute for military service. It developed from fines for non-attendance at musters under the Carolingian kings in France, but in England by the 12th century it had become a purely fiscal measure designed to raise money to finance mercenary armies, reflecting the decline in the military significance of feudalism.

SDLP abbreviation for ◊*Social Democratic Labour Party*, a nationalist political party in Northern Ireland.

Sèvres, Treaty of the last of the treaties that ended World War I. Negotiated between the Allied powers and the Ottoman Empire, it was finalized Aug 1920 but never ratified by the Turkish government.

The treaty reduced the size of Turkey by making concessions to the Greeks, Kurds, and Armenians, as well as ending Turkish control of Arab lands. Its terms were rejected by the

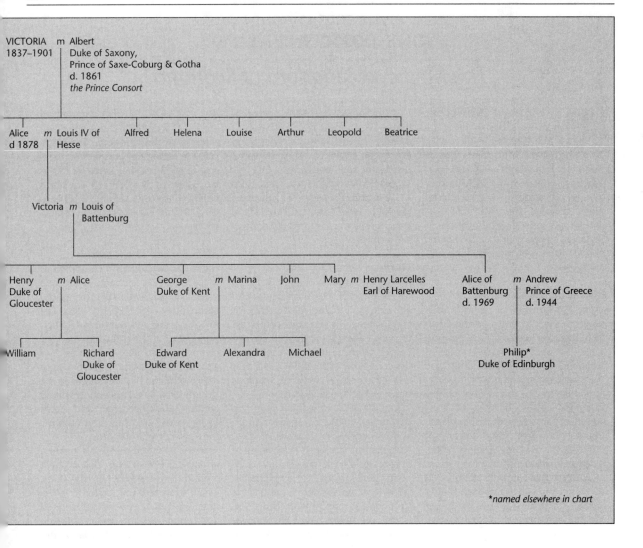

VICTORIA m Albert
1837–1901   Duke of Saxony,
              Prince of Saxe-Coburg & Gotha
              d. 1861
              the Prince Consort

Alice   *m* Louis IV of   Alfred   Helena   Louise   Arthur   Leopold   Beatrice
d 1878   Hesse

Victoria *m* Louis of
               Battenburg

Henry   *m* Alice   George   *m* Marina   John   Mary *m* Henry Larcelles   Alice of   *m* Andrew
Duke of   Duke of Kent   Earl of Harewood   Battenburg   Prince of Greece
Gloucester   d. 1969   d. 1944

William   Richard   Edward   Alexandra   Michael   Philip*
                   Duke of   Duke of Kent   Duke of Edinburgh
                   Gloucester

named elsewhere in chart

newly created nationalist government and the treaty was never ratified. It was superseded by the Treaty of Lausanne 1923.

Sedgemoor, Battle of 6 July 1685, battle in which ◊Monmouth's rebellion was crushed by the forces of James II, on a tract of marshy land 5 km/3 mi southeast of Bridgwater, Somerset.

Selden John 1584–1654. English antiquarian and opponent of Charles I's claim to the divine right of kings (the doctrine that the monarch is answerable to God alone), for which he was twice imprisoned. His *Table Talk* 1689 consists of short essays on political and religious questions.

select committee any of several long-standing committees of the House of Commons, such as the Environment Committee and the Treasury and Civil Service Committee. These were intended to restore parliamentary control of the executive, improve the quality of legislation, and scrutinize public spending and the work of government departments. Select committees represent the major parliamentary reform of the 20th century, and a possible means – through their all-party membership – of avoiding the automatic repeal of one government's measures by its successor.

self-denying ordinance in the Civil War, proposal 3 April 1645 that all New Model Army officers who were peers or members of Parliament should be obliged to resign. The measure was introduced after the Parliamentary army's failure at the second Battle of ◊Newbury and

THE LONG RIVALRY

The Medieval Kingdom of Scotland

The only royal rivals of the medieval English kings in the British Isles lay in the north. The kings of the Scots claimed to be the heirs to a line of over 100 royal forebears, rulers of a people unconquered by invaders. From 1300, relations between the two realms of Britain were dictated by rival claims to land and power in the north of the island, claims which fuelled long-running war.

Clients and rivals

After the emergence of both kingdoms in the 9th century, Anglo-Scottish relations rested on a balance: between an English desire to bring Scotland into its political orbit, and Scottish territorial ambitions in northern England. These ambitions had by the 11th century encouraged Scotland's expansion from its heartlands north of the Forth. The annexation of Strathclyde and of English-settled Lothian marked out Scotland as an aggressive power with designs on Cumbria and Northumberland. After 1058, Scotland, unlike the other Celtic kingdoms, was ruled by a single dynasty; though challenged by rival claimants, the Canmores moved from being kings of an unruly federation to masters of their kingdom.

The Normans recognized this situation and there was no Norman conquest of Scotland. Instead the Norman kings sought to increase their influence with the Canmores. David I (1124–1153), as brother-in-law and vassal of Henry I of England, was part of the Anglo-Norman world. The politics and culture of twelfth century Scotland were transformed by the arrival of the personnel and practices of Norman nobility, church, government, and trade. If change was not entirely peaceful, in Scotland it did not sweep away native power.

The Canmores used the new techniques of war and administration to increase royal authority. Although influenced heavily by their powerful neighbour, neither David I nor his successors became vassal rulers; from 1124 to 1286, designs on northern England were still pursued and English claims to be lords of Scotland still resisted.

The long war

In the last decades of the 13th century, the end of the Canmore dynasty and Edward I of England's search for real influence in Scotland combined to sweep away the balance between English claims and Scottish independence. From 1296 until 1560 war was the normal state of relations between the two kingdoms.

English aims varied between the destruction of the Scottish kingdom and its reduction to a vassal-state. The greatest efforts to achieve these goals came in the half-century up to 1346, but claims to overlordship were never abandoned. English kings continued to press these claims and from 1544 union based on war was revived in the 'Rough Wooing' of Scotland by Henry VIII.

The demands of a war for survival shaped late medieval Scotland. The language of resistance to Edward I and his heirs stressed the existence of Scotland as a community whose rights were under threat. The usurpation of Robert the Bruce 1306 harnessed effective royal leadership to this sense of grievance. Bruce's military success against English forces was exploited to create a bond between his kingship and the aristocratic community. This bond was cemented by the rise of families, like the Stewarts and Douglases, who had been closest to Bruce's cause. In the century after his death in 1329, when the Scots lacked a similar royal leader, these noble fam-

ilies combined private aggrandizement with a patriotic cause, the maintenance of the kingdom. Scotland's place in diplomacy was defined by a role as the hereditary enemy of England and as the ally of England's enemy, France. By the mid-14th century, British conflict and European conflict had become intertwined.

Kingdom and community

History and geography combined to make medieval Scotland seem little more than a collection of provinces by comparison with England. Areas like Argyll, Moray, and Galloway retained significance and identity into the 15th century. While the Canmores had added Caithness and the Hebrides to their realm, the highland areas of the kingdom remained under only limited control. Sustained war and, from 1329, weak kingship strengthened the power of regional lords.

In the west and north this meant a resurgence of Gaelic power built around the Lordship of the Isles, which stretched from Ulster to Inverness. The threat from the Isles fostered a growing cultural divide between lowland and highland Scotland after 1400.

Traditions of kingship did not sit comfortably in a realm which by 1400 was dominated by great lords. The subsequent century witnessed a series of aggressive rulers of the Stewart dynasty asserting the rights of the Crown to the full. Two of the five kings between 1406 and 1542 died at their subjects' hands, and all faced opposition. However, they ultimately restored royal primacy. By 1500 Scotland seemed secure as a small but stable kingdom with connections in diplomacy, trade, and culture which stretched beyond the British Isles.

MICHAEL BROWN

provided an expedient means of dismissing ineffectual Parliamentary commanders, such as the Earl of Manchester, without causing individual bitterness. Cromwell was reappointed to his position.

Selkirk Alexander 1676–1721. Scottish sailor marooned 1704–09 in the Juan Fernández Islands in the South Pacific. His story inspired Daniel Defoe to write *Robinson Crusoe*.

Sepoy Rebellion alternative name for the ◊Indian Mutiny, a revolt of Indian soldiers against the British in India 1857–58.

Septennial Act 1716 act extending the term of a parliament from three to seven years. It was designed to bolster the Whig government, by postponing the election due 1718 to 1722, but in the long term it led to greater stability but also increased the opportunities for corruption. The ◊Parliament Act 1911 reduced the life of a parliament to five years.

serfdom the legal and economic status of peasants under ◊feudalism. Serfs could not be sold like slaves, but they were not free to leave their master's estate without his permission. They had to work the lord's land without pay for a number of days every week and pay a percentage of their produce to the lord every year. They also served as soldiers in the event of conflict. Serfs also had to perform extra labour at harvest time and other busy seasons; in return they were allowed to cultivate a portion of the estate for their own benefit. Serfdom died out in England between the 14th and 17th centuries.

Settlement, Act of a law passed 1701 during the reign of King William III, designed to ensure a Protestant succession to the throne by excluding the Roman Catholic descendants of James II in favour of the Protestant House of Hanover. Elizabeth II still reigns under this act.

Sevastopol, Siege of during the Crimean War, successful British and French siege Oct 1854–Sept 1855 of Sevastopol, a fortified Russian town on the Black Sea. The Russian fleet was based in Sevastopol harbour, so the town was the prime objective of the main Allied attack in the Crimea.

seven bishops, trial of in 1688 trial of William Sancroft, archbishop of Canterbury, and six other bishops on charges of seditious libel after they objected to James II's order that the ◊Declaraton of Indulgence should be read from the pulpit of all Anglican churches on two successive Sundays May–June 1688. They were found not guilty of sedition 29 June, a severe blow to James' authority.

Seven Years' War known as the ***French and Indian War*** in North America, war 1756–63 arising from the conflict between Austria and Prussia, and between France and Britain over colonial supremacy. Britain and Prussia defeated France, Austria, Spain, and Russia and gained control of India and many of France's colonies, including Canada.

Spain ceded Florida to Britain in exchange for Cuba. Fighting against great odds, Prussia was eventually successful in becoming established as one of the great European powers. The war ended with the Treaty of Paris 1763, signed by Britain, France, and Spain.

Britain's part in the war, under the direction of William Pitt the Elder, was mainly confined to operations at sea, notably the victory of Quiberon Bay, Brittany, 1759, and in the colonies, where the victories of ◊Wolfe and ◊Clive resulted in the conquest of Canada and the foundation of the Indian empire.

Severus Lucius Septimius 146–211. Roman emperor, the only African to become emperor. He was commanding an army on the Danube when the emperor Pertinax was murdered 193. Proclaimed emperor by his troops, Severus proved an able administrator. He came to Britain 208 to lead an invasion of the Caledonians' territory in Scotland. He made peace 210 and divided the country into Upper and Lower Britain. He died at York the following year.

Seymour Jane *c.* 1509–1537. Third wife of Henry VIII, whom she married in 1536. The sister of Lord Protector ◊Somerset, she was a lady-in-waiting to Henry's previous two wives. She died soon after the birth of her son Edward VI.

Shackleton Ernest 1874–1922. Irish Antarctic explorer. He was a member of Scott's Antarctic expedition 1901–04 and in 1907–09, he commanded an expedition that reached 88° 23' S latitude, located the magnetic South Pole, and climbed Mount Erebus.

I will drive a coach and six horses through the Act of Settlement...

ACT OF SETTLEMENT
politician Stephen Rice (attributed remark)

Is this country to wage eternal war upon wild imaginary schemes of conquest?

SEVEN YEARS' WAR
Earl of Hardwicke, speech in the House of Lords, 1760

Shaftesbury Anthony Ashley Cooper, 1st Earl of Shaftesbury 1621–1683. English politician, a supporter of the Restoration of the monarchy. He became Lord Chancellor in 1672, but went into opposition 1673 and began to organize the ◊Whig Party. He headed the Whigs' demand for the exclusion of the future James II from the succession, secured the passing of the Habeas Corpus Act 1679, then fled to Holland when he was accused of treason 1681.

Shaftesbury Anthony Ashley Cooper, 7th Earl of Shaftesbury 1801–1885. British Tory politician and social reformer. He strongly supported the Ten Hours Act of 1847 and other factory legislation, including the 1842 act forbidding the employment of women and children underground in mines. He was also associated with the movement to provide free education for the poor.

Sharp Granville 1735–1813. English philanthropist. He was prominent in the anti-slavery movement and in 1772 secured a legal decision 'that as soon as any slave sets foot on English territory he becomes free'.

Sheffield Outrages sensational reports in the British press 1866 of summary justice exercised by trade unions to secure subscriptions and obtain compliance with rules by threats, removal of tools, sabotage of equipment at work, and assaults.

Dramatic accounts of action taken against a strike-breaking worker in the cutlery trade led to a Royal Commission inquiry into trade-union activity. This coincided with a campaign by trade unionists to obtain the reform of the Master and Servant Act, which discriminated between employer and employee in cases of breach of contract. The Majority and Minority Reports favoured the legalization of trade unions, and the repeal of the Master and Servant Act. This was implemented in the Trade Union Act and the Criminal Law Amendment Act, both 1871.

Shelburne William Petty FitzMaurice, 2nd Earl of Shelburne 1737–1805. British Whig politician. He was an opponent of George III's American policy, and as prime minister in 1783, he concluded peace with the United States of America. He was created Marquess of Lansdowne in 1784.

shell scandal furore in the British press 1915 over supplies of ammunition to artillery units in the field. Sir John French, British commander at Neuve Chapelle, cited lack of ammunition as the reason for his failure to the *Times* journalist Col Repington. Encouraged by Lloyd George, both the *Times* and the *Daily Mail* ran headline stories on the 'shell scandal', claiming War Office inefficiency was depriving front-line troops of ammunition. By this time, the difficulties had largely been overcome and the story had little lasting impact, although Lloyd George was appointed minister for munitions in the coalition government formed in May.

Sheppard Jack 1702–1724. English criminal. Born in Stepney, East London, he was an apprentice carpenter, but turned to theft and became a popular hero by escaping four times from prison. He was finally caught and hanged.

Sheridan Richard Brinsley 1751–1816. Irish dramatist and politician. His social comedies include *The Rivals* 1775, celebrated for the character of Mrs Malaprop, and *The School for Scandal* 1777. He entered Parliament 1780 as an adherent of Charles ◊Fox. A noted orator, he directed the impeachment of the former governor general of India, Warren Hastings, and was treasurer to the Navy 1806–07. His last years were clouded by the burning down of his Drury Lane Theatre 1809, the loss of his parliamentary seat 1812, and by financial ruin and mental breakdown.

sheriff (Old English *scīr* 'shire', *gerēfa* 'reeve') in England and Wales, the Crown's chief executive officer in a county for ceremonial purposes; in Scotland, the equivalent of the English county-court judge, but also dealing with criminal cases.

In England, the office (elective until Edward II) dates from before the Norman Conquest. The sheriff, who is appointed annually by royal patent, and is chosen from the leading landowners, acts as returning officer for parliamentary elections, and attends the judges on circuit. The duties of keeping prisoners in safe custody, preparing panels of jurors for assizes, and executing writs, are supervised by the under-sheriff. The City of London has two sheriffs elected by members of the livery companies.

Sheriffmuir, Battle of during the Jacobite rebellion of the ◊Fifteen, inconclusive engagement 13 Nov 1715 between the Earl of ◊Mar's 10,000-strong Jacobite army and 3,300 royalist troops under the Duke of Argyll. Although not actually defeated, Mar was forced to retreat to Perth and the rising collapsed shortly after.

Shetland Islands group of islands off the north coast of Scotland, beyond the Orkney Islands. The islands were a Norse dependency from the 10th century to 1469, when they were pledged to James III of Scotland in lieu of a dowry for Margaret, daughter of King Christian of Denmark, when she married James 1470. Mary, Queen of Scots, granted the islands to her half-brother, Earl Patrick 1564, but after his death they were assimilated into the rest of the Scottish kingdom. The islands were officially called Zetland until 1974.

shilling English coin worth 12 ◊pennies (there were 20 shillings to one pound), first minted under Henry VII. Although the denomination of a shilling was abolished with the advent of decimalization 1971, the coins remained in circulation as five-pence pieces.

ship money tax for support of the navy, levied on the coastal districts of England in the Middle Ages. Charles I's attempts to levy it on the whole country 1634–36, without parliamentary consent and in time of peace, aroused strong opposition from the member of Parliament John Hampden and others, who refused to pay. Ship money was declared illegal by Parliament 1641.

shire administrative area formed in Britain for the purpose of raising taxes in Anglo-Saxon times. By AD 1000 most of southern England had been divided into shires with fortified strongholds at their centres. They were replaced by ◊counties after the Norman conquest but the Midland counties of England are still known as **the Shires**; for example Leicestershire and Northamptonshire.

Short Parliament the English Parliament that was summoned by Charles I 13 April 1640 to raise funds for his war against the Scots. When it became clear that the parliament opposed the war and would not grant him any money, he dissolved it 5 May and arrested some of its leaders. It was succeeded later in the year by the ◊Long Parliament.

Shovell Cloudesley c. 1650–1707. English admiral who took part, with George Rooke (1650–1709), in the capture of Gibraltar 1704. In 1707 his flagship *Association* and four other ships of his home-bound fleet were wrecked off the Isles of Scilly and he was strangled for his rings by an islander when he came ashore.

Shrewsbury, Battle of or **Battle of Hateley Field** decisive royal victory 21 July 1403 over rebels led by Sir Henry 'Hotspur' Percy north of Shrewsbury. The rebellion was crushed and Henry IV promoted the Neville family in the North to counterbalance the Percies.

Sicilian Business Henry III's campaign in Siciliy 1254–58. Henry joined the crusades 1250 but became involved in Sicily 1254 when the pope decreed that he could fulfill his crusading vows by ejecting Rome's enemies, the Hohenstaufen emperors of Germany, from the island. Henry accepted the island as a papal fief on behalf of his son, Edmund, but by 1258 he faced difficulties at home and was forced to accept the ◊Provisions of Oxford by the barons. Part of the problem was the huge cost of the Sicilian adventure and consequent financial exactions on the nobility and Henry was forced to withdraw from the campaign.

Sidmouth, Viscount title of Henry ◊Addington, British Tory prime minister 1801–04.

Sidney Algernon 1622–1683. English Republican politician. He was a cavalry officer in the Civil War on the Parliamentary side, and was wounded at the Battle of ◊Marston Moor 1644. He was elected to the ◊Long Parliament 1646, but retired from politics when ◊Cromwell dissolved the ◊Rump 1653. After the ◊Restoration he lived in exile on the Continent, but on returning to England 1677 continued to oppose the monarchy. He was arrested after the ◊Rye House Plot 1683, convicted of high treason, and executed.

Sidney Philip 1554–1586. English poet and soldier. He wrote the sonnet sequence *Astrophel and Stella* 1591, *Arcadia* 1590, a prose romance, and *Apologie for Poetrie* 1595, the earliest work of English literary criticism.

Sidney was born in Penshurst, Kent. He entered Parliament 1581, and was knighted 1583. In 1585 he was made governor of Vlissingen in the Netherlands, and died at Zutphen, fighting the Spanish.

Thy necessity is yet greater than mine.

PHILIP SIDNEY
on giving his water-bottle to a critically wounded soldier at the Battle of Zutphen, 1586

Sierra Leone former British colony, West Africa. Settlements for runaway and freed slaves were set up on the coast here by English philanthropists 1787, with Freetown established as 'capital' 1788 on land purchased from a local chief. The settlement became a British colony 1808 and the territory was gradually extended into the hinterland. After a clash with the French 1893 the region was acquired for Britain by treaty 1895 and proclaimed a protectorate 1896. It gained independence 1961.

Silbury Hill steep, rounded artificial mound (40 m/130 ft high) of the Bronze Age 2660 BC, in Wiltshire, near ◊Avebury, England. It was previously believed to be a barrow (grave), but excavation on the site has shown this is not the case.

Silchester archaeological site, a major town in Roman Britain. It is 10 km/6 mi north of Basingstoke, Hampshire.

Silures Celtic tribe in southeast Wales which joined with ◊Ordovices in resisting the Romans. They were eventually subjugated c. AD 75 and were recognized as a ◊civitas, with their capital at Venta Silurum (Caerwent).

Simnel Lambert c. 1475–c. 1535. English impostor, a joiner's son who under the influence of an Oxford priest claimed to be Prince Edward, one of the ◊Princes in the Tower. ◊Henry VII discovered the plot and released the real Edward for one day to show him to the public. Simnel had a keen following and was crowned as Edward VI in Dublin 1487. He came with forces to England to fight the royal army, and attacked it near Stoke-on-Trent 16 June 1487. He was defeated and captured, but was contemptuously pardoned. He is then said to have been put to work in the king's kitchen.

Simon John Allsebrook, Viscount Simon 1873–1954. British Liberal politician. He was home secretary 1915–16, but resigned over the issue of conscription. He was foreign secretary 1931–35, home secretary again 1935–37, chancellor of the Exchequer 1937–40, and lord chancellor 1940–45.

Simpson James Young 1811–1870. Scottish physician, the first to use ether as an anaesthetic in childbirth 1847, and the discoverer, later the same year, of the anaesthetic properties of chloroform, which he tested by experiments on himself. It was Queen Victoria's endorsement of Simpson's use of chloroform during the birth of her seventh child 1853 that made his techniques universally adopted and he was eventually appointed her physician.

Singapore former British colony, at the southern end of the Malay Peninsula. Sir Stamford Raffles set up a trading post here 1819 and it was incorporated with Penang and Malacca as the Straits Settlements 1826. The Straits Settlements, with Singapore as its capital from 1836, became a British Crown Colony 1867. Singapore became a state of Malaysia 1963 but left the federation to become an independent sovereign state within the British Commonwealth 1965.

Sinn Féin ('Ourselves alone') Irish nationalist party founded by Arthur Griffith (1872–1922) in 1905; in 1917 Eámon ◊de Valera became its president. It is the political wing of the Irish Republican Army (IRA), and is similarly split between comparative moderates and extremists. In 1985 it gained representation in 17 out of 26 district councils in Northern Ireland. Its president from 1978 is Gerry ◊Adams. In 1994, following a declaration of a cessation of military activities by the IRA, Sinn Féin was poised to enter the political process aimed at securing lasting peace in Northern Ireland.

Six Acts 1819 acts of Parliament passed by Lord Liverpool's Tory administration to curtail political radicalism in the aftermath of the ◊Peterloo massacre and during a period of agitation for reform when ◊habeas corpus was suspended and the powers of magistrates extended.

The acts curtailed the rights of the accused by stipulating trial within a year; increased the penalties for seditious libel; imposed a newspaper stamp duty on all pamphlets and circulars containing news; specified strict limitations on public meetings; banned training with guns and other arms; and empowered magistrates to search and seize arms.

Six Articles act introduced by Henry VIII 1539 to settle disputes over dogma in the English church. The articles affirmed belief in transubstantiation, communion in one kind only, auricular confession, monastic vows, celibacy of the clergy, and private masses; those who rejected transubstantiation were to be burned at the stake. The act was repealed in 1547, replaced by 42 articles in 1551, and by an act of Thirty-Nine Articles in 1571.

slave trade the transport of slaves from one country to work in another. British slaves were taken to Rome during the Roman occupation of Britain, and slaves from Ireland were imported to work in Bristol before the 11th century. The transportation of slaves from Africa to work in plantations in the New World began in the early 16th century. This stimulated a lucrative trade in slaves and the need for slaves to work the British plantations in the Americas led to the development of the Atlantic triangle trade. By the late 17th century, when sugar plantations in the West Indies had become profitable, much of the slave trade was being organized by the British.

From the late 17th century gradual opposition to the slave trade began in Britain. The ◊Mansfield judgment 1772 held that a slave held on a ship on the Thames after escaping had become free on setting foot in Britain. The Society for the Abolition of the Slave Trade was founded 1787 with William ◊Wilberforce as a leading member. After persistent campaigning by abolitionists, an Act of Parliament 1807 made it illegal for British ships to carry slaves or for the British colonies to import them. Finally the Abolition Act 1833 provided for slaves in British colonies to be freed and for their owners to be compensated.

SLD abbreviation for ◊*Social and Liberal Democrats*, British political party.

Slim William Joseph, 1st Viscount 1891–1970. British field marshal in World War II. He served in the North Africa campaign 1941 then commanded the 1st Burma Corps 1942–45, stemming the Japanese invasion of India, and then forcing them out of Burma (now Myanmar) 1945. He was governor general of Australia 1953–60.

Sluis, Battle of (or *Sluys*) 1340 naval victory for England over France which marked the beginning of the Hundred Years' War. The English fleet, under the personal command of Edward III, took control of the English Channel and seized 200 great ships from the French navy of Philip IV; there were 30,000 French casualties but Edward did not follow up on the victory.

Smith Henry George Wakelyn 1787–1860. British general. He served in the Peninsular War (1808–14) and later fought in South Africa and India. He was governor of Cape Colony 1847–52. The towns of Ladysmith and Harrismith, South Africa, are named after his wife and himself respectively.

Smith John 1580–1631. English colonist. After an adventurous early life he took part in the colonization of Virginia, acting as president of the North American colony 1608–09. He explored New England in 1614, which he named, and published pamphlets on America and an autobiography. His trade with the Indians may have kept the colonists alive in the early years.

During an expedition among the American Indians he was captured, and his life is said to have been saved by the intervention of the chief's daughter Pocahontas.

Smith John 1938–1994. British Labour politician, party leader 1992–94. He entered parliament 1970 and served in the administrations of Harold Wilson and James Callaghan. He was Trade and Industry Secretary 1978–79 and from 1979 held various shadow cabinet posts, culminating in that of shadow chancellor 1987–92. As Leader of the Opposition, he won a reputation as a man of transparent honesty and a formidable parliamentarian. His sudden death from a heart attack shocked British politicians of all parties.

Smithfield site of a meat market from 1868 and poultry and provision market from 1889, in the City of London. Formerly an open space, it was the scene of the murder of Wat Tyler, leader of the Peasants' Revolt 1381, and the execution of many Protestant martyrs in the 16th century. The annual Bartholomew Fair was held here 1614–1855.

Smuts Jan Christian 1870–1950. South African politician and soldier; prime minister 1919–24 and 1939–48. During the Second ◊South African War (1899–1902) Smuts commanded the Boer forces in his native Cape Colony. He subsequently worked for reconciliation between the Boers and the British. He supported the Allies in both world wars and was a member of the British imperial war cabinet 1917–18.

SNP abbreviation for ◊*Scottish National Party*.

snuff finely powdered tobacco for sniffing up the nostrils (or sometimes chewed or rubbed on the gums) as a stimulant or sedative. Snuff taking was common in 17th-century England

The movement of the middle classes for the abolition of slavery was virtuous, but it was not wise. It was a very ignorant movement.

Slave Trade
Benjamin Disraeli,
Lord George Bentinck;
A Political Biography
1851

and the Netherlands, and spread in the 18th century to other parts of Europe, but was largely superseded by cigarette smoking.

socage Anglo-Saxon term for the free tenure of land by the peasantry. Sokemen, holders of land by this tenure, formed the upper stratum of peasant society at the time of the ◊Domesday Book.

Social and Liberal Democrats official name for the British political party formed 1988 from the former Liberal Party and most of the Social Democratic Party. The common name for the party is the ***Liberal Democrats***. Its leader (from July 1988) is Paddy Ashdown.

Social Democratic Federation (SDF) in British history, a socialist society, founded as the Democratic Federation 1881 and renamed in 1884. It was led by H M Hyndman (1842–1921), a former conservative journalist and stockbroker who claimed Karl Marx as his inspiration without obtaining recognition from his mentor. In 1911 it became the British Socialist Party.

Social Democratic Labour Party (SDLP) Northern Irish left-wing political party, formed 1970. It aims ultimately at Irish unification, but has distanced itself from violent tactics, adopting a constitutional, conciliatory role. The SDLP, led by John Hume (1937–   ), was responsible for setting up the ◊New Ireland Forum 1983, and for initiating talks with the leader of Sinn Féin (the political wing of the IRA), Gerry Adams, 1993, which prompted a joint UK-Irish peace initiative and set in motion a Northern Ireland cease-fire 1994.

Social Democratic Party (SDP) British centrist political party 1981–90, formed by members of Parliament who resigned from the Labour Party. The 1983 and 1987 general elections were fought in alliance with the Liberal Party as the ***Liberal/SDP Alliance***. A merger of the two parties was voted for by the SDP 1987, and the new party became the ◊Social and Liberal Democrats, leaving a rump SDP that folded 1990.

SOE abbreviation for ◊***Special Operations Executive***.

Solemn League and Covenant alliance between the Scots and English Parliamentarians 25 Sept 1643; both sides agreed to abolish episcopacy and introduce Presbyterianism. In return for £30,000, the Scots provided another army against Charles I, and their cavalry was instrumental in the royalist defeat at ◊Marston Moor 1644.

Solomon Islands former British protectorate, a group of islands in the west Pacific. Following visits by European navigators, missionaries and traders from the 16th century, the islands were divided between Britain and Germany 1886, the latter receiving the northern islands. The southwestern islands came under British dominion 1893, and Britain's possessions here were declared a protectorate then. The German islands were taken by Australian forces 1914 and became an Australian mandate, as part of New Guinea. The British islands achieved independence 1978.

Solway Moss, Battle of crushing defeat 24 Nov 1542 of the Scots by an invading English force under the Duke of Norfolk. Some 500 Scottish prisoners were captured including two earls and five barons, and the shame is said to have led to James V's death three weeks later. The ◊Treaty of Greenwich, by which the infant ◊Mary Queen of Scots would marry Edward, Prince of Wales, was signed in the aftermath of the battle.

Somerset Edward Seymour, 1st Duke of Somerset c. 1506–1552. English politician. Created Earl of Hertford after Henry VIII's marriage to his sister Jane, he became Duke of Somerset and protector (regent) for Edward VI in 1547 and defeated the Scots at the Battle of ◊Pinkie later in the year. His attempt to check ◊enclosure (the transfer of land from common to private ownership) offended landowners and his moderation in religion upset the Protestants. He was overthrown by his rival, the Duke of ◊Northumberland, and beheaded on a fake treason charge in 1552.

Somersett's Case see ◊Mansfield judgment.

Somme, Battle of the Allied offensive in World War I July–Nov 1916 on the river Somme in northern France, during which severe losses were suffered by both sides. It was planned by the Marshal of France, Joseph Joffre, and UK commander-in-chief Douglas Haig; the Allies lost over 600,000 soldiers and advanced 13 km/8 mi. It was the first battle in which tanks

This is to make an end of all wars, to conclude an eternal and perpetual peace.

DUKE OF SOMERSET
*justifying his invasion of Scotland.
letter, 1548*

were used. The German offensive around St Quentin March–April 1918 is sometimes called the Second Battle of the Somme.

South Africa former British colony, southern Africa. The Cape of Good Hope Colony was founded by the Dutch 1652 and remained a Dutch colony until Britain took possession of it 1795. An increasing British presence in the colony led to the 'Great Trek' of the Boers (descendants of Dutch settlers) north and east of the Orange River 1836. Natal was annexed to the Cape Colony 1844, and in 1877 Britain annexed the South African Republic, which had been guaranteed its independence by the Sand River Convention 1852. Transvaal and the Orange Free State (as the Orange River Colony) became British colonies after the Boer defeat in the Second Boer War 1899–1902. The self-governing colonies of Cape of Good Hope, Natal, Transvaal and Orange River Colony were united 1910 as the Union of South Africa. Independence within the British Commonwealth was gained 1931. South Africa left the Commonwealth 1961 to became a republic.

South African Wars or *Boer Wars* two wars between the Boers (settlers of Dutch origin) and the British; essentially fought for the gold and diamonds of the Transvaal.

The *War of 1881* was triggered by the attempt of the Boers of the ◊Transvaal to reassert the independence surrendered 1877 in return for British aid against African peoples. The British were defeated at Majuba, and the Transvaal again became independent under the terms of the Pretoria Convention.

The *War of 1899–1902*, was precipitated by the armed Jameson Raid into the Boer Transvaal; a failed attempt, inspired by the Cape Colony prime minister Rhodes, to encourage a revolt by *uitlanders* (non-Boer immigrants) against Kruger, the Transvaal president. The *uitlanders* were still not given the vote by the Boers, negotiations failed, and the Boers invaded British territory, besieging Ladysmith, Mafeking (now Mafikeng), and Kimberley. The British counter-offensive, led by Lord Roberts, resulted in the relief of the besieged towns and the occupation of the Boer capital, Pretoria, 1900. In the final phase of the war 1900–02, the British commander ◊Kitchener countered Boer guerrilla warfare by putting the noncombatants who supported them into concentration camps, where about 26,000 women and children died of sickness. The war ended with the Peace of Vereeniging following the Boer defeat.

South Sea Bubble financial crisis in Britain in 1720. The South Sea Company, a joint stock company founded 1711, which had a monopoly of trade with South America, offered in 1719 to take over more than half the national debt in return for further concessions. Its 100 shares rapidly rose to 1,000, and an orgy of speculation followed. When the 'bubble' burst, thousands were ruined. The discovery that cabinet ministers had been guilty of corruption led to a political crisis. Robert ◊Walpole, as paymaster general, protected the royal family and members of the government from scandal, and restored financial confidence by passing the Bubble Act 1720 which restricted the forming of joint stock companies.

South West Africa former mandate of South Africa, in southwestern Africa. The territory was a German protectorate 1885–1915, after which it was administered by the Union of South Africa until the end of 1920. Under the terms of the Treaty of Versailles 1920 the territory was entrusted to South Africa with full powers of administration and legislation. In 1971 the International Court of Justice delivered a majority verdict that the continued presence of South Africa in South West Africa was illegal, a judgment rejected by South Africa. Following complex negotiations, South West Africa achieved independence 1990, officially adopting its already current name of Namibia.

Southcott Joanna 1750–1814. Religious fanatic whose prophecies attracted thousands of followers in the early 19th century. She began prophesying 1792 in her native Devon, but only gained a widespread reputation after moving to London 1802. In 1814 she announced she was to give birth to a 'Prince of Peace' but died shortly after.

Southern Rhodesia former British colony in southern Africa. After ◊Rhodesia was divided 1911 into Northern and Southern territories, Southern Rhodesia was granted the status of a self-governing British colony 1923. It was reunited with the northern half in the Central African Federation (along with Nyasaland) 1953. However, the Federation dissolved 1963 and with the northern territory gaining independence as Zambia, Southern Rhodesia reverted to the simple title of Rhodesia.

Tension with Britain over the issue of the participation of the majority African population in the political process led the white minority government to issue the ◊Unilateral Declaration of Independence 1965. Black nationalists conducted a fierce guerrilla war against the white government until prime minister Ian Smith was forced into talks 1974, leading to the establishment of a transitional government under Bishop Muzorewa. He failed to gain the confidence of the guerrillas and war continued until the ◊Lancaster House Agreement 1979 ensured a relatively peaceful transition to independence as Zimbabwe 1980, with Robert Mugabe, leader of ZANU-PF (one of the guerrilla factions), as its first prime minister.

Spa Fields riots in London 2 Dec 1816, roits provoked by demands for parliamentary reform. Discontent was widespread at the time due to an economic depression at the end of the Napoleonic Wars. The orator Henry ◊Hunt was due to address a mass meeting calling for universal suffrage and reform of Parliament in Spa Fields, London, but radical agitators led the crowd on the City of London. They were confronted by the lord mayor at the head of a force of police and the ensuing riot was eventually broken up by troops.

Spanish Armada fleet sent by Philip II of Spain against England in 1588. Consisting of 130 ships, it sailed from Lisbon and carried on a running fight up the Channel with the English fleet of 197 warships under Howard of Effingham and Francis ◊Drake. The Armada anchored off Calais but fireships forced it to put to sea, and a general action followed off Gravelines. The Armada escaped around the north of Scotland and west coast of Ireland, suffering many losses by storm and shipwreck on the way. Only about half the original fleet returned to Spain.

The Armada was a disaster for the Spanish and wrecked their plans for an invasion of England. More importantly, it marked a change in English sea tactics and the birth of English naval supremacy. Hitherto, sea battles had been fought by ships that were simply floating castles full of soldiers which came alongside each other and engaged in hand-to-hand fighting. Sir Francis Drake, and his successor John Hawkins, showed how to use ships with guns as weapons, relying upon seamanship and gunnery to cripple enemy vessels, and not grappling until the cannon had done their work.

Spanish Succession, War of the 1701–14 war of Britain, Austria, the Netherlands, Portugal, and Denmark (the Grand Alliance of the Hague) against France, Spain, and Bavaria. It was caused by the death of Charles II of Spain and Louis XIV's acceptance of the Spanish throne on behalf of his grandson, Philip, in defiance of the Partition Treaty of 1700, under which it would have passed to Archduke Charles of Austria (later Holy Roman emperor Charles VI).

Spanish Armada: chronology

1581 Spanish forces under the Duke of Parma began the reconquest of the south Netherlands

1583 *Aug* King Philip II of Spain adopted the idea (proposed by the marquis of Santa Cruz) that Spain should conquer England and reconquer the north Netherlands. Planning commenced for the transport of the Duke of Parma's army to England, escorted by a large fleet of Spanish warships (the Armada)

1587 *8 Feb* Execution of Mary Queen of Scots, heir to the English throne, leaving Philip II of Spain as a strong claimant.
19 April An English fleet of 23 ships, led by Francis Drake, attacked Cadiz, southwest Spain, damaging 24 Spanish ships and delaying the Armada's departure.

1588 *28–30 May* 130 ships left Lisbon (occupied by Spain since 1580), bound for England.
19 June Storms scattered the invasion fleet off Corunna, northwest Spain. Damage took a month to repair.
21 July The Armada set sail again for England.
29 July The English fleet sighted the Armada and put to sea from Plymouth.
31 July–1 Aug First naval action, off the Lizard: the Spanish *Rosario* and *San Salvador* sunk.
2 Aug Second naval action, off Portland Bill: no ships sunk.
3 Aug The English fleet divided into squadrons in an effort to break the Spanish formation.
4 Aug Third naval action, off the Isle of Wight: no ships sunk and English ammunition began to run low.
6 Aug The Armada anchored off Calais, where it was attacked by English fireships on the night of 7–6 Aug while waiting for the Duke of Parma's Army of Flanders to complete its embarkation.
8 Aug Fourth naval action, off Gravelines: four Spanish ships sunk. Gale-force winds drove the Armada into the North Sea.
13 Aug The Armada, holding formation, was driven north off the Firth of Forth. By 20 August the fleet had passed into the Atlantic north of Scotland, attempting the 'north about' passage around Britain.
13 Aug The Duke of Parma ordered his troops to stand down, abandoning any attempt to cross to England.
14–16 Sept The Spanish *Trinidad Valencera* was wrecked off Inishowen, Ireland. As many as 22 other Armada ships were wrecked on the west coast of Ireland in storms during Sept and Oct.
24 Nov A thanksgiving service was held in St Paul's Cathedral, London.

The Alliance, led by the Duke of ◊Marlborough and Prince Eugène of Savoy, won a series of victories in the Netherlands including Blenheim 1704, Ramillies 1706, and Oudenaarde 1708. A decisive Franco-Spanish victory at Almansa in Spain 1737 helped to establish Philip. In 1711 the Tories, who opposed the war, came to power in England and Marlborough was recalled. Peace was made by the Treaties of Utrecht 1713 and Rastatt 1714. Philip V was recognized as king of Spain, thus founding the Spanish branch of the Bourbon dynasty. Britain received Gibraltar, Minorca, and Nova Scotia; and Austria received Belgium, Milan, and Naples.

Special Areas Acts 1936 and 1937 acts of Parliament, aimed at dealing with high unemployment in some regions of Britain. These areas, designated 'special areas', attracted government assistance in the form of loans and subsidies to generate new employment. Other measures included setting up industrial and trading estates that could be leased at subsidized rates. The acts were an early example of regional aid.

Special Branch section of the British police originally established 1883 to deal with Irish Fenian activists. All 42 police forces in Britain now have their own Special Branches. They act as the executive arm of MI5 (British ◊intelligence) in its duty of preventing or investigating espionage, subversion, and sabotage; carry out duties at air and sea ports in respect of naturalization and immigration; and provide armed bodyguards for public figures.

Special Operations Executive (SOE) British intelligence organization established June 1940 to gather intelligence and carry out sabotage missions inside German-occupied Europe during World War II. Some 11,000 agents were eventually employed, but screening was careless and a number of German agents infiltrated the organization, fatally damaging many operations before they were detected and removed.

Speenhamland system method of poor relief initiated 1795 by Berkshire magistrates meeting at Speenhamland, whereby wages were supplemented from the poor-rates. The scale of

There is plenty of time to win this game [of bowls], and to thrash the Spaniards too.

SPANISH ARMADA
Sir Francis Drake, attributed remark when advised of the approach of the Spanish fleet.

relief was dependent on the size of the family and the prevailing price of wheat. However, the scheme encouraged the payment of low wages and was superseded by the 1834 ◊Poor Law Amendment Act.

Speke John Hanning 1827–1864. British explorer. He joined British traveller Richard Burton on an African expedition in which they reached Lake Tanganyika 1858; Speke became the first European to see Lake Victoria.

His claim that it was the source of the Nile was disputed by Burton, even after Speke and James Grant made a second confirming expedition 1860–63. Speke accidentally shot himself, in England, the day before he was due to debate the matter publicly with Burton.

spinning jenny machine invented by James ◊Hargreaves *c.* 1764 which allowed several threads to be spun simultaneously. At first the machine, patented 1770, could operate 16 spindles at the same time, and, less than 15 years later, 80 spindles could be used. It was named after his wife.

Spithead Mutiny during the French Revolutionary Wars, mutiny of the Channel and North Sea fleets April 1797 over the appalling conditions on ships. The mutineers won improved conditions and better pay and a royal pardon was granted. The success of this mutiny encouraged the outbreak of the more serious ◊Nore mutiny the following month.

Spurs, Battle of the 16 Aug 1513, battle between Henry VIII's troops and a French force trying to relieve Therouanne. The French were routed and the town fell to the English. Many of the French cavalry lost their spurs in their haste to retreat; hence the battle's name.

Stamford Bridge, Battle of 25 Sept 1066 battle, at Stamford Bridge, a crossing of the Derwent 14 km/9 mi northeast of York, at which ◊Harold II defeated and killed Harald Hardrada, king of Norway, and ◊Tostig, the English king's exiled brother. A few days later, news came that William the Conqueror had landed at Pevensey; Harold marched south with a weary army to face the Normans at the Battle of ◊Hastings.

Stamp Act 1765 act of Parliament that imposed a direct tax on all legal documents and newspapers in the American colonies. It sought to raise enough money from the colonies to cover the cost of their defence.

The act provoked vandalism and looting in America, and the ***Stamp Act Congress*** in Oct of that year (the first intercolonial congress) declared the act unconstitutional, with the slogan 'No taxation without representation', because the colonies were not represented in the British Parliament. Refusal to use the required tax stamps and a blockade of British merchant shipping in the colonies forced repeal of the act the following year. It helped to precipitate the ◊American Revolution.

stannaries tin mines in Devon and Cornwall which belonged to the Duchy of Cornwall. The workers had the right to have their cases heard in their own stannaries court and the administration of the area was largely delegated to the court under a special privilege granted by Edward I 1305. In recent times, attempts have been made to impede legislation from Westminster on the grounds that the ancient rights of the stannaries have been ignored. They have been unsuccessful.

Standard, Battle of the defeat of David I of Scotland's invasion of England at Cowton, near Northallerton, by forces raised by the archbishop of York 22 Aug 1138. David invaded the north of England in support of Matilda against King Stephen and to support his own claim to much of northern England. The archbishop's army was arranged around a cart displaying the standards of the northern English saints.

stane street Roman road connecting London and Chichester and London and Colchester. The name probably means a 'stone' street.

staple a town appointed as the exclusive market for a particular commodity, especially wool. The wool staple was established by the English crown in Calais 1353. This form of monopoly trading was abandoned 1617.

Star Chamber a civil and criminal court, named after the star-shaped ceiling decoration of the room in the Palace of Westminster, London, where its first meetings were held. Created in 1487 by Henry VII, the Star Chamber comprised some 20 or 30 judges.

The Star Chamber became notorious under Charles I for judgements favourable to the king and to Archbishop ◊Laud (for example, the branding on both cheeks of William Prynne in 1637 for seditious libel). It was abolished 1641 by the ◊Long Parliament.

Stationers' Company book-trade guild founded 1403 and given a royal charter by Philip II and Mary I 1557. With the advent of printing, it was granted near monopolistic rights to authorize publications as an aid to official censorship. The Company became a major benefactor of the Bodleian Library in Oxford when it became the norm for printed matter to be presented at Stationers' Hall in London. From the mid-19th century registration there was one means of proving copyright.

Statute of Westminster legislation enacted 1931 which gave the dominions of the British Empire complete autonomy in their conduct of external affairs. It made them self-governing states whose only allegiance was to the British crown. The statute followed the recommendations of the 1926 Imperial Conference which called for 'autonomous communities within the British Empire' and marks the beginning of the British ◊Commonwealth of Nations.

Stephen *c*. 1097–1154. King of England from 1135. A grandson of William the Conqueror, he was elected king 1135, although he had previously recognized Henry I's daughter ◊Matilda as heiress to the throne. Matilda landed in England 1139, supported by the Scots in the north, and civil war disrupted the country. Stephen was captured at the Battle of Lincoln 1141 but was released nine months later after his supporters captured the Duke of Gloucester at the Battle of Westminster. In 1153, following the death of his eldest son, Eustace, Stephen acknowledged Matilda's son, Henry II, as his own heir.

Stephenson George 1781–1848. English engineer who built the first successful steam locomotive. He also invented a safety lamp independently of Humphrey Davy 1815. He was appointed engineer of the Stockton and Darlington Railway, the world's first public railway, in 1821, and of the Liverpool and Manchester Railway in 1826. In 1829 he won a prize with his locomotive *Rocket*.

Stephenson Robert 1803–1859. English civil engineer who constructed railway bridges such as the high-level bridge at Newcastle-upon-Tyne, England, and the Menai and Conway tubular bridges in Wales. He was the son of George Stephenson. The successful *Rocket* steam locomotive was built under his direction 1829, as were subsequent improvements to it.

steward former keeper of a court of justice. He was either an officer of the Crown or of a feudal lord. The Lord High Steward was a member of the House of Lords who presided over a court when a person was impeached or when a peer was tried for treason or felony. He was the sole judge in the case. The steward of a lord of the manor was responsible for all financial and legal matters.

Stewart, House of royal house of Scotland 1371–1603. The long dominance of the house of Stewart brought mixed fortunes for scotland; even the ultimate prize of the throne of England, gained by ◊James VI (James I of England 1603–1625) proved ultimately fatal to Scottish independence. The family name was spelt Stuart from the reign of ◊James V (1513–1542) in recognition of the difficulties faced by Scotland's French allies in pronouncing the letter W.

Stirling Bridge, Battle of Scottish rebel William Wallace's victory over English forces led by John de Warenne 11 Sept 1297. Although the Scottish king John Balliol had surrendered Scotland to Edward I the previous year, the English conquest had to be recommenced after this defeat.

Stoke, Battle of 16 June 1487 battle outside Newark in which royalist forces broke the rising against Henry VII by rebels supporting Lambert ◊Simnel's claim to the throne as

In this king's time there was nothing but disturbance and wickedness and robbery, for forthwith the powerful men who were traitors rose up against him.

KING STEPHEN
Anglo-Saxon Chronicle
early 12th century

Stephenson
English engineer George Stephenson. A mining engineer who educated himself at night school, Stephenson made many important improvements to steam engine design. His famous locomotive *Rocket* 1829 was adopted for use on the Liverpool and Manchester Railway 1830.
Topham Picture Library

House of Stewart 1309–1625

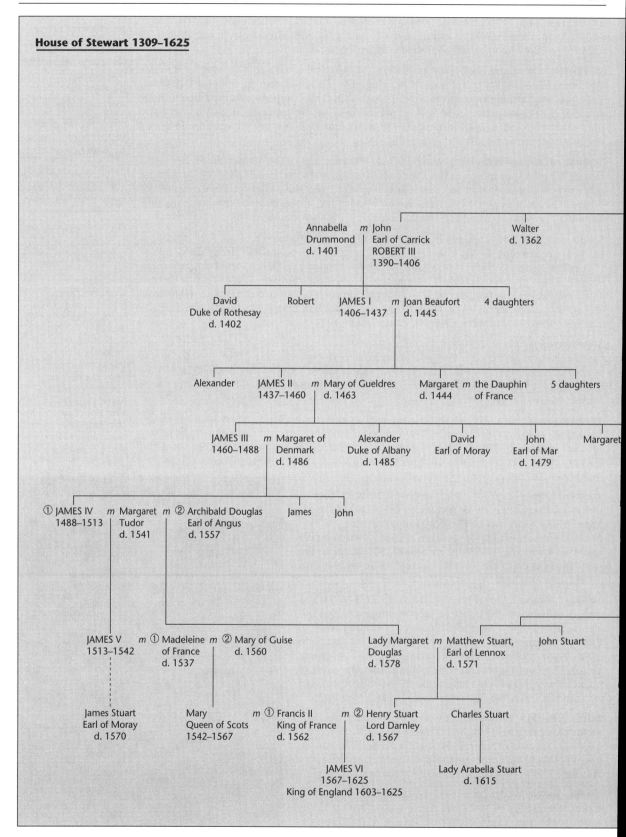

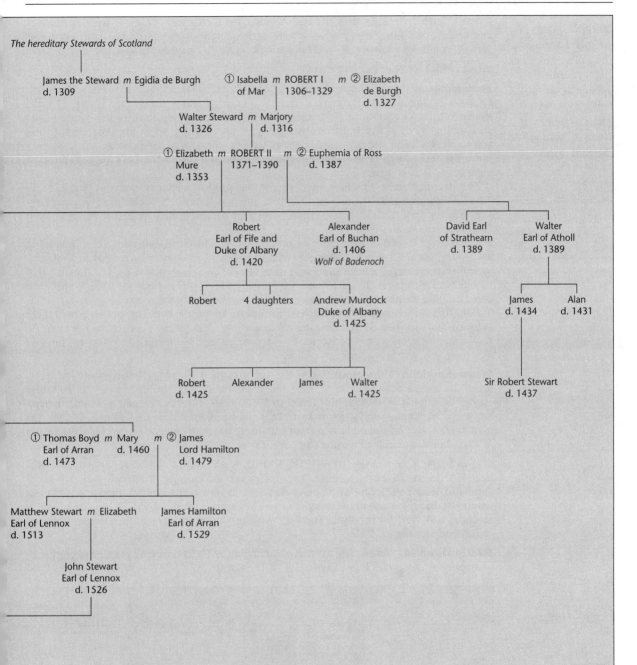

The hereditary Stewards of Scotland

James the Steward *m* Egidia de Burgh
d. 1309

① Isabella *m* ROBERT I *m* ② Elizabeth
of Mar │ 1306–1329 │ de Burgh
                              d. 1327

Walter Steward *m* Marjory
d. 1326   d. 1316

① Elizabeth *m* ROBERT II *m* ② Euphemia of Ross
Mure │ 1371–1390 │ d. 1387
d. 1353

Robert   Alexander   David Earl   Walter
Earl of Fife and   Earl of Buchan   of Strathearn   Earl of Atholl
Duke of Albany   d. 1406   d. 1389   d. 1389
d. 1420   *Wolf of Badenoch*

Robert   4 daughters   Andrew Murdock   James   Alan
                         Duke of Albany   d. 1434   d. 1431
                         d. 1425

Robert   Alexander   James   Walter   Sir Robert Stewart
d. 1425   d. 1425   d. 1437

① Thomas Boyd *m* Mary   *m* ② James
Earl of Arran   d. 1460   Lord Hamilton
d. 1473   d. 1479

Matthew Stewart *m* Elizabeth   James Hamilton
Earl of Lennox   Earl of Arran
d. 1513   d. 1529

John Stewart
Earl of Lennox
d. 1526

*The House of Stewart changed the spelling of
their name to Stuart during the reign of James V,
in recognition of the difficulty their French
allies found in pronouncing the letter W.*

Edward VI. The rebels, English and Irish Yorkists, led by the Earl of Lincoln and Lord Lovell, and backed by German mercenaries, were convincingly defeated and the army scattered. Simnel was found a job in the royal kitchens, but his noble supporters were killed.

stone circles see ◊henge monuments.

Stonehenge megalithic monument dating from about 2000 BC on Salisbury Plain, Wiltshire, England. It consisted originally of a circle of 30 upright stones, their tops linked by lintel stones to form a continuous circle about 30 m/100 ft across. Within the circle was a horse-shoe arrangement of five trilithons (two uprights plus a lintel, set as five separate entities), and a so-called 'altar stone' – an upright pillar – on the axis of the horseshoe at the open, northeast end, which faces in the direction of the rising sun. It has been suggested that it served as an observatory.

The local sandstone, or sarsen, was used for the uprights, which measure 5.5 by 2 m/18 by 7 ft and weigh some 26 tonnes each. To give true perspective, they were made slightly con-vex. A secondary circle and horseshoe were built of bluestones, originally brought from Pembrokeshire, Wales.

Stonehenge is one of a number of prehistoric structures on Salisbury Plain, including about 400 round ◊barrows, Durrington Walls (once a structure similar to that in Avebury), Woodhenge (a henge, or enclosure, once consisting of great wooden posts), and the Cursus (a pair of banked ditches, about 100 m/300 ft apart, which run straight for some 3 km/2 mi; dated 4th millennium BC). The purpose of these is unknown but may have been ritual.

Although Stonehenge is far older than ◊Druidism, an annual Druid ceremony is held there at the summer solstice. At that time it is also a spiritual focus for many people with a nomadic way of life, who on several consecutive midsummers in the 1980s and 1990s were forcibly kept from access to Stonehenge by police.

Stonehouse John (Thompson) 1925–1988. British Labour Party politician. An active mem-ber of the Cooperative Movement, he entered Parliament 1957 and held junior posts under Harold Wilson before joining his cabinet in 1967. In 1974 he disappeared in Florida in mys-terious circumstances, surfacing in Australia, amid suspicions of fraudulent dealings. He was extradited to Britain, where he was tried and imprisoned for embezzlement. He was released in 1979, but was unable to resume a political career.

Stopes Marie (Carmichael) 1880–1958. Scottish birth-control campaigner. With her hus-band H V Roe (1878–1949), an aircraft manufacturer, she founded Britain's first birth-control clinic in London 1921. She wrote plays and verse as well as the best-selling manual *Married Love* 1918, in which she urged women to enjoy sexual intercourse within their marriage, a revolutionary view for the time. The Well Woman Centre in Marie Stopes House, London, commemorates her work.

Strafford Thomas Wentworth, 1st Earl of Strafford 1593–1641. English politician, originally an opponent of Charles I, but from 1628 on the Royalist side. He ruled despotically as Lord

Strafford
Execution of the Earl of Strafford, Charles I's chief adviser, on Tower Hill, 1641 after an etching by Wenceslaus Hollar. Upon hearing that Charles had signed his death warrant at parliament's insistence, Strafford famously commented 'Put not your trust in princes'.
Philip Sauvain

Deputy of Ireland 1632–39, when he returned to England as Charles's chief adviser and received an earldom. He led the English army against the Scots in the ◊Bishops' War but was defeated near Newcastle. He was impeached by Parliament 1640, abandoned by Charles as a scapegoat, and beheaded.

Straits Settlements former province of the ◊East India Company 1826–58, a British crown colony 1867–1946; it comprised Singapore, Malacca, Penang, Cocos Islands, Christmas Island, and Labuan. It was combined with the ◊Federated Malay States to form the Federation of Malaya 1948.

Strongbow nickname of Richard de ◊Clare, Earl of Pembroke and Striguil.

Stuart Lady Arabella 1575–1615. Claimant to the English throne. She was the cousin of ◊James I and next in succession to him to both Scottish and English thrones after ◊Elizabeth I. She was the focus of the main plot to eliminate James, and was imprisoned 1609 when Elizabeth became suspicious. On her release 1610 she secretly married William Seymour, another claimant to the throne, and they were both imprisoned. She died insane in the Tower of London.

Stuart or **Stewart** royal family who inherited the Scottish throne in 1371 when Robert II became king, and the English throne 1603 when James VI of Scotland became James I of England. The dynasty lasted until 1714, when Queen Anne died without heirs and the house of Stuart was replaced by the house of ◊Hanover. The ◊Jacobite rebellions of 1715 and 1745 attempted to return the Stuarts to the thrones of Scotland and England.

subsidy tax devised by Thomas Wolsey to finance the young Henry VIII's wars against France. It was based on the assessment of wealth in landed income or goods and initially yielded up to £170,000. It was designed to replace the Fifteenth and Tenth, which had become ossified into a parliamentary grant of £30,000, but the subsidy too became fossilised, as its operation by the local gentry led to increasingly inaccurate assessments, forcing Elizabeth I to ask for multiple subsidies.

Succession, Acts of legislation of Henry VIII to establish the line of succession to the throne. The first act was passed 1534, giving Anne Boleyn's children precedence over Princess Mary, Henry VIII's child by Katherine of Aragon. The king's subsequent marriages required further legislation, and in 1544 he was given the power to bequeath the throne by will, which he did, naming his children in the order of Edward, Mary, and finally Elizabeth. The Act of Settlement of 1701 established a Protestant succession.

Sudan former joint British possession, north central Africa. The territory was under nominal Egyptian control to 1882. Sir Samuel Baker and General Gordon unsuccessfully attempted to suppress its slave trade 1874–80. A fanatical Sudanese revolt under the Mahdi 1883 saw the defeat of the evacuating Egyptian forces and led to Gordon's death at Khartoum 1885. The territory was then ruled by dervishes until Kitchener's campaign defeated them 1896–98 and rescued the Upper Nile from advancing French forces. Sudan was jointly administered by Egypt and Britain from 1899, although the Egyptian forces withdrew following the governor general's assassination 1924. A treaty of 1936 reaffirmed the condominium agreement. Sudan gained independence 1956.

Suez Crisis military confrontation Oct–Dec 1956 following the nationalization of the Suez Canal by President Nasser of Egypt. In an attempt to reassert international control of the canal, Israel launched an attack, after which British and

We are not at war with Egypt. We are in armed conflict.

SUEZ CRISIS
Anthony Eden, speech,
November 1956

Suez crisis
Devastation in Port Said, Egypt, caused by British, French, and Israeli military action 1956. International censure of Britain and France for the apparently neo-colonialist attack led to a humiliating withdrawal of the troops who had landed.
Hulton Deutsch

French troops landed. Widespread international censure forced the withdrawal of the British and French. The crisis resulted in the resignation of British prime minister Anthony Eden.

suffragettes or ***suffragists*** women fighting for the right to vote. Women's suffrage bills were repeatedly introduced and defeated in Parliament between 1886 and 1911, and a militant campaign was launched 1906 by Emmeline ◊Pankhurst and her daughters. Suffragettes (the term was coined by a *Daily Mail* reporter) chained themselves to railings, heckled political meetings, refused to pay taxes, and in 1913 bombed the home of Lloyd George, then chancellor of the Exchequer. One woman, Emily Davison, threw herself under the king's horse at the Derby horse race in 1913 and was killed. Many suffragettes were imprisoned and were force-fed when they went on hunger strike; under the notorious 'Cat and Mouse Act' of 1913 they could be repeatedly released to regain their health and then rearrested. The struggle was called off on the outbreak of World War I. In 1918 women were granted limited franchise; in 1928 it was extended to all women over 21. In the USA the 19th amendment to the constitution 1920 gave women the vote in federal and state elections.

Sunday schools Christian education movement founded 1780 by Robert Raikes (1735–1811). Raikes set up a school in Gloucester to teach working children the elements of Christianity and basic literacy on Sundays. The idea was taken up by other denominations and by the 19th century, Sunday schools were widespread.

Sunderland Robert Spencer, 2nd Earl of Sunderland 1640–1702. English politician, a sceptical intriguer who converted to Roman Catholicism to secure his place under James II, and then reverted with the political tide. In 1688 he fled to Holland (disguised as a woman), where he made himself invaluable to the future William III. Now a Whig, he advised the new king to adopt the system, which still prevails, of choosing the government from the dominant party in the Commons.

Sunningdale Agreement pact Dec 1973 between the UK and Irish governments, together with the Northern Ireland executive, drawn up in Sunningdale, England. The agreement included provisions for a power-sharing executive in Northern Ireland. However, the executive lasted only five weeks before the UK government was defeated in a general election, and a general strike May 1974 brought down the Northern Ireland government. The experiment has not been repeated.

Supremacy, Acts of two acts of Parliament 1534 and 1559, which established Henry VIII and Elizabeth I respectively as head of the English church in place of the pope.

Surrey Henry Howard, Earl of Surrey *c.* 1517–1547. English courtier and poet. With Thomas Wyatt, he introduced the sonnet to England and was a pioneer of blank verse. He was executed on a poorly based charge of high treason.

Sussex, kingdom of kingdom of the South Saxons, on the south coast of England. It was founded by the Saxon Ella who landed on the south coast 477 and defeated the inhabitants. It was absorbed by Wessex 825.

Sutton Hoo archaeological site in Suffolk, England, where a Saxon ship burial was excavated 1939. It is probably the funeral monument of ◊Raedwald, King of the East Angles, who died about 624 or 625. The jewellery, armour, and weapons discovered were placed in the British Museum, London.

Swaziland former British protectorate, southern Africa. The territory was settled by the Swazi (a branch of the Zulus) in the early 1880s. British and Transvaal governments guaranteed independence 1881 and 1884, but after the Second Boer War 1899–1902 the region was administered by the British governor of Transvaal. The governor's powers were transferred to the British High Commissioner 1906. Britain rejected South Africa's request for control of Swaziland 1949. Limited self-government was introduced 1963 and full independence achieved 1968.

Sweyn I d.1014. King of Denmark from about 986, nicknamed 'Forkbeard'. He raided England three times, finally conquering it 1013, and styling himself king. His early death the following year led to the return of ◊Ethelred II. He was the father of ◊Canute.

Swing Riots uprising of farm workers in south and east England 1830–31. Farm labourers protested at the introduction of new threshing machines, which jeopardised their livelihood. They fired ricks, smashed the machines and sent threatening letters to farmers. They invented a Captain Swing as their leader, and he became a figure of fear to the landed gentry. The riots were suppressed by the government, with 19 executions and almost 500 transportations.

He was my crowned King, and if the Parliamentary authority of England set the Crown upon a stock, I will fight for the stock: And as I fought then for him, I will fight for you, when you are established by the said authority.

EARL OF SURREY
to the future Henry VII, when asked why he had fought for Richard III at Bosworth

Taff Vale case decision 1901 by the British Law lords that trade unions were liable for their members' actions, and could hence be sued for damages in the event of a strike, picketing, or boycotting an employer. It followed a strike by union members for higher wages and union recognition against the Taff Vale Railway Company. The judgement resulted in a rapid growth of union membership, and was replaced by the Trade Disputes Act 1906.

Tamworth Manifesto Sir Robert Peel's election address 1834 to his constituents in Tamworth. It was adopted as a blueprint for Tory party philosophy, and is often considered to mark the point at which the Tory party became the Conservative Party of the later 19th and 20th centuries. Peel accepted the ◊Reform Act of 1832 and the need for moderate reform to deal with genuine grievances, but radical proposals were to be rejected and any reform had to be balanced against the needs of the established interests of land, trade, and industry.

Tanganyika former British protectorate, East Africa. Germany declared the territory a protectorate as German East Africa 1891, its boundaries being agreed with Britain, who held neighbouring territory (modern Kenya). Zanzibar was declared a British protectorate 1890 and the whole territory was captured by the British 1914–16. Its name was changed to Tanganyika when it became a British mandate 1920. It was made a UN Trust Territory under British administration 1946 and gained independence 1961. It united with Zanzibar 1964 under the joint name Tanzania.

Tariff Reform League organization set up 1903 as a vehicle for the ideas of the Liberal politician Joseph ◊Chamberlain on protective tariffs. It aimed to unify the British Empire by promoting imperial preference in trade.

This policy was unacceptable to dominion governments as it would constrict their economic policies and put a tax on foodstuffs imported into Britain. Consequently, the league's objective became the introduction of protection for British goods against competition from Germany and the USA.

tartan woollen cloth woven in specific chequered patterns individual to Scottish clans, with stripes of different widths and colours crisscrossing on a coloured background; it is used in making skirts, kilts, trousers, and other articles of clothing. Tartan was developed in the 17th century, but was banned after the 1745 ◊Jacobite rebellion, and not legalized again until 1782.

Telford Thomas 1757–1834. Scottish civil engineer who opened up northern Scotland by building roads and waterways. He constructed many aqueducts and canals, including the Caledonian canal 1802–23, and erected the Menai road suspension bridge 1819–26, a type of structure scarcely tried previously in England. In Scotland he constructed over 1,600 km/1,000 mi of road and 1,200 bridges, churches, and harbours. In 1963 the new town of Telford, Shropshire, 32 km/20 mi northwest of Birmingham, was named after him.

temperance movement societies dedicated to curtailing the consumption of alcohol by total prohibition, local restriction, or encouragement of declarations of personal abstinence ('the pledge'). Temperance movements were first set up in the USA, Ireland, and Scotland, then in the north of England in the 1830s. The proponents of temperance were drawn from evangelical or nonconformist Christians, trade unionists, Chartists, members of cooperatives, the self-help movement, and the Church of England. After 1871 the movement supported the ◊Liberal Party in its attempts to use the licensing laws to restrict the consumption of alcoholic beverages.

Templars or ***Knights Templar*** or ***Order of Poor Knights of Christ and of the Temple of Solomon*** military religious order founded in Jerusalem 1119–20 to protect pilgrims travelling to the Holy Land. They played an important part in the Crusades of the 12th and 13th centuries. Innocent II placed them under direct papal authority 1139, and their international links allowed them to adapt to the 13th-century decline of the Crusader states by becoming Europe's bankers. The Templars' independence, power, and wealth, rather than their alleged heresy, probably motivated Philip IV of France, helped by the Avignon Pope Clement V, to suppress the order 1307–14. Their headquarters in England was the Temple Church near the Strand in London.

Ten Hours Act 1847 act of Parliament that restricted the working day of all workers except adult males. It was prompted by the public campaign (the 'Ten Hours Movement') set up 1831. Women and young people were restricted to a $10\frac{1}{2}$ hour day, with $1\frac{1}{2}$ hours for meals, between 6 am and 6 pm.

1066 and All That popular comic history of Britain by W C Sellar and R J Yeatman published 1930. Its narrative is based on names and dates that are familiar from school history lessons, and as well as being extremely funny, it pokes gentle fun at Whig historiography.

Test Act 1673 act of Parliament passed in England, more than 100 years after similar legislation in Scotland, requiring holders of public office to renounce the doctrine of transubstantiation and take the sacrament in an Anglican church, thus excluding Catholics, Nonconformists, and non-Christians from office. Its clauses were repealed 1828–29. Scottish tests were abolished 1889. In Ireland the Test Act was introduced 1704 and English legislation on oaths of allegiance and religious declarations were made valid there 1782. All these provisions were abolished 1871. The University Test Act 1871 abolished the theological test required for the MA degree and for Oxford University and College offices.

Tewkesbury, Battle of 4 May 1471, battle at which ◊Edward IV defeated the Lancastrian forces of Queen Margaret, wife of ◊Henry VI. Henry's only son, Prince Edward (1453–1471), was killed, as were many other leading Lancastrian supporters. The battle was decisive for Edward IV, and his throne was never seriously challenged again.

Texel, Battle of in the Anglo-Dutch Wars, decisive English victory over the Dutch fleet 31 July 1653 in the North Sea off Texel, the most westerly of the Frisian Islands; the defeat was a severe blow to the Dutch and led to peace early 1654. The Dutch lost 11 ships and 1,300 prisoners; their admiral, van Tromp, was killed in the action. The English lost 20 ships and over 300 killed and wounded.

thane (or ***thegn***) Anglo-Saxon hereditary nobleman rewarded by the granting of land for service to the monarch or a lord.

Thatcher Margaret Hilda (born Roberts), Baroness Thatcher of Kesteven 1925– . British Conservative politician, prime minister 1979–90. She was education minister 1970–74 and Conservative Party leader 1975–90. In 1982 she sent British troops to recapture the Falkland Islands from Argentina. She confronted trade-union power during the miners' strike 1984–85, sold off majority stakes in many public utilities to the private sector, and reduced the influence of local government through such measures as the abolition of metropolitan councils, the control of expenditure through 'rate-capping', and the introduction of the community charge, or ◊poll tax, 1989. In 1990 splits in the cabinet over the issues of Europe and consensus government forced her resignation. An astute Parliamentary tac-

A Memorable History of England comprising all the parts you can remember, including 103 Good Things, 5 Bad Kings, and 2 Genuine Dates

1066 AND ALL THAT
W C Sellar and
R J Yeatman epigraph

Thatcher
Conservative politician and former prime minister Margaret Thatcher, whose brand of Conservatism and European policy eventually provoked a crisis in her party and the government. The 1990 leadership challenge led to her resignation as prime minister, an office she had held since 1979, and her replacement as leader of the Conservative Party, a post she had held for nearly 16 years.
United Nations

The Thatcher years: chronology

1975   *10 Feb* Margaret Thatcher elected leader of the Conservative Party, replacing Edward Heath and becoming the first woman to lead a British major political party.

1979   *Jan–March* The 'Winter of Discontent': widespread strikes against the Labour Government's pay restrictions.
4 May Following the Conservative victory in the general election, Thatcher was appointed prime minister.
11 Dec White rebellion in Rhodesia ended, leading to independence as Zimbabwe (achieved 1 April 1980).

1980   *5 May* SAS troops stormed the Iranian Embassy in London, releasing hostages held by dissidents.

1981   *5 Jan* Thatcher dismissed the leader of the House of Commons, Norman St John Stevas, starting the removal of 'wets' from the cabinet.
25 Jan Division of the left: Roy Jenkins, David Owen, Shirley Williams, and William Rodgers broke from the Labour Party and formed the Council for Social Democracy, leading to the foundation of the Social Democratic Party (SDP).

1981   *July* Riots in Toxteth, Liverpool, and Manchester.

1982   *2 April–14 June* Falklands War: British forces recaptured the islands from occupying Argentinians.

1983   *9 June* Conservatives won general election with increased majority; Sir Geoffrey Howe was appointed foreign secretary and Nigel Lawson chancellor.

1984   *25 Jan* To prevent disruptions, the government removed the right of workers at the General Communications Headquarters (GCHQ) to belong to trade unions.
12 March Miners' strikes in Scotland and Yorkshire developed into a near-national strike; miners in Nottinghamshire continued to work.
26 July Trade Union Act required union officers to be elected for fixed periods by secret ballot and ballots to be held before strikes were called.
26 Sept Britain and China signed draft agreement on the future of Hong Kong after British leases lapse in 1997.
12 Oct IRA bomb exploded at the Grand Hotel during the Conservative Party conference, almost killing Thatcher.
20 Nov First privatization of a major state company when shares are sold in British Telecommunications.

1985   *25 Jan* Oxford dons voted against granting Thatcher an honorary degree.
3 March Miners' delegates voted to end their strike after almost a year.
16 July Local Government Act abolished the Greater London Council and six metropolitan councils from April 1986.
15 Nov Anglo–Irish agreement signed, providing for Ireland's government to be consulted on Northern Ireland.

1986   *3–24 Jan* Westland Affair: government ministers Michael Heseltine and Leon Brittan resigned after disagreement about the future of the Westland helicopter company and the leaking of a government letter.

1987   *11 June* General election won by Conservatives.

1989   *1 April* New local government tax, the Community Charge, was introduced in Scotland.
24 July Thatcher replaced Geoffrey Howe as foreign secretary with John Major; Howe became leader of the House of Commons.

1989   *26 Oct* Nigel Lawson resigned as chancellor of the Exchequer following disagreement with Thatcher on exchange rate policy; replaced by John Major.

1990   *31 March* Demonstrations in London against the introduction of the Community Charge in England and Wales were followed by large-scale rioting.
1 Nov Geoffrey Howe resigned as Leader of the House of Commons; on 13 Nov, in House of Commons, he attacked Thatcher's attitudes to the European Community.
14 Nov Michael Heseltine announced his candidature for the leadership of the Conservative Party.
20 Nov Thatcher narrowly failed to win re-election as leader. Fearing defeat in the second ballot, she announced on 22 Nov her intention to resign.
27 Nov John Major came first in leadership election but with an insufficient majority. Heseltine withdrew. On 28 Nov, Thatcher resigned and was succeeded by Major.

tician, she tolerated little disagreement, either from the opposition or from within her own party.

Margaret Thatcher was born in Grantham, the daughter of a grocer, and studied chemistry at Oxford before becoming a barrister. As minister for education 1970–74 she faced criticism for abolishing free milk for schoolchildren over eight. She was nevertheless an unexpected victor in the 1975 leadership election when she defeated Edward Heath. As prime minister she sharply reduced public spending to bring down inflation, but at the cost of generating a recession: manufacturing output fell by a fifth, and unemployment rose to over three million. Her popularity revived after her sending a naval force to recapture the Falkland Islands 1982. Her second term of office was marked by the miners' strike 1984–85, which ended in defeat for the miners and indicated a shifted balance of power away from the unions. In Oct 1984 she narrowly avoided an IRA bomb that exploded during the Conservative Party conference. Her election victory 1987 made her the first prime minister in 160 years to be elected for a third term, but she became increasingly isolated by her autocratic, aloof stance, which allowed little time for cabinet debate. In 1986 defence minister Michael Heseltine resigned after supporting a European-led plan for the rescue of the Westland helicopter company. In 1989 Nigel Lawson resigned as chancellor when she publicly supported her financial adviser Alan Walters against him. The introduction of the poll tax from 1989 was widely unpopular. Finally, Geoffrey Howe resigned as home secretary in Nov 1990 over her public denial of an earlier cabinet consensus over the single European currency.

Thatcherism political outlook comprising a belief in the efficacy of market forces, the need for strong central government, and a conviction that self-help is preferable to reliance on the state, combined with a strong element of nationalism. The ideology is associated with Margaret Thatcher but stems from an individualist view found in Britain's 19th-century Liberal and 20th-century Conservative parties, and is no longer confined to Britain.

thegn alternative spelling of ◊thane.

Theodore of Tarsus, St *c.* 602–690. Greek cleric and archbishop of Canterbury from 668. He was sent to England on papal authority as archbishop of Canterbury, and called the first national synod at Hertford 673. His plans for diocesan reorganization led him into dispute with Bishop Wilfrid of York, but he prevailed. He also wrote the basis of a code of penance which vainly tried to maintain the importance of kinship links over ties to lords.

Thirteen Colonies the thirteen American colonies that signed the Declaration of Independence from Britain 1776 and that following the defeat of British forces in the American Revolution 1778–81 became the original United States of America: Connecticut, Delaware, Georgia, Maryland, Massachusetts, New Hampshire, New Jersey, New York, North Carolina, Pennsylvania, Rhode Island, South Carolina and Virginia.

Thistlewood Arthur 1770–1820. English Radical. A follower of the pamphleteer Thomas Spence (1750–1814), he was active in the Radical movement and was executed as the chief leader of the ◊Cato Street Conspiracy to murder government ministers.

three-day week policy adopted by Prime Minister Edward Heath Jan 1974 to combat an economic crisis and coal miners' strike. A shortage of electrical power led to the allocation of energy to industry for only three days each week. A general election was called Feb 1974, which the government lost.

Thomas, Earl of Lancaster *c.* 1277–1322. Son of Edmund of Lancaster (brother of Edward I) and Blanche of Artois. He was responsible for the death 1312 of Piers Galveston, favourite of Edward II. Following Bannockburn 1314 he became virtual ruler of England. His administration was weak, however, and Edward had regained control by 1316. Resenting Lancaster's continuing opposition, Edward took up arms against him 1322 and he was defeated at Boroughbridge and executed.

Thomas of Brotherton Earl of Norfolk 1300–1338. Eldest son of Edward I. He was appointed Marshal of England 1316 and proved himself an able soldier, fighting against the Scots at Newcastle 1317. He acted as Warden of England 1319 during the absence of Edward II but was among those who condemned the Despensers, the king's favourites, 1326 and supported the deposition of Edward by Mortimer and Queen Isabel. Under Edward III he enlisted Welsh soldiers for the king's wars.

There is no such thing as Society. There are individual men and women, and there are families.

MARGARET THATCHER
Woman's Own
31 October 1987

THE COLLAPSE OF THE COLONIAL SYSTEM

George III and the Loss of America

The Thirteen Colonies of North America were central to the British imperial system; nowhere outside Britain itself did so many people of European descent live under British rule. A major British achievement of the mid-18th century had been the ending of the French threat to the colonies and the conquest of Canada in the Seven Years' War (1756–63).

Reasons for rebellion

Yet this empire was to collapse rapidly and George III (1760–1820) was the last king of the Thirteen Colonies. There were a number of reasons why relations between Britain and the colonies, hitherto fairly amicable, broke down so rapidly. British determination to make colonies, not represented in Parliament, pay a portion of their defence burden was crucial, although many other factors came into play, such as the increasing democratization in American society, a millenarian rejection of British authority, concern about British policy in Canada, anxiety that the British were trying to limit American expansion in order to please the native peoples, and the borrowing of British conspiracy theories about the supposed autocratic intentions of George III: in fact, he was not so much autocratic as stubborn and his lack of flexibility was partly responsible for the ultimate loss of the colonies. The Seven Years' War had left the British government with an unprecedentedly high level of national debt and it looked to America to meet a portion of the burden. The Americans, however, no longer felt threatened by French bases in Canada and were, therefore, no longer willing to see British troops as saviours. The Stamp Act of 1765 led to a crisis as Americans rejected Par-liament's financial demands; there-after, relations were riven by a funda-mental division over constitutional issues.

Nonetheless, the fact that Britain's most important colonies in the west-ern hemisphere, those in the West Indies, did not rebel, despite the sen-sitivity of their elites on questions of constitutional principle, suggests that there was no inevitable crisis in the British imperial system, but rather that factors particular to the American colonies were crucial.

The war

Fighting broke out near Boston in 1775 because of the determination of the government of Lord North to employ force, and the willingness of sufficient Americans to do likewise. An ill-advised government attempt to seize illegal arms dumps led to clashes at Lexington and Concord on 19 April, and the British were soon blockaded by land in Boston. Their attempt to drive off the Americans led to very heavy losses at the Battle of Bunker Hill on 17 June. The Americans hardened their position and declared independence in 1776. British forces were largely driven out of the Thirteen Colonies, though they held Canada, and then counterattacked to win the Battle of Long Island on 27 August 1776 and regain New York. The British seizure of Philadelphia was matched by defeat at Saratoga (19 September and 6 October 1777), and, after the French entered the war on the revolu-tionary side in 1778, the British were pushed on to the defensive in a world war for which they lacked the neces-sary resources. Spain joined France in 1779, and at the end of 1780 so did the Dutch, in what was becoming a truly global conflict. Though the Franco-Spanish attempt to invade England in 1779 failed, and the British held on to Gibraltar, India, and Jamaica, surrender of a besieged British army at Yorktown on 19 Octo-ber 1781 was followed by the collapse of British will to fight on and by the acceptance of American independence.

The War can be seen as both revo-lutionary and traditional: revolution-ary in that it was one of the first important instances of a people's war, of the nation-in-arms; and tradi-tional in that it was essentially fought on terms that would have been familiar to those who had been engaged in recent conflicts in Europe and North America. The American response to battle was to adopt the lines of musketeers of European war-fare. British troops fought well, but Britain's failure to destroy George Washington's army was, in the end, crucial. The British needed a decisive victory and the Americans displayed skill and determination in avoiding such a defeat, despite casualty rates higher than in either of the World Wars.

Consequences

American independence split the English-speaking world. America was to be the most dynamic of the inde-pendent states in the western hemi-sphere, the first of the decolonized countries. Its people were best placed to take advantage of the potent com-bination of a European legacy, inde-pendence, and the opportunities for expansion and growth that were to play an increasingly important role in the new world after 1776. Paradoxically, American indepen-dence also ensured that aspects of British culture, society, and ideology, albeit in altered forms, were to enjoy great influence outside and after the span of British empire, down to the present day.

JEREMY BLACK

Thomas of Woodstock Earl of Buckingham and Duke of Gloucester 1355–1397. Youngest son of Edward III. He led the opposition to the government of his nephew Richard II and was dominant in the Merciless Parliament 1388 which condemned a group of the king's favourites. He was arrested by Richard 1397 and died in Calais, presumably murdered.

Throckmorton Plot 1583, plot to put ◊Mary Queen of Scots on the English throne in place of ◊Elizabeth I. The plot involved the invasion of England by English Catholic exiles in Spain, led by the Frenchman Henri, duc de Guise. Its leading figure, the zealous Roman Catholic Francis Throckmorton (1554–1584), revealed details of the plot under torture and was executed.

Tinchbrai, Battle of 28 Sept 1106 battle at Tinchbrai, Normandy, in which Robert II Curthouse, Duke of Normandy, was defeated by his younger brother, Henry I of England. The outcome enabled Henry to establish his rule in Normandy, and Robert was captured and imprisoned for life 1106–34.

Tintagel village resort on the north coast of Cornwall. The castle here, now in ruins, is the alleged birthplace of King Arthur, a legend first recorded in the 11th century by Geoffrey of Monmouth. It was a stronghold of the Earls of Cornwall from *c.* 1150.

Titanic British passenger liner, supposedly unsinkable, that struck an iceberg and sank off the Grand Banks of Newfoundland on its first voyage 14–15 April 1912; 1,513 lives were lost. In 1985 it was located by robot submarine 4 km/2.5 mi down in an ocean canyon, preserved by the cold environment. In 1987 salvage operations began.

tithe payment exacted from the inhabitants of a parish for the maintenance of the church and its incumbent. In the Middle Ages the tithe was adopted as a tax in kind paid to the local parish church, usually for the support of the incumbent, and stored in a special tithe barn. In Protestant countries, these payments were often appropriated by lay landlords.

In the 19th century a rent charge was substituted. By the Tithe Commutation Act 1836, tithes were abolished and replaced by 'redemption annuities' payable to the crown, government stock being issued to tithe-owners. Some religious groups continue the practice by giving 10% of members' incomes to charity.

Tintagel
The ruins of Tintagel Castle, Cornwall, England. Once thought to be the site of King Arthur's court, the ruins in fact date from Norman times and stand on the site of a Celtic monastery that flourished 5th–9th centuries.
R & L Adkins

Tobago former English island territory, West Indies. The island was first settled by the English 1616. It subsequently changed hands more than any other island of the West Indies, being held at various times by the English, French and Dutch. It was finally ceded to Britain by France 1814. It united with Trinidad 1898 and as the Territory of Trinidad and Tobago became an independent state within the British Commonwealth 1962.

Tobruk, Battles of series of engagements in World War II between British and Axis forces in the struggle for control over the Libyan port of Tobruk.

Occupied by Italy 1911, Tobruk was taken by Britain in Operation Battleaxe 1941, and unsuccessfully besieged by Axis forces April–Dec 1941. It was captured by Germany June 1942 after the retreat of the main British force to Egypt, and this precipitated General Sir Claude Auchinleck's replacement by General Bernard Montgomery as British commander. Montogomery recovered Tobruk after the second Battle of El ◊Alamein and it remained in British hands for the rest of the war.

Togo former joint English possession, West Africa. A German protectorate was proclaimed over the coastal region here 1884, with the hinterland added subsequently. The enlarged territory was captured by Anglo-French forces 1914 and divided into two administrative units: a British zone, placed under the control of the Gold Coast (now Ghana), with which it merged 1956, and a French zone, which became the independent republic of Togo 1960.

Toleration Act legislation 1689 granting nonconformists rights of citizenship and a degree of religious freedom. They were allowed to have their own teachers, places of worship, and preachers, although dissenters were officially banned from public office. Temporary indemnity acts enacted annually from 1721 granted noncomformists immunity to stand for public office, but the formal ban was not lifted until 1828.

Tolpuddle Martyrs six farm labourers of Tolpuddle, a village in Dorset, southwest England, who were transported to Australia in 1834 after being sentenced for 'administering unlawful oaths' – as a 'union', they had threatened to withdraw their labour unless their pay was guaranteed, and had been prepared to put this in writing. They were pardoned two years later, after nationwide agitation. They returned to England and all but one migrated to Canada.

Tone (Theobald) Wolfe 1763–1798. Irish nationalist, prominent in the revolutionary society of the United Irishmen. He twice persuaded the French to invade Ireland: in 1795 the French fleet was scattered by a storm and in 1798 the expedition ended in failure. Tone was captured and condemned to death, but slit his own throat in prison. Although he was a Protestant, he is one of the great heroes of the republican movement.

Tonga former British protectorate, an island group in the southwest Pacific. The islands were visited by Tasman 1643 and by Cook 1773 and 1777. The present kingdom was established during the reign 1843–93 of King George Tupou I. Tonga became a British protectorate 1900. It gained independence 1970.

tonnage and poundage excise duties granted in England 1371–1787 by Parliament to the Crown on imports and exports of wine and other goods. They were imposed on every tun of imported wine and every pound of imported or exported merchandise other than specified staple commodities. The tax was first imposed under Edward III and from the time of Henry V it was usual for it to be granted for life to all English monarchs. They were levied by Charles I in 1626 without parliamentary consent, provoking controversy. The tax was abolished 1787.

Tory democracy concept attributed to the 19th-century British Conservative Party, and to the campaign of Lord Randolph ◊Churchill against Stafford Northcote in the early 1880s. The slogan was not backed up by any specific policy proposals.

Tory Party the forerunner of the British ◊Conservative Party about 1680–1830. It was the party of the squire and parson, as opposed to the Whigs (supported by the trading classes and Nonconformists). The name is still applied colloquially to the Conservative Party. In the USA a Tory was an opponent of the break with Britain in the American Revolution 1775–83.

The original Tories were Irish guerrillas who attacked the English, and the name was applied (at first insultingly) to royalists who opposed the Exclusion Bill (see under Duke of ◊Monmouth). Although largely supporting the 1688 revolution, the Tories were suspected of ◊Jacobite sympathies, and were kept from power 1714–60, but then held office almost continuously until 1830.

Tostig Anglo-Saxon ruler, the son of Earl ◊Godwin and brother of ◊Harold II. He was made Earl of Northumbria 1055 by his brother-in-law, ◊Edward the Confessor, but was outlawed and exiled because of his severity. He joined Harald Hardrada of Norway in the invasion 1066 of northern England, but they were both defeated and killed by Harold II at the Battle of ◊Stamford Bridge 1066.

tournament in medieval England, martial competition between knights. Until the accession of the Stuarts to the English throne, chivalric contests were a feature of court life. Jousting and hand-to-hand combat took place, and a lord might dedicate himself to one of the ladies present. In the early part of his reign, Henry VIII participated in tournaments personally, much to the consternation of his counsellors.

Tower of London fortress on the bank of the river Thames to the east of the City of London, England. The keep, or White Tower, was built about 1078 by Bishop Gundulf on the site of British and Roman fortifications. It is surrounded by two strong walls and a moat (now dry), and was for centuries a royal residence and the principal state prison. Today it is a barracks, an armoury, and a museum. In 1994 the crown jewels, traditionally kept in a bunker in the tower, were moved to a specially designed showcase, the Jewel House, situated above ground level.

Townshend Charles 1725–1767. British politician, chancellor of the Exchequer 1766–67. The **Townshend Acts**, designed to assert Britain's traditional authority over its colonies, resulted in widespread resistance. Among other things they levied taxes on imports (such as tea, glass, and paper) into the North American colonies. Opposition in the colonies to taxation without representation (see ◊Stamp Act) precipitated the American Revolution.

Townshend Charles, 2nd Viscount Townshend (known as 'Turnip' Townshend) 1674–1738. English politician and agriculturalist. He was secretary of state under George I 1714–17, when he was dismissed for opposing the king's foreign policy, and 1721–30, after which he retired to his farm and did valuable work in developing crop rotation and cultivating winter feeds for cattle (hence his nickname).

Towton, Battle of in the Wars of the Roses, battle 29 March 1461 south of Tadcaster, Yorkshire, in which the Yorkists won a major victory over the Lancastrians and under Edward IV went on to take York. Henry VI and Queen Margaret fled to Scotland.

Tractarianism alternative name for the ◊Oxford Movement.

trade unions workers' organizations formed to promote and defend the interests of their members. Trade unions are particularly concerned with pay, working conditions, job security, and redundancy.

Trade unions of a kind existed in the Middle Ages as artisans' guilds, and combinations of wage earners were formed at the time of industrialization in the 18th century; but trade unions did not formally (or legally) come into existence in Britain until the Industrial Revolution in the 19th century. The early history of trade unions is one of illegality and of legislation to prevent their existence. Five centuries of repressive legislation in Britain culminated in the passing of the ◊Combination Acts 1799 and 1800 which made unions illegal. The repeal of these 1824–25 enabled organizations of workers to engage in collective bargaining, although still subject to legal restrictions and with no legal protection for their funds until the enactment of a series of Trade Union Acts 1871–76. In 1868, 34 delegates representing 118,000 trade unionists met at a 'congress' in Manchester; the Trades Union Congress (TUC) gradually became accepted as the central organization for trade unions.

Under the Trade Union Act of 1871 unions became full legal organizations and union funds were protected from dishonest officials. Successive acts of Parliament enabled the unions to broaden their field of action; for example, the Trade Disputes Act of 1906 protected the unions against claims for damages by their employers (see ◊Taff Vale judgement); and the 1913 Trade Union Act allowed the unions to raise a political levy (see ◊Osborne Judgement). The TUC was for many years representative mainly of unions of skilled workers, but in the 1890s the organization of unskilled labour spread rapidly. Industrial unionism (the organization of all workers in one industry or trade) began about this time, but characteristic of the so-called New Unionism at the time of the 1889 dock strike was the rise of general labour unions (for example, the Dock Workers and General Labourers in the gas industry).

During World War I the leading trade unions cooperated with the employers and the government, and by 1918 were stronger than ever before with a membership of 8 million. In 1926, following a protracted series of disputes in the coal industry, the TUC called a general strike in support of the miners; this collapsed and after nine days it was called off, leaving the miners' union to continue the strike alone for a further six months. Under the Trade Disputes and Trade Union Act of 1927 general strikes or strikes called in sympathy with other workers were made illegal.

Is not this house as nigh heaven as my own ?

TOWER OF LONDON
Thomas More, on entering the Tower; quoted in Roper's Life of Sir Thomas More.

trade unions
National Union of Clerks demonstration demanding better working conditions 1913, the year the use of union funds for political purposes was legalized by the Trade Union Act. *Hulton Deutsch*

British trade unions: chronology

1799 The Combination Act outlawed organizations of workers combining for the purpose of improving conditions or raising wages. The act was slightly modified 1800.

1811 Luddite machine-breaking campaign against hosiers began; it was ended by arrests and military action 1812.

1818 Weavers and spinners formed the General Union of Trades in Lancashire.

1824 The Combination Act repealed most of the restrictive legislation but an upsurge of violent activity led to a further act 1825. Trade unions could only bargain peacefully over working hours and conditions.

1830 The General Union of Trades became the National Association for the Protection of Labour; it collapsed 1832.

1834 Formation of the Grand National Consolidated Trade Union, which lasted only a few months. Six agricultural labourers from Tolpuddle, Dorset, were convicted of swearing illegal oaths and transported to Australia.

1842 The 'Plug Plot' (removing plugs from boilers) took on the appearance of a general strike in support of a People's Charter.

1851 The foundation of the Amalgamated Society of Engineers marked the beginning of the 'New Model Unionism' of skilled workers.

1866 The 'Sheffield outrages' (attacks on nonunion labour) led to a royal commission. The Hornby v Close case cast doubt on the legal status of unions.

1867 Amendments to the Master and Servant Act gave more scope for trade unions, and the royal commission recommended they be given formal legal status.

1868 The first Trades Union Congress (TUC) was held in Manchester.

1871 The Trade Union Act gave unions legal recognition.

1888 Beginnings of 'new unionism' and the organization of unskilled workers.

1901 Taff Vale case re-established union liability for damage done by strikes; this was reversed by the Trade Disputes Act 1906.

1909 Osborne judgements ruled against unions using funds for political purposes; this was reversed by the Trade Union Act 1913.

1918–20 Widespread industrial unrest on return to a peacetime economy.

1926 A general strike was called by the TUC in support of the miners.

1930–34 Union membership fell as a result of economic recession. The Transport and General Workers replaced the Miners Federation as the largest single union.

1965 The Trade Disputes Act gave unions further immunities.

1969 The TUC successfully stopped the Labour government white paper *In Place of Strife*.

1971 The Conservative government passed the Industrial Relations Act, limiting union powers.

1973–74 'Winter of Discontent'. Strikes brought about electoral defeat for the Conservative government. Labour introduced the 'social contract'.

1980 The Conservatives introduced the Employment Act, severely restricting the powers of unions to picket or enforced closed shop; this was extended 1982.

1984 The miners' strike led to widespread confrontation and divisions within the miners' union.

1984–90 The Conservative government continued to limit the powers of trade unions through various legislative acts.

During World War II a number of trade-union leaders served in the coalition government and membership of trade unions had again risen to 8 million by 1944. The restrictive 1927 Act was repealed under the Labour government in 1946. The postwar period was marked by increased unionism among white-collar workers. From the 1960s onwards there were confrontations between the government and the trade unions, and unofficial, or wildcat, strikes set public opinion against the trade-union movement. The Labour governments' (1964–70) attempts to introduce legislative reform of the unions was strongly opposed and eventually abandoned in 1969. The Conservative government's Industrial Relations Act 1971 (including registration of trade unions, legal enforcement of collective agreements, compulsory cooling-off periods, and strike ballots) was repealed by the succeeding Labour government 1974, and voluntary wage restraint attempted under a social contract. The Employment Protection Act 1975 and the Trade Union Act 1976 increased the involvement of the government in industrial relations. ACAS was set up 1975 to arbitrate in industrial disputes.

The Thatcher government, in the Employment Acts of 1980 and 1982, restricted the closed shop, picketing, secondary action against anyone other than the employer in dispute, immunity of trade unions in respect of unlawful activity by their officials, and the definition of a trade dispute, which must be between workers and employers, not between workers. The

Trade Union Act 1984 made it compulsory to have secret ballots for elections and before strikes. Picketing was limited to the establishment at which strikes were taking place. The Employment Act 1988 contains further provisions regulating union affairs, including further requirements for ballots; rights for members not to be unfairly disciplined (for example, for failing to support a strike); and prohibiting use of union funds to indemnify union officers fined for contempt of court or other offences.

Trades Union Congress (TUC) organization which represents the trade union movement as a whole in the UK. Trade unions join (or are 'affiliated to') the TUC and pay an annual subscription according to the number of members they have. The TUC employs full-time paid workers to give individual trade unions legal and economic advice, as well as liaising with trade unions internationally and acting as a pressure group.

After World War II, governments regularly consulted the TUC about economic policy in general and employment policy in particular. However, since the election of a Conservative government 1979, trade unions and the TUC have lost all influence over government. Moreover, in the 1980s the government passed a series of laws which restricted trade union power, for example by limiting the right to strike.

Trafalgar, Battle of during the ◊Napoleonic Wars, victory of the British fleet, commanded by Admiral Horatio Nelson, over a combined French and Spanish fleet 21 Oct 1805; Nelson was mortally wounded during the action. The victory laid the foundation for British naval supremacy throughout the 19th century. It is named after nearby Cape Trafalgar, a low headland in southwest Spain, near the western entrance to the Straits of Gibraltar.

The British fleet consisted of 27 ships of the line mounting 2,138 guns; the Franco-Spanish fleet consisted of 33 ships with 2,640 guns under Admiral Pierre de Villeneuve. The French were sailing in a loose line formation and Nelson divided his force into two parts which he intended to drive through the French line at different points. The manoeuvre was successful, Nelson's flagship *Victory* passing the stern of the French flagship *Bucentaure* and discharging its broadside at 10 yds range, causing 400 casualties, and other British ships used similar tactics of close-quarter gunnery. The battle commenced at about 12 noon, and at 1.30 p.m. Nelson was mortally wounded by a musket-shot. By 3 p.m. the battle was over, and the surviving French and Spanish ships were concentrating on escape. Of their number, 15 had been sunk, and of the 18 which escaped two were wrecked 24 Oct and four taken by a British squadron 3 Nov. The British lost no ships and sustained casualties of 449 killed and 1,242 wounded; French and Spanish casualties amounted to about 14,000.

trainbands civil militia first formed in 1573 by Elizabeth I to meet the possibility of invasion. Trainbands consisted of about 100 men who were supposed to meet at least once a year. They were used by Charles I against the Scots 1639, but their lack of training meant they were of dubious military value.

Transjordan former British mandate, southwest Asia. Present-day Jordan was created 1921 out of former Turkish territory and proclaimed an independent state 1923 but

Trafalgar, Battle of Contents bill used by news vendors selling pirated copies of the Trafalgar issue of the *Times*. Although the battle took place 21 Oct 1805, detailed news of the battle did not reach England for another two weeks.
Hulton Deutsch

THE TIMES

For 7th NOVEMBER. 1805

BATTLE OF TRAFALGAR

CAPTURE OF FRENCH AND SPANISH FLEETS

DEATH OF NELSON

List of Killed and Wounded

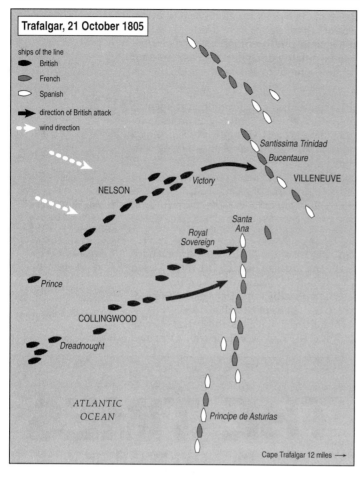

Trafalgar, 21 October 1805

ships of the line
- British
- French
- Spanish

→ direction of British attack
⋯▸ wind direction

Santissima Trinidad
Bucentaure
VILLENEUVE

NELSON
Victory

Santa Ana
Royal Sovereign

Prince

COLLINGWOOD

Dreadnought

ATLANTIC OCEAN

Principe de Asturias

Cape Trafalgar 12 miles →

Trafalgar, 21 October 1805
Nelson's victory over the combined Franco-Spanish fleet at Trafalgar was a decisive moment in the Napoleonic Wars and the culmination of a career of tactical innovation at sea by Nelson himself. In two squadrons to windward, the British ships crowded on sail and cut the enemy line at two points. Neither the combined fleet's van nor rear squadron was able to intervene effectively, and Villeneuve's fleet was shattered.

simultanously a mandate under British protection. The mandate was revoked 1946 and by a treaty of 22 March that year became an independent kingdom. The name Jordan was adopted 1949.

transportation punishment of sending convicted persons to overseas territories to serve their sentences. It was introduced in England toward the end of the 17th century and although it was abolished 1857 after many thousands had been transported, mostly to Australia, sentences of penal servitude continued to be partly carried out in Western Australia up until 1867. Prior to the American Revolution, convicts were also shipped to North America.

Trevithick Richard 1771–1833. English engineer, constructor of a steam road locomotive, the *Puffing Devil*, 1801, the first to carry passengers, and probably the first steam engine to run on rails 1804. Trevithick also built steamboats, river dredgers, and threshing machines.

trial by battle decision in a legal case arrived at by fighting between litigants or their champions, the assumption being that God would not let the innocent be vanquished. It was introduced by the Normans and had largely fallen into disuse by the late Middle Ages but it was not formally abolished until 1819 after an isolated attempt to invoke the right to this method of trial.

trial by ordeal in the Middle Ages, a test of guilt or innocence; see ◊ordeal, trial by.

Triennial Act three 17th century acts, attempting to ensure parliaments met at least once in three years. The first statute 1641 required that Parliament should meet every three years, for at least 50 days. The measure fell into abeyance and was re-instated by an act of 1664. The final act 1694 stipulated that Parliament should meet at least once every three years and not last more than three years.

Trinidad former British island territory, West Indies. Following its discovery by Columbus 1498 and subsequent Spanish settlement, the island was occupied by the British 1797 and ceded to Britain by the Treaty of Amiens 1802. It united with Tobago 1898 and as the Territory of Trinidad and Tobago became an independent state within the British Commonwealth 1962.

Triple Entente alliance of Britain, France, and Russia 1907–17. In 1914 this became a military alliance and formed the basis of the Allied powers in World War I against the Central Powers, Germany and Austria-Hungary.

Troubridge Ernest Charles Thomas 1862–1926. British admiral. He joined the navy 1878, was naval attaché in Vienna, Tokyo, and Madrid 1901–04, captain and Chief of Staff Mediterranean fleet 1907–08, chief of Admiralty war staff 1911–12, and commanded the Mediterranean cruiser squadron 1912–13. In 1914 he was second-in-command of the Mediterranean fleet and was severely criticized for allowing the *Goeben* to escape. He was court-martialled and acquitted of any fault but in 1915 was made head of the British naval mission to Serbia and he remained in this backwater for the rest of the war. In 1918 he was made president of the International Danube Commission, was knighted and promoted to admiral 1919 and retired 1921.

Trucial States group of emirates on the southern shore of the Persian Gulf that formerly had a special agreement with Britain. The Portuguese were the first European power to settle here in the 16th century, taking advantage of the Gulf's location for trade with the East. By 1650 they had been replaced by the British as a result of Britain's supremacy in India. With the aim of ending piracy and the slave trade, Britain signed a treaty 1820 with the five emirates of Abu Dhabi, Sharjah, Ajman, Umm-al-Quwain and Fujairah to observe peace at sea and refrain from piracy and slave trading. The five were collectively known as the Trucial States. Ras-al Khaimah and Dubai were formed from Sharjah 1866. The seven states formed the independent federation of the United Arab Emirates 1971.

Truck acts four acts of Parliament introduced 1831, 1887, 1896, and 1940 to prevent employers misusing wage-payment systems to the detriment of their workers. The legislation made it illegal to pay wages with goods in kind or with tokens for use in shops owned by the employers.

True Leveller member of a radical Puritan sect that flourished 1649–50; see ◊Digger.

Tudor dynasty English dynasty 1485–1603, descended from the Welsh Owen Tudor (*c.* 1400–1461), second husband of Catherine of Valois (widow of Henry V of England). Their son Edmund married Margaret Beaufort (1443–1509), the great-granddaughter of ◊John of Gaunt, and was the father of Henry VII, who became king by overthrowing Richard III 1485. The dynasty ended with the death of Elizabeth I 1603.

Tull Jethro 1674–1741. English agriculturist who about 1701 developed a drill that enabled seeds to be sown mechanically and spaced so that cultivation between rows was possible in the growth period. His chief work, *Horse-Hoeing Husbandry*, was published 1733. Tull also developed a plough with blades set in such as way that grass and roots were pulled up and left on the surface to dry. Basically the design of a plough is much the same today.

tunnage and poundage alternative spelling of ◊tonnage and poundage.

Turnham Green, Battle of in the Civil War, early encounter 13 Nov 1642 between royalist and parliamentary forces at Turnham Green, on the western outskirts of London. Neither side opened hostilities, and Charles I retreated to Oxford, which became his capital for the remainder of the war.

turnpike road gated road with a barrier preventing access until a toll had been paid, common from the mid-16th to 19th centuries. The turnpikes were administered by turnpike trusts which were permitted to levy tolls in order to maintain the roads. Many new and improved roads were built but the scheme was never popular and with the advent of railways in the 19th century, revenue from the tolls started to decline. In 1991, a plan for the first turnpike road to be built in the UK since the 18th century was announced: the privately funded Birmingham northern relief road, 50 km/31 mi long.

turnpike road
Turnpikes on the site of the old gallows at Tyburn, from Ackerman's *Microcosm of London* 1813. The Toll House. where the toll-keeper lived, is the octagonal building on the left.
Image Select

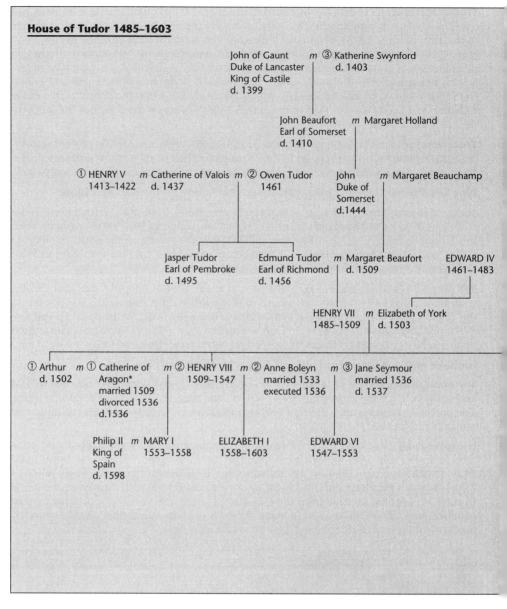

House of Tudor 1485–1603

John of Gaunt _m_ ③ Katherine Swynford
Duke of Lancaster   d. 1403
King of Castile
d. 1399

John Beaufort _m_ Margaret Holland
Earl of Somerset
d. 1410

① HENRY V _m_ Catherine of Valois _m_ ② Owen Tudor   John _m_ Margaret Beauchamp
1413–1422   d. 1437   1461   Duke of
Somerset
d.1444

Jasper Tudor   Edmund Tudor _m_ Margaret Beaufort   EDWARD IV
Earl of Pembroke   Earl of Richmond   d. 1509   1461–1483
d. 1495   d. 1456

HENRY VII _m_ Elizabeth of York
1485–1509   d. 1503

① Arthur _m_ ① Catherine of _m_ ② HENRY VIII _m_ ② Anne Boleyn _m_ ③ Jane Seymour
d. 1502   Aragon*   1509–1547   married 1533   married 1536
married 1509   executed 1536   d. 1537
divorced 1536
d.1536

Philip II _m_ MARY I   ELIZABETH I   EDWARD VI
King of   1553–1558   1558–1603   1547–1553
Spain
d. 1598

Turpin Dick 1706–1739. English highwayman. The son of an innkeeper, he turned to highway robbery, cattle-thieving, and smuggling, and was hanged at York, England.

His legendary ride from London to York on his mare Black Bess is probably based on one of about 305 km/190 mi from Gad's Hill to York completed in 15 hours in 1676 by highwayman John Nevison (1639–84).

Tyburn stream in London near which (at the junction of Oxford Street and Edgware Road) Tyburn gallows stood from the 12th century until 1783. The Tyburn now flows underground.

Tyler Wat. English leader of the ◊Peasants' Revolt of 1381. He was probably born in Kent or Essex, and may have served in the French wars. After taking Canterbury, he led the peasant army to Blackheath, outside London, and went on to invade the city. At Mile End King Richard II met the rebels and promised to redress their grievances, which included the imposition of a poll tax and the ◊Statute of Labourers. At a further conference at Smithfield, London, Tyler was murdered by the mayor of London, Sir William Walworth.

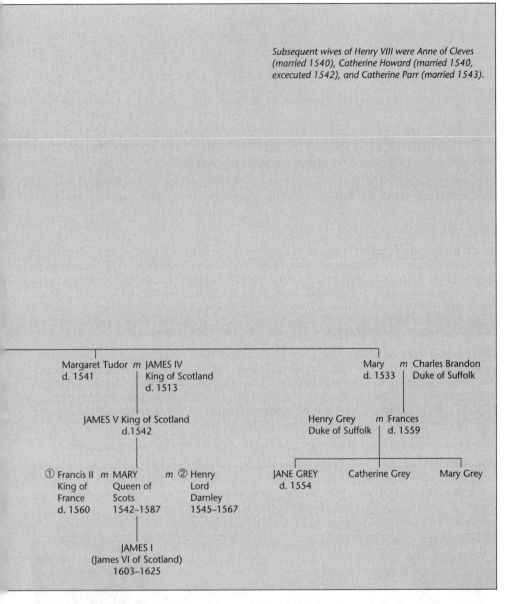

Subsequent wives of Henry VIII were Anne of Cleves (married 1540), Catherine Howard (married 1540, executed 1542), and Catherine Parr (married 1543).

Tyndale William 1492–1536. English translator of the Bible. The printing of his New Testament (the basis of the Authorized Version) was begun in Cologne 1525 and completed in Worms. Tyndale introduced some of the most familiar phrases to the English language, such as 'filthy lucre', and 'God forbid'. He was burned as a heretic at Vilvorde in Belgium.

Tynwald, court of legislative assembly of the Isle of Man consisting of the lieutenant-governor representing the crown, a legislative council, and the 24 elected members of the House of Keys. The Tynwald can enact laws, subject to the royal assent, and laws passed at Westminster only affect the island if specifically so provided. The Tynwald's origins are obscure but appear to be Norse – the House of Keys is recorded as long ago as 1422.

Tyrconnell Richard Talbot, Earl of Tyrconnell 1630–1691. Irish general, a personal friend of James II. He was granted command of the Irish army 1684, was created Earl of Tyrconnell on James's accession 1685, and appointed Lord Deputy of Ireland 1687. He held Ireland for James after the king's fall 1688 but was defeated by William III at the Boyne 1690. He died soon after the final Jacobite defeat at Aughrim 1691.

U

UDI acronym for ◊*Unilateral Declaration of Independence*.

Uganda former British protectorate, East Africa. Following visits by English explorers and missionaries, agents of the British East India Company arrived in the region 1890 and a British protectorate was formally proclaimed 1894. Independence was achieved 1962.

Uladh Irish name for the kingdom of ◊Ulster.

Ulster, kingdom of ancient kingdom of Ireland, mainly in what is now Northern Ireland. In the 5th century AD it was the most powerful of the five kingdoms. It was conquered by the English in the 13th century and turned into a feudal earldom. By 1461 it had passed to the Crown, and in the 16th century was divided into nine counties: Antrim, Armagh, Down, Fermanagh, Londonderry, Tyrone, Cavan, Donegal and Monaghan. The first six of these (the 'six counties') remained in the United Kingdom 1921, while the other three became the province of Ulster in the Republic of Ireland.

Ulster Defence Association (UDA) Northern Ireland Protestant paramilitary organization responsible for a number of sectarian killings. Fanatically loyalist, it established a paramilitary wing (the Ulster Freedom Fighters) to combat the ◊Irish Republican Army (IRA) on its own terms and by its own methods. No political party has acknowledged any links with the UDA. In 1994, following a cessation of military activities by the IRA, the UDA, along with other Protestant paramilitary organizations, declared a cease-fire.

Ulster Freedom Fighters (UFF) paramilitary wing of the ◊Ulster Defence Association.

underground rail service that runs underground. The first underground line in the world was in London, opened 1863; it was essentially a roofed-in trench. The London Underground is still the longest, with over 400 km/250 mi of routes. Many large cities throughout the world have similar systems, and Moscow's underground, the Metro, handles up to 6.5 million passengers a day.

underground
Construction of the junction of the Metropolitan and St John's Wood Railway at Baker Street, London, 18 April 1868, from the *Illustrated London News*. The underground railways revolutionized public transport in Victorian London.
Image Select

The Population of Greater London from 1563	
year	*population*
1563	over 90,000
1583	c. 120,000
1600	less than 200,000
1666	c. 350,000
c. 1700	650,000
1800	865,000
1821	over 1,000,000
1830	1,500,000
1888	less than 5,000,000
1900	4,500,000*
1951	8,346,000
1961	7,992,600
1971	7,452,500
1981	6,696,200
1991	6,679,700
1993	6,933,000

* county of London

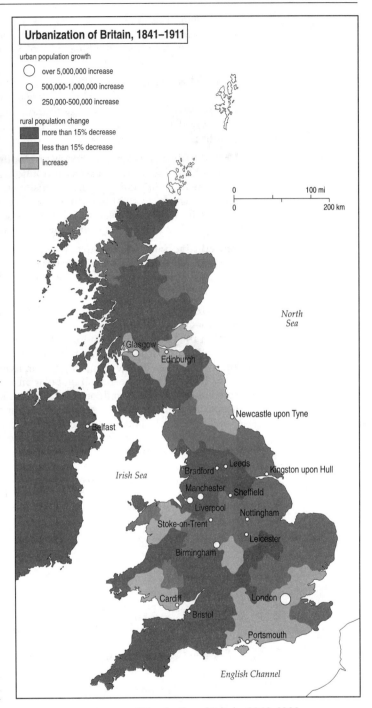

Urbanization of Britain, 1841–1911

urban population growth
- ○ over 5,000,000 increase
- ○ 500,000–1,000,000 increase
- ○ 250,000–500,000 increase

rural population change
- more than 15% decrease
- less than 15% decrease
- increase

Uniformity, Acts of four acts of Parliament that attempted to impose religious uniformity in the Church of England through the use of an official prayer book. The first 1549 required the use of ◊Cranmer's *Book of Common Prayer*, but only imposed small fines on those who failed to do so. The 1552 Act was more severe, penalizing Catholic ◊recusants and those who failed to attend church. The third act 1559 imposed the Prayer Book on the whole English kingdom; the last 1662 required the Prayer Book to be used in all churches, and some 2,000 ministers who refused to comply were ejected.

Unilateral Declaration of Independence (UDI) the declaration made by Ian Smith's Rhodesian Front government 11 Nov 1965, announcing the independence of Rhodesia (now Zimbabwe) from Britain.

Smith unilaterally declared Rhodesia an independent state, to resist sharing power with the black African majority. It was a move condemned by the United Nations and by the UK, who imposed sanctions (trade restrictions and an oil embargo). With the support of the UN, Britain also imposed a naval blockade, but this was countered by the South African government breaking sanctions. Negotiations between British prime minister Harold Wilson and Smith foundered. It was not until April 1980 that the Republic of Zimbabwe was proclaimed.

Union, Act of 1707 act of Parliament that brought about the union of England and Scotland; that of 1801 united England and Ireland. The latter was revoked when the Irish Free State was constituted 1922.

Urbanization of Britain, 1841–1911
Against an overall population increase from 27 million to 45 million, the 70 years before World War I saw a huge change in the relative distribution of British people. The industrial centres of Central Scotland, the Northeast, the Northwest, South Wales, the Midlands, and London expanded rapidly, while the rural population in many areas actually declined. Since World War I the relative changes have been much less marked.

union flag British national flag, popularly called the ***Union Jack***, although, strictly speaking, this applies only when it is flown on the jackstaff of a warship. It combines the red cross of St George (England), the blue cross of St Andrew (Scotland), and, after 1801, the white cross of St Patrick (Ireland).

Union Movement British political group. Founded as the ***New Party*** by Oswald ◊Mosley and a number of Labour members of Parliament 1931, it developed into the ***British Union of Fascists*** 1932. In 1940 the organization was declared illegal and its leaders interned, but it was revived as the Union Movement 1948, characterized by racist doctrines including anti-Semitism.

United Irishmen society formed 1791 by Wolfe ◊Tone to campaign for parliamentary reform in Ireland. It later became a secret revolutionary group. Inspired by the republican ideals of the French Revolution, the United Irishmen was initially a debating society, calling for reforms such as the right of Catholics to vote in Irish elections, but after an attempt to suppress it in 1793, the organization became secret, looking to France for military aid. An attempted insurrection 1798 was quickly defeated and the leaders captured.

United Kingdom (UK) country in northwest Europe off the coast of France, consisting of England, Scotland, Wales, and Northern Ireland. The term 'United Kingdom' became official 1801, but was in use from 1707, when the Act of Union combined Scotland and England into the United Kingdom of Great Britain. The Act of Ireland 1801 united Britain and Ireland.

urbanization process by which the proportion of a population living in or around towns and cities increases through migration as the agricultural population declines.

With the exception of London, which grew rapidly from Tudor times onward, urbanization in Britain occurred mainly from the early 19th century to the early 20th. Between 1841 and 1911 the percentage of the population living in cities increased from 37 to 74, against an overall increase in the British population from 27 to 45 million. London's population increased from under 2 million to over 6.5 million over the same period, and the numbers of people living in Glasgow, Liverpool, Manchester, and Birmingham grew to nearly or just over 1 million in each. These cities were all in the growing industrial areas of Britain. In general, the people who moved to them came from the surrounding regions, but London in particular attracted immigrants from all over Britain. People from Ireland, where the overall population declined from 8.5 million in 1845 to 4.4 million in 1911, moved to all the British cities.

Since World War I the relative decline of the British rural population has been much less, and the cities, particularly in the Southeast, have expanded considerably in area but very little in population, a phenomenon known as urban sprawl.

Vane Henry 1613–1662. English politician. He went to New England 1635 and was governor of Massachusetts 1636–37. Elected a member of the ◊Long Parliament 1640, he was prominent in the impeachment of Archbishop ◊Laud and in 1643–53 was in effect the civilian head of the Parliamentary government. He opposed Cromwell's Protectorate and retired from politics until Cromwell's death 1659. At the Restoration of the monarchy he was executed.

vassal person who paid feudal homage to a superior lord (see ◊feudalism), and who promised military service and advice in return for a grant of land. The term was used from the 9th century. The relationship of vassalage was the mainstay of the feudal system and declined along with it during the transition to bastard feudalism.

Verneuil, Battle of in the Hundred Years' War, devastating English victory 17 Aug 1424 over a joint French and Scottish army. The Scots were decimated: they suffered some 7,000 casualities including the 4th Earl of Douglas. The French failed to retake Normandy and the Earl of Bedford was able to seize Maine.

Verney Edmund 1590–1642. English courtier, knight-marshal to Charles I from 1626. He sat as a member of both the Short and the Long Parliaments and, though sympathizing with the Parliamentary position, remained true to his allegiance: he died at his post as royal standard bearer at the Battle of ◊Edgehill.

The ***Verney papers***, a collection of his memoirs and other personal papers, are a valuable record of this and later periods. His son Ralph (1613–96) supported the Parliamentarians.

Vernon Edward 1684–1757. English admiral who captured Portobello from the Spanish in the Caribbean 1739, with a loss of only seven men. He prevented the French from supporting the ◊Jacobite rebellion of 1745 by blockading their Channel ports.

Versailles, Treaty of peace treaty after World War I between the Allies and Germany, signed 28 June 1919. It established the League of Nations. Germany surrendered Alsace-Lorraine to France, and large areas in the east to Poland, and made smaller cessions to Czechoslovakia, Lithuania, Belgium, and Denmark. The Rhineland was demilitarized, German rearmament was restricted, and Germany agreed to accept responsibility for causing the war and pay reparations for war damage. The treaty was never ratified by the USA, which made a separate peace with Germany and Austria 1921.

Verulamium important Roman-British town whose remains have been excavated close to St Albans, Hertfordshire.

vestiarian controversy 16th century dispute over the use of clerical vestments. The Puritans opposed clergy wearing the surplice which they felt had overtones of a Catholic priesthood, and the issue was hotly contested under Edward VI and then especially in the first years of Elizabeth I's reign. Matthew Parker, archbishop of Canterbury, ordered conformity to the *Book of ◊Common Prayer* 1566, signalling the Queen's determination not to reform the Church further.

Victoria 1819–1901. Queen of the UK from 1837, when she succeeded her uncle William IV, and empress of India from 1876. In 1840 she married Prince ◊Albert of Saxe-Coburg and Gotha. Her relations with her prime ministers ranged from the affectionate (Melbourne and Disraeli) to the stormy (Peel, Palmerston, and Gladstone). Her golden jubilee 1887 and diamond jubilee 1897 marked a waning of republican sentiment, which had developed with her withdrawal from public life on Albert's death 1861.

I have eaten his bread, and served him near thirty years, and will not do so base a thing as to forsake him ...

EDMUND VERNEY
pledging allegiance to King Charles I, 1642

Only child of Edward, Duke of Kent, fourth son of George III, she was born 24 May 1819 at Kensington Palace, London. She and Albert had four sons and five daughters. After Albert's death 1861 she lived mainly in retirement. Nevertheless, she kept control of affairs, refusing the Prince of Wales (Edward VII) any active role. From 1848 she regularly visited the Scottish Highlands, where she had a house at Balmoral built to Prince Albert's designs. She died at Osborne House, her home in the Isle of Wight, 22 Jan 1901, and was buried at Windsor.

Victoria Cross British decoration for conspicuous bravery in wartime, instituted by Queen Victoria 1856. It is bronze, with a 4 cm/1.5 in diameter, and has a crimson ribbon. Until the supply was exhausted 1942 all Victoria Crosses were struck from the metal of cannon captured from the Russians at Sevastopol; they are now made from gunmetal supplied by the Royal Mint.

Victory battleship, the flagship of Admiral Nelson at ◊Trafalgar; 2,198 tonnes/2,164 tons, launched 1765, and now in dry dock in Portsmouth harbour, England.

Vienna, Congress of international conference held 1814–15 that agreed the settlement of Europe after the Napoleonic Wars. National representatives included the Austrian foreign minister Metternich, Alexander I of Russia, the British foreign secretary Castlereagh and military commander Wellington, and the French politician Talleyrand. Its final act created a kingdom of the Netherlands, a German confederation of 39 states, Lombardy-Venetia subject to Austria, and the kingdom of Poland. Monarchs were restored in Spain, Naples, Piedmont, Tuscany, and Modena; Louis XVIII was confirmed as king of France.

The congress also condemned the slave trade, recommended extending the rights of Jews, and established the modern system of diplomacy.

Viking or ***Norseman*** the inhabitants of Scandinavia in the period 800–1100. They traded with, and raided, much of Europe, and often settled there. In their narrow, shallow-draught, highly manoeuvrable longships, the Vikings penetrated far inland along rivers. They plundered for gold and land, and were equally energetic as colonists – with colonies stretching from North America to central Russia – and as traders, with main trading posts at Birka (near Stockholm) and Hedeby (near Schleswig). The Vikings had a sophisticated literary culture, with sagas and runic inscriptions, and an organized system of government with an assembly ('thing'). Their kings and chieftains were buried with their ships, together with their possessions.

In France the Vikings were given Normandy. Under Sweyn I they conquered England (where they were known as 'Danes') 1013, and his son Canute was king of England as well as Denmark and Norway. In the east they established the first Russian state and founded Novgorod. They reached the Byzantine Empire in the south, and in the west sailed to Ireland, Iceland, Greenland, visited by Eric the Red, and North America, by his son Leif Ericsson who named it 'Vinland'. As ◊'Normans' they achieved a second conquest of England 1066.

THE SCOURGE FROM THE NORTH

The Vikings in Britain

The Viking Age in the British Isles began in the late 8th century with a series of raids by Scandinavian pirates on coastal monasteries such as Lindisfarne (sacked 793) and Iona (sacked 795). These hit-and-run raids were virtually impossible to prevent: by the time an army had gathered to counterattack, the Vikings had taken their plunder and set sail for home.

In the 840s Viking activity intensified. The Vikings came in larger numbers and founded permanent bases, such as Dublin in 841, from which they could campaign all year round. They were now interested as much in settlement as in plunder. The first areas to be settled were Scotland's northern and western isles, but the largest settlements took place in eastern and northern England after the Danes overran the Anglo-Saxon kingdoms of East Anglia, Northumbria, and Mercia in 865–74. The Vikings were greatly aided in this period by the disunity of the native kingdoms in Britain and Ireland, which failed absolutely to bury their differences and unite against the common enemy.

As the 9th century drew to a close, Viking activity declined. This was partly because many Vikings had now settled down as farmers and partly because of stiffening native resistance, such as that of Wessex under the leadership of Alfred the Great. Once the Vikings had settled down they lost their main advantage over the natives: their mobility. Between 912 and 954 Wessex conquered the Danelaw, as the Viking-settled area of eastern England was known, and the Viking kingdom of York. In Ireland the Vikings of Dublin struggled to maintain their independence and often paid tribute to Irish kings.

The late 10th century saw a resumption of large-scale Viking raiding, directed mostly at England. At first the raiders were content to extract Danegeld (protection money) but as English defences crumbled, the Danish king Sweyn I Forkbeard conquered the country in 1014. A resurgence of English resistance was put down by his son Canute in 1016 and England remained under Danish rule until 1042. The last major Viking invasion of the British Isles was Norwegian King Harald Hardrada's attempt to seize the English throne in 1066: he was defeated and killed by Harold I Godwinson at Stamford Bridge just days before William the Conqueror launched his own successful invasion.

The cultural impact

Most of our historical sources for Viking Age Britain were written by monks. Monasteries were the main cultural centres of early medieval Britain and Ireland: they were also wealthy and unprotected and this made them a favourite target of Viking raids. Not surprisingly therefore, monastic chroniclers dwelt mainly on the violence and destruction wrought by the Vikings. Some modern historians have argued that these chroniclers were prejudiced against the Vikings because of their paganism and greatly exaggerated the violence of their raids. However, contemporary accounts of Viking raids from Francia, the Byzantine empire, and the Islamic lands, and Viking poetry, all agree that Viking raiders were extremely violent and destructive. Much of the damage caused by Viking raids was temporary, but their attacks on monasteries were devastating for cultural life: works of art and literature were destroyed, and the communities of learned monks were dispersed. In England, monasticism made a strong recovery in the 10th century, but the brilliant monastic civilization of early Christian Ireland, which had produced masterpieces like the *Book of Kells*, never recovered from the Viking raids.

Perhaps the most important effect of the Viking invasions was that they broke up the existing power structures of the British Isles. Viking raids on western Scotland encouraged the Scots to expand inland, conquering the Picts, thus creating the kingdom of Scotland. By destroying their rivals the Vikings also greatly aided the creation of a unified English kingdom by the kings of Wessex in the 10th century.

The abiding influence

The Vikings were not only warriors and pirates, however, but also merchants, farmers and settlers, and skilled craftsmen. Viking traders stimulated the growth of trading centres like York and the foundation of new towns like Dublin. Viking art styles influenced and enriched Celtic and Anglo-Saxon art. The English language was also greatly enriched by Danish loan words, including 'sky', 'egg', and 'sister'. After the initial violence of conquest, the Viking settlers farmed peacefully alongside their Celtic or Anglo-Saxon neighbours and, through conversion to Christianity and intermarriage, were quickly assimilated.

The Viking settlements have left few physical remains, but their locations and density can be inferred from the distribution of Scandinavian placenames. For example, Danish placenames (typically ending in '-by' or '-thorpe') are common in much of eastern England, while Norwegian placename elements (such as 'fell') are common in northwest England and the Hebrides. In Orkney and Shetland almost all placenames are of Scandinavian origin, pointing to a particularly dense Viking settlement.

JOHN HAYWOOD

Viking invasions: chronology

793	First recorded Viking attack on Britain, on Lindisfarne monastery in northeast England.
795–830	Viking raids on Ireland.
c. 800.	Settlement of Norse in Orkneys.
830s	Norse settlement in Ireland; strongholds established on east coast, including Dublin.
835	Danes made large-scale raid on the Isle of Sheppey, Kent, southeast England.
850–1	Danes first wintered in England.
865	The Danish 'great army' landed in Britain, led by Ivar and Halfan, leading to colonization.
866	Danes occupied York.
867	Danes established control over Northumbria.
869	Danes killed King Edmund of East Anglia.
871	Alfred became king of Wessex.
874	Division of the Danish 'great army'; some members settled in the east and north Ridings of Yorkshire, others in the east Midlands after driving out King Burgred of Mercia.
878	Danes led by King Guthrum overran much of Wessex, but were defeated by King Alfred at Edington in Wiltshire. In the ensuing Treaty of Wedmore, Guthrum accepted Christianity.
879	Start of large-scale Danish settlement in East Anglia.
886	King Alfred recaptured London from the Danes.
899	Death of King Alfred. Succeeded by Edward the Elder.
910	Battle of Tettenhall (Staffordshire): Vikings defeated by Wessex forces.
919	Ragnald founded the Norse kingdom of York; lasted until 927.
937	King Athelstan of Wessex defeated Norse and Scots at the Battle of Brunanburh (location unknown).
939	Olaf Guthfrithson re-established the Danish kingdom of York.
950	Scandinavians attacked Wales.
954	Last Norse king of York was deposed.
973	Edgar, king of Wessex since 959, was crowned in Bath, symbolizing the creation of a united kingdom of England.
980	Danes renewed raids on England.
991	Battle of Maldon: Danish raiders defeated an English army in Essex (the battle was later the subject of an Old English poem). Afterwards, King Ethelred paid the Danes to depart – the first payment of Danegeld.
997	Widespread Danish raids in England.
1002	St Brice's Day massacre: Danes in England were killed on order of King Ethelred.
1002–14	In Ireland, reign of Brian Boru who captured Dublin from the Vikings in 999 and later defeated Vikings at the Battle of Contarf 1014.
1012	Danes murder Archbishop Aelfheah in Canterbury Cathedral.
1013	Danes in the Danelaw area of England accepted King Sweyn of Denmark as ruler.
1014	Death of King Sweyn of the Danelaw; the Danish army elected Canute as successor.
1016	Battle of Ashingdon: Danes under King Canute defeated the English; Canute became king of England.
1035	Death of King Canute; succeeded by Harold I Harefoot (regent 1035–37, king 1037–40) and HarthaCanute (1040–42).
1042	Accession of Edward the Confessor, restoring English kings to the throne.
1066	Invasion of King Harald Hardrada of Norway; defeated by King Harold at the Battle of Stamford Bridge.
1069–70	King Sweyn II Estrithson of Denmark landed in east England to aid rebels against the Norman king, William I, but was bought off.
1098	Final intervention of Vikings in Wales, when they helped to defeat Norman invaders.

Viking raids on the British Isles started with the sacking of the monastery of Lindisfarne 793. Soon Viking rule was established in the Orkneys, Shetlands, Hebrides, and parts of north and western Scotland, in parts of Ireland, and increasingly in England, where the Vikings controlled most of the Anglo-Saxon kingdoms, an area known as the **Danelaw**. The kingdom of Wessex under Alfred the Great resisted strongly, however, and was victorious in 899. The need for organized resistance accelerated the growth of the feudal system. In the 10th century the Scandinavian settlers in England lost their power, reflecting the civil war then raging in Scandinavia, but toward the end of the century raids from Denmark increased, culminating in the invasion and conquest of England under Sweyn I and Canute. They created permanent settlements, for example in York, and greatly influenced the development of the English language.

In Ireland the Vikings founded the cities of Dublin (840), Cork, and Limerick. They were halted, however, by their defeat at the Battle of Clontarf, 1014.

villein see ◊serfdom.

Vinegar Hill, Battle of 21 June 1798 battle during the Irish rebellion, in which General Lake, defending Irish loyalist possessions in County Wexford, defeated Catholic rebels.

Virginia former British colony in North America; see ◊Thirteen Colonies.

viscount the fourth degree of British nobility, between earl and baron.

Vittoria, Battle of in the ◊Peninsular War, French defeat by the Duke of Wellington 21 June 1813, near Vittoria, a north Spanish town. This battle effectively ended French influence in Spain, and after clearing out French stragglers from the border area, the British were able to march on into France.

Vortigern 5th century AD. English ruler, said by ◊Bede to have invited the Saxons to Britain to repel the ◊Picts and Scots, and to have married Rowena, daughter of ◊Hengist.

Vote of No Address decision of the the Long Parliament 17 Jan 1648 to break off negotiations with the king. The vote was a response to news of Charles II's ◊Engagement with the Scots. However, by this time power had already passed to the army and the measure was repealed Sept 1648.

English conquest of Wales, 1070–1300

As in Ireland, and in contrast to Anglo-Saxon England, Norman penetration of Wales took place very gradually after 1066, and was largely undertaken by the individual marcher lords. Only with the reign of Edward I was north Wales systematically conquered, reorganized into counties, and secured by major royal castles. Edward's campaigns effectively ended the last hope of an independent Welsh state.

Wade George 1673–1748. Hanoverian soldier. As Hanoverian commander-in-chief in Scotland from 1724–38, he built roads and bridges to assist military communications and formed a Highland militia which later became the Black Watch. He returned to England, but was dismissed 1745 after he failed to prevent the Scots invading the North in the Jacobite ◊Forty-Five rebellion.

Waitangi, Treaty of 1840, treaty negotiated in New Zealand between the British government and the indigenous Maori. The treaty guaranteed the Maori their own territory and gave them British citizenship. The British claimed sovereignty over the territory and the treaty is seen as the establishment of modern New Zealand.

Wakefield Edward Gibbon 1796–1862. British colonial administrator. He was imprisoned 1826–29 for abducting an heiress, and became manager of the South Australian Association, which founded a colony 1836. He was an agent for the New Zealand Land Company 1839–46, and emigrated there in 1853. His son **Edward Jerningham Wakefield** (1820–1879) wrote *Adventure in New Zealand* 1845.

Wakefield, Battle of in the Wars of the Roses, battle 30 Dec 1460 in which a superior Lancastrian force defeated and killed Richard of York, who was besieged at Sandal Castle, near Wakefield. Richard was trying to secure the North's acceptance of him as the official heir to Henry VI. His severed head was decorated with a paper crown and taken to York.

Wales principality of (Welsh *Cymru*) constituent part of the UK, in the west between the Bristol Channel and the Irish Sea.

Wales, Church in the Welsh Anglican church; see ◊Church in Wales.

Wales, Prince of title conferred on the eldest son of the UK's sovereign. Prince ◊Charles was invested as 21st prince of Wales at Caernarvon 1969 by his mother, Elizabeth II. The title was established 1301 when Edward I conferred it on his eldest son Edward of Caernarfon alone with the lands of the prinicipality.

Wallace William 1272–1305. Scottish nationalist who led a revolt against English rule 1297, won a victory at Stirling Bridge, invaded northern England, and assumed the title 'governor of Scotland'. Edward I defeated him at Falkirk 1298, and Wallace was later captured and executed in London.

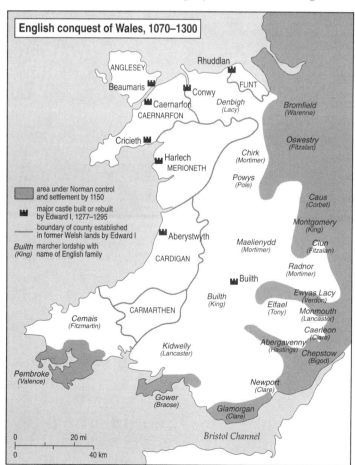

English conquest of Wales, 1070–1300

ANGLESEY
Rhuddlan
Beaumaris
Conwy
FLINT
Caernarfon
CAERNARFON
Denbigh (Lacy)
Bromfield (Warenne)
Cricieth
Oswestry (Fitzalan)
Harlech
MERIONETH
Chirk (Mortimer)
Powys (Pole)
Caus (Corbet)
Montgomery (King)
Aberystwyth
Maelienydd (Mortimer)
Clun (Fitzalan)
CARDIGAN
Radnor (Mortimer)
Builth
Ewyas Lacy (Verdon)
CARMARTHEN
Builth (King)
Elfael (Tony)
Monmouth (Lancaster)
Cemais (Fitzmartin)
Caerleon (Clare)
Kidwelly (Lancaster)
Abergavenny (Hastings)
Chepstow (Bigod)
Pembroke (Valence)
Newport (Clare)
Gower (Braose)
Glamorgan (Clare)
Bristol Channel

area under Norman control and settlement by 1150

major castle built or rebuilt by Edward I, 1277–1295

boundary of county established in former Welsh lands by Edward I

Builth marcher lordship with
(King) name of English family

0   20 mi
0   40 km

Wales 844–1282: chronology

844–78 Reign of Rhodri Mawr (the Great) of Gwynedd (northwest Wales), who acquired Powys (northeast Wales) in 855 and absorbed Seisyllwg (west Wales); he was forced into exile by Vikings in 877 and died fighting Mercians.

***c.* 904–50** Reign of Hywel Dda (the Good), a grandson of Rhodri Mawr, who acquired Dyfed by marriage and extended his rule over most of Wales. He is reputed to have codified Welsh law.

1039–63 Reign of Gruffydd ap Llywelyn of Gwynedd and Powys; in 1055 he had Gruffydd ap Rhydderch of south Wales killed; he also acquired English territory.

1066 Norman invasion of England; King William I established earldoms along the Anglo–Welsh border, based on Hereford, Shrewsbury, and Chester; their Norman inhabitants soon started pushing into Wales.

1081 Battle of Mynydd Carn: the exiled claimant to Gwynedd, Gruffydd ap Cynan, in alliance with the claimant to Deheubarth (southwest Wales), Rhys ap Tewdwr, defeated their rivals. Gruffydd was then captured and imprisoned by the Normans. Possibly at this point, the Norman Robert of Rhuddlan seized Gwynedd.
William I of England visited St David's; Rhys ap Tewdwr of Deheubarth may have submitted to William; William may have founded Cardiff.

***c.* 1088–90** Normans led by Arnulf of Montgomery swept across central Wales and then the south, founding Pembroke.

1088 Gruffydd ap Cynan killed Robert of Rhuddlan; Gruffydd ruled Gwynedd until 1137.

1090s Normans conquered and settled in the Vale of Glamorgan (south Wales).

1093 The Norman Bernard of Neufmarché killed King Rhys ap Tewdwr at Aberhonddu (later called Brecon) and established a castle there.

1102 King Henry I of England broke the Bellême family, involving the loss of their Welsh lands.

***c.* 1103–35** King Henry I sponsored large-scale Norman settlement in south Wales; the first royal castle in Wales was founded at Carmarthen in 1109.

1135 In England, disputed accession of King Stephen; war broke out in south Wales, enabling Welsh rulers to retake land from the Normans. In 1136, Gruffydd ap Rhys reconquered most of Deheubarth.

1137–*c.*70 Following the death of Gruffydd ap Cynan, king of Gwynedd, reign of his son Owain Gwynedd, who extended Gwynedd's territory in the northeast (towards Chester).

1155–97 Reign of Rhys ap Gruffydd, king of Deheubarth. From 1170 Deheubarth became the major kingdom in Wales. Rhys supported Henry II of England, serving as Henry's justiciar in south Wales. On Rhys's death, the succession was disputed, causing the disintegration of the kingdom.

***c.* 1194–1240** Reign of Llewelyn ab Iorwerth of Gwynedd (possibly a grandson of Owain Gwynedd). Starting *c.* 1190, Llewelyn reunited Gwynedd and in 1204 married Joan, the illegitimate daughter of King John of England. He acquired Powys (1208, 1216) and in 1216 held an assembly in Aberdyfi at which other Welsh rulers may have done homage to him.

1240–46 Reign of Dafydd ap Llewelyn of Gwynedd (son of Llewelyn ab Iorwerth). In 1241 Henry III invaded north Wales and forced Dafydd to cede land conquered by Llewelyn ab Iorwerth. Around 1244, when trying to make Wales a papal fiefdom, Dafydd styled himself 'prince of Wales'.

1246 Accession of Llewelyn ap Gruffydd of Gwynedd (one of four nephews of Dafydd ap Llewelyn). Following campaigns through Wales, most Welsh rulers acknowledged him as 'prince of Wales' in 1258. In 1265, Simon de Montfort agreed to recognize Llewelyn as prince; in 1267 King Henry III extended recognition to Llewelyn's successors.

1272 *16 Nov* Death of King Henry III of England; accession of Edward I.

1276 *12 Nov* Following a series of disputes with Llewelyn ap Gruffydd, Edward I declared war; three armies invaded Wales.

1277 *9 Nov* Treaty of Aberconwy: Llewelyn agreed to Edward's harsh terms, including the loss of territories outside Gwynedd.

1282 *21 March* Llewelyn's brother Dafydd began revolt against the English in northeast Wales, which was joined by other Welsh rulers. Edward responded with an invasion.
11 Dec Llewelyn was killed.

1283 *25 April* English suppressed Welsh resistance; in June they captured Dafydd (who was later tried and executed).

1284 *19 March* Edward I issued the Statute of Wales at Rhuddlan, providing for English government in Wales.

Sovereigns and Princes of Wales 844–1282

844–78	Rhodri the Great
878–916	Anarawd
915–50	Hywel Dda (Hywel the Good)
950–79	Iago ab Idwal
979–85	Hywel ab Ieuaf (Hywel the Bad)
985–86	Cadwallon
986–99	Maredudd ab Owain ap Hywel Dda
999–1008	Cynan ap Hywel ab Ieuaf
1018–23	Llywelyn ap Seisyll
1023–39	Iago ab Idwal ap Meurig
1039–63	Gruffydd ap Llywelyn ap Seisyll
1063–75	Bleddyn ap Cynfyn
1075–81	Trahaern ap Caradog
1081–1137	Gruffydd ap Cynan ab Iago
1137–70	Owain Gwynedd
1170–94	Dafydd ab Owain Gwynedd
1194–1240	Llywelyn Fawr (Llywelyn the Great)
1240–46	Dafydd ap Llywelyn
1246–82	Llywelyn ap Gruffydd ap Llywelyn

English Princes of Wales from 1301

1301	Edward (II)
1343	Edward the Black Prince
1376	Richard (II)
1399	Henry of Monmouth (V)
1454	Edward of Westminster
1471	Edward of Westminster (V)
1483	Edward
1489	Arthur Tudor
1504	Henry Tudor (VIII)
1610	Henry Stuart
1616	Charles Stuart (I)
c. 1638	Charles (II)
1688	James Francis Edward (Old Pretender)
1714	George Augustus (II)
1729	Frederick Lewis
1751	George William Frederick (III)
1762	George Augustus Frederick (IV)
1841	Albert Edward (Edward VII)
1901	George (V)
1910	Edward (VII)
1958	Charles Philip Arthur George

Waller Sir William c. 1597–1686. Parliamentary general in the Civil War. He was a member of the Long Parliament from 1640 and made a colonel on the outbreak of hostilities 1642. He was promoted general and captured Hereford, but was defeated at Roundway Down 1643. He resigned his commission following the formation of the New Model Army 1645. As a leading Presbyterian in Parliament he came into conflict with the army and was imprisoned 1648–51. He conspired against Richard Cromwell 1659 and was a member of the Convention Parliament that brought about the Restoration 1660.

Walpole Robert, 1st Earl of Orford 1676–1745. British Whig politician, the first 'prime minister' as First Lord of the Treasury and chancellor of the Exchequer 1715–17 and 1721–42. He helped to restore financial stability after the ◊South Sea Bubble, encouraged trade and tried to avoid foreign disputes but was forced into the War of Jenkins's Ear with Spain 1739.

Opponents thought his foreign policies worked to the advantage of France and his attempt to extend excise duties to wine and tobacco was successfully opposed. He held favour with George I and George II, struggling against ◊Jacobite intrigues, and received an earldom when he eventually retired 1742.

Walsingham Francis c. 1530–1590. English politician who, as secretary of state to Elizabeth I from 1573, advocated a strong anti-Spanish policy and ran the efficient government spy system that made it work. The plots of Ridolfi 1570–71, Throckmorton 1583, and Babington 1586 were all uncovered by his network of spies.

Walter Hubert d. 1205. Archbishop of Canterbury 1193–1205. As justiciar (chief political and legal officer) 1193–98, he ruled England during Richard I's absence and was chancellor under King John. He introduced the offices of coroner and justice of the peace.

Walter Lucy c. 1630–1658. Mistress of ◊Charles II, whom she met while a Royalist refugee in The Hague, Netherlands, 1648; the Duke of ◊Monmouth was their son.

Wansdyke ('Woden's Ditch') Anglo-Saxon defensive earthwork, probably built in the 5th century as a defence against British (Welsh) raids. It runs from Bristol to Wiltshire, and may have had a wooden wall or staves for some of its length.

wapentake (Scandinavian 'weapon-taking') subdivision of a county in the ◊Danelaw, corresponding to the ◊hundred in counties outside the Danelaw.

War of 1812 war between the USA and Britain 1812–14 caused by British interference with US merchant shipping as part of the economic warfare against Napoleonic France. US sailors were impressed from American ships, and a blockade was imposed on US shipping by Britain. In North America, British assistance was extended to Indians (such as Tecumseh) harassing the northwest settlements and there was increasing tension over the British presence in Canada. President Madison authorized the beginning of hostilities against the British on the high seas and in Canada but military success was limited to the capture and burning of York (now Toronto) and a few notable naval victories. In 1814, British forces occupied Washington, DC, and burned the White House and the Capitol. A treaty signed in Ghent, Belgium, Dec 1814 ended the conflict but before news of it reached the USA, American troops under Andrew Jackson defeated the British at New Orleans 1815.

Warbeck Perkin c. 1474–1499. Flemish pretender to the English throne. Claiming to be Richard, brother of Edward V, he led a rising against Henry VII 1497, and was hanged after attempting to escape from the Tower of London.

Wardens of the Marches officials responsible for the security of the Anglo-Scottish border from the 14th century. They were appointed separately in England and Scotland for the East, West, and Middle Marches. Usually local noblemen, their duty was not only to defend their respective borders but, more usually, to maintain peace and settle disputes. The offices lapsed with James VI's accession to the English throne 1603.

wardrobe financial department of the royal household, originally a secure place for royal robes and other valuable items. As the Exchequer became a formal department of state, monarchs needed to maintain a privy treasury under their personal supervision and the wardrobe was secure enough to hold money. By the time of Henry III's reign, the wardrobe was so important that the barons demanded all income should be officially accounted for in the Exchequer. Under Edward I, it became a war treasury and was used to pay the armies on major expeditions. However, from the time of Edward IV, and more especially the Tudors, it was largely replaced by the Chamber as a form of 'current account'.

wardship and marriage the right of the Crown to supervise minors who were tenants-in-chief. Since those who held land of the Crown did so as long as they performed military service, the king was entitled to control both minors and their land, as well as their choice of marriage partner. The tenants were considered to be minors until the age of 21 in case of boys and 14 for girls. The Magna Carta prohibited the despoiling of minors' estates, but wardships were frequently sold by monarchs, though often to relatives, and by the 16th and 17th centuries it was purely a financial expedient.

Warwick Richard Neville, Earl of Warwick 1428–1471. English politician, called *the Kingmaker*. During the Wars of the ◊Roses he fought at first on the Yorkist side against the Lancastrians, and defeated and captured Henry VI at Northampton 1460, placing Edward IV on the throne. Having quarrelled with Edward, he restored Henry VI 1470, but was defeated and killed by Edward at Barnet, Hertfordshire.

Waterloo, Battle of final battle of the Napoleonic Wars 18 June 1815 in which a coalition force of British, Prussian, and Dutch troops under the Duke of Wellington defeated Napoleon near the village of Waterloo, 13 km/8 mi south of Brussels, Belgium. Napoleon found Wellington's army isolated from his allies and began a direct offensive to smash them, but the British held on until joined by the Prussians under Marshal Gebhard von Blücher. Four days later Napoleon abdicated for the second and final time.

Wellington had 67,000 soldiers (of whom 24,000 were British, the remainder being German, Dutch, and Belgian) and Napoleon had 74,000. The French casualties numbered about 37,000; coalition casualties were similar including some 13,000 British troops.

Napoleon's 120,000-strong army was amassed on the French–Belgian frontier 12 June; Wellington had about 90,000 troops at Brussels, of whom 30,000 were British, and was expecting Napoleon to march on Brussels to attack him. However, on their way to attack Wellington, the French fought the Prussians at Ligny, and also fought a combined Dutch–Belgian army at Quatre Bras, all of which delayed Napoleon and enabled Wellington to concentrate his forces at Waterloo, in anticipation of the arrival of Marshal Blücher with the Prussian army. Napoleon despatched the Marquis de Grouchy with 33,000 troops to block the road upon which the Prussians were expected to arrive and took the rest of his army to face the Allies.

The French opened the battle at 11.30 a.m. 18 June, and a fierce struggle developed for Hougoumont Farm. On the left, a long bombardment by French artillery, followed by an infantry assault, forced the Dutch and Belgians to give way, but the situation was saved by a charge of British cavalry under Lord Uxbridge. In the centre, the action revolved around the farmhouse of La Haie Sainte, where the British stubbornly beat off the French until about 6

> *... it was ordained that the winding ivy of a Plantagenet should kill the true tree itself.*
>
> Perkin Warbeck
> *Francis Bacon,*
> The Life of Henry VII

Warwick
Richard Neville, Earl of Warwick, known as 'the Kingmaker'. He all but ruled England in the first three years of Edward IV's reign, but his influence declined when Edward married Elizabeth Woodville and he began intrigues to restore the former king, Henry VI.
Philip Sauvain

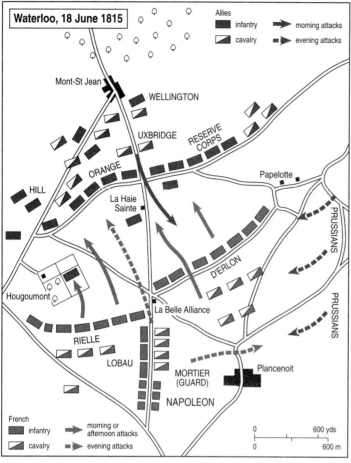

Waterloo, 18 June 1815

Allies
- infantry
- cavalry
- morning attacks
- evening attacks

Mont-St Jean
WELLINGTON
UXBRIDGE
RESERVE CORPS
ORANGE
HILL
La Haie Sainte
Papelotte
PRUSSIANS
D'ERLON
Hougoumont
La Belle Alliance
RIELLE
LOBAU
MORTIER (GUARD)
Plancenoit
NAPOLEON
PRUSSIANS

French
- infantry
- cavalry
- morning or afternoon attacks
- evening attacks

0   600 yds
0   600 m

Waterloo, 18 June 1815
The final Allied defeat of Napoleon at Waterloo owed little to tactical imagination, but was one of the most decisive battles in modern European history. D'Erlon's initial assault was thrown back by Allied musketry and Uxbridge's heavy cavalry, after which traditional British line and square formations held off repeated French infantry and cavalry attacks. Blücher's advance on Plancenoit in the evening sealed the fate of Napoleon's army.

p.m., when the French managed to seize the farmhouse, although they were evicted from it shortly afterwards. The French cavalry, meanwhile, was expending its energy against the British infantry squares: they failed to break the formations but inflicted heavy casualties. The first elements of Blücher's Prussians arrived in the afternoon, but Grouchy managed to push them back. Napoleon then made his last attempt, ordering the Guard, under Marshal Michel Ney, to advance against the British Guards division. These stood firm until the French were very close, then at Wellington's orders fired a devastating volley, followed by a bayonet charge. The French attack was thrown into confusion, and at this moment Blücher's main force thrust Grouchy aside and came on to the field. British cavalry charged forward, the French broke, and were pursued off the field by the Prussians.

Watling Street Roman road running from London to Wroxeter (Viroconium) near Chester, northwest England. Its name derives from *Waetlingacaester*, the Anglo-Saxon name for St Albans, through which it passed.

Watt James 1736–1819. Scottish engineer who developed the steam engine in the 1760s. He made Thomas Newcomen's steam engine vastly more efficient by cooling the used steam in a condenser separate from the main cylinder.

Wavell Archibald, 1st Earl 1883–1950. British field marshal in World War II. As commander in chief in the Middle East, he defended Egypt against Italy July 1939 and successfully conducted the North African war against Italy 1940–41. He was transferred as commander-in-chief in India July 1941, and became Allied Supreme Commander after Japan entered the war. He was unable to prevent Japanese advances in Malaya and Burma and Churchill became disillusioned with him. He was made viceroy of India 1943–47.

Waverley John Anderson, 1st Viscount Waverley 1882–1958. British administrator. He organized civil defence for World War II, becoming home secretary and minister for home security in 1939. **Anderson shelters**, home outdoor air-raid shelters, were named after him. He was chancellor of the Exchequer 1943–45.

Webb (Martha) Beatrice (born Potter) 1858–1943 and Sidney (James), Baron Passfield 1859–1947. English social reformers, writers, and founders of the London School of Economics (LSE) 1895. They were early members of the socialist ◊Fabian Society, and were married in 1892. They argued for social insurance in their minority report (1909) of the Poor Law Commission, and wrote many influential books, including *The History of Trade Unionism* 1894, *English Local Government* 1906–29, and *Soviet Communism* 1935.

Sidney Webb was professor of public administration at the LSE 1912–27. He was a member of the Labour Party executive 1915–25, entered Parliament 1922, and was president of the Board of Trade 1924, dominions secretary 1929–30, and colonial secretary 1929–31. Beatrice wrote *The Co-operative Movement in Great Britain* 1891, *My Apprenticeship* 1926, and *Our Partnership* 1948.

Wedgwood Josiah 1730–1795. English pottery manufacturer. He set up business in Staffordshire in the early 1760s to produce his agateware as well as unglazed blue or green stoneware (jasper) decorated with white Neo-Classical designs, using pigments of his own invention.

Wei-Hai-Wei former British territory, northeastern China. Following Japanese occupation of the Chinese port here 1895 the territory was leased to Britain 1898 and used as a naval base. It was returned to China 1930.

welfare state political system under which the state (rather than the individual or the private sector) has responsibility for the welfare of its citizens. Services such as unemployment and sickness benefits, family allowances and income supplements, pensions, medical care, and education may be provided and financed through state insurance schemes and taxation.

In Britain, David Lloyd George, as chancellor, introduced a National Insurance Act 1911. The idea of a welfare state developed in the UK from the 1942 Beveridge Report on social security, which committed the government after World War II to the provision of full employment, a free national health service, and a social-security system. The wartime coalition government accepted its main provisions and they were largely put into effect by the Labour government 1945–51. Since then, economic stringencies and changes in political attitudes have done something to erode the original schemes but the concept remains as an ideal. In Oct 1994 a Commission on Social Justice, established by the Labour Party, recommended a radical review of the welfare state.

Wedgwood
English potter Josiah Wedgwood in a portrait by Joshua Reynolds (1782). Responsible for the development of several new wares, Wedgwood's most famous contribution was the production of unglazed blue jasper ware, which he decorated with Neo-Classical figures.
J Wedgwood & Sons

Wellesley family name of dukes of ◊Wellington; seated at Stratfield Saye, Berkshire, England.

Wellesley Richard Colley, Marquess of Wellesley 1760–1842. British administrator; brother of the 1st Duke of Wellington. He was governor general of India 1798–1805, and by his victories over the Marathas of western India greatly extended the territory under British rule. He was foreign secretary 1809–12, and Lord Lieutenant of Ireland 1821–28 and 1833–34.

Wellington Arthur Wellesley, 1st Duke of Wellington 1769–1852. British soldier and Tory politician. Wellington was born in Ireland, the son of an Irish peer, and sat for a time in the Irish parliament. He was knighted for his army service in India and became a national hero with his victories of 1808–14 in the ◊Peninsular War and as general of the allies against Napoleon. He defeated Napoleon Bonaparte at Quatre-Bras and Waterloo 1815, and at the Congress of Vienna he opposed the dismemberment of France and supported restoration of the Bourbons. As prime minister 1828–30, he modified the Corn Laws but became unpopular for his opposition to parliamentary reform and his lack of opposition to Catholic emancipation. He was foreign secretary 1834–35 and a member of the cabinet 1841–46. He held the office of commander-in-chief of the forces at various times from 1827 and for life from 1842. His home was Apsley House in London.

Wentworth Peter *c.* 1530–1596. Puritan politician. As an MP he was a strong defender of parliamentary freedom during the reign of Elizabeth I. He vigorously supported Parliament's right to discuss religious matters 1571 and was imprisoned three times for his outspokenness: 1576, for attacking attempts by the Crown to influence Parliament through the Speaker; 1587, for challenging the Queen's supremacy over the Church; and again 1593–96, for petitioning Elizabeth to name her successor.

wergild or *wergeld* in Anglo-Saxon and Germanic law during the Middle Ages, the

Wellington
Arthur Wellesley, 1st Duke of Wellington, a portrait 1814 by Thomas Lawrence. After a successful campaign against the French in Spain and Portugal, Wellington – known as 'the Iron Duke' – met Napoleon for the first time at Waterloo 1815, where he finally crushed the French emperor's attempt to regain his former power.
E T Archive

compensation paid by a murderer to the relatives of the victim, its value dependent on the social rank of the deceased. It originated in European tribal society as a substitute for the blood feud (essentially a form of vendetta), and was replaced by punishments imposed by courts of law during the 10th and 11th centuries.

Wesley John 1703–1791. English founder of ◊Methodism. He was born at Epworth, Lincolnshire, where his father was the rector, and went to Oxford University together with his brother Charles, where their circle was nicknamed Methodist because of their religious observances. He was ordained in the Church of England 1728 and returned to his Oxford college 1729 as a tutor. In 1735 he went to Georgia, USA, as a missionary. On his return he experienced 'conversion' 1738, and from being rigidly High Church developed into an ardent Evangelical. When the pulpits of the Church of England were closed to him and his followers, he took the gospel to the people. For 50 years he rode about the country on horseback, preaching daily, largely in the open air. His sermons became the doctrinal standard of the Wesleyan Methodist Church. His *Journal* gives an intimate picture of the man and his work.

Wessex, kingdom of former kingdom of the West Saxons in Britain, said to have been founded by Cerdic about AD 500, covering present-day Hampshire, Dorset, Wiltshire, Berkshire, Somerset, and Devon. Its chief towns were Winchester and Hamwic

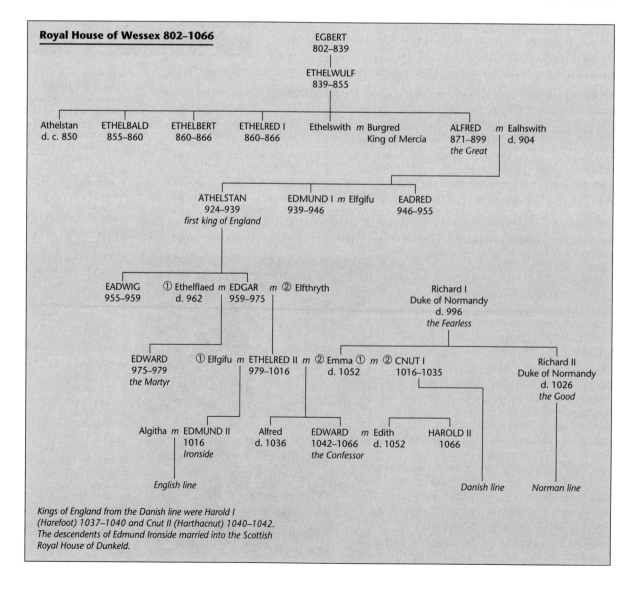

Royal House of Wessex 802–1066

Kings of England from the Danish line were Harold I (Harefoot) 1037–1040 and Cnut II (Harthacnut) 1040–1042. The descendents of Edmund Ironside married into the Scottish Royal House of Dunkeld.

(Southampton). In 829 Egbert established West Saxon supremacy over all England and under Alfred it was the only kingdom that successfully resisted the Viking invasion.

West Cameroon former British colony in West Africa. The whole territory of the Cameroons was a German protectorate 1884–1916. It was occupied by Anglo-French forces 1914, and divided between France and Britain 1916. The League of Nations granted East Cameroon as a mandate territory to France 1922, and West Cameroon to Britain. Both regions became UN Trust Territories 1946, East Cameroon remaining with France, West Cameroon (divided as North Cameroon and South Cameroon) with Britain. East Cameroon achieved independence as Cameroon 1960. South Cameroon voted for union with Cameroon 1961, and North Cameroon for union with Nigeria.

Western Rebellion peasant rising in Devon and Cornwall 1549, partly in response to sheep tax and inflationary pressures but mainly against Edward IV's reformation laws. The rebels besieged Exeter and captured Plymouth, but were defeated by Lord Russell and crushed. The rebels particularly complained that the Cornish speakers among them could not understand the new *Book of Common Prayer*. This claim was rebuffed with the answer they could not understand Latin either.

Western Samoa former joint British territory, a group of islands of Samoa in the southwest central Pacific. The Samoan Islands were jointly administered by Britain, the United States and Germany 1889–99. They were occupied by New Zealand forces 1914–20 and became a mandate of New Zealand 1920 and UN Trust Territory (administered by New Zealand) 1947. They gained independence 1962.

Westminster, Palace of see ◊parliament, houses of.

Westminster Abbey Gothic church in central London, officially the Collegiate Church of St Peter. It was built 1050–1745 and consecrated under Edward the Confessor 1065. The west towers are by Nicholas Hawksmoor, completed after his death 1745. Since William I nearly all English monarchs have been crowned in the abbey, and several are buried there; many poets are buried or commemorated there, at Poets' Corner; and some 30 scientists, including Isaac Newton, Lord Kelvin, and James Prescott, are either buried or commemorated there.

The Coronation Chair includes the Stone of Scone, on which Scottish kings were crowned, brought here by Edward I 1296. Poets' Corner was begun with the burial of ◊Spenser 1599. Westminster School, a public school with ancient and modern buildings nearby, was once the Abbey School.

Whig Party predecessor of the ◊Liberal Party. The name was first used of rebel ◊Covenanters and then of those who wished to exclude James, Duke of York, (later James II) from the English succession (as a Roman Catholic). They were the political party behind the ◊Glorious Revolution 1688 and subsequently concentrated on defending the ◊Bill of Rights. They were in power continuously 1714–60 and pressed for industrial and commercial development, a vigorous foreign policy, and religious toleration. During the French Revolution, the Whigs demanded parliamentary reform in Britain, and from the passing of the Reform Bill in 1832 became known as Liberals.

Whitby, Synod of council summoned by King Oswy of Northumbria 664, which decided to adopt the Roman rather than the Celtic form of Christianity for Britain.

Westminster Abbey
View of Westminster by Wenceslaus Hollar 1647. Parliament is housed in St Stephen's Chapel and Westminster Abbey is outside its twin towers which were added by Hawksmoor 1745.
Philip Sauvain

White Horse any of several hill figures in England, including the one on Bratton Hill, Wiltshire, said to commemorate Alfred the Great's victory over the Danes at Ethandun 878; and the one at Uffington, Berkshire, 110 m/360 ft long, and probably a tribal totem of the early Iron Age, 1st century BC.

White Ship ship carrying Henry I's only legitimate son, Prince William, and some 300 other passengers which sank 25 Nov 1120 on its way from Normandy to England. William's death led to a disputed succession and civil war between Stephen I and Matilda.

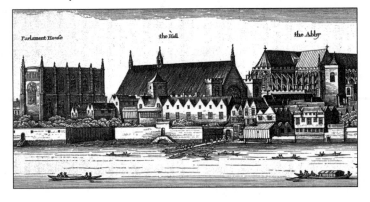

Whiteboys Irish Catholic peasant socieies in the 18th century. They terrorized the south, destroying the property of landlords and Protestant clergy, and protested vigorously against unjust rents and tithes. Their name refers to their custom of assembling at night wearing white shirts.

Whitehall street in central London between Trafalgar Square and the Houses of Parliament, containing many government offices and the Cenotaph war memorial.

It was the site of a royal palace, bought by Henry VIII from Cardinal Wolsey until most of it burnt down in the 1690s. The banqueting hall, which still survives, was the site of Charles I's execution.

Whittington Dick (Richard) d. 1423. English cloth merchant who was mayor of London 1397–98, 1406–07, and 1419–20. He was sufficiently wealthy to lend money to Richard II, Henry IV, and Henry V. According to legend, he came to London as a poor boy with his cat when he heard that the streets were paved with gold and silver. His cat first appears in a play from 1605.

Wight, Isle of island and county off the south coast of England. The Romans conquered it AD 43 and knew it as *Vectis*, the meaning of which is disputed. (Modern 'Wight' evolved from it.) The Jutes settled here in the 5th century AD and were defeated by the Saxons 661, although remaining to rule. The island formed part of the estate of Godwin, Earl of Wessex until his death 1053. After the Norman Conquest 1066 it was governed by a succession of lords. Charles I fled to the island from the Parliamentarian army 1647 and was imprisoned in Carisbrooke Castle. Queen Victoria purchased the Osborne estate here 1845 and used it as a winter residence. The island was part of Hampshire until 1974 when it was made a separate county (England's smallest, in both area and population).

Wilberforce William 1759–1833. English reformer who was instrumental in abolishing slavery in the British Empire. He entered Parliament 1780 and with other members of the ◊Clapham Sect founded the Society for the Abolition of the Slave Trade. In 1807 his bill for the abolition of the slave trade was passed, and in 1833, largely through his efforts, slavery was abolished throughout the empire.

Wild Jonathan *c.* 1682–1725. English criminal who organized the thieves of London and ran an office that, for a payment, returned stolen goods to their owners. He was hanged at Tyburn.

Wilfrid, St 634–709. Northumbrian-born bishop of York from 665. He defended the cause of the Roman Church at the Synod of ◊Whitby 664 against that of Celtic Christianity. He introduced the ◊Benedictine order to Anglo-Saxon monasteries. Feast day 12 Oct.

Wilkes John 1727–1797. British Radical politician, imprisoned for his political views; member of Parliament 1757–64 and from 1774. He championed parliamentary reform, religious toleration, and US independence.

Wilkes, born in Clerkenwell, London, entered Parliament as a Whig 1757. His attacks on the Tory prime minister Bute in his paper *The North Briton* led to his being outlawed 1764; he fled to France, and on his return 1768 was imprisoned. He was four times elected MP for Middlesex, but the Commons refused to admit him and finally declared his opponent elected. This secured him strong working- and middle-class support, and in 1774 he was allowed to take his seat in Parliament.

Wilkinson (Cecily) Ellen 1891–1947. Journalist and Labour politician. She was an early member of the Independent Labour Party and an active campaigner for women's suffrage. As a member of Parliament for Jarrow in 1936, she led the ◊Jarrow Crusade of 200 unemployed shipyard workers from Jarrow to London.

William four kings of England:

William (I) the Conqueror c. 1027–1087. King of England from 1066. He was the illegitimate son of Duke Robert the Devil and succeeded his father as Duke of Normandy 1035. Claiming that his relative King Edward the Confessor had bequeathed him the English throne, William invaded the country 1066, defeating ◊Harold II at Hastings, Sussex, and was crowned king of England.

He was crowned in Westminster Abbey on Christmas Day 1066. He completed the establishment of feudalism in England and placed Normans in all key administrative positions. He compiled detailed records of land and property in the Domesday Book, and kept the barons firmly under control. He married his cousin Matilda of Flanders 1053; they had four children. He died in Rouen after a fall from his horse and is buried in Caen, France. He was succeeded by his son William II.

William (II) Rufus ('the Red') c. 1056–1100. King of England from 1087, the third son of William the Conqueror. He spent most of his reign attempting to capture Normandy from his brother ◊Robert II, Duke of Normandy. His extortion of money led his barons to revolt and caused confrontation with Bishop Anselm. He was killed while hunting in the New Forest, Hampshire, and was succeeded by his brother Henry I.

William (III) of Orange 1650–1702. King of Great Britain and Ireland from 1688, the son of William II of Orange and Mary, daughter of Charles I. He was offered the English crown by the parliamentary opposition to James II. He invaded England 1688 and in 1689 became joint sovereign with his wife, ◊Mary II. He spent much of his reign campaigning, first in Ireland, where he defeated James II at the battle of the Boyne 1690, and later against the French in Flanders. He was succeeded by Mary's sister, Anne.

Born in the Netherlands, William was made *stadtholder* (chief magistrate) 1672 to resist the French invasion. He forced Louis XIV to make peace 1678 and then concentrated on building up a European alliance against France. In 1677 he married his cousin Mary, daughter of the future James II. When invited by both Whig and Tory leaders to take the crown from James, he landed with a large force at Torbay, Devon. James fled to France, and his Scottish and Irish supporters were defeated at the battles of Dunkeld 1689 and the Boyne 1690.

William IV 1765–1837. King of Great Britain and Ireland from 1830, when he succeeded his brother George IV; third son of George III. He was created Duke of Clarence 1789, and married Adelaide of Saxe-Meiningen (1792–1849) 1818. During the Reform Bill crisis he secured its passage by agreeing to create new peers to overcome the hostile majority in the House of Lords. He was the last monarch to dismiss a prime minister when he replaced Melbourne with Peel 1834. He was succeeded by his niece Victoria.

William of Malmesbury c. 1080–c. 1143. English historian and monk. He compiled the *Gesta regum/Deeds of the Kings* c. 1120–40 and *Historia novella*, which together formed a history of England to 1142.

William of Wykeham c. 1323–1404. English politician, bishop of Winchester from 1367, Lord Chancellor 1367–72 and 1389–91, and founder of Winchester College (public school) 1378 and New College, Oxford 1379.

William the Lion 1143–1214. King of Scotland from 1165. He was captured by Henry II while invading England 1174, and forced to do homage under the terms of the Treaty of Falaise. Richard I abandoned the English claim to suzerainty in return for a money payment 1189. In 1209 William was forced by King John to renounce his claim to Northumberland.

William the Marshall 1st Earl of Pembroke c. 1146–1219. English knight, regent of England from 1216. After supporting the dying Henry II against Richard (later Richard I), he went on a crusade to Palestine, was pardoned by Richard, and was granted an earldom 1189. On King John's death he was appointed guardian of the future Henry III, and defeated the French under Louis VIII to enable Henry to gain the throne.

William (I) the Conqueror
The Great Seal of William I, the Norman duke who mounted the last successful conquest of England. He successfully subdued the country and imposed a new system of government dominated by an aristocratic Norman elite.
Philip Sauvain

By the splendour of God I have taken possession of my realm; the earth of England is in my two hands.

WILLIAM THE CONQUEROR
attributed remark when he fell as he landed in England

Wilson (James) Harold, Baron Wilson of Rievaulx 1916–1995. British Labour politician, party leader from 1963, prime minister 1964–70 and 1974–76. His premiership was dominated by the issue of UK admission to membership of the European Community (now the European Union), the social contract (unofficial agreement with the trade unions), and economic difficulties.

Wilson, born in Huddersfield, West Yorkshire, was president of the Board of Trade 1947–51 (when he resigned because of social-service cuts). In 1963 he succeeded Hugh Gaitskell as Labour leader and became prime minister the following year, increasing his majority 1966. He formed a minority government Feb 1974 and achieved a majority of three Oct 1974. He resigned 1976 and was succeeded by James Callaghan. He was knighted 1976 and made a peer 1983.

Wilson ('Jumbo') Henry Maitland, 1st Baron Wilson 1881–1964. British field marshal in World War II. He was commander-in-chief in Egypt 1939, led the unsuccessful Greek campaign of 1941, was commander-in-chief in the Middle East 1943, and in 1944 was supreme Allied commander in the Mediterranean.

Winchester, Battle of or ***rout of Winchester*** defeat 14 Sept 1141 of Matilda's forces, which were besieging the episcopal residence of Wolvesey Castle, by a royalist relief force. Her forces were themselves besieged, and were defeated as they tried to break out. Robert, Earl of Gloucester was captured, forcing Matilda to release King Stephen, who had been held since the Battle of ◊Lincoln in exchange for him.

window tax levy on windows imposed in England 1696, replacing ◊hearth tax. Scotland was exempt under terms of the Union 1707. Houses with fewer than seven (later eight) windows were exempted 1792, but this led to windows being blocked up and new houses being built with few windows. It was abolished 1851.

Windsor, House of official name of the British royal family since 1917, adopted in place of Saxe-Coburg-Gotha. Since 1960 those descendants of Elizabeth II not entitled to the prefix HRH (His/Her Royal Highness) have borne the surname Mountbatten-Windsor.

Wingate Orde Charles 1903–1944. British soldier. In 1936 he established a reputation for unorthodox tactics in Palestine. In World War II he served in the Middle East and organized guerilla forces in Ethiopia, and later led the Chindits, the 3rd Indian Division, in guerrilla operations against the Japanese army in Burma (now Myanmar).

Winstanley Gerrard *c.* 1609–1660. Civil War radical, leader of the ◊Diggers. Born in Lancashire, he was an unsuccessful cloth merchant in London. He advocated common ownership of land, and in 1649–50 he led the Diggers in their cultivation of common land in Walton-on-Thames and in Cobham. After the commune had been broken up, he tried to spread his ideas by pamphlets such as *The Law of Freedom in a Platform* 1652, dedicated to Oliver Cromwell, which expounded the view that the struggle with the king was a class war. He condemnned priests and lawyers along with the monarchy.

Wishart George *c.* 1513–1546. Scottish Protestant reformer burned for heresy on the orders of Cardinal ◊Beaton. He probably converted John ◊Knox to Calvinism.

Witan or ***Witenagemot*** council of the Anglo-Saxon kings, the forerunner of Parliament, but including only royal household officials, great landowners, and top churchmen. Its role was technically just advisory, but it served as a useful check on the power of the king.

Wolfe James 1727–1759. British soldier who served in Canada and commanded a victorious expedition against the French general Montcalm in Québec on the Plains of Abraham, during which both commanders were killed. The British victory established their supremacy over Canada.

Wolfe fought at the battles of ◊Dettingen, Falkirk, and ◊Culloden. With the outbreak of the Seven Years' War (the French and Indian War in North America), he was posted to Canada and played a conspicuous part in the siege of the French stronghold of Louisburg 1758. He was promoted to major-general 1759.

Wollstonecraft Mary 1759–1797. British feminist, member of a group of radical intellectuals called the English Jacobins, whose book *A Vindication of the Rights of Women* 1792 demanded equal educational opportunities and economic independence for women. She married William Godwin and died giving birth to a daughter, Mary (later Mary Shelley).

Wolseley Garnet Joseph, 1st Viscount Wolseley 1833–1913. British army officer. He fought in the Crimean War 1853–56 and then commanded in both the Ashanti War 1873–74 and last part of the Anglo-Zulu War 1879. He campaigned in Egypt, but was too late to relieve Charles ◊Gordon at Khartoum.

Wolsey Thomas *c.* 1475–1530. English cleric and politician. In Henry VIII's service from 1509, he became archbishop of York 1514, cardinal and lord chancellor 1515, and began the dissolution of the monasteries. He organized an alliance against France with the Holy Roman Emperor Charles V 1521. He was Henry's a chief adviser but his reluctance to further Henry's divorce from Catherine of Aragon, partly because of his ambition to be pope, led to his downfall 1529. He was charged with high treason 1530 but died before being tried.

Women's Land Army organization founded 1916 for the recruitment of women to work on farms during World War I. At its peak Sept 1918 it had 16,000 members. It re-formed June 1939, before the outbreak of World War II. Many 'Land Girls' joined up to help the war effort and, by Aug 1943, 87,000 were employed in farm work.

women's movement the campaign for the rights of women, including social, political, and economic equality with men. Early European cam-

NATIONAL SERVICE
WOMEN'S LAND ARMY

APPLY FOR ENROLMENT FORMS AT YOUR NEAREST POST OFFICE OR EMPLOYMENT EXCHANGE

paigners of the 17th–19th centuries fought for women's right to own property, to have access to higher education, and to vote (see ◊suffragette). Once women's suffrage was achieved in the 20th century, the emphasis of the movement shifted to the goals of equal social and economic opportunities for women, including employment. A continuing area of concern in industrialized countries is the contradiction between the now generally accepted principle of equality and the demonstrable inequalities that remain between the sexes in state policies and in everyday life.

Pioneer 19th-century feminists, considered radical for their belief in the equality of the sexes, include Mary ◊Wollstonecraft and Emmeline ◊Pankhurst in the UK. Since 1975 discrimination against women in employment, education, housing, and provision of goods, facilities, and services to the public has been illegal under the Sex Discrimination and Equal Pay Acts. The economic value of women's unpaid work has been estimated at £2 trillion annually. In the UK 1971, £1 in every £4 of household income went to women; in 1991 the figure had risen to £1 in £3. The average British woman's income 1991 was £100 a week, of which almost 25% from social-security benefits. In the civil service, 90% of the highest-paid jobs were held by men, while in the lowest-paid jobs (typing, catering, and cleaning) women far outnumbered men.

In the UK in 1993, women made up 49.5% of the workforce (5% of judges, 9% of members of Parliament, and 5% and 7% of professors at Oxford and Cambridge universities respectively), but the average female worker earned nearly 40% less than the average male earner, and women managers (9.8% of all managers) earned 16% less than their male counterparts. British companies had on average 3.7% women board members. In 1994 girls outperformed boys at every level of education.

Woodville Elizabeth 1437–1492. Queen consort of Edward IV. She married Edward 1464 when she was already a widow with children. She was unpopular because of her Lancastrian links and her advancement of her own family. After Edward's death 1483, her sons were murdered (see ◊Princes in the Tower). Her eldest daughter, Elizabeth of ◊York, married Henry VII.

Wookey Hole natural cave near Wells, Somerset, England, in which flint implements of Old Stone Age people and the bones of extinct animals have been found.

woolsack the seat of the Lord High Chancellor in the House of Lords: it is a large square bag of wool and is a reminder of the principal source of English wealth in the Middle Ages. The woolsack was introduced in the reign of Edward III.

Worcester, Battle of in the Civil War, final victory of Oliver Cromwell's Commonwealth forces over Charles II 3 Sept 1651. Charles invaded England at the head of a Scottish royalist army which was routed by Cromwell, forcing him to hide before fleeing to France the following year. The defeat was a crushing blow to the Royalists.

workhouse former institution to house and maintain people unable to earn their own living. Groups of parishes in England combined to build workhouses for the poor, the aged, the disabled, and orphaned children from about 1815 until about 1930.

Sixteenth-century poor laws made parishes responsible for helping the poor within their boundaries. The 19th-century parish unions found workhouses more cost-effective. An act of Parliament 1834 improved supervision of workhouses, where conditions were sometimes harsh, and a new welfare legislation in the early 20th century made them redundant.

Workmen's Compensation Act legislation 1897 that conferred on workers a right to compensation for the loss of earnings resulting from an injury at work.

Women's movement in Britain: chronology

1562   The Statute of Artificers made it illegal to employ men or women in a trade before they had served seven years' apprenticeship. (It was never strictly enforced for women, as many guilds still allowed members to employ their wives and daughters in workshops.)

1753   Lord Hardwick's Marriage Act brought marriage under state control and created a firmer distinction between the married and unmarried.

1803   Abortion was made illegal.

1836   Marriage Act reform permitted civil weddings and enforced the official registration of births, deaths, and marriages.

1839   The Custody of Infants Act allowed mothers to have custody of their children under seven years old.

1840s   A series of factory acts limited the working day and occupations of women and children. A bastardy amendment put all the responsibility for the maintenance of an illegitimate child onto its mother.

1857   The Marriage and Divorce Act enabled a man to obtain divorce if his wife had committed adultery. (Women were only eligible for divorce if their husband's adultery was combined with incest, sodomy, cruelty, etc.)

1857–82 The Married Women's Property Acts allowed them to own possessions of various kinds for the first time.

1860s   Fathers could be named and required to pay maintenance for illegitimate children.

1861   Abortion became a criminal offence even if performed as a life-saving act or done by the woman herself.

1862–70 The Contagious Diseases Acts introduced compulsory examination of prostitutes for venereal disease.

1864   Schools Enquiry Commission recommendations led to the establishment of high schools for girls.

1867   The Second Reform Act enfranchised the majority of male householders. The first women's suffrage committee was formed in Manchester.

1869   Women ratepayers were allowed to vote in municipal (local) elections.

1871   Newham College, Cambridge, was founded for women.

1872   The Elizabeth Garrett Anderson Hospital for women opened in London.

1874   The London School of Medicine for women was founded.

1878   Judicial separation of a married couple became possible. Maintenance orders could be enforced in court.

1880   The Trades Union Congress (TUC) adopted the principle of equal pay for women.

1882   The Married Women's Property Act gave wives legal control over their own earned income.

1883   The Contagious Diseases Acts were repealed.

1885   The age of consent was raised to 16.

1887   The National Union of Women's Suffrage Societies became a nationwide group under Millicent Fawcett.

1903   The Women's Social and Political Union (WSPU) was founded by Emmeline and Christabel Pankhurst.

1905–10 Militant campaigns split the WSPU. Sylvia Pankhurst formed the East London Women's Federation.

1918   The Parliament (Qualification of Women) Act gave the vote to women householders over 30.

1923   Wives were given equal rights to sue for divorce on the grounds of adultery.

1925   The Guardianship of Infants Act gave women equal rights to the guardianship of their children.

1928   The 'Flapper' Vote: all women over 21 were given the vote.

1937   The Matrimonial Causes Act gave new grounds for divorce including desertion for three years and cruelty.

1944   The Butler Education Act introduced free secondary education for all.

1946   A Royal Commission on equal pay was formed.

1948   Cambridge University allowed women candidates to be awarded degrees.

1960   Legal aid became available for divorce cases.

1967   The Abortion Law Reform Act made abortion legal under medical supervision and within certain criteria.

1969   Divorce reform was introduced that reduced the time a petitioner needed to wait before applying for a divorce.

1973   The Matrimonial Causes Act provided legislation to enable financial provision to be granted on divorce.

1975   The Sex Discrimination and Equal Pay Acts were passed. The National and Scottish Women's Aid Federations were formed.

1976   The Domestic Violence and Matrimonial Proceedings Act came into effect. The Sexual Offences (Amendment) Act attempted to limit a man's defence of consent in rape cases.

1977   The employed married women's option to stay partially out of the National Insurance system was phased out. Women qualified for their own pensions.

1980   The Social Security Act allowed a married woman to claim supplementary benefit and family income supplement if she was the main wage earner.

1983   The government was forced to amend the 1975 Equal Pay Act to conform to European Community (now European Union) directives.

1984   The Matrimonial and Family Proceedings Act made it less likely for a woman to be granted maintenance on divorce. It also reduced the number of years a petitioner must wait before applying for a divorce to one.

1986   The granting of invalid-care allowance was successfully challenged in the European Court of Justice. The Sex Discrimination Act (Amendment) allowed women to retire at the same age as men, and lifted legal restrictions preventing women from working night shifts in manufacturing industries. Firms with less than five employees were no longer exempt from the act.

1990   The legal limit for abortion was reduced to 24 weeks.

1991   Rape within marriage became a prosecutable offence in the UK.

World War I 1914–18. War between the Central Powers (Germany, Austria-Hungary, and allies) on one side and the Triple Entente (Britain and the British Empire, France, and Russia) and their allies on the other side. An estimated 10 million lives were lost and twice that number were wounded. It was fought on the eastern and western fronts, in the Middle East, in Africa, and at sea. In 1917, Russia withdrew because of the Russian Revolution; in the same year the USA entered the war on the side of Britain and France. The peace treaty of Versailles 1919 was the formal end to the war.

The war was set in motion by the assassination in Sarajevo of the heir to the Austrian throne, Archduke Franz Ferdinand, by a Serbian nationalist in June 1914. Tension had already been mounting over many years between the major European powers who were divided, by a series of alliances, into two rival camps: one led by Germany and Austria-Hungary and the other containing France, Britain and Russia. Germany and Britain had both recently modernized their navies, and imperialist rivalries had led to a series of international crises: Russia against Austria over Bosnia 1908–09, and Germany against France and Britain over Agadir 1911. When Austria declared war on Serbia 28 July 1914, Russia mobilized along the German and Austrian frontier. Germany then declared war on Russia and France, taking a short cut in the west by invading neutral Belgium; on 4 Aug Britain declared war on Germany. The war against Germany was concentrated on the Western Front; the German advance was initially halted by the ◊British Expeditionary Force under Sir John French at Mons and, following an Allied counterattack at the Marne, the Germans were driven back to the Aisne River. The opposing lines then settled into trench warfare with neither side advancing more than a few miles over the next three years. Poison gas was first employed by the Germans at the 2nd battle of Ypres 1915 and the British introduced tanks at the Battle of the Somme 1916.

On the Eastern front the major Allied offensive was the ◊Gallipolli campaign 1915 which attempted to break through the Dardanelles and open up a route to assist Russia in its fight against the Turks. The failure of the campaign and the great loss of mainly Australian and New Zealand troops led to Winston Churchill's resignation as First Lord of the Admiralty. The Turks were also under attack in Mesopotamia, with Baghdad finally falling in 1917, and in Palestine where General ◊Allenby, assisted by the Arab revolt, won a series of victories that resulted in the Turkish armistice Oct 1918.

The war at sea involved, almost exclusively, the British and German navies but the major sea battle at ◊Jutland 1916 was indecisive. The main impact at sea was by German U-boats (submarines) which from Jan 1917 attempted to destroy Britain's merchant fleet and succeeded in bringing the country close to starvation. They were countered by the introduction of the convoy system, by British prime minister Lloyd George, in which groups of vessels were protected by warships. As a result of the submarine threat the USA entered the war in April 1917.

In the spring of 1918, Germany launched a major offensive on the Western Front which was halted at the second Battle of the Marne Aug 1918, while in Italy the Austro-Hungarian army was defeated at Vittorio-Veneto. German capitulation began with naval mutinies at Kiel Oct 1918, followed by uprisings in the major cities. Kaiser Wilhelm II abdicated, and on 11 Nov the armistice was signed. The peace conference at Versailles began Jan 1919 and the treaty was signed by Germany June 1919.

The terms of peace were negotiated separately with each of the Central Powers in the course of the next few years:

Treaty of ◊Versailles between the Allies and Germany, signed 29 June 1919, ratified at Paris, 19 Jan 1920;

Treaty of ◊St Germain-en-Laye between the Allies and Austria, signed 10 Sept 1919, ratified in Paris, 16 July 1920;

Treaty of Trianon between the Allies and Hungary, signed 4 June 1920;

Treaty of ◊Sèvres, between the Allies and Turkey, signed 10 Aug, 1920, not ratified and superseded by

Treaty of ◊Lausanne between the Allies and Turkey, signed 24 July 1923, and ratified in the same year.

World War II 1939–45. War between Germany, Italy, and Japan (the Axis powers) on one side, and Britain, the Commonwealth, France, the USA, the USSR, and China (the Allied powers) on the other. The main theatres of war were Europe, the USSR, North Africa, and the

Fifty years were spent in the process of making Europe explosive. Five days were enough to detonate it.

<small>WORLD WAR I
historian Basil Liddell Hart,
The Real War 1914–1918
1930</small>

World War I: chronology

1914   *June:* Assassination of Archduke Franz Ferdinand of Austria 28 June.

July: German government issued 'blank cheque' to Austria, offering support in war against Serbia. Austrian ultimatum to Serbia. Serbs accepted all but two points. Austria refused to accept compromise and declared war. Russia began mobilization to defend Serbian ally. Germany demanded Russian demobilization.

Aug: Germany declared war on Russia. France mobilized to assist Russian ally. Germans occupied Luxembourg and demanded access to Belgian territory, which was refused. Germany declared war on France and invaded Belgium. Britain declared war on Germany, then on Austria. Dominions within the Empire, including Australia, automatically involved. Battle of Tannenburg between Central Powers and Russians. Russian army encircled.

Sept: British and French troops halted German advance just short of Paris, and drove them back. First Battle of the Marne, and of the Aisne. Beginning of trench warfare.

Oct–Nov: First Battle of Ypres. Britain declared war on Turkey.

1915   *April–May:* Gallipoli offensive launched by British and dominion troops against Turkish forces. Second Battle of Ypres. First use of poison gas by Germans. Italy joined war against Austria. German submarine sank ocean liner *Lusitania* 7 May, later helping to bring USA into the war.

Aug–Sept: Warsaw evacuated by the Russians. Battle of Tarnopol. Vilna taken by the Germans. Tsar Nicholas II took supreme control of Russian forces.

1916   *Jan:* Final evacuation of British and dominion troops from Gallipoli.

Feb: German offensive against Verdun began, with huge losses for little territorial gain.

May: Naval battle of Jutland between British and German imperial fleets ended inconclusively, but put a stop to further German naval participation in the war.

June: Russian (Brusilov) offensive against the Ukraine began.

July–Nov: First Battle of the Somme, a sustained Anglo-French offensive which won little territory and lost a huge number of lives.

Aug: Hindenburg and Ludendorff took command of the German armed forces. Romania entered the war against Austria but was rapidly overrun.

Sept: Early tanks used by British on Western Front.

Nov: Nivelle replaced Joffre as commander of French forces. Battle of the Ancre on the Western Front.

Dec: French completed recapture of Verdun fortifications. Austrians occupied Bucharest.

1917   *Feb:* Germany declared unrestricted submarine warfare. Russian Revolution began and tsarist rule overthrown.

March: British seizure of Baghdad and occupation of Persia.

March–April: Germans retreated to Siegfried Line (Arras–Soissons) on Western Front.

April–May: USA entered the war against Germany. Unsuccessful British and French offensives. Mutinies among French troops. Nivelle replaced by Pétain.

July–Nov: Third Ypres offensive including Battle of Passchendaele.

Sept: Germans occupied Riga.

Oct–Nov: Battle of Caporetto saw Italian troops defeated by Austrians.

Dec: Jerusalem taken by British forces under Allenby.

1918   *Jan:* US President Woodrow Wilson proclaimed 'Fourteen Points' as a basis for peace settlement.

March: Treaty of Brest-Litovsk with Central Powers ended Russian participation in the war, with substantial concessions of territory and reparations. Second Battle of the Somme began with German spring offensive.

July–Aug: Allied counter-offensive, including tank attack at Amiens, drove Germans back to the Siegfried Line.

Sept: Hindenburg and Ludendorff called for an armistice.

Oct: Armistice offered on the basis of the 'Fourteen Points'. German naval and military mutinies at Kiel and Wilhelmshaven.

Nov: Austria-Hungary signed armistice with Allies. Kaiser Wilhelm II of Germany went into exile. Provisional government under social democrat Friedrich Ebert formed. Germany agreed armistice. Fighting on Western Front stopped.

1919   *Jan:* Peace conference opened at Versailles.

May: Demands presented to Germany.

June: Germany signed peace treaty, followed by other Central Powers: Austria (Treaty of St Germain-en-Laye, Sept), Bulgaria (Neuilly, Nov), Hungary (Trianon, June 1920), and Turkey (Sèvres, Aug 1920).

THE EMBATTLED ISLAND

Britain in the World Wars

War is often cited as a catalyst for change, and Britain's experience during the World Wars seems to prove the maxim. If World War I saw the birth of modern British society, World War II, to continue the analogy, saw its maturation.

'The War to End all Wars'

The events of July 1914 caught most of Britain by surprise. Despite Sir Edward Grey's apocalyptic remark 'the lamps are going out all over Europe; we shall not see them lit again in our lifetime', the majority of British people adhered to the popular belief that the European war would be over by Christmas. This belief goes some way to explain why the military encounter which consumed the next four years was so difficult for Britain; it proved to be a war of stalemate which established military thinking was powerless to break.

Reactions to the new reality of war were slow; neither British military nor political leaders were equipped for a major challenge to their accepted ideas. The prime minister, Asquith, was at first unwilling to treat the war as 'total', and then unable to implement the necessary control measures. The creation of Lloyd George's coalition in 1916 saw the first real political incursion into civilian life, ending the 'business as usual' attitude which had hampered the war effort until then.

The length of the conflict meant that resources were paramount, especially as Britain had traditionally been an importer of raw materials. Great efforts were made from 1916 to co-ordinate the country's requirements with industry's capabilities, and the rapid technical development which accompanied the war was effectively harnessed. The success of British agriculture is best shown in the delay of rationing until 1918, despite the threat of starvation caused by the German U-boat campaign of 1917.

Britain's most valuable resource in a war of attrition was its population. Kitchener's volunteer army had raised half a million by September 1914, but it was necessary to introduce conscription in 1916 for all males aged between 18 and 41. The labour market was filled by the allocation of women to the agricultural and industrial sectors, and their achievements gave weight to the call for emancipation, finally met in 1918.

The First World War is remembered for its horrific casualties. It is estimated that of those who served 40% were either killed or suffered serious injuries. Both the reality and the image of these casualties haunted British society for decades afterwards.

The interwar years

'What is our task? To make Britain a fit country for heroes to live in.' Lloyd George's slogan of 1918 reflected an admirable sentiment, but it proved unobtainable in the postwar world. By 1917, the war was costing Britain £7 million per day, the money coming largely from American loans. By 1918, the country was economically exhausted, and the impact of the war upon the international economy meant that Britain's usual revenue from exports was severely curtailed. The worldwide interwar depression further diminished Britain's economic standing, leaving the country facing the threat of Hitler in 1939 with limited resources, but at least with the experience of total war gleaned from the earlier conflict.

The Finest Hour

During the 1930s, despite the policy of appeasement, Britain had been preparing for war; this is clearly demonstrated by the issue of gas masks as early as 1937. In May 1940, a coalition government was formed, with a War Cabinet of five. Led by Winston Churchill, this administration proved to be the most competent since the turn of the century. Conscription was introduced as soon as war broke out. In 1940 the Emergency Powers Act was enacted, effectively giving the government unlimited powers.

Although military casualties in World War II were about one third of those suffered in the First War, the home population also faced direct attack. Fear of invasion and the horrors of the Blitz greatly increased civilian hardship caused by strict rationing, but tight government control of information ensured that no social breakdown occurred. Churchill's carefully contrived morale-boosting broadcasts also helped to maintain a spirit of national unity which transcended social divisions. As in the First War, effective management of resources was essential, and in Ernest Bevin Britain had an ideal minister of labour, directing workers nationally. Despite significant wage increases, inflation was prevented by strict controls.

The financial consequence of a lengthy war was nevertheless a bankrupt Britain, and the war had highlighted huge social problems. Beveridge, working from the premise that 'warfare necessitates welfare', produced a report in 1942 which formed the blueprint for the Welfare State. Central to this plan was the creation of a system of universal secondary education, achieved by the 1944 Education Act, but many other welfare provisions were also floated. Thus on VE Day the British people really believed that they were entering a period of prosperity.

PETER MARTLAND

World War II: chronology

1939   *Sept* German invasion of Poland; Britain and France declared war on Germany; the USSR invaded Poland; fall of Warsaw (Poland divided between Germany and USSR).
Nov The USSR invaded Finland.

1940   *March* Soviet peace treaty with Finland.
April Germany occupied Denmark, Norway, the Netherlands, Belgium, and Luxembourg. In Britain, a coalition government was formed under Churchill.
May Germany outflanked the defensive French Maginot Line.
May–June Evacuation of 337,131 Allied troops from Dunkirk, France, across the Channel to England.
June Italy declared war on Britain and France; the Germans entered Paris; the French prime minister Pétain signed an armistice with Germany and moved the seat of government to Vichy.
July–Oct Battle of Britain between British and German air forces.
Sept Japanese invasion of French Indochina.
Oct Abortive Italian invasion of Greece.

1941   *April* Germany occupied Greece and Yugoslavia.
June Germany invaded the USSR; Finland declared war on the USSR.
July The Germans entered Smolensk, USSR.
Dec The Germans came within 40 km/25 mi of Moscow, with Leningrad (now St Petersburg) under siege. First Soviet counteroffensive. Japan bombed Pearl Harbor, Hawaii, and declared war on the USA and Britain. Germany and Italy declared war on the USA.

1942   *Jan* Japanese conquest of the Philippines.
June Naval battle of Midway, the turning point of the Pacific War.
Aug German attack on Stalingrad (now Volgograd), USSR.
Oct–Nov Battle of El Alamein in N Africa, turn of the tide for the Western Allies.
Nov Soviet counteroffensive on Stalingrad.

1943   *Jan* The Casablanca Conference issued the Allied demand of unconditional surrender; the Germans retreated from Stalingrad.
March The USSR drove the Germans back to the river Donetz.
May End of Axis resistance in N Africa.
July A coup by King Victor Emmanuel and Marshal Badoglio forced Mussolini to resign.
Aug Beginning of the campaign against the Japanese in Burma (now Myanmar); US Marines landed on Guadalcanal, Solomon Islands.
Sept Italy surrendered to the Allies; Mussolini was rescued by the Germans who set up a Republican Fascist government in N Italy; Allied landings at Salerno; the USSR retook Smolensk.
Oct Italy declared war on Germany.
Nov The US Navy defeated the Japanese in the Battle of Guadalcanal.
Nov–Dec The Allied leaders met at the Tehran Conference.

1944   *Jan* Allied landing in Nazi-occupied Italy: Battle of Anzio.
March End of the German U-boat campaign in the Atlantic.
May Fall of Monte Cassino, S Italy.
6 June D-day: Allied landings in Nazi-occupied and heavily defended Normandy.
July The bomb plot by German generals against Hitler failed.
Aug Romania joined the Allies.
Sept Battle of Arnhem on the Rhine; Soviet armistice with Finland.
Oct The Yugoslav guerrilla leader Tito and Soviets entered Belgrade.
Dec German counter-offensive, Battle of the Bulge.

1945   *Feb* The Soviets reached the German border; Yalta conference; Allied bombing campaign over Germany (Dresden destroyed); the US reconquest of the Philippines was completed; the Americans landed on Iwo Jima, south of Japan.
April Hitler committed suicide; Mussolini was captured by Italian partisans and shot.
May German surrender to the Allies.
June US troops completed the conquest of Okinawa (one of the Japanese Ryukyu Islands).
July The Potsdam Conference issued an Allied ultimatum to Japan.
Aug Atom bombs were dropped by the USA on Hiroshima and Nagasaki; Japan surrendered.

Pacific and Atlantic seaboards. An estimated 55 million lives were lost, including 20 million citizens of the USSR and 6 million Jews killed in the holocaust. Germany surrendered May 1945 but Japan fought on until the USA dropped atomic bombs on Hiroshima and Nagasaki in Aug.

The war's origins lay in Germany' s reluctance to accept the frontiers laid down at the peace of Versailles, and in the highly aggressive foreign policy of Adolf Hitler (German Chancellor from 1933). Britain and France declared war on Germany 3 Sept 1939, two days after German forces had invaded Poland. In the following months (the 'phoney' war) little fighting took place until April 1940 when the Germans invaded Denmark and Norway. The failure of the Allied resistance led to the replacement of British prime minister Neville Chamberlain by Winston Churchill. By the end of May, Germany had invaded Holland, Belgium, and France, and 337,131 Allied troops had to be evacuated from the beaches of ◊Dunkirk to England. Following the aerial bombardment of British cities known as the ◊Blitz, German air attacks on British air bases were successfully resisted by the RAF in the Battle of ◊Britain and the planned invasion of Britain was abandoned.

The Germans then moved east, invading Yugoslavia and Greece April 1941, and launching an attack on the Russian front in June; by the end of the year they had come within 40 km/ 25 mi of Moscow and had begun to besiege Leningrad (now St Petersburg). After their initial success in the USSR, the Germans were gradually repulsed; Leningrad lost about a third of its population while resisting the German siege for nearly two years. The Germans were finally expelled from the USSR Aug 1944.

The USA entered the war Dec 1941 following the Japanese bombing of the US naval base at Pearl Harbor, Hawaii. The Japanese then took control of southeast Asia and Burma, capturing some 90,000 British and Commonwealth prisoners. They were only checked June 1942 with a series of US naval victories culminating in the defeat of the Japanese fleet at Leyte Gulf in Oct 1944. The major turning point for the Allies occurred in North Africa where German successes under Rommel were reversed when the British Eighth Army under ◊Montgomery won the decisive Battle of El ◊Alamein Oct–Nov 1942; by May 1943 the German army in Africa had surrendered. This left the Allies free to invade Sicily, and after the fall of the Italian dictator Mussolini July 1943, mainland Italy. Rome fell June 1944, and the Germans in Italy finally surrendered after the fall of Trieste May 1945. The Allies launched the successful D-Day invasion of Normandy 6 June 1944 under the command of Eisenhower; Paris was liberated by August and in spite of the setback at Arnhem, the Allies pressed forward across the pre-war German frontier to link up April 1945 with the Soviet Army on the Elbe. The Germans surrendered at Rheims 7 May. The Japanese continued to fight, despite the loss of Burma and the Philippines in 1945, and only surrendered after US atom bombs were dropped on the cities of Hiroshima and Nagasaki.

Wulfstan, St *c.* 1009–1095. Anglo-Saxon cleric, bishop of Worcester from 1062. He supported William the Conqueror and so was the only Anglo-Saxon bishop allowed to retain his see. He helped compile the *Domesday Book* and may have been involved in the *Anglo-Saxon Chronicle*. His sermons against the slave trade in Bristol were instrumental in bringing an end to the trade from the port. He was canonized 1203 and his feast day is 19 Jan.

Wyatt's Rebellion Protestant uprising in Kent Jan–Feb 1554 led by Sir Thomas Wyatt, in protest against Mary I's proposed marriage to Philip II of Spain. He marched on London with about 3,000 men early Feb but Mary remained firm and the rebellion was put down. Wyatt had written to Princess Elizabeth, but the government could not prove she was implicated, though she went to the Tower briefly. Wyatt was executed and the 'Spanish Match' went ahead along with the restoration of Roman Catholicism.

Wycliffe John *c.* 1320–1384. English religious reformer. Allying himself with the party of John of Gaunt, which was opposed to ecclesiastical influence at court, he attacked abuses in the church, maintaining that the Bible rather than the church was the supreme authority. He criticized such fundamental doctrines as priestly absolution, confession, and indulgences, and set disciples to work on translating the Bible into English. He was denounced as a heretic, but died peacefully at Lutterworth. His followers were later referred to as ◊Lollards.

Yalta Conference in 1945, a meeting at which the Allied leaders Churchill (UK), Roosevelt (USA), and Stalin (USSR) completed plans for the defeat of Germany in World War II, the foundation of the United Nations, and the position of the Polish–Russian border which largely followed the ◊Curzon Line. In a secret agreement between the USA and the USSR, Stalin agreed to declare war on Japan when the European war ended. It took place in Yalta, a Soviet holiday resort in the Crimea.

yeoman small landowner who farmed his own fields. This farming system formed a bridge between the break-up of feudalism and the agricultural revolution of the 18th–19th centuries.

Yeomanry English volunteer cavalry organized 1794, and incorporated into regiments which became first the Territorial Force 1908 and then the Territorial Army 1922.

York, archbishop of metropolitan of the northern province of the Anglican Church in England, hence Primate of England. Next in rank to the Lord High Chancellor. Initially, it was envisaged that the office would hold equal weight with that of the archbishop of Canterbury, but the latter came into the ascendancy in the 16th century (see ◊archbishop).

York, Duke of. Title often borne by younger sons of British sovereigns, for example George V, George VI, and Prince Andrew from 1986.

York, House of English dynasty founded by Richard, Duke of York (1411–60). He claimed the throne through his descent from Lionel, Duke of Clarence (1338–1368), third son of Edward III, whereas the reigning monarch, Henry VI of the rival house of Lancaster, was descended from the fourth son. The argument was fought out in the Wars of the ◊Roses. York was killed at the Battle of Wakefield 1460, but next year his son became King Edward IV, in turn succeeded by his son Edward V and then by his brother Richard III, with whose death at Bosworth the line ended. The Lancastrian victor in that battle was crowned Henry VII and consolidated his claim by marrying Edward IV's eldest daughter, Elizabeth.

Yorktown, Battle of decisive British defeat in the American Revolution Sept–Oct 1781 at Yorktown, Virginia, 105 km/65 mi southeast of Richmond. The British commander Lord Cornwallis had withdrawn into Yorktown where he was besieged by 7,000 French and 8,850 American troops and could only wait for reinforcements to arrive by sea. However, the Royal Navy lost command of the sea at the Battle of Chesapeake and with no reinforcements or supplies forthcoming, Cornwallis was forced to surrender 19 Oct, effectively ending the war.

Young England group of Cambridge-educated English aristocrats, newly elected to Parliament 1841, who shared a distaste for the growth of democracy and manufacturing industry in contemporary England, and who promoted instead a revived traditional church and aristocracy to preserve society. The movement faded within five years, but its spirit was captured by Benjamin ◊Disraeli, the future prime minister, in his novel *Coningsby* 1844.

Young Ireland Irish nationalist organization, founded 1840 by William Smith O'Brien (1803–1864), who attempted an abortive insurrection of the peasants against the British in Tipperary 1848. O'Brien was sentenced to death, but later pardoned.

Young Pretender nickname of ◊Charles Edward Stuart, claimant to the Scottish and English thrones.

Ypres, Battles of (Flemish *Ieper*) in World War I, three major battles 1914–17 between German and Allied forces near Ypres, a Belgian town in west Flanders, 40 km/25 mi south of

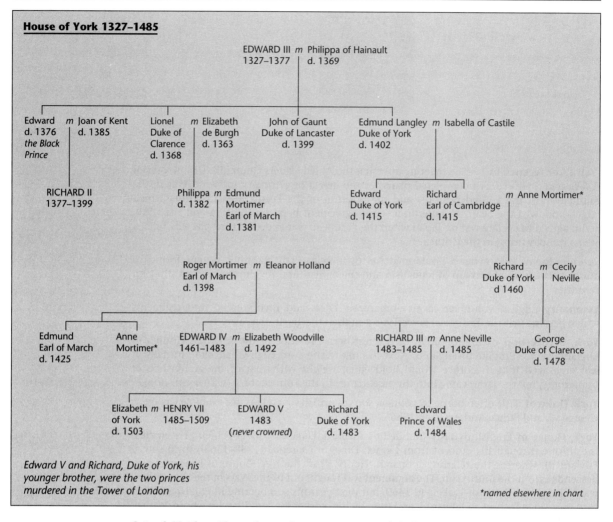

House of York 1327–1485

EDWARD III *m* Philippa of Hainault
1327–1377 | d. 1369

Edward *m* Joan of Kent
d. 1376 | d. 1385
the Black
Prince

Lionel *m* Elizabeth
Duke of | de Burgh
Clarence | d. 1363
d. 1368

John of Gaunt
Duke of Lancaster
d. 1399

Edmund Langley *m* Isabella of Castile
Duke of York
d. 1402

RICHARD II
1377–1399

Philippa *m* Edmund
d. 1382 | Mortimer
Earl of March
d. 1381

Edward
Duke of York
d. 1415

Richard
Earl of Cambridge
d. 1415

m Anne Mortimer*

Roger Mortimer *m* Eleanor Holland
Earl of March
d. 1398

Richard *m* Cecily
Duke of York | Neville
d 1460

Edmund
Earl of March
d. 1425

Anne
Mortimer*

EDWARD IV *m* Elizabeth Woodville
1461–1483 | d. 1492

RICHARD III *m* Anne Neville
1483–1485 | d. 1485

George
Duke of Clarence
d. 1478

Elizabeth *m* HENRY VII
of York | 1485–1509
d. 1503

EDWARD V
1483
(never crowned)

Richard
Duke of York
d. 1483

Edward
Prince of Wales
d. 1484

Edward V and Richard, Duke of York, his
younger brother, were the two princes
murdered in the Tower of London

*named elsewhere in chart

Ostend. Neither side made much progress in any of the battles, despite heavy casualties, but the third battle in particular (also known as ◊*Passchendaele*) July–Nov 1917 stands out as an enormous waste of life for little return. The Menin Gate 1927 is a memorial to British soldiers lost in these battles.

Oct–Nov 1914 a British offensive aimed at securing the Channel ports of Dunkirk and Ostend clashed with a German offensive aimed at taking those ports. The subsequent fighting was extremely heavy and ended with the Germans gaining the Messines Ridge and other commanding ground but with the British and French holding a salient around Ypres extending into the German line. German losses were estimated at 150,000 troops, British and French at about the same number.

April–May 1915 battle opened with a German chlorine gas attack; this made a huge gap in the Allied lines but the Germans were unprepared for this success and were unable to exploit it before the Allies rushed in reserves. More gas attacks followed, and the British were driven to shorten their line, so making the Ypres Salient a smaller incursion into the German line.

July–Nov 1917 an Allied offensive, including British, Canadian, and Australian troops, was launched under British commander-in-chief Field Marshal Douglas Haig, in an attempt to capture ports on the Belgian coast held by Germans. The long and bitter battle, fought in appalling conditions of driving rain and waterlogged ground, achieved an advance of only 8 km/5 mi of territory that was of no strategic significance, but the Allies alone lost more than 300,000 casualties.

Ypres, 1st Earl of title of Sir John ◊French, British field marshal.

Z batteries British anti-aircraft rocket batteries in World War II. First employed 1942, they were usually operated by units of the ◊Home Guard. The British began work on air defence rockets 1936 and perfected a 3-in solid-fuel rocket carrying a 12 kg/28 lb high-explosive warhead. A simple two-rocket launcher was produced and these were organized into 56-launcher batteries around ports and other important targets.

Zanzibar former British protectorate, East Africa. The islands of Zanzibar, Pemba and adjacent smaller islands became a British protectorate 1890 having previously been part of the mainland holdings of the German East Africa Company. Zanzibar became an independent state within the British Commonwealth 1961 and united with Tanganyika 1964 under the joint name Tanzania.

Zinoviev Letter forged letter dated 25 Oct 1924 allegedly from Grigory Zinoviev, chairman of Comintern, inciting British Communists to rebellion. It was printed in the British press just before the General Election, and drew an official protest from the Foreign Office to the Soviet Union. In 1966 it was proved to be a forgery perpetrated by a group of White Russian émigrés with the aim of damaging the Labour Party. Although the Labour Party lost the 1924 election, the letter probably made little difference.

Zion Mule Corps in World War I, a wholly Jewish unit of the British Army. It served with distinction in Gallipoli 1915, carrying rations and ammunition to the forward troops, and after the evacuation of the peninsula the corps was merged with the Jewish Regiment 1917.

Zulu War see ◊Anglo-Zulu War.

Thematic Chronology
of British and Irish History

Events involving Britain and Ireland	Other events

before AD 1

55 BC First Roman expedition to Britain.
54 BC Second Roman expedition to Britain.

27 BC Augustus established as ruler of the Roman Empire.
30 Crucifixion and claimed resurrection of Jesus Christ.
46–62 Missionary journeys of Saint Paul to Mediterranean countries.

AD 1–200

43 Roman invasion of Britain.
c. **50** Foundation of Londinium (London) and Verulamium (St Albans).
60 Revolt of Iceni tribe, led by Boudicca.
71 Foundation of York.
74–84 Governor Agricola's six military campaigns in Scotland.

66–73 First Jewish revolt against Roman rule.
79 In Italy, eruption of Mt Vesuvius, burying the towns of Pompeii and Herculaneum.
117 Roman Empire reached its largest extent.

122 Start of construction of Hadrian's Wall across N England.

139–42 Recapture of Scotland lowlands and construction of the Antonine Wall across the Clyde–Forth isthmus.
163 or 164 Final withdrawal from the Antonine Wall. Hadrian's Wall again became the northern border.
197 Possible date of division of Britain into two provinces.

132–35 Second Jewish revolt against Roman rule; Jews dispersed from Judaea.

188 Romans suppress revolt in Germany.

200–400

210 Revolt of Maeatae in Scotland; crushed by Romans.

259–74 Britain part of the Gallic Empire formed by Postumus.
276–82 Construction of Saxon Shore forts.
286–96 Britain part of rebel Empire founded by Carausius; suppressed by Emperor Constantius.
296–314 Britain's two provinces each divided in two.

226 In Persia, foundation of the Sassanian Empire.
268 Goths attacked Athens, Sparta, and Corinth in Greece.
285 Division of the Roman Empire into two halves for administration.
311 Breakup of the first Chinese empire.
313 Constantine issued the Edict of Milan, granting toleration to Christianity in the Roman Empire.
330 Foundation of Constantinople as new capital of Eastern Roman Empire.
360 Huns invaded Europe.

360s Barbarian attacks on Britain; order restored by Count Theodosius.
383–88 Rebellion of Magnus Maximus; Maximus killed in Gaul.

395 Division of Roman Empire into Western and Eastern Empires with separate rulers.

400–600

401, 407 Troops withdrawn from Britain to deal with crises elsewhere.
409 Possible expulsion of imperial Roman officials from Britain.
c. **430** Start of settlement of Germanic people in E and SE England.
432 Traditional start date of St Patrick's mission in Ireland.
450–600 Expansion of area settled by Germanic peoples in England.

410 Sack of Rome by Goths.

451 Fourth ecumenical council of the Christian Church held at Chalcedon.
455 Vandals attacked Rome.
470 Withdrawal of Huns from Europe.
476 Deposition of the last emperor of the Western Roman Empire.
486–507 Clovis, king of the Franks, conquered Gaul.
527–65 Reign of Byzantine Emperor Justinian, who conquered former Roman lands in NW Africa, Italy, and SW Spain.
568 Lombards invaded NE Italy.

597 Arrival in SE England of Christian mission from Rome, led by Augustine.

600–800

601 Augustine enthroned as first archbishop of Canterbury.

627 King Edwin of Northumbria accepted Christianity.

635 Monastery and bishopric founded on Lindisfarne island, NE England, by the monk Aidan.
655 Battle of the Winwaed: the Christian King Oswy of Northumbria killed the pagan King Penda of Mercia.
664 Synod of Whitby.

622 In Arabia, flight of the Prophet Muhammad from Mecca to Medina, marking the start of the Islamic era.
632 Death of the Prophet Muhammad; his followers spread Islam through Arabia, N Africa, and W Asia.

661 Muawiya founded the Omayyad dynasty of caliphs, ruling the Muslim empire from Damascus.

711 Muslims from N Africa invaded Spain.

716–57 Reign of King Ethelbald, who expanded the kingdom of Mercia.

720 Muslims invaded France.
732 Charles Martel, ruler of France, defeated the Muslims at the Battle of Tours.

Society, economy and science	Cultural history
	before AD 1
	AD 1–200
	70s Building of palatial villa at Fishbourne, S England.
	97–98 Roman historian Tacitus wrote the *Agricola*.
by 100 Most *civitas* capitals founded.	
c. 150 Theatre built at Verulamium (St Albans).	
150–270 Walls built around most Roman towns in Britain.	
late 2nd century Early Christian communities probably established in Britain.	
200–300 Cult of Mithras reached height in Roman Britain.	**200–400**
209–11 Possible time of martyrdom of St Alban.	
301 Emperor Diocletian fixed prices of British woollen goods and beer in price edict.	**early 300s** greatest period of Romano-British mosaic art.
c. 397 St Ninian founded monastery at Candida Casa (Whithorn) in SW Scotland.	**400–600**
402 Last issue of Roman coins to be found in Britain.	
400–430 Decline in industry and town life.	
	475–89 Gildas, *On the Ruin of Britain* (Latin).
604 Earliest recorded Saxon land charter.	**600–800**
625–40 Period when first English coins issued.	**625** Death of King Raedwald of East Anglia, who may have been buried in the magnificent ship burial at Sutton Hoo, Suffolk.
672 Theodore of Tarsus held Council of Hertford.	**675–700** Ruthwell and Bewcastle crosses erected.
674 Benedict Biscop founded monastery at Monkwearmouth (followed by Jarrow in 681 or 682).	**c. 680** Caedmon of Whitby Abbey wrote earliest Christian poetry in English.
688–726 Reign of Ine of Wessex, who issued earliest surviving laws.	**late 7th century** Book of Durrow, the earliest surviving decorated English book.
	698–721 Lindisfarne Gospels.
	c. 700 Tara Brooch, Ardagh Chalice; *Beowulf* written down.
	731 Bede completed the *Ecclesiastical History of the English People* (Latin).
735 Archbishopric created at York.	

Events involving Britain and Ireland	Other events
	750 Abul Abbas founded the Abbasid dynasty of caliphs, who ruled the Islamic world from 762 onwards from Baghdad. **751** Deposition of King Childeric III of the Franks by Pepin the Short, who founded the Carolingian dynasty. **771** Charlemagne becomes sole king of the Franks.
757–96 Reign of King Offa of Mercia.	
793–95 First recorded Viking raids on Britain. **795–830** Vikings raided Ireland.	
830s Norse settlement in Ireland; Norse town foundation included Dublin. **843** Formation of Scotland when King Kenneth MacAlpin of the Scots becomes king of Pictland. **844–78** Reign of Rhodri Mawr (the Great) of Gwynedd. **850–51** Danes wintered in England for the first time.	**800** Charlemagne, king of the Franks, crowned Holy Roman Emperor by Pope Leo III. **843** Treaty of Verdun: division of the Frankish Empire into three for Charlemagne's grandsons.
865 Arrival in England of the 'great army', which started Viking settlement in England. **869** Danes killed King Edmund of East Anglia. **878** Battle of Edington: King Alfred of Wessex defeated Danes. **886** King Alfred recaptured London from the Danes.	**862** Mission of Saints Cyril and Methodius to the Balkan slavs. **870–930** Large-scale migration of Norwegians to Iceland.
c. 904–50 In Wales, reign of Hywel Dda (the Good), grandson of Rhodri Mawr.	
937 Battle of Brunanburh: King Athelstan of Wessex defeated Danes.	
973 Coronation of King Edgar of Wessex, symbolizing completion of Wessex conquest of England. **991** Danish victory at the Battle of Maldon, leading to first payment of King Ethelred's first payment of Danegeld.	**955** Battle of the Lech: King Otto I of Germany defeated the Magyars. **962** Otto I, king of Germany, is crowned Holy Roman Emperor by Pope John XII. **988** Prince Vladimir of Kiev adopted Christianity.
1014 Battle of Clontarf: High King Brian Boru of Ireland defeated Vikings. **1016** Battle of Ashingdon: Danes defeated English and Canute became king of England. **1039–63** Reign of Gruffydd ap Llywelyn of Gwynedd and Powys. **1042** Death of Danish King Harthacanute of England; succeeded by Edward the Confessor. **1066** Norman invasion of England, led by William the Conqeror. **1069** Normans suppressed widespread rebellions.	**1054** Schism between Latin (Western) and Greek Christian churches. **1071** Battle of Manzikert (E Turkey), leading to Turkish control of Asia Minor. **1075** Beginning of the Investiture Dispute between papacy and Holy Roman Empire. **1085** In Spain, Christians recaptured Toledo.
1085 William the Conqueror orders the compilation of Domesday Book. **1088–90** Normans moved through central Wales and founded Pembroke in the southwest . **1103–35** Large-scale Norman settlement in S Wales. **1106** Battle of Tinchebrai in Normandy; Henry I took Normandy from brother Robert Curthose. **1120** 'White Ship' disaster: Henry I's male heir drowned.	**1096–99** First Crusade. **1122** Concordat of Worms, providing temporary peace in Investiture Dispute. **1127** Normans completed their conquest of Sicily
1139–53 Civil war in England during Stephen's reign.	**1147–49** Second Crusade. **1147** Christians recaptured Lisbon.
1167 Arrival of first Normans in Ireland. **1170** Murder of Thomas Becket. **1173–74** Major rebellion against Henry II.	**1171** Saladin conquered Fatimid-ruled Egypt. **1177** Peace of Venice between Pope and Holy Roman Emperor. **1187** Saladin recaptured Jerusalem. **1189–92** Third Crusade.
1203–04 Loss of Normandy and most other French lands of king of England. **1208–14** Papal interdict in England.	**1204** Fourth Crusade, in which crusaders sacked Constantinople. **1210–29** Crusade against the Albigensians in S France. **1212–50** Reign of Frederick II, emperor and king of Sicily.

800–1000

1000–1200

1200–1300

Society, economy and science

757–96 Reign of King Offa of Mercia, who issued high-quality silver pennies.

803 Synod at Clofesho suppressed rival archbishopric at Lichfield.

890s Likely period when King Alfred created system of *burhs* in Wessex.

c. 930 King Athelstan appointed ealdormen as royal agents.
940 Start of refoundation of the monastery of Glastonbury, leading to refoundation or reform of other monasteries.

c. 970 Compilation of the *Regularis concordia*.

1017 King Canute reorganized England as four earldoms.

1102 Marriage of clergy forbidden by Council of London.

1129 Foundation of first Cistercian house in England, Waverley Abbey.
1142–44 Adelard of Bath wrote treatise on the Astrolabe.

1152 Synod of Kells reorganized Church in Ireland.

1176 Assize of Northampton.

1179 Richard Fitznigel, *Dialogue of the Exchequer* (Latin).
1180 *Treatise on the Laws and Customs of England* (Latin) attributed to Ranulf de Glanville.

1199 Start of English chancery rolls.

1209–14 'Great Dispersion' of Oxford University following dispute with townspeople; some clerks start Cambridge University.

Cultural history

c. 820 Athelwulf completed *On the Abbots* (Latin poem), about the abbots of Lindisfarne.
c. 835 Nennius, *History of the Britons* (Latin).

c. 885 King Alfred of Wessex commissioned translation (from Latin to English) of the *History of the World* by Orosius.

c. 890 *On the Consolation of Philosophy* by Boethius translated from Latin into English, possibly by King Alfred.
893 *Anglo-Saxon Chronicle* started.

970 Apogee of Winchester School of art.

1093 Start of building of present Durham Cathedral.

c. 1129 Simeon of Durham, *Deeds of the Kings* (Latin).
c. 1136 Geoffrey of Monmouth wrote *History of the Kings of Britain* (Latin), featuring King Arthur.

1175 Rebuilding of choir of Canterbury Cathedral.
1176 First Eisteddfod held in Wales.

c. 1200 *Brut*, a verse history of England in English, by Layamon.

800–1000

1000–1200

1200–1300

Events involving Britain and Ireland

1215 King John accepted Magna Carta; followed by civil war.
1216–17 Invasion of Prince Louis of France.

1235 Anglo-Normans complete conquest of W Ireland.

1258 Welsh rulers acknowledge Llewelyn ap Gruffydd of Gwynedd as 'prince of Wales'.
1264–65 Civil war in England.
1265 Simon de Montfort holds parliament in England.

1276 English invasion of Wales.

1284 Statute of Wales issued, providing for English government in Wales.
1290 Death of Queen Margaret in Scotland causes succession crisis.
1296 English invasion of Scotland.

1300–1400 **1306** Robert Bruce crowned king of Scotland.

1314 Scots defeated English at Battle of Bannockburn.
1328 Edward III of England recognized Robert the Bruce as king of Scots.
1337 Start of Hundred Years' War between England and France.
1346 English defeat French in Battle of Crécy.

1360 Treaties of Brétigny and Calais.

1369 Renewal of Hundred Years' War.
1371 In Scotland, accession of Robert II, the first Stewart ruler.

1396 Anglo–French truce agreed for 28 years.

1400–1500
1414 English restart the Hundred Years' War.
1415 English defeat French in Battle of Agincourt.
1420 Treaty of Troyes.

1449–53 French retake English-ruled territory in France apart from Calais.
1455 Battle of St Albans, marking start of the Wars of the Roses between supporters of King Henry VI (Lancastrians) and the dukes of York and supporters (Yorkists).
1461 Edward, duke of York, took throne from Henry VI and was proclaimed King Edward IV.

1470 Restoration of Henry VI.
1471 Restoration of Edward IV.

1485 Invasion of Henry Tudor; killed Richard III at Battle of Bosworth and became King Henry VII, founding the Tudor dynasty.

1500–1600
1513 Battle of Flodden: English defeated Scots.

1527 Henry VIII sought papal agreement to divorce from Catherine of Aragon.

Other events

1213 Genghis Khan begins conquest of N China.

1235–48 Christians recaptured Cordoba and Seville.
1237–40 Mongol conquest of Russia.
1241 Mongol invasion of Europe.

1273 Rudolf of Habsburg is elected king of Germany.

1291 Last Christian states in the Holy Land are recaptured.

1309 Papacy moved to Avignon, S France, from Rome.

1326 Ottoman Turks captured the Byzantine city of Bursa.

1356 Ottoman Turks entered Europe.

1378–1417 Great Schism of papacy.

1389 Battle of Kosovo: Ottoman Turks defeated the Serbs, gaining control of Balkans.

1397 Kalmar Union, uniting Denmark, Norway, and Sweden.
1402 Battle of Ankara.

1415–17 Council of Constance.
1419–36 Hussite wars in Bohemia.

1453 Ottoman Turks captured the Byzantine capital of Constantinople (Istanbul).

1477 Death of last duke of Burgundy.
1479 Marriage of Ferdinand of Aragon and Isabella of Castile.
1480 Ivan III, prince of Moscow, stopped payment of tribute to the Mongols.
1492 Fall of Granada, ending Muslim rule in Spain; Christopher Columbus discovered the Americas.
1498 Vasco da Gama reached India.

1516 Martin Luther attacked indulgences, starting the Reformation.
1521 The Ottoman Sultan Suleiman the Magnificent captured Belgrade

1526 Battle of Moha#1cs: Ottoman Turks defeated the Hungarians.

Society, economy and science

1215 Court of Common Pleas established at Westminster.

1224 Franciscan friars arrived in England.
1236 Statute of Merton (earliest declaration of points of law in England).

c. **1250** Walter of Henley, *Hosebondrie* (treatise on estate management).

1268 Henry de Bracton, *On the Laws and Customs of England* (Latin).
1279 Statute of Mortmain, forbidding alienation of land to religious corporations without licence.
1283 Statute of Acton Burnell provided procedures for merchants to recover debts.

1320 University founded in Dublin.
c. **1324** *Modus tenendi parliamentum.*

1366 Statutes of Kilkenny legislating relations in Ireland between English and Irish.

c. **1375** Start of Lollard translations of the Bible into English.
1376 First recorded performance of Corpus Christi play cycle in York.
1382 Foundation of Winchester College

1410 First university in Scotland formed in St Andrew's (given charter 1412).

1430 Electors of County MPs to English parliaments required to have freehold land worth 40 shillings per annum.
1441 Foundation of Eton College.

1456 Reginald Pecock, *The Book of Faith.*

1468 Statutes against livery and maintenance and various games.
1476 William Caxton established printing press in Westminster.

1481 Thomas Littleton, *Of Tenures.*

1507 First printing press in Scotland.

1517 Commissioners investigated enclosures in English counties.
1523 Anthony Fitzherbert, *Book of Husbandry.*
1525 Cardinal Wolsey founded Ipswich School and Cardinal College (now Christ Church), Oxford.

Cultural history

1220 Start of building of Salisbury Cathedral on new site.

1245 Start of rebuilding of Westminster Abbey.
c. **1250** Song *Sumer is icumen in* first written down.

c. **1264** *The Song of Lewes* (Latin poem).

c. **1295** *The Harrowing of Hell*, earliest surviving miracle play in English.
1303 Robert Mannyng began writing *Handlyng Synne*.   **1300–1400**

1362 First version of *Piers Plowman* by William Langland.

c. **1375** *Sir Gawain and the Green Knight; The Cloud of Unknowing.*

1390 John Gower, *Confessio amantis.*
c. **1393** Julian of Norwich, *Revelations of Divine Love.*
c. **1396** Walter Hilton, *The Scale of Perfection.*
1400 Death of Geoffrey Chaucer, leaving his *Canterbury Tales*   **1400–1500**
unfinished.
1412 John Lydgate, *The Troy Boook.*

c. **1423** James I of Scotland, *The King's Quair.*
c. **1432–36** *The Book of Margery Kempe.*

1453 Death of the influential English composer John Dunstable.

c. **1470** Sir Thomas Malory completed *Le Morte d'Arthur* (printed 1485).

1480 William of Worcester wrote his *Itineraries.*

1503–19 Henry VII's chapel, Westminster Abbey.   **1500–1600**

Events involving Britain and Ireland	*Other events*
1529 Fall of Lord Chancellor Cardinal Wolsey.	
1534 Act of Supremacy confirmed Henry VIII in powers formerly exercised by the pope in England.	**1536** Jean Calvin published *The Institutes of the Christian Religion*.
1539–40 Larger religious houses in England were dissolved.	
1541 Irish parliament acknowledged Henry VIII as king of Ireland and head of the Irish Church.	**1545–63** Council of Trent.
1549 First English prayer book introduced.	**1555** Peace of Augsburg, ending religious wars in Germany.
1559 In Scotland, John Knox attacked idols, marking start of Scottish Reformation.	**1562–98** Wars of Religion in France.
	1567–1609 Revolt of the Netherlands against Spanish rule.
	1571 Battle of Lepanto: Spanish and Venetians defeated the Ottoman fleet.
	1572 St Bartholomew's Day massacre of Protestants in France.
1587 Execution of Mary, Queen of Scots, by order of Queen Elizabeth of England.	
1588 Spanish Armada sent against England.	**1598** Edict of Nantes issued in France, granting liberties to Huguenot Protestants.

1600–1700

1603 James VI of Scotland crowned James I of England.	
1605 Gunpower Plot: Guy Fawkes captured while preparing explosion for opening of parliament.	
1609 In Ireland, rebellion of the Northern Earls, followed by establishment of Scottish plantations.	**1609** Dutch republic became independent.
	1618–48 Thirty Years' War.
1629–40 Personal rule of Charles I.	
1642–46 First Civil War.	
1648 Second Civil War.	
1649 Execution of Charles I; republican government established.	**1648–53** *Fronde* civil wars in France.
1653–58 Protectorate of Oliver Cromwell.	
1660 Restoration of monarchy, with Charles II as king.	**1654** Russia acquired Ukraine from Poles.
	1661 Effective start of rule of Louis XIV of France (king since 1643).
1679–81 Exclusion Crisis: produced Whig and Tory parties.	
	1683 Unsuccessful Turkish siege of Vienna.
	1685 In France, revocation of the Edict of Nantes.
1688 'Glorious Revolution': flight of Catholic James II; accession of Protestants William III and Mary.	**1686** Hungarians and Habsburgs recaptured Buda from the Ottoman Turks.
1690 Battle of the Boyne: William III defeats Irish and French army.	
1694 Triennial Act: maximum length of English parliament to be three years.	**1699** Peace of Karlowitz: leaves Habsburg emperor ruling most of historic Hungary.

1700–1800

1701–14 War of Spanish Succession.	**1700–21** Great Northern War between Russia and Sweden.
1701 Act of Succession settles succession to English throne on Electress Sophia of Hanover and her descendants.	**1703** Foundation of St Petersburg (capital of Russia from 1712).
1704 Battle of Blenheim: British and Allies defeated French and Bavaria.	
1707 Union of Scotland and England.	
	1709 Battle of Poltava: Russians inflicted major defeat on Swedish invaders.
1715 Jacobite Rebellion.	
1716 Septennial Act: maximum length of English parliament extended to seven years.	
1720 South Sea Bubble.	

Society, economy and science	Cultural history

1540 Race course opened in Chester.

1562 Bishop Jewel, *Apologia Ecclesiae Anglicanae*.
1564–66 Exeter Canal dug, including first pound locks in Britain.

1575 Publication of *County Atlas of England and Wales* by Christopher Saxton; *Cantiones Sacrae* by William Byrd and Thomas Tallis.
1576 William Lambarde, *A Perambulation of Kent*.
1577 Raphael Holinshed, *History of England*.

1578–80 Sir Francis Drake circumnavigates the globe.

1586 William Camden, *Britannia*.
1590 First known production of plays by William Shakespeare.
1597 Francis Bacon, *Essays: Civil and Moral*.

1598 Poor Law Act in England and Wales.

1600 Foundation of the East India Company.

1600–1700

1607 Ben Jonson, *Volpone, or The Fox*.

1607 First successful English settlement on American mainland at Jamestown, Virginia.
1611 James VI and I created first baronets; Authorised Version of the Bible published.
1620 Voyage of the Pilgrims on the Mayflower to the USA.
1622 First turnpike act in England.

1614 Sir Walter Raleigh, *History of the World*.

1621 Robert Burton, *Anatomy of Melancholy*.
1623 Posthumous publication of the 'First Folio' of William Shakespeare's collected plays.
1628 William Harvey published discovery of the circulation of the blood.
1633 Posthumous publication of *The Temple* by George Herbert.
1636 Anthony van Dyck, *Charles I on Horseback*.

1651 Thomas Hobbes, *Leviathan*.
1653 Izaak Walton, *The Compleat Angler* (–1676).

1662 Foundation of the Royal Society.
1666 Great Plague and Fire of London.
1675 Greenwich Observatory founded; Isaac Newton, *Opticks*.

1667 John Milton, *Paradise Lost*.

1688 Regular meetings of insurance underwriters held at Lloyd's Coffee House, London.
1689 John Locke, *Two Treatises of Government*.
1691 Foundation in Tower Hamlets, London, of the first Society for the Reformation of Manners.
1694 Foundation of the Bank of England.

1689 Henry Purcell, *Dido and Aeneas*.

1700–1800

1700 William Congreve, *The Way of the World*.

1700–1800

1705 John Vanbrugh, Blenheim Palace.
1706 George Farquhar, *The Recruiting Officer*.

1706 Sun Fire Office insurance company founded in London.

1709 Abraham Darby used coke to smelt iron.

1710 George Berkeley, *A Treatise Concerning the Principles of Human Knowledge*.

1712 Last execution for witchcraft in England.

1712 Alexander Pope, *The Rape of the Lock*.

1719 Daniel Defoe, *Robinson Crusoe*.

Events involving Britain and Ireland	Other events
1721–42 Second ministry of Sir Robert Walpole.	
1745 Jacobite Rebellion.	**1740** War of Austrian Succession: Prussia conquered Silesia.
1756–63 Seven Years' War.	**1756–63** Seven Years' War, ending with the Treaty of Paris. **1772** First Partition of Poland.
1776 American Declaration of Independence from Britain. **1781** Americans forced British army to surrender at Yorktown.	
	1789 Outbreak of French Revolution.
1793 Revolutionary government in France declared war on Britain. **1798** Battle of the Nile: Royal Navy defeated French navy in Egypt.	**1793, 1795** Second and Third Partitions of Poland. **1792–97** War of the First Coalition. **1798–1801** War of the Second Coalition. **1799** In France, Napoleon overthrew the Directory.

1800–1900

Events involving Britain and Ireland	Other events
1801 Union of Britain and Ireland. **1802** Britain made peace with France. **1805** Battle of Trafalgar: Royal Navy defeated French and Spanish fleets.	**1805–07** War of the Third Coalition.
1815 Battle of Waterloo: Britain and allies defeated French.	**1813–14** War of the Fourth Coalition, ending with the abdication of Napoleon. **1815** Napoleon's 'Hundred Days' as restored emperor of France; Treaty of Vienna.
1829 Catholic Emancipation. **1832** Great Reform Act.	**1829** Greek kingdom established. **1830** July Revolution in France: Louis Philippe replaced Charles X.
1845–46 Great Potato Famine in Ireland. **1846** Abolition of Corn Laws; Conservative Party split. **1854–56** Crimean War: Britain and France fought Russia.	**1848** Revolutions in Europe; republic established in France.
	1861–65 American Civil War. **1861** Kingdom of Italy proclaimed.
1867 Second Reform Act.	**1870–71** Franco–Prussian War. **1871** German Empire proclaimed; Third Republic established in France.
1884 Third Reform Act. **1885** Redistribution Act creates single-member constituencies. **1886** Gladstone's first Home Rule Bill for Ireland defeated; Liberal Party split.	**1894** Franco–Russian Alliance formed.
1899–1902 Boer War.	

Society, economy and science

1721 Lady Mary Wortley Montague introduced inoculation for smallpox into England.

1733 James Kay patented the 'flying shuttle', for use in weaving.
1738 John Wesley received call to evangelism.

1750 Foundation of the English Jockey Club and of the Hambledon Cricket Club.
1754 Foundation of the Royal and Ancient Golf Club, St Andrew's.
1768–71 James Cook's first voyage of discovery.

1773–79 Construction of the cast-iron bridge at Ironbridge, Shropshire.
1774 Joseph Priestley discovered oxygen.
1776 Adam Smith, *An Inquiry into the Nature and Causes of the Wealth of Nations*.
1787 Marylebone Cricket Club (MCC) founded.
1789 Jeremy Bentham, *Introduction to the Principles of Morals and Legislation*.
1790 Edmund Burke, *Reflections on the Revolution in France*.

1798 Thomas Malthus, *Essay on the Principle of Population*.

1802 John Dalton proposed atomic theory and compiled tables of atomic weights; William Paley, *Natural Theology*.
1811 Luddite attacks on textile machinery in Nottingham and Yorkshire.

1825 Opening of the Stockton and Darlington Railway.
1829 Foundation of the Metropolitan Police force (London).

1833 John Keble begins the Oxford Movement in the Church of England.
1834 Poor Law Amendment Act.
1838 Working Men's Association draws up the People's Charter.
1840 Introduction of Penny Postage.

1843 Great Disruption in Scottish Church.
1844 Foundation of the Cooperative Society.

1851 Great Exhibition held in Hyde Park, London, in Joseph Paxton's Crystal Palace.

1857 Matrimonial Causes Act established divorce courts in England and Wales.
1859 Charles Darwin, *The Origin of Species*; J S Mill, *On Liberty*.

1865 Debut of W G Grace, cricketer.
1867 Karl Marx, *Das Kapital*, Vol. 1 (Vol. 2, 1885; Vol. 3, 1895).
1871 Bank Holidays introduced in England and Wales.

1882 Married Women's Property Act.

Cultural history

1724 Foundation of Three Choirs Festival (for choirs in Gloucester, Hereford, and Worcester).
1726 Jonathan Swift, *Gulliver's Travels*.
1728 John Gay, *Beggar's Opera*.

1739 David Hume, *Treatise on Human Nature*.
1741 George Frederick Handel, *Messiah*.
1749 Henry Fielding, *The History of Tom Jones, A Foundling*.

1759 Opening of British Museum.

1776 Edward Gibbon, *Decline and Fall of the Roman Empire* (–1788).

1791 James Boswell, *Life of Johnson*.

1800–1900

1813 Jane Austen, *Pride and Prejudice*.

1817 Foundation of *The Scotsman*.
1818 Lord Byron, *Don Juan* (–1823); Mary Shelley, *Frankenstein*.
1821 John Constable, *The Hay Wain*.
1824 Foundation of the National Gallery, London.

1836 Charles Dickens, *Sketches by Boz* and start of *Pickwick Papers*.

1841 Publication of *Punch*.

1847 W M Thackeray, *Vanity Fair* (–1848).

1857 Anthony Trollope, *Barchester Towers*.

1865 Lewis Carroll, *Alice's Adventures in Wonderland*.

1871 George Eliot, *Middlemarch* (–1872).
1872 Thomas Hardy, *Under The Greenwood Tree*.

1889 J K Jerome, *Three Men in a Boat*.
1892 A Conan Doyle, *The Adventures of Sherlock Holmes*.
1895 Oscar Wilde, *The Importance of Being Earnest*; first series of Promenade Concerts at Queen's Hall, London, conducted by Henry Wood.
1899 Edward Elgar, *Enigma Variations*.

	Events involving Britain and Ireland	**Other events**

1900–1920

1902 Anglo–Japanese Alliance formed.
1904 Anglo–French entente.

1905 Attempted Revolution in Russia.

1907 Anglo–Russian entente.

1908 Austria-Hungary annexed Bosnia-Herzegovina.

1909 Rejection of David Lloyd George's 'People's Budget' by Lords started constitutional crisis.
1911 Parliament Act reduced power of Lords.
1914 Irish Home Rule Act on statute book, but was suspended.
1914 Start of World War I: British forces involved in campaigns in NE France.

1914 Assassination of Austrian Archduke Franz Ferdinand in Sarajevo led to outbreak of World War I.

1915 Dardanelles campaign.
1916 Easter Rising in Dublin; Battle of Jutland; Battle of the Somme.

1915 Italy joined War on Allied side.
1916 Battle of Verdun on Western Front; Brusilov Offensive on Eastern Front.

1917 Third Battle of Ypres (Passchendaele).

1917 'February Revolution' in Russia (March), followed by the Bolshevik (Communist) 'October Revolution' (Nov) and civil war; USA entered War.

1918 Counteroffensive against the Central Powers.

1918 Treaty of Brest–Litovsk between Russia and Germany; end of War with Armistice of 11 Nov.
1919 Treaty of Versailles, including creation of the League of Nations.
1920 Russian Civil War ended with Bolshevik victory.

1920–1940

1921 Partition of Ireland with separate governments in the north and the Irish Free State.

1922 Benito Mussolini appointed prime minister of Italy.

1924 First Labour government, with Ramsay MacDonald as prime minister.

1925 Locarno Pact: Rhineland made a demilitarized zone.

1926 General Strike.

1929 Second Labour government, with Ramsay MacDonald as prime minister.

1929 Wall Street Crash and start of the Great Depression.

1931 Formation of coalition National Government, with Ramsay MacDonald as prime minister.

1933 Adolf Hitler appointed chancellor of Germany.
1934 Stalin started purge of political enemies and others in USSR.
1936–39 Spanish Civil War.
1937 Japanese invasion of China.

1936 Abdication crisis: Edward VIII abdicates.

1938 Munich crisis: Prime Minister Neville Chamberlain agreed to Hitler's demands on Czechoslovakia.
1939 Following German invasion of Poland, Britain declared war on Germany.

1939 Soviet–German Pact; outbreak of World War II.

1940–1960

1940 Churchill appointed prime minister of coalition government; British withdrawal from Dunkirk; Battle of Britain.

1940 German invasion of Low Countries and France.
1941 German invasion of USSR; Japan bombed Pearl Harbor and occupied SE Asia.
1942 US Navy defeated Japan in Battle of Midway.

1942 Battle of El Alamein: British army defeated Germans under Erwin Rommel.
1943 Anglo–American invasion of Italy.
1944 D-Day invasion of France.
1945 End of World War II.

1943 German army surrendered to Russians at Stalingrad.
1945 Foundation of United Nations; end of World War II in Europe; atomic bombs halted war in Asia.
1946–48 Communist governments established in E European countries.

1947 Britain granted independence to India, Pakistan, and Burma.
1949 Formation of NATO with Britain as member; southern Ireland became fully independent.
1951 Festival of Britain.

1955 Warsaw Pact signed.

1956 Suez crisis.

1957 Creation of the European Economic Community.

Society, economy and science

1901 Guglielmo Marconi transmitted wireless message from Poldhu, Cornwall, to Newfoundland.
1902 Balfour Education Act provided state secondary education and integrated state and church schools.
1905 Foundation of the Automobile Association.

1907 Formation of Boy Scouts (Girl Guides formed 1909).

1911 Ernest Rutherford identified nuclear atom.
1914 British government granted emergency powers.

1916 Marie Stopes, *Married Love*.

1918 School leaving age increased to 14.

1919 John Maynard Keynes, *The Economic Consequences of the Peace*.

1922 Foundation of the British Broadcasting Company (Corporation from 1927).

1925 UK divorce laws made inoperative in Irish Free State.

1926 John Logie Baird demonstrated television.

1929 Most Scottish Presbyterian churches united as Church of Scotland.
1930 First British Empire Games held (in Canada).

1932 James Chadwick discovered the neutron.
1933 Controversial 'bodyline' MCC cricket tour of Australia.

1935 First successful experiments with radar.
1936 Billy Butlin opened first holiday camp, near Skegness; BBC started television broadcasting.

1940 Howard Florey developed penicillin for medical use.

1942 William Beveridge, *Social Security and Allied Services* (the Beveridge Report); William Temple, *Christianity and the Social Order*.
1944 'Butler' Education Act, creating three-school system of secondary education.

1946 London Airport opened at Heathrow.

1949 Maiden flight of the Comet, the first jet airliner.

1953 Francis Crick and James Watson announced double-helix structure of DNA.
1954 Roger Bannister's four-minute mile.

1956 Nuclear power station at Calder Hall opened.

1958 Munich air crash killed eight Manchester United players.
1959 Mini Minor on sale.
1960 Trial ruled that *Lady Chatterley's Lover* by D H Lawrence is not obscene.
1961 First betting shop opened; Michael Ramsey became 100th archbishop of Canterbury.

Cultural history

1902 Publication of the *Times Literary Supplement*.
1903 G E Moore, *Principia Ethica*.

1906 John Galsworthy, *The Man of Property* (Vol. I of The Forsyte Saga).
1908 Kenneth Grahame, *The Wind in the Willows*.

1911 Max Beerbohm, *Zuleika Dobson*.

1918 Lytton Strachey, *Eminent Victorians*.

1919 Edward Elgar, *Cello Concerto*.

1922 T S Eliot, *The Waste Land*; James Joyce, *Ulysses*.
1923 William Walton, *Façade*.

1926 A A Milne, *Winnie the Pooh*.
1928 Virginia Woolf, *Orlando*.
1929 Noel Coward, *Bitter Sweet*; Robert Graves, *Goodbye to All That*.
1930 W H Auden, *Poems*.

1932 Aldous Huxley, *Brave New World*.

1936 A J Ayer, *Language, Truth and Logic*.

1938 Graham Green, *Brighton Rock*.

1943 T S Eliot, *Four Quartets*.

1945 Benjamin Britten, *Peter Grimes*.

1947 First Edinburgh Festival of the Arts.
1949 George Orwell, *Nineteen Eighty-four*.

1954 Kingsley Amis, *Lucky Jim*; William Golding, *Lord of the Flies*.
1955 Samuel Beckett, *Waiting for Godot*; Philip Larkin, *The Less Deceived*.
1956 John Osborne, *Look Back in Anger*.
1957 Richard Hoggart, *The Uses of Literacy*.
1958 John Betjeman, *Collected Poems*.

1961 Debut of The Beatles.

	Events involving Britain and Ireland	**Other events**
1960–1980	**1962** 'Night of Long Knives': Prime Minister Macmillan dismissed 7 of 21 cabinet ministers.	**1962** Cuban missile crisis.
	1963 British application to join European Common Market vetoed by France; Profumo Scandal.	**1963** In USA, assassination of President John F Kennedy.
	1964 Creation of the Welsh Office.	**1964** Growth of US involvement in Vietnam War.
	1965 Rhodesia made Unilateral Declaration of Independence from Britain.	**1965** Cultural Revolution in China.
	1967 Sterling devalued.	**1967** Six-Day War between Israel and Arab countries.
	1968 Enoch Powell's 'rivers of blood' speech advocating repatriation of immigrants.	**1968** Student unrest in France.
	1969 Outbreak of 'the troubles' in Northern Ireland.	
	1973 Britain joined the European Economic Community.	**1973** USA withdrew from Vietnam War.
	1974 Britain established direct rule of Northern Ireland.	
		1975 In Spain, death of General Franco; succeeded by King Juan Carlos.
	1979 'Winter of discontent': widespread strikes by public workers discredited Labour government; Margaret Thatcher elected first woman prime minister.	**1979** Peace Treaty between Egypt and Israel; USSR invaded Afghanistan.
1980–1994		**1980** Death of President Tito of Yugoslavia; Ronald Reagan elected president of the USA.
	1981 Riots in Brixton (London) and Toxteth (Liverpool).	**1982** Martial Law declared in Poland and Solidarity Union suppressed.
	1982 Falklands War.	
	1984–85 Miners' strike.	**1984** Prime Minister Indira Gandhi of India assassinated.
	1985 Anglo–Irish Agreement.	**1985** Mikhail Gorbachev appointed secretary general of Soviet Communist Party.
		1989 Tiananmen Square massacre in Beijing, China.
		1989–90 Collapse of Communism in E Europe.
	1990 Resignation of Margaret Thatcher; succeeded by John Major.	**1990–91** Gulf War.
		1991 Collapse of Soviet Union; formation of the Confederation of Independent States; Maastricht Treaty agreed.
	1992 Conservative Party's fourth consecutive victory in general election.	
	1994 Paramilitary organizations declared ceasefire in Northern Ireland.	**1994** Non-racial general election held in South Africa.

Society, economy and science

1963 Beeching Report proposed closure of quarter of railway network.

1966 England won World Cup.
1967 Completion of Cathedral of Christ the King, Liverpool; colour television introduced.

1969 Maiden flights of Concorde supersonic airliner; Open University founded.
1970 Age of majority reduced from 21 to 18.

1973 Introduction of commercial radio.

1975 Equal pay for both sexes compulsory.
1978 First 'test-tube' baby born.

1982 First papal visit to Britain.

1986 GCSE examinations replaced O level and CSE.
1989 Ayatollah Khomeini of Iran issued fatwa sentencing British writer Salman Rushdie to death for blasphemy in his novel *The Satanic Verses*.
1991 Polytechnics permitted to become universities.

1992 Church of England voted to allow ordination of women to the priesthood.
1993 Queen Elizabeth II and Prince of Wales volunteered to pay income tax; Buckingham Palace was opened to the public.
1994 Privatization of British coal mines.

Cultural history

1962 Anthony Burgess, *A Clockwork Orange*; BBC broadcast *That Was The Week That Was*.
1963 John le Carré, *The Spy Who Came in from the Cold*.

1960–1980

1969 *Civilisation*, television series presented by Kenneth Clark; Rupert Murdoch purchased *The Sun*.
1970 Ted Hughes, *Crow*.
1972 Frederick Forsyth, *The Day of the Jackal*.

1978 *Evita*, musical by Tim Rice and Andrew Lloyd Webber.

1980–1995

1982 *Gandhi*, film directed by Richard Attenborough.

1984 First payments to authors on library loans under Public Lending Right.
1985 *Triumph of the West*, television series on world history presented by J M Roberts.
1989 John Tavener, *The Protecting Veil* for cello and string orchestra.
1990 Glasgow 'Cultural Capital of Europe'.
1991 Closure of the *Listener* magazine (founded 1929).

1993 Rachel Whitehead awarded Turner Prize for *House* (plaster cast of inside of London house).

Bibliography

Celtic Britain

Martin Henig

Cunliffe, Barry *Iron Age Communities in Britain* 1974 This is the standard work on the subject, especially good on settlement and the economy.

Cunliffe, Barry *Iron Age Britain* 1995 A more concise and accessible version of Professor Cunliffe's views, even better illustrated.

Green (ed), Miranda J *The Celtic World* 1995 This is a massive compendium by numerous authors discussing all aspects of the Celts, but very properly with an insular bias.

James, Simon *Exploring the World of the Celts* 1993 Although the production is sometimes irritatingly trendy, this is the best general book on all aspects of the Celts, in Britain and beyond.

Ross, Anne *The Pagan Celts* 1986 The wide learning and enthusiasm of Dr Ross are very apparent in this book, originally published in 1970 with the more accurate title of *Everyday Life of the Pagan Celts*.

Raftery, Barry *Pagan Celtic Ireland. The Enigma of the Irish Iron Age* 1994 La Tène culture was confined to the northern half of the island of Ireland, and Iron Age Irish culture shows strong continuity from the Bronze Age past. This is a very important book, showing that invasion is not necessarily a sign of cultural change.

Piggott, Stuart *The Druids* 1968 The classic study of the well known priestly caste and its place in Iron Age society, together with the story of the re-invention of the Druids in much more recent times.

Megaw, Ruth, and Megaw, Vincent *Celtic Art from its beginnings to the Book of Kells* 1989 The best book on Celtic Art in general, including insular art. It is superbly illustrated.

Youngs (ed), Susan *'The work of Angels'. Masterpieces of Celtic Metalwork. 6th–9th centuries AD* 1989 The catalogue of one of a series of major exhibitions. No better proof is needed that the greatest achievements of the Celts lay in post-Roman times.

Webster, Graham *The Roman Conquest of Britain* 1993 A classic trilogy exploring through archaeology and historical sources the epic clash between Celts and Romans. It comprises revised editions of *The Roman Invasion of Britain* 1980, *Rome against Caratacus* 1981, and *Boudica* 1978.

Roman Britain

Martin Henig

Salway, Peter *The Oxford Illustrated History of Roman Britain* 1993 The revised and illustrated edition of the fullest and most readable overview of the subject, with many photographs in black and white and colour.

Millett, Martin *Roman Britain* 1995 Dr Millett focusses on the subtle processes of cultural change. His book is both thoughtful and accessible.

Tacitus, Cornelius (translated by H Mattingly as *The Agricola and the Germania* 1948, revised 1970) 1970 One of the classics of Latin literature, Tacitus' encomium on his father-in-law offers a near contemporary account of one of Roman Britain's most influential governors.

Breeze, David J, and Dobson, Brian *Hadrian's Wall* 1987 A lively account of Britain's most famous Roman monument. It deals with life on the Wall as well as military topics, and should accompany any visitor.

Wacher, John *The Towns of Roman Britain* 1974 This book has proved its worth over the years by bringing together all the evidence from place names, topography, inscriptions, and archaeology.

Birley, Anthony *The People of Roman Britain* 1988 By skilled use of inscriptions and other written sources, Professor Birley introduces us, albeit fleetingly, to the actual inhabitants of the province.

Henig, Martin *Religion in Roman Britain* 1995 In this book I have tried to show that Roman tolerance towards and encouragement of religion was an important agent of cultural change in Britain.

Thomas, Charles *Christianity in Roman Britain to AD 500* 1981 The author assembles the evidence for Christianity in the province and makes an unassailable case for continuity into the so-called 'Dark Ages'.

Henig, Martin *The Art of Roman Britain* 1995 Here I have attempted to show that the art of Roman Britain has the same dynamism and originality as Celtic and Anglo-Saxon art and that it is one of the best indicators of the pagan, literary culture of the 4th-century British gentry.

Anglo-Saxon England

Martin Henig

Bassett (ed), Steven *The Origins of Anglo-Saxon Kingdoms* 1989 Diverse essays by different authors showing that not all kingdoms had the same origin, and showing the part played by indigenous Britons as well as the Germanic newcomers.

Bede (translated by Leo Sherley-Price 1955; revised 1990 as *The Ecclesiastical History of the English People*) *A History of the English Church and People* 1955 A warm and moving account of politics and religious conversion by a great and highly readable historian, born AD 673.

Webster, Leslie, and Backhouse (eds), Janet *The Making of England. Anglo-Saxon Art and Culture AD 600–900* 1991 Here, in a catalogue to a British Museum exhibition, is all the visual evidence for Bede's world and beyond, down to the reign of Alfred. There are excellent introductory essays.

Backhouse, Janet, Turner, D H, and Webster (eds), Leslie *The Golden Age of Anglo-Saxon Art 966–1066* 1984 The cultural achievements of the late Anglo-Saxon period were stupendous. This is another very important offering from the British Museum.

Dodwell, C R *Anglo-Saxon Art: A New Perspective* 1982 An excellent study of Anglo-Saxon artistic achievement in its European context.

Campbell, James, John, Eric, and Wormald, Patrick *The Anglo-Saxons* 1982 A fine, illustrated, general study of the Anglo- Saxons, written by three of the leading authorities on the subject.

Keynes, Simon, and Lapidge, Michael (translated with introduction and notes) *Alfred the Great. Asser's Life and Other Contemporary Sources* 1983 A collection of texts, the most important of which is Asser's *Life of Alfred*.

Richards, Julian D *Viking Age England* 1991 A concise and well written account of the northmen who harried and invaded but also settled and traded in England.

Medieval Britain

Simon Hall

Poole, A L *The Oxford History of England: From Domesday Book to Magna Carta* 1955

Powicke, Maurice *The Oxford History of England: The Thirteenth Century* 1962

McKisack, May *The Oxford History of England: The Fourteenth Century* 1959

Jacob, E F *The Oxford History of England: The Fifteenth Century* 1961 Together these four volumes form the standard, large-scale conventional guide to the whole field of English medieval history.

various *English Historical Documents, vols II–V* various A monumental, accessible, and always fascinating collection of the major (and some minor) primary sources.

Le Patourel, John *The Norman Empire* 1976 The magisterial culmination of the career of the greatest modern authority on the world of the Normans.

Clanchy, M T *From Memory to Written Record* 1979 An analysis of the development of literacy and a literate mentality in Britain which demonstrates that the most exciting new approaches to medieval history are not necessarily French.

Warren, W L *Henry II* 1973 An outstanding biography of one of the most important medieval kings of England.

DuBoulay, F R H *An Age of Ambition* 1970 An thematic approach to later medieval England, charting many areas (marriage, sex, status of women) now being thoroughly explored.

Davies, Rees *Domination and Conquest: The Experience of Ireland, Scotland and Wales 1100–1300* 1990 A good starting point for the history of the non-English kingdoms of medieval Britain.

Tudor and Early Stuart England

Glyn Redworth

Elton, Sir Geoffrey *England Under the Tudors* 1974 This classic textbook first appeared in the 1950s and portrays a Tudor state which is effectively ruled by usually exceptionally strong monarchs.

Guy, John *Tudor England* 1990 Incorporates the latest research and gives a greater insight into the mechanics of Tudor government.

Davies, C S L *Peace, Print, and Protestantism* ?? A wonderfully succinct account of English history from the Wars of the Roses to the mid-16th century, revealling how early Tudor history is best studied with an understanding of the Middle Ages.

Rowse, A L *Bosworth Field and the Wars of the Roses* 1966 A thoroughly well written account of how, by fair means and foul, the Tudors seized the English throne.

Haigh, C A *The English Reformations* ?? A so-called revisionist account of the Reformation not as an event but as a series of processes. This work encapsulates the new consensus.

Starkey, David *The Court of Henry VIII* 1985 A well illustrated and vividly written account of the behind-the-scenes history of the king's reign. By emphasizing faction and not policy, Starkey brings alive the cut and thrust of the age.

Marius, Richard *Thomas More* 1985 A highly controversial account of the martyr's life. Seeing him as much sinner as saint, this is one of the more engaging of psychobiographies.

Russell, Conrad *The Causes of the English Civil War* 1990 A forensic account of early Stuart history, in which the son of the philosopher Bertrand Russell dissects what we mean by causes.

Civil War

Glyn Redworth

Gardiner, S R *History of England from the Accession of James I to the Outbreak of the Civil War* These ten volumes, originally published in the 1880s, remain the best account of the lead-up to the Civil War. Gardiner's stock rises and falls, but successive generations of historians can never quite escape from his shadow.

Russell, Conrad *The Fall of the British Monarchies 1637–1642* 1991 A bold attempt to use narrative detail to explain the Civil War, focussing in part onthe difficulty faced by Charles I in ruling together an Anglican England, a Presbyterian Scotland, and a largely Catholic Ireland.

Hexter, J A *The Reign of King Pym* 1941 A powerful account despite its age of one of Charles I's most brilliant opponents.

Hibbard, Caroline *Charles I and the Popish Plot* 1983 Details not only the anti-popish fears in England, but also Charles's somewhat naive attempts at diplomatic rapprochement with Rome.

Coward, B *Oliver Cromwell* 1991 The most fair-minded and unsensational account of a character who still arouses much controversy.

Kishlansky, Mark *The Rise of the New Model Army* 1979 This is the new military history at its best, demonstrating that military studies cannot be divorced from a wider understanding of politics and society.

Hill, Christopher *The English Bible and the Seventeenth Century Revolution* A subtle study of the role of ideology in 17th-century England by the greatest Marxist authority on the period.

Strong, Sir Roy *Charles I on Horseback* 1972 A fascinating account of the image of a king.

Wooton, D (ed) *Divine Right and Democracy* 1986 A comprehensive selection of writings, ranging from James I's views on kingship to the radical thoughts of the Interregnum.

Restoration to Hanoverian Britain

Glyn Redworth

Jones, J R *Court and Country 1658–1714* 1978 An excellent introduction to the politics and culture of the age.

Hutton, Ronald *The Restoration* 1987 A highly intelligent account of the return of the House of Stuart.

Gregg, Edward *Queen Anne* Deals with a much neglected monarch, in whose reign the relative decline of the monarchy is particularly apparent.

Hatton, Ragnhild *George I. Elector and King* 1978 Probes how a Hanoverian monarch came to occupy the British throne and how his distance from the minutiae of English politics was a fillip to the growth of parliamentary government.

Monod, P K *Jacobitism and the English People* 1989 An analysis the role of those who never quite came to terms with the Glorious Revolution, also casting much light on Scotland's absorption into the British kingdom.

Derry, John *English Politics and the American Revolution* 1976 Deals with the loss of the American colonies and the divisions in England which precipitated it.

Mathias, Peter *The Transformation of England* 1979 Remains the best introduction into the problems behind the notion of an Industrial Revolution.

Langford, P *A Polite and Commercial Society* 1989 This has become almost an instant classic, detailing the social transformation of England.

Ross, A (ed) *Selections from the Tatler and the Spectator* 1982 The liveliness of journalistic commentary in its first, golden, age is apparent on every page of these short extracts from the two leading journals of the 18th century.

19-century Britain

Peter Martland

McCord, N *British History 1815–1906* 1991 A narrative that is easy to follow and absorb coupled with a comprehensive bibliography and useful appendices make this the ideal introduction to 19th-century British history.

Briggs, Asa *The Age of Improvement 1783–1867* 1959 Standing the test of time, this seminal work is still 'total history' at its most accessible..

Shannon, R T *The Crisis of Imperialism 1865–1915* 1974 A lucid rendering of a period full of imperial confrontations and complicated diplomacy, helped by a very useful chronology and biographical notes on the major figures in foreign affairs.

Gash, N *Aristocracy and People 1815–65* 1979 A very readable account of British political history, going beyond the major characters to produce a fascinating insight into the working of a political system.

Young, G M *Portrait of an age: Victorian England* 1953 Young's account of the bewildering changes in all spheres of life during the Victorian era creates a vivid picture that places him amongst the greatest of writers.

Perkin, H *The Origins of Modern British Society 1780–1880* 1969 Convincingly arguing that the industrial revolution initiated a social revolution, Perkin expounds the theory that just as technology is one step ahead of industry so was society ahead of politics in the 19th century.

Matthew, H C G *Gladstone 1809–74* 1986 Towering over the second half of the century, Gladstone left copious diaries which provide rich pickings for the biographer. Matthew makes a complex man understandable without ever divorcing him from his age.

20-century Britain

Peter Martland

Lloyd, T O *Empire, Welfare, Europe: English History 1906–1992* 1993 A well structured book covering the predominant historical themes in a chronological order. Ideal as an introduction, with a comprehensive bibliography and a very useful set of factual appendices.

Taylor, A J P *English History 1914–1945* 1976 Taylor's outstanding answer to his critics' accusations of 'popularism'; here his erudition shines through without ever obscuring a fascinating story of rapid political change, told in his ever readable style.

Morgan, K O *The People's Peace: British History 1945–1990* 1992 A rare example of recent events being treated as historical occurrences rather than current affairs, and an objective, lucid, and entertaining account of post-war Britain.

Pollard, S *The Development of the British Economy 1914–1980* 1993 A book which makes economics understandable without recourse to complex theory. Pollard charts the relative decline of Britain's economy in all too vivid detail.

Gilbert, Martin *Churchill: A Life* 1991 An elegant account of Britain's most eminent politician of the century and the overseas affairs in which he made his reputation.

Marwick, Arthur *British Society since 1945* 1982 A stimulating analysis of Britain's fluctuating social structure, charting the erosion of social class in the face of economic segregation.

Robbins, K *The Eclipse of a Great Power: Modern Britain 1870–1975* 1983 An excellent account of the demise of the British Empire and the various strategies Britain has adopted since in an attempt to keep a place on the world stage.